Currents

FROM THE

Dancing

River

ALSO BY RAY GONZALEZ

Anthologies

CROSSING THE RIVER:
POETS OF THE WESTERN U.S.

TRACKS IN THE SNOW:
ESSAYS BY COLORADO POETS

AFTER AZTLAN:
LATINO POETS IN THE NINETIES

WITHOUT DISCOVERY:
A NATIVE RESPONSE TO COLUMBUS

MIRRORS BENEATH THE EARTH:
CHICANO SHORT FICTION

THIS IS NOT WHERE WE BEGAN:
ESSAYS BY CHICANO WRITERS

Essays

MEMORY FEVER

Poetry

FROM THE RESTLESS ROOTS

TWILIGHTS AND CHANTS

THE HEAT OF ARRIVALS

Currents

FROM THE

Dancing River

CONTEMPORARY LATINO FICTION, NONFICTION, AND POETRY

EDITED BY

Ray Gonzalez

A Harvest Original
Harcourt Brace & Company
SAN DIEGO NEW YORK LONDON

Permissions, which constitute a continuation of the copyright page,
appear following page 567.

Library of Congress Cataloging-in-Publication Data
Currents from the dancing river: contemporary Latino fiction,
nonfiction, and poetry/edited by Ray González.—1st ed.
p.   cm.
ISBN 0-15-123654-2   0-15-600130-6 (pbk.)
1. American literature—Hispanic American authors.
2. Hispanic Americans—Literary collections.
3. American literature—20th century.   I. González, Ray.
PS508.H57C87   1994
810.8'0868—dc20   94-4327

This text was set in Galliard.

Printed in the United States of America

Designed by Kaelin Chappell

First edition

A B C D E

This book is dedicated to the memory of the late Arturo Islas, Ernesto Trejo, and Reinaldo Arenas, three writers whose voices are part of our history.

Contents

Preface

Currents from the Dancing River gathers some of the outstanding Latino writers living in the United States today. As a contemporary collection, it represents several of the most vibrant cultures in the emergence of multicultural literature. Over the last twenty-five years, Mexican Americans, Puerto Ricans, and Cuban Americans have produced writers who have influenced the political and artistic evolution of American literature. By presenting well-known writers together with lesser-known, younger authors, *Currents from the Dancing River* becomes one of the first books to show that Latinos are at the forefront of the vast changes in writing in recent decades.

As we approach the twenty-first century, the term *multicultural* may be used less often, because the kind of writing in this collection will no longer be part of forgotten or "minority" cultures. It will no longer be necessary to remind readers, writers, and critics that the canon of American arts and letters must be representative of this country's cultural wealth. The true triumph of multiculturalism is evident in the fact that Latino writing is now part of mainstream American literature. *Currents from the Dancing River* celebrates that redefinition of the American literary canon.

The Latinos contributing to new American writing with poetry, fiction, and essays make clear how far they have come from the rhetorical poetry that fueled the emergence of many "ethnic" writers in the sixties and seventies. The stereotype of the Mexican American writing only angry poetry about marching at mass political rallies is long obsolete. The notion that Cubans growing up in exile in the United States, or those born here, had no original literature is disproved in the recent successes of many Cuban American writers. While Puerto Ricans still call for the independence of their homeland, their writers have established, in their communities on the East Coast, a completely different way of life and of looking at the world.

Although cultural differences remain between Mexican Americans, Puerto Ricans in the United States, and Cuban Americans, Latino writers are coming together in a cohesive yet exciting and unpredictable whole. *Currents from the Dancing River* presents the three genres of poetry, fiction, and nonfiction in order to offer the reader many voices. Each poem, story, and essay stands on its own, but throughout the book a Latino perspective on today's world echoes and builds. While this anthology is not a historical overview of Latino literature over the last twenty-five years, it is the kind of book that firmly establishes contemporary Latino authors in their *active* roles as artists, historians, collectors of tales, and observers of political change. Combining the three genres creates its own lyrical and meta-phorical music to evoke and define a body of Latino writing.

The work in the present volume showcases Latino literature for the largest audience it has ever had through writing that preserves cultural and familial traditions, and although clearly rooted on the American continent, recognizes as well the historical clash of cultures. Its contents comes from writers who are not afraid to blend their native language with English to create new ways of speaking. Most important of all, Latino literature today is more political than it has ever been—not because its writers are relying on the rhetoric of the past to communicate their mes-sages or their stories but because the multicultural movement has forced doors to open for them. It has also allowed these voices to express their timeless struggle for social justice at a time when there are more options and more advocates for progress. Thus the political message need not be sacrificed or compromised in order to reach an audience outside a Latino culture.

Currents from the Dancing River presents Latino writing in its strong-est period. It is no coincidence that this book is appearing at the turn of the century. As we rid ourselves of words once necessary but no longer useful—words like *multicultural*—the poetry, fiction, and nonfiction in this collection will speak for itself. It vibrates with Latino voices who have been speaking for a long time through the small presses, while making way for younger artists who write for a large, attentive audience curious about today's Latino poetry and prose—an ever-growing audi-ence who realizes that the rich gathering of writers in this book must be read, listened to, and spoken about before we go on to the year 2000.

Acknowledgments

I would like to thank the following individuals for their spiritual support during the gathering of this anthology. My thanks to Alane Mason at Harcourt Brace for her belief in this project and to her staff for the detailed work on the book. For their ideas, their own contributions, and suggestions for finding new writers, I thank Juan Felipe Herrera, Rudolfo Anaya, Dagoberto Gilb, Pat Mora, Francisco Alarcon, and Virgil Suarez. None of my anthologies would be possible without the continuing friendship and support of Phil Woods, Tom & Marilyn Auer, Peter Ashkenaz, Bill Broadwell, Pat Doyle, Betty Chancellor, Cathy Bowman, Jesse Cardona, Lalo Delgado, Don Eron, John Bradley, George Kalamaras, Leroy Quintana, John Ellison, Leslie Link, Tino Villanueva, Bill Johnson Gonzalez, my agent Susan Ginsburg and my wife, Ida Steven.

Currents

FROM THE

Dancing
River

Salsa x 2

Salsa music coming out of Puerto Rico. Tito Puente. Gloria Estefan comes out of Miami and she sweeps the country. Los Lobos and Little Joe y La Familia play New York. . . . Bigger than our political accomplishments, which are going to be significant, and our business accomplishments, which are going to be significant, is the cultural dimension. Many changes are going to take place in America over the next fifteen years, but one of the most dramatic is what I have called the Hispanization of the United States. The country will have a sense that there is something new here in the culture. And it's going to be very pervasive. It's going to be in Seattle, in Minneapolis, in Chicago, in Indianapolis, in Cleveland, in Boston, as much as in Miami or Houston. . . . The first phase is going to be sensory awareness: enjoyment. Music, literature, architecture, women's clothing, food . . . Already, the New York Times *tells me, salsas have superseded ketchup as the favorite condiment on American foods, and nachos are more popular at the Chicago Cubs baseball stadium than hot dogs. . . .*
— HENRY CISNEROS IN AN INTERVIEW
WITH ENRIQUE FERNÁNDEZ

Salsa + salsa. Salsa × 2. Latin music and Latin food. Culture moves and expands through the same process as demographic growth, through seduction. Hear my music, eat my food, you are mine, you are me. Politics shakes its angry fist, theorists polemicize. Culture keeps on cooking. Culture just happens, and it happens most suavely when it tastes good.

Taste. *Sabor.* Food and music must have it. *Sabor*—flavor—is what Latino life is about. It is the quality of our difference. The flavor of salsa, both the spicy dance and the spicy dip for tortilla chips. The flavor of passion, the flavor of an everyday life that is not life if it is not highly spiked with pleasure. Highly. Every day.

"Why does your mother cook with such little seasoning?" asks Miami salsa star Hansel in his hit song "Americana Americana," a song lamenting the differences between a Latino boy and an Anglo girl. *¡Qué rico!* is the phrase most heard in Spanish-language food commercials. It's also the words most heard in Spanish-language beds. *¡Ay, qué rico!* Salsa means "sauce" and *mutatis mutandi* it means saucy Latin music. At first it was

1

a purely commercial term of no musical significance, invented by record labels intent on marketing the dance grooves that had evolved from the Cuban mambo and taken root among New York's Puerto Rican community in the 1940s and 1950s, the era of the mambo kings. By the seventies, when this Latin dance music really came into its own, African-American music was called not by a specific beat or genre but by an ineffable quality: soul. Eager to cash in on a marketable, simple word, the Latin labels came up with a somewhat more concrete metaphor. If black music had soul, Latin music had . . . sauce! . . . salsa!

In the eighties, another Latin music genre with a culinary metaphor for a name invaded New York: merengue, from the Dominican Republic, brought in by a massive immigration that would only get larger. In Spanish the word meant "meringue," and it was an appropriate term for a groove that was frothy, rich, and, as anything from the Caribbean, filled your veins with sugar energy. It wasn't new or exclusively Dominican; one finds merengues in the folk music of other Latin American countries, though they sound quite different. But Dominican merengue is the only one internationally popular for dancing, one of the Latin classics like the Cuban rhumba, mambo, and cha-cha. As far back as my childhood I could remember merengues that swept the Latin American hit parades. Particularly one superhit titled "El negrito del batey," with lyrics like "I like to dance sideways / dance good and tight / with a very yummy Negress."

I have deliberately translated the lyrics as literally as possible to underscore certain cultural attitudes. One is a casualness toward race. The word *negrito* in the title means something like "little black boy." Words like *negrito* and *negrita* are used among some Latinos with the same nonchalance as "nigger" in the street talk of African Americans. Except that it lacks the ugly violence of American racial language; in fact, *negro, negra,* the gentler diminituves *negrito* and *negrita,* and the humorously sexy augmentatives *negrón* and *negrona* are common terms of endearment in the Spanish Caribbean, used by black and white folk alike to address loved ones of either race.

But what about the *"negra bien sabrosa,"* the yummy Negress the singer wants to dance the sideways step of the merengue, holding her good and tight? We have entered that curious chamber of the Latin house: the bedroom/kitchen, where sex and food fuse in an insouciant synaesthesia. *Comer,* "to eat," is the verb of choice in some Spanish-speaking countries for sexual intercourse; not oral sex, as in colloquial English, just sex. *Quiero comerte,* I want to eat (fuck) you—you're good enough to eat—you're a *negra bien sabrosa*—your body is flavorful—I want to taste you and in our love the senses run into one another—your mouth—my mouth—your sex—my sex—our flavors—*¡Ay, qué rico!*

A Dominican lady, twice burned in the fires of matrimony, told me recently that if she had known years ago what she knows now, the first thing she would have asked a man is "Do you like *plátanos?*" A man who doesn't like *plátanos,* she has learned the hard way, is quirky and untrustworthy. One who does is a regular guy. Not perfect, but regular. A Latino mensch.

To love *plátanos* is to be a good old boy, since they are the quintessential *criollo* food. When a Spaniard goes native in the Caribbean, he is said to be *aplatanado*—all plantained up. Though *plátanos* is another name for bananas, we're talking plantains, bananas' tougher, bigger cousins, always served cooked and seldom for dessert. Plantains can be a full main course when stuffed with a spicy ground-beef *picadillo* mixture. Or they can be chopped into Caribbean stews, along with cassava, peppers, and corn. Mashed with vegetables and meats, they are shaped into the tamalelike dish Puerto Ricans call *pasteles* and South Americans *huayacas.* They can be sliced paper-thin and fried like potato chips.

Treasonous as it may sound to my compatriots—and to my Dominican lady friend—I have never loved ripe *plátanos.* My mother's cooking was more Spanish than *criollo* and my taste buds are not sufficiently *aplatanado.* The cloying sweetness of fried ripe plantains insinuates itself on my tongue like a corruption. Still, most Cubans die for that taste. To experience the difference between Spanish and *criollo* food, try a basic *tortilla española,* an austere dish of eggs, potatoes, onions, olive oil, and salt. Then sample a *tortilla de plátanos,* which uses ripe plantains instead of potatoes. Can you just taste how all that Spanish austerity is seduced by the *plátanos?*

Latin food, Latin music. I walk the full length of Miami's massive Latino street party, Calle Ocho, named after the center strip of Little Havana, S.W. 8th Street. As I emerge my ears are ringing with clanging cowbells, slapped drums, rasping gourds, blaring trumpets, and the aggressively nasal come-ons of feisty *soneros.* My skin is covered with a thick layer of garlic-scented pork fat from hundreds of steaming Cuban sandwiches. I am so saturated in *sabor* that I need to switch on the Evian-water-flavored jazz-fusion station on the car radio in order to detox.

But I go back for more. The nearest Latino restaurant to my midtown Manhattan office is almost a mile away. There are days when I just have to walk it. On a visit to San Antonio I can't resist ordering a side bowl of *menudo* to my breakfast of *huevos con carne seca*. More flour tortillas, señora, please. And when a conjunto accordion begins to moan, I just want to feel this way forever. Virgen de Guadalupe, if I must die in your Amerindian soil instead of fanned by my Afro-Caribbean breezes, let it be like this, among frijoles and chiles, *acordeones y cervezas*.

Cross the threshold of Latin music and food and everything changes. Your heart expands, your soul relaxes, if you're not careful you'll break down and cry. What is styled, camera-ready has no place here. Artifice is blatantly artificial. Sexuality is lurid as hell. And if anything is revved up it's moist sentimentality and Hotspur machismo, not cool attitude.

Twenty-five million Latinos in the U.S., probably more. By the year 2010, more Latinos than African Americans. Latino Cassandras predict that Latinos will become the country's underclass, peons to our aging, glutted, conceited generations of Anglo baby boomers. Latino Pollyannas predict the Hispanization of the U.S. More likely, the future will be dialectical. There will be some of both the bleak and the joyful. There will be serious trials. Where African Americans provoke powerful emotions in the Anglo-American soul, deep fears and deep guilts, Latinos provoke mere disdain. Like pests. Like something that shouldn't be there in the first place. Already, Latinos are at the bottom of any social problem one can think of: the most destitute homeless, the least-cared-for aged, the most-troubled war veterans, the highest school dropout rate, not to mention Latino casualties in the gang and drug wars that ravage our cities.

Among the findings of the Latino National Political Survey, a study of our political attitudes undertaken by important Latino researchers, is the lack of identification with labels like *Latino* and *Hispanic,* with each group preferring designations like *Cuban, Puerto Rican,* and *Mexican-American,* or *mexicano.* The implication is that we don't bond with each other; we are assimilating. We are not Latinos; we are almost Americans. What could unite a light-skinned Cuban settled in a deluxe condo in Miami's Key Biscayne and a dark-skinned Puerto Rican living in the projects of the south Bronx?

Yet we have in common a Caribbean variant of Spanish. A nostalgia for the very same landscape and climate. A shared history of nationalist struggle against Spain and against Uncle Sam. Practically the same food (except the Puerto Rican love of cilantro and the Cuban preference for black beans over *gandules*). The same body language. The same music.

The mix of Spain and Africa (unless one subscribes, as far too many people of all races do, to fascist notions of ethnicity, one must conclude that all Cubans and all Puerto Ricans are, culturally, mulatto).

No two Latino groups could be more different or more at odds with one another than Mexicans and Cuban Americans: Chicanos forged their political identity in a revolutionary civil rights struggle based on a dispossession by Anglo-American foes. Cuban Americans forged their political identity in a struggle against revolutionaries that led them to the warm embrace of Anglo Americans when they were dispossessed by leftist ideologues who think and talk suspiciously like Chicano activists. Chicanos and Cuban Americans compete fiercely in the business and political arenas; in the arts and academia, they are, at best, distant. Some Chicanos hate Cuban Americans, and vice versa.

Yet they share a language lost or beleaguered. A Roman Catholic background infused with and deconstructed by non-European belief systems. A Spanish sense of formality and, most important, honor. An ease with the realm of the passions. A common vocabulary of pop culture dating from the day when Cuban music invaded Mexico and Mexican film invaded Cuba. The geographical proximity of both home countries that has always made travel and exchange frequent and common. A baroque sensibility.

Ah, but how do you translate loss, nostalgia, honor, passion, never mind the flash of pop culture or the twists of the baroque into the discourse of social science? What is the language of your tenderness, your wrath, your lusts—Spanish or English? What is the language of your dreams? What do you feel like or want to be, *americano* or *latinoamericano*? When a Mexican says *pinche gringo,* do you identify with the speaker or the object of the speech? What is your desire? My questionnaire to Latinos would ask not "What are your attitudes?" but "Where lie your passions?"

Unlike African Americans, Latinos do not share a visible sign of bonding, and because our presence in this country is both ancestral (we were here earlier) and recent (we just crossed the border), we are not a cohesive group. But I believe we are seeking—we will seek—each other. A common culture binds us. Those who fear the emergence of one more bothersome and populous minority must feel reassured by our apparent disunity. I am here to tell you that you should not rest easy. We are not about to dissolve into manageable microminorities. Our currents run deep.

———

So what is the Hispanic heritage, or at least that part of what we inherited from Spain, that we should be proud of? Here is my list of what's Hispanic worth celebrating.

1. HONOR. If anyone wants to understand what makes Hispanics tick, they should go read Spanish seventeenth-century honor plays—or catch them at the Spanish Repertory Theater on East Twenty-seventh Street in New York.

In the Spanish worldview, honor is a human being's essence. Without it, you're not even human. You're nothing. Only the honorable deserve to have rights, never mind privileges. In our society, where everyone is clamoring for their rights, it might make sense to demand honor in return.

2. FORMALITY. The word *formal* is downright negative in modern American society: "Oh, he's so formal." Not so in the Spanish-speaking world.

First of all, it has nothing to do with wearing black tie. It means that you live up to your word—that honor again—and do what must be done.

To accomplish in modern English means to excel in order to fulfill your personal ambitions, while *cumplir* in Spanish means to excel in fulfilling your obligations to others. In Spanish, no one wants to be *informal,* or be around anyone who is.

3. HEART. I never understood all that New Age blarney about "getting in touch with your feelings." To be unfeeling has always been an aberration in the Spanish-speaking world: typically, Spaniards attribute it to their archenemies, the English.

Of course you feel. Of course your heart breaks. This, however, does not mean you loosen up your formality and disregard the demands of honor. On the contrary, the great tragedy of being alive is that one must do the right thing and feel, to the hilt, the pain that inevitably follows.

4. HUNGER FOR THE EARTH. Death is the big no-no in American life, the big nuisance. In traditional Spanish life, death has been a faithful companion. From Spain's bullfights to Mexico's laughing skulls. Hispanic culture not only accepts but celebrates death, even plays with it. In southern Spain, wrote the poet García Lorca, some people never are as alive as the day they are carried out of their houses dead.

Morbid we are, but never depressed. One reason Hispanic humor is so difficult to translate into English is because it's nearly always black humor, cruel and terrible. However, if you swing with it, it's very funny: We're all gonna die someday, so why take it seriously?

Hispanic tastes are deliciously morbid. Centuries before New York downtowners imposed their fashion on the world, King Philip I made it *de rigueur* to wear all black, not only at the Spanish court but at all the great courts of Europe, where Spanish black was aped.

And Hispanic food: the passion for reconstituted food—brought back to life—like beans and salt cod, and for ham and sausages and cheeses dried into a state of voluptuous mummification. And music: The pained wail of flamenco or the woeful songs of Spain's Celtic north. In Spanish culture, death is rich with life.

5. LOVE. Spanish is a loving tongue, as the old cowboy song says. That making love is better in Spanish is such a cultural stereotype that one should rush to deny it. Instead, one is likely to rush to try it.

Certainly those of us who live bilingually will tell you that Spanish love songs release feelings that are hard to express in English. I've interviewed both Gloria Estefan and Linda Ronstadt on why they sing in Spanish when they're big pop stars in English and, well, they just gotta do it.

So, let's let this be our finest Hispanic heritage: A language unabashed in lovemaking. We don't have a patent on it. We got it from Spain and, like all languages, it's there for the taking, for the talking, for the singing, for the loving. It's yours, *mi amor, mi corazón.*

"Which language comes most naturally to you?" a Latin American writer asked me not long ago, "Spanish or English?" "Neither and both," I replied. "My natural language is Spanglish." The writer, who was fairly fluent in English, urged me to try some Spanglish on him. I couldn't. He was not a Spanglish speaker. Only with another like myself could I speak this yet uncodified tongue. With Spaniards and Latin Americans I use, not without some strain, a curiously formal Spanish of uncertain origin. But with my fellow Hispanics here in the entrails of the monster, I can relax into our *nuevo* creole.

Like all languages, Spanglish comes in many different flavors and shapes. Tex-Mex and East Harlem variants sound nothing like each other. You don't use the same Spanglish to sell dope uptown as to discuss metalinguistics at Yale. But Spanglish, like Don Juan, has made it in the humblest cabins and the loftiest palaces, east and west, all around the town, the country, even the world. How does it work? How do two languages fuse?

The most obvious mix is in vocabulary. English and Spanish words are juxtaposed. In a business transaction you could ask *¿donde está el invoice?* That new person you met was *bien* nice. Or you can take an English word and add a Spanish suffix, as in *coolear,* Spanglish for *to cool* *out,* or, my fave, *hanguear* for "to hang out," whence comes the word *hangueadores,* the people you find in clubs night after night. That's not all. You can start a sentence in one language, switch to the other one, then back again, and so on. And that's *el* Spanglish, man, a language *que es bien* nice if you know how to *usarlo, ¿comprendes?*

But why *usarlo* at all when you've got *dos* languages *que son perfectamente* fine *para expresar* what you mean? Well, you might not have the words in one language. No sooner does an immigrant arrive on these shores than the media begins its bombardment. So, *¿cómo se dice* Brillo pad, Dolby sound, Miller Lite *en español?* The answer is *no se dice en español,* you say it in English. There are Spanish words that have perfect equivalents in English but lack the emotional ring, to a Hispanic American, of the words we learned at home from *la familia.* Or we may use the Spanish words because of their power of identification, a way of drawing others like ourselves into a circle and keeping out whoever doesn't share this bilingualism. This works in two ways. Interjecting Spanish words in an English discourse proclaims one's Latin-ness; interjecting English into Spanish proclaims one's hipness.

I'm making it sound like everyone is highly conscious of the language they use, when, in fact, we open our mouths and words come out. We barely know what we're saying until we've said it. If we, speakers of Spanglish, paid attention to our discourse we might notice, to our horror, that when we switch from one language to another we're switching worldviews, attitudes, personalities. Schizophrenia? On the contrary, Spanglish is an emotional safety valve for the strain of straddling two different, often antagonistic cultures. I believe the switch comes when the pressure of one language reaches a critical level and it's necessary to seek the shelter of the other worldview.

Some years ago, the brilliantly written bilingual sitcom *Que Pasa USA?* explored these cultural and linguistic turns within a three-generation Cuban-American family. The grandparents spoke Spanish and knew only a handful of English words. The kids spoke English and could muster only a few phrases in Spanish. And the parents switched constantly back and forth, mixing the two. The funniest bits in the show came when the oldest or the youngest generation made comments in their main language that the other end of the generational spectrum could not understand. These outbursts were pure comic relief. Relief from the pressure of being too Latin in an American world or too American in a Latin family. This show, which still stands as the best TV presentation of U.S. Hispanics, was written in Spanglish, a clever, fresh, deliberate Spanglish. Though it touched bilingual Hispanics in a particular way, it could be appreciated by anyone. And it proved that Spanglish was a viable language.

Not everyone finds this phenomenon charming, however. The reaction against bilingual education reflects a fear among Anglo-Americans that their linguistic heritage is being eroded. And that's nothing compared to the concerns that English-Spanish fusion has raised on the other side of the Atlantic. Spaniards, who have seen their language gradually submit to the English invasion provoked by Spain's entry into the modern world in the last few decades, are now raising a cry of alarm as the computer revolution threatens to deform the shape of their beautifully archaic tongue. Technotalk is rampant in Spain and there's a lively debate over what to do about it.

Some of the smartest Spanish writers on the subject have pointed out something that should be obvious if one knows linguistics but can be easily overlooked. Language, as the semioticians explain it, works along two axes of signification, two ways of meaning—vocabulary and syntax. A U.S. Latino and a Spanish technocrat will mix Spanish and English words, but, most significantly, they will also arrange the words of one language using the syntax of the other. In the case of Spain's mother tongue, the new technology has meant that the lovely curves of Spanish syntax are being replaced by the sharp-edged word order of English. The result is an awkward Castilian that would make the great writers of the Spanish Baroque spring from their graves, sword in hand, to punish the offenders.

But if this is true for anglicized Castilian, it must also be the case for our homegrown Spanglish. I know so from my own experience. I can tell a U.S. Hispanic from a Latin American by the former's awkward syntax in Spanish, an *English* syntax. My own Spanish is the same, though thanks to the good fortune of higher education and a lifetime of reading Spanish literature, I compensate by adding rococo flourishes to my *español*. It works the other way too, as my editors well know. I bend and twist English in unnatural ways. Editing my copy requires a hot iron and a firm hand. Editing as conk job.

Therefore, if the massive Hispanic immigration has some influence on the American language, this will be more than just Spanish words entering English, like the *hoosegow, calaboose,* and *desperado* of the Old West. Look for exuberant shapes missing from the Queen's English since the Elizabethan era. Look for hyperbatons, redundancies, excess. Look for the death of economy, pithiness, terseness. Look for rhetoric. Look for a new language that will sound like a *concierto barroco*. Look for too much. More *es más*.

Those spices . . . that beat. Latino culture beckons. It promises to fill the sensory vacuum of Anglo America. The frightening nothingness inherited from Puritan England and northern Europe. In an American novel a black character pressed by a white lover to explain how white folk smell answers that what's unpleasant about them is that they don't smell. No-funk. Likewise, when Latinos are pressed to explain what they find lacking in American food and American sexual attractions, the answer is *no tiene sabor*. No-*sabor*. *Horror vacuii*. Come fill me.

How does *sabor*/seduction work? In that gorgeous morality play, John Ford's *The Searchers*, the John Wayne character relentlessly pursues his kidnapped niece in hope of catching up with her and her Indian abductors before she comes of age, before she can be tainted by miscegenation, before she becomes a mother of a *mestizo*, a mother of an *hijo de la chingada*. After a good long time his search is more of a reflex than an obsession. And somewhere in *la frontera*, the searcher relaxes. His clothes are loose, his drink is Mexican, his body language Latino. Of course, it is at the very precise moment of his *mestizaje*-through-assimilation that he finds his niece: ripe *y bien chingada*. But it's too late for righteousness. The Puritan knight who began the search has yielded to the seduction of the Other. Is the Other. As was the Duke himself, that Latinophile, tequila head, *mestiza* lover. The searcher has found himself.

Chiles

From *The Rain God*

Miguel Chico's godmother Nina was a practical woman. The otherworldly side of her came to the surface before her son's death, and she explored it with the care and precision she used to prepare the annual income tax accounts of various business firms in town.

Money and cards fascinated her and Fortune followed her, if not abundantly, certainly with cheer. But it was not until her children were well into adolescence that she looked casually over her shoulder one day and recognized a greater power smiling at her from behind Fortune's face. This same power that would take away her son began training her early on to endure, rather than resign herself to, the deprivation.

Nina had always been afraid to die. The very idea of being buried in the earth filled her heart with terror. No matter that she would be dead and insensate by that time, the funeral rites passed through in a silence as complete as that of the chrysanthemums surrounding her corpse, Nina knew she would feel the desert trickling down her throat, and that knowledge was unbearable to her. At best, it made her irritable and anxious during the many ordinary activities of her busy days; at worst, it caused her unalleviated fits of depression.

"I don't care what you say," Nina said to her sister Juanita, "I know I'm going to feel it."

"But how? You'll be dead. You won't feel anything," Juanita replied. She was disturbed by how much Nina had been drinking lately. To Miguel Chico's mother, more than one drink was too much. Juanita had known about Nina's fears for a long time. When they were children sleeping in the same bed, she would get Nina a glass of water in the middle of the night and distract her by singing the latest Mexican ballads until she went back to sleep. Years later, when their children were babies, their endless and elaborate card games allayed Nina's terror but did not get rid of it.

"Let me get another scotchito," Nina said as Juanita dealt out another hand of five hundred rummy.

"You're being ridiculous, Nina. Sit down and play."

It was not until she discovered the spirit world that Nina began to recognize that death might not exist as she imagined it in her terror. At the biweekly séances in the basement of her friends' Mexican food restaurant, her nose itching from the Aqua Velva they sprinkled into the air to induce serenity, Nina gradually became aware of two women waving at her from a strange and unknown region. They were about the same age, and Nina saw with joy that one of the women was her sister Antonia, who had died in her late twenties. The other woman was her mother, who at twenty-nine had died giving birth to Nina. She awoke from her trance weeping, greatly relieved and peaceful, her initial skepticism about spiritualism gone forever. She did not see the women again, but the possibility that she might gave her courage and kept alive her faith in some kind of practical afterlife. "Imagine," she said to Juanita, "the two of them at the same age. They were like sisters, not like mother and daughter."

Juanita, more dominated by Church doctrine than was her younger sister, did not approve of these "spook" gatherings, though when she saw how effectively they helped Nina overcome her childhood fears she decided to overlook the heresy and defend her sister against the family's ridicule. Nevertheless, Juanita staunchly refused Nina's repeated invitations to join her in exploring the afterlife, even if she was secretly and guiltily attracted to it.

Nina's own humor, lively and persistent even during her moments of anxiety, grew, and she was able to bring happiness to everyone except her own family. Her husband, Ernesto, and their three children could not understand or accept her enthusiasm for the impalpable, and they were jealous of her time away from them.

Ernesto, a silent and calm man, brought up to believe in the teachings of the Church, expressed his disdain by becoming even more quiet after she returned from one of her encounters with the spirits. When Nina tried to share with him her excitement, Ernesto asked her not to talk to him about such things. She honored his request because she loved and respected him for his already serene nature, and she sensed that his soul was more highly evolved than hers.

Ernesto Garcia was a hardworking, responsible man. The children adored him with an affection they did not extend to Nina. She had married him because he was honest and because she liked the way he laughed.

Like her, he could lose his temper, but unlike her, he was able to recover it quickly and not bear grudges. He was as stubborn as she, but his obstinacy showed itself in the determined way he provided for his family without allowing himself to get into debt. For a man of Mexican origin, coming of age and marrying during the Depression, that was an accomplishment. Then, too, Ernesto was different from other men she knew. He was not given to bragging or lording it over others. From the start, she had recognized his superiority.

"Come on, Neto, just go to one meeting with me."

"No, and stop telling me about them." He refused her invitations without anger. From that time on, when anyone phoned for her while she was at a séance, Ernesto said, "She's with the spirits right now. But don't worry, when she gets home, I'll bring her back down to earth."

In this period, Anna, their oldest child, had stopped quarreling with her mother and was too preoccupied with her school activities and boyfriends to pay much heed to Nina's idiosyncrasies. Their youngest child, Cristina, was still too young to give her parents much trouble. But Nina and her son, Antony, almost fifteen, were beginning to disagree with each other about everything in stubborn and exaggerated ways. Usually Ernesto sided with his wife in these arguments, but at times he wondered aloud if she were not living too much with her head in the clouds. When Ernesto took Tony's part against her, Nina felt betrayed.

"I live with three rams and a crab in this house," Nina said to Juanita, who did not understand astrology or accept it as valid. "I'm nothing but air. What can I do?" She cooked her chile jalapeño.

Only three people could eat it: their lifelong friend El Compa, her son, and herself. For the remainder of humanity, her green chile sauce was fire itself. "Ay, Nina, why do you make it so hot?" Juanita asked, exasperated. She did not like being left out, but she no longer made valiant attempts to taste the stuff. Her nose began watering the minute she walked into Nina's kitchen on those days when she toasted the chiles. Water, tortillas, bread and butter, aspirin and other remedies had not been able to calm Juanita's digestive tract after those times she had gamely swallowed a spoonful.

"I don't make it hot. Do I grow the chiles? I only choose them at the market like everybody else. How can I help it if they come out tasting like that after I prepare them?"

"But how can you eat it? It's going to kill you."

Nina laughed at her sister. "It will prepare me for the devil." In those days, she believed in the devil.

Juanita and Ernesto watched El Compa, Antony, and Nina eat the chile sauce as if it were chicken soup. The only evidence the two outsiders had of its power was in the tears the eaters shed without restraint as they said over and over like a rosary, "It's so good, it's so good."

"You're crazy," Ernesto said to them and went into the living room to read the afternoon paper. But Juanita stayed to the end and participated vicariously in their ability to enjoy the extremes in life.

"Let me tell you a joke I heard about chile," El Compa said one winter evening as they sat down to eat.

"Is it dirty?" Juanita asked.

"No, *comadre,* would I tell a dirty joke in front of you?"

"That's what my husband always says before he goes ahead and tells one."

"Leave him alone, Juanita. Go on, Compa, tell it. I love stories about chiles," Nina said with a little girl's smile on her face. She could be salacious without being obscene, and Juanita watched her carefully because she wanted to learn that talent. Juanita's best friend, Lola, who was married to El Compa, had the same skill.

"I'm not talking about that kind of chile," El Compa said. "I'm talking about the kind we're eating."

"Go on, get it over with," Tony said, resigned to having to listen to another bad joke.

"Well, there was this gringo who was in Mexico for the first time. At a restaurant he ordered a mole poblano that was real hot. I mean hot, hotter than this."

"Impossible," Nina said, offended.

"Well, almost, *comadre.* Anyway, the poor guy sat there awhile after he ate a couple of mouthfuls, flames coming out of his ears, and when he could talk he asked the waitress to come over to his table. She saw right away from his face what was wrong, and she brought him some ice cream. 'What good will that do?' the guy asked her. 'It'll help take away the burn,' she told him."

"It never worked for me," Juanita said.

"Well, the next day," El Compa went on.

"Here it comes, the corny punch line," Tony said.

"Shut up, both of you," Nina said.

"The next day, the gringo is sitting on the toilet, and you know what he is saying?"

"No, what?" Juanita asked, taken in once again by El Compa's charm.

" 'Come on, ice cream, come on!' "

"Ay, *pelado!*" Juanita said, blushing and enjoying herself immensely. Nina and Tony laughed at both of them.

Nina was the youngest child in her family. Her mother was Mexican, but her father was half French and half Mexican. Unable to accept the death of his wife, he had not forgiven Nina for destroying what he had loved most in the world. He died when Nina and Juanita were in their teens, and Nina had been secretly glad because she had resented her father's authoritarian ways. Unfortunately for her own children, that tendency to be uncompromisingly strict survived in her methods of disciplining them.

"You hit them too much," Juanita said to her when the children were almost adolescents. She knew she was breaking their agreement not to interfere in how they brought up their children.

"They've got to learn," Nina replied, "I can't stand spoiled brats."

"You sound just like Papá, Nina. I can't believe it."

Their father's oldest child, a brother they never knew, had died as an infant in San Francisco. Their parents had sailed north from the Mexican fishing village on the Pacific where they had met and married. Seeing his son's death as divine retribution for his having left Mexico, their father, a cigar maker, gradually moved his family toward the homeland, settling in an obscure New Mexican town first and finally in the Texas border town where his three daughters were born.

"So you see, Miguelito," Nina said to her godson, "that's why you live in San Francisco. Your uncle's spirit is still there. He would be over seventy years old now, unless of course he's learned his lessons and progressed farther into the spirit world. Look for him in the clouds, Mickie."

"Oh, Nina, you know I don't believe in those things. And they're not clouds. It's just plain fog." He was a graduate student at the time and was therefore a literal young man who took himself and others very seriously.

Antonia, the oldest sister and the aunt Miguel Chico never knew, was their father's favorite. She died of tuberculosis. Nina and Juanita nursed her at home for a time, then went to see her at the sanatorium every day for five years until her death. After they buried her, Nina did not go to another funeral until her own son was buried in the new cemetery at the outer edge of the desert on the north side of town.

After that, Nina visited his grave on his birthday, on holidays, and on the Day of the Dead. She did so conscientiously, indulged in self-reproach over his tombstone, and tried to keep horror from overwhelming her as she imagined him beneath her with the desert in his mouth. She stopped paying homage to her guilt and grief on the day she realized Antony was no longer lying in wait for her.

"Aren't you going to the cemetery to visit Tony?" Juanita asked Nina on his birthday. He would have been twenty years old.

"What for?" Nina replied casually. "He's not there. He never was."

Juanita was puzzled but dropped the matter. She did look very carefully at her sister's face to make sure she was not in some kind of trance. As a gesture of good will toward Nina's interest, Juanita had begun attending classes in mind control. It was her way of seeing to it that Nina did not ascend into heaven without her.

Nina and Juanita had loved each other deeply from the beginning. Their passage through the illness and death of their older sister, their suffering from their father's arbitrary nature, their constant sharing even after their marriages and the setting up of separate lives in separate households had bound them irrevocably. If they were unable to see each other during the day, they would speak on the phone as if they had been apart for years. Nina was the pragmatic one for all her later spiritual adventures; Juanita was the idealist and romantic. Nina's poetic nature expressed itself in the subtle mixture of spices with which she served up whatever had been plain meat or poultry.

"My God, Nina, this is delicious. What is it?" Miguel Chico asked her, tasting a dish that satisfied all but his sense of hearing.

"Roast chicken. Eat it before it gets cold."

After their father's death, Nina and Juanita were left alone in the small house on the south side of town six blocks from the border. Nina cooked all the meals for them and the occasional relatives and friends who stopped by. Juanita cleaned house and did the laundry. Both already had part-time jobs which they kept, but only Juanita finished high school. Nina thought school a waste of time for industrious people with common sense. Unless they had some practical value, books bored her, and she could not bring herself to read novels or stories because daily life and real people were infinitely more interesting to her. Juanita, who joined a book club shortly after she married, could never get Nina to read the latest best seller that arrived monthly and which she read immediately. After thumbing through a few of them, Nina judged them boring and "pure trash." Stories about the endless suffering of southern belles left her unmoved.

"Why don't they write about us?" Nina asked her sister.

"Who wants to read about Mexicans? We're not glamorous enough. We just live," Juanita answered. She was getting ready to go out to the annual policemen's ball with Miguel Grande. Four-year-old Miguel Chico watched his mother show off her new dress. He and the two women were reflected in the mirror of her dressing table.

"Not glamorous enough, huh?" Nina said. "Look at yourself."

Juanita did and saw a tall, slender woman with a long, pale face and dark hair. She was wearing a burgundy-colored dress with a pleated skirt in the style of the early forties, and she delighted her son by turning gracefully from one end of the room to the other so that her dress ballooned out and displayed her beautiful legs. "My mother has glamour legs," he liked to tell the neighborhood.

"The new book came this week," she said to Nina. "Read it after Mickie goes to sleep."

"No thanks. I've got better things to do."

"You're going to remain an illiterate Mexican all your life," Juanita told her as she kissed her son good night.

"I can read what I need to know. Anyway, in this country, all you really need to know is how to count."

Their aunt Antoinette came up from Mexico City to be with them after their father's death. She was too delicate and ladylike for Nina, but Juanita was delighted with her wardrobe and the few jewels she had brought with her. Antoinette was in her mid-forties and had not married. Mysteriously, she hinted that she had more jewels at home and left the source to Juanita's fancy. Her niece begged her to tell them about the dances and young men of the capital, and the aunt, flattered by the attention, made up stories that satisfied at least one of her brother's daughters. Nina saw through her aunt's pretensions but, so as not to spoil Juanita's pleasure, did not share her insights. After a few months Antoinette was convinced that the girls were safe and could take care of themselves, and she returned to the capital, where she lived in a poor section of town, far removed from the fancy dress balls and the pretty young men now part of Juanita's imagination.

Their aunts on their mother's side had families of their own to care for and called infrequently. Nina and Juanita enjoyed their independence immensely. Now they could attend the Saturday night social events sponsored by the Church without having to sneak away and then suffer from the punishments of discovery when they returned home.

"Devil's daughters!" their father had bellowed at them when he found out that they had been to a social and not a religious function. "You are lost!" He, like others from the provinces, was unable to separate the body from the soul.

Their father could be vicious in his rage and was capable of beating them severely when he drank too much. Though she could bear it for herself when he hit them, Nina could not stand to see him hurt her sister. Once she attempted to strike him as he was taking the strap to Juanita. He was so shocked by Nina's temerity that he stopped in the middle of the whipping and walked out of the room without a word. Stunned, the girls could only look at each other in disbelief.

Nina trembled for the rest of the day, waiting in dread to suffer from the consequences of her boldness. The punishment did not come. At the table they sat in their customary silence, a silence broken only by the sounds of their father's eating. They were not permitted to begin their meal until he finished his. As the days went by without his saying or doing anything to her, Nina understood that her punishment was the constant fear of reprisal under which she lived. He was a clever man, she granted him that. But she was his daughter, and her strategy, once she understood, was to pretend to be afraid. Now they sneaked away at will, and their father never touched them again.

On his deathbed, he called for them both and looked at them sadly. Juanita was crying and Nina wondered why. She was glad to be rid of him at last, a sentiment for which she would feel residual guilt until she came upon the spirit world.

"Crybaby, Juanita. What's the matter with you? Remember how he treated us?" To think of him already in the past tense relieved Nina, and she refused to give him the satisfaction of her tears. She looked back at him with a straight, impassive face.

"Daughters," he said. "Behave yourselves." He reached for their hands, recoiled from the contact, and died with his mouth and eyes open.

Nina wanted to burst out laughing, but she restrained herself. "Behave yourselves!" It struck her as ridiculous that a man's last words to his children should be so stupid. She hazarded a comment to Juanita as they were being led out of the room by their aunts. "What else have we ever done?"

"Shut up," Juanita said. "Have respect for the dead." She had stopped crying at least. With their aunts' permission, they agreed not to tell Tonia that their father was dead. Antonia had stopped asking for him after the time he had visited her in the sanatorium crazy drunk and cursing her for having abandoned him.

Years later, when they told her that Antony was dead, Nina was standing in her kitchen looking out the window at the desert that came right to their back door. Tony had not wanted to move to this house so far away from his friends and favorite cousins. It meant a change in schools for him, and he did not like the idea of having to adjust to new teachers (he had the reputation of being a gifted but "difficult" student) or of leaving his girlfriend behind.

"Now I'll be more isolated than ever," Tony said to his mother. "Is that what you want?" He was sixteen, handsome like his father, with Gallic features from Nina's side of the family. His Mexican school friends called him "Frenchie" and teased him for being so good-looking.

"You'll get used to it. And you'll make new friends," Nina said, unwilling to be swayed from her determination to buy the house. "The money we save will put you through college." Tony, like his father, was interested in electrical engineering.

"I don't want to go to college, and your whole life revolves around money."

"Listen to you. If it weren't for the fact that your father and I have worked all our lives to see that you and your sisters live decently, you wouldn't have that car you run around in so much." Nina had been against his having a car at so young an age.

"I bought that car on my own, so don't start in on how grateful I'm supposed to be to you for supporting me. I didn't ask to be born." He was a sophomore in high school.

"If you keep talking to me like that, I'll have your father take that car away from you whether you bought it or not. And you'll go to college because you've got the chance to make something of yourself. Do you hear me, Tony?"

"You never finished high school and you did all right," he said to her.

"It's different now. Besides, I still have to work hard to make ends meet. So does your father."

"It's different now, all right. Everybody's going to college so that they can make more money, and for what? The country's so fucked up, it'll send me to Vietnam before I can even get into college."

"Don't you use bad language in front of me." Nina was not prudish, but she did not like her children to speak that way in her presence. She saw it as an indication of their disrespect for authority, and she wondered what her children were learning in school.

"If you make me change schools, I won't study."

"Don't threaten me. You'll change schools if you have to, and you'll study if I have to lock you in your room and throw away the keys to it and your car."

Tony walked away from her.

"Where are you going?"

"Out."

"That's no answer."

"That's the only answer I'm going to give you."

Nina went ahead with the deal for the new house. It was an extraordinarily good buy. In a few years, they could sell it for ten times as much and move back to the part of town they liked best. The money they gained would help put Tony through college. They owned a lot next to the house they were in, and Ernesto was a good engineer. He had built all the homes they had owned. He was as taken by the bargain as she and agreed with her readily over Tony's protests.

The house was one of those new, prefabricated structures that were going up everywhere on the northern and eastern ends of the town. If the economy continued as it had for the last five years, the house would be practically in the middle of town in the next five. At the time they bought it, however, its rear windows looked eastward onto miles of sand and tumbleweed.

Their move was hard on Juanita, who was afraid to drive that far on the highway even in the daytime. "Are you crazy, Nina? You're going to be shoveling sand out of your bathtub."

"What do I care? As long as it doesn't get into my beans, let it do whatever it wants." They moved in during the last days of August. The children changed schools, and Tony fulfilled his threats to stop studying. Nina threatened him in turn with whatever she thought might get him to stop being so obstinate. Juanita was disturbed by their struggle and she tried to interfere once again.

"You're being as stubborn as he is, Nina. Let him have his car so that he can at least get out of the house once in a while. Tony's young and healthy. You'll make him sick if you continue to coop him up out here in the middle of nowhere."

"I'll let his father give him the keys to the car when he decides to start doing his homework again."

Juanita saw that it was hopeless to argue with her sister about it. She saw obstinacy and grudge bearing as the main flaws in Nina's character, and she was trying to keep them from doing too much damage. She went up to Tony's room.

"Tony, it's your tía Juanita. May I come in?"

"Sure," he said and giggled. "You have to unlock the door from your side. She put in a deadbolt the other day."

Juanita went into his room. Tony was in bed listening to the radio and smoking a forbidden cigarette. His sister, in league with him against their mother, had smuggled it into his room.

"Tony, I know it's none of my business," Juanita began.

"If you're going to try to talk me into doing what she wants, you're wasting your time," he said very quietly.

Instead, she talked to him about her youngest son, Raphael, Tony's favorite cousin, and how much they all missed his visits to their house across town. Juanita saw the same faults in her nephew as in her sister and decided that her only course was to pray for them both and hope for the best. But when she went downstairs she said firmly to Nina, "You'd better think very carefully about what you're doing to that boy."

"I have. It's for his own good," Nina said.

The following Easter Sunday they came to tell her that he was dead, drowned at the smelter lake with all his clothes on. She had allowed Ernesto to give Tony the keys to his car for the holiday. As he had walked out the door, she had told him to behave himself.

Nina thought of her father in that moment before she began howling. "Damn you, Father," she said, inhaling the words, "why do you keep punishing me?" Juanita was holding her tightly from behind, and the two of them rocked together in a slow, horrible dance. She let her go when Nina said she wanted to sit down. Nina walked out of the kitchen, chile still toasting on the burner, and made her way into the living room. Her daughters and husband's relatives were there. She stared at them blindly, sat on the sofa, and resumed her weeping. Her sister-in-law Carmela, Tony's godmother, sat next to her but did not touch her.

In the kitchen, Juanita turned off the burners and, glancing out the window, saw Ernesto standing on the sand, his back to the house. The spring light was still in the sky; the evening would be lovely. Behind her, she heard Miguel Grande say, "Don't go out there. Leave him alone," but she was already out the door and halfway to where Ernesto stood. Looking at the side of his face, for he did not turn to greet her, she sensed that his expression was as dry as the earth beneath them. It chilled her, and all of her instincts could not bear the silence. Quietly, she said to him, "And you, Ernesto? Why don't you cry too?"

He turned to look at her, and she thought he was going to strike her. At that moment, he was the loneliest creature she had ever seen. He took her hand and slowly, guided by her, began to feel his loss.

"My son," he said. The desert was in his eyes.

Tony appeared in the sand before him as he had looked on the floor of the emergency room. The medics had taken off all but his trousers, and Ernesto tried to revive him without knowing that the firemen had pronounced him dead by the lake an hour earlier. Miguel Grande and the doctors had to use force to get him away from his son. Police and newspaper photographers were taking flash photos. Juanita showed one of them to Miguel Chico the following Christmas when he was home for the holidays. As he looked at the photograph, Miguel Chico was struck by his cousin's youth, his athletic chest, the handsome face.

"I don't remember him as grown up as this," he said.

"You didn't bother to see him," his mother answered.

"Don't start, Mother. He didn't exactly care that much for me, you know. He told Raphael that he thought I was a phony."

"That's not true. He loved you."

"It's too late, Ernesto. He's gone," Miguel Grande had told him when he had calmed down somewhat. After the identification forms were signed, he and Miguel Grande walked out of the hospital into the late mid-April afternoon. The day was sunny and warm.

Miguel had parked his police vehicle next to Tony's car. Ernesto noticed it. "Get that car out of my sight," he said angrily to his brother-in-law. "I don't care what you do with it."

They got into the police car. Raphael was waiting in the backseat, having refused to go into the emergency room. None of them said anything during the drive to the house on the east side. Miguel stopped once at a precinct station to phone Juanita and give her instructions. When they arrived, Juanita, Lola, and some of Ernesto's relatives were waiting in their cars. Together they walked to the front door of Nina's house. It was open, the screen door unlatched; the aroma of roasting chiles caused Ernesto to stop dead. He looked at Miguel and Juanita and then walked around the side of the house by himself.

"God damn it," Miguel Grande said for Juanita and Lola to hear, "I'm going to have to tell her." The women followed him into the house.

Ernesto was in the backyard looking at the desert. Seeing it at its most beautiful in the sunset of the holy day, he felt its desolation for the first time in his life. He thought he had always loved it, but now he understood that he had accepted it as a given fact, like breathing. From this day, he could no longer take anything for granted, though his duty as a man was to pretend to do so until the day he died. The vision was overwhelming, and bitterness and despair wrestled with his soul. Both were as dry and timeless as what he was gazing at; only his uncertainty was mortal.

"Why did you swim with all your clothes on? How many times, Antony, have I told you not to go in deep water unless there is someone on the shore?"

After a while, an angel stood beside him. It asked him in a familiar voice why he did not weep. He thought it a strange question from a creature he had been taught had no emotions. He would ask Nina about it; she would be able to explain it to him. He turned to look at the angel. When he took its hand, it vanished and he saw his sister-in-law Juanita.

The two of them sat side by side on the sand like children, knees drawn up to their chests, until the first stars appeared. They astonished him. He was seeing them as if for the first time. A few moments later, he and Juanita got up and went into the house through the kitchen. Ernesto began to weep when he saw the chiles on the stove. Their smell filled the house and he went from room to room opening all the windows.

Puertoricanness

It was Puerto Rico waking up inside her. Puerto Rico waking her up at 6:00 A.M., remembering the rooster that used to crow over on Fifty-ninth Street and the neighbors all cursed "that damn rooster," but she loved him, waited to hear his harsh voice carving up the Oakland sky and eating it like chopped corn, so obliviously sure of himself, crowing all alone with miles of houses around him. She was like that rooster.

Often she could hear them in her dreams. Not the lone rooster of Fifty-ninth Street (or some street nearby . . . she had never found the exact yard though she had tried), but the wild careening hysterical roosters of 3:00 A.M. in Bartolo, screaming at the night and screaming again at the day.

It was Puerto Rico waking up inside her, uncurling and shoving open the door she had kept neatly shut for years and years. Maybe since the first time she was an immigrant, when she refused to speak Spanish in nursery school. Certainly since the last time, when at thirteen she found herself between languages, between countries, with no land feeling at all solid under her feet. The mulberry trees of Chicago, that first summer, had looked so utterly pitiful beside her memory of flamboyan and banana and . . . . No, not even the individual trees and bushes but the mass of them, the overwhelming profusion of green life that was the home of her comfort and nest of her dreams.

The door was opening. She could no longer keep her accent under lock and key. It seeped out, masquerading as dyslexia, stuttering, halting unable to speak the word which will surely come out in the wrong language, wearing the wrong clothes. Doesn't that girl know how to dress? Doesn't she know how to date, what to say to a professor, how to behave at a dinner table laid with silver and crystal and too many forks?

Yesterday she answered her husband's request that she listen to the whole of his thoughts before commenting by screaming, "This is how we talk. I will not wait sedately for you to finish. Interrupt me back!"

She drank pineapple juice three or four times a day. Not Lotus, just Co-op brand, but it was *piña,* and it was sweet and yellow. And she was letting the clock slip away from her into a world of morning and afternoon and night, instead of "five-forty-one and twenty seconds—beep."

There were things she noticed about herself, the Puertoricanness of which she had kept hidden all these years, but which had persisted as habits, as idiosyncracies of her nature. The way she left a pot of food on the stove all day, eating out of it whenever hunger struck her, liking to have something ready. The way she had lacked food to offer Elena in the old days and had stamped on the desire to do so because it was Puerto Rican: *Come, mija . . . ¿quieres café?* The way she was embarrassed and irritated by Ana's unannounced visits, just dropping by, keeping the country habits after a generation of city life. So unlike the cluttered datebooks of all her friends, making appointments to speak to each other on the phone days in advance. Now she yearned for that clocklessness, for the perpetual food pots of her childhood. Even in the poorest houses a plate of white rice and brown beans with calabaza or green bananas and oil.

She had told Sally that Puerto Ricans lived as if they were all in a small town still, a small town of six million spread out over tens of thousands of square miles, and that the small town that was her country needed to include Manila Avenue in Oakland now, because she was moving back into it. She would not fight the waking early anymore, or the eating all day, or the desire to let time slip between her fingers and allow her work to shape it. Work, eating, sleep, lovemaking, play—to let them shape the day instead of letting the day shape them. Since she could not right now, in the endless bartering of a woman with two countries, bring herself to trade in one-half of her heart for the other, exchange this loneliness for another perhaps harsher one, she would live as a Puerto Rican lives *en la isla* right here in north Oakland, plant the *bananales* and *cafetales* of her heart around her bedroom door, sleep under the shadow of their bloom and the carving hoarseness of the roosters, wake to blue-rimmed white enamel cups of *jugo de piña* and plates of *guineo verde,* and heat pots of rice with bits of meat in them on the stove all day.

There was a woman in her who had never had the chance to move through this house the way she wanted to, a woman raised to be like those women of her childhood, hardworking and humorous and clear. That woman was yawning up out of sleep and into this cluttered daily routine of a northern California writer living at the edges of Berkeley. She was taking over, putting doilies on the word processor, not bothering to make appointments, talking to the neighbors, riding miles on the bus to buy *bacalao,* making her presence felt . . . and she was all Puerto Rican, every bit of her.

Immigrants

For years after we left Puerto Rico for the last time, I would wake from a dream of something unbearably precious melting away from my memory as I struggled desperately to hold on, or at least to remember that I had forgotten. I am an immigrant, and I forget to feel what it means to have left. What it means to have arrived.

There was hail the day we got to Chicago, and we joked that the city was hailing our arrival. The brown brick buildings simmered in the smelly summer, clenched tight all winter against the cold and the sooty sky. It was a place without silence or darkness, huddled against a lake full of dying fish whose corpses floated against the slime-covered rocks of the south shore.

Chicago is the place where the slack ended. Suddenly there was no give. In Indiera there was the farm: the flamboyan tree, the pine woods, the rain-forest hillsides covered with *alegría,* the wild joyweed that in English is called impatiens. On the farm there were hideouts, groves of bamboo with the tiny brown hairs that stuck in your skin if you weren't careful. Beds of sweet-smelling fern, drowsy making under the sun's heat, where the new leaves uncurled from fiddleheads and tendrils climbed and tangled in a spongy mass six feet deep. There were still hillsides, out of range of the house, where I could watch lizards hunt and reinitas court, and stalk the wild cuckoos, trying to get up close. There were mysteries and consolations. There was space.

Chicago was a wasteland. Nowhere to walk that was safe. Killers and rapists everywhere. Police sirens. Ugly, angry looks. Bristling hostility. Worst of all, nowhere to walk. Nowhere to go if it was early morning and I had to get out. Nowhere to go in the late afternoon or in the gathering dusk that meant fireflies and moths at home. Nowhere to watch animal life waking into a new day. The animal life was rats and dogs, and they were always awake because it never got dark here: always that sickly purple and orange glow they call sky in this place. No forest to run wild in. Only the lot across Fifty-fifth Street with huge piles of barren earth, outlines of old cellars, and a few besieged trees in a scraggly row. I named one of them Ceres, after the goddess of earth and plenty who appeared in my high school production of *The Tempest:* bounteous Ceres, queen of the wasteland. There were no hills to race down, tumbling into heaps of fern, to slide down, on a slippery banana leaf: no place to get muddy. Chicago had grime, but no mud. Slush, but no slippery places of the heart, no genuine moistness. Only damp alleyways, dank brick, and two little humps in the middle of Fifty-fifth Street over which grass had been made to grow. But no real sliding. No slack.

There are generations of this desolation behind me, desolation, excitement, grief, and longing all mixed in with the dirty air, the noise, seasickness, and the strangeness of wearing a winter coat.

My grandmother Lola was nineteen the day she married my grandfather and sailed away to Nueva York in 1929. She had loved someone else, but his family disapproved and he obeyed their orders to leave for the States. So her family married her to a son of a neighboring family because the family store was doing poorly and they could no longer support so many children. Two months after her first love left, she found herself married and on the boat. She says: "I was a good Catholic girl. I thought it was my duty to marry him, that it was for the good of my family." I have pictures of her, her vibrant beauty wrapped up but not smothered in the winter coats and scarves. In my grandfather's violent possessiveness and jealousy. She is standing in Central Park with her daughters, or with her arms around a friend or cousin. Loving the excitement. Loving the neighbors and the hubbub. In spite of racist landlords. In spite of the girdle factory. In spite of Manolin's temper and the poverty and hunger. Now, retired to Manolin's dream of a little house in Puerto Rico with a yard and many plants to tend, she longs for New York or some other U.S. city where a woman can go out and about on her own, live among many voices speaking different languages, out of the stifling air of that house, that community, that family.

My mother, the child in that Central Park photo, grew up an immigrant child among immigrants. She went to school speaking not a word of English, a small Puerto Rican girl scared out of her wits, and learned fast: learned accentless

English in record time, the sweet cadence of her mother's open-voweled words ironed out of her vocabulary, the edges flattened down, made crisp, the curls and flourishes removed. First generation.

The strangeness. The way time worked differently. The way being on time mattered. Four second bells. Four minutes of passing time between classes. A note from home if you were ten minutes late, which you took to the office and traded for a late pass. In Indiera the classroom emptied during coffee season, and they didn't bother to send the inspector up unless we were out for longer than four or five weeks. No one had a clock with a second hand. We had half days of school because there were only four rooms for six grades. Our room was next to the bakery, and the smell of the warm *pan de agua* filled our lungs and stomachs and mouths. Things happened when they were ready, or "*cuando Dios quiere.*" The *público* to town, don Paco's bread, the coffee ripening, the rain coming, growing up.

The stiffness. The way clothing mattered with an entirely different kind of intensity. In Indiera, I wore the same wine-colored jumper to school each day with the same white blouse, and only details of the buttons or the quality of the cloth or the presence or absence of earrings, only the shoes gave information about the homes we left at dawn each day, and I was grateful to be able to hide my relative wealth. In Chicago, there were rituals I had never heard of. Knee socks and plaid skirts and sweaters matching each other according to a secret code I didn't understand. Going steady and wearing name tags. First date, second date, third date, score. The right songs to be listening to. The right dances. The coolness.

In the middle of coolness, of stiffness, of strangeness, my joyful rushing up to say, "I come from Puerto Rico, a nest of beauty on the top of a mountain range." Singing "beauty, beauty, beauty." Trying to get them to see in their minds' eyes the perfected edge of a banana leaf against a tropical blue sky, just wanting to speak of what I longed for. Seeing embarrassed faces turning away, getting the jeering voices, singing "Puerto Rico, my hearts devotion . . . let it sink into the ocean!" Learning fast not to talk about it, learning excruciatingly slowly how to dress, how to act, what to say, where to hide. The exuberance, the country-born freshness going quietly stale. Made flat. Made palatable. Made unthreatening. Not different, really. Merely "exotic."

I can remember the feelings, but I forget to give them names. In high school we read novels about immigrant families. In college we discussed the problems of other first generations, talked about displacement, talked about families confused and divided, pride and shame. I never once remembered that I was an immigrant, or that both my parents are the first U.S.-born generations of their families.

Kitchens

I went into the kitchen just now to stir the black beans and rice, the shiny black beans floating over the smooth brown grains of rice and the zucchini turning black, too, in the ink of the beans. Mine is a California kitchen, full of fresh vegetables and whole grains, bottled spring water and yogurt in plastic pints, but when I lift the lid from that big black pot, my kitchen fills with the hands of women who came before me, washing rice, washing beans, picking through them so deftly, so swiftly, that I could never see what the defects were in the beans they threw quickly over one shoulder out the window. Some instinct of the fingertips after years of sorting to feel the rottenness of the bean with a worm in it or a chewed-out side. Standing here, I see the smooth red and brown and white and speckled beans sliding through their fingers into bowls of water, the gentle clicking rush of them being poured into the pot, hear the hiss of escaping steam, smell the bean scum floating on the surface under the lid. I see grains of rice settling in a basin on the counter, turning the water milky with rice polish and the talc they use to make the grains so smooth; fingers dipping, swimming through the murky white water, feeling for the grain with the blackened tip, the brown stain.

From the corner of my eye, I see the knife blade flashing, reducing mounds of onions, garlic, cilantro, and green peppers into *sofrito* to be fried up and stored, and best of all is the pound and circular grind of the *pilón: pound, pound, thump, grind, pound, pound, thump, grind. Pound, pound* (the garlic and oregano mashed together), THUMP! (the mortar lifted and slammed down to loosen the crushed herbs and spices from the wooden bowl), *grind* (the slow rotation of the pestle smashing the oozing mash around and around, blending the juices, the green stain of cilantro and oregano, the sticky yellowing garlic, the grit of black pepper).

It's the dance of the *cocinera:* to step outside
fetch the bucket of water, turn,
all muscular grace and striving,
pour the water, light dancing in the pot,
and set the pail down on the blackened wood.
The blue flame glitters in its dark corner,
and coffee steams in the small white pan.
Gnarled fingers, *mondando ajo,*
picando cebolla, cortando pan,
colando café,
stirring the rice with a big long spoon
filling ten bellies
out of one soot-black pot.

It's a magic, a power, a ritual of love and work that rises up in my kitchen, thousands of miles from those women in cotton dresses who twenty years ago taught the rules of its observance to me, the apprentice, the novice, the girl child: "Don't go out without wrapping your head, child, you've been roasting coffee, *y te va' a pa'mar!*" "This much coffee in the *colador,* girl, or you'll be serving brown water." "Dip the basin in the river, so, to leave the mud behind." "Always peel the green bananas under cold water, *mijita,* or you'll cut your fingers and get *mancha* on yourself and the stain never comes out: that black sap stain of *guineo verde* and *plátano,* the stain that marks you forever."

So I peel my bananas under running water from the faucet, but the stain won't come out, and the subtle earthy green smell of that sap follows me, down from the mountains, into the cities, to places where banana groves are like a green dream, unimaginable by daylight: Chicago, New Hampshire, Oakland. So I travel miles on the bus to the immigrant markets of other people, coming home laden with bundles, and even, now and then, on the plastic frilled tables of the supermarket, I find a small curved green bunch to rush home, quick, before it ripens, to peel and boil, bathing in the scent of its cooking, bringing the river to flow through my own kitchen now, the river of my place on earth, the green and musty river of my grandmothers, dripping, trickling, tumbling down from the mountain kitchens of my people.

1930

My grandmother Lola, with her beautiful sagging face and her fine, black and silver hair, sits on the bed weeping as she tells me the story, tears and words spilling slowly. She loves the weeping and telling and the gestures she incorporates, rolling her eyes to heaven, casting them down. But the story is nonetheless true, and I don't move, so as not to break the thread.

The images, once heard, are unforgettable. My *abuelo* walking ninety blocks to look for work, saving the nickel so he could take the trolley home. The janitor's job opening up just in time, *mijita*. There was a group of Puerto Ricans, *tú sabes,* people who all knew each other and looked out for each other, not *familia,* but *parecido,* because, you know, there weren't so many of us in New York then. They said, "Who should get this job?" and someone said, "Manolin, because he has a new baby." So they sent for him and took him down there at night and taught him how to use the vacuum cleaner, one of those big industrial ones, and the next day he got the job. As soon as they paid him, he went straight to the store and bought food. We hadn't eaten in three days. *Imaginate!,* with Sari nursing. She was taking all that milk out and nothing was going in. I was *así* (she holds up her pinkie to show me how thin and laughs), *así*. He brought home a couple of eggs and a little butter. He had to cook them for me because I was too weak to get up, and then he fed them to me because I couldn't even hold the spoon. Sari and I just lay on the bed together. She'd be drinking the milk and I'd be just lying there, too weak to move. And she heaves a deep quavering sigh, absentmindedly scratching the skin of my bare leg.

There is a memory of hunger in me, a hunger from before birth that aches in the hollows of my fingers, my hands, my arms, bones caving in on themselves from hunger, stomach swelling, teeth falling out. My mother is there, too, tiny and dark haired and black eyed, her mouth sucking and sucking.

This is a story I make up from the scraps my mother and grandmother have let fall, a story I tell myself over and over, embroidering it, filling in the missing details of wind and weather and smells, of how my grandfather's hands clutch at the coat against the cold, how he leans forward into the wind like a steamboat; the way my grandmother's face is drawn and thin, the dim light of the bedroom where she lay, and the sharp urgency of my mother's cries; the smell of those eggs cooking and how they felt in Lola's stomach, those first few bites. My mother is the infant in the picture, but this is not my mother's story. It is my story for her, told to myself as I invent the details of her history, the foundations of my own. I lean on my grandmother's bed in the heat and humidity of Bayamon in summer, gathering material.

"I had a brown dress," she says after a moment. "That's all I had to wear. *Sí, mija!* One dress. When I had to wash it, I took it off and wore my slip until it was dry. We called it 'wash and wear.' " She laughs again, that snorting laugh of my grandmother's that I love so much, the one that erupts into the middle of her best dramas. "I'll never forget that brown dress."

And I think of my mother loving brown, the rich, comforting earthy warmth of that color which was the only one her mother wore during the first year of Sari's life: and I think of Lola's closet now, packed to the point of explosion with clothing of brilliant colors mixed wildly, a tropical rainbow of rayon and cotton and polyester blends: knit pants and cotton housedresses and silky negligees and satiny synthetic blouses, never again just one brown dress.

There is this picture: my thin grandmother with her suckling child lying half starved together on a bed in a dark old tenement building. There is also another picture: long limbed and graceful as a young stork, radiant with life, she stands on the roof with neighbors and cousins, her place near the sky. We look at it in silence, then, "I always wanted to sing," she says. "I used to pray that I would wake up able to sing. I always had this crooked little squeaky voice. *Las nenas se burlaban de mí.* But if I could wake up one morning singing, I would die happy."

Let's Begin the Day

The day has just begun, put on your coat.
—CESAR VALLEJO

If I can't be a saint
I'll be a mirror in your room
where you can see yourself.
I'll be a man on the street
giving chrysanthemums to passersby.
Come to me,
for if I can't be a saint
the music will start again
and I'll be suffering badly.
Let me touch you
for I feel blind.
Let me cover your face with kisses
for it is necessary to begin the day
with enthusiasm and the bravado
of the bullfighter.
There is nothing wrong,
just the crazy boredom
which follows us into the night
like a sad creature from the sea.

Prayer to the Child of Prague

My mother prays to the Child
of Prague and the spring days
go by like lonely women
on their way to the cemetery.
These days of philosophers
and swallows looking for a better
life prey on my mind.
And the Child of Prague in his
sweet sleep cannot imagine
bitterness like I can,
though even in the worst saint
one can find comfort.
Being full of fear in a sanitarium,
I too need your solace,
Child, in my bitter castle,
in my rootless abode.
Shelter me from the cynical,
the faithless and arrogant,
all the weeds grown up
around the weak heart.
Give me courage and strength
to bear up and let me believe
for much strife comes
bundled up like an old man
who holds his shoes
in his hands for sale.

Courtship of Darkness

The world dresses like an orphan
as the night falls,
waking up ghosts.
The eyes of darkness
roam the countryside
and animals are becoming devout.
Madness sings in the tune
of an old man
playing a mouth-harp,
and children are weeping
along the side street
to the church.
The wind enters through
the window like memory
fleeing the rocks of desire.
And so the future walks
idly by, despite someone
in the distance playing
the violin as if there were
still hope. I must hurry
with these words
and not be taken unaware.
Death is dragging
through the valley,
and as always
above the roofs
I think I hear
a beautiful woman
moaning childlike.

ABRAHAM RODRIGUEZ, JR.

The Lotto

From *The Boy Without a Flag*

Another sleepless night.

Dalia kept having the same bad dream. She wished she could tell her mother about it, but she couldn't. She sat by the window and bit her lip.

Her mother was always asking her if she'd had any Lotto dreams, especially this week, with the fifty-million-dollar pot in the balance. Dalia would run through her dream bit by bit while her mother whipped some eggs into froth. "You said there were how many men with beards?" she'd ask, deriving a number from inane symbols. Her mother believed in the power of dreams. She believed God was going to disclose to her the winning numbers.

Dalia wasn't so sure about dreams, but now that this horrible dream kept coming back, she couldn't help feeling that God was trying to tell her something. Three times in seven days she'd had the dream. In the dream, she was sitting in a waiting room that looked like a small theater. On a stage facing her were several doctors in white smocks and surgical masks. In front of them was a table on which sat three top hats. The doctors kept reaching into the hats, pulling out babies with resounding pops. The babies were handed to nurses who waited nearby and wore elbow-high surgical gloves. Dalia always began to cry with horror and to scream for Ricky, but he was nowhere to be found. This last time she was whimpering like a puppy when she woke up. She sat by the window, listless breezes caressing her. Definitely one dream she couldn't tell her mother about.

The street below was alive with activity even though it was three-thirty in the morning. Dealers leaned into double-parked cars. A young girl with a scarred face swung her ass at passing cars, her silver shorts sparkling as headlights swept past. Next to her was a guy in ratty jeans that Dalia recognized. He was a quiet kid with a cratered face named Careta, which is Spanish for "funny face." He was the first person she had seen since Ricky vanished five days ago who might know where he was.

Dalia quickly slipped on some clothes. She scooped her keys off the dresser and slipped out on sneakered tippytoes, creeping quietly past her parents' room, her father's snoring coming through the shut door. She didn't want to think of what would happen if they discovered her sneaking out like that. She thought instead of the glistening baby bodies coming out of top hats. That made her walk faster. She came right up to Careta and put it to him, but Careta was evasive. He hardly looked her in the eyes and made cigarette smoke clouds that swirled around her like fog. (Dalia hated cigarettes.) He was a kid of few words, but he managed to get irritated enough to spit out a torrent of them before he jetted. "Lookit," he said, finally nailing her with his cave-dweller eyes, "I don't know where he is. I know he's hidin, thass all. You shunt ax why. He's juss involved in some shit, thass all. He bit off more than he could chew." The words seemed to be aimed right at her, like torpedoes.

She thought of the last time she had seen Ricky, five days ago. It was just after the first time she had the dream. They were both standing in the building stairwell after a disastrous date where she wouldn't let him touch nothin. She told him about the dream. When he didn't get the message, she told him more, about throwing up and being weak-kneed and dizzy and scared. His answer was to light a cigarette. He never did that in front of her because he knew she hated it. She wouldn't kiss him, and he'd have to suck on breath mints. Now he was puffing away and the smoke screen engulfed her.

"When you gonna know bout this shit f' sure?" he asked petulantly.

"I don't know."

"You don't know? Wha kinda shit is that? A girl's suppose t' take care a' this shit, man. You blew it big time, you stupid . . ."

"It's not all my fault," she said, hating the way her voice quivered. "I din't do it alone." She stared at his contorted face, disgusting smoke pouring out of his mouth. She hated him, hated that she had made love to him. She shoulda neva opened her legs for him! She fought off the tears. She didn't want him to think she was crying for him, she was just angry with herself for letting such a bastid fuck her. The tears started coming out just as a whole family came trooping down the stairs. Plump chattering adults clacked past, children in thumping sneakers bringing up the rear. They all turned to look as they passed.

"Come on, man! Don't cry, you embarrassin me," Ricky whispered angrily. He leaned on the far wall as if he didn't know her. He waited for all the noise to die down, for the vestibule door to screech shut. Then he said, "I gotta go." He dutifully kissed her, then briskly hopped down the stairs with quick clumpings. And that was the last time she had seen him.

As she sneaked back upstairs into her dark room, she thought of how much time she had spent trying to decide if she was going to fuck him or not.

"I say go for it," Elba had said to her in "their" pizzeria on Wales Avenue. Elba, a short, curvy girl with dark, curly hair tumbling down to her shoulders, was in Dalia's homeroom. This past semester they had become close friends, holding unofficial races to see who would get a boyfriend first. Dalia lost, but when she caught up they began exchanging notes and observations. Elba's first boy was a thin basketball player named Jose, while Dalia smooched with a pudgy jock named David. They soon grew bored and moved on, always comparing like shoppers. Elba always got more boyfriends, but that was because she was a loudmouth and wore tight blue slacks that showed off her sweet ass like the taut skin on a plum. She talked real loud, catty and chatty, and if you din't like it, fuck you, she'd say, eyes flashing a challenge. Dalia was meek. Maybe she braided her shiny hair and wore skirts with the panty hose that had designs on the thighs, but she wasn't catty or chatty. Her prettiness was more of a private affair, something you'd spot in the way she smiled or the way she put her face close to the paper whenever she wrote anything, her hair cascading gently. She was pickier than Elba. This was because she read a lot of romance books. The young toughs who tamed their streetwalk around her and bought her slices of pizza before locking her in a half nelson in the balcony at the Prospect didn't stand much of a chance, which was why Ricky was such a problem. She wondered if maybe she had done it with him because of Elba's decision one night to up the ante in their contest by having sex. She had, by this time, been seeing the same guy for close to a year, on and off.

"But do you love the guy?" Dalia had asked as they sat at a greasy table in the pizzeria, a nearby video game whirring and beeping.

"I don't know," Elba said, munching thoughtfully on her slice. "It's nah tha easy to tell an shit."

"But you should know, shouldn't you?"

Elba shrugged. "I been wif the guy long enough, girl. I know I'm crazy about him. But he's gettin antsy."

"Antsy?"

"Yeah, you know." Her eyes flashed. "Yesterday I caught him inna hall outside Mr. Baumann's class. His hands were holdin Teresa Del Rio." Dalia frowned. Teresa was the junior-high tramp. She got up to yawn one day in math class, stretching her catlike body, rubbing her ass against the desk behind her. "I love sex," she said, "can't get enough." Every boy in class heard it. The scores for the surprise quiz on polynomials that morning were abysmal. "If I don't do it, he'll go somewhere else," Elba said with a mouthful of pizza. One of her long curls fell into the slice as if tasting it.

"But that's no reason to do it, is it?" Dalia waited for an answer, wide-eyed, but Elba only munched and grinned and shook hair off a shoulder. The video game buzzed and beeped, the young guy in front of the screen swerving, his hand banging into buttons. "He that important to you? You get boyfriends all the time. When you fight with him, you go on the prowl. Why does he matter so much now?"

Elba shrugged. She was biting into her slice and suddenly froze, a dazed look on her face. "I don't know," she said.

"What if you get pregnant?"

The video game let out a series of loud explosions. "Damn!" the young guy yelled, slamming his palm against the dashboard of his dead star cruiser. There was a funeral march.

Elba scowled. "I won't get pregnant. You see too much 'General Hospital.' "

Elba didn't get pregnant. She had sex and liked it and had more sex and began liking it more and more. She urged Dalia to find someone to do it with. Was that why she had done it with Ricky? This question kept popping up. It was like indigestion. Dalia didn't want to admit to herself that maybe she did it so she wouldn't lose Elba, who was now walking on a higher plane. All she talked about was fucking. She hung out with other girls now too, even Teresa Del Rio. It seemed like some exclusive club, this womanhood deal. Dalia felt left out, the younger sibling tagging along with the bigger girls.

So maybe that's why she had chosen Ricky. So what? She knew him from seeing him hanging out on Prospect Avenue with his goon pals. There they were, shattering the glass on a bus stand, their peals of laughter echoing down Southern Boulevard. There they came, running past her window, chasing a skinny Mexican kid from the fifth floor who had his paycheck punctually stolen every Friday. Ricky always smiled at her. He winked. He had a mustache, but it was baby fuzz. They began exchanging words. He had a childlike way of pointing with his chin, eyes twinkling luminously. Whenever he popped up in front of her on the street, she'd get a nervous look in her eyes. She'd look down as if trying to hide her smile behind her shoulder.

One day she was in the pharmacy taking in her mother's Lotto forms when he crept up behind her and gave her a huge red lollipop. He offered to take her to the movies. "Which one?" she asked, not looking at him. He leaned against the counter and didn't look at her either. "Somethin romantic. Maybe *Rambo III*." Dalia told her mother she was going to Elba's house, even though she hadn't seen Elba for two weeks. Elba was too busy with her steady boyfriend and the world of sex to be much excited by one of Dalia's schoolgirl status reports.

Ricky met her on the stoop wearing a clean big shirt and gray chinos. Even his wild bushy hair was combed neatly. A batch of his friends watched them from their spot by the bodega, faces solemn. "For you," he said, handing her a new pack of Starbursts. She remembered seeing parts of *Rambo III* in between all the kissing and pressing, the taste of lipstick and popcorn. On the way back, her legs felt weak and springy, her eyes dreamy and stoned. Despite the petting, Ricky was pretty respectful. His hands roamed but stayed in all the roaming places, and this made her like him even more. It took two weeks before she got into bed with him. By that time, she had already spoken to Elba about it. They had one of their special meetings, slices of pizza steaming on their table.

"Go for it," Elba said nonchalantly. "It's no big deal once you get used to it." She was examining her long red nails. "You scared?"

"No," Dalia lied. She laughed and Elba gripped her hands. Elba seemed like an older sister now. She wore makeup and cut her hair some and took to wearing more skirts with glittering panty hose and pumps. Her eyes looked kind of chinky from the eyeliner. "Go for it," she said. "Lemme know wha happens."

Ricky took her to some guy's house, a crack dealer who worked nights. His tiny crib was on Jackson Avenue, overlooking the el. The sun was still out when Ricky first got a look at her frilly see-through panties, which she had bought with Elba at Alexander's on Third Avenue. Ricky was real gentle. He hadn't smoked all day, so his kisses tasted like cherry Chapstick. He cradled her like a little girl and stopped when it hurt. They stopped and started all night without even eating, and it felt better and better. Just before midnight he was still fucking her, and the clattering trains that passed filled the dark room with flickering strobe lights.

"Ma?" she said into the phone, trying to pull Ricky's mouth away from one of her nipples. "Yeah, I know. Elba's ma says I could maybe stay over tonight? It got later than I planned."

"Did you drop off the Lotto forms for me?"

"Yes."

"Don't lose the stubs. The drawing is tomorrow."

The next night, she felt sick. She didn't know if it was guilt over all that fucking, or whether it was just nerves because she had read about morning sickness and she had had that, puking up quietly in the bathroom with the door shut and the tap water running. She looked at her mother's wrinkled face and wondered if God would snitch on her.

"I had a dream last night," she could hear her mother saying with a grim face. "I had a dream you did something very bad, and maybe now you're sick." She sat on the couch beside her father, who was reading *El Diario* while the TV blared; it was the start of the World Series. Dalia's mother, in the kitchen washing dishes, occasionally stepped over into the living room, gripping a dripping pan. "Don't forget, the drawing," she'd say every ten minutes. Her father, paragon of patience, kept quiet, but finally he yelled, "Cut it out already. I can't stand you going on about this shit." He had a stern rock-hard face. Like a president's face on Mount Rushmore.

"Watch the way you talk!" she yelled from the doorway. "You want God to punish us for your lack of faith?" He looked up from his paper. She came closer, pointing a dripping pan at him. "God punishes us every time you let loose with that mouth of yours. Remember last week? Two numbers short! If only you'd believe a little."

"I can't believe," he yelled, tossing down the paper, "that I sit behind a little window eight hours a day and sell people stamps so you can spend ten bucks a week on the fucking Lotto." He glared at Dalia, who felt like puking. "I hope you're not getting like your mother. I hear you every morning, telling her your Lotto dreams. Does God send you secrets in your dreams, too, or what?" He shook Dalia's arm. "You getting as cracked as Rosa here?"

"Camilo!" Dalia's mother screamed. She had gone back to the kitchen during his harangue but now returned. "It's time! The drawing!" She ran over to the TV, drying her hands on her apron frantically.

"I'm scared," Dalia told Elba a week later. They were sitting in a children's park across the street from their school. She told Elba about being sick and scared and about the way Ricky was losing his interest in her, and it was good in a way because he was a stupid dipshit, and she shoulda neva done it with him, but it was bad because she had and now she was like this.

Elba leaned back against the bench and stared up at the murky sky. "Oh boy," she said, her hands buried in her jacket pockets.

"You think I did a 'General Hospital'?" Dalia asked softly. They both watched a trio of boys jump up on a slide, toppling down its silvery smoothness one right after the other.

Elba sighed, pursing her lips as if she were sucking on a lemon. "You better tell this jerk real quick," she said quietly.

The morning Dalia met Ricky to tell him, she had the dream. She figured it was just nerves. She had called his house several times to leave messages. That was the only way to get him. He was never there. Somehow he always got the messages, always called back. But what if he didn't want to? When he got back to her, they set up a date, but it was more like a pretend date. They had pizza and walked around and even did some necking, but he tasted like Winstons, and she was too nervous to get into it. They ended up in the stairwell. After he vanished, the dream came back. She kept seeing the slick, quivering baby bodies and kept hearing Rosa's voice: "Whenever God wants to tell you something, he'll put it in a dream, and if you don't get the hint, he'll make it come back again and again. So let me know if you have any dreams like that, because it could be God trying to give us Lotto numbers."

After Careta failed her, Dalia lay in bed staring at the ceiling until dawn came. "I've got to see Elba," she thought. She hadn't seen her since Ricky went poof. "She'll know what to do."

She slept late, got up at one with her eyes feeling like prunes. When she walked into the kitchen, she found her mother sitting at the kitchen table with her magic box. It was a wooden box with carved angels on it and rusty latch that Rosa had found in the mountains of Jayuya when she was twelve. It was a lucky box, filled with a lifetime of lucky trinkets, a rabbit's foot and a rooster claw that burned evil spirits and a pair of dice her brother Martino had won four thousand dollars with in Korea. She had a batch of Lotto tickets in there. This was because whenever she felt uncertain about something, she'd stick it in the box with the lucky things. Dalia remembered that Rosa had done it once with an electric bill Camilo had been worried about. She had put it in the box the minute Dalia brought it in. The next morning, after Camilo had left for work, she brought the box over and took the envelope out of it and told Dalia to open it. Inside Dalia found a notice informing them that because of a computer error they had overpaid their last bill and now had credit.

"You see?" Rosa had said, petting her hand. "You must have faith! Too bad your father isn't here to see this!"

Dalia sat down beside her, rubbing her eyes while Rosa fiddled with her Lotto forms. "You look tired," she said. She held up two of the forms. "Any Lotto dreams?"

Dalia bit her lower lip. "Nah. Nothing." She blushed. She felt as if her mother would be able to sense God was sending her signals of some kind, but her mother just handed her a pair of forms.

"I had one the other night," Rosa whispered. "I've never had such an intense dream. Migdalia, it's going to happen! Fifty million dollars!" Dalia smiled, chin in hand, Lotto forms blurring in front of her. "Let me tell you about this dream. I'm standing by this huge scaffold with all these people from my town, even dead ones, like Nydia Fernandez, who was hit by a cement mixer. Anyway, we're standing around, and these soldiers appear, bringing with them this bearded man. It dawns on all of us that he is being put to death! So, as the noose is going around his neck, he stoops over to where I am and says, 'Look, this is the only time I'll get to tell you, so listen well: sixteen, two, four, seventeen . . .' And then there was this other dream where I'm on the street playing marbles, only I'm fully grown, and—"

"Ma, I gotta make a call," Dalia cut in, not wanting to stay for the punch line.

"What I want to ask you is can you take these Lotto forms over to the pharmacy today?" Her mother's eyes gleamed. She was holding up the Lotto forms as if they were train tickets.

"Sure. No problem." Dalia gave her a kiss on the head, declining offers of food. Her stomach was still rumbling, her head dizzy. She phoned Elba's, but only got her mother, who said Elba had left the house looking grim. Dalia left a message and got dressed. She started thinking of how her parents would take the news that she was about to have the baby of a street punk. Her father would get angry and yell, her mother would cry and ask God why. She hated the feeling in her head, the weakness in her limbs. She could almost feel something growing inside of her, like a plum pit stuck in her throat. She called Ricky's. He wasn't there. "Do you know when he'll be back?" she asked in her jittery Spanish. "No *tengo* idea," the terse wheezing voice replied. The line went dead.

She left the stuffy apartment with the Lotto cards in her hand. She wandered up Southern Boulevard, looking into pizzerias and bodegas where she knew Ricky sometimes hung out. She stopped by a laundromat on Avenue St. John where she had caught him many times rapping to girls. She crossed through an empty lot and went down Prospect all the way to the el station because she knew sometimes Ricky and posse terrorized passengers coming off trains by swinging sticks at them and shoving them down stairs. Nothing. Not a single face tied to Ricky. He had disappeared and taken all his friends with him.

She came back down Prospect, up 149th Street. She was heading for the pizzeria on Wales, where she and Elba always had their chats. She was just reaching it when she saw Elba in a black skirt and large jacket, hair tumbling down onto her shoulders in dark round coils. She seemed distraught, almost shivering as she stood outside the pizzeria, arms folded across her chest. Dalia's heart began to pump loudly in her ears. She raced across the street. The minute Elba spotted her, she let out a tiny yell. "Damn, I was thinkin boutchu right now," she said. "Thass weird."

"What are you doing here?"

"I don't know. How'd it go wif yuh boyfriend?"

Dalia's face darkened. "Ever since I told him, he's been gone. Even his friends." She shrugged. "Five days ago."

"Didju find out if yuh—"

"Don't even say it."

"Butchu don't even know?"

"I don't think I wanna."

Elba grabbed her by the arm and steered her into the warm pizzeria. "Come on. Pizza time."

Dalia sat down by the warbling, humming video game while Elba ordered some slices. She thought that Elba looked a little funny around the eyes, like maybe she hadn't been sleeping. As Elba sat down, she also noticed that the polish on her nails was chipped, something very un-Elba-like. "Look," Elba said commandingly, "we can't fuck around. This is real serious shit, okay? I love you an everythin, but you can't sit around. You gotta take a test."

Dalia sighed. "Planned Parenthood?"

Elba's face seemed to shrink for a fraction of a second. "Nah," she said, playing with her straw wrapper. "You ain't got time. You gotta get a quick test. One of those instant things, like in the pharmacy. I shoulda done that. Shit." She looked away disgustedly.

"You?" Dalia's eyes widened.

"Come on, try the fucken slice. Paid money for it, you know." She bit down on the crust with a crunch. Elba always started with the crust.

Dalia stared at her slice and felt as if she were falling into that greasy sea of sauce and cheese. She couldn't. "Tell me what's going on, Elba."

Elba grinned tiredly, her eyes evasive. She suddenly gripped Dalia's hand, then took another bite of the crust. She wasn't looking at Dalia at all. "I got an appointment," she said.

"Really?" There was fear and admiration in Dalia's voice. It made Elba look at her for a moment, but not for too long, because she was in that fragile place where any small thing might bring tears. Her eyes were sore from that stuff already. She inhaled deeply. "Yeah. Today at three. I've rescheduled twice. I keep chickenin out, but I got to go. I was standin outside, thinkin maybe I wanted t' call you, an there you are." Something in her voice broke. Her eyes got watery. She tried not looking at Dalia, but Dalia got up and sat beside her and pulled her closer, and that did it. Elba began to sob convulsively. It only lasted a moment, because of the pizza guy twirling his dough, and the two guys by the window chomping on slices, and that counterboy in the red-striped shirt munching gum and staring. In no time, she was wiping her face and shaking her head and half-laughing. She caught the sparkle in Dalia's eyes for a moment, but Dalia quickly applied the pizza napkin. "You want I should come with you?"

Elba patted her hand. "Nah. Betta if I go alone, I think. But maybe I drop by yuh house later?"

"Yeah, you better."

"An you girl, we gonna getchu a test. We do it now, while I'm around. We'll go to the pharmacy an buy it. Butchu gotta take it tonight. When I go ova t' yuh house, if you din't take it, I won't tell you about my . . . news."

Dalia sighed. "Okay. You got a deal." They shook on it. They both walked to the pharmacy, feeling a little quiet. When they got to the corner of Southern Boulevard and 149th, they saw the Lotto line stretching from the pharmacy entrance to the supermarket doorway three stores down. Dalia got right in line while Elba went in to buy the test for Dalia. This was because Dalia was known by a lot of people in the store, and if they saw her buying that, they'd talk, and the talk might get to her mother. Elba didn't have that problem. She bought the test and came right back. "No sweat," she said, handing her the package. "This one takes thirty minutes." She was going to take it out of the bag for Dalia to show her, but Dalia yanked it away.

"Damn man," Elba said, laughing, "it's not like you got leprosy an shit."

After that little laugh, Elba got kind of grim because her appointment was coming up. Dalia gave her a hug and reminded her to come by the house. Elba rolled her fingers under Dalia's chin as if tickling her. "See ya wif the verdick." Dalia watched Elba walk off down the street, getting smaller and smaller until the traffic seemed to swallow her up. She stood in that line for close to forty minutes, behind a fat man who kept blowing his nose with pink tissues that he dropped on the sidewalk. Rosa was waiting for her when she got home. She took the ticket stubs and tucked them right into her box. She made a funny face and crossed her fingers. "Tonight's the night," she said.

Dalia went into her room. She took the package out of her jacket pocket and stuck it deep inside a drawer, as if she planned never to see it again. She knew she had made a deal with Elba and all, but she was thinking that maybe she could take the test when Elba arrived. After all, it took only thirty minutes! She changed into her bummy clothes and went into the kitchen to help her mother prepare dinner. Camilo worked until noon on Saturdays, but then came the weekly domino tournament outside Pellin's bodega on Southern Boulevard, he and three others sitting on crates, downing beers, playing for money. It was an outdoor event that sometimes moved to the back room when it was chilly.

By the time he tramped in wearing his weary face, Dalia had already taken the test. She had done it in the bathroom because she was sick of the babies coming out of hats while she was peeling potatoes and chopping onions. She hid the little vial behind a pair of old paint cans under the basin.

"I tell you," Camilo said, searching in the refrigerator for a beer, "we better win that fucking Lotto tonight because I didn't have a good night at dominoes."

Rosa frowned. "I don't believe you! How could you? Tonight being so special."

"Special? Get out of here with that. There's a drawing every damn Saturday."

"Not for fifty million dollars! And you, gambling!"

"What the hell you think a Lotto is, a religious event? The damn World Series is on."

"Camilo, put the drawing on," Rosa said urgently. "Put it on now, before the game, please! I don't want to miss it. We can't." Camilo popped his beer open and took a sip and went into the living room.

"I live in a nuthouse," he muttered, flipping on the TV.

Rosa hurried into the kitchen to retrieve her magic box, which was on the refrigerator and had the stubs inside.

"You'll miss the Lotto, honey," Rosa said urgently to Dalia, who was turning the rice.

Her stomach was churning. She knew that her test results were waiting. The verdict was already in. She stood by the doorway to the kitchen, watching as her parents sat in front of the TV, the blazing screen bouncing light off the walls. Rosa was holding all her ticket stubs in her hand.

"Give me the tickets." Camilo made a grab for them.

"No. I'll hold them. Camilo!"

"Get a paper! Write the numbers down!" he screamed. The two of them fumbled over each other as Dalia stood behind them, her senses twitching. Her hands involuntarily grasped her tummy where all the trouble was.

On the screen was a blond woman, pale features stark against the orange and blue background. In front of her was a huge machine resembling a corn popper. Inside hopped and spun dozens of white golf balls, each printed with a number. When the woman pressed a button, a ball would be sucked up a thin tube, appearing atop a kind of funnel.

"And the first number is three," she said.

"*Ay Cristo,*" Rosa moaned, waving one of the many tickets she was holding. Camilo was trying to snatch it. "*Carajo,* I don't believe it," he said loudly.

"Shut up with the cursing!" Rosa screamed, punching him. "You'll blow it for all of us!"

"The next number is sixteen." The camera zoomed in on the ball.

"Goddamn," Camilo said, shaking the ticket. He was hopping up and down, inching closer to the screen. He shot Dalia an amazed look.

"Seven, the next number is seven."

Camilo turned up the volume on the set. The cheesy Lotto electronic music boomed through the room. It was like a video game theme.

"*Ay Dios, ay Dios* . . ." Rosa was chanting, her nails digging deep into Camilo's wrist.

"I'll never laugh at your dreams again," he vowed in a deep voice, "if only . . . oh Jesus . . ."

Dalia backed away from it. She ran into the bathroom. The cheesy Lotto music was still playing. She shut the door hard and turned on the tap water full blast, until she couldn't hear anything but the roar of the water and her heart hammering away in her head. She knelt down under the basin, her hand searching for the vial. Her fingers closed in on its smoothness. Her heart seemed to jump for just a second. The room filled up with steam. She held the vial up to the light. Short gasps escaped her. She stared and stared at it from all sides, her hands trembling. Then she climbed up on the toilet and forced the tiny window open, her eyes clouding with tears. Gusts of cold air struck her face like hard slaps. She checked the vial one last time, then threw it as hard as she could. She shut the window and turned off the water and watched it glisten in the tub. She pulled open the door, cool air sweeping over her as she stepped out of the humidity and into the living room. It was almost as if she were coming out of some dream.

A massive cheer greeted her. It filled the whole room. A stadium of people were standing on their feet, stomping and screaming, players rounding the bases. On the couch sat Camilo, face drawn, staring at the game vacantly. A beer sweated in one hand. The torn scraps of the Lotto tickets lay scattered all over the couch beside him. He turned to look at Dalia and noticed her face was all wet.

"Ah shit, not you too. I'm stuck with a pair of loonies. You and your stupid dreams," he said resentfully. The words made her start gasping for breath again, her chest racked with sobs.

Rosa appeared at the door, her face also red. She came over to Dalia and hugged her. "It's okay, it's okay," she said in English. "God still cares." At the sound of those words Dalia exploded, tears of relief and gratitude overwhelming her. She was laughing and crying at the same time, so that Rosa pulled back to look at her.

"It was so close," Dalia said, but she looked relieved.

"Next time it's the real thing," her mother said soothingly. "Just have faith." Rosa shot Camilo a look, but he was facing the baseball game as if they didn't exist.

When the door buzzer sounded, Dalia jumped. "I'll get it," she told Rosa, scampering past the kitchen into the hall, where the intercom was.

"Guess who," Elba's voice came over the speaker.

"Come on up. Hurry!" Dalia said, unlocking the door, standing out in the hallway listening to Elba's sneakers thumping up the stairs. In no time, Elba was standing in front of her. She gripped Dalia's arms anxiously. "Well?"

"You tell me first!" Dalia almost screamed.

"Fuck you! I came up here," Elba said angrily. "Now spill it, girl!"

"I'm not, I'm not, I'm not!" Dalia jumped in the air and gave Elba a tight, tight hug that made her let out a kind of squeaking noise. Elba's arms wrapped slowly around her, fingers gripping. "I knew it," she said into her ear. "I knew you wasn't! Din't I tell you not t' worry? I gotta instic' about this shit! I'm happy f' you, runt!"

They embraced, Dalia letting out victorious peals of laughter until she noticed something change in the way Elba was holding her. It was almost as if Elba's arms, having been prepared to carry her, suddenly lost strength and now needed support. Dalia began pulling back, trying to look into Elba's face. Elba avoided it. "Elba," Dalia said, trying to disentangle herself, but Elba gripped her closer. It was about a minute before she loosened her grip. Dalia could hear her sniffing, feel something warm through her shirt.

"Elba," Dalia whispered slowly, "how about you?" She pulled her back and saw it written on Elba's face, which seemed all sunken in. The old Elba might've turned around so Dalia couldn't see. This Elba bit her lip and stared at the floor. "Fuck it," she said, sniffling, her fingers stabbing at the tears quickly. "I don't like school anyway."

"Elba," Dalia whispered softly, tears coming back to her.

Elba looked as if she had just lost fifty million dollars, her lower lip quivering. She covered her eyes with both hands and tried to make her face harden, taking a deep breath. "Nah," she said. "I gotta go."

"Elba, wait," Dalia said desperately. She reached out, but Elba spun away from her.

"I'll call you later," Elba said as she raced down the stairs, her sneakers thumping as if they belonged to a happy little kid on her way to play house.

Bringing Her Back

Tonight you watch your sister undress
in that perfectly white room,
and a memory falls through the air
between you.

Beautiful Ana stepping out
of a blue dress. You were fourteen
and you remember everything.
The way the light fell on her bare shoulders,
the dressing table full of sleep,
the names of the boys she had danced with.

That was years ago, before the last stroke,
before her mind began to go, light
and dark, a constant circling.
She holds the blank mirror up
before the shifting landscape of her face
while you fill in the odd details—
the lake in summer, the white and green
shutters of a Victorian house, the tabby
curled up in the blue chair.

She runs the comb through her hair.
Nothing. The house is wind,
the cat is voicelessness,
pure sleep, an empty place
the color of regret.
It isn't cruelty that changes
the constant shape of things,
reeling our lives in
one moment at a time.

The way our memories choose us,
tie us to nothing we can actually keep.
An old woman unfolds her handkerchief
to lay that whiteness open. *Remember this?*

You say *cat, house, chair*
working the words slowly through themselves
until the smallest glint of recognition
widens in her brown eyes and she says, *yes,*
yes, I remember, the memory falling
around her like a ruined dress,
a gesture as simple as light
touching a window. The ghosts
of hands pulling back the drapes.

Lunes de Revolución

for Tania Díaz Castro, under house arrest

I used to stand with my face to that wall.
Imagine my surprise when certain
words you spoke became doors opening and closing.
I was a child then, I have a child's memories.
I have nothing to say
about it and the wind lifting my coat

                    will lift my coat
and nothing else. Brick by brick the metaphors became a wall
around me until everything you said
landed back in my face. I want to remember certain
things and forget others. Memory
is a fool's hunger. *Swallow this, sister.* I close

my eyes and try to imagine that dream like a mouth closing
around a crust of bread. A fresh coat

of paint over the crumbling house of memory,
the cracked and rotting walls
of the new Revolution, that certain
hunger you said

would save us. I don't know what to say.
In Cuba there are no heroes left and history has moved in too close
for comfort, until certain
days you walk past the writers' union with your coat
wrapped tightly around you and a strange chill in your heart,
        looking for a wall
to lean against. Whatever memories

sustained you then won't save you now. Memory
is the proof that after all is said
and done we live behind our eyes, our vision nailed to a wall
of blood and silence. The truth is closer
than you know. The dream coating
your tongue has a certain

bitterness. But life has no certainty
beyond the pull of memory
or faith. What you know of this place covers your words like a coat
of sorrow until you cannot say
even the names of your closest
friends. History has become a wall

of fear and memory, the thin arms of the past closing
around all the things left unsaid—the chill inside your coat,
the same four walls that surround what can never be certain.

Floating

When you have no brothers
you are more than you are.
You carry your own flashlight.

Every oncoming storm brings another
blackout and a hot wind you can feel
from way down the road.
In the dark every stone is
an animal. You learn to touch
things without knowing the
difference. *A silverfish*
is not a rose, and who wants to know?
For weeks the rain is one long prayer.
Some nights the river runs to
your back door with its cargo
of bottles, cigarette butts, stones.
You know the places you're falling
toward and how to land there,
how in five years your black hair
will float all the way down
your back. The river is old
and deep. The beautiful crimes
of childhood lift you out of
the water, out of your bed all night.
You touch your small breasts
like a benediction. A tender
rain falls over everything you know.
Your grandfather writes elaborate
love letters to the wife of a dead
president. The envelopes drift
out of his shirt pockets when
you think he's asleep, her name
like a cup you drink from in the dark.

Paying Respects

El antiguo camposanto San Fernando.
The final majesty of stones
in all the years and years of stones.
Stones of small children buried
while they ran at play.
Stones of aproned grandmothers resting
under transplanted front-porch ferns.
Near the iron fences, stones of
incontinent old men in khakis
left over from Villa's days.
Near the rosebushes, stones of young lovers
with the right to sleep together at last.
Nearest the sun, stones of mothers
and fathers stilled in their prime.

And the stones of the unknown dead.
The ones I kiss and kiss because their names
and times are so worn away that only
my lips are able to feel them out.
Leal, Ferreyro, Gonzaba.
Araceli, Seferina, Rafael.
They ask what I want of them.
They say this is an encampment of saints
whose beds have long been made,
that I disturb the peace with
my infernal comings and goings,
my talk of choices.
Who gave them a choice?
They have no patience with a woman
only flirting with the living,
only flirting with the dead.

Taking the Air

*For now I no longer recognized it, and I became uneasy, as though I were in a
room in some hotel or furnished lodging, in a place where I had just arrived, by
train, for the first time.*

—MARCEL PROUST

When you walk out of my room
the air stops dead in its tracks,
then begins to dart around
in the spaces you just were,
not knowing what to do with itself.
Finally it sniffs you out
and rushes after you,
pulling all memory with it.
This air that does your bidding is
the same air that makes off with my name,
leaves me gasping
stripped down to my shadow.
It absconds with everything.
The candle I light for my grandmother
at Immaculate Heart of Mary.
My great-aunt Sophia waiting
tables at Bar America.
The seasonal butcher and treasure
hunter at El Paso Meat Market.
My grandfather's café on Produce Row.
La Rosita Grocery, its stock and its
faithful old couple dwindling away.
Our Lady of Guadalupe Church with its
photograph of some mother's
junkie offspring hopelessly pinned
to a bleeding Christ.

My own mother and the hands
I inherited from her.
The air after your going
takes it all. My heart,
my words, my eyes, my past.
How easily you call it to you,
admitting everything without shame.
This is what it means to love you.
This air that keeps the sweetness
from dissolving in any of my cups,
from staying with me.
This air that leaves me nothing
to breathe,
nothing to remember,
nothing to write that is not already yours.
Proust hangs blindfolded on my wall.

Ariadne Seven Years Later

for G.

I suppose I don't have to tell you. You
already know it's my turn. And you must also
know it's been exactly seven years to the day
since you began learning, slowly you said,
the hatred I required of you, my eyes
that would not open, the mazes that would not end,
your fear that I was collecting you, that I rattled
the walls of the labyrinth only when it suited me.
Do you remember saying these things? June 16, 1976.

Yes, it's my turn. The minotaur is gone, the *real*
monster has fled. (You were never that, Theseus, no
matter what I've ever seemed to be telling you.)
The minotaur is gone. My love
has finally and violently tired of too many questions,
too much waiting for me to make
of him the lamb, the man, the *whole,*
the one thing or the other.

And so, he has crushed through the walls in a blind rage.
And the bellowing and howling is terrible. Since even
now, at his moment of breaking free, he cannot
speak, cannot say how I have failed him. Even now
when he gores me deep, decorating his wedding crown
with my blood. Even now when he tries to root out
my heart, that imperfect chalice, and offer it back
to my father in some kind of unholy tribute.
I'm telling you, he can't *speak.*

It has come to this: I have never left my father's
island. A shade followed you to Naxos, gave herself
to Dionysios, wears the garland of stars. I spend most
days lying on the floor of the maze, trying to stanch
the flow of my blood down all its blind alleys. My
only gauze is my one pitiful thread, recalled now
into a hopelessly tangled mess. Sometimes, in the early
mornings, I limp into the palace gardens and cut red
and yellow carnations, some fragrant basil, try to keep
them safe in the still turquoise vase of the sea.

                           Twilights are the worst.
That is when I stand at my father's highest window
watching the water for the tiniest sign of a swimmer,
keeping the tense vigil for the shaggy head coming back
to me. It is at twilight that I have shattered
my entire collection of spyglasses. Their salty
splinters are lodged in my hands, the hands you
always found so beautiful as they reeled out, reeled
in my little string.

                    No, Theseus, I tell you I am dying.
And yet I cannot. As you know perhaps better than

anyone. There are these words that must be spoken.
There are heroes to be remembered, heroines to be recreated.
The bloodletting has to stop. I need to lie on my back
in the sand, the white sun in my mouth, on my breasts.
I need to flap my arms the way children do in the snow
of colder climes. Make a sand angel. Watch her fly.

The Black Virgin

From *Silent Dancing*

In their wedding photograph my parents look like children dressed in adult costumes. And they are. My mother will not be fifteen years old for two weeks; she has borrowed a wedding dress from a relative, a tall young woman recently widowed by the Korean War. For sentimental reasons they have chosen not to alter the gown, and it hangs awkwardly on my mother's thin frame. The tiara is crooked on her thick black curls because she had bumped her head coming out of the car. On her face is a slightly stunned, pouty expression, as if she were considering bursting into tears. At her side stands my father, formal in his high-school graduation suit. He is holding her elbow as the photographer has instructed him to do; he looks myopically straight ahead since he is not wearing his wire-frame glasses. His light brown curls frame his cherubic, well-scrubbed face; his pale, scholarly appearance contrasts with his bride's sultry beauty, dark skin, and sensuous features. Neither one seems particularly interested in the other. They are posing reluctantly. The photograph will be evidence that a real wedding took place. I arrived more than a year later, so it was not a forced wedding. In fact, both families had opposed the marriage for a number of reasons only to discover how adamant children in love can be.

My parents' families represented two completely opposite cultural and philosophical lines of ancestry in my hometown. My maternal relatives, said to have originally immigrated from Italy, were all farmers. My earliest memories are imbued with the smell of dark, moist earth and the image of red coffee beans growing row after row on my great-grandfather's hillside farm. On my father's side there is family myth and decadence. His people had come from Spain bringing tales of wealth and titles, but all I was aware of as a child was that my grandfather had died of alcoholism and meanness a few months before my birth, and that he had forbidden his wife and children ever to mention his family background in his house, under threat of violence.

My father was a quiet, serious man; my mother, earthy and ebullient. Their marriage, like my childhood, was the combining of two worlds, the mixing of two elements—fire and ice. This was sometimes exciting and life-giving and sometimes painful and draining.

Because their early marriage precluded many options for supporting a wife, and because they had a child on the way, Father joined the U.S. Army only a few months after the wedding. He was promptly shipped to Panama, where he was when I was born, and where he stayed for the next two years. I have seen many pictures of myself, a pampered infant and toddler, taken during those months for his benefit. My mother lived with his mother and learned to wait and to smoke. My father's two older brothers were in Korea during the same period of time.

My mother still talks nostalgically of those years when she lived with Mamá Nanda, as her grandchildren called her, since her name, Fernanda, was beyond our ability to pronounce during our early years. Mamá Nanda's divorced daughter, my aunt Felícita, whom I am said to resemble, also lived with us. The three women living alone and receiving Army checks were the envy of every married woman in the pueblo.

My mother had been the fourth child in a family of eight, and had spent most of her young life caring for babies that came one after the other until her mother had exiled her husband from her bed. Mamá Pola had been six months pregnant with her last child at my parents' wedding. My mother had been resentful and embarrassed about her mother's big belly, and this may have had some effect on my grandmother's decision.

Anyway, my mother relished the grown-up atmosphere at her mother-in-law's house, where Mamá Nanda was beginning to experiment with a new sense of personal freedom since her husband's death of alcohol-related causes a couple of years before. Though bound by her own endless rituals of religion and superstition, she had allowed herself a few pleasures. Chief among these was cigarette smoking. For years, the timid wife and over-worked mother had sneaked a smoke behind the house as she worked in her herb garden where she astutely grew mint to chew on before entering the house. Occasionally she would steal a Chesterfield from her husband's coat pocket while he slept in a drunken stupor. Now she bought them by the carton, and one could always detect the familiar little square in her apron pocket. My mother took up the smoking habit enthusiastically. And she, my aunt Felícita, and Mamá Nanda spent many lazy afternoons smoking and talking about life—especially about the travails of having lived with the old man who had been disinherited by his father at an early age for drinking and gambling, and who had allowed bitterness for his bad fortune to further dissipate him. They told family stories, stories which moralized or amused according to whether it was Mamá Nanda or the New York-sophisticated Felícita who told them. They were stories my mother would later repeat to me to pass the time away in colder climates while she waited to return to her island. My mother never adopted the United States, she did not adapt to life anywhere but in Puerto Rico, although she followed my father back and forth from the island to the mainland for twenty-five years according to his tours of duty with the Navy. She always expected to return to *Casa*—her birthplace. And she kept her fantasy alive by recounting her early years to my brother and me until we felt that we had shared her childhood.

At her mother-in-law's, Mother learned the meaning of scandal. She considered the gossip created by Felícita's divorce in New York and subsequent return to the conservative Catholic pueblo yet another exciting dimension in her new adventure of marriage. After her young husband had left for Panama, she had had trouble sleeping, so Aunt Felícita had offered to sleep in the same bed with her. Felícita had desperately wanted a child of her own, but her body had rejected three attempts at pregnancy—one of the many problems that had helped to destroy her marriage. And so my mother's condition became Felícita's project; she liked to say that she felt like the baby was hers too. After all, it was she who had felt the first stirrings in my mother's belly as she soothed the nervous girl through difficult nights, and she who had risen at dawn to hold her up while she heaved with morning sickness. She shared the pregnancy, growing ever closer to the pretty girl carrying her brother's child.

She had also been the one to run out of the house in her nightgown one night in February of 1952 to summon the old midwife, Lupe, because it was time for me to make my entrance into the world. Lupe, who had attended at each of Mamá Nanda's twelve deliveries, was by that time more a town institution than an alert midwife. That night she managed to pull me out of my mother's writhing body without serious complications, but it had exhausted her. She left me wrapped up in layers of gauze without securing my umbilicus. It was Felícita, ever vigilant of her babies, my mother and myself, who spotted the blood stain soaking through my swaddling clothes. I was rapidly emptying out, deflating like a little balloon even as my teenage mother curled into a fetal position to sleep after her long night's work.

They say that until my father's return, the social pariah, Felícita, cared for me with a gentle devotion that belied all her outward bravura. Some years before my birth, she had eloped with a young man whom her father had threatened to kill. They had married and gone to New York City to live. During that time, all her letters home had been destroyed in their envelopes by the old man who had pronounced her dead to the family. Mamá Nanda had suffered in silence, but managed to keep in touch with her daughter through a relative in New York. The marriage soon disintegrated, and Felícita explored life as a free woman for one year. Her exploits, exaggerated by gossip, made her legendary in her hometown. By the time I could ask about such things, all that was left of that period was a trunk full of gorgeous party dresses Felícita had brought back. They became my dress-up costumes during my childhood. She had been a striking girl with the pale skin and dark curly hair that my father's family could trace back to their ancestors from northern Spain.

Piecing her story together over the years, I have gathered that Felícita, at the age of sixteen, had fallen madly in love with a black boy a little older than herself. The romance was passionate and the young man had pressed for a quick marriage. When he finally approached my grandfather, the old man pulled out his machete and threatened to cut Felícita's suitor in half with it if he ever came near the house again. He then beat both his daughter and wife (for raising a slut), and put them under house arrest. The result of his actions was an elopement in which half the town collaborated, raising money for the star-crossed lovers and helping them secure transportation and airline tickets to New York. Felícita left one night and did not return for many years, after her father's death.

But the tale is more complex than that. There was talk at the time that the groom may have been fathered by the old man, who kept mistresses but did not acknowledge their children. For his pleasure, he nearly always chose black women. There was no way to prove this awful suspicion one way or another. Felícita had been struck and blinded by a passion that she could not control. The marriage had been tempestuous, violent, and mercifully short. Felícita was a wounded person by the time I was born; her fire was no longer raging, but smoldering—just enough to keep me warm until my mother came out of her adolescent dream to take charge of me.

The three women and a baby girl then spent the next two years waiting for their soldier to come home. Mamá Nanda, a deeply religious woman, as well as superstitious, made a *promesa* for the safe return of her three sons. She went to early mass every day at the famous Catholic church in our town, the site of a miraculous appearance by the Black Virgin during the Spanish colonial period. Mamá Nanda also climbed the one hundred steps to the shrine on her knees once a week, along with other women who had men in the war. These steps had been hewn out of a hillside by hundreds of laborers, and a church had been constructed at the top, on the exact spot where a woodcutter had been saved from a charging bull by the sudden vision of the Black Lady floating above a treetop. According to legend, the bull fell on its front knees in a dead halt right in front of the man paralyzed by fear and wonder. There is a fresco above the church altar depicting this scene. Pilgrims come from all over the island to visit the shrine of the Black Virgin. A statue imported from Spain representing the Lady sits on a portable ark, and once a year, during her *fiestas patronales,* she is taken on her dais around the town, followed by her adorers. She is said to have effected many miraculous cures, and her little room, off to the side of the nave, is full of mementos of her deeds, such as crutches and baby garments (she can induce fertility in barren women). It was to her that Mamá Nanda and other women prayed when their men were in wars and during domestic crises. Being a woman and black made Our Lady the perfect depository for the hopes and prayers of the sick, the weak, and the powerless.

I have seen the women dressed in black climbing the rough steps of *la escalinata* to the front portals of the church, and I have understood how the act itself could bring comfort to a woman who did not even know exactly where on earth her son or husband was, or even the reasons why he was risking his life in someone else's war. Perhaps God knew, and surely Our Lady, a woman, wife, and mother herself, would intercede. It was a man's world, and a man's heaven. But mediation was possible —if one could only get *His* attention. And so there were *promesas,* ways to make your requests noticed. Some women chose to wear *hábitos* until their prayers were answered, that is, a plain dress of the color that represented their favorite saint, such as light blue for the Holy Mother or red for the Sacred Heart. The *hábito* was cinched at the waist with a cord representing Christ's passion. The more fervent would wear sackcloth underneath their clothes, a real torment in the tropical heat. The *promesa* was only limited by the imagination of the penitent and her threshold for pain and discomfort. In many households women said rosaries nightly in groups, and this brought them together to share in their troubles. Mamá Nanda did it all, quietly and without fanfare. She wore only black since the death of her husband, but mourning and penance had become an intrinsic part of her nature long before; of her twelve children only six had survived; the other six died in infancy from childhood diseases which were prevented a generation later by a single vaccine or simple antidote. She had buried each little corpse in the family graveyard with a name and a date on the headstone—sometimes the same date for birth and death—and she had worn black, kept *luto* for each. The death of her babies had made her a melancholy woman, yet one who was always ready to give God another chance. She lobbied for His favors indefatigably.

At Mamá Nanda's house, my young mother and her baby were treated like royalty. Having served a demanding husband and numerous children, the older woman now found herself in a practically empty house with a new grandchild she could dote on and a daughter-in-law that was no more than an adolescent herself. My mother's only job was to play with the baby, to take me for strolls in fancy clothes bought with Army checks, and to accompany Mamá Nanda to mass on Sundays. In the photographs taken of my mother and me during this period, I can see the changes wrought on the shy teenage bride in the short span she was taken care of by Nanda and Felícita: she is chubby and radiant with good health, she seems proud of the bundle of ruffles and bows in her arms—her baby doll—me.

By the time Father returned from Panama, I was out of diapers and ambulatory, Mother had regained her svelte figure, and Mamá Nanda had thick calluses on her knees which kept her from feeling the pain she thought was necessary to get results from heaven. The safe homecoming of her son was proof that her sacrifices had been worthwhile, and she applied her fruitful mind to even greater penances toward credit for the other two who would both be wounded in an ambush while traveling in a jeep in Korea and would soon be back in Puerto Rico—slightly damaged, but alive. Nanda's knees bore the scars like medals received in many wars and conflicts. Aunt Felícita found herself suddenly displaced as my "other parent" and returned to her own life. All changed.

My first memory is of Father's homecoming party and the gift he brought me from San Juan—a pink iron crib like an ornate bird cage—and the sense of abandonment I felt for the first time in my short life as all eyes turned to the handsome stranger in uniform and away from me in my frilly new dress and patent leather shoes, trapped inside my pink iron crib, screaming my head off for *Mami, Tía, Mamá Nanda,* anybody . . . to come lift me out of my prison.

When I ask about the events of that day, my mother still rolls her eyes back and throws her hands up in a gesture of dismay. The story varies with the telling and the teller, but it seems that I climbed out of my tall crib on my own and headed for the party in the backyard. The pig was on the spit and the beer was flowing. In the living room the Victrola was playing my father's Elvis Presley records loudly. *I may have imagined this*. My mother is sitting on his lap. She is gorgeous in the red silk dress he has given her. There is a circle of people around him. Everyone is having a good time. And everyone has forgotten about me. I see myself slipping through the crowd and into flames. Immediately, I am pulled out by a man's strong hands. No real damage: my abundant hair is a little singed, but that is all. Mother is crying. I am the center of everyone's attention once again. Even *his*. Did I sleep between them that night because my mother had finally realized that I was not a rubber dolly but a real flesh-and-blood little girl? When I ask, she says that she remembers only staying awake listening to me breathe on the night of "the incident." She had also been kept up by the unaccustomed noise of my father's snoring. She would soon get used to both facts of life: that everyone of her waking hours would belong to me from then on, and that this solemn stranger—who only resembled the timid young man she had married two years before—would own her nights. My mother was finally coming of age.

The Witch's Husband

My grandfather has misplaced his words again. He is trying to find my name in the kaleidoscope of images that his mind has become. His face brightens like a child's who has just remembered his lesson. He points to me and says my mother's name. I smile back and kiss him on the cheek. It doesn't matter what names he remembers anymore. Every day he is more confused, his memory slipping back a little further in time. Today he has no grandchildren yet. Tomorrow he will be a young man courting my grandmother again, quoting bits of poetry to her. In months to come, he will begin calling her Mamá.

I have traveled to Puerto Rico at my mother's request to help her deal with the old people. My grandfather is physically healthy but his dementia is severe. My grandmother's heart is making odd sounds again in her chest. Yet she insists on taking care of the old man at home herself. She will not give up her house, though she has been warned that her heart might fail in her sleep without proper monitoring, that is, in a nursing home or a relative's care. Her response is typical of her famous obstinacy: "*Bueno,*" she says, "I will die in my own bed."

I am now at her house, waiting for my opportunity to talk "sense" into her. As a college teacher in the United States I am supposed to represent the voice of logic; I have been called in to convince *la abuela,* the family's proud matriarch, to step down—to allow her children to take care of her before she kills herself with work. I spent years at her house as a child but have lived in the States for most of my adult life. I learned to love and respect this strong woman who with five children of her own had found a way to help many others. She was a legend in the pueblo for having more foster children than anyone else. I have spoken with people my mother's age who told me that they had spent up to a year at Abuela's house during emergencies and hard times. It seems extraordinary that a woman would willingly take on such obligations. And, frankly, I am a bit appalled at what I have begun to think of as "the martyr complex" in Puerto Rican women, that is, the idea that self-sacrifice is a woman's lot and her privilege. A good woman is defined by how much suffering and mothering she can do in one lifetime. Abuela is the all-time champion in my eyes. Her life has been entirely devoted to others. Not content to bring up two sons and three daughters as the Depression raged on, followed by the war that took one of her sons, she had also taken on other people's burdens. This had been the usual pattern with one exception that I knew of: the year that Abuela spent in New York, apparently undergoing some kind of treatment for her heart while she was still a young woman. My mother was five or six years old, and there were three other children who had been born by that time, too. They were given into the care of Abuela's sister, Delia. The two women traded places for the year. Abuela went to live in her sister's apartment in New York City while the younger woman took over Abuela's duties at the house in Puerto Rico. Grandfather was a shadowy figure in the background during that period. My mother doesn't say much about what went on during that year, only that her mother was sick and away for months. Grandfather seemed absent, too, since he worked all of the time. Though they missed Abuela, they were well taken care of.

I am sitting on a rocking chair on the porch of her house. She is facing me from a hammock she made when her first baby was born. My mother was rocked on that hammock. I was rocked on that hammock, and when I brought my daughter as a baby to Abuela's house, she was held in Abuela's sun-browned arms, my porcelain pink baby, and rocked to a peaceful sleep, too. Abuela sits there and smiles as the breeze of a tropical November brings the scent of her roses and her herbs to us. She is proud of her garden. In front of the house she grows flowers and lush trailing plants; in the back, where the mango tree gives shade, she has an herb garden. From this patch of weedy-looking plants came all the remedies of my childhood, for anything from a sore throat to menstrual cramps. Abuela had a recipe for every pain that a child could dream up, and she brought it to your bed in her own hands smelling of the earth. For a moment I am content to sit in her comforting presence. She is rotund now—a small-boned brown-skinned earth mother—with a big heart and a temper to match. My grandfather comes to stand at the screen door. He has forgotten how the latch works. He pulls at the knob and moans softly, rattling it. With some effort Abuela gets down from the hammock. She opens the door, gently guiding the old man to a chair at the end of the porch. There he begins anew his constant search for the words he needs. He tries various combinations, but they don't work as language. Abuela pats his hand and motions for me to follow her into the house. We sit down at opposite ends of her sofa.

She apologizes to me as if for a misbehaving child.

"He'll quiet down," she says. "He does not like to be ignored."

I take a deep breath in preparation for my big lecture to Grandmother. This is the time to tell her that she has to give up trying to run this house and take care of others at her age. One of her daughters is prepared to take her in. Grandfather is to be sent to a nursing home. Before I can say anything Abuela says, "*Mi amor,* would you like to hear a story?"

I smile, surprised at her offer. These are the same words that stopped me in my tracks as a child, even in the middle of a tantrum. Abuela could always entrance me with one of her tales.

I nodded. Yes, my sermon could wait a little longer, I thought.

"Let me tell you an old, old story I heard when I was a little girl.

"There was once a man who became worried and suspicious when he noticed that his wife disappeared from their bed every night for long periods of time. Wanting to find out what she was doing before confronting her, the man decided to stay awake at night and keep guard. For hours he watched her every movement through half-closed eyelids with his ears perked up like those of a burro.

"Then just about midnight, when the night was as dark as the bottom of a cauldron, he felt his wife slipping out of bed. He saw her go to the wardrobe and take out a jar and a little paintbrush. She stood naked by the window, and when the church bells struck twelve, she began to paint her entire body with the paintbrush, dipping it into the jar. As the bells tolled the hour, she whispered these words: *I don't believe in the Church, or in God, or in the Virgin Mary*. As soon as this was spoken, she rose from the ground and flew into the night like a bird.

"Astounded, the man decided not to say anything to his wife the next day, but to try to find out where she went. The following night, the man pretended to sleep and waited until she had again performed her little ceremony and flown away, then he repeated her actions exactly. He soon found himself flying after her. Approaching a palace, he saw many other women circling the roof, taking turns going down the chimney. After the last had descended, he slid down the dark hole that led to the castle's bodega, where food and wine were stored. He hid himself behind some casks of wine and watched the women greet each other.

"The witches, for that's what they were, were the wives of his neighbors and friends, but he at first had trouble recognizing them, for, like his wife, they were all naked. With much merriment, they took the meats and cheeses that hung from the bodega's rafters and laid a table for a feast. They drank the fine wines right from the bottles, like men in a cantina, and danced wildly to eerie music from invisible instruments. They spoke to each other in a language that he did not understand, words that sounded like a cat whose tail has been stepped on. Still, horrible as their speech was, the food they prepared smelled delicious. Cautiously placing himself in the shadows near one of the witches, he extended his hand for a plate. He was given a steaming dish of stewed tongue. Hungrily, he took a bite: it was tasteless. The other witches had apparently noticed the same thing because they sent one of the younger ones to find some salt. But when the young witch came back into the room with a salt shaker in her hand, the man forgot himself and exclaimed, 'Thank God the salt is here.'

"On hearing God's name, all the witches took flight immediately, leaving the man completely alone in the darkened cellar. He tried the spell for flight that had brought him there, but it did not work. It was no longer midnight, and it was obviously the wrong incantation for going *up* a chimney. He tried all night to get out of the place, which had been left in shambles by the witches, but it was locked up as tight as heaven is to a sinner. Finally, he fell asleep from exhaustion and slept until dawn, when he heard footsteps approaching. When he saw the heavy door being pushed open, he hid himself behind a cask of wine.

"A man in rich clothes walked in, followed by several servants. They were all armed with heavy sticks as if out to kill someone. When the man lit his torch and saw the chaos in the cellar, broken bottles strewn on the floor, meats and cheeses half eaten and tossed everywhere, he cried out in such a rage that the man hiding behind the wine cask closed his eyes and committed his soul to God. The owner of the castle ordered his servants to search the whole bodega, every inch of it, until they discovered how vandals had entered his home. It was a matter of minutes before they discovered the witch's husband, curled up like a stray dog, and—worse—painted the color of a vampire bat, without a stitch of clothing.

"They dragged him to the center of the room and beat him with their sticks until the poor man thought that his bones had been pulverized and he would have to be poured into his grave. When the castle's owner said that he thought the poor wretch had learned his lesson, the servants tossed him naked onto the road. The man was so sore that he slept right there on the public *camino,* oblivious to the stares and insults of all who passed him. When he awakened in the middle of the night and found himself naked, dirty, bloody, and miles from his home, he swore to himself right then and there that he would never, for anything in the world, follow his wife on her nightly journeys again."

"*Colorín, colorado.*" Abuela claps her hands three times, chanting the childhood rhyme for ending a story, "*Este cuento se ha acabado.*" She smiles at me, shifting her position on the sofa to be able to watch Grandfather muttering to himself on the porch. I remember those eyes on me when I was a small child. Their movements seemed to be triggered by a child's actions, like those holograms of the Holy Mother that were popular with Catholics a few years ago—you couldn't get away from their mesmerizing gaze.

"Will you tell me about your year in New York, Abuela?" I surprise myself with the question. But suddenly I need to know about Abuela's lost year. It has to be another good story.

She looks intently at me before she answers. Her eyes are my eyes, same dark brown color, almond shape, and the lids that droop a little:

called by some "bedroom eyes"; to others they are a sign of a cunning nature. "Why are you looking at me that way?" is a question I am often asked.

"I wanted to leave home," she says calmly, as though she had been expecting the question from me all along.

"You mean abandon your family?" I am really taken aback by her words.

"Yes, *hija*. That is exactly what I mean. Abandon them. Never to return."

"Why?"

"I was tired. I was young and pretty, full of energy and dreams." She smiles as Grandfather breaks into song standing by himself on the porch. A woman passing by with a baby in her arms waves at him. Grandfather sings louder, something about a man going to his exile because the woman he loves has rejected him. He finishes the song on a long note and continues to stand in the middle of the tiled porch as if listening for applause. He bows.

Abuela shakes her head, smiling a little, as if amused by his antics, then she finishes her sentence. "Restless, bored. Four children and a husband all demanding more and more from me."

"So you left the children with your sister and went to New York?" I say, trying to keep the mixed emotions I was feeling out of my voice. I look at the serene old woman in front of me and cannot believe that she once left four children and a loving husband to go live alone in a faraway country.

"I had left him once before, but he found me. I came back home, but on the condition that he never follow me anywhere again. I told him the next time I would not return." She is silent, apparently falling deep into thought.

"You were never really sick," I say, though I am afraid that she will not resume her story. But I want to know more about this woman whose life I thought was an open book.

"I *was* sick. Sick at heart. And he knew it," she says, keeping her eyes on Grandfather, who is standing as still as a marble statue on the porch. He seems to be listening intently for something.

"The year in New York was his idea. He saw how unhappy I was. He knew I needed to taste freedom. He paid my sister Delia to come take care of the children. He also sublet her apartment for me, though he had to take a second job to do it. He gave me money and told me to go."

"What did you do that year in New York?" I am both stunned and fascinated by Abuela's revelation.

"I worked as a seamstress in a fancy dress shop. And . . . *y pues, hija*"—she smiles at me as if I should know some things without being told—"I lived."

"Why did you come back?" I ask.

"Because I love him," she says, "and I missed my children."

He is scratching at the door. Like a small child he has traced the sound of Abuela's voice back to her. She lets him in, guiding him gently by the hand. Then she eases him down on his favorite rocking chair. He begins to nod; soon he will be sound asleep, comforted by her proximity, secure in his familiar surroundings. I wonder how long it will take him to revert to infantilism. The doctors say he is physically healthy and may live for many years, but his memory, verbal skills, and ability to control his biological functions will deteriorate rapidly. He may end his days bedridden, perhaps comatose. My eyes fill with tears as I look at the lined face of this beautiful and gentle old man. I am in awe of the generosity of spirit that allowed him to give a year of freedom to the woman he loved, not knowing whether she would ever return to him. Abuela has seen my tears and moves over on the sofa to sit near me. She slips an arm around my waist and pulls me close. She kisses my wet cheek. Then she whispers softly into my ear, "And in time, the husband either began forgetting that he had seen her turn into a witch, or believed that he had just dreamed it." She takes my face into her hands. "I am going to take care of your grandfather until one of us dies. I promised him when I came back that I would never leave home again unless he asked me to: he never did. He never asked any questions."

I hear my mother's car pull up into the driveway. She will wait there for me. I will have to admit that I failed in my mission. I will argue Abuela's case without revealing her secret. As far as everyone is concerned she went away to recover from problems with her heart. That part is true in both versions of the story.

At the door she gives me the traditional blessing, adding with a wink, "*Colorín, colorado.*" My grandfather, hearing her voice, smiles in his sleep.

What We Don't Know
About the Climb to Heaven

Ariel Zurita was the second illegal who paid Daisy to marry him so he could get his green card and, like the first, was also her boarder. In the five months he lived in her small apartment, their paths crossed only on Saturday mornings. From the kitchen area, separated from the living room by a dining table, she wished him a good morning as, in a bathrobe, he came out of his room to take a shower or returned, fragrant with after-shave. She would prepare breakfast. After eating hers, she knocked on his door. Unlike his predecessor, Zurita never opened it in his underwear. She let him eat alone, reading his newspaper, as she imagined he preferred. Except for those weekly brushes, each kept a private life. She didn't know what he did with his days, or why he came in late every night or was gone for the weekend to be back on Monday morning, and at first thought she didn't care.

Daisy had met him that spring, a year after she was rid of Jorge, a Mexican who entered her life giving every appearance of being a godsend. She needed to pay off the loan to ship her father's body to Puerto Rico. But to earn that money she invested dearly. The perfumed, gentlemanly Jorge turned out to be involved in shady dealings. She lived in constant fear of a visit by a stranger with a machine gun. And he was a *machista,* who presumed his rent also leased her body. The nights she didn't sleep upstairs, at her motherly neighbor Martina's, she slept beside a carving knife wrapped in a towel. So when Jackie, a Cuban coworker at the dress factory, approached her sewing machine to make a pitch for a Salvadoran friend offering to pay a United States citizen to marry him, Daisy said no. Jackie, Cubanly persistent, personally vouched for this man's decency. He sometimes preached at her Pentecostal church. "Besides, how else would you earn good money so easily. Aren't you saving to retire in your own house in Puerto Rico?"

At work's end the following afternoon, Jackie rushed to catch up with Daisy by the elevators. On the sidewalk, in the sunlight behind the factory's steel doors, a man in a dark blue suit smiled as if he had been waiting for them. Sucked-in cheeks gave his Indian face a determined demeanor. Jackie acted surprised and introduced Ariel Zurita. "You remember, the man I spoke to you about."

Zurita offered his hand. "I'm so glad we are finally being introduced."

Daisy threw ocular flames at Jackie, who apologized for having to hurry home to cook for her hungry husband, and took off. Left alone with Zurita, she forced a courteous smile. "Well, it was nice meeting you, but I have to take a long subway ride home." She started to walk away.

"Can I accompany you to the Bronx?"

Jackie must have told him where she lived. This truly annoyed her. "Oh, do you live up there too?"

"No, but I don't mind."

"I don't think it's necessary."

"Please, I really do need your help."

Urgency radiated from his eyes. Surprising herself, she consented. On the subway ride he explained that in El Salvador, opposing the government endangered one's life as much as actually being a guerrilla. Being related to revolutionaries also put you in danger. His brother, a doctor, was a guerrilla officer. Because their family belonged to a social class that should know better, the government was certain to make an example of them. Zurita suspected the death squad would eventually try to use the family to capture his brother. If they discovered his own connections, they wouldn't hesitate to kill him. But because the squad had yet to make a move against him or his family, the United States refused to give him a visa as a political exile. An American priest had helped him get a tourist visa. Daisy enjoyed his polished manner and cultured vocabulary.

Zurita's exiting the train by her side brought on butterflies. At the top of the station stairs, she was about to say that he shouldn't bother to walk the three blocks to her building at the very second that he invited her to dinner at the Cuban-Chinese restaurant in front of them. His graciousness caught her off guard, weakened her apprehension. They ordered from the daily specials. She inquired about his preaching at Jackie's church. "I don't see it as preaching, really. Jackie exaggerated. Maybe once or twice the minister invited me to speak." The food came fast. Eating and his curiosity about her Caribbean background lengthened their digression from the topic that had brought them together. Over coffee, Daisy took the initiative. "How long have you known Jackie?"

"Just this last month."

"Do you plan to sell drugs?"

He laughed. "No, no drugs."

"Where do you get the money to travel?"

"From my father. He's a dental surgeon."

He was obviously educated. "Do you have formal training in something?"

"I used to be a minister."

"Why did you stop?"

"Politics. Then I became a professor."

"How do you plan to earn a living? Can you speak English?"

"Only a little. I'm thinking of driving a taxi, a night shift for a gypsy cabdriver, a member of Jackie's church."

Daisy read his eyes. This Zurita was everything Jackie said he was. He was too good a person to have to negotiate a marriage for pay. "Where are you staying now?"

"With other illegals crowded in a basement on the Lower East Side. Everybody who is staying there is selfish and vindictive. A few hate each other and are capable of avenging an enemy at their own and everybody else's expense. I need to move out. Can we get married soon?"

"How soon?"

"Next week. I can get the license this week. I know a Colombian doctor who will sign the blood test certificates."

"I need a couple of days to think this over." But she knew she would say yes. He called two evenings later. He agreed to her terms of payment and the monthly rent, then asked her questions pertinent to the license. A week later, she took Friday afternoon off and met him at City Hall. Jackie witnessed. Zurita moved into her "Husband Room," filling it with his silence and his books.

That first week he established his pattern of arriving late and staying out on the weekend. Not expecting him back till Monday, on Saturday afternoons she cleaned his room, the vacuum cleaner tube a giant key to his privacy. Inside, the bedclothes were always tucked in, the pillows fluffed up, his several shirts and three suits neatly on hangers, his three pairs of shoes abreast on the closet floor. Rows of books stood on every free surface: the floor, the windowsill, the top of the dresser. The books especially fascinated her. Books filled the closet shelves and boxes under the bed. How could somebody read so many books? They were all about religion, some in English, most in Spanish; a few, she guessed, were in French. From the variety, however, she couldn't pin down his religion. Jewish mysticism. Christian spiritualism. Books with glossy photographs of divine Hindu leaders or statues of Buddha. Books on African tribal gods. Books on Mayan temples. After vacuuming, she always dusted them, taking her time to linger in the peace Zurita's presence had added to this room. If the book she was dusting was in Spanish, she would try to read something from it, invariably finding its vocabulary over her head.

Browsing in this way, she came upon *What We Don't Know About the Climb to Heaven* by Ariel Zurita. According to the brief preface, he wrote it in Venezuela, on the offshore island of Margarita. She couldn't get over her surprise. Zurita had not mentioned he was a writer. She wanted very much to read it. Pressing the row of books filled in the missing tooth of its absence. She hoped to have it read before he noticed it was missing. After storing the vacuum cleaner, she sat on the sofa to read Zurita's book. His Spanish prose was far more hospitable than the impenetrable words of the other books in his room. The Introduction, "Why We Need to Imagine Heaven," began simply, "Heaven is what all religions help us find. They are our guides and Faith is the glorious mountain. Heaven is the kingdom we see once we climb to the top. But our guides only help us once we have started climbing. Something else motivates us to begin. We come into the world crying inside with this yearning to experience the wondrous vision from Faith's highest peak. Unless we listen and tend to this soundless crying, we will not begin to look for our mountain of faith." She tried to continue reading but kept hearing Zurita's voice repeat the image of the mountain. She went into her bedroom and placed the book on the night table, at arm's reach, then devoted the afternoon to cleaning the bathroom and kitchen.

That evening, as she did every Saturday, Daisy watched television at Martina's. While they waited for Mrs. Graham, the elderly woman from the second floor who always joined them, Martina inquired why Daisy didn't seem herself. Daisy confessed that her arrangement with Zurita was making her unhappy.

"I don't understand, if he's such a good man who doesn't give you problems."

"That's what I mean. Treating this kind man in a businesslike way, no different than the one before, feels wrong."

"Why don't you try to get close to him, make him your guest, cook for him."

But Daisy knew those Saturday morning encounters were too brief. Later that night, after brushing her shoulder-length black hair, she contemplated her reflection in the mirror. She had not studied herself in a long time. At the age of forty-six, her vanity had become dormant. She would have wanted to be pretty. As a young woman, only her long Indian hair, cascading to the small of her back, used to catch some eyes. The young men in her town called her "La India," the Indian girl. She pressed the sides of her nightgown against her broad hips, then released the gown, resigned. She got into bed with Zurita's book. His opening sentences again engulfed her in his voice. She found it impossible to concentrate. From then on, she would just open the book to any page and read passages. That night she dreamed of standing on a peak as high as Everest and hearing God speak with Zurita's voice.

In the coming weeks, on the subway to and from work and in bed before sleeping, she read from Zurita's book. When a passage especially moved her, she recited it to herself over and over. In time she learned several by heart. Having Zurita so present gave her a solace that evolved into sadness. Her devotion began to trouble her. She decided to stop thinking about Zurita. She returned his book to its place. She would see him as a good person and no more. The following three Saturday mornings she prepared breakfast, knocked on his door, wished him a good morning, and returned to her room, as before, with no other expectations. Later she vacuumed his room and left it immediately. On the fourth Saturday, she forgot her resolve. After vacuuming, she lingered in the room's order. She dusted the rows of standing books, finding Zurita's. She opened it and read sentences here and there, as if taking gulps at an oasis.

That Monday, before leaving for work, she thought of leaving him brewed coffee, but decided against it. At the factory, as her fingers rapidly joined zippers to dresses, she broke her self-imposed censorship. She realized that thinking about Zurita infused in her soul the same sense of order she experienced in his room. In her private silence in the din of the factory, she ran over the list of questions she knew she had no right to ask. What does he do all day? Where does he stay all weekend? What was he doing in Venezuela? Where is he going? Just before lunch break, Jackie came around and wanted to know how Daisy liked living with Zurita, insinuating amorous fringe benefits. Daisy answered insipidly, without interrupting her sewing. She really didn't know how he was. She hardly ever saw him for that matter. Jackie, on the other hand, gushed with things to say about him. He had spoken again at her church and he was magic. "I don't know what that man has, but it is very special and you should feel very blessed." *Blessed*. Jackie had put her finger on Daisy's feeling.

It had taken Daisy those five months to work up the courage to plan a casual, coincidental breakfast together. That Saturday, she rose early, put on a dress, made herself up, prepared coffee, and baked aromatic little bread rolls. She hadn't heard him arrive during the night, but assumed he was in his room. Late into the morning, she had not heard a rustle. She tapped on his door. Daring to open it, she discovered he wasn't there and that the room had an air of not having been slept in. She never imagined such a painful disappointment. She changed into pants and trained her mind on her chores: sorting out dirty clothes, purchasing a lottery ticket on the way to the coin laundry, doing the wash.

She pulled her shopping cart with two bulging pillowcases of dirty clothes through the Saturday laundry crowd of mostly women and children. No machine was free, a sloshing in every porthole. She waited on the wall-long bench. The woman on her right shouted at a pair of children chasing each other. The woman at her left complained to another one about her exploitative landlord. Daisy removed Zurita's book from one of the pillowcases and opened it at random. Her eyes, initially at sea, swam to the boldly printed section heading. "Angels, With and Without Wings." Angels, according to Zurita, captain the hands of good works on earth. "We don't have to wait for our wings to perform our role, if we decide to join God's highest officers." Surprised by her improving ability to retain his ideas, she read on, unable to differentiate who, according to Zurita, was an angel and who merely a good person in life. She was interrupted by the mother reprimanding her kids for playing tag around and behind people trying to do their laundry.

The washer directly in front suddenly stopped. The woman who had complained about her landlord piled her clothes into a plastic basket, then threw the window door shut. In the circular window, Daisy's reflection was obese as a Buddha's. The business of throwing the clothes into the tumbler evicted the Buddha from her mind. Unable to read Zurita amidst the laundry's distractions, she picked up a copy of that day's *El Diario* left on the bench. A report on the civil war in El Salvador touched her as if on a personal tragedy befalling Zurita.

Back in her apartment, as she folded her clothes, a bubble burst in her consciousness: Zurita's woman. It would only be natural that he had one. He didn't look like a man who liked men, even though *she* obviously didn't arouse any curiosity in him. Her clothes put away, she straightened up in the dresser mirror. She was heavy, but not the Buddha in the washer window. She removed the pins holding back her hair and brushed, extracting some luster. A dab of moisturizer softened her brown skin. A touch of rouge highlighted her cheeks. She was forming a red circle on her arced lips when keys jingled at the apartment door. She went out to the living room. When the door opened, her hand jumped to her heart. "My God, you frightened me." Zurita didn't look right, rigid as a robot. "Ay, did something happen?"

"My family was killed last week. Government soldiers."

"Oh, Blessed Jesus," she said, making the sign of the cross. She wrapped his limp arm around her shoulder, crutching his few steps to the sofa.

"The soldiers went after my brother. They accused my parents of protecting him."

His eyes looked ancient. He had probably not slept for days. Daisy went to her kitchen cabinet and returned with a bottle of sherry and a drinking glass. Beside him, she poured an inch of sherry. Zurita thanked her but just held the glass with both hands. Stroking wide circles over his back, she put her other palm under the glass and lightly pushed up. "Drink it." He looked at the glass as if it had suddenly materialized in his hands. He drank the sherry in one swig, and she put the glass on the floor. His eyelids started to droop. Daisy's hand circled up to the nape of his neck and gently pulled him toward her. His head was almost on her shoulder when, losing her nerve, she moved out of the way and positioned it on a cushion against the sofa arm. She stretched out his legs and removed his shoes, then called Martina. "He's lying on the sofa like a corpse, the poor thing."

Martina invited Daisy to dinner and suggested bringing Zurita along, so he wouldn't be alone. After hanging up, Daisy felt lost. Zurita's book was on the bed. She opened to a page near the end and read the first complete sentence. "The commission of an angel is for eternity. Each of us, with or without wings, must covet its prestige by carrying out our mission to do good every second of life and in the afterlife, whether as a Hindu, Jew, Mayan, Yoruba, Buddhist, Moslem, or Christian. Every act in the universe, however miserable it may seem in our time, redeems itself in the history of the cosmos and is good; every molecular change is sacred." A well of sympathy for his grief began to overpower her. The telephone rang.

She rushed before the ringing awakened Zurita, then covered the mouthpiece, pausing a second to compose herself. Someone sniffled on the other end. "Hello," a woman said in Spanish. "Hello, can I speak with señor Ariel Zurita?"

"Well, señor Zurita is sleeping right now. Would you like to leave him a message?"

"No, well, yes. Please tell him that it is urgent he call Marisol Contreras."

The speaker sounded like an educated woman. "If you will excuse me, señora, but does this have to do with his family's death?"

"No, well, indirectly. It's complicated. It's extremely important that I reach him soon."

A faint voice whispered in her mind, and she heard a buzzing, like at a door, only in her heart. "He's sleeping right now. Why don't you come here?"

"Oh, señora . . . I don't think it would be correct."

"Don't worry. It's all right. Come over now."

Marisol Contreras lived in Manhattan. It would take her less than an hour. She knew the address.

The invitation from her own lips now struck Daisy as perverse. She did feel sorry for this weeping Contreras woman, but she also wanted to meet her and compare. Intuiting a strong blow, she took a shower, put on the dress she had worn that morning, and touched up her face. She was steaming milk for coffee when there was a knock at the door.

Daisy looked through the peephole. Besides being educated, Marisol Contreras was pretty, with a young Indian girl's face. Daisy patted her hair with her hand and opened the door. Marisol Contreras met her, holding out her hand. Her petite, well-proportioned figure was discreetly displayed by her dark blue dress. A matching sweater hung over her arm. Daisy put a finger to her lips and pointed to the sofa. Marisol nodded. Daisy seated her at the dining table, with her back to Zurita.

As Daisy served coffee, Marisol kept looking back. The necessary "How dark?" and "How many sugars?" broke the ice and fixed Marisol's attention on Daisy. They spoke in a whisper.

"I don't know if Ariel told you about me. He said he was going to."

"No, but I imagined you existed."

"We met at church. I had just come from Colombia . . ."

"Look, I don't really have a right to know anything. He's a decent man and we have a business arrangement, that's all. You don't have to tell me anything. If you want to wake him, I can let you talk in private."

"Ariel says you are one of those people he calls angels. He tried to stay out of your way as much as possible because he was ashamed he had to impose himself on you."

Daisy didn't know what to say. That Zurita should consider her an angel came as a shock.

"But what I have to tell him may affect you. So you should know too." She paused. It was hard for her to begin. Daisy, nervous, excused herself, got up, and opened the refrigerator. She removed a bakery box and lumped a handful of cookies on a small dish. Holding a cookie between her teeth, she offered the cookies to Marisol, who shook her head. "I am not divorced yet. My husband refuses to give me a divorce. He is waiting for me to go back to him. He says that if it's necessary he has friends who can provide evidence that I am involved in cocaine. Either I go back to him or he will report me. I am supposed to be living alone while I decide. I met Zurita at my church. My husband found out about him and insists it's a long-running affair, that I really left him for Zurita. My husband paid a detective to investigate him. He knows about Zurita's political problems and about your arrangement. If Zurita tries to register as a political exile, he says he'll pull strings so it won't work. He wants to get Zurita deported and is willing to do anything against you and him or anybody. I can't bear to think I can cause so much harm to this man or to someone like you. I was going to run away, leave Zurita, tell my husband I had broken with Zurita, then disappear to Florida. I was preparing my mind to do it. I planned to avoid him, but when I didn't hear from him in three days, I started to worry. Nobody knows about Zurita and me, so I wasn't informed. Today at church Jackie told me what happened to his family and that nobody knew where he was."

She was about to cry. Daisy reached over and pressed the back of her folded hands. "Your husband, what is he?"

"Arcadio's a citizen. He's Cuban. He swears the detective can prove Zurita's a Communist terrorist, so you can imagine how he feels about getting him deported. Zurita devotes his time to helping his priest friends get persecuted people out of his country. The priests feed him. They give him a little money. He could not kill like his brother, but he has the same commitment. He didn't want you to be afraid, or hurt by his work. He stayed in my apartment to protect you from Arcadio."

"And you? What's your status?"

"I have the green card."

Daisy didn't know what to say or do. "Why don't you wake him up. I'll go to my room." As she rose from the chair, Daisy saw Zurita already sitting up. He rubbed his face as if realigning disjointed parts.

"Daisy, you don't have to leave the room."

Marisol's rushing to sit beside him pierced Daisy with jealousy.

"There's only one answer." His head shook off sleep. "We have to leave together." Marisol's hand was stroking wide circles over his back.

"No." Marisol shot up, transformed from a tender nurse into a formidable opponent. "You have invested too much time. I don't want these gringos to kick you out." Her back to him, arms folded, she fumed determination.

Daisy remembered a passage she had memorized but hadn't fully understood until now: "Angels measure their acts cosmically. If an Angel cups a hand, it may not fill with water for months, decades, or centuries, and might take eons to comfort the waiting, burning lips for which that hand was raised."

"You don't understand, my love. Just because you leave, Arcadio won't believe we have broken up. His detective has probably told him every detail of our life together. You'll leave and, after I get my green card, I'll follow you. That will be his logical theory. The only way he can short-circuit that is to get me deported now, and that would mean Daisy will also suffer. She can be accused of conspiracy. I can't allow that and neither can you."

That danger had never crossed Daisy's mind. Now that Zurita described it so clearly, she wanted to defend him whatever happened. Her words came out like breath. "Zurita, please don't worry about me."

"Daisy, my decision is the only right one. With Marisol I know I will survive, but without her I would simply lose my sense of place. I'm not afraid of starting over. Time is endless. I'm just afraid of losing her and not recovering her in this lifetime."

Listening to him, Daisy heard the voice in his book. Zurita went into his room. Daisy listened to the banging of empty suitcases, the locks snapping open. Marisol hadn't moved, her arms still folded, her stare aimed at the floor. Daisy came up behind her and gently squeezed her arms. "If he stays I'll take care of him for you. I don't think you would lose him if he waits until he gets his green card. It's just a question of three or four months. But he wouldn't be happy without you. And maybe he can work things out later on. He has friends who help him. Look, deep down he doesn't care if he lives in this country or any country. He carries the universe inside, you know that. He always has that green card."

Marisol nodded, letting her arms fall. "I should be helping him."

"Oh, tell Zurita I have his book."

Marisol spun around, rejoicing. "Oh, thank God. He thought he had lost it. It's the only copy he brought with him. And now, who knows what happened to the others."

Marisol helped Zurita, and Daisy steamed more milk. Their movements in the other room evoked in Daisy the days ahead, after they had decided where to hide, when they had emptied out Marisol's apartment, moved out the boxes of his books. Every foreseen stage excavated an old inner cavity she would have to refill with something else, as she had managed all her life. "Who can say," she mentally recited in Zurita's voice, "the purpose of a lonely life, a quiet solitude that for years must witness the joys of companionship bestowed on others. A protracted solitude can be the long prologue to a redemption in some glorious future." The words began the process of replenishing her emptiness. That's when she remembered. Zurita had agreed to pay in full, whether or not he obtained his green card. But she could not accept his money. Instead she would request, so he would always know where to find it, to remain the keeper of his book.

La Calle del Niño Perdido

I find him, just an infant,
lying at the curb
playing with water, his brow
radiant with rain.

"Great," I say, "just what I need,
a baby." "Don't worry," he says,
"tiny as I am, I can speak,
and I know everything."

I carry him through the supermarket.
While I poke through grapefruit
he talks and talks,
sometimes in rhymed iambic pentameter,
telling me about his past lives,
transformations, famous battles,
and how the grapefruits remind him
of the asteroids
beyond Alpha Centauri.

We are interviewed on television.
He sits on my lap,
but will not say one word.
But I talk, my finger
strumming my lips, "blewrm, blewrm,
da da do, do," spittle
dribbles down my chin.

It is raining
on the Street of the Lost Child.
He rides my back
and whispers in my ear,
"Don't be sad,

I'll tell you a story."
Two bald men.
One very small.
Lost.

Doing the Tarantella with Lola Montez

Using their webs like sails, spiders rise
into the stratosphere.
Their webs stick to other webs
forming clouds, whispy mare's tails
that twist across the sky.
When they get too heavy,
they fall back to earth
in silvery clumps
that frighten school children.

Some women make love like spiders.
With their tongues they cover you
in thin webs of pleasure.

Nothing can make you so sad
as the bite of certain tarantulas.
You can die from sadness.
Only frantic dancing can save you.
People who see you
start dancing too—
as if they were tied
to invisible strings.

But I am the happiest of all.
I have danced with Lola Montez,

Queen of the Barbary Coast,
who stamped her heels
on the floorboards
at the small rubber spiders
that bounced beneath her dress.

Open Letter
to My Friends

Today I learned that black smoke glowing red
at its base is a new fire. White means
the firemen are there with ropes of water.
Large flakes of ash drift by my window, dark gray
with a fringe of white, like expensive lettuce
or the edge of surf seen from an airplane.

Down below, whole families run by my front gate
carrying shopping bags full of shoes. Everything
anyone ever wanted is free. Gang members
who live across the street are more methodical,
military in their short haircuts, white T-shirts
and black baggy pants. They stride two by two
out of the alley and into their cars, returning later
with trunks full of electronic equipment.

I am becoming a connoisseur of night sounds:
the distant chatter of automatic rifles,
the popping of a .22, a car alarm.
I can tell the difference between the whoosh
of Molotov cocktails and the rip a shotgun
makes in the air. This city manufactures
its own clouds—solid, symmetrical, metallic.

They press against the sky from horizon to horizon
propped up by twirling pylons.

The streets are lined with trees bursting with purple blossoms.
But you probably don't believe me—accustomed to my lies,
you never believe me when I tell the truth.

A Case of Mistaken Identities: The Human Body

The first thing I learned was how to grunt—I'd like to learn how to float.
—SEAMUS HEANEY

Since art was informed by something beyond its power, all we could enact was a dance of doubt.
—DEREK WALCOTT

Duermo en mi cama de roca
Mi sueño dulce y profundo:
Roza una abeja en mi boca
Y crece en mi cuerpo el mundo.
—JOSÉ MARTÍ

I remember it clearly, because I heard it while we were trying very hard to cut something out. The surgeon's arms were almost shoulder deep within the abdominal cavity, and he seemed to struggle against being swallowed up by the gaping incision in the patient. His forehead was lightly beaded with perspiration. My grasp on the retractors kept slipping, because my latex gloves were covered with a thin film of blood. They had told me to feel the spleen and the liver. As I stood on the verge of slipping into blackness myself—I had heard many stories of medical students fainting in the OR—I found myself desperately attaching myself to a sound. I hadn't even been aware of how intently I was listening to it, and how it seemed to be the only level ground upon which I could stand, until the moment I tried to identify its source. It comforted me eternally and seemed to buoy me up. It steadied my balance, defining the outline of my tired back like a perfect hand cupped along the length of my spine. Finally, I looked up from the abyss of the sterile field, feeling my neck muscles flex, my eyes reaching toward what was saving me: the rhythmic sound of the respirator. In a small, protective glass chamber misted with condensation, its fragile black balloon collapsed and refilled, inhaled and exhaled, made its fist and opened to its blossom, over and over again.

I have been trying to answer this question for as long as I can remember. It is the surgery I have been performing on myself since I began writing poems, as if I too required assisted breathing the way a patient undergoing an operation to remove a malignant tumor requires the temporary artificial imposition of the innate breathing rhythms. My parents, my premedical advisers, my colleagues in medicine all have wondered why I write poetry, and especially why I bother with so-called formal poetry. They want a clear answer, as much as I do.

I hear this question as an echo of the external world's ongoing question of me. It is the question that appears explicitly on every application and every test, medical school applications and tests of standard written English included. It is the question implicitly asked whenever I pass an attractive man in the street on my way to school, or when the professor addresses my pathophysiology class in English. "Identify yourself—" this question always demands, "who are you?"

I began by trying to look inwardly at my internal organs to articulate my answer, but my spleen is no different in its contours from any other human spleen, and my brain is just about as convoluted and primitive looking as the next person's. (I know because I looked beneath another's cranium in anatomy class.) Some of my bones may be a little weaker because a skiing accident in high school broke my left humerus. But it is not until I explore the incision that I am—I sometimes feel myself being cut into the world when I walk into the wind—or step away from the gurney to examine my exterior features, that I discover the soft places where the question so easily pierces me.

I have green eyes that seem unusually light against the contrast of my dark complexion. I had many girlfriends before I fell in love with a man. My closet contains blood-spotted surgeon's scrubs shouting their orders and the collegiate cardigans that discuss literature; one desk drawer is full of fragments of poems I've written, and another holds the snake of a stethoscope that listens to their rhythms and cadences. I see these contradictions every day in the huge mirror of the world, but especially on the clearest days, and I can't escape seeing myself. I know I stared blankly at my own body in the wood-framed mirror in my bedroom when I was a teenager, trying to figure out which parts I wanted, and which differentiated me from other people and thus should be amputated. Except I didn't know how to amputate then.

I grew up in an affluent New Jersey suburb. I was the darkest note in the white harmony of classroom after antiseptic classroom—I worried I made discordant sounds when I smiled or played. So I listened very carefully, to whatever was humming and throbbing in the environment at all times, as a way of validating my existence. Maybe this is more simply called heightened alertness. I wondered at what I heard; I became fascinated, even obsessed by sounds. But I often wonder whether it was Spanish murmuring rhythmically in my head, an incessant replaying of those horrible yet oddly comforting albums my father played, filling the evenings up to the stars with warm hands. The merengue singers' laments seemed directed at me personally, their sadness related somehow to my absence, their energy the arms that could pull me almost gravitationally back to Cuba—the only place, it seemed, that I had never visited.

I was also continuously embarrassed by who I might be then, as if my classmates had invisible ears pressed to my family life, so that they might hear the Spanish blaring from the crack under my door. I remember the fluorescent lights in those eerie classrooms, laid together in the shallow, upside-down graves of the ceiling. I felt backward and exposed in their light, as they buzzed all the time their commentary on me, telling me not to sing aloud because it was America all around me. "Don't be proud or pompous. Don't be different. Don't be musical. Don't be a sissy. Don't speak Spanish." These strange lights seemed the condensation of the absence of a tropical landscape, a sort of eternal snow raining down, a cold light of winter.

As a sad child I learned voraciously, eating up knowledge to fend off the starvation of my spirit. I knew I was "different," so I learned my new language very well. I began telling unbelievable stories and writing poems early in life, and I wonder whether my impulse to write was at first rebellious, engendered by a desire to revise the world according to my own internal reality. My cardboard report cards, like my bed and all windows and every classroom, were a series of squares which contained me. My parents rewarded me for all the As which were held, like me, in careful, tiny square boxes.

My favorite sport in those days was soccer (it seemed vaguely important to me that this was a popular sport in Latin America). I was happy American kids liked it. It was a game with straightforward rules, yet I discovered I could create with the movement of my own body. I played the game passably well. While running on the cold autumnal continent of playing field with the trees on fire out of control all around me, I fixed my mind on getting the beautiful arc right by my powerful kick so that the bouncing patchwork soccer ball would enter the rectangle of the goal, to the applause of the crowd. The wild ball would finally rest, caught and seeming terribly deflated in the thousands of boxes that made the net.

In a sense, in spite of myself I have always wanted to enter the squares of New England. I wanted to fit like the square peg fit into the board of the very earliest of my preschool toys. (It was not until I moved to Venezuela that I played with iguanas and cracked open coconuts.) Even now, I can still stare at the pattern of the red bricks in the buildings of Amherst College when I return there as an alumnus. I like to stand in the middle of the main quadrangle, and from this vast square look out over the playing fields to the panoramic pulsations of mountains, the language of the land, along the horizon. It was these that made me choose to attend Amherst.

When I was still a child my family moved to Venezuela rather un-expectedly, with the news of my father's transfer to manage a subsidiary company owned by the larger corporation for which he worked. "A good opportunity for you to learn Spanish," he said/threatened. I was terrified by the prospect of traveling to a place that might more closely resemble a home, where I could unpack and breathe more definitively. The move precipitated violent headaches in me, the last of which attacked me on my final airplane ride back to the United States.

I recall those headaches vividly—they were the atomic explosions of all that sun and the new environment into my head, the heat and the gigantic sun, my subterraneous language of Spanish now suddenly spoken loudly everywhere, the unpredictability everywhere, even in the shapes of leaves. The playgrounds where iguanas suddenly dropped from the trees and the sky. Suddenly there were horrible metaphors and invisible creatures in the very sounds of the exotic language I was speaking. The words touched each other in forbidden ways, in the ways I was discovering I wanted to touch and be touched. I was only nine or ten at the time, so I may have been demanding attention, or pleading to be returned to the flat pavement of the playgrounds in America that had begun to give form to my imagination. Though I do not remember feeling uprooted or homesick, I know I was afraid—afraid, perhaps, to be set free in a place where I was expected to know the way, but where I feared not having the right directions. I was afraid of my own home, I was afraid of what I desired intensely. I was afraid my stomach might swell up, even explode, like the bellies of the malnourished children running naked in the street of Caracas, who in other ways resembled me more than did my friends in suburban New Jersey. Despite intensive medical and psychological study—including the oddly reassuring experience of having my brain imaged by a machine whose walls enclosed me in a space not more than six inches beyond my nose—the experts my parents consulted never found anything wrong with me.

When I returned after several years to New Jersey with my family, all that had really changed was that I had glimpsed a jungle. I compared what I had seen to the jungle boiling inside me. I began to perceive consciously that my task in growing up, like that of anyone born into an unfamiliar environment which they by necessity call home, was to transpose somehow the internal onto the external. I needed to create a safe nest that would bear me in its heart through the long, white winters, where I could have the brick walls on which I had come to depend, but which could be lined with bits and shreds of my jungle. My most private, innermost bed, I allowed myself, could take the shape of the wildly unpredictable leaf that I saw beckoning in Venezuela. The obscenities of Spanish words that I brought back and continued to speak in my head, reassembled by the ceaselessly modulating, echoing container of my English voice box—my mouth, my stroking tongue, the most sensual organs in my body—from these together I had the fantasy of describing my own secure habitat.

So, where I had been called Ralph all through grammar and high school, I suddenly was transformed to Rafael in college. Where I had been clean shaven, I let grow a bushy mustache my mother said made me "look like a Mexican." And as for the flamboyant orchid of my sexuality—I had been attracted to men for as long as I could remember—I stopped plucking it before it could open its magnificent arms. Most important, however, was the very self-conscious writing of poetry I attempted during this time. It was a way of deliberately applying boundaries and squares to these "new" aspects of myself. I wrote terrible poems, but at least I was writing. At the same time, I prepared myself for a career in medicine—the largest, and most rigid, box of all those I had encountered and could construct—in another effort to contain my blossoming. Perhaps the glowing image of the CAT scanner, and the way it investigated me so effortlessly and painlessly, its invisible fingers combing through my murky interior, attracted me. And if either of these paths could lead to the respect and admiration of others, then that was even better. The mere superficial idea people in general might come to have of me by such means was comforting in its flatness, in its two dimensions, in the frame of the simple word "Doctor" preceding my name.

So at Amherst (but even more at Boston University's graduate Creative Writing program, later) writing workshops became the stethoscopes through which I could hear more clearly the sounds poems were making; medical school then allowed me to ultrasound the human body. The two, I pretended as I filled in blanks on my medical school applications, were connected. I tried to fashion a single school of high-walled Gothic architecture in my mind, an uninterrupted hallowed hallway in which I could flow in one directed process of learning. Full of the youthful arrogance my parents labeled idealism, I enrolled in medical school with the conscious purpose of helping to heal the medically indigent populations in this country—the shadows of the taut-bellied children still haven't left me—and to keep the human body from failing to keep time.

I know I wrote my first poem to my mother because I wanted her to stop crying—so she could breathe more easily, the way she did when she carried me in her body. In the time that's passed, these rather unsophisticated impulses still seem closely related to me. Both are attempts, I think, to reintroduce that familiar sense of order into an environment gone out of my control. They were ways of reinforcing the concrete in my walls, the walls that sheltered my nest and allowed it to exist. They were attempts to create a figure of my design, for once, upon painful experience. In short, they were responses to the question of who I was.

I am still in love with the muscularity of formal verse, the way it can wring meaning from the patchwork cloth that I still fear is always wiping away my life in a society desperate for homogeneity. Writing iambic pentameter feels like putting stitches into the anonymous, eternally gaping wound of being human, and rhymes can be intertwined like surgical knots. To write formal poetry is sometimes even a way of sewing myself into the body of traditions from which I feel excluded, as if I were an amputated clubfoot yearning to have its blood supply restored. If I can make English rhyme and sing, if I can be graceful and clean, I can touch the gleaming shell that rests on the beach of my Cuban heritage, the conch that, when blown, has always seemed to produce a melody of Spanish sounds. If I can write a sonnet, I can bring my hand to my lover's chest, and stroke it with the same passion an English gentleman felt as he passed his warm hands across his lover's breasts.

I am startled often by the moments when I glimpse my imagination pedaling along in its rhythms like a child on a bicycle; I am startled when I observe these rhythms corresponding to the exterior world. I dream that these rhythms are all fundamentally the same. I want to become part of these rhythms, and to strike only harmonious chords. I want my language to be the same, I want my sexuality to be a normal variation. I want to be a good son and a good American, and I want to be my own hero, the armored Spanish sailor who never sank and drowned with the Armada but washed up miraculously upon England's shore, and at the same time the red-bearded Celt who gave my father's Spanish grandparents their blue eyes—I know these imaginary historical people are all versions of the same history I want to reincarnate. I want life to be like science class, so it makes sense and I will not go crazy. I want to learn the rules and conventions of formal verse the way I learned chemical reactions. I want to hear myself think clearly, and I want my parents to listen—I want to catch the ear of others around me. I want to be heard, to stand on the stage at the center of human attention, where all the drums are beating. I desperately want everyone to understand Spanish—rhythm, meter, and rhyme can make these wishes of a child come true.

I have adult reasons too for why I continue to be drawn in the direction of formal poetry. It too is a complex science, with its own elegant arguments. It is also a practical system with rules I can trust. I can measure my experience with it; I can use it to plot a graph of my emotions, that I can hold up later to study more carefully. I may make connections with it to other artists, when I quote Wordsworth and Traherne and Herbert.

In a similar way, in a parallel universe, medical science is also a way of controlling and understanding the physical processes of the human body. Perhaps I saw a way to wrap my hands around life, my own particular, peculiar life feeling so unanchored at times. In laying my hands upon the bodies of patients, I could touch my own body. I could purge their bodies of infestations with antibiotics, and I could be a whole, unitary, cleansed person myself. In curing them, I could cure myself. This was when I imagined medical school was a place where illnesses were simply diagnosed and treated.

What had been growing inside me throughout medical school, however, is a relationship to language I did not expect. The stirrings I feel inside me are not necessarily the viable fetus of my desires given flesh, but some unborn potential in me waiting to be expressed, the expectant language to which I still want to give voice, the rhythmic contractions of birth empowering my mouth.

So, once I arrived at Harvard Medical School, I reinventoried my needs. I desperately wanted to learn the inner language of the human body, and have the kind of fluency that comes from tracing the surface of the liver, in the way the Venezuelan heat which hummed with the Spanish language felt like living, even waiting to be born, inside my own body. I wanted to mend my broken arm, to make from words the skeleton to give shape to the body of my experience—I wanted to make a cast to protect myself, to keep myself straight and correctly aligned. I wanted to hear the rhythms of breathing amplified by my stethoscope. I wanted to examine the vocal cords through a laryngoscope, and see the anatomy of the ear drum and the tiny protruding ossicles through an otoscope. I wanted to descend even closer, even smaller, and step down the tunnel of a microscope to hear the ions ebbing and flowing across cell membranes, and the incessant beating of cilia. I wanted, in short, a scientific explanation for the mystery of my voice—a distorted, pathological corollary to my wanting to create that voice. More and more, I wanted my own voice to be defined by objective, physical constraints.

But at the end of three years of medical school, I had never seen Cuba through the microscope; in fact, I needed a telescope for that. Science seemed to be failing me. The equations I memorized began taking up the space of poems I had learned in college. The sheer amount of material I was expected to learn was staggering, and I was being flattened—again, but in a different way since now I was actively cooperating. Some of the horror stories I had heard about medical school were beginning to come true.

Especially distressing to me during this time was the fact that I objected internally to giving voice to these feelings—for the first time, I forbade myself the application of language, even internal dialogue, to what I was doing. The more I feared that medical school was not providing the supports I needed to define myself, the more I avoided the very mechanisms set in place by the medical school to assist students. Control became the medium in which I was entrapped, rather than my art—like a sculptor entering his stone, but never returning with what he's found. My beautiful Gothic architecture was becoming a garish disguise for a bleak prison.

My writing itself became transformed, and like a medical student who begins to diagnose in himself the diseases he is studying, so too did my poems become diseased. Some of the rhyming mnemonics I employed were vulgar and distasteful. I began to conceal the fact that I wrote poems, because for the first time it felt not like a private activity but more like a devious thing to do. Poetry became my dirtiest secret, an entirely nonmedical enterprise that was interfering with my career goals—and I feared being exposed as a poet, more than I ever did seeing "send back the wetbacks" or "die faggot" spray-painted on the brick walls around Harvard Square. (Even now as I write, I still shudder slightly at the thought of "coming out"—as an artist.)

After the first two years, I stopped writing altogether. I concentrated all my energies on saving the container I wanted medical school to be for me. I worked harder than ever, and, paralleling the pattern of my early childhood, did well in my rotations.

It was my surgery rotation that jolted me away from my path toward relentless self-enclosure. Ironically, at first it must have been the labyrinth of the surgical floor that attracted me to surgery—its rooms within rooms filled with tiles, the locker room brimming with locked compartments, literally to the ceiling. The surgical floor, with its automatically closing doors always sealing tightly behind me, transmitted the unconscious message of "everything is under wraps"—the ultimate in a controlled environment, where even microorganisms were screened out of the ORs by the infinitesimal meshwork of air filters. The strong hierarchy of the surgical team also appealed to me, and I convinced myself that their homophobic jokes were funny and the abuse was deserved—after all, I desperately needed to be controlled.

Then came the day in the OR that I discovered myself clinging to the respirator like it was my own heartbeat and I hadn't ever been born. By the end of that lengthy operation, I felt as though the huge tumor had finally been cut out of me. I looked at it: a bloody, contorted mass lying in a perfectly sterile, square, mirrorlike metal pan. At that moment, I didn't know which was worse, to live recklessly as the tumor did, exceeding its own walls and almost killing the patient who carried it— or to have brutally excised it the way the surgeons had, placing it like a prize framed in a cold specimen dish to confirm that it was now incapable of hurting anyone.

What I saw was an excised tumor in a sterile specimen dish. My staring began to transform it, until I saw the shape of an island bloodied by revolution in a dazzling sea. Then I saw the castrated penis of a homosexual cast upon the cold stone floor of the Inquisitors' jail. Then, with the same suddenness and heaving effort of the patient as he came up coughing from the depths of anesthesia, I understood what I needed to do.

Now I realize that for a long time I had feared my own humanity— the sound of my own voice had frightened me, as if I had been walking along a dark alleyway alone at night. I realize now that by singing and whistling to myself I only imitated life, instead of creating it, when I wrote poems. The point was, and still is, I had never been controlled by my environment at all—I created the illusion that I was. I began without the hope of being the peg that fit into the board—when I was the monstrous, pink-mouthed iguana lurking in the closet. The most affluent suburb in America could not change that. Years of classrooms could not change that, nor could peering out into the razor sunlight from half-shut doors and windows. Even "returning" to Venezuela was a long-winded lie, told by an airplane that transported me so close to, without ever actually reaching, the sun.

My schizophrenias are what I am, the active process itself. There is no medication to cure me, and only boxes of my own construction to contain me, whose walls allowed me to smash my own head against them.

That day I decided to answer the question, putting all the facile answers of history, and genealogy, and careerism aside. The very act of passing through a door, and the expectations on the way to my art were the source of energy to write poems. Music and language were suddenly my instruments, not enslavers to be appeased. I could scream in my voice like hands all over their golden words and grammatical rules, in the way I had once dreamed of touching them. Spanish and English were immediately the same, they had the same sounds, they were spoken in the same mouth, and they lived in confluent gyri on my temporal lobe. Being gay was joyfully not to have a country of origin at all, only a place in my heart where a man was extending his arms toward me. I could take possession of each sound in my own mouth, and they could lift me up to a new hilltop that was in no particular country, but one I could visit and demonstrate to the world. I did not need medical school to show me that my eyes see into the world by their own physiology, my own neurons encode and transmit my experience; and I have been seeing and seeing all along.

I can see that I am something new, and that from me I can extend my naked arm. The form of the bone, which healed long ago, gives it a peculiar shape. I do not want to amputate it, or rebreak it and set it in a better cast. Now I give myself the parts of me I never understood or never liked. As a poet, my challenge is to create myself, in my own image, using the materials common to all speakers of English. Words are indistinguishable from my physical body now. As a physician, I hope to perform a similar role for my patients: hand them back, as I examine them and talk with them, their own bodies with their distinct, troubling features attended to, cared for, studied, and discussed. Sometimes, they will be cured—a spine set straight, an abscess drained. Sometimes they will die unexpectedly and suddenly. But these extremes identify only small corners in the drama of healing. In the middle of a single life, and in so many other cases, what I am naming may be their real need: someone to listen at first to their breathing, then to their heart, and hear the universal human sound each one alone creates.

LUIS ALBERTO URREA

Father's Day

From *Across the Wire: Hard Times on the U.S.-Mexican Border*

January 10. My father, in a red American Motors 440, drives north through the Sonora desert, ticking off towns as the sun rises to his right: Santa Ana, Caborca, Tajito. He is on his way to Tijuana, to his mother's house, where he has lived on and off since my mother threw him out of our home. He left Culiacán yesterday, in the morning. He's been driving alone, nonstop, pausing for gas and two terrible roadside meals. The cheap tape recorder nestled among packs of cigarettes on the seat beside him has been playing Mexican songs that call forth all his ghosts and memories. Miguel Prado, Agustín Lara, Pedro Infante, Lola Beltrán. Mile upon mile, the car has gradually filled with the dead and forgotten. The backseat is crowded with a hundred girlfriends, lovers, and wives. Time swirls around him like smoke. His dentures fit badly—the pain keeps him awake. He has spent Christmas in his hometown, in the farthest southern corner of Sinaloa, and he has recognized no one. All of them are old and strange to him. Their concerns are foolish, their laughter painful to his ears. He has retrieved a thousand dollars from the bank on Morelos Street, a gift for me. My father is sixty-one years old.

San Luis Río Colorado appears in the shimmering early light. He is driving fast—he always drives fast. Far away, Yuma, Arizona, suggests itself through the haze. The Mexican checkpoint is outside of town. Bored and aggressive Mexican Immigration and Federal Judicial Police officers wave cars over and inspect papers. They deny passage randomly, confiscate valuable-looking goods, exact "tolls" from gringos and border Mexicans who lack the papers or the conviction to convince the officers they may proceed. My father is Mexican, but he is also blond and blue eyed. (His blond hair has gone white, but his skin is still pale pink, and his eyes behind his glasses are still bright.) He has California plates on his car. He is going fast.

This is where the thing happens.

No one knows exactly what, or if it happened before the *aduana* (customs inspection) huts or after. But somehow, my father—Mexican ballads rattling through the cheap speakers, all those voices in his head, smoking a cigarette, smoke trailing from his mouth like he's burning already and going down—leaves the road and sails into the desert dawn.

His car sails for a dreadful instant, forever. Angles off the road and lifts into the air. Unimaginable movement of fists on the wheel, trying to right the car after it has taken flight. Dust and gravel cresting beneath him like a wave, as he catapults over the edge of a drop-off. Everything in the car—tapes, cigarettes, ashes, coins, recorder, my father's glasses— comes to life and eddies around him. The car tips. Its front corner digs into the ground. It flips once, twice. Later, rumors suggest it rolled six times. The wheel breaks off in his hands. The windshield vanishes. He goes out the window. The car rolls on him. He is dragged back in by the lurching force of the crash. All around, his things scatter across the sand and sage.

It is easy to imagine the silence returning then. Increments of peace. The wind can be heard again, then the calling of crows and jays. In the distance, a siren.

I am not brought into this story until late.

Without me, my father goes about the business of dying. He tries not to die, of course. My father would not surrender easily to death. But the Mexicans manage to convince him.

Before they take him to the hospital, various agents of the Mexican Republic help themselves to the sudden flea market my father has set out for them. As he bleeds on the gurney, blind and mute, pissing his pants, they sift through the goods: there are a lot of tapes, after all. Someone nabs his recorder. Someone else takes a fancy to his new shoes, bought for him by my favorite cousin and given to him only two days before.

His wallet and my thousand dollars are safe—soaked in urine in his pockets. Nobody cares to fish for them at the moment. Because nobody wants to reach into all that mess, they don't find out he's a Mexican citizen, a retired army officer, late of the presidential staff of Mexico, and a retired federal cop. He can't talk to tell them. They drive off, blue lights inconsequential against the sun.

In town, they strip him naked and call in a Mexican doctor.

The doctor says something along the lines of "My God, it's Beto!"

One of the attendants says something else, like "What do you mean, *Beto?*"

The doctor looks around him. He can't believe it. This is too strange. Just days ago, he was at a party with my father in Sinaloa. He'd asked my father for a ride to this very town. My father turned him down, saying, cryptically, "I don't want to be responsible for your life."

"I know this man," the doctor says. "He's a Mexican."

Somebody calls the police. The Federales are on their way. Something strange is going on here, and the doctor wants nothing to do with it. He snaps some orders to the staff of the clinic, then plunges his hand into my father's pockets. He is no doubt startled to find a thousand dollars there, in new bills. He takes my father's wallet out of the back pocket and flees. For reasons that will remain unclear, the Federales will spend the rest of the day trying to find him to get all these things back from him. He will be so busy avoiding them that he will not see my father again.

Once the doctor leaves, they wheel my father, naked, into a room. He is beginning to struggle, to writhe around in his bed. His ribs are cracked; his internal injuries bleed within him; his chin is split, and he might have a concussion; he has some brain injuries and might have suffered a stroke. Nobody's quite sure what's wrong with him. They decide to quiet him down and shoot him with morphine.

My father, drugged, settles back into a velvet haze. All his ghosts swarm to him and begin to smother him.

I have siblings whom I know and don't know: Juan, Alberto, Octavio, Leticia, and Martha. The circumstances of my father's life took him from them at an early age, and they were left to struggle with their mother. I am younger than all of them, and have never lived with any of them. Like me, they fear him and worship him and miss him even when he's with us. Somehow, word gets out on the border that Alberto Urrea has been seriously hurt in a car wreck. But people think it's my brother Alberto. People start looking for my brother's family to tell them he's dying.

In the meantime, in our old neighborhood in Tijuana, my aunt Lety and cousin Hugo are in the family house on Rampa Independencia. They are waiting for Beto to arrive from Sinaloa. Hugo has built him a small bedroom where he keeps all his tokens—love letters, bowling trophies, moldering *Playboy* magazines, a box of photographs. In those photos, my father is a skinny boy with a heart-shaped mouth. He looks sad in every one. The years have tinted them all brown.

My aunt hears my father's car idling in front of the house. She glances out and sees a red shape pull up to her gate.

"It's Beto!" she calls. My grandmother, gone mad with age, blinks in her chair like a pudgy bird.

"Who?" she says.

"Beto," says my aunt. "*Beto ya llego*." (Beto has arrived.)

She steps outside to greet him. There is no car there. She steps into the street. Looks both ways. No red car in sight.

"Beto's dead," she says.

Word spreads—the doctor calls my aunt. Somehow, she and Alberto make contact, and they, along with my cousin Hugo and my father's former wife, Emilia, head east in Alberto's car. Strangely enough, it is a vast black Cadillac: they rush to my father's death in a hearse.

Other relatives go into a Mexican version of action: one branch grabs the first plane they can that flies to Arizona. In their panic, they don't realize the ticketing agent has sent them to the wrong part of Arizona. The flight leaves them farther from my father than if they'd stayed in Tijuana.

Somebody finally calls me in San Diego. I have been listening to music—something as ridiculous as Uriah Heep. Everyone has left for San Luis Río Colorado. Everything is happening. I am asked to hold steady. Someone will get right back to me. Nobody does.

My cousin Hugo, the most feared member of the family, is the one who finally tells me what it was like to find my father in the clinic. Hugo was raised by him and knows him better than some of his own sons. Hugo calls him "Papa."

Family legend has it that once, when Hugo was driving through Tijuana late at night, a carload of *cholos* began to harass him, trying to push him off the road, yelling taunts. Hugo calmly pulled over, took a homemade broadsword out from under the seat, and proceeded to chop pieces off their car. He split their hood with it, pulled it out, and said, "All right, come on."

They abandoned their car and ran into the night.

Hugo pushes his way into the room and sits on the bed, holds my writhing father down. Tells him, "Don't worry, Papa. We're here. We'll get you out."

My father cannot say anything to him, but Hugo senses he understands. He calms down, lies back. Hugo talks to him for a moment more.

According to what faction of the Urrea family you consult, either of the following occurs:

Arrangements are made to transport my father to the border, and there, an American ambulance will carry him into Yuma. Hugo knows my father will die if left in this clinic. The American ambulance arrives at the border crossing and waits, off to the side, doors open, light circling.

No Mexican unit arrives. Repeated calls reveal nothing: nobody knows what happened to the ambulance. Isn't it there? It ought to be there. How curious.

It never arrives. Hugo and my father wait for an hour. It has been eight hours since the accident.

Or:

Hugo and my aunt Lety and my brother Alberto and his mother, Emilia, gather and make the evacuation plans. But my aunt, seeing too clearly what is about to happen, convinces them to abandon hope. *Beto is going to die,* she tells them. *Can't you see?*

Finally, the ghosts convince my father. He settles back in the bed, eyes looking at nothing in particular. Without a word or a gesture, my father dies.

A few miles away, the Americans close their doors, turn off their lights, and drive back to Yuma.

Too late to do any good, I enter the picture.

Hugo's sister, Margo, picks me up on her way to Tijuana. A family friend has called me and told me the news. Margo's car is crammed with silent people as we ride into Tijuana and rise up to Independencia, shoulders digging into each other as the car hits the ruts and half-buried boulders in the road.

We gather in the dirt street outside the family home: Hugo, Aunt Lety, Margo, the riders, me. Dogs behind the fence think we're having a party. They think the fun's about to begin. They dance on their back legs, eagerly watching us in the street.

"Let's go," Hugo says. He means to the funeral home: Funeraria González.

I get in Hugo's truck. Hugo has been the closest to the thing. He has accumulated a kind of evil grace. I hope he can tell me if anything special happened. If there were any apparitions, sounds, lights, angels.

"He died," he says. For him, that's enough.

We drive downtown. The funeral home is nondescript, in the middle of a run-down block. But then, most blocks in Tijuana are run-down, all cobbled together with no plan in mind, facade after mid-fifties facade leaning into each other, paint coming away from the walls on thin wedges of stucco.

The brothers are waiting for me outside. We don't want to take a step without each other. Nobody knows how to grieve. We stand apart from each other with a strange military precision, two feet between each man. We shuffle. We grin: the old man's dead. We shake our heads, sigh. We laugh. Nobody can fit the fact into the day. They have my father's money and wallet. The doctor has turned them over to somebody, I don't know who, and they have appeared here, in front of the family house. My eldest brother, Juan, hands me the cash. It's floppy. Wet, it feels like felt.

"It must have rained," Octavio says. "Do you think it rained? Everything's all wet."

Hugo looks at me. He says nothing. I know why it's wet. Hugo and Juan know why it's wet. Juan and I stare into each other's eyes.

I say, "I guess they had an early morning shower."

Everybody nods.

Juan gives me the wallet. Inside: driver's license, green card, social security card, notes, slips of paper, useless cards in various shades of blue and yellow. In his picture, my father looks small and old. He has a pouch under his chin. You can see the curve of his skull under the diminishing front rank of his hair.

"Okay," I say.

We turn as one and enter the door.

Hugo grabs my arm as the brothers start upstairs. "Down here," he says.

"What?" I say.

"The body's down here," he says.

"So?"

"So you're going to look at it."

"No I'm not."

"Yes you are. You're going to look at it."

"No."

Hugo has a habit of always speaking English to me. For some reason, I insist on speaking Spanish to him. I'm not sure what it is we're trying to convince each other of.

"It's up to you," he says. "He's all banged up. You've got to decide if it's an open casket or not. That's what he'd want. Come on."

His grip is bony as a talon as he pulls me into the little room. The casket is on a stone bench, about three feet off the ground. Mexican floral arrangements have begun to surround the coffin: horseshoes on stands, wreaths, all of them draped in *faux*-satin sashes with family names and condolences written across them in glue and glitter. They look like entrants in a retirement home flower-arranging contest, or good luck displays at a high school reunion.

Hugo uses his pocketknife to unscrew the lid. The screw rises, rises, interminably coming up until it wiggles loose, and he says, "Look," and I put my hands on the lid and wait. "Go on," he says. I resent his manliness more than anything on earth at that instant, then I lift the lid. For some reason, I hold my breath, like my father is going to smell. But he's encased in glass. In fact, he probably does smell—he's been dead now for two days with no embalming. Many Mexican funeral homes just clamp a sheet of glass over the body to prevent any problems, and you look down at them as though you were in a glass-bottomed boat, drifting across the shoals of Hell. It's alarming. You think, *He can't breathe in there.*

I look in. He's small as a ten-year-old boy in a faded brown photograph. He's unimaginably sad, his lips turned a little around his injured mouth, looking as though he's about to say a word that begins with *m*. I stare down at my father, my only father, and my breath fogs the glass and steals his face.

Open wounds turn black after death.

"Close it," I say.

Hugo shuts the lid gently.

"Don't screw it down," I say. "He wouldn't want people to see him like that, but I think they have a right to say good-bye, if they want to. So they can lift the lid for themselves."

It is my first decision as a grown man.

"Good," Hugo says. "That's the right choice."

Upstairs, my brother Juan is waiting for me. The others stand behind him.

"There's a problem," he says.

"What problem?"

"We owe some money," he says, "for the body."

"We what?"

A pleasant short man steps up. He has a tan police uniform, but no badge or gun. He's a lackey for the San Luis Río Colorado cops.

"I brought the body," he says.

"Thank you," I tell him.

"They said to tell you," he glances away, "that the body is still in custody."

We all look at each other, eyes clicking in steady sweeps of all the faces.

"You're kidding," I say.

"No, señor," he says. "The police department still has possession of your father. I have been instructed to ask you for the fee to release him to you."

"You want me to pay bail for a corpse?"

The man is uncomfortable. He says nothing.

"How did my father come here?"

"In my station wagon."

"I see."

This whole scene is so bizarre that I don't know how to respond. There's no one to ask what to do. My brothers just stand there. Hugo is as inscrutable as a stone carving. I reach into my pocket.

"How much?"

"Seven hundred and fifty dollars, American."

I pull out the wet bills and count out eight hundred dollars. He hands me fifty back in change. He smiles. Everybody's relieved. He shakes all our hands. He tells me it's sad, what happened, and how hard it is for all of us when these things befall us. I'm thinking, *Fuck you, fuck you, fuck you*.

The funeral director steps up. He's unctuous, in a suit and hair oil and cologne. His workers are short Indian men in tan work clothes. It's like an optical illusion: the police toady steps away and three reflections of him appear in his absence.

I still have the change in my hand. He starts in—*tragic losses, at rest now, gone to glory, deepest sympathies*—but there is the small matter of the funeral costs.

"How much?" I say.

"Five hundred and fifty dollars," he says. "Unfortunately."

I hand him my change.

"We'll come up with the rest," one of my brothers says.

"We'll take up a collection," says another.

On our way back downstairs, Hugo says, "So much for your present."

I am so confused, I want to cry. I cannot. For years afterward, I will try to cry and be unable to. On some nights, I will take spit on the tips of my fingers and draw tears down my cheeks, trying to find relief.

We Mexicans wake the dead. We *give wakes* to the dead. Hugo and I agree that my shift will be at around two in the morning. He leads me to my father's room and goes off to bed. My aunt still shares a room with her mother. I can hear the women in there, snoring. The sounds of Tijuana carry up the hills, somehow different from the sounds of the United States. The dogs, the car horns, the traffic rumble, the whistles, the trumpets are all in a different language. Their pitch and timbre are as distinctive as is Chinese, or Russian. Or Spanish.

I sit in my father's room, listening. All that noise, and the whole world dead. His pillow is still streaked with his hair pomade—he wore it trim, short, combed straight back off his forehead, always as slick as Jerry Lewis'. I can't sleep in his bed. Everything smells like him. I am naked. I am unbelievably aroused. All I can think about is sex. I keep hoping the family's cleaning woman will wake up and come to my room. I want to eat, make love, climb a mountain, have a fistfight. I talk to Jesus. I sit in the middle of the floor and sift through layers of paper: report cards, citations, letters from women in Sinaloa, divorce papers, poems, tax forms, INS papers, bowling certificates, sheets with numbers on them, military records, a letter from the president of Mexico. Silverfish and roaches come forth from my father's pages, where they have lived safely, eating his past.

I pull the string attached to the bare bulb above my head. The dark claps shut around me. Years later, it seems, Hugo speaks from the greater darkness of the doorway.

"It's time."

I get dressed.

We go to his truck.

Everything's quiet. You can even hear crickets. He starts up, puts it in gear. We drive down the dark hill. Everybody's lights are out as we descend.

"God damn it," Hugo finally says. "It's not fair."

He drops me off at the door.

"See you in the afternoon," he says.

"All right."

"Somebody will be by in a few hours," he says.

"All right."

He drives away. I step inside. It's bright, pleasant. Old carpets have loops tugged loose. Inexplicably, there is an electric clock with a soft-drink logo on it. Chapel A has a forgotten casket in it. My father waits in Chapel B.

It's a dull little room with dull little drapes at the end. There are about eight rows of pews. A plywood lectern stands before the raised coffin. And there are all those flowers. Their colors are basically white and carmine beneath the fluorescent lights; the greens look like rubber.

I try sitting in a pew, looking at the coffin. It looks like a gigantic throat lozenge. I prowl the building. Periodically, the Indian men come downstairs. They apparently sleep up there, because their hair is in disarray and their eyes are red and puffy. "Do you want some coffee?" they ask.

"No thank you."

"Coke? Water?"

"No, I'm fine."

They nod, go back up. Occasionally, one will pat my elbow.

I lift the curtains from the wall and look behind them. There is a door near the head of the coffin. I open it. I step into a small parking area behind the funeral home. A dark station wagon is crunching in on the gravel, backing up to a wooden chute that runs down at an angle from the second floor. One of the workers steps out. He and the driver exchange murmurs. They open the back and pull a figure out by its feet. A motor begins to whirr. They wrestle the drooping corpse in its shroud into the chute. Apparently, there is a conveyor belt inside. The body rises and seems to float, going up to the sky, feetfirst.

I step back inside and close the door.

I lift the lid on my father. I can count the tiny white whiskers growing in the blackness of his chin and throat. Stains smaller than dimes dot the front of his shirt—stains he would have never allowed in life. One of my sisters wants him dressed in a jacket. A funeral parlor worker tells me they'll have to go at my father's arms with a mallet to get them loose enough to put the coat on him. Nobody else knows. He wants to make sure I understand. I do. "What does it matter now?" is what I say.

I go to my pew again.

I wait.

A woman who is notorious as a "bad girl" in our family comes in silently. It is nearly four A.M. She is with a florid American. Her hair is as huge as Tina Turner's, her eyes surrounded by hedges of lashes. She seems startled to see me, caught.

"Come in," I say.

"I'm sorry," she says.

It turns out she didn't want to make any scandal, just to pay her respects privately.

The American hangs around at the back of the room. When I nod at him, he says, " 'Zit goin'?"

Inanely, I say, "Pretty good."

She sits with me. She says, "He was always kind to me."

"He loved you," I say.

I am in love with her. I look at the tiniest of wrinkles beside her mouth, I smell her musky perfume and look at her dangerous nails and tight skirt, and I think I will marry her on the spot. She is the only person in the world who is alive with me at that moment. I smell her, sit close to her. We hold hands.

"I'm not what they think," she says.

She kisses me. Gets up to leave. Says, "Can I see him?"

I let her go up there alone. She opens the box, looks down at him. The muscles in her legs clench tight as fists. She speaks softly. She lowers the lid. When she comes back, she is crying.

"Good-bye," she says.

I nod. The American says, "Take it easy." They walk out the door. I can smell her all over the room.

My father was a big stud. Though he was five seven, you thought he was six feet tall. My mother chased him out of the house when I was about twelve. He was probably the first Mexican to ever rub shoulders with the neighbors on our suburban San Diego street. They weren't that crazy about it. Neither was he.

One day, the lady from across the street came over and told my mother that he was seeing a string of women while she was at work. The neighbor wanted to know if they were prostitutes, or what. That was it for my mother. He left in disgrace, and they never spoke to each other again. When he came by the house to see me, she hid in her room, wanting him to think she was gone.

Every Friday night, we went to the Tu-Vu drive-in to watch movies and eat hot dogs.

All these memories come at me, and I wait. I try to sleep—on the pew, on the floor. I can't. I wait all morning. Finally, around two or three in the afternoon, people start to show up at the funeral home. I've been waiting with my father for twelve hours. I'm eager to get it over with.

People shuffle in, avert their eyes. Halfhearted embraces happen all over the room, everybody avoiding the embarrassment of the coffin. My sisters go up and look. A Mexican Pentecostal evangelist takes the podium and begins to harangue us. It's a pattern I have begun to notice at funerals lately: the preacher takes countless cheap shots at the crowd, which is presumably softened up by the recent death and is busy hoping it won't be next. I feel disinterested. Lack of sleep and hunger have made the insides of my ears feel swollen.

We drag my father off to a dismal little hillside cemetery. He takes his last car ride nestled in pointless plushness; satin pillows cradle him inside the darkness of the box. The hearse is muted and stately. We are led by my uncle, Carlos Urrea, heroic motorcycle cop in the stunning Tijuana uniform. Cars stop and wait for us to drive by. Inside, people are watching the procession, saying "There goes the dead guy" through the glass.

On the hill, his box descends. I back away, then turn around. I watch clouds, heavy as trucks, driving across Tijuana.

When the death certificate comes, it says my father died of a stroke. The insurance company will not pay us a cent, since auto coverage is for car wrecks. They insist on proof.

Hugo goes back to San Luis Río Colorado. He enters the police compound and finds my father's car. It's beat to hell—the tires are twisted, the roof collapsed. He shoots a roll of film, then comes home unscathed.

"Somebody killed Papa," he says. "I know it."

I look at the pictures.

"One side of the car's all bashed in," he says. "There's black and white paint in the door."

"So?"

"Cops. They chased him and ran him off the road. Where would he get black and white paint on a red car that crashed out in the desert?"

I don't know—it sounds farfetched, then it doesn't. Mexican relatives tell me I'm crazy. They tell me to deal with reality. My uncle tells me the authorities wouldn't behave in such a manner.

Since we buried my father, his mother has died. Hugo called me one morning and said, "You know Grandma? She's dead."

My own mother is trapped in a financial catastrophe that continues to deepen. Within three years of my father's death, she is living in a house without heat, without plumbing in the kitchen, with broken plumbing in the bathroom, and without a stove or oven. She cooks on a hot plate.

Months later, Hugo shuffles through his pictures. The car looks red as blood. It looks, at turns, vast and minuscule. I stare at the crooked seats and see my own ghosts and memories, my own hundreds of miles sitting *right there*.

I can't get my eyes off the roof of the car. It's bent down. All the windows are broken. Hugo is right. There's black and white paint smashed into the passenger door. Or are they simply scrapes?

We send the photographs to the insurance company, and we contact the American consulate for help in investigating the accident. The insurer returns the photos and refuses to pay us a settlement, suggesting the pictures could have been taken after my father died from his stroke. Besides, they tell us, there's no proof that it's even his car.

The consul contacts me a few days later. After a full investigation into the death of my father, the facts seem to indicate that there can be no investigation of the death of my father. In the months subsequent to his death, the entire police force of San Luis Río Colorado has apparently retired. No officer can be found who was on active duty at the time of the accident, and since the ones who were on duty have retired and left San Luis to enjoy their leisure time, there is no one to talk to. The case is closed. Official cause of death: stroke.

In a final act of desperation, I write to the chief of police of the town. Hugo, when he hears about it, says, "Hey. You'd better not go to San Luis. Ever." He laughs.

An answer comes: the chief calls me on the phone. Or he claims to be the police chief. I realize now, he could have been anyone. In response to my inquiry, he says, he has only one thing to say. And I should remember this thing, I should take it to heart. "It is over, señor Urrea," he tells me. "It is better for all of us that you forget it and move on with your life. It is better for all of us," he says, "if there was no accident. Am I clear? There was no accident."

"Yes, sir," I say. "You are extremely, perfectly, clear."

"Good," he says. Then "Good" again.

He hangs up the phone so quietly, there isn't even a click.

Within a month of my final conversation with the police, I receive an envelope in the mail. It is from the head office of the chief of municipal police of San Luis Río Colorado, Sonora. The information is printed on the envelope with various official swirls of ink and a seal of some sort. I expect it's a letter, but it's not.

I find instead a bill on flimsy paper. The bill is requesting the immediate payment of twelve hundred dollars in American currency. This sum will cover, in full, the damages my father caused to city property on the date of January 10, 1977. There is no mention of how these damages came about. When people ask me, I make a joke out of it. I tell them, "I don't know—maybe he fell out of bed really hard." Nobody laughs but me.

On the Day They Buried My Mother...

The wind pushed the sun
behind the moon
and
in the dark of light I saw
shadows trailing the cool

Autumn shook hands with winter
just before it died
Summer leaves bloomed
and ran away on a spring ride

coulda wrote an epithet
on a mountain tombstone for an
ant
a deer laid dead on a fresh water stream
and the hunter cursed
beneath his breath at the spirits of
the stars who caused the deer's death . . .

The earth shook with laughter
as the spades tickled its side
and gleamed so pretty with
so many forgotten flowers
from those final cadillac brides

My hat fell in the open grave
my feet inside my shoes swayed
my gloves were wet with sweat
looked quickly in the mirror of my heart
sign a relief . . .
and calmly smiled my fears aside . . .

This Is Not the Place
Where I Was Born

puerto rico 1974
this is not the place where i was born
remember—as a child the fantasizing images my mother planted
within my head—
the shadows of her childhood recounted to me many times
over welfare loan on crédito food from el bodeguero
i tasted mango many years before the skin of the fruit
ever reached my teeth
i was born on an island about 35 miles wide 100 miles long
a small island with a rain forest somewhere in the central
regions of itself
where spanish was a dominant word
& signs read by themselves
i was born in a village of that island where the police
who frequented your place of business-hangout or home came as
servant or friend & not as a terror in slogan clothing
i was born in a barrio of the village on the island
where people left their doors open at night
where respect for elders was exhibited with pride
where courting for loved ones was not treated over confidentially
where children's laughter did not sound empty & savagely alive
with self destruction . . .
i was born on an island where to be puerto rican meant to be
part of the land & soul & puertorriqueños were not the
minority
puerto ricans were first, none were second
no, i was not born here . . .
no, i was not born in the attitude & time of this place
this sun drenched soil

this green faced piece of earth
this slave blessed land
where the caribbean seas pound angrily on the shores
of prefabricated house/hotel redcap hustling people gypsy taxi cab
fighters for fares to fajardo
& the hot wind is broken by fiberglass palmtrees
& highrise plátanos mariano on leave & color t.v.
looneytune cartoon comicbook characters with badges
in their jockstraps
& foreigners scream that puertorriqueños are foreigners
& have no right to claim any benefit on the birthport
this sun drenched soil
this green faced piece of earth
this slave blessed land
where nuyoricans come in search of spiritual identity
are greeted with profanity
this is insanity that americanos are showered
with shoe shine kisses
police in stocking caps cover carry out john wayne
television cowboy law road models of new york city detective
french connection/death wish instigation ku-klux-klan mind
panorama screen seems
in modern medicine is in confusion needs a transfusion quantity
treatment if you're not on the plan the new stand
of blue cross blue shield blue uniform master charge
what religion you are
blood fills the waiting room of death
stale air & qué pasa stares are nowhere
in sight & night neon light shines bright
in el condado area puerto rican under cover cop
stop & arrest on the spot puerto ricans who shop for the flag
that waves on the left-in souvenir stores—
puertorriqueños cannot assemble displaying the emblem
nuyoricans are fighting & dying for in newark, lower east side
south bronx where the fervor of being
puertorriqueños is not just rafael hernández
viet vet protest with rifle shots that dig into four pigs
& sociable friday professional persons rush to the
golf course & martini glasses work for the masses
& the island is left unattended because the middle class

bureaucratic cuban has arrived spitting blue eyed justice
at brown skinned boys in military khaki
compromise to survive is hairline length
mustache trimmed face looking grim like a soldier
on furlough further cannot exhibit contempt for what is
not cacique born this poem will receive a burning
stomach turning scorn nullified classified racist
from this pan am eastern first national chase manhattan
puerto rico . . .

Ghost Trap

A woman was building a ghost trap to catch the ghost of her *marido,* who had recently died. She wanted to keep him from coming into her house. At first she had been devastated by his death. She had thrown herself into the grave on top of his coffin wailing like *la llorona,* the ghost woman who wandered in the dark. She would wake in the middle of the night in a sweat, turn to him to share a dream or a fear, and find an emptiness. She would walk from room to room at night feeling like a ghost. The loneliness turned into anger at his desertion.

One night the second week after his death she woke to find him in bed with her, or rather his ghost. "*¡Viejo!*" she cried out, smiling for the first time since his death. But suddenly she frowned and felt fear squeeze her heart.

During the day he would follow her around the house and to the backyard, but he would never go beyond the front gate when she left to run errands. She began to spend more time away from the house. She realized that she missed her solitude. Instead of making her feel wanted and protected, as his presence had before his death, his constant hovering now stifled her.

"*Viejo,* why do you keep coming back every night? Did you leave something unfinished? Is there some business you want to complete? Tell me and I'll help you do it."

"*Vieja, viejita linda,* bring me clean clothes," he said to her in a wisp of a whisper.

"*Ba, estás muerto, ¿pa' qué necesitas ropa?* You're dead, you have no need of clothes," she whispered back. His repeated request, which seemed to get louder and louder, finally drove her to the closet. Of course his clothes were missing; she'd given them away. Now she would have to go into the shop and buy men's things and face the look of censure in the shopkeeper's face at how fast she had replaced her husband with another man.

"*Vieja, vieja,* fix me some dinner," he said in a harsh mutter. She fixed him carnitas, his favorite dish, and set it on the table. But a ghost can't eat, and the food sat on the table gathering flies. "*Vieja, viejita linda,* bring me a beer." Off she would go to the market to get the beer. *La gente* began to talk about how her grief had driven her to drink. She would pull the lid and place the can of beer on the table by "his" chair. "You know I only drink Dos Equis," he growled. The beer went flat. She was tempted to drink his beer to alleviate her increasing irritation.

Tending to his ghost seemed to take all her time. She began to resent all the washing and cooking and trimming of his hair and toenails when he was alive. Just when she thought herself free, the pisser was back and more trouble now that he was dead. Her only consolation was that she didn't have to wash his smelly socks and dirty underwear. But her two-week-old *vida* was no longer her own and she wanted it back. How could she stop her *marido muerto* from returning?

One day she got inspired. She made a little model of her house with Popsicle sticks and glue and placed it in a safe spot halfway between his grave in the nearby cemetery and her home. She had heard that ghosts don't have a sense of perspective. Rocking back and forth, her chair creaked on the porch as she waited for *el espanto* to enter the model house thinking it was the real one.

That night she did not awaken. In the morning when she woke, she turned toward the side where her husband had been sleeping the past thirty years. His ghost was not there, nor was he there the following night. She sat up waiting for him, worrying about what to do with the ghost house. Suppose someone found *la casita* and accidentally opened the door and let the ghost out. Conceivably some element of nature—a strong wind or a fire—could destroy the flimsy house and her dead husband could get out. The tiny house was too fragile to be buried— the earth would crush it and the ghost would escape. She had to put it somewhere safe and out of the reach of others. After several days of deliberation she carefully carried the ghost trap into her house and placed it under the bed where mischievous nieces and nephews could not find it. That night a voice woke her up. It called out, no longer whispering, "*Vieja, vieja quiero hacerte el amor.*" She thought she felt his body stirring under the bed covers. Half-dreaming, half-awake, she pushed him away, but he kept climbing on top of her. All night she refused to open her legs to him.

Next morning she woke with deep grooves down the corners of her mouth and bruises on her mouth, breasts, arms, and inner thighs. She peered under the bed and saw that the door of the *casita* was open. She walked from room to room looking for *el pinche desgraciado* and muttering to herself, How am I going to get rid of that fucker? She considered going to the local *curandera* and asking her to drive his soul into *el pozo*, better yet, to hell. Huh, or she could look through the yellow pages to find a ghostbuster. Ah, no, she'd do it herself—with words and curses.

She decided to be prepared should her words fail. That night she plugged in the vacuum cleaner and put it by her bed. She tugged on two of her sturdiest corsets, several pairs of pants, and three shirts, turned off the lights, got into bed, and waited. She jumped out of bed, fetched her heavy iron skillet, and hid it under the bed covers just in case he'd taken on more substance than the vacuum could handle. Come on *cabrón, vente chingón,* she said under her breath.

Puddles

for Rodrigo Reyes and Jaye Miller

The gay man always left a puddle on his chair, along with the tip on the table. It got so Prieta ceased being surprised. With one hand she'd wipe it up with a towel (the puddle wasn't very big) and with the other, pocket the quarter. The tip was always a quarter no matter whether it was coffee he'd ordered or a full meal. After half a dozen times of wanting to, Prieta finally dipped her finger in. The puddle, Prieta decided after sniffing it, was not piss. Nor was it water, though it looked clear. She put the wet finger in her mouth—it didn't taste like wine or coffee.

The next morning, as she washed her face she noticed that the tip of her tongue had turned green. She scrubbed it with her toothbrush. She rinsed it with mouthwash. No changes. She was running late for work. Never mind the green tongue. She planned to confront the man whose puddle had turned her tongue green. Was he carrying some weird disease? Come to think about it, he was a bit strange. Along with the pink triangle and earring in his left ear, he always wore an olive green parka that covered him to his knees. Though he never spoke to her, just pointed at the menu when he ordered, nodded or shook his head when she came around with the coffee carafe, a look of recognition would pass between them. Did he have a reason for always picking one of her tables instead of one of Amy's? Both were dykes, but Amy was the one who smiled and cracked jokes with the customers while Prieta complained about the twenty-five wars—imagine, twenty-five—being fought on the planet. Now that she thought about it, he always sat at the same table. *Jíjole, qué curioso.* How long had he been coming in? Two weeks?

"What's wrong with your finger?" asked her friend Amy when she got to Les Amis. "Why is it green?"

"My finger? *¡Ayno!*" she said looking at her finger and giving a small yipe.

"Would you believe I have a way with plants? *Tu sabes,* a green thumb?"

Amy looked at her funny. "You've never showed you've had a sense of humor—until now that is. Your face is all lighted up. You wearing some kind of fluorescent makeup? The color's all wrong, got sort of a greenish tinge. Oh, and your knees look sort of wrinkled," she said bending down to get a closer look. Prieta craned her head to look at her knees.

Though a voice called, "Oh, waitress," she snuck into the washroom and peered into the broken and dirty mirror over the sink. Yeah, her face looked different even though she couldn't pinpoint the changes. The green had begun to creep from her finger to the back of her hand.

All day as she bustled from table to counter to kitchen she kept an eye on the door. But the man who made puddles did not come in that day, nor the next. She noticed the customers kept eyeing her knees. *Su piel se convertía en cuerpo de lagarto.*

By the fourth day she *knew* what each customer was going to order before they opened their mouths. She also knew that the "green man" was never coming back—he didn't have to, he'd done his deed. On the fifth day she had to wear trousers, long-sleeved shirts that buttoned all the way to her neck, and heavy beige makeup. But it was her gloved hands that cast suspicion on her, and at the end of the week, her boss told her he had to let her go because she was spooking the customers. By then she had only to cast her eyes over some man hunched over his lunch or dinner and she'd know if he was sticking it to his daughter. She would slap the check, along with a napkin, face down on the table. The bold green letters on the napkin would read, "I know what you are doing to your daughter. If you do it again your thing will turn green and fall off." By the end of the week she did not need this particular waitressing job. A few days later her green skin began to flake off. Underneath it she could see her original brown skin emerge. She began to get glimpses of other "afflicted" people—something in their eyes marked their difference.

She decided to drop by Les Amis to see if Amy was ready. If she was, Prieta would leave her the gift and say good-bye. Prieta had found out what her real work was—to move from town to town, work in restaurants, keep her knees covered, and when no one was looking touch an exposed knee to a chair and let slide a puddle of tears.

The Cassettes

for Manuel Mancilles

The cassettes play music
the hoarse voice of earthquakes bones and crippled guitars
the stoplights with a yellow eye/open wishing black
the streets with a hospital wheelchairs waiting ready
the church with crossed legs trembling tiny ancient
the hand floating down without arm or shoulder demanding a body
the bread wrapped in plastic smothered pure brown moist
the oils on the chest staining piercing the suit
the silent sleepwalking wheel running over the rain
the embryos folded in sheets beating against rumors
the man with a fork and necktie awaiting makeup
the movie theater sweating awakened navies the adolescent juice
the open windows loaded with knowing alcohol

the cassettes play music
they play in front of the strip of figures.

Notes on Other Chicana & Chicano Inventions

for all middle-school teachers

Like I said,
Cilantro aftershave.

Hominy &
peanut butter Burritos

Sanwishes
de Sardinas con Ketchup.

(I am not going
to mention the low-rider,
actually created in Tijuas in the 40's,
Jose Samuel Flores told me
mecánico de primera)

Huevos for empacho & mal ojo
Plantillas for bad fiebres
Bendiciones for a good day
Migajón for enojos

Arroz con leche with pasas
Ponchis de huevo con canela

The art of eating Vicks VapoRub with your dedos.
The art of sucking an egg w/o breaking the shell
The art of splashing yourself with alcohol & ruda

Sobadas
Aceitadas

Hueseras & Curanderos
Mamberos & Merenguidas

Tepaches & Tardeadas
Lunadas & Barbekiadas

Jalapeños in a Circle K bag

(you can use these words
when you sing the Twelve Days
of X-mas at your in-laws, cuñao
Louie wrote it)

How to wear your khakis high up to your chin w/o chopping
    your nachas
How to roll up your catholic pleated skirt & look favorable
How to make braids out of anything, even masa, or calcetines
How to take a two by four and make skates, surfboards
How to make parches & remendadas & empanadas de camote
How to make velas take your wishes to the universe
How to make salsa with stones, fire and box wood
How to make a chicken say por favor, si señor, si señora
How to feed the cat estek con papas, refrieds & espinaca
How to bang on the roof to get the tapa de la olla down
How to wear your hair high up so it looks like a tipi

The word Machaca
The word Fayukero
The word Garabato
The word Chocholukos
The word Brekas
The word Chorreada
The word Apestosidad
The word Huevonetes
The word Achicopalado
The word Mixtiada
The word Berruga
The word Estinche

Code words like caldo, like pelotas, like ojos de rata

Phrases like
You better wash those dishes Juan, or I'll give you a wamazzo.

Phrases like
I said, you better wash those trastes o te torzo el hosiko boy.
Phrases like
You better not hang around with that bola de marijuanos or arranco
that branch off el arbol y te curo las centaderas.
Phrases like
Keep on painting your carota de chankla like that & you're gonna
get granotes the size of a calabaza, you hear, esquinckla?

Rodney King, the Black Christ of Los Angeles and All of Our White Sins— May 1, 1992

The verdict came down. Four White cops beat King
—found not guilty.

Rodney went down for all of us.
This alley guitar pours its juice into my veins.
I can feel it.

His jawbone moved, he spoke
the words of our origin, our names.

The blue-black night sticks came down
to his plump flesh, across the face and the bones inside.
The bones wavered into the heart and they exploded for us,

I am kneeling down.

In East Los, *La Raza* is contemplating *Cinco de Mayo*
and the French skin that still covers our nakedness.

A cloud with the face of WB DuBois hangs
over the Sherman Williams paint store in South Central LA—
WB said the crises of the 20th century would be the color line.

Churn up more blackness through the windows.
Two Chicanas run out of a busted mall, one loaded
with bags of Pampers, the other with loaves of bread.

Beneath the Harbor Freeway bridge, a tired man
who looks like Ho Chi Minh spits at the fire trucks going by.

The burn of kerosene comes up from the apartments
and *chile Piquín* peppers on the black asphalt grill.

Streets smell like Guadalajara
where there is a giant crutch being built by the politicos.

They are chanting about *la tierra mojada*—
"the earth has the aroma of rain," they say.
That's what they sing at the Mariachi festivals.

This is the *colonia* that blew up a few weeks ago.
Pemex let the gasoline burst underground. Said
it was too expensive to fix the line leaks.

So, they let gas run beneath
the bedroom floors of the Mexicans

—oil and gasoline.

These are the psychic sheets
of our penitence and liberation.

A Harley
—on fire

at the Martin Luther King Blvd. intersection
a few blocks from the Sports Arena. A blonde
woman in jeans—pushed out of her Toyota pickup,
a reddish 84. The Harley is melting

into a chrome praying mantis. Crackle and spit.
Hundreds of oblong bodies rush.

My cousin Vincent
who spent 20 years in the pen sits in his beat-up sofa,
laughs at the blue flash in the corner of his living room.

He picks his nose
laughs at the news woman who is beginning
to stumble on the teleprompter.

More choppers and tanks.
Tomorrow is paycheck day.

La lana,
la piola,
la rifa,
el cartón,
la feria,

except this time
la gente will cash their welfare checks in a chopper.

Or a National Guard tank,
just maybe.

I am behaving like a Mexican,
the kind you see in Cheech & Chong movies.

The post offices are down
and the banks in San Bernardino are down.

Longo is going up in flames too.
Money is worth a bowl of beans today.

The supermarkets are open and everything is free.
Ginsberg was wrong about the supermarket

—Whitman
and Lorca are elsewhere.

This is my atonement,
this is my resurrection,
this is the way of the black cross,
the brown crown of thorns.

The liquor stores are ours. The laundries are ours.
Shirts we never wore are finally pressed, ready
for church and the toasters

with extra-wide slots are ours too.
There is a pearl white Mercedes being kicked in
by six kids with Adidas and torn faces.

A bloody Chicano is taking pot shots
at my neighbor, Taiji, as he swerves
into an onramp going west. The Guard
is on the way, the *Federales* are on the way.

A cop shoots mace into a White boy's eyes
—how does it feel, how does it?

Another guy fondles his own breasts
as he looks at a VCR behind the window.

A pack of Michelob,
a gold suit and a helmet,
badges

& justice
& rachets.

Sirens come for Rodney's spirit. Someone gets run over,
the legs are crushed on Normandy avenue–

a young *vato's* brains slide down
the head rest of his 59 Biscayne;

on the way back from a soccer game
he met a bullet with his name.

Rodney has answered all the silences.
It is a tender voice, a cavernous tenderness.

Greenish smoke curls toward Hollywood Blvd.
Edward James Olmos comes out to clean up with brooms.

David Gardner, ex-UC Pres, knows
this is God's work too.

A month ago he ripped off the State
bringing in the Speaker of the House to Berkeley
made sure he got his $800,000 house

and a quarter-million-a-year stub
—his retirement package from the UC campus.

This is the way of Presidents.

There is a crew of White students
huddled in a hamburger diner called Burgertime,
they are saying—

Blacks and minorities got their share already
"Why are they doing this?" "Why?" they say.

& another newscaster uses the word *animal*
as he peeks through the tube.

And Rodney's White lawyer's face stretches
as he becomes Black in an uncanny way.
He is looking for more words about justice.

There is no Black Christ.

I said it to get myself going. I was loaded
with stupor and complacency. Because
I live in the suburbs of North Fresno.
Because I see fat tractors and rigs

smooth the ground
for more cells of silence.

Now, I have spilled my guts
in a Mexican way.

Need more fuel now;
thought I was clean. Thought I could do

with the other things,
but I need the fuel now, need the cheap kind.

My wife Margarita is upstairs taking a shower.
The water is churning through the ceiling
making high-pitched sounds,
shredding sounds.

More smoke. Another line of dead,
nameless dead with one name for all of them.
Maybe our name, maybe

it is my name and your name they are calling.
An old woman in an oversized sweater,

in denims, drinks
a hot Gatorade from the mess of a 7-Eleven.
A Korean cat and a Mexican dude are fingering their mouths

—their stores are in ashes. These are the ashes.
Cross your foreheads on this Ash Friday,

this Ash Saturday of black palms and talkative gutters
full of the rainbow juice, the kind that comes from radiators,
skulls and cracked batteries. This year we had a long Easter.

It got caught up in a bad cycle of drought, earthquakes,
blood, glue, and pregnant cats and bird nests thrown open
by a car crash. The broken birds are soapy without skin,

there is a tiny purple ball still
ticking inside their stomachs;

the beaks are too yellow
—the color of emergency plastic tape,

the type cops put around a murder scene.
Don't step on them, if there is anything you do
—please don't step on them.

At Union Square, in San Francisco,
they are ripping down the neon signs,

right across from the St. Francis Hotel. My mother
worked there as a salad girl in the forties,

right after the war;
that's when Lawrence Welk was the main feature
on weekends, and they are on Market street too

by the Embassy theater
where you can see a porno show for one dollar.

I am carrying a triple landscape in my head.
Walking around with tears on my ragged face.
Congas and *timbales* by the trash cans.

I can see everything—San Francisco, Guadalajara and the city
which was an empire once upon a time. I used to go there
as a kid and look at my hands to make sure

I was there—
to remember myself there by the shape of my hands.

This is the way of the Gods in the Streets, this is the Gospel
of Rodney King and the Black & Brown Wand of Inspiration.

Zoot Suit on a
Bed of Spanish Rice

From *Listening to Santana*

When one of us dies you can tell.

A swarm of children in black. Notice how El Greco paints us into the
barrio scene. The men are short, then elongated, going up into the turbulent skies, stilled by a crazy figure inside and outside: a charcoal ma-
donna with the face of Martha Graham, except more oval and with a
seductive mouth. Their bent, tiny heads glimmer. For a second or two.
A couple of shots are heard. Four shots—a military salute for the wrap
in the casket—the way my uncle Geno went down into the ground
in '57.

Behind tombstones.

Hide & go seek with Chente, my cousin. Both of us have buck teeth
and we laugh like girls. Mama is the only one crying, she leans down
into the soft earth and pulls up the bluish pit in her soul. When I cry
—silence. Sometimes it comes in little beeps. Gets jammed somewhere
on my upper back, near the neck. Useless, most of the time. A few
years ago I made peace with another uncle, Roberto Q. Five carnations. We never talked. Made candy, pink-striped bars wrapped in cel-
lophane in his basement. Got busy, later—a poet with four kids.

Riding around Stanford in a 1954 yellow Ford pickup. Wore bell bottoms and aced the classes. Except Collier's statistics; you can always catch a Chicano flunking statistics. This was my first folly at Stanford. The second was disappearing for an entire summer in Mexico to live the life of Cagney in Cuernavaca and Brando in Acapulco. At 5 am, hang out the window of the Hotel Regency Presidente—eight floors up. Gaze over the bay, baby, inhale the green air, love the sweetness from the sky. Alcohol from my ledge and gasoline from speedboats and the helicopters, the ones that take you up in a nylon kite for four hundred pesos. Come down and drink gin gimlets in the pools. Make love to a secretary from Tegucigalpa. An accident. That's what I said when I got back.

When my mother died my shirt tightened. Cried for six years. Shaved my mustache. Shaved my head. Wanted to cut myself down to size. Strip the skin off. Because I couldn't feel it. Think of ukuleles, I told myself. Oblong brown chocolate ones with good strings. Or Hawaiian shirts at the National Dollar store in San Diego where we used to go shopping in the fifties; Jergens, Three Roses pomade, khakis for fifth grade. Airplane glue in a sock hanging out with Raymond & Arnold & Miguel. Every ghost boy I know. They show up with my uncles now—smoke rings on my bruised face.

The therapist says Just a couple of visits. I show my teeth. Is it a peppermint flavor inside my lips? Or is it fire? Sport a flat top now. Think on the days—original flat top days & Roman Meal bread, soft speckled stuff the doctors prescribe for my mother. My father was alive then too. Makes me laugh when he does his special imitation of a gun going off. Does this the same way he makes dove sounds. Pulls his lower lip down with his thumb and forefinger. Then he breathes backward.

Cook at least three things, learn, he said.

Rice, the long red pointed kind buried with burnt tomatoes. Enchiladas, the apartment kind, folded with onions and Kraft cheese. They can be served anywhere to anyone. Char the salsa too, on an iron grill. Mash the green-black pulp inside a stone bowl. The one that rocks on three legs.

Milagros & Angels

At an early age my mother warned me You have a star on your forehead, then she pointed at the reddish patch near the inside of my left knee.

This is what saves me. You just don't know how many times I've been saved. Saved from the emptiness sweltering all around us.

Solorzano, a buddy from East Los, sensed it.

He said he wanted to get away from it—ended up as a receptionist in the emergency room at General Hospital. Reading Popular Mechanics and looking at blood spurt from matted heads saved me, he says, twisting the pages of the magazine with speaker wiring and lumber on the cover.

Fell into a twenty-foot well, in Mexico.

This was 1961, in Atizapan de Zaragoza, a village that specialized in haircuts, tortillas flattened with a dog-head shaped stone, and pulque. A shaft of wind across the back of my legs pushed me forward to the other side by the pig pen. The smooth complexioned animals were my favorites; they never let me trick them into eating raw bulbous jalapeños even when I mixed the seeds with corn slush.

Milagros are sudden.

In '70, I walked into South Tepic, Mexico, with Mendoza and Mancillas. A Huichol Indian asked us why are you late? I've been waiting for you for a while, he said. How could he know? Three crazy Chicanos from Venice and East Los. No way, I jived. Then he pointed up to the sky as he sat cross-legged on the outskirts of the city, pasting pink yarn on a slab of plywood. Because *Tauyepá*, Father Sun told me, he whispered.

Four years later: jammed down a dusty road on the way to Guatemala City; a small troop of soldiers stopped the bus in the middle of the jungle. Pulled me out. The driver jumped in, said leave 'em alone.

Made it back again—to the US of A.
Began to drink more carrot juice.

Drank so much I turned into a copper-shoe version of Wayne Newton. My hands were orange peanut shells. A tapioca fondue, a mango Maharishi phenomenon. Turned mango so bad one of my anthro profs, an Australian aborigine scholar at UCLA, called me down from the auditorium in Haines Hall.

You better see a doctor, he stammered on his armchair. Things couldn't be better, I told him—tonight I got tickets to Sonny & Terry at the Ashgrove. Things are going all right. Next week, Richie Havens and Taj Majal.

Milagros are hard to talk about—you can't clock them or pin them down.

My mother told me stories of men who kicked their wives and then on the following Sunday hobbled on her knees to the Zócalo in Mexico, all the way to the altar of the church. When I got there years later, I stood on the bloody granite and concrete square.

The cathedral sank to one side.

A young girl played her harmonica with a sudden gentleness. The breathy sweetness mixed with the clouds and the violet striped shawls and the leather of the tourists. An old man in brown jeans, with long sideburns and a thick back, dragged himself into that blackness, below the steeple, into that broken viola of fright and silvery rays, silvery with reddish squares and octagons of stained window faces and on the long varnished counters, a head of a dead saint, bony hands and fingers in a vinegar jar—next to the confessional. Marble slime on the pillars and torso statues. The man said he wanted to go down into the abyss where one of the saints was buried—for all of us to see. He pinned a gold leaf metal heart on the flannel mantle of Saint Judas. This was the necessary cargo.

Now they have another church close by where you can toss your *milagros* on a conveyor belt. This one doesn't smell of bloody pillows and frenzy, the quiet kind, the kind that gets the job done.

Ritual & pneumonia are the key ingredients.

When you break away you will begin to look at yourself in a tender and evil way. This is the starting point of the *milagro*.

My mother charged me to the care of an ancient angel figure. I am forbidden to mention the name. She told me this after I sliced seven inches into my knee. A safety pin did it while I was sleeping. Good that it happened in the dark. Just wetness on my right hand and my legs. The same knee with the red patch—the one my mother said a friend of hers had read while I was a baby. The gypsy turned to my mother and said things. All I can tell you is this: *milagros* have to do with a system of star-shapes on the body. If you trace the shapes, they will lead you to the miracles. Solorzano didn't know this.

This tiny formula saves me from burning—the fire that consumes me, the fire across the world. And I have seen the fire-starters, the men in beige, green, and blue with their pointed faces and flint noses, swiveling their eyes through fences, from undercover vans.

Mariachi Drag Star

Air guitar on Lincoln Blvd.
Call me Freddy this time. Freddy B. Good in mariachi drag.

Got my father's grape-picking knife, the one with a hooked blade dangling from my sequins belt made in Jalisco, a wavy turf that takes you into the sky and drops you on a flat-bed mango truck. Hauling fast. You have to see my boots. Like the ones my uncle Beto sent me when I was five years old living on the outskirts of Escondido. See me bomb the anthills in my chopper—a can of kerosene in one hand, a match in the other, my left one. There I am chewing grapefruit, sitting on a wooden bench, the meat is diced and spiced with sugar and cinnamon. My feet stick out. The little spiral arabesque designs by the ankles can barely be seen. And my pants—this is what counts and makes me loose: velveteen black canvas drapes, used for Elvis Presley or John F. Kennedy posters and sold a few blocks down, at La Fulton mall. And my shirt. It hasn't changed. Have a Boycott Coors and a Boycott Grapes and US out of El Salvador & Apartheid buttons running down the sides of my embroidered sleeves. The hat really is the best item. Size of a New York pizza, with a gourd for the head. Bought the gourd on Olvera Street where the artists hang out and go to blues shows at night. That's all they have here is blues shows. My face is rusty. This is the way I look when I swagger down the avenues. Say things like fuck a duck *cabrón,* I am a capricorn. Sometimes they rhyme like that. Malls are my hangouts. Cross-legged on the linoleum in Radio Shack to tease the store manager. Where are your radios? Or slide by the Mitsubishi dealer and push the color intensity to black on the 40 inch demonstration model. I am deep inside now. Standing next to the *licuados*—Indian energy drinks made out of local weeds. *Chilacayote* and *flor de calabaza. Flor de calabaza* is good for hangover quesadillas and *chilacayote* is a cure-all especially if you happen to get poison ivy *pito* or as they say in English, poison ivy dick. This is what beaner men get when they mess with their genitals while hiking around Topanga Canyon in cut-off Friscos. Chicano men always dress the same whether they are at the beach or in the mountains: cut-off black Friscos with ragged Fruit of the Loom T-shirts. It has nothing to do with class or gender. The women are more creative.

Believe me, I know about poison ivy. When I was a kid, I got a bad case of *chile huero pito.* This time it was the yellow wax pepper that did me in. What a mess. My mom had to yank me out of the trailer and haul me over to a *tina,* an extra large tin bucket in the middle of the dirt yard next to the killing post used for wild turkey on special Saturdays. My father, Emilio, did that stuff.

Now I am next to a fashionable men's store, a European joint that sells French tweeds with orchid ties. Six hundred to fifteen hundred dollars. These are starting prices.

I spin to a foreign tune; Trini Lopez sings Farsi in my head. Milling my arms round and round doing a disjointed hula, skating up the granite and onyx open-air restaurant floors. There is a man whispering to an oval faced Mexican Penelope. His reddish face looks up & down at her from his tiny seat. Two white dudes shuffle into the sports shop where two black *vatos* are holding up a Bulls jacket. Moving fast.

My leathery heart burns up its last jelly drop. I sing—picking grapes the way my father did. Pull up my roman nosed knife. Same shape as my nose. Pasolini strolling to the Caracalla baths in Rome. Waltzing through the mud, holding a little boy's hand who pulls a Ducati bike with the other. The mother in a greenish tunic looks on at me in the rain. Her hands go up and rest at the hips. I pull the bike faster than the other kid next to me. He is wearing the same outfit. Where did he get it? Maybe it's my lost brother. The one whose hands they would tie to the pews at Saint Ann's. The brother I thought I always had. The one that likes kosher pickles and peanut butter burritos. And who's that below him? She is rolling on the ground. She is uncontrollable, bursting with tears of laughter or is it sweat? No, she's laughing. I don't know her. I don't want to look at her. Whose sister would wear headphones in this heat? You can hear Wilson Pickett's jagged falsetto belting out of her ears. To my left, a Filipino man is hoeing. Fast. Red cap and striped canvas gloves. He is anxious. Looks like my father. I recognize the nerves.

Bobbing and weaving. Skating. Burning ants.
Luring the juice out from the bulbous violet fruit. My spurs are somewhere, tumbling below the skylights.

My spurs emit little swishing sounds so I won't lose my step. I am falling. This is downtown Venice. I've been here for ages, it seems. Next to the La Cabaña Café, the place I have bumped into. I am in there, drinking coffee and eating a caraway cheese sandwich with bologna from Chicago. My cigaret burns and spits a spark. Sister Leila comes out of the back in her woolly brown skirt. She reminds me it is time to go to work at Ellison Tire. Look out the window—there is a guy spilling his snow cone trying to figure where he's headed. His legs shoot out from under him into the glassy street. His face wiggles too, like Fred Flintstone, like the rest of us. Picks at a tiny address book in his shirt pocket, the one thing his mother left him wrapped in a rum-colored scarf before she died. Now, he rubs his finger on it, reads it like a novel.

Adonde Vive Dios?

From *Barrio Stories*

Lupe Reyes's fingers moved constantly, going around and around, fingering each of the beads as she repeated her *oración*, painfully, earnestly, moving her lips along with the prayers. The random-curtained windows of shacks like hers were worse than blind. They shouted emptiness and hunger, and the kind of despair that comes only after honest effort results in nothing but failure. If they could have mourned the silence, the death, they would have seemed more alive, less abandoned. But the abandoned living within the gouged walls, the dry splintering wooden doors breathed only endings. Nothing new could be born from their hearts. Even endurance seemed like a sin, here, obscene, rotting. Only Lupe Reyes still believed in miracles. Because she deserved a miracle. She deserved to have God reveal Himself to her. Hadn't He promised . . . she didn't know what . . . but surely the believers, the doers of all the things He ordered, could at last expect, and receive, mercy. Mercy in the form of recognition. Recognition that would bring just one little act of vengeance on all the bad evildoers and, it goes without saying, a little something for the others to enjoy, to stretch out over, after all the diligence, all the paying attention to His will.

Otherwise, what was all the pain for?

Lupe Reyes left the candle burning. In the dark, it was something to look at. Something to give her eyes something to do, following the flickering golden light as it cut the darkness, filled the bare walls and empty corners. So she was not so alone. And then she might sleep. The walls were gray, the candle fluttering in a yellow puddle, when she opened her eyes again. Except for that, nothing had changed. She sighed, kissed the crucifix on the rosary around her neck, and got up. It was harder to do each day, *pero, ahí Dios dira*. She went out and dumped the can of piss in the ravine behind the shack and then washed her hands with a cup of water from the bottle. She'd have to go down to the gas station at the fork, or better the other one, the one way down at La Quinta—she hadn't been there lately—with her bottle to get water from their hose. If there was nothing to eat that morning, *pues,* her *panza* was getting too big anyway.

When she got to the gas station, *el gringo dueño* was there. She watched from behind a clump of saguaros across the road, her *tapalo* covering her face to keep away the *moscas* that were eating the dog shit a few feet away. She waited and watched, and when she didn't see him for a while, she walked over gingerly and started filling her bottle. She was almost done when, *anda, cabrón,* there he came from around the back, carrying a dirt-covered tire in each hand. When he saw her, he started yelling. She let the hose go and tried to run, but the water bottle was too heavy, and it almost slipped from her fingers, as the *maldito* let the tires roll and, picking up the hose, aimed it at her back. The water was like the shock of a striking fist on her shoulders, while the fat pig of a *dueño* squealed with loud, phlegm-filled laughter. When she heard him coughing and spitting, she looked back and saw the hose snaking in his hands and the water going all over his feet. "*Anda, se lo pago Dios,*" said Lupe Reyes, satisfied. After that, the bottle did not seem so heavy, nor the way so long. She cut through the mesquites near Obregon, and stopped to pick some *quelites* that had sprouted in the shallow ditches beneath some trees. There were even some *verdolagas* creeping along the rocky ground: what a nice tangy flavor they would add to the *quelites.* Holding her *mantel* with the greens to her breast, she followed the trail across Obregon. Dust covered her huaraches, and when she got home she used a few precious drops of water to wash and cool her feet. When Jesus had washed the disciples' feet, it was not only humility, she knew. After all, if He expected them to walk so far, He had to show them how to take care of their feet. Then she went down to the arroyo and gathered a few pieces of wood brought down by the flash floods. Then she used one of the matches in the *librito* from the crossroads diner. Quintero, the bartender, was her friend. He always said, take as many as she needed. But she never took more than two books at a time. So he would see she was careful. She looked, like she always did, at the picture on the matchbook. A young and beautiful naked woman with nothing but stars on her *chee-chees,* who bent over nicely so one could light the match on her *nalgas. Hombres cochinos,* she thought, like she always did, and folded the matchbook and put it safely away in the empty can by the *comal.*

After she had eaten the *quelites* and *verdolagas,* it was not so hard. She could believe again that she would live through this day too, and that a miracle was coming soon. It was descending from the skies, from God's favorite place, the one just between the peaks that always looked golden and glowing with a special light, like *la Virgensita*'s cheek above the roster of candles. Then this miracle would skim the *lomitas,* gathering force as it came speeding over the boulders, flying down the sandy wash like a sudden flash flood on an August afternoon. And when it reached her *jacal,* this miracle would burst open, absorbing the land, the house, and her in it, in one stupendous cataclysmic light that transformed everything forever. And then what, she didn't know, except that she would never be alone again and her life would cease to be painful. The aging woman in ragged black dress, with the callused, tired feet, the fingers distorted by labor, the crooked teeth with more spaces than teeth, the deep sorrowful eyes that nonetheless took joy in seeing; the strong body that slept and woke, that moved and yearned to rest: this whole *mujer* would rush toward heaven, pulled by an ecstacy of recognition, with total forgiveness, total love, and somehow she would never experience her old life in this world again, and somehow she would be alive forever. That is what God promised; that was the miracle she waited for, knew would come, had to come. God would not disappoint her. She only had to wait long enough.

But her friend, old señora Quiroz, who lived some ways west and beyond the arroyo, did not see things this way. "*Gozar de la vida*" is what señora Quiroz always said. But it was easy for her to do who had a big healthy grandson coming around with bags of groceries. Of course, that was nice for Lupe Reyes too, because then señora Quiroz would come to the edge of the gulley and call, "Lupita, Lupita, *ven a tomar cafesito con migo,*" and there was always sugar in it too, and señora Quiroz never let her leave with empty hands. "*Mira,* Lupita," señora Quiroz would always say, as they sat on orange crates under the ramada, noisily sipping the hot black café with pleasure. "*Mira,* Lupita, what you need to do is find yourself a man, *un buen hombre.*"

"*Callate,* Carmelita," Lupe Reyes would say. "What do I need a man for? *Y ya sabes,* that with a man around, miracles never come close."

"*Ahí, tu y tus miracoles,*" señora Quiroz would scoff. "Miracles are not as good as flesh and bone, ever."

"The solace of the flesh is gone for me forever," said Lupe Reyes. "From now on until God takes me, I know nothing of the flesh."

"A big strong woman like you?" said señora Quiroz, but she knew better than to continue. She'd have to go visit Maria Tiburon down on *la cinquenta,* if she wanted to discuss pleasure, and that was a long walk away.

"My miracle is on its way. I know it," said Lupe Reyes, getting that bright streak in her dark eyes again. "I feel it right here in my heart. But I promise—when it comes I won't go without saying adios."

"*¡No, ningunos adioses quiero yo!*" señora Quiroz snapped, petulantly. The very idea that Lupe would be going anywhere, leaving her behind, was unspeakable, and she refused to even consider it.

Lupe Reyes smiled, remembering this last conversation with old señora Quiroz. Then she got up and went to the arroyo to wash her dishes with sand. When she was finished, she went on sitting there. She wasn't just sitting, but she wasn't exactly looking or listening to anything either. It was more like watching and waiting. And not that either—like making an agreement of some kind, to be a certain thing, a person of substance, but without a name, without identification, just Lupe-with-sand-between-her-toes, or Lupe-with-sun-on-her-skin. And between one breath and the next, she wasn't even that. The arroyo was on fire! The mesquites along the banks of the arroyo were burning! The sand exploded into diamonds in front of her eyes. And then she felt a cool breeze lift the hair from her forehead, and she felt herself breathing, just the same, felt the rocks under her feet, and she thought she heard her name. It was. It was señora Quiroz's voice sounding far away.

"Lupita, Lupita, *¡ayudame!* Lupita," the voice called again. Lupe Reyes stood up quickly, looking this way and that down the arroyo. There was nothing to be seen.

"Carmelita! Señora Quiroz!" she called, and waited, but there was no sound. Nothing. Suddenly, terror gripped her heart. Without going to find her huaraches, she went hurriedly down the arroyo, trying to step in the soft sand between the rocks and boulders. As she climbed up to the trail that left the arroyo and went south, the thorny branches of a palo verde lifted the *tapalo* from her head, but she didn't stop to untangle it. She left it stuck on the tree, a black piece of cloth, and went as quickly as she could, through the grove of barrel cactus to the old horse path from Rancho Acequia. Margaritas still bloomed there, now gone wild, among the cholla and tall grass. Now that the way was free, she almost ran in the soft cool dirt of the horse path until she reached *los portales*. From the broken-down gates, she could see down the slope to señora Quiroz's shack. It sat like a small square of life next to a vast piece of open ground that had once been the rancho's grazing land, now peppered with locoweed and wild grass rippling in the wind.

There was no sign of life. No smoke came from the *comal*. The palm branches that made up the ramada roof lifted here and there as the winds blew, and somewhere metal clanged against metal.

"Carmelita, ¿adonde estas?" Lupe called, descending the slope. No one answered. She reached the door out of breath, and it was closed. She tried it, expecting to find it locked, but the door flew open and banged against the wall. Frightened, she looked quickly inside the small room, but it was dark—the windows were still covered—and there was nothing to be seen. It smelled like tortillas, and there was a bowl filled with dried oatmeal the old woman liked to eat. Lupe closed the door and looked toward the clapboard outhouse. She knew there was no one there, but she went and looked in it anyway. Then she came back and sat on an orange crate under the ramada. She felt calmer now and thought perhaps she had imagined what she heard, but she knew she was not one who imagined such things.

"Señora Quiroz, ¿estas aquí?" She stood and called once more. As if in answer, she heard the sound of metal clanging against metal again and tried to tell where it came from. She walked slowly past the outhouse, down the steep side of a hill toward the old citrus orchard that grew on the lower slope. The trees, old and crippled, bent in strange forms toward the ground, their leaves sparse and wrinkled, dry. There, along the thistle-covered, but still evident, rows between the trees, she saw what was making the noise. Cans, Folger coffee cans, the cans señora Quiroz kept her provisions in—and the contents themselves—scattered nearby. Pinto beans lay in a pile on a pillow of flour, the aroma of coffee rose to her head, black grains mixed up with white grains of arroz, the empty cans moving and shifting, rolling back and forth against each other. The metallic sounds were not as loud as before, and they were sweeter than those she had first heard, as though, now that she was there, they didn't have to shout for her anymore. They became like musical notes, strung haphazardly together, but correctly, by the wind. "Tinkle, tinkle, rrrrr," the cans said, scraping gently against each other, round holes of them looking back at the mounds of their previous contents.

Lupe Reyes's eyes and feet followed the sweet voices of the rolling cans down through the rows of trees, noting scattered bunches of dried peas, lentils, and, finally, the remains of gorditas already partially eaten by pack rats or other small animals, until at last she found what she was looking for.

The Mexican policeman at the diner at la cinquenta was sucking nachos and cleaning his fingernails with a toothpick, when una señora de años, pero bien hecha, appeared beside him.

"Huh!" he grunted, quickly establishing his authority over underlings.

"*Señor policia,* I must talk to you," said Lupe Reyes, not at all timidly. She was already moving through the swinging door, and he had to follow, resentful and bored. After she told him what she had to say, he made her stand outside, waiting, until another car arrived with more police and a plainclothes detective. In the orchard, the same grunting policeman nosed around the piles of rice and coffee like a *javalina* pawing the ground in search of roots, until the plainclothes nodded him off with a curt gesture. The plainclothes, a clean-shaven mixed blood, wearing Levi's and a silver concho belt, went with her to her house and sat down with Lupe Reyes and talked to her.

"There are those who prey upon women living alone," he said. "Se-ñora Albura, right on the corner of *la cinquenta-tres,* brutally assaulted and robbed; the old woman, a white woman, who lived in a small trailer by the fork, *golpiada,* almost killed, and Cristina Gaspacho from the barrio, attacked while walking home with her groceries, her fingers cut off with a knife because she would not release her bag." Lupe Reyes listened to all this respectfully, even when he said, "You *mujeres* are easy to damage. That's just how it is. Is there no place I can take you?" he added, his face closing down again, becoming impersonal, when she declined. "At least put a lock on your door," he threw back in parting. Lupe Reyes sat looking at her *jacal* after he was gone. The door didn't even fit in the opening, cracks showing around it. The door itself was nothing, but hidden by the lintel was a frame of steel—the doubtful gift of a possessive and paranoid man who thought once that he could lock Lupe Reyes in her own house. Her mind went to the windows next. There was no glass on two of them—she had nailed a torn piece of screen across them, only to keep the flies out. The other two windows wouldn't go up or down, jammed about three inches from the bottom. She welcomed the breeze that entered through them on hot nights. She thought about all these things, but they were just thoughts passing through. The rest of her mind was deep in her soul, curled up around the picture of her friend, her head twisted at an impossible angle, *su bulto* stretched out and covered with dry citrus leaves, as if the tree had shaken with her agony and scattered its leaves to cover her nakedness, and the blood. All the paths to Lupe Reyes's heart had been closed. If there was a miracle coming, it would never be able to arrive, because she could no longer receive it, she knew now, and this hurt her as much as the rest.

All that afternoon, she sat, unmoving, by the palo verde tree in front of the *jacal.* She could not have said where she went, but it was a way strewn with thorns and her feet were bare. When finally she reached deliverance from this anguish of the soul, the sun had left, but the sky still burned, and the mountains were becoming huge with the mystery of darkness. She made her preparations with the door. Then Lupe Reyes lit a candle—her last one—and set it on a box near the door. Next, she moved the rocks aside, one by one, until the ground in front of the entrance was only dirt. She dug at it with her fingers until they revealed an iron box that had once been painted yellow, but now was rusted and encrusted with chunks of hardened earth. She pulled the box away from its hole a little at a time because it was very heavy, and then she took the rosary that was around her neck, kissed the crucifix, inserted it, headfirst, into the lock. The lock turned, as smooth as oil.

Even before Lupe Reyes finished with everything she had to do, night came on with a rush, stars licking the tops of trees, seeping to the ground in liquid light. She was there, waiting in the darkness, but only the wild animals knew it, and accepted it, as they did the presence of rocks or the bodies of cactus. The waning moon had risen and sunk quickly behind the hills before an aged coyote with withered flanks and patchy fur came up the trail from the arroyo, sniffing the air for something to eat. He sniffed the strange smells and, identifying them, slunk away without a sound like a silken shadow. And Lupe Reyes waited. She waited that night and the next, and the next. On the third night, she felt him and smelled him long before he was even close. He came forward, drifting out of a curtain of morning-glory vines at the eastern edge of the ravine. He moved toward the *jacal,* unaware that he was being drawn to it like a magnet drawing a poisoned nail from a bleeding wound. Lupe Reyes was pulling him in with her personal power, step by step, winding him around his own mistakes, his mind vacant, his lips pulling away from small sharp teeth like those of a rat. He raised the knife in his hand as the other hand reached out and touched the door and then froze in place, as he listened, licking his lips. She even heard him swallow twice against a dry throat, as he gently, so slowly, almost imperceptibly, opened the door. With one swift motion, he was inside, the door shutting behind him. She leaped up, dropping the iron bars into place; with an extension of the same springing motion, putting match to kerosene, running as lightly as a deer around the *jacal,* creating fire as she ran. Within seconds, the dry wood was blazing like tinder. It took time for the sounds to pierce the invincible armor of himself, seconds to identify the sounds for what they were. She heard the sounds of breaking glass, the scream of rage as he realized he could not fit through the windows, and the mighty kicking and shattering of the door, the snarling of a wild beast as he tore the wood from its hinges and pressed forward, but was prevented by the iron bars and the flames already rising to the height of a man. He tried to grasp and shake them, but the heat cast him back, twisting his body in vain. Then he screamed the words "It is you, O God, who needs forgiveness!" and then he had time to plead for his life only once before it became a plea for death. He never heard the gunfire that shattered his mind, ending the fear a second before everything was consumed in flames.

She sat through the night keeping vigil, the instrument of her mercy, a Colt .45 with a shining silver stock, held in her hands. The silver was engraved with a beautiful woman's face, half in light, half in shadow, and the metal was warm and loving from the heat of her hands.

The sun had risen long ago, and the little sparrows had returned to play in the nearby trees, before the ashes had cooled enough to walk on. She gathered the knife and the charred bones that were left, and carried them to the citrus orchard and buried them on the spot where Carmelita Quiroz had fallen. When she returned, she remembered her *tapalo*. But when she took it from the palo verde tree, she saw that the center of the black square was bleached white as if by an intense light, and for a moment, beneath the moving shadows of the tree, Lupe Reyes saw her own face among the threads.

Tears on My Pillow

Mama Maria learned me about *la llorona*. *La llorona* is the one who doing all the crying I've been hearing all this time with no one to tell me who it was til Mama Maria. She told me *la llorona*'s this mama, see, who killed her kids. Something like that. How does it goes? Something like there's this girl and some soldiers take her husband away and she goes to the jail to look for him, asses why these soldiers took him. And she gots I don't member how many kids all crying cause their daddy's gone, you know. And the soldier being mean and stupid and the devil inside him (but that's okay cause God knows everything says Mama Maria), he points a gun to her head and says "I gonna kill you." But she looks at him and says "Do me the favor." That's like something Arlene would say, you know. But the girl she don't know when to stop. "You kill everything so go ahead and kill me," she tells the soldier, "but first kill my kids cause I don't want 'em hungry and sick and lone without no ama or apa or TV." So the devil says "okay," and shoots all the kids, bang, bang bang. But you know what? He don't kill her. Cold shot, huh? She goes coocoo and escapes from the nuthouse like my grandpa Ham used to do before he got dug in at Evergreen. And to this day, the girl all dressed up in black like Mama Maria cause she killed her kids and she walks up and down City Terrace with no feet, crying and crying and looking for her kids. For reallies, late in the dark night only.

You could hear her crying, for reals, I swear. When you hear her crying far away that means she's real close so don't go out at night. She's as close as your bed, so don't sleep with your feet to the window cause even she can pull you out. She'll get you, I swear. Ask Mama Maria. She's too old to lie.

Arlene don't believe me either. Not til she's home on a Friday night with nowhere to go but here. She heared it, too, herself, covered my ears. Ssshhh, my mama Arlene said. Make it stop, I told her. Make it stop. I wished to God for Gregorio to come home. He's mean and can kick *la llorona*'s ass to the moon. Arlene took me to her bed, and I pulled up my feet real close to her. She smelled like cigarettes and warm beer and Noxzema cream. Her chichis was soft and cool under her slip, where I put my head. Please, mama, make it stop. I asses her to put the TV on real loud, do something, cause *la llorona* was crying so crazy, she was breaking windows.

Ssshh, Arlene said, turning off the light, ssshhh.

La llorona only comes at night. When it's day, Veronica will always stay. That's what I say. I don't like Veronica. Not cause her skin was all scaly and yellow and pusy 'round the elbows and neck and behind her knees. Not even cause she's been hold back a few grades and just gets taller, or the way spit always dried at the corners of her mouth and turned white. I'm ascared of her cause her mama died a few months back, when the hot so hot you could fry your toes on the tar street. And every time I seen her, I remember if it's possible for my mama to die too. And my stomach burns bad to see her, tall and ugly and bad luck stuck to her like dried pus.

I have to sit next to Veronica on account of both our last names begin with G, no relation. She smells like pee and no one talk to her 'cept for Miss Smith, but she don't answer to nobody, not even Miss Smith. Veronica forgets that her name begins with V, puts spit on her eraser to erase the T on paper. Watching her smear the T all greasy black, then seen her scratching, scratching makes me want to tear out to anywheres. But Veronica, she lives close to me too.

Veronica and the brat brothers live 'cross the street from us in City Terrace Flats. Everybody ugly in her family, 'cepting her mama, Lil Mary G. Arlene knew her mama cause they went to Belvedere Jr. High together and hung around at Salas drugstore afterward. Then they got old.

Once when Arlene and me are in the bra section, First Street Store, cuz Arlene needs a new bra cause the thing that makes the straps go up and down broke and so her chichis hang down like a cow's she told Pancha, Veronica came up with Lil Mary G. For the first time, I seen Veronica's mama up front. She was short, kinda lumpy in a Arlene sorta way, which even made Veronica look more longer and ropey with knots for hands. Arlene said:

"Hey Lil Mary G! Member when we had to wear these, member?" Meaning Arlene picked up this kinda crippled bra for beginner chichis to show her. Lil Mary G. don't look like she even related to Veronica. I'm thinking about how someone so purty could have someone so ugly for a kid. She had glued, black Maybelline falsie lashes, black liner on top and at the bottom of her eyes, raccoon style. And she gots these gray eyes like rain clouds. Ain't never seen color in eyes like that before. She wore her hair beehive teased, looked bitch'n cause you couldn't even see the bobby pins. But even, I seen the way Veronica looked at me staring at her mama, the way I check her out her skin so tissuey and Veronica gets all proud at her mama.

"Ain't buying this for Veronica," said Lil Mary G, and grabbed Veronica's chichis and Veronica gets all bareassed, unknots her hands and flapped Lil Mary G. chichis back, kinda laughing, kinda pushed out of shape. "Its for me," and Arlene and Veronica's mama had a good laugh between the rows of boxes with them bra girls pushing out their starched up tits, thinking they all look Hot. No one 'cepting me don't even pay no attention to the way Veronica always scratching, scratching her arm, behind her legs, or the spit all white on her mouth even in the bra section at the First Street Store.

Arlene was in the kitchen. Got her rollers the size of candles all waxed stiff with Deb gel. She looked to be a shadow at the kitchen window, sitting in the dark, and for a snap of a minute, cause maybe I woke up all sleepyhead, I think it's a ghost. Mama? but she don't answer me, just the radio real low, a man singing Arlene's favorite song. You don't member me, but I member you, was not so long ago, you broke my heart in two—I peek over her to see what she's looking at.

"Crying shame" was all I heard, shaking her head like she does when Grandpa escaped and no one ever knowed where he was. The peoples down below all grouping next to Lil Mary G.'s house, the ambulance doors scream open and the bed rolls out like a tongue. I seen a plastic bag and lots of tubes, red period spots on white sheets, the tongue swallowed up by the ambulance mouth. I don't see Veronica nowheres, and I stick my head out to look for her but Arlene grabbed me back in real hard, like she's piss at me for something. "I hope they blow his fucking dick off," she tells no one.

Veronica don't talk to no one, and purty soon no one talk to her. She just wants to be left alone til everybody forgets she's around. I think that's what it is. Then she can disappear like Lil Mary G. without no one paying no attention. You don't need bras or nuthin' when you just air.

But to me, she just gets taller and rashier and her scratching sounds louder, like someone always rubbing sandpaper together. For reals.

Miss Smith yelled to me in a voice coming from a deep cave, "Ofelia, answer my question!" cause she been calling me and who cares, I don't know the answer anyways and I said "I dunno the answer anyways" and the bell rings. I ain't allowed to stay after school and play with Willy on account of he bit me like a dog, and Arlene and Tía Olivia had a fight, sos I ain't allowed to go to Tía's house either, and I dunno where my brother Gregorio is sos I guess I just go straight home, put the TV on loud or something.

When the door opens and its Arlene, my stomach burns stop. Her face makeup is all shiny sweat. Last week, me and Arlene and Pancha, who can drive a pickup truck, go to where Arlene works on account of I might get this job there pulling pant pockets inside out and getting money for it. Pancha can't find no parking so its just me and Arlene that goes into this big room with pipe guts for ceilings and no windows. All these sewing machines buzzing, buzzing, eating up big balls of string about big as my head spinning dizzy and so much dust flying 'round, makes it hard to breathe where Arlene works. Even I sneeze to no God bless yous. Nobody even to look up to say hello, not even Mr. Goldman who's so red he's pink 'n' says I'm too young anyways. Arlene said everyone at the machines ascare to go pee cause when you come back, might some other girl be in your place and no more job for you. Sos she got to hold her piss—'til my pussy 'bout to pop—she said to Pancha at the Kress lunch counter and I heard.

"Turn off the TV," she always says before hello. "Get me some aspirins." And I does both. I know it takes a long time for the buzzing of the machines in your head to stop. I know it after last week. Arlene kicks off her tennies, goes straight for the couch. The gummy black mascara lashes close like venetian blinds, puts her arm over her forehead, asses me, "Where's Spider?"

"I dunno."

"Was he home?"

"I dunno."

"Did he go to school?"

"I dunno." And in a snap of a minute, she's asleep.

Sos not to wake her, I go to the kitchen, look out the window for Gregorio. I see Veronica across the street, sitting on the porch, licking her lips, and I act like I don't see nuthin'. She act like she don't see nuthin' either.

———

"What the fuck's wrong?" Arlene yells, running into the bathroom, her hair wrapped in a towel like a vanilla Foster Freeze ice cream. "Well?" She's pissed, unwraps her towel, bows to rewrap it.

"Oh," I says, wiping my nose with the back of my hand, feeling stupid. "It's nuthin' ama. I just thought you . . ."

"Cheezes, *mi'ja*. Don't do me that again, *sabes?*"

I dunno what to say. One minute I seen her in the tub, next minute I run into the bathroom and stand there and the tub is empty and I only seen the water circling and circling into the drain and I screamed for I dunno why. Ain't nothing worser could happen than for a mama to die, you know. They ain't supposed to. Not even with such a purty name like Lil Mary G.

Just they never say hello and they never say good-bye. Mama Maria never said good-bye, she just left and that's that and nobody to tell me why Tío Benny don't live with Tía Olivia any more or when is Gregorio gonna come home or if Arlene is fixed up to go dancing at the Paladium tonight. No one to say nuthin'.

Arlene is getting ready in front of the mirror, pulls the top of her hair up, teases it with a brush, brushes it back, forks it high with her comb. I trip out cause she can do this and blow bubble gum at the same time without missin' a beat. Sprays Aqua Net back and forth, back and forth til her hairdo as shiny and hard as candied apples.

See what I mean? They just never say hello and never say good-bye. They just disappear, leaving you alone all ascared with your burns and *la llorona* hungry for you.

Nicanor, Saturday

Where is it that a man can find no reason to weep in secret, in secret because he is ashamed to weep from pain, ashamed because he can recall no mention of other men weeping, no mention of his father or his grandfather ever weeping? It is not here. And it is not anywhere else that any of the neighbors he thought of had been, they had been only here. But only here was not the only place. The Incredible Mr. Balance had said so and who could not believe such a man, such a man among men—a man among children. Children, thought Nicanor, nothing more, for he was one of these men and he should know. What Nicanor knew was that he wept, openly but in that secret way of his that was only his because his shame had made it his. Nicanor laughed.

And laughed and laughed at all the things the Incredible Mr. Balance could do, and laughed at all the things he talked about, things he said were not magic at all, not even special or hard to get and own, and the can opener that was electric and had a knife sharpener in back? Well, that was one of the easiest. But not here. And women anyone can have, if you've got money, and sometimes, even if you don't. Women, and nobody knows. Nobody cares, nobody but you. You.

"Who are you, Incredible Mr. Balance?"

"Here I am God. I am God today."

Nicanor stared at God.

"Tomorrow I may change my mind. I may change my mind because you have changed your mind."

"Can God change His mind? Can God not be God?"

"Yes. Yesterday I was not God, and tomorrow I will not be God. You can be God tomorrow."

"No, tomorrow I cannot. Tomorrow I must work, tomorrow I will yell when I come home, tomorrow I might cut these fingers picking the prickly pears off the cactus for dinner. Tomorrow my skin sweats."

"Here, lick my skin."

Nicanor licked His skin and shrugged his shoulders.

"I am the taste of all things."

The taste of the Incredible Mr. Balance was salty, good on food but not off the skin, good and not good, but salt and nothing else. The taste was gone and nothing else filled his mouth. Nicanor closed his mouth and walked away. He walked until his throat, his mouth chuckled, until his mouth became full of the laughing that now he did not want to understand, full of the laughing that made tears fall down the back of his throat because he could let no one else see them in his eyes, tears that made his mouth salty. Nicanor tried to pull the tears out of his mouth with his hands, his fingers, but they, too, were salty, his hands and his fingers were pure salt, more than his tears, but no, that couldn't be. Nicanor could not be God, he could not, he had no time, he had no skills, no balance, no magic.

No, he laughed, no, God must be God, he cried then, please, God must be God, and tomorrow, tomorrow especially, tomorrow is Sunday.

How the Mouth Works

I

A sound, laughter
fell from her mouth
out carelessly
in the manner of those
women who have lived
longest, who have been
forever our aunts,
fell as a liquid
goatmilk still warm
onto her pale blouse
then skirt,
which was long,
and so it went

but without wetness
without the dark
marks of rain
down to the floor
over to its particular
corner, staying there,
seeping into the wood,
almost always too quiet
but for the *moments*
when it was not,
and each time someone
suggests as someone
must always do
that this room is not
truly hers,
not her, that the walls
are not her skin,
that the laughter
at such a *moment* in the room
is a squeaking board
come loose, or some such idea—
when this is said at last
laughter comes, then,
from our mouths, which work
this way, this laughter
unmistakable, having come
up from where we have stepped
in this tired room,
from the particular place
in the corner of the floor,
laughter
which has come up the legs
of these blue pants,
up the shirt and higher,
this laugh
which is hers
as much as our eyes are,
then—this is the *moment*—
having moved up
into the mouth

my mouth this time,
she does laugh, yes.
We can hear it,
hear that it is long
and for nothing funny.

2

Her dream in the sheets
of the night drawn up
right next to her face,
next to where she breathed,
had been recurring.
It came like blood,
always the same, always
about the first time
she had seen a ball
for bowling, that game
where all the men were
for all those years,
and how the ball was held
precisely, and this was
what her dream was,
how this ball was held
just so, with the three
fingers inserted,
but rather into the head
of a large half-black cat,
her second Miguelito,
the one that ran away.
Into his two eyes
and his sad mouth.
This was her one dream
and in it, then, she
became the cat.
This was why her mouth
was falling and sad
on these last mornings,
two fingers of a bad dream
going into her, but upside down

so she could see,
two fingers going into
her, instead of babies
coming out, and the third
into her stomach
pushing out the breath.
That is how her navel
must have gotten there,
someone in the night
as she was asleep
and too young to speak
must have done this,
and in her dream
these were her scars,
made bigger again, and
again, three fingers
into them, her first
Miguelito, his fingers,
the man who ran away.

3

And then one morning
as I slept in her bed
to comfort her, her
baby that never came,
she sat up like an L
and I saw her, saw
that the dream this time
had not ended.
She spoke to me
in the words of her dream,
so that the words
of this world
must have gone
with her. To help her.
Our names, the names of salt
and *chile,* salt
y las papas
cociendo en la mañana.

She spoke, and I held
her new word in my hands,
held the moan
to comfort it,
I held it in both hands
because I had to.
The sound of this thing
I had watched,
how it pulled out, long,
as if her tongue
all the while
all the years I had seen her,
had been the plain
and thin head
of a fisherman's eel
finding its chance now
to go, get out, but slow
in the only way
it could move
through a small mouth
after so much waiting.
I held it, this word,
held it across
the palms of my two hands
and it was longer
than any man's arm.

The Vietnam Wall

I
Have seen it
And I like it: The magic,
The way like cutting onions
It brings water out of nowhere.

Invisible from one side, a scar
Into the skin of the ground
From the other, a black winding
Appendix line.
    A dig.
    An archaeologist can explain.
The walk is slow at first
Easy, a little black marble wall
Of a dollhouse,
A smoothness, a shine
The boys in the street want to give.
One name. And then more
Names, long lines, lines of names until
They are the shape of the U.N. building
Taller than I am: I have walked
Into a grave.
And everything I expect has been taken away, like that, quick:
    The names are not alphabetized.
    They are in the order of dying,
    An alphabet of—somewhere—screaming.
I start to walk out. I almost leave
But stop to look up names of friends,
My own name. There is somebody
Severiano Ríos.
Little kids do not make the same noise
Here, junior high school boys don't run
Or hold each other in headlocks.
No rules, something just persists
Like pinching on St. Patrick's Day
Every year for no green.
    No one knows why.
Flowers are forced
Into the cracks
Between sections.
Men have cried
At this wall.
I have
Seen them.

Mother of Shrines

Mother has paid tribute to her dead relatives
with shrines—candles, plastic flowers, plastic saints,
set on altars draped with lace doilies and satin—
since time immemorial. The real motives
for this hobby? Could it be genetic:
some ancient impulse to preserve the remains
of loved ones against decay, against Satan?
In return the dead are empathic,
and can be called upon in times of need.
After all, some of the dead were real brains;
they're flattered you seek their superior reason.
And they're bored—can't read, can't feed, can't breed.
So, it's a racket. What isn't these days?
Light a candle, close your eyes. Call out a name.

Mother of the Long Good-bye

Mother arrives at a small airport
carrying only a small suitcase. She comes
to say good-bye to her dying sister.
They talk of where they will be. This is important.

These are memories I've never had. Next
is the part that repeats like a film, that runs
and runs, over and over. A small gesture:
she turns, I see her face full of sadness.
My mother, with the knowledge of her own death
in her eyes, is saying good-bye. Nothing blunts
this scene. Now I wish I had caressed her
when I had the chance, before her last breath.
These are the right things in the right order.
Waking is a bullet right through me; I shudder.

Mother of the Historical Tree

Mother sent me this picture: it's summer
in Crystal City, Texas, and she wears
a sleeveless dress, her bare arms raised above
her head, raised and reaching behind her,
touching a tree planted forty years ago.
She rests against the tree, while the air
accepts her smile, accepts her loyal love,
my little mother in this brazen pose;
her armpits showing, her body given over
to dreams. Does the driver in the passing truck care
that her father planted this tree? Her blood
responds as the memory grows bolder.
The colors of the instant photograph
are sexy and vivid: her epitaph.

Psalm for Your Image

Lord,
You gave the indians tobacco
You gave the white man alcohol
You gave the arabs caffeine
You gave the chinese gunpowder

Lord, I can't shake the tobacco
Can't leave the alcohol
Can't imagine a world
Without coffee

And as for the gunpowder
Which I could do without
It's always popping around me

Lord,
If we are in your image
You must be a coffee guzzling
Gunslinger with a serious hangover
And a cigarette cough.

Sonnet for Mars

Mars. I loved you once as much as I now grieve.
I envied your two moons, red planet. But now I see
Red blood, the color of armaments rusting and
Buried nuclear waste erupting, corroding the soil.

Face ripped by mining, face tracked by trenches
Blew open the ozone, cannons shredded the leaves
Hydrogen fire boiling the water to meager icecaps
Impotent warrior; cannot make mists or spit clouds.

Mars. Where is the poet's song to the simultaneous
Eclipses of Phobos and Deimos, the painting with
The anemic greens of your last sterile spring?

Mighty warrior parched. Mighty warrior breathless.

      Mars.
      Now I understand the meaning of your desolate face.

Sonnet for Angelo Monterosa

Monterosa, your body is dead on Avenue A. Angelo,
They found you eyes open staring at the beer
Soaked floorboards. Did you want that? Did
You mind them filling your back with buckshot?

Angelo, I am angry with them all, and you Monterosa
Killed and killers, killing and dealing dope. No good
You were, no good they are. Still, I wish their fate
To be bodies stacking under the same blue smoke.

Monterosa, there is blood on your song, blood on the juke
Box; the cowbell, the conga, and your corpse form the trio
That is the rhinestone pin of my failure, your failure,
Our failure, who loved, but did not rescue Angelo.

  Angel, hold him, while I bury him in these clean words,
  And pray to see the resurrection of the rose mountain.

Look on the Bright Side

The way I see it, a man can have all the money in the world but if he can't keep his self-respect he don't have shit. A man has to stand up for things even when it may not be very practical. A man can't have pride and give up his rights.

This is exactly what I told my wife when Mrs. Kevovian raised our rent illegally. I say illegally because, well aside from it being obviously unfriendly and greedy whenever a landlord or lady wants money above the exceptional amount she wanted when you moved in not so long ago, here in this enlightened city of Los Angeles it's against the law to raise it above a certain percentage and then only once every twelve months, which is often enough. Now the wife argued that since Mrs. Kevovian was a little ignorant, nasty, and hard to communicate with, we should have gone ahead and paid the increase—added up it was only sixty some-odd bones, a figure the landlady'd come up with getting the percentage right, but this time she tried to get it two months too early. My wife told me to pay it and not have the hassle. She knew me better than this. We'd already put up with the cucarachas and rodents, I fixed the plumbing myself, and our back porch was screaming to become dust and probably would just when one of our little why nots—we have three of them—snuck onto it. People don't turn into dust on the way down, they splat first. One time I tried to explain this to Mrs. Kevovian, without success. You think I was going to pay more rent when I shouldn't have to?

My wife offered the check for the right amount to the landlady when she came to our door for her money and wouldn't take it. My wife tried to explain how there was a mistake but when I got home from work the check was still on the mantle where it sat waiting. Should I have called her and talked it over? Not me. This was her problem and she could call. In the meantime, I could leave the money in the bank and feel that much richer for that much longer, and if she was so stupid I could leave it in the savings and let it earn interest. And the truth was that she was stupid enough, and stubborn, and mean. I'd talked to the other tenants, and I'd talked to tenants that'd left before us, so I wasn't at all surprised about the Pay or Quit notice we finally got. To me, it all seemed kind of fun. This lady wasn't nice, as God Himself would witness, and maybe, since I learned it would take about three months before we'd go to court, maybe we'd get three free months. We hadn't stopped talking about moving out since we unpacked.

You'd probably say that this is how things always go, and you'd probably be right. Yeah, about this same time I got laid off. I'd been laid off lots of times so it was no big deal, but the circumstances—well, the company I was working for went bankrupt and a couple of my paychecks bounced and it wasn't the best season of the year in what were not the best years for working people. Which could have really set me off, made me pretty unhappy, but that's not the kind of man I am. I believe in making whatever you have the right situation for you at the right moment for you. And look, besides the extra money from not paying rent, I was going to get a big tax return, and we also get unemployment compensation in this great country. It was a good time for a vacation, so I bunched the kids in the car with the old lady and drove to Baja. I deserved it, we all did.

Like my wife said, I should have figured how things were when we crossed back to come home. I think we were in the slowest line on the border. Cars next to us would pull up and within minutes be at that red-light green-light signal. You know how it is when you pick the worst line to wait in. I was going nuts. A poor dude in front of us idled so long that his radiator overheated and he had to push the old heap forward by himself. My wife told me to settle down and wait because if we changed lanes then *it* would stop moving. I turned the ignition off then on again when we moved a spot. When we did get there I felt a lot better, cheerful even. There's no prettier place for a vacation than Baja and we really had a good time. I smiled forgivingly at the customs guy who looked as kind as Captain Stubbing on the TV show "Love Boat."

"I'm American," I said, prepared like the sign told us to be. My wife said the same thing. I said, "The kids are American too. Though I haven't checked out the backseat for a while."

Captain Stubbing didn't think that was very funny. "What do you have to declare?"

"Let's see. A six-pack of Bohemia beer. A blanket. Some shells we found. A couple holy pictures. Puppets for the kids. Well, two blankets."

"No other liquor? No fruits? Vegetables? No animal life?"

I shook my head to each of them.

"So what were you doing in Mexico?"

"Sleeping on the beach, swimming in the ocean. Eating the rich folks' lobster." It seemed like he didn't understand what I meant. "Vacation. We took a vacation."

"How long were you in Mexico?" He made himself comfortable on the stool outside his booth after he'd run a license plate check through the computer.

"Just a few days," I said, starting to lose my good humor.

"How many days?"

"You mean exactly?"

"Exactly."

"Five days. Six. Five nights and six days."

"Did you spend a lot of money in Mexico?"

I couldn't believe this, and someone else in a car behind us couldn't either because he blasted the horn. Captain Stubbing made a mental note of him. "We spent some good money there. Not that much though. Why?" My wife grabbed my knee.

"Where exactly did you stay?"

"On the beach. Near Estero Beach."

"Don't you work?"

I looked at my wife. She was telling me to go along with it without saying so. "Of course I work."

"Why aren't you at work now?"

"Cuz I got laid off, man!"

"Did you do something wrong?"

"I said I got *laid off,* not *fired!*"

"What do you do?"

"Laborer!"

"What kind of laborer?"

"Construction!"

"And there's no other work? Where do you live?"

"No! Los Angeles!"

"Shouldn't you be looking for a job? Isn't that more important than taking a vacation?"

I was so hot I think my hair was turning red. I just glared at this guy.

"Are you receiving unemployment benefits?"

"Yeah I am."

"You're receiving unemployment and you took a vacation?"

"That's it! I ain't listening to this shit no more!"

"You watch your language, sir." He filled out a slip of paper and slid it under my windshield wiper. "Pull over there."

My wife was a little worried about the two smokes I never did and still had stashed in my wallet. She was wanting to tell me to take it easy as they went through the car, but that was hard for her because our oldest baby was crying. All I wanted to do was put in a complaint about that jerk to somebody higher up. As a matter of fact I wanted him fired, but anything to make him some trouble. I felt like they would've listened better if they hadn't found those four bottles of rum I was trying to sneak over. At this point I lost some confidence, though not my sense of being right. When this other customs man suggested that I might be detained further if I pressed the situation, I paid the penalty charges for the confiscated liquor and shut up. It wasn't worth a strip search, or finding out what kind of crime it was crossing the border with some B-grade marijuana.

Time passed back home and there was still nothing coming out of the union hall. There were a lot of men worried but at least I felt like I had the unpaid rent money to wait it out. I was fortunate to have a landlady like Mrs. Kevovian helping us through these bad times. She'd gotten a real smart lawyer for me too. He'd attached papers on his Unlawful Detainer to prove *my* case, which seemed so ridiculous that I called the city housing department just to make sure I couldn't be wrong about it all. I wasn't. I rested a lot easier without a rent payment, even took some guys for some cold ones when I got the document with the official court date stamped on it, still more than a month away.

I really hadn't started out with any plan. But now that I was unemployed there were all these complications. I didn't have all the money it took to get into another place, and our rent, as much as it had been, was in comparison to lots still cheap, and rodents and roaches weren't that bad a problem to me. Still, I took a few ugly pictures like I was told to and had the city inspect the hazardous back porch and went to court on the assigned day hoping for something to ease out our bills.

Her lawyer was Yassir Arafat without the bedsheet. He wore this suit with a vest that was supposed to make him look cool, but I've seen enough Ziedler & Ziedler commercials to recognize discount fashion. Mrs. Kevovian sat on that hard varnished bench with that wrinkled forehead of hers. Her daughter translated whatever she didn't understand when the lawyer discussed the process. I could hear every word even though there were all these other people because the lawyer's voice carried in the long white hall and polished floor of justice. He talked as confidently as a dude with a sharp blade.

"You're the defendant?" he asked five minutes before court was to be in session.

"That's me, and that's my wife." I pointed. "We're both defendants."

"I'm Mr. Villalobos, attorney representing the plaintiff."

"All right! Law school, huh? You did the people proud, eh? So how come you're working for the wrong side? That ain't a nice lady you're helping to evict us, man."

"You're the one who refuses to pay the rent."

"I'm disappointed in you, compa. You should know I been trying to pay the rent. You think I should beg her to take it? She wants more money than she's supposed to get, and because I wanna pay her what's right, she's trying to throw us onto the streets."

Yassir Villalobos scowled over my defense papers while I gloated. I swore it was the first time he saw them or the ones he turned in. "Well, I'll do this. Reimburse Mrs. Kevovian for the back rent and I'll drop the charges."

"You'll drop the charges? Are you making a joke, man? You talk like I'm the one who done something wrong. I'm *here* now. Unless you wanna say drop what I owe her, something like that, then I won't let the judge see how you people tried to harass me unlawfully."

Villalobos didn't like what I was saying, and he didn't like my attitude one bit.

"I'm the one who's right," I emphasized. "I know it, and you know it too." He was squirming mad. I figured he was worried about looking like a fool in the court. "Unless you offer me something better, I'd just as soon see what that judge has to say."

"There's no free rent," he said finally. "I'll drop these charges and reserve you." He said that as an ultimatum, real pissed.

I smiled. "You think I can't wait another three months?"

That did it. He charged the court and court secretary, and my old lady and me picked the kids up from the babysitter's a lot earlier than we'd planned. The truth was I was relieved. I did have the money, but now that I'd been out of work so long it was getting close. If I didn't get some work soon we wouldn't have enough to pay it all. I'd been counting on that big income tax check, and when the government decided to take all of it except nine dollars and some change, what remained of a debt from some other year and the penalties it included, I was almost worried. I wasn't happy with the US Govt and I tried to explain to it on the phone how hard I worked and how it was only that I didn't understand those letters they sent me and couldn't they show some kindness to the unemployed, to a family that obviously hadn't planned to run with that tax advantage down to Costa Rica and hire bodyguards to watch over an estate. The thing is, it's no use being right when the US Govt thinks it's not wrong.

Fortunately, we still had Mrs. Kevovian as our landlady. I don't know how we'd have lived without her. Unemployment money covers things when you don't have to pay rent. And I didn't want to for as long as possible. The business agent at the union hall said there was supposed to be a lot of work breaking soon, but in the meantime I told everyone in our home who talked and didn't crawl to lay low and not answer any doors to strangers with summonses. My wife didn't like peeking around corners when she walked the oldest to school, though the oldest liked it a mess. We waited and waited but nobody came. Instead it got nailed to the front door very impolitely.

So another few months had passed and what fool would complain about that? Not this one. Still, I wanted justice. I wanted The Law to hand down fair punishment to these evil people who were conspiring to take away my family's home. Man, I wanted that judge to be so pissed that he'd pound that gavel and it'd ring in my ears like a Vegas jackpot. I didn't want to pay any money back. And not because I didn't have the money, or I didn't have a job, or that pretty soon they'd be cutting off my unemployment. I'm not denying their influence on my thinking, but mostly it was the principle of the thing. It seemed to me if I had so much to lose for being wrong, I should have something equal to win for being right.

"There's no free rent," Villalobos told me again five minutes before we were supposed to swing through those doors and please rise. "You don't have the money, do you?"

"Of course I have the money. But I don't see why I should settle this with you now and get nothing out of it. Seems like I had to go outa my way to come down here. It ain't easy finding a babysitter for our kids, who you wanna throw on the streets, and we didn't, and we had to pay that expensive parking across the street. This has been a mess of trouble for me to go, sure, I'll pay what I owe without the mistaken rent increase, no problem."

"The judge isn't going to offer you free rent."

"I'd rather hear what he has to say."

Villalobos was some brother, but I guess that's what happens with some education and a couple of cheap suits and ties. I swore right then that if I ever worked again I wasn't paying for my kids' college education.

The judge turned out to be a sister whose people hadn't gotten much justice either and that gave me hope. And I was real pleased we were the first case because the kids were fidgeting like crazy and my wife was miserable trying to keep them settled down. I wanted the judge to see what a big happy family we were so I brought them right up to our assigned "defendant" table.

"I think it would be much easier if your wife took your children out to the corridor," the judge told me.

"She's one of the named defendants, your honor."

"I'm sure you can represent your case adequately without the baby crying in your wife's arms."

"Yes ma'am, your honor."

The first witness for the plaintiff was this black guy who looked like they pulled a bottle away from him the night before, who claimed to have come by my place to serve me all these times but I wouldn't answer the door. The sleaze was all lie up until when he said he attached it to my door, which was a generous exaggeration. Then Mrs. Kevovian took the witness stand. Villalobos asked her a couple of unimportant questions, and then I got to ask questions. I've watched enough lawyer shows and I was ready.

I heard the gavel but it didn't tinkle like a line of cherries.

"You can state your case in the witness stand at the proper moment," the judge said.

"But your honor, I just wanna show how this landlady . . ."

"You don't have to try your case through this witness."

"Yes ma'am, your honor."

So when that moment came all I could do was show her those Polaroids of how bad things got and tell her about roaches and rats and fire hazards and answer oh yes, your honor, I've been putting that money away, something which concerned the judge more than anything else did.

I suppose that's the way of swift justice. Back at home, my wife, pessimistic as always, started packing the valuable stuff into the best boxes. She couldn't believe that anything good was going to come from the verdict in the mail. The business agent at the hall was still telling us about all the work about to break any day now, but I went ahead and started reading the help-wanted ads in the newspaper.

A couple of weeks later the judgment came in an envelope. We won.

The judge figured up all the debt and then cut it by twenty percent. Victory is sweet, probably, when there's a lot of coins clinking around the pants pockets, but I couldn't let up. Now that I was proven right I figured we could do some serious negotiating over payment. A little now and a little later and a little bit now and again. That's what I'd offer when she came for the money, which Mrs. Kevovian was supposed to do the next night by five P.M., according to the legal document. "The money to be collected by the usual procedure," were the words, which meant Mrs. Kevovian was supposed to knock on the door and, knowing her, at five exactly.

Maybe I was a tiny bit worried. What if she wouldn't take anything less than all of it? Then I'd threaten to give her nothing and to disappear into the mounds of other uncollected debts. Mrs. Kevovian needed this money, I knew that. Better all of it over a long period than none of it over a longer one, right? That's what I'd tell her, and I'd be standing there with my self-confidence more muscled up than ever.

Except she never came. There was no knock on the door. A touch nervous, I started calling lawyers. I had a stack of junk-mail letters from all these legal experts advising me that for a small fee they'd help me with my eviction procedure. None of them seemed to understand my problem over the phone, though maybe if I came by their office. One of them did seem to catch enough though. He said if the money wasn't collected by that time then the plaintiff had the right to reclaim the premises. Actually the lawyer didn't say that, the judgment paper did, and I'd read it to him into the mouthpiece of the phone. All the lawyer said was, "The marshall will physically evict you in ten days." He didn't charge a fee for the information.

We had a garage sale. You know, miscellaneous things, things easy to replace, that you could buy anywhere when the time was right again, like beds and lamps and furniture. We stashed the valuables in the trunk of the car—a perfect fit—and Greyhound was having a special sale which made it an ideal moment for a visit to the abuelitos back home, who hadn't been able to see their grandkids and daughter in such a long time. You have to look on the bright side. I wouldn't have to pay any of that money back, and there was the chance to start a new career, just like they say, and I'd been finding lots of opportunities from reading the newspaper. Probably any day I'd be going back to work at one of those jobs about to break. Meanwhile, we left a mattress in the apartment for me to sleep on so I could have the place until a marshall beat on the door. Or soon

I'd send back for the family from a house with a front and backyard I promised I'd find and rent. However it worked out. Or there was always the car with that big backseat.

One of those jobs I read about in the want-ads was as a painter for the city. I applied, listed all this made-up experience I had, but I still had to pass some test. So I went down to the library to look over one of those books on the subject. I guess I didn't think much about the hours libraries keep, and I guess I was a few hours early, and so I took a seat next to this pile of newspapers on this cement bench not that far away from the front doors. The bench smelled like piss, but since I was feeling pretty open-minded about things I didn't let it bother me. I wanted to enjoy all the scenery, which was nice for the big city, with all the trees and dewy grass, though the other early risers weren't so involved with the love of nature. One guy not so far away was rolling from one side of his body to the other, back and forth like that, from under a tree. He just went on and on. This other man, or maybe woman—wearing a sweater on top that was too baggy to make chest impressions on and another sweater below that, wrapped around like a skirt, and there were pants under that, cords, and unisex homemade sandals made out of old tennis shoes and leather, and finally, on the head, long braided hair which wasn't braided too good—this person was foraging off the cemented path, digging through the trash for something. I thought aluminum too but there were about five empty beer cans nearby and the person kicked those away. It was something that this person knew by smell, because that's how he or she tested whether it was the right thing or not. I figured that was someone to keep my eye on.

Then without warning came a monster howl, and those pigeons bundled up on the lawn scattered to the trees. I swore somebody took a shot at me. "Traitor! You can't get away with it!" Those were the words I got out of the tail end of the loud speech from this dude who came out of nowhere, who looked pretty normal, hip even if it weren't for the clothes. One of those great, long graying beards and hair, like some wise man, some Einstein. I was sure a photographer would be along to take his picture if they hadn't already. You know how Indians and winos make the most interesting photographs. His clothes were bad though, took away from his cool. Like he'd done caca and spilled his spaghetti and rolled around in the slime for a lot of years since mama'd washed a bagful of the dirties. The guy really had some voice, and just when it seemed like he'd settled back into a stroll like anyone else, just when those pigeons trickled back down onto the lawn into a coo-cooing lump, he cut loose again. It was pretty hard to understand, even with his volume so high, but I figured it out to be about patriotism, justice, and fidelity.

"That guy's gone," John said when he came up to me with a bag of groceries he dropped next to me. He'd told me his name right off. "John. John. The name's John, they call me John." He pulled out a loaf of white bread and started tearing up the slices into big and little chunks and throwing them onto the grass. The pigeons picked up on this quick. "Look at 'em, they act like they ain't eaten in weeks, they're eatin like vultures, like they're starvin, like vultures, good thing I bought three loafs of bread, they're so hungry, but they'll calm down, they'll calm down after they eat some." John was blond and could almost claim to have a perm if you'd asked me. He'd shaven some days ago so the stubble on his face wasn't so bad. He'd never have much of a beard anyway. "They can't get enough, look at 'em, look at 'em, good thing I bought three loafs, I usually buy two." He moved like he talked—nervously, in jerks, and without pausing—and, when someone passed by, his conversation didn't break up. "Hey good morning, got any spare change for some food? No? So how ya gonna get to Heaven?" A man in a business suit turned his head with a smile, but didn't change direction. "I'll bury you deeper in Hell then, I'll dig ya deeper!" John went back to feeding the birds, who couldn't get enough. "That's how ya gotta talk to 'em," he told me. "Ya gotta talk to 'em like that and like ya can back it up, like ya can back it up."

I sort of got to liking John. He reminded me of a hippie, and it was sort of nice to see hippies again. He had his problems, of course, and he told me about them too, about how a dude at the hotel he stayed at kept his SSI check, how he called the police but they wouldn't pay attention, that his hotel was just a hangout for winos and hypes and pimps and he was gonna move out, turn that guy in and go to court and testify or maybe he'd get a gun and blow the fucker away, surprise him. He had those kind of troubles but seemed pretty intelligent otherwise to me. Even if he was a little wired, he wasn't like the guy that was still rolling under the tree or the one screaming at the top of his lungs.

While we both sat at the bench watching those pigeons clean up what became only visible to them in the grass, one of the things John said before he took off was this: "Animals are good people. They're not like people, people are no good, they don't care about nobody. People won't do nothing for ya. That's the age we live in, that's how it is. Hitler had that plan. I think it was Hitler, maybe it was somebody else, it coulda been somebody else." We were both staring at this pigeon with only one foot, the other foot being a balled-up red stump, hopping around, pecking at the lawn. "I didn't think much of him gettin rid of the cripples and the mentals and the old people. That was no good, that was no good. It musta been Hitler, or Preacher Jobe. It was him, or it musta been somebody else I heard. Who was I thinkin of? Hey you got any change? How ya gonna get to Heaven? I wish I could remember who it was I was thinkin of."

I sure didn't know, but I promised John that if I thought of it, or if something else came up, I'd look him up at the address he gave me and I filed it in my pocket. I had to show him a couple of times it was still there. I was getting a little tired from such a long morning already, and I wished that library would hurry up and open so I could study for the test. I didn't have the slightest idea what they could ask me on a test for painting either. But then jobs at the hall were bound to break and probably I wouldn't have to worry too much anyway.

I was really sleepy by now, and I was getting used to the bench, even when I did catch that whiff of piss. I leaned back and closed the tired eyes and it wasn't so bad. I thought I'd give it a try—you know, why not?—and I scooted over and nuzzled my head into that stack of newspaper and tucked my legs into my chest. I shut them good this time and yawned. I didn't see why I should fight it, and it was just until the library opened.

The Graduation

Above the merengue playing on the radio, Glori heard a motorcycle stall and quick footsteps on the walkway to her house. She was stretched across the living room couch in a blue nylon nightgown, partly listening to the music, more intently examining her cuticles. The knock came. She sat up and reached over to the end table beside the sofa to turn down the transistor radio. "Who is it?" she asked uneasily. Glori slighted the caller by not properly answering the door. She would not be seen, by anyone, dressed as she was.

"Alina's brother," a voice responded. "Don't bother opening up." A green envelope slipped under the wooden door. Its appearance startled her, like a lizard did when it suddenly ran across a wall. She grabbed the robe that had doubled as a pillow and shook it out to cover herself with before going to the open window to see if she could get a glimpse of him.

She lifted the nightgown above her ankles, slid into matching blue slippers, and crossed the old Spanish-tiled floor to the one window on the side of the house, a favorite lookout. She had tacked Polaroid photographs of an assortment of relatives on each horizontal wooden board that met the lengths of the window frame. The snapshots flanked the window and kept her company.

Glori stepped quickly onto the brick which her husband, Henry, had placed beneath the window. Barely five feet tall, she had been a little too short for the post. Glori found it hard to see out without straining, even in high heels. Henry had resolved the problem. Now her chin hovered comfortably above the sill. She liked the brick so much she had bought a remnant of upholstery fabric and sewn a cloth cover for it, so it did not look odd in the living room. The move was her first inspired effort that morning.

Glori saw three motorcycles zoom down the long hill toward the plaza; no doubt Alina's brother was on one of them. One driver, the one carrying a military man, had a red helmet on. She frowned. Glori scanned the sidewalks and street for a few moments to see if anyone unusual was on Maximo Gomez Avenue. The vegetable man and his dusty donkey and cart were coming up the slope. Two of the six children who lived in one of the other wooden houses left on the block played on the concrete floor. Those kids are always naked, she thought. Then, as if to prove her wrong, the ten-month-old boy crawled past the open door wearing a shirt, his mother laughing, following right behind him.

Turning from the window, Glori stepped down carefully and went to get the green envelope. She was waiting to hear from a certain cousin Matilda in Puerto Rico and hoped it was a message from her. She paused there for a moment, thinking about the exciting possibilities. But Alina's brother had brought it. That confused her. She picked it up, returned to the sofa, and poured more Coca-Cola into a glass. With a nail file she opened the envelope, which contained an invitation.

It wasn't what she had hoped for, but the notice was good. She clapped her hands and brought them to her breast. "Alina is graduating!" Glori called out to her mother-in-law, Magda, who was preparing lunch for the household.

"What did you say?" Magda called back from the kitchen in the back of the small house.

"It's Alina's turn this time!" she almost yelled.

"I'm coming." After fifteen years of sharing the same house, Magda knew something of her daughter-in-law's capricious ways. "What is it now?" Magda didn't bother to lay down the cooking spoon when she went to see what Glori wanted.

Glori repeated the news and held out the invitation.

"So, Alina is graduating." Magda chuckled softly. "Which Alina?"

"Clara's third. Don't you remember, mama?" Irritation had brought a tenseness into her voice. Glori stood up to look directly into the older woman's eyes. She expected an answer.

"Don't you?"

"How could I know? With three Alinas in the family." The older woman's face relaxed when she thought about the girls. She was startled by Glori's steady stare and looked right back into her eyes.

"No, I have not lost track of the numbers, just of which one is moving on," she said. Magda suspected the two daughters-in-law of choosing the same name to cause confusion. Crafty women. With so many other names to choose from.

"Where did they find that name, anyway?" the old woman asked. "I haven't heard of any Saint Alina. Alina Maria, Alina Beatrice, Alina Caridad." Magda tasted what was left on the spoon. Would Glori be kind enough to clarify the mystery? She waited.

"She's a manicurist now, mama." Glori softened her voice, recalling the spiral notebook in the kitchen drawer. Magda had written down all her grandchildren's names and birthdates. Glori was grateful for the record. She often took it out to refer to it. Magda had twelve children. And they had all had so many that, frankly, it was hard to keep track of the in-laws. Glori was careful to buy cards on their birthdays for the ones who lived closest. Glori knew she would not have remembered which Alina it was either if she hadn't seen her working at the beauty parlor last week. She extended one hand and spread her fingers to show off the manicure.

Magda took one of Glori's fingers between two of hers as if it were a strange cookie and brought it closer to inspect the polish. "I see."

"Aren't they beautiful?"

"The color is pretty." Magda returned to the kitchen smacking the wooden spoon against the palm of her free hand.

The sympathy toward her mother-in-law's confusion was temporary. It had passed by the time Glori settled back on the sofa. She took long sips of soda, until she could see the front door through the cleared bottom of the glass. She should have jumped at the old woman to see if she'd drop the spoon and come to her senses. She would, once again, instruct her about the importance of keeping kitchen utensils in their proper place. Magda had not gone to school, but she would have to learn somehow. After all these years, why hadn't she learned? Dense. She'd tell Henry about his mother later. Was she so senile that she didn't remember it was wrong to walk into a formal living room with a spoon dripping with broth?

Glori put the glass back down next to the radio and stood up. She too could be as stubborn as an old mule. Why, the old lady was not concerned at all about the family. Determined to teach her, to show Magda how she had failed the family in a new way, Glori walked through the narrow dining room to the kitchen to confront her.

"You don't seem excited about going," she began.

The old woman didn't answer.

"Why not?"

She continued stirring the soup.

"I can't wait to see Alina in a cap and gown."

Magda glanced at her daughter-in-law, who was leaning against the kitchen wall. I don't owe Glori an explanation, Magda thought. I was taught to ask my parents for permission and their blessings. Then I did what they said. When I was married, I talked things over with my husband. Her parents, her husband, Magda trusted the three people who never misled her; she loved and missed them.

Magda turned a knob and bent to watch the burner's flame go down. For my actions, she thought, I am now accountable only to God.

Glori respected her silence and stayed to watch her mother-in-law finish cooking. She knew Magda would not be going Saturday; it was useless to press it. Magda had gone to the first few ceremonies, glad that the grandchildren, especially the girls, had attended three—or six was it?—courses at the institute to prepare them to do something other with their lives than spending them sitting across the threshold of a door cuddling babies or jumping up to fetch an unemployed husband a glass of water.

After a while, Magda decided there were better ways to spend a Saturday afternoon. A nap was of particular interest to an old woman who rose at five to prepare for the day. Besides, at home she wouldn't be in the sun.

Magda lifted a lid to check how the rice was doing. She gave the white grains a big stir, hit the spoon against the side of the aluminum pan, and covered it. "It's ready. Get the cantina out so your husband will have some food ready when he drives by for it, will you?"

Glori stopped to consider the request, then did what was asked.

The meal packed, Glori heard Henry's car motor in front of the house. She left the three-tiered lunch pail on the counter. Magda had set a place for herself at the dining room table. She poked through the pots, making selections for her own plate.

Glori smoothed her hair down, adjusted the top of her robe, and went to greet Henry. He pushed open the door. Glori looked past him at the beat-up blue Datsun. Its front half was on the sidewalk. She started to remind him to move it, but he sensed the reprimand coming, took off his cap, and planted a kiss on her mouth.

"You are a bold one," she said, and started to smile. He pinched her thigh. She grunted. He quickly pulled a small bag of cashews out of his shirt pocket.

"Thanks," she said, and went over to the sofa to enjoy what she preferred for lunch. Glori wanted to wipe the sweaty kiss away but decided against it. Henry was, after all, her husband of fifteen years, who drove a public car for their living in the hot sun. He was ten years older than Glori. Some said he looked older because he had started balding early.

Glori had heard women say he had a very sexy smile. She thought he did. And it was always in his favor. But Glori noticed that as he aged, much like the mother who had borne him, he became coarser in his manners.

Henry heard his mother's call, but he stopped to watch how Glori relished each curved nut and each sip of Coca-Cola. He'd been buying the American soft drink for three months now, though it was more expensive than the Dominican brand. He did not worry about the extra expense. It was money he would have spent bringing surprises home to a child. He hoped the treats kept her happy—anything to keep her home, happy.

Henry placed his hand briefly on his mother's shoulder in greeting when he passed her for his lunch. He thought about how he didn't like Glori to go into town much—too much gossip, too many strange ideas in the air. One time Glori had come home talking about a job in a fabric store, and he had told her to get the idea right away right out of her head.

"Listen, Alina is graduating Saturday," she told Henry as he hurried back through the room and out the door. He ate in his car, parked under a large tree at the edge of town near the baseball stadium. During the early years of their marriage, Glori had constantly argued with Henry about his eating lunch away from the house. Long ago, Henry had gotten and kept his way. He didn't nap, though it was the custom, but continued making the same run, picking up and dropping off people who in time ceased to be strangers. Although he never counted the trips, Henry guessed he made more than a hundred a day and was proud he knew, at least by sight, every family on the route. Before he had been introduced to Glori, he had seen her dressed in a school uniform talking with friends on the porch of her father's house.

He had driven girls who had grown into beautiful adolescence, then disappeared inside their husbands' houses. He missed some of them. During his twenty years of driving he had also seen new shops open, and close after a few months of halfhearted business. Others had started in one small room and expanded, like the English language school, which now earned enough money to renovate the old square concrete building that housed it.

"Which one is she?" he asked.

"Clara's third," said Glori. She did not blame Henry for not remembering. He had enough on his mind.

"I'll be working that Saturday," Henry said.

"That's what you always say," she complained. "I want you to come with me. Your mother won't go. I may have to go alone."

"Glori, my love"—he took her hand and raised it up to kiss it—"every month someone from our family graduates. We have a manicurist, a professional waiter, a bilingual typist who refuses to speak English. Now, one more manicurist. I am a simple driver. That's what I'll be doing then." He smacked a kiss loudly onto her hand and left, singing.

She can go alone, Henry thought. People would be watching the graduation and concerned with their own family members, for once. He slammed the car door shut out of necessity, not anger. As he drove off, Henry recalled the last accident, unfortunately with another public car driver. The car door wouldn't stay closed unless it got a good bang. Henry knew the car embarrassed Glori, though no one else in town seemed to mind its looks. Every now and then he reminded her she was eating well because of it. That quieted her. He drove off.

The ten days until the Saturday of Alina's graduation passed without much fanfare. Glori looked forward to the change the ceremony would bring. On the morning of the big day, Glori got out of bed early and pulled on a comfortable dress. She had an appointment to have her hair styled. Henry had left money for her on the dining room table. Fortified by a glassful of hot milk with coffee, she walked the four blocks down the hill to the beauty parlor.

The shop doors opened at exactly eight in the morning. The beautician was setting up for the day's work. In one corner, a tall standing fan was twirling and blowing hard. She motioned Glori to the swivel chair. The beautician washed and rolled her client's hair, since she was not allowed to cut it. Glori loved her curly shoulder-length hair, good hair that it was, everyone noted. It was as fine as any Spaniard's. She would have to spend a couple of hours under a big electric hair dryer, one of two in the salon. Time would go slowly.

Usually she shunned the other women in the shop. She talked only to Alina, who worked there part-time, gaining experience. She was obviously at home today preparing for the ceremony. "Thank God there's electricity this morning," Glori said finally to the woman next to her. The woman was asleep.

Glori looked at her image in the round mirror hanging across from her on a dirty pink wall. She gently massaged her face like Alina had taught her. Henry loved her smooth, light brown complexion. It was one of the reasons he had married her. He wouldn't like her any darker, though he often commented on the appeal of women who were. Her thin frame was outlined under the white cotton dress. While many women grew uncomfortably fat after marriage, Glori weighed exactly the same as the day she had married—101 pounds. She looked attractive, even in rollers.

Another reason Henry had married her, besides love, of course, was to have children. But none had been conceived. In the early years of their marriage, Glori remembered, Magda had almost demanded grandchildren. Glori knew she had failed the family in that way. Henry still wanted children. There was nothing she could do.

Glori grew tired of her own thoughts. But stuck under the dryer for at least another hour, she had little else for entertainment. She paged through the greasy magazine that had been on the end table for months. She tossed it back. Then she decided to watch the cars and people pass the open door of the shop. She might spot Henry. A Mercedes, plenty of motorcycles, loud, even above the noise of the dryer. No Henry, though this was his route. She started counting soldiers. Five in different vehicles. Two on foot. She was tired of them too.

The beautician turned off the dryer. Glori returned to the swivel chair to have her hair combed and sprayed. Above her, the beautician talked loudly to anyone who would listen. Satisfied with the style, Glori paid the woman and gladly, carefully, under a wide blue sky, headed home.

"Mama, where are you?" she asked as she walked through the rooms of an empty house to the kitchen's back screen door. Magda finished hanging the last of her hand washing. "I'm home."

"I'm coming in." With a few plastic pins clutched in one hand, the old woman came inside. She looked at Glori. The only comment she made when Glori did a pirouette to show it off was "You didn't cut it."

"No, combed differently." Glori retreated to the bathroom to check the hair style again, hurt by the lack of admiration. There was some consolation in the fact that Magda was barely literate. What could she possibly know about elegance, beauty, and style?

After a quick lunch, Glori started dressing for the graduation. She dressed slowly, putting on stockings, a slip, and, over these, her best yellow dress. She snapped a belt made of the same material around her waist and searched the portable closet in the kitchen for a pair of yellow high heels. A handkerchief and some money in her purse, good-bye to Magda, who was snoring on her cot in the dining room, and Glori was out the front door and on her way.

The moment she left the avenue and turned the corner onto a smaller side street, a man whistled at her. She felt good about it, attractive; Henry would be angry if he found out. She quickened her pace. She neared a bar on the next corner, which was across from the institute. A man drinking beer in the doorway pulled the dark green bottle away from his mouth just to call her a sweet little Arab. Glori kept her eyes fixed on the institute.

She was damp when she got to her favorite spot right across from the institute—a black awning in front of a clothing boutique. Last year an Italian man had opened the shop. A huge awning hung over the display window to protect the colorful garments, arranged on a black backdrop, from fading. If the procession lagged, Glori could inspect the clothes and shoes brought from Venezuela and Italy. She imagined wearing one of those short skirts that she knew Henry noticed on certain women when he was driving.

The Italian man was a little odd, and Glori was relieved he wasn't around. He had good taste as a buyer, no doubt about it, she had seen nothing in town before like the clothes in his shop, only in magazines. (She had not dared walk into the boutiques in the capital.) What she thought was strange was his habit of always wearing black.

Despite these misgivings, the shop made an excellent background for graduation pictures. Glori had taken several and tacked them to a wall in her living room. Pictures of her educated in-laws were better than post-cards, although she had noticed that sometimes the young people looked uncomfortable under those white polyester robes. In one photograph, the Italian peered out the door at them.

The ceremonial music from a portable tape player started. Under the awning, she watched the students file out in twos through the red doors of the institute. She stood at attention. A few of the young men seemed to think it was funny to tug off the women's mortarboards. Others flapped their arms, the sleeves on their robes as big as angel's wings. The women laughed and talked; one pulled out the middle of the big robe to pretend she was pregnant.

Glori was relieved when the director of the institute cut the foolish-ness. He reminded the group it was a solemn occasion. The students adjusted their robes and hats, then dropped their hands to their sides, arranging themselves quietly on the sidewalk. The two-block walk to the church at the top of the plaza, where the ceremony would be held, would be dignified. They began the ascent.

Along with the other spectators, Glori moved slowly from under the shade to find a place behind the soon-to-be graduates. The sun had a bite to it. She was startled by the thought that perhaps Henry was right. The procession to the church, the mass, much longer on these occasions, and the long ceremony—it was almost unbearable. Then Alina turned around to look at the crowd behind the graduates. Older, more habitual desires overshadowed the doubt. Glori waved.

Glori took pride in Alina's accomplishment and was glad she was there to let the town know it. Her family was rising in rank. She was bettering her lot along with them. She wanted to be seen as someone who, in the near future, would be wearing fashionable ready-made dresses, becoming more and more like the Europeans.

The ceremony was much like any other of its kind. The priest had spoken very well about what was expected from the town's newly skilled youth. By the time the mass was over and everyone had a diploma in hand, the sun had started losing some of its strength. Glori went to the simple reception in the plaza that followed. She made sure to greet and give her best wishes to every graduate. It was nearing dusk when she returned home.

Magda had moved a chair to the open doorway and was enjoying the cooler evening air. She fanned herself with a cardboard notebook cover. "How was it?" Magda asked Glori.

Gloria came up next to her and bent to kiss her on the cheek. "Beautiful, mama. I wish you'd come."

Magda kept rocking.

"Where's my husband?"

"I don't know," Magda said.

"He hasn't come by?"

"Yes, he came home from work," she responded. It was the truth.

"And?"

"He bathed, put on the guayabera I washed and ironed earlier."

"Where did he go?"

"He said, 'I'm gone,' and left." Magda didn't know what else to tell her.

But Glori sensed that the mother knew more than she was telling. The old woman was deaf on occasion. When convenient, Magda was blind, unable to sew a button on Henry's shirt. Now she appeared to be acting dumb.

Glori hung onto the rocker, letting her arm follow its rhythmic movement. She wanted to ask why she thought Henry had gone out again.

Magda was inclined to warn her.

But neither of them said a word.

The old woman stopped rocking and laid the fan on her lap. She reached deep into the front of her dress for something. A letter.

"One of your relatives who got back from Puerto Rico dropped it off."

"Thanks." Glori took it inside the house. She lit the kerosene lamp above the sofa, sat down, and tore the envelope open. Her cousin Matilda's son would be graduating from kindergarten to first grade. A formal ceremony and dinner was planned for the El San Juan Hotel on a Friday evening in June. It was a black-tie affair. Matilda had sent for her.

She went directly into the kitchen. In the dark, she sifted through a drawer and pulled out paper and an envelope. She returned to the sofa and began writing. "I will be there," she wrote. "Make all preparations on your side."

The application for a visa would be in the government office Monday. Glori swore she would go inside the Italian's boutique to get an idea for a formal dress, no matter how strange he was. She'd take the express bus to the capital to buy the right fabric. The visit to Puerto Rico would go well indeed.

She would go alone. Even if she had to cross the Mona Passage in a wooden boat to get there, she thought, then laughed out loud at the idea of her doing so. It was a step in the right direction. She was not afraid to start at the bottom, even cleaning Puerto Rican houses for a living, to get to where she was going.

Gravity

I take an animal trail down a sheer hillside
to a rush of trees blurring inside a river.
Gnats spin crazily on coded commands,
scraps of molecule rest on stone, then shoot off
when the first green needles slip through the webbings.

Through echoing splinters of sun
my mind enters the horizon. Clouds whimper
under the scuff of my heel, and I scar
the blue with my leaving.

But I return as I must, to fists of dirt clinging
to roots of an upturned cedar. Seasons
twine beneath the bark and break their hold
and I kneel, touching the years. A sliver of wood
sparks, and I know the pain of gravity
in a globe of blood.

The Seed Must Kill

The future that flares from a pistil is the seed
scorching to earth. While darkness leans
against the wind, and trees arrive
on the lip of distance the sun spreads on the road
for travelers, the seed makes itself known.

It demands water, and so reservoirs open
in a cloud. It discovers navigation in the stars,
begins the spinning journey through an intestine
or on a wing, between the brotherhood of dust
and heaven on a hill of dung.

Sure the moon gives its zero percent
the sun its measure and water its spoon
but the seed is at war with History
that wants to consume it, with Astronomy
that seeks to count its graves.

What does it matter that a man cradles under
a tree and celebrates with worms? Who cares
that ink fails? The seed must keep on
with its endless quarrel between ovule and sperm,
and with crowbar arms peel up the crusts of asphalt
and pop like corn on the sidewalk,
because the tumors of the city must be
destroyed, above all they must
be annihilated.

A Letter from My Mother

My mother writes me in an alphabet born from letters
that bite acid into the leather of her bible.
She stitches commas, dots periods exact as the rules
demand; her exclamations are more resolute than weeds.

My mother sits and writes of funerals that have shrunk
her youth down into a tight clarity of wrinkles.
Her days are shards of sun piercing through the leaf's rage,
a root is her pillow, the skies a dead shore far from
the rains that flung her and my father, directionless.

She talks of prayers unleashed when uncle was handcuffed
to a squad car and led away to confess his own teeth,
and how father says our masters uptown are lessons
from a bruise. And this is why
happiness is stuck in her throat
by grief and its commanding fist.

Son . . . she says, Hijo . . . and I know that all the sorrows
of what my mother could never stomach
except as children will pour from her hands.
Ink will brood and speak its mind
and each word will be pressed, each letter folded
into those paper angels
that won't protect us ever again.

Miguelito, Miguelito

"Miguelito, Miguelito, *sin pantalones*. Shame, shame on Miguelito *sin pantalones!*"

It has been hell for Miguelito to hear the children's chants. One night La Amelia threw him out of her house without his pants and not even his shorts. Only his shirt, which he failed to think of as a way to cover his nakedness. That is, not until it was too late and half of the village had seen him in his nakedness. It was during the day of a religious procession. And that religious procession happened to be passing in front of La Amelia's house when she threw him out, naked for the world to see.

That was her revenge for his refusal to marry her.

Miguelito's mother was not in the procession, but it was only a matter of minutes before she heard that her son was running down the street butt naked. Poor woman was too shocked to say anything for a while, and when she finally spoke she asked, "Are you sure it was my Miguelito?"

And for weeks the children have been playing their game of Miguelito. Suddenly they'll turn to one of their own and strip that child's pants and run swiftly away chanting, "Shame, shame, Miguelito *sin pantalones!*" And the poor child will burst into tears and run home and cry to his parents that La Amelia took his pants away.

Well, after several children reported this offense, a committee of angry parents descended on La Amelia's door and threatened her with violence if she didn't immediately leave town.

La Amelia stood her ground. She placed her hands with their many rings on her wide hips, and she stared every one of them down. She had them bring the children so they could accuse her to her face. The children were more frightened of her than were their parents. It quickly became apparent that La Amelia had never stripped them of their pants, and what they were referring to was a game they were playing with reference to Miguelito. Everyone got a good laugh out of this, not least of whom was La Amelia.

"That *tontito,*" La Amelia said loud enough for everyone to hear, and by this time a good part of the village was in attendance, including Miguelito's mother. "That *tontito*," she repeated for effect. "I don't know why I wasted my time with him. He should wear a dress."

That caused everyone to whisper. Poor Miguelito's mother. She fled as if from bees.

Backward Facing Man

The result of Miguelito's breakdown, of his being thrown into the street by La Amelia, is that he became a backward facing man. What I mean by that is that he began wearing his pants and shirts backward, and when a person spoke to him, Miguelito faced away, that is his face faced away, but the way he wore his clothes, it made it seem that he was facing you, except for the odd exception of his face, which was not his face but the back of his head.

Fortunately La Amelia took him back after a few weeks, and this corrected his outward appearance, but inwardly he remained a backward facing man, so upsetting had been his experience of having to fend for himself in the streets, realizing how alone he could be, rejected even by his own mother who felt he had caused her grievous shame by his running down the street butt naked in front of a religious procession, a procession for Our Lady no less! That had been the last straw. So she kept a careful watch at her window, and whenever she saw him approaching her house, she'd lock the door.

"Mamacita," he'd say, "I need some money for food. I need a place to stay."

This went on for a number of days until the shock of finding himself so alone in the world (his friends' wives made sure that their husbands kept away from Miguelito) changed him, almost overnight, into a backward facing man. And having made this transformation, he stopped bothering his mother and just went about aimlessly, wearing his clothes backward and muttering. And this saved his life, because people started leaving food out for him. And from then on, his friends' wives didn't mind if their husbands spent a little time with Miguelito, in fact they encouraged it.

"Look at what a *tontito* he's become," they'd say to their husbands. "La Amelia wanted to marry him and make a man out of him, and look at where his refusal has gotten him. He's become a backward facing man."

And when the wives would see Miguelito on the street, they'd engage him in conversation. They'd stick out their tongues at him because he always faced away.

At first, Miguelito's friends tried to straighten him out, but soon they saw they could have fun at his expense. When Miguelito got drunk, he talked backward, and his friends found this hilarious, but not anywhere as funny as when he was full of beer and needed to relieve himself. He would piss upward instead of down and always got the front of his clothes wet. The men laughed and laughed at this and so did their wives when they were told. "*¡Que tontito!*" they'd giggle.

And it was true. He was a bona fide *tontito*. And in the end it was only La Amelia who cared enough for him to save him. But even so, damage had been done to his psyche, and his backward facing character slipped out at times much to La Amelia's amusement. Like the time La Amelia had the mayor over to her house for dinner. For years she had been politically active and she had played an important role in getting the mayor elected. And also she had contributed money to his campaign. What offended the mayor was not that from time to time Miguelito would reach over to the mayor's plate and help himself to what he wanted; nor was he unsettled by Miguelito opening his mouth to say something but instead making the sound of water being flushed down a toilet. No, these things didn't bother him. What made the mayor blow up and rush out of La Amelia's house was Miguelito sitting on the mayor's lap and giving the mayor a big wet kiss on the lips. La Amelia found this greatly amusing though she wouldn't have been able to say why.

"Come here and give me a big, wet kiss," she demanded of Miguelito.

And like the *tontito* that he was, a backward facing man, he did as she had asked, except he kissed her on the nose instead of on the lips. And this La Amelia found so funny that she couldn't resist great bellyfuls of laughter.

"Come, Miguelito," she'd demand, "a big, wet one on the lips."

And Miguelito would kiss and kiss and kiss. Everywhere but the lips. And La Amelia would laugh and laugh and laugh.

But eventually La Amelia did tire of Miguelito. He had become backward even in matters of sex. He kept trying to mount her from the back, and La Amelia didn't like that at all. *"Que tontito,"* La Amelia would say night after night in great exasperation, and finally one night she kicked him out of the house. For good this time. But this time Miguelito was fully clothed. He had learned his lesson the first time and had kept his clothes on when he went to bed with La Amelia.

From *The Devil in Texas*

Benito smiles as he walks among the dark houses. Not even any dogs are barking, or maybe he can't hear them. He smiles with triumph written on his lips. His smile, made from a grimace that fools no one, is as clear as an X-ray. The rider moves among the blocks of prosaic adobe. Adobes that were made at one time from new straw and that now look like useless cornstalks. Anybody who'd want to make poetry of this is a liar. All the houses lack is a cross in front of them to be cemeteries. Nevertheless, now and then one of them wards off death with little flowers and a veranda in front. Then the dusty, unblacktopped street. The green devil smiles because they've all been tricked. The devil manipulates puppets. The devil plays with human life. And human beings never understood how he made it into their midst. He was like a gust of wind that blows between their legs, making them trip. Others say that it was a dream from which they had awakened naked. When they awoke, they had placed themselves in the hands of the gentleman, who had promised them relief and had made good. He had given them work on their own land, and the people began to feel life again in their stomachs. Then he paid them in advance, and they paid it back into his hands. "Every family gets a box of food as a Christmas gift, and I'll have a barbecue when the harvest is over. But don't forget, vote for me, vote Democratic." In two years, the vassals had crowned a king they called the "Green Devil."

A stifling night, an oppressive night, a night that chokes people. Pale skulls of squeezed-out sap, skulls lost on the dry land of the cotton fields. False plants watered with sweat. Stuffed worms. Presidio, prison, hell. A devil laughing silently. Shhh!

Benito appeared like a ghost at the door of the house. Then he glued his lips to the jamb and called quietly, "Pst! Lorenzo!"

The barking of the dog inside the porch answered him, and Benito jumped back.

"Shut up, you bastard!"

"Hey, who's there?"

"It's me, Ben."

"Wayda momen."

"That's okay, Lorenzo. Don't get up. I'm only here about the pickers. They're near the river. Go by later, okay?"

"Okay, don Benito."

The Green Devil moved away like a shadow.

Lorenzo did not go to bed then. The appearance of Ben at this hour had left him restless, so he went outside to smoke a cigarette. Crafty old guy, bastard. If he weren't paying my salary, I would have bailed out already. The problems he brings me. One of these days I'm going to wake up stretched out in the river, plugged by my own people. And people are right, I'm bad to them, but the fact is that they get you from all sides. If the old goat helped the poor people instead of paying them shit, he wouldn't have any problems. Jerk. Someday he'll change, after I'm good and dead.

Already in the middle of the field ten riders appear and surround old Ben. He tells them the basics: the pickers will be in the section indicated by the fat poplar, but to be on the safe side, wait for Lorenzo. The latter didn't need a pistol to convince him he should serve as guide. Just don't go too far. Then we'll see what happens, he tells them.

The man digs his spurs in and disappears into the night. It's been a long day.

The whistle on the other side of the river shatters the silence. It reaches the ears on the Mexican side. Quickly various figures jump into the river and lose themselves among the cotton fields. Like frightened criminals they run toward the poplar tree to grab the bags and disappear again into the ditches. They tie the bags to their waists and begin to devour the plants like locusts. Bush after bush is stripped. Shas. Shas. Shas. The bags fill up. They cast the bags over their shoulders like giant sausages and place them alongside the ditch.

This night the pickers are especially wary and move filled with fear. Worse, they don't know if it's the waiting or not being sure if the Coyote will come. For that reason some of them have started in the middle of the rows and have picked toward the river.

The men drag themselves along under the moonlight. They twist and turn among the plants. The green plants, with their white buds, look like Christmas trees. The pickers try to climb to the top just like elves. But they can't escape the long tail that ties them to the ground. Now the serpent, tied to their waists, tries to devour them with its open maw, but it can't. The picker stuffs it with cotton, cocoons that will leave it full so it will leave the people alone. The rapid, rapid hands get all scratched. Perhaps some miracle will transform the cocoons into small gold coins. But it's all no use. The devil carts them away. The devil multiplies. Then another serpent comes along, as hungry as the other one, and then another and another, until one night God's blessing pays them for the misery they don't deserve. For now the platinum-colored pickers will continue to slither among the green sea and white serpents. White tufts, poof, green-backs. Green eyes, green teeth. Rotten, the soul rotten, green, green. Green sea, green bodies, green death, decomposition.

Fresh death in an upholstered coffin is nice and warm. The body can lie down in it, enjoy the warmth of an electric blanket. But these moments are short-lived because then the evening's dew takes its place and envelops the body in cold. That is when the soul emerges with the will to prolong life. It slips along the upholstery like a cat seeking warmth, but it's all useless; the coffin's no longer warm or tender. The soul is like a mother who loses her son in a storm, and the wind carries her far away from her lost child. That's what happens with Chente. The dawn's breeze trans-forms his soul into a long trail of cigarette smoke, blowing it over toward the fort, where so many other souls have been deposited.

Outside, behind the hut, the men squatted on their haunches around a bottle. As the couples would arrive at the house of the deceased, men and women would separate and go off in different directions. The women would go in; the men would enlarge the circle. With the warmth of the bottle and Levario's animated tongue, the men often forgot why they were there.

Inside, there is a wafting odor of wax, but it is soon blanketed by the dust rising from the dirt floor. No faces can be seen in the dying light of the candle. Rather, there are bodies wrapped in black dresses and shawls like fishnets. The women who were able to find a seat stare off into space. They are like mummies, tired of fingering their rosaries. It looks like they are trying to make the beads rounder and at times, as if someone had wound them up, they begin to pray out loud. The murmuring lasts only a few minutes; then there is a leaden silence, a silence interrupted by a huge and bothersome fly. The fly buzzes twice around the coffin of the deceased and lands. Silence takes over again. The women get up to go out for some air and others come in to take their places on the benches.

Shrouded rows contrast with recently whitewashed walls. Roberto, Eduvije's fiancé, comes and goes, comes in and goes out, asking the men to help him bring chairs from their houses because more people are likely to show up. Thanks to Chito, Levario, don Francisco, and Reyes, who came and left early, everyone's helped him out. Poor Vicke didn't even have time to make her dress, sweep, make arrangements. But everyone helped out. The coffin, placed on top of two buckets, was donated by Levario, despite the fact that he was so repulsive. You had to know him to stand him. He was one of those persons who only need to open their mouths to give you a pain in the ass. The announcement on the door of his "coffin factory" says it all: DIE IN STYLE . . . WITH LOMELI COFFINS. But he had a good heart. Roberto remembers the time he went to fetch a coffin for the little angel.

"Who was it this time?"

"Chentito, Vicke's brother."

"Ah! May he rest in peace, since he never got anywhere. The kid was born sick. He almost died when he was six months old, and the worst part is that all they gave him to eat was crackers with coffee. Let's see, how about these, they're the best ones. He'll sure go to heaven in style with this one, right? Heh, heh. With this upholstery he can fly pretty damn good. Take it, no charge, and tell Vicke many happy returns, hah, hah. That's right, tell her I'll stop by to see her tonight." (That's the reason, you talk too much, and because you are what you are, you rub people the wrong way, jerk. Maybe also because you joke about death, making fun of it. Look at you, dressed in your best, with your bottle of tequila, ready to yak all night long. That's what you'll do until your wife, Virginia, stops you cold and drags you drunk off home. I don't like you because you're a parasite of death.)

"Thanks, Levario. God bless you."

The hut is little, but the whitewash makes the two rooms look bigger. The percale curtain covers the opening where the door should be, although the light shines through as it does from the priest's side of the confessional. Vicke, sitting on her bed, observes the movements with dull eyes and then casts her gaze on a candle that threatens to go out as it projects the heart of Jesus along the wall. Christ accompanies Vicke in her suffering, a suffering that flickers in tune with the dancing light. The Holy Child, with his luxurious garment, is also present. Now Vicke moves her gaze to the portrait of the dead little angel and then to the image of the Holy Child. Once, twice, three times. Many times, until the two images become one. She studies and compares them. The curly hair, the smile, the joined hands. "Ay, no, no, the picture is missing a hand!" And she recalls that it was because of the wind last night. She remembers that when the statue fell, her brother was dying, the poor thing. She had picked the statue up from the floor, as he had ordered her to do, and no sooner had she done it when the child became very talkative. When she brought him the warm cloth he'd requested, he asked her to take him by the hand, and then he began to remember things. "Let's see, Vicke, I'll bet you don't remember this: there's the moon . . . What's that business about the moon eating prickly pears if it's made of cheese? I believe that if it were true, it would've already melted, don't you think so, Vicke? There's the sun drinking sotol . . . Listen, Vicke, do you think things in heaven are like us? That's why I'm not afraid of the night, are you? When you go outside, I don't . . . the snake in the sea, in the sea, around here you can . . . Listen to me, Vicke, do you remember the song about the pretty little fish? . . . in clear water flowing from the fountain . . . playing with my hoop . . . my mama told me not to go outside or I'd die right away . . ." And that's how Vicke had spent the night. Listening to him, singing to him, answering him, making his lips into a smile until the wee hours when he slipped off to sleep. When he could no longer awaken, the smile still stamped on his little face, she sent for Roberto. Her love came as quick as . . . "My God, give me strength. I only want to know why you do these things to little children. You know they are little angels and do no harm. Why did you take this little boy instead of me? Punish us, kill us adults, but not them. Why do you do it? Why have you left me so alone, alone, alone?"

Levario's jokes become more and more gross and drunken. They filter through the window as though making fun of Our Fathers and the Hail Marys. Like a gas chamber, the hut is suffocating in bodies, candles, night, nausea. Dizziness. Vicke feels sick. "My deepest sympathy, no. My deepest sympathy, no. My deepest sympathy, NO! My deepest sympathy, NO! NO!" The NO grows larger like two inflated balloons. NO. They slowly grow larger in Vicke's mind until the balloons cannot fit in the two rooms. Then they spill out through the window and get even bigger. Finally the thorn of suffering pops them. "Noooo!" Vicke begins to cry. Long sobs mixed with NO. Outside the conversation stops to receive Vicke's suffering through the ears, but liquor has already stopped them up. Is that not why they drink on these occasions? Ah, old cowards! Why aren't you men enough, like the women? Why can't you take it like they can? Only Levario's dog answers as though he were mindful of the suffering. His howling accompanies the woman.

"Shhht! Shut up, mangy dog!" Levario kicks him. The dog, with his tail between his legs, moves around the drunken men and then lies down again alongside his master. The talking drops in pitch.

"Poor woman, her parents died just two years ago, one right after the other."

"At the time of the long trek to Marfa?"

"Yes, then. I also remember that the kid got real sick. His face was all red from coughing so much."

"What was it?"

"Well, no one knows, but they say he picked it up over there. Others say that he caught something in the mines when he worked there."

"Poor kid. They should never have let him go."

"Poor Vicke, because she's the one who always took care of him."

"They say that don Benito and doña Rosa were over to see her earlier."

"Good grief! The boss?"

"Yes. When he wants to be, the old guy is okay. He's the one who built these rooms for Vicke on his own property."

"Sure. There's no doubt about it. I helped him do it, although at the time he told me it was to store alfalfa bales, but since it didn't work out . . ."

"So, there you are. I heard just the opposite, that he built them for Vicke because he owed something to her dead parents."

"Really? And what was that?"

"No one knows, but I believe that there's something to it, because when the soldiers came, they didn't cart her off to El Paso. I mean, only to Marfa, but then Ben went over and brought her and Chentito back."

"Well, who knows what the deal is, but if they came to see her, there must be something . . ."

Thus the night fills with life, while inside the remains of death beat against people's breasts. They jab, wounding like a pin. Vicke dozes off from being so worn out, and she dreams nightmares. A luminous little point that turns into an indecisive bat. Then it drops down on the wake like a blind comet. Vicke sees it first as tiny, but then it grows larger, more and more and more, then *plop!* It smashes into her forehead. The beating of its wings in her eyes and on her arms makes her tremble. The bat departs. The woman opens her eyes. Levario stumbles in and goes over to Chente's body. "My God, get that drunk out of here, get him home to bed. Make him respect the little angel, for God's sake." The drunk draws near, while the eyes of the women try to stop him but can't. He begins to feel the coffin. With a sensual pleasure he runs his hands over the cloth. No, it isn't the body that moved him to draw near. It's his work, his coffin. He's so fascinated that he forgets that the coffin is mounted on two pails, and he leans against it. The body moves to one side. The man attempts to stop it, but he's drunk. The two fall to the ground with a dry thud.

"Aaaaaaay! Have pity, don't hit him. It'll hurt him! No! Chentito, my beloved Chentito!"

Roberto, who has just come in, runs to help the women who are helping to resettle the coffin on the pails. Then he takes Levario by the arm and pulls him outside.

"Go on, now, Levario. It's time to go. And don't come back." His tone of voice is that of repressed anger.

"All I tried to do was to touch the coffin . . ."

"Go on, I told you!"

His wife, Virginia, comes out mortified, saying over and over again how sorry she is, and takes him home. Meanwhile, inside they are rubbing Vicke's neck with alcohol to calm her. She cries for a few moments and then falls back into the snares of sleep.

MARY HELEN PONCE

The Day Rito Died

From *Hoyt Street*

I remember well the day my brother Rito died. He died of tuberculosis in Olive View Sanitarium, where he had been confined for as long as I could remember. I often forgot I had such a brother, except when on Sundays I was left at home while my parents and older siblings visited him.

Rito had caught cold, *frío,* as we said in the barrio, which settled in his lungs. He lost weight, and when the tuberculosis set in, he became weak. I only saw him a few times. I remember most that he wore blue cotton pajamas.

My parents visited Rito each Sunday. When he became worse after lung surgery, they visited during the week too. Soon afterward his condition became critical, and he was moved to a private room in the infirmary, to make sure he would not contaminate others. When he took a turn for the worse in the winter, my father arranged to be notified, day or night, of his condition.

We had no telephone. Few folks in the neighborhood, other than local merchants and the Anglos who lived across the tracks, had telephones. All emergency calls from the sanitarium were relayed to our parents by Mr. Jameson, owner of the Pacoima General Store, and Mr. Tamez, of the Tamez Grocery Store. They were good, kind men who did more than sell food. They extended food credit to *la gente mexicana,* those unemployed or sick. Sometime previously both men agreed to relay to my father any message they received from the sanitarium.

One night or early morning, Mr. Tamez came with the message that Rito was near death. I woke up when el Duque began to bark at the car that drove up and woke our household. Doña Luisa immediately got up, lit the kerosene lamp kept on the metal trunk, and got dressed. I saw the lights come on in our house; the kitchen bulb illuminated my father's form. I heard voices coming from my mother's room, soft, murmuring;

there was never panic in our house. The engine of the Dodge sputtered, then came to life. I heard the car pull out of the driveway, my father at the wheel, the tires crunching on the hard dirt. I then went back to sleep, lulled by doña Luisa, held tight in her thin arms. When I awoke the car was back. A deadly silence permeated our home, broken only by the sound of muffled crying.

I don't remember who told me Rito had died. I don't remember if I cried. I was a child and barely remembered the handsome stranger with eyes so like my father's, who had been in Olive View half of his life. In the morning I saw shadowy figures enter and leave our house: friends, neighbors, and relatives, dressed in dark clothes, came to give my parents *el pésame*. The women brought food, which was put on the kitchen table next to the enamel coffeepot that was kept filled by Elizabet. Inside the large kitchen, neighbor women warmed tortillas and beans for those who were hungry, but first they fed us hot cereal and toast. Quietly they shooed us out the kitchen door.

Curious as I was, I refused to stay in the backyard, so I found my way to the side of the house near my mother's bedroom window. I heard whispers, muffled crying, comforting words in both Spanish and English. Within minutes Uncle Louie, my mother's cousin (who wore bib overalls all his life), came to the door dressed in a dark shirt and pants. I barely recognized him. He came and left through the kitchen door, a red handkerchief held to his face. That afternoon Uncle Nasario, that jovial, outgoing man who always made me smile, drove up in his shiny car, his handsome face strained and lined. He went to my mother, held her tight, then turned away to hide the tears that filled his light brown eyes.

I didn't see my mother for the rest of the day. She remained in her room, where sad-eyed women, most of whom I knew, arms laden with rubbing alcohol and hand towels, entered and left, as if on cue. Outside, near the garage, the men stood, among them my father and uncles, who huddled together. They spoke in Spanish; their short, muted sentences were hard to hear, but appeared to comfort my father.

Among the men was Berney, now in his early teens, a tall, strapping boy who, because of the seriousness of this occasion, was allowed to be *con los hombres*. Some of Berney's friends stood in the circle, among them Danny, a handsome boy who it was said had a crush on Ronnie. Norbert stayed in the men's rooms, talking with friends who cut school to be with him. Ronnie and Trina, in clean dresses, remained indoors, helping with the guests that filled our house. Josey, I believe, slept most of the day. Now and then, tired of the inactivity (and knowing well I had to be quiet), I scrambled up on a chair to peek outside. Except for Uncle Nasario and a bibless Uncle Louie, I failed to recognize the men with my father.

Toward evening a small fire was built in the backyard where the men congregated. From the kitchen door I saw one of them sip from a small bottle, which was passed around to the others. When the bottle was offered to Berney, he declined the whiskey with a jerk of his curly head. My father, I knew, did not encourage his sons to drink, not even on this somber occasion. Around suppertime the women who earlier had ministered to my mother went home to feed their own families, saying they would return for the wake. Uncle Nasario and my father came indoors to eat the food prepared by Elizabet and two cousins from Oxnard whom I had never seen before.

The men remained around the fire, warming their hands and softly talking, as el Duque circled them. The yellow flames cast deep shadows on the men; their sad faces took on an eerie, deathly pallor. The Mexican tradition was that they remain until late at night, out of respect for my father.

Mexican families like ours had little money to spend on wakes or funerals. The funeral mass was offered free of charge; the cemetery plot was paid for in installments. The mortuary bill, which included *la carroza* and the coffin, was also to be paid in installments. Funerals were kept simple, not because of tradition but due to lack of money. The viewing of the body was done in the home; this was not only convenient but less expensive. Early on it was decided that Rito's wake would be held in our front room. My siblings and cousins put things in order. They cleaned and dusted, wanting the *sala* to look worthy of my brother. Once more I was shooed out the back door.

That evening I went to sleep with doña Luisa as usual. She tossed and turned all night long and in the morning continued to sniffle, her dark eyes full of sadness. She put on her best black dress, one that came to her ankles, fed me *avena y pan tostado,* then went to our house to help prepare for Rito's wake.

I was playing hopscotch toward the back of the house, where I wouldn't be seen or heard, when the hearse came to deliver my brother's body. I was about to jump a square when I looked up to see a long black sedan, the length of two regular cars, approaching. The driver leaned out and asked, "Is this 13011 Hoyt Street?" "Yes," I answered. Before I could ask what it was they wanted, I heard movement inside the house. Suddenly the front door opened; out came Elizabet and cousin Mary, dressed in dark clothing. Cousin Mary, who was most proper, wore a navy blue dress with a white collar and cuffs; a short string of pearls was at her throat. Their loud and clear voices, so unlike the crying of before, drifted across the yard to where I stood. The driver, a pale man wearing thick glasses, backed up the hearse until it was parallel to the front door, then slammed on the brakes. The hearse appeared to let out a sigh, then came to a stop. The driver got out, door slamming loudly, then opened the back door and pushed back his hair, as if about to make a delivery. By now my father and my uncles Louie and Nasario were on hand to pull out the long silvery box that I knew was the coffin in which Rito lay. They yanked it halfway out, squeezed it through the door, then carried it inside.

Anxious to see everything, I kept getting in everyone's way. Rather than stand aside, I walked alongside the men, my hand resting on Rito's box. When we neared the porch steps, I stumbled, nearly tripping Uncle Louie. Elizabet pulled me aside and began to scold.

"Stay in the back."

"But I want to see!"

"This is only for grown-ups."

"But . . ."

Doña Luisa came to the rescue; with promises of lemon drops, she convinced me to stay in the backyard. Accompanied by the faithful Duke, who for all the sadness of the day still wagged his tail, I went toward my favorite fig tree, then waited for Josey to join me.

When next I looked, the black car was gone. Relieved of its cargo, it slipped away down Hoyt Street, raising no visible dust, and onto Van Nuys Boulevard. I played with my dolls, one eye on the kitchen door, hoping to be called inside where the grown-ups were. In the cold, wintry yard everything seemed so still. Duke lay on the dirt, his tail looped around his scruffy legs, his long ears dropping across his face. Not a branch moved in the eucalyptus trees that cast huge shadows over our house. High above, a lone cloud drifted across the blue sky, then disappeared.

I heard crying from inside the house. Soft, forlorn. From near the fig tree, I heard my mother's anguished cries. *Hijo mio. Ay hijo mio.* Her cries came and went like waves. Even el Duque was subdued. He kept to the back of the house, his tail between his legs.

Toward afternoon neighbors and relatives came to pay their respects: the Garcias, Jaramillos, Montaños, Solises, Reyes, and others. Among them was Mrs. Goodsome, principal of Pacoima Elementary School, which my siblings attended. She was a good, kind lady who liked our family, especially Rito, who she claimed was an excellent student. When I saw her inside, I too wanted to be part of the crowd. I pushed my way in between the mourners to the front of the room. It was then I saw Rito.

He lay inside a silver coffin lined in white material. The quiltlike material looked soft, comfortable. Rito's coffin was on top of the wooden bench that normally sat near the garage. The upper half was open, so that we could peek at him. Rito was dressed in a dark jacket and a snowy white shirt. I think he wore a tie. His curly hair shone with pomade and was combed to the side, with one limp curl over his clear forehead. His lovely green eyes, now closed forever, were fringed by dark lashes that brushed his fair cheeks. His pale hands were clasped together as if in prayer; the tapered fingers were intertwined with a black rosary.

Behind the coffin and on both sides of the wall hung crisp white sheets. Pinned to them were velvety gardenias, their dark green leaves shiny and fragrant. Large candles were set at the head and foot of the casket; inside the dim room they glowed warm and bright. Next to the casket and on the floor stood zinc buckets and cans with fresh flowers: roses, carnations, gladiolus. The flowers, brought by friends and neighbors, were surrounded by crespón, a mossy green fern that grew in our backyards. From a distance the home-grown flowers looked quite pretty, and not at all like the stiff, formal arrangements found at most wakes. I think Rito would have liked them.

On top of the closed half of the coffin lay a small silver crucifix. Next to it was a funeral wreath of gardenias and white stock. A white ribbon inscribed in gold letters lay across the wreath: *Nuestro Hijo Quierido.* Bowls of buttercups, called *tasa en plato,* sat close by; they were pretty but gave off a strong smell. Their aroma, combined with that of the creamy gardenias, was what we kids referred to as *olor a muerto,* smell of the dead. The stifling odor and the sad eyes of the mourners forced me to leave the room, but not before I sidled up to Mrs. Goodsome, who hugged me, called me a sweet child, and admonished me to obey my mother.

That night Father Juanito came to pray the rosary. He first gave my parents *el pésame,* then knelt to recite the rosary. He prayed the Ten Soulful Mysteries. The women who throughout the day had been praying inside my mother's room gave the response. "*Ruega por el,* pray for him." When he finished with the rosary, Father Juanito recited the Litany of the Saints, then concluded *el velorio* with the prayers for the dead. "Requiescat en pace," he intoned. "Amen," we responded. He then took his hat with the pom-poms (brought from his native France), set it on his graying head, and left.

That night I was allowed to sleep in my mother's bed. There was no room elsewhere, or so I was told. The relatives from Oxnard who remained overnight were given my spot on doña Luisa's lumpy bed. Excited about the attention I was now getting, I began to jump up and down on the bed, until doña Raquel (mother of my friend Romey) came into the room, tucked me in, and in a gentle voice told me to go to sleep. She stayed with me until I did.

In the morning everyone looked haggard and somber in their mourning clothes. Even Uncle Nasario's ruddy cheeks and friendly eyes appeared sad and drawn. Inside the kitchen my sisters and cousins served hot chocolate from an enamel pot atop the stove. They filled platters with the sweet Mexican bread brought earlier by Uncle Louie. Just then the church bell began to peal. Everyone began to gather coats and hats for the walk to church. Without being told, Uncle Nasario and our male relatives went into the living room. They pushed aside the limp sheets with the wilted gardenias and smelly buttercups that had made me sick. They picked up the silver coffin and Rito, hoisted it onto their shoulders, and went out the door, followed by my mother, now dressed in a dark winter dress and her best hat. Neighbor women, black dresses to their knees, huddled around my mother, then escorted her down the porch steps and to the street. My older siblings checked our clothes and hair, then herded us children out the door toward Hoyt Street. I stumbled along with doña Luisa, who appeared to lack her usual vigor. We caught up with the procession at the church door. Suddenly the bells began to peal again. Dong. Dong. Dong. Even the bells sounded sad.

At the entrance to the church, Father Juanito awaited Rito's body, which he blessed, while we crowded around. The high requiem mass followed, beginning with the "Liberame Domine." During communion friends and relatives received the host, which was offered for the soul of our dearly departed one, and which I knew would ensure that Rito's soul would ascend straight to heaven.

When mass was ended, we followed Father Juanito and the silver coffin down the aisle. Once more our pastor blessed my dead brother, then sang "In Paradisum." This last hymn signaled the end of the service and was something like *la despedida,* the farewell sung at Mexican parties. The coffin was then placed in the waiting hearse, the same one that had brought Rito home for the last time.

I did not attend the funeral; they said I was too young. I walked home trailing after my mother, who did not go to the cemetery. "I cannot bear to see my son interred," she whispered to my father, her voice lost and forlorn; my sisters, however, went in her place. My mother now walked with my cousin Mary, who appeared to hold her up; their dark listless forms inched their way down the empty street.

When the big black hearse went by, my mother wavered in her step, then stopped. She stood deathly still until the hearse had passed, then slowly pulled back her hat veil. "*Adios hijo mio*," she murmured, then resumed the long, slow walk.

I stayed behind, slowly picking my way between the rocks and grass on the path next to the street, my eyes glued on the big black car that finally turned left and disappeared.

Black Hair

There are two kinds of work: one uses the mind and the other uses muscle. As a kid I found out about the latter. I'm thinking of the summer of 1969 when I was a seventeen-year-old runaway who ended up in Glendale, California, to work for Valley Tire Factory. To answer an ad in the newspaper I walked miles in the afternoon sun, my stomach slowly knotting on a doughnut that was breakfast, my teeth like bright candles gone yellow.

I walked in the door sweating and feeling ugly because my hair was still stiff from a swim at the Santa Monica beach the day before. Jules, the accountant and part owner, looked droopily through his bifocals at my application and then at me. He tipped his cigar in the ashtray, asked my age as if he didn't believe I was seventeen, but finally, after a moment of silence, said, "Come back tomorrow. Eight-thirty."

I thanked him, left the office, and went around to the chain link fence to watch the workers heave tires into a bin; others carted uneven stacks of tires on hand trucks. Their faces were black from tire dust, and when they talked—or cussed—their mouths showed a bright pink.

From there I walked up a commercial street, past a cleaners, a motorcycle shop, and a gas station where I washed my face and hands; before leaving I took a bottle that hung on the side of the Coke machine, filled it with water, and stopped it with a scrap of paper and a rubber band.

The next morning I arrived early at work. The assistant foreman, a potbellied Hungarian, showed me a time card and how to punch in. He showed me the Coke machine, the locker room with its slimy shower, and also pointed out the places where I shouldn't go: the ovens where the tires were recapped and the customer service area, which had a slashed couch, a coffee table with greasy magazines, and an ashtray. He introduced me to Tully, a fat man with one ear, who worked the buffers that resurfaced the whitewalls. I was handed an apron and a face mask and shown how to use the buffer: lift the tire and center, inflate it with a foot pedal, press the buffer against the white band until cleaned, and then deflate and blow off the tire with an air hose.

With a paintbrush he stirred a can of industrial preserver. "Then slap this blue stuff on." While he was talking a coworker came up quietly from behind him and goosed him with the air hose. Tully jumped as if he had been struck by a bullet and then turned around cussing and cupping his genitals in his hands as the other worker walked away calling out foul names. When Tully turned to me smiling his gray teeth, I lifted my mouth into a smile because I wanted to get along. He has to be on my side, I thought. He's the one who'll tell the foreman how I'm doing.

I worked carefully that day, setting the tires on the machine as if they were babies, since it was easy to catch a finger in the rim that expanded to inflate the tire. At the day's end we swept up the tire dust and emptied the trash into bins.

At five the workers scattered for their cars and motorcycles while I crossed the street to wash at a burger stand. My hair was stiff with dust, and my mouth showed pink against the backdrop of my dirty face. I then ordered a hot dog and walked slowly in the direction of the abandoned house where I had stayed the night before. I lay under the trees and within minutes was asleep. When I woke my shoulders were sore and my eyes burned when I squeezed the lids together.

From the backyard I walked dully through a residential street, and as evening came on, the TV glare in the living rooms and the headlights of passing cars showed against the blue drift of dusk. I saw two children coming up the street with snow cones, their tongues darting at the packed ice. I saw a boy with a peach and wanted to stop him, but felt embarrassed by my hunger. I walked for an hour only to return and discover the house lit brightly. Behind the fence I heard voices and saw a flashlight poking at the garage door. A man on the back steps mumbled something about the refrigerator to the one with the flashlight.

I waited for them to leave, but had the feeling they wouldn't because there was the commotion of furniture being moved. Tired, even more desperate, I started walking again with a great urge to kick things and tear the day from my life. I felt weak and my mind kept drifting because of hunger. I crossed the street to a gas station, where I sipped at the water fountain and searched the Coke machine for change. I started walking again, first up a commercial street, then into a residential area where I lay down on someone's lawn and replayed a scene at home—my mother crying at the kitchen table, my stepfather yelling with food in his mouth. They're cruel, I thought, and warned myself that I should never forgive them. How could they do this to me.

When I got up from the lawn it was late. I searched out a place to sleep and found an unlocked car that seemed safe. In the backseat, with my shoes off, I fell asleep but woke up startled about four in the morning when the owner, a nurse on her way to work, opened the door. She got in and was about to start the engine when I raised my head up from the backseat to explain my presence. She screamed so loudly when I said "I'm sorry" that I sprinted from the car with my shoes in hand. Her screams faded, then stopped altogether, as I ran down the block where I hid behind a trash bin and waited for a police siren to sound. Nothing. I crossed the street to a church where I slept stiffly on cardboard in the balcony.

I woke up feeling tired and greasy. It was early and a few streetlights were still lit, the east growing pink with dawn. I washed myself from a garden hose and returned to the church to break into what looked like a kitchen. Paper cups, plastic spoons, a coffee pot littered on a table. I found a box of Nabisco crackers which I ate until I was full.

At work I spent the morning at the buffer, but was then told to help Iggy, an old Mexican, who was responsible for choosing tires that could be recapped without the risk of exploding at high speeds. Every morning a truck would deliver used tires, and after I unloaded them Iggy would step among the tires to inspect them for punctures and rips on the sidewalls.

With a yellow chalk he marked circles and Xs to indicate damage and called out "junk." For those tires that could be recapped, he said "goody" and I placed them on my hand truck. When I had a stack of eight I kicked the truck at an angle and balanced them to another work area where Iggy again inspected the tires, scratching Xs and calling out "junk."

Iggy worked only until three in the afternoon, at which time he went to the locker room to wash and shave and to dress in a two-piece suit. When he came out he glowed with a bracelet, watch, rings, and a shiny fountain pen in his breast pocket. His shoes sounded against the asphalt. He was the image of a banker stepping into sunlight with millions on his mind. He said a few low words to workers with whom he was friendly and none to people like me.

I was seventeen, stupid because I couldn't figure out the difference between an F 78 14 and 750 14 at sight. Iggy shook his head when I brought him the wrong tires, especially since I had expressed interest in being his understudy. "Mexican, how can you be so stupid?" he would yell at me, slapping a tire from my hands. But within weeks I learned a lot about tires, from sizes and makes to how they are molded in iron forms to how Valley stole from other companies. Now and then we received a truckload of tires, most of them new or nearly new, and they were taken to our warehouse in the back where the serial numbers were ground off with a sander. On those days the foreman handed out Cokes and joked with us as we worked to get the numbers off.

Most of the workers were Mexican or black, though a few redneck whites worked there. The base pay was a dollar sixty-five, but the average was three dollars. Of the black workers, I knew Sugar Daddy the best. His body carried two hundred and fifty pounds, armfuls of scars, and a long knife that made me jump when he brought it out from his boot without warning. At one time he had been a singer, and had cut a record in 1967 called "Love's Chance," which broke into the R and B charts. But nothing came of it. No big contract, no club dates, no tours. He made very little from the sales, only enough for an operation to pull a steering wheel from his gut when, drunk and mad at a lady friend, he slammed his Mustang into a row of parked cars.

"Touch it," he smiled at me one afternoon as he raised his shirt, his black belly kinked with hair. Scared, I traced the scar that ran from his chest to the left of his belly button, and I was repelled but hid my disgust.

Among the Mexicans I had few friends because I was different, a *pocho* who spoke bad Spanish. At lunch they sat in tires and laughed over burritos, looking up at me to laugh even harder. I also sat in tires while nursing a Coke and felt dirty and sticky because I was still living on the street and had not had a real bath in over a week. Nevertheless, when the border patrol came to round up the nationals, I ran with them as they scrambled for the fence or hid among the tires behind the warehouse. The foreman, who thought I was an undocumented worker, yelled at me to run, to get away. I did just that. At the time it seemed fun because there was no risk, only a good-hearted feeling of hide-and-seek, and besides it meant an hour away from work on company time. When the police left, we came back and some of the nationals made up stories of how they were almost caught—how they outraced the police. Some of the stories were so convoluted and unconvincing that everyone laughed *mentiras,* especially when one described how he overpowered a policeman, took his gun away, and sold the patrol car. We laughed and he laughed, happy to be there to make up a story.

If work was difficult, so were the nights. I still had not gathered enough money to rent a room, so I spent the nights sleeping in parked cars or in the balcony of a church. After a week I found a newspaper ad for a room for rent, phoned, and was given directions. Finished with work, I walked the five miles down Mission Road looking back into the traffic with my thumb out. No rides. After eight hours of handling tires I was frightening, I suppose, to drivers, since they seldom looked at me; if they did, it was a quick glance. For the next six weeks I would try to hitchhike, but the only person to stop was a Mexican woman who gave me two dollars to take the bus. I told her it was too much and that no bus ran from Mission Road to where I lived, but she insisted that I keep the money and trotted back to her idling car. It must have hurt her to see me day after day walking in the heat and looking very much the dirty Mexican to the many minds that didn't know what it meant to work at hard labor. That woman knew. Her eyes met mine as she opened the car door, and there was a tenderness that was surprisingly true—one for which you wait for years but when it comes it doesn't help. Nothing changes. You continue on in rags, with the sun still above you.

I rented a room from a middle-aged couple whose lives were a mess. She was a schoolteacher and he was a fireman. A perfect setup, I thought. But during my stay there they would argue with one another for hours in their bedroom.

When I rang at the front door both Mr. and Mrs. Van Deusen answered and didn't bother to disguise their shock at how awful I looked. But they let me in all the same. Mrs. Van Deusen showed me around the house, from the kitchen and bathroom to the living room with its grand piano. On her fingers she counted out the house rules as she walked me to my room. It was a girl's room with lace curtains, scenic wallpaper of a Victorian couple enjoying a stroll, canopied bed, and stuffed animals in a corner. Leaving, she turned and asked if she could do laundry for me and, feeling shy and hurt, I told her no; perhaps the next day. She left and I undressed to take a bath, exhausted as I sat on the edge of the bed probing my aches and my bruised places. With a towel around my waist I hurried down the hallway to the bathroom where Mrs. Van Deusen had set out an additional towel with a tube of shampoo. I ran the water in the tub and sat on the toilet, lid down, watching the steam curl toward the ceiling. When I lowered myself into the tub I felt my body sting. I soaped a washcloth and scrubbed my arms until they lightened, even glowed pink, but still I looked unwashed around my neck and face no matter how hard I rubbed. Back in the room I sat in bed reading a magazine, happy and thinking of no better luxury than a girl's sheets, especially after nearly two weeks of sleeping on cardboard at the church.

I was too tired to sleep, so I sat at the window watching the neighbors move about in pajamas and, curious about the room, looked through the bureau drawers to search out personal things—snapshots, a messy diary, and a high school yearbook. I looked up the Van Deusens' daughter, Barbara, and studied her face as if I recognized her from my own school—a face that said "promise," "college," "nice clothes in the closet." She was a skater and a member of the German Club; her greatest ambition was to sing at the Hollywood Bowl.

After a while I got into bed and as I drifted toward sleep I thought about her. In my mind I played a love scene again and again and altered it slightly each time. She comes home from college and at first is indifferent to my presence in her home, but finally I overwhelm her with deep pity when I come home hurt from work, with blood on my shirt. Then there was another version: home from college, she is immediately taken with me, in spite of my work-darkened face, and invites me into the family car for a milk shake across town. Later, back at the house, we sit in the living room talking about school until we're so close I'm holding her hand. The truth of the matter was that Barbara did come home for a week, but was bitter toward her parents for taking in boarders (two others besides me). During that time she spoke to me only twice: once, while searching the refrigerator, she asked if we had any mustard; the other time she asked if I had seen her car keys.

But it was a place to stay. Work had become more and more difficult. I not only worked with Iggy, but also with the assistant foreman who was in charge of unloading trucks. After they backed in I hopped on top to pass the tires down by bouncing them on the tailgate to give them an extra spring so they would be less difficult to handle on the other end. Each truck was weighed down with more than two hundred tires, each averaging twenty pounds, so that by the time the truck was emptied and swept clean I glistened with sweat and my T-shirt stuck to my body. I blew snot threaded with tire dust onto the asphalt, indifferent to the customers who watched from the waiting room.

The days were dull. I did what there was to do from morning until the bell sounded at five; I tugged, pulled, and cussed at tires until I was listless and my mind drifted and caught on small things, from cold sodas to shoes to stupid talk about what we would do with a million dollars. I remember unloading a truck with Hamp, a black man.

"What's better than a sharp lady?" he asked me as I stood sweaty on a pile of junked tires. "Water. With ice," I said.

He laughed with his mouth open wide. With his fingers he pinched the sweat from his chin and flicked at me. "You be too young, boy. A woman can make you a god."

As a kid I had chopped cotton and picked grapes, so I knew work. I knew the fatigue and the boredom and the feeling that there was a good possibility you might have to do such work for years, if not for a lifetime. In fact, as a kid I imagined a dark fate: to marry Mexican poor, work Mexican hours, and in the end die a Mexican death, broke and in despair.

But this job at Valley Tire Company confirmed that there was something worse than field work, and I was doing it. We were all doing it, from foreman to the newcomers like me, and what I felt heaving tires for eight hours a day was felt by everyone—black, Mexican, redneck. We all despised those hours but didn't know what else to do. The workers were unskilled, some undocumented and fearful of deportation, and all struck with an uncertainty at what to do with their lives. Although everyone bitched about work, no one left. Some had worked there for as long as twelve years; some had sons working there. Few quit; no one was ever fired. It amazed me that no one gave up when the border patrol jumped from their vans, baton in hand, because I couldn't imagine any work that could be worse—or any life. What was out there, in the world, that made men run for the fence in fear?

Iggy was the only worker who seemed sure of himself. After five hours of "junking," he brushed himself off, cleaned up in the washroom, and came out gleaming with an elegance that humbled the rest of us. Few would look him straight in the eye or talk to him in our usual stupid way because he was so much better. He carried himself as a man should—with that old world "dignity"—while the rest of us muffed our jobs and talked dully about dull things as we worked. From where he worked in his open shed he would now and then watch us with his hands on his hips. He would shake his head and click his tongue in disgust.

The rest of us lived dismally. I often wondered what the others' homes were like, I couldn't imagine that they were much better than our workplace. No one indicated that his outside life was interesting or intriguing. We all looked defeated and contemptible in our filth at the day's end. I imagined the average welcome at home: Rafael, a Mexican national who had worked at Valley for five years, returned to a beaten house of kids who were dressed in mismatched clothes and playing kick-the-can. As for Sugar Daddy, he returned home to a stuffy room where he would read and reread old magazines. He ate potato chips, drank beer, and watched TV. There was no grace in dipping socks into a washbasin where later he would wash his cup and plate.

There was no grace at work. It was all ridicule. The assistant foreman drank Cokes in front of the newcomers as they laced tires in the afternoon sun. Knowing that I had a long walk home, Rudy, the college student, passed me, waving and yelling "Hello," as I started down Mission Road on the way home to eat out of cans. Even our plump secretary got into the act by wearing short skirts and flaunting her milky legs. If there was love, it was ugly. I'm thinking of Tully and an older man whose name I can no longer recall fondling one another in the washroom. I had come in cradling a smashed finger to find them pressed together in the shower, their pants undone and partly pulled down. When they saw me they smiled with their pink mouths but didn't bother to push away.

How we arrived at such a place is a mystery to me. Why anyone would stay for years is even a deeper concern. You showed up, but from where? What broken life? What ugly past? The foreman showed you the Coke machine, the washroom, and the yard where you'd work. When you picked up a tire, you were amazed at the black it could give off.

Dear Frida,

1

We're stuck on you, on the thorns you press
into your swan neck, black swan, *niñita*
limping on a stubborn withered leg.

"Frida, pata de palo. Frida, pata de palo,"

You cover the skinny ankle, skirts long
even when the sweat slides down your legs
like blood, *sangre,* your paint, Frida.

You make us taste it, the blood that burst
everywhere, your bones crushed in a bus crash,
a rod shoved through you   pelvis to spine.

Perfect aim, your clothes ripped away
the young swan plucked clean, limp skin
gleaming in the sun, blood and gold, powdered gold

burst into the air with wheels, eggs, bones
and screams, their screams wild at the glitter
of your mangled red and gold body.

"¡La bailarina, la bailarina!" they shouted.

2

Round your bed, she dances round
your stiff white cast, your stiff white room,
La Pelona dances round your body tomb.

Clakati, clak-clak, clakati, clak-clak.

Bald Death watches surgeons carve,
below your swan neck—knives, needles, cut,
stitch, pinch skin together, but your body falls apart.

They mold you stiff, but still you slip out,
head first escape from boring ceilings through
your fingertips, through the smell of paint.

3

We're stuck on him, Frida, on your old fat toad-frog,
your "*Sapo-Rana*" croaking, "*Yo, yo, yo,*" into your neck,
with perfect aim stroking each of your scars until

it opens, bleeds. How his thick lips suck on you,
your Diego, immense baby bending your crooked
spine while your babies melt and slip away.

Clakati, clak-clak, clakati, clak-clak.

Your dolls and the hungry black monkeys
curled around your neck watch you slowly brand
yourself, stamp Diego right between your

eyes. We want to erase him, Frida, but he's stuck
on you, the man you love more than your own sad bones,
the hungry toad who likes a woman in each hand.

He is your sun and moon, your dance, your laugh,
your flowers, your brandy and bread, his sweat
sweet as watermelon on your nervous tongue.

You drink his breath heavy as a storm. Lightning
sizzles through you pelvis to spine, his hands
mold you until you hide in his slow folds.

No others will do. "*¡Chingado!*" you cry
and try men and women, bite them so hard
they bleed, but always you taste Diego, Diego.

You love the ones he went to. You chew
the lips he'd kissed hungry for some shred
of him, smelling him on their willing breasts.

4

La Pelona Tonta dances while you paint
yourself, smear the familiar red smell
on floors, legs, breasts, sheets white as milk.

Your paintings don't laugh like you did,
Frida, that laugh smelling of curses
rough as cactus tossed at sour faces.

Small skulls must have floated in your bath
like white soaps, *La Pelona* grinning at herself
in your mirror when you soaked your scars.

Clakati, clak-clak, clakati, clak-clak.

Why are your wounds always open, Frida,
why can't you hide stabs, gashes, corsets?
Why can't you vomit in private, like a lady?

5

You come to your last show in an ambulance,
drugged but on fire, you drink, sing in your large bed.
You are your art, and you make the crowd see you dying.

Frida, *pata de palo,* we still hear you scream,
"NO!" But your withered leg has to go.
Clakati, clak-clak, clakati, clak

6

When your bloodless body slides into its last
burning, it bolts up in the oven's hungry heat.
Clak. Around your face, your hair blazes.

The Itch

Three weeks after my return from Central America, the big bites still itch, the discomfort remains. What got under my skin, continues to disturb me. It is the persistent sadness at seeing and feeling injustice, whether on our holiday streets as I write this in that period of consumer frenzy between Thanksgiving and Christmas or in the struggling countries to the south, countries which admit with resignation that they are our "backyard farm."

I sit and eat an ample breakfast of eggs, black beans, plátanos fritos, tortillas, served by the enthusiastic and grateful employees of a large banana plantation who tell us how well they are treated by their absent landlords, international business executives, the phone-and-faxers, men who work in multiple time zones from multiple homes and contribute generously to worthy causes for which they are honored and respected as global donors whose decisions and ideas control the lives of the unseen.

In Honduras, a country in which eight out of ten persons live in poverty, company employees have jobs, health care, schools, of sorts. As we walk toward the lush rows of banana plants, the erotic flowers drooping to rich, fungus-free soil, we see a plane spraying chemicals in the wide, blue sky. "Are there workers in that area?" someone asks. "Oh, yes, but all we use is safe," the response.

Standing in the shade of the broad banana leaves, my feet begin to itch wildly. I try to apply my insect repellent discreetly as I wobble a bit on the leafy mulch, listen to the plantation foreman describe the care given each banana to be exported. He explains how on each mature plant one "hijo" is selected for pampering, the next generation. All remaining sprouts are removed. I ask why the future is labeled "hijos" and "hijas." He laughs and continues.

Although he never states it in these terms, it's obvious that the fussiness of banana buyers in this country, in Italy, Germany, Japan, will be satisfied. Those clean, manicured hands that use phones and faxes know about quality control. Their bananas will be ready to ripen, with their skin a bruiseless, smooth yellow. I think of the children I've seen in Honduras, hungry, scantily dressed, as I hear this man explain a process that must seem logical to him, his livelihood. He shows us how the clusters of bananas are carefully covered with plastic bags to create a perfect microenvironment. No leaf ever touches the fruit, to avoid unsightly marks. Women measure, grade, and wash the bananas brought by cables and pulleys to the packing station, press them into plastic bags with a vacuum hose, remove all air, and box the thick green fingers for the boat trip to our friendly stores.

That's part of the itch, the *comezón* eating away at me as I sit here in Cincinnati's winter cold, remembering the Honduran heat and the statement that to satisfy buyers like me, men check each of the countless banana plants to assure that no leaf ever blemishes a fruit. And those children?

Who protects the boy, and the many like him, asleep face down on a street corner of the city of San Pedro Sula, probably victims of glue sniffing? He is not an exportable commodity. He is as discardable as the bananas that don't qualify for the small status stickers, the marketing ploy that produced designer bananas. Who creates perfect microenvironments for children and families taken from their homes and dumped in an empty plot far from any city, from water, electricity?

We visit such a group, ride past houses made of twigs, children and cattle climbing mounds of garbage as buzzards circle above, stop to hear the brave words of the members of Esperanza el Rancho, as they call their community. It had rained the night before and the mosquitoes made the night a long one; children whimper as adults thank us for coming to visit. We squirm. Most families have stacked wooden boxes, hung faded bed sheets for walls. They know they have been thrown into an open field like "garbage," taken from the coconut and mango trees they had nurtured for seven years. *"Aquí un compañero no vale nada."*

The issue is land. Honduras imports its staples: corn, beans, rice. Its land is not used to feed its citizens but to produce our pleasures: coffee, sugar, bananas, a dessert economy.

I walk with doña Feliciana, a widow who never had a family. She shows me the house she built alone at sixty-three, two rooms. How could anyone help her when each family struggles against such odds? Outside the house, she's hung a blue tin pot, planted a scraggly plant in it. Hope.

We drive to the coast, see roads being constructed to the beaches by foreign companies. Can tourists be far behind? We visit a group that fears this definition of development. The Garifuna are blacks who came to Honduras from San Vicente over two hundred years ago. This community of Tornable, like the other Garifuna communities, has a culture closely tied to the ocean. They live in its sound, fish from its waters. We walk past grand palms whose trunks arch from the base like curved arms. We walk on the land the Garifuna treasure. *"La tierra es fuente de vida,"* they tell us. We walk through the village, which looks much like an island village, hear dogs, roosters, see thatched houses, barefoot women, their heads wrapped in scarves; but we hear Spanish, see children swinging at a pumpkin-shaped piñata.

"Buenas tardes," a woman says, bending, as she has for centuries, into the smell of bread, into the blaring heat of her makeshift oven, the red smolder of rocks and coconut shells. Her arms, which can lift mountains, raise a blazing tin slab, show you innocence—bread browning under the trees, hot round puffs sweet with coconut oil and the power of this black Garifuna woman.

Like many groups in Central America and in this country, the Garifuna speak of the importance of bilingual and bicultural education, of having Garifuna teachers working with their children. A joy for a Chicana or Chicano who travels in the Americas, this hemisphere colonized by the Spanish, Portuguese, French, and British, is experiencing the energy and determination of the many people from traditionally ignored groups who share our desire to participate in shaping the future of our countries and region. The decision by the United Nations to make 1993 the Year of Indigenous Peoples, after the Nobel Peace Prize was awarded to the brave and eloquent Guatemalan Quiché writer and leader Rigoberta Menchú, can serve as a symbol that those without financial power can occasionally be heard. In one of her poems she describes what I so felt, *"Cruce la frontera empapada de tristeza."*

We drive through the green hills under purple clouds that tumble and roll on the road to Tegucigalpa. For two days I live with the Alvarados in a marginal community outside the city. I had expected a rural setting, the old voices I so cherish. Instead I find myself in a low-income urban area. How glad my host, Rey, is that I speak Spanish. *"La suere de Dios,"* he calls it. Dressed casually, I wear my tennis shoes for the climb up the rocky road so that the visit will be informal. The Alvarados, however, are dressed up to meet me, frilly dresses on the girls, their mother in red high heels. After all, I am from the United States. Although the banana plantations have elaborate irrigation and sprinkler systems, marginal communities like Colonia Flor del Campo have no running water. No running water or sewer system for thirteen thousand inhabitants. The Alvarado house has a TV, stereo, and video machines, which are Rey's business. He's also very active in his Pentecostal church and has the decal "*Misionero de Dios*" placed boldly on his truck windshield.

Nights I sleep in the bottom bunk in the children's room. Three children sleep above me. Candy—note the name—the youngest, sleeps with her parents. I hear mosquitoes buzz and rub on more insect repellent in the dark, trying not to make any noise and wake the children. The first night is a teary one for me. Suddenly, I am in a young family like mine must have been, the same configuration, three daughters and one son. I watch Rey Alvarado joking with his children and think, That's what my teasing father, now so confused and mentally limited, was like.

Mornings I lie in bed for a few minutes listening to Xiomora and Rey speaking in soft tones. I remember how my friend, the writer Arturo Islas, used to talk about the pleasure of returning home as an adult and listening to his parents' morning conversations, that return to childhood's sounds. Soon Xiomara's sweeping, and Rey's rock religious music begins, hip rhythms about "*Cristo y la biblia*" and "*Jesús, Jesús, Jesús.*"

Rey has many questions about my country and is anxious to visit it. He enjoys practicing the few English words he knows. He lies on the hammock stretched across the small living room with his son Roger lying on his stomach. He tells me about wanting to go to parts of the United States where there are few Latinos. "We're so much alike," he says. "I want to go learn about how other people live." And indeed we are alike. I sit visiting or watching TV with this young Alvarado family, finally feeling at ease. Initially, of course, it is a bit uncomfortable for a feminist like myself to adjust to Xiomara's habit of retreating from the living room, but I learn to seek her out and hear her story. She was raised by her grandmother who, she says, is "*anciana*" now. "How old is she?" I ask. The answer: fifty-five.

Our group is taken to walk around the community, to help us understand the work being done there and its difficult realities. Juan Hernandez, one of the community organizers, says, "You have us in your heads or in your books, but not in your hearts." Juan repeats what we hear from many Central Americans, that they do not want our charity. They want us to encounter one another as fellow human beings seeking common solutions.

We see boys trying to fly kites made from newspapers. We visit a tiny shoemaking project, three men working in a small, broiling room full of glue fumes. We visit a health clinic, watch a local troupe's play on AIDS prevention. At night I return to my family. How grateful I am for the thoughtfulness of the Alvarados and for their words that they feel as if they were losing a member of the family when I leave.

During my last afternoon in Honduras, I see a woman with one leg who has stopped halfway across a street and is leaning on her crutch. I can understand why, given her personal condition and the conditions around her, she might be too weary to take the next step, to move on.

Our group flies to Costa Rica, a country with a small remaining indigenous population, the least economically stressed of the Central American countries. I take a small plane to visit the rain forest, but spend most of my time wiping perspiration from my face, rubbing repellent on my wrists and ankles, trying to recover from what I witnessed in Honduras, including the arrogance of U.S. officials and my personal ignorance about Central America, its history of violence and repression and economic domination.

A group of us find our way to a nearby bay to try to escape from the heat. I sit on an underwater rock, only my head above the surface, and gaze at the tropical vegetation, the clouds. Ping. I slap my neck when I feel a sharp sting and soon hear my companions slapping their arms and faces. We can't escape the bites even in the water.

Fortunately, before we leave the region, our group hears Father Xavier Gorostiaga, rector of the Universidad Centroamericana in Managua. I learn much from him: the need for a return to Central American integration to diminish domination from foreign countries, lending agencies, multinationals; the need for a "respectful" relationship between the United States and Central America; the need to democratize the media which control our images, including our images of other countries. Father Gorostiaga quotes a women's group in Lima, El Vaso de Leche, who say, *"Tenemos que pasar de protesta sin propuesta a propuesta con protesta."* (We must protest without proposing to protest.) He is not bitter, but alive with passionate commitment, and cautions that "comfort is the best narcotic." Over and over he reminds me that we have to pose the right questions and thus frame the discussion. In spite of his caring, exuberant manner, his words sting.

———

I was in Central America after the rainy season in October of 1992, that now infamous anniversary of Columbus's arrival in the Americas, with a group exploring the topic of leadership development. Honduras was far greener and far prettier than I had expected, but it was difficult to enjoy the beauty. The visible presence of the military, the hidden presence of ours defined as an "indefinitely temporary" one, the eager desire on the part of the local elite to lure investors were as oppressive as the heat. Is globalization the colonization process of 1992?

I think of the Greek notion of the need for gadflies in society. Maybe that's what I can learn from these persistently red and itching bites as this year of the quincentenary ends: that creatures perceived as small and unimportant, even as nuisances, have power. Unlike insects that respond through instinct, we humans need hope. Only with hope can we use our personal and collective strength, which may be the reason so many of the intriguing speakers on this difficult trip spoke of the necessity of optimism. I think of doña Feliciana, building her own house at sixty-three, planting her frail plant in the sun.

Seals

Like gloves stacked on a shelf
then dropped, the seals arc
the lead beach. All thumbs,
their barks climb the stark
cliff walls to reach us, broken,
a code no attention could sew.
No gesture moves them, except
the light twitch of loud heads
we know for sure dispatch
these sounds up the funneling bluffs
toward our view point.

They are in season, like dark
fruit opportunely plump.
And yet they are rare.
Past a dozen viewing points
no sign of them till now, although
a mile ago we stared at a seal-like rock
until waves failed
to awaken it more than once,
and then we called it a rock for sure.

The certainty of the nameless lies
everywhere. Each rock, leaf, and beast
has a name we ignore, despite the park signs
that conjure silhouettes of poison oak
or breaching whales. We are from the city
and in love, and so we find
in this terrain the heart's echo,
where knowledge is too fast for names.

There feeling dips into the torn mantels of foam,
half woman and half fish, the sea lion
which deceived the Pinta's sailors.
I call them seals. The heart seals.
And as it does, it binds nothing.

Swirling Lines

A brain, a tree heart,
the cellular meltings
of a galaxy, a fly's wing,
a torpedo's bubbly void,
a moire dress shifting,
leaf, ear, onion, fist,
blood's canopy, rolled newspaper,
a knot of hair, a dozing
cat-o'-nine-tails, a ring
of cigar ash, grasses
on the river, a face diluted
on a concave, marble's calcium strings,
a snake nest, an astrolabe,
smoke writing or clenching,
a pineapple's crown, estuary
sand settling like pastry shells,
run-on opalescences, hamburger,
the acrobatics of streaks on glass,
geology's veils, a rippling pond,
a disemboweled wire, a bowl of pasta,
a peacock feather, cloud fronds,
the citadel of a care engine,
a star-of-Bethlehem, a bouquet
of cathodes and filaments,
squid embracing, genes,

an agate word, a project
for a cabbage, combed sand,
the lace of oil on water,
plywood, a terraced slope,
the penmanship of dance,
watermarks, a vortex of moss,
the ways of meaning, wet fur,
fire's filigree, a plowman's world,
an artichoke halved, a nautilus echo,
a deck of handkerchiefs arching
like papyrus heads, the mother-of-pearl
undulations of a porch screen,
brushstrokes, climate mapped
from a satellite, a labyrinth,
this thumb against the pane—
the face of touch—
on the first morning of spring.

Minas de Cobre

Beneath the tobacco fields
of Pinar del Río the map says
there is copper. Two men
bludgeon an ore clump with hammers.
The Spaniards never came this far
or deep, it seems. The miners
work between Cuba and Yucatán
on the sea Cortéz conquered before the Aztecs.
Now they open the Cuban earth
for better metal. The times have changed

their clothing and instruments, lights
have replaced plumes on their helmets, ore

beneath their blows instead of natives' heads.
They dig into the map above
the Península de Guanahacabibes,
a toppled question mark on the wrong
side of the glass, pointing to Mexico.

They dig in the azure space,
their bodies punctually curved to
lift while the other drops the sledge hammer.
The thing becomes many, then more,
fragments, images, like fluids
which science says are made up of tiny solids.
Which reminds me that when you dig
and hit blood you know
you've gone beyond memory.

R U T H   W A R A T

Love and Hunt
in the Dark Room

After photographs by Emmet Gowin

I stir the waters
where your mouth must dawn
and I capture you,
or rather I give birth to you
between my fingers.
Ten different grays and a successful black
reflect the volumes of your face,
the roundness and chinks
where my lips should glide.
I admonished you before to love me
and in spite of your suspicions
I've made you eternal.

The tongs hold the print
and I jiggle the paper somehow tenderly
after every bath and, yes, I cradle the trays.

Since I cannot acknowledge my self as cruel
I imagine this chemical ritual as a path.
Slabs in an Oriental garden
along which I smell your skin,
and a soft dizziness overtakes me
every time you get near to help me jump.

Since I am precise,
I'll conceive it a hopscotch
because, like a child,
it is a territory I can master.
It's in truth a lair where I retire

amidst the images I have stalked
and savor your contempt.

I know that when I multiply you
I renounce in the orgy of infinite copies
to make you intimate, mine.
Give me a son, a daughter,
I'll decree tender darkness outside
and turn on the light in hell.
I'll burn the photographs.

Inquisitors, Dead and in Power. Their Use of Torture Is Abominable, but Is the Sensuality They Employ in Purloining What Makes Them Hateful?

for Dr. Helen Fagin

An attempt by Hasidic Jews to reclaim 12,000 sacred books from Russia's largest library erupted into a brawl. Fighting broke out when a library officer ordered the Jews to leave and called on the police to force them out.
—*New York Times,* FEBRUARY 18, 1992

It is not because I paid ransom for my flesh.
It's just because you changed into a person
of highly delicate taste,
and anyway the smell of burnt bodies would not accomplish
the joy that a caress

of your fingers can discover
while tracing voluptuously
the curves of black flames,
the outlines of my alphabet.
Calligraphy sickens you with nostalgia
for a power that you surmise
lies somewhere between the shape of the letters
and the pages you grasp,
but it is as elusive for you,
although you pile up our manuscripts,
as it is a yoke for us.

Escaping from Poland, Castilla, and Buenos Aires,
I saw a love dance with a carcass on a plain,
the scavenger kissed and tore
entrails and words.
Life tried to hide in the marshes,
but failed and decomposed
in a thousand printed fragments.
The scavenger was still adoring the bones.
I saw you watching the scene, clad in linen,
young, sacred. A candle immemorial.
You deemed it obscene that tenderness
will dissolve in stench and leave written pages
as proof of its madness.
Murmurs of obscure consciences
that of course would be more coherent if dead.
But the texts remained immaculate and you wondered
if there was a miracle inscribed in them,
some whisper missed in torment,
some quality of the soul kneaded in the pulp of paper
like in the wafer. You commenced to collect.

I don't accumulate. We can't but take
a violin by its waist and wander perplexed.
I am, we are, pathetic and peripatetic.
And we keep falling in love
with dark heavens while we flee.
It is not, then, because some inconspicuous virtue of ours,
or some minor merit of mine,
or because we are at a loss without them;

the texts have been walked for centuries,
and nothing in the prophesies is unknown to us.
It is because we learned from your gluttony
and we relinquished too much to your desire,
that we demand our books back.

RAFAEL BARRETO-RIVERA

The Marriage
of the Prostitute
in Puerto Rican Folklore

the lights we saw were not
the lights of houses on a distant mountainside
at night
but, in another country,
they were the lights of light-haired girls
enjoying ice cream
or sitting on a wall in short skirts
   at the return of spring

  Impossible to listen after this
    If there were honesty, he said
and the moon shone in a peculiar way
over our low-lying shining heads
  In silence we smoked our ration
    the canal shacks on stilts
above the stench of the city

  The songs of the whores
audible, audible,

Lights shone on the smelly water
like cosmetics
So I said, why don't you stay
  and he wiggled his loins like a fan
over the edge of the bridge
buildings rose and fell like bottles
the city, fluid
radiance of the city, women

El Fanguito,
La Perla,
Los Bravos de Boston,
El Condado,
        soul slum

For sale, she said
        the best meat of the island

                In the ripples of my brain
smell of her loins appeared
fish-like
the heat rose and the humidity
I felt as if I had no arms
and tried to feel my way like hands
across the nighttime

        (she said
                Feel!
        Taste before trying!)

until I realized
there were no victims rending anything
near the ends of sleep

Where do you live? she said
I said on the cliffs of Guajataca

Now, she said
                You coming with me?
Negroes were weeping, reclining
on the balconies
        Under the bridge the water
flowed like semen

        And the city, island city, wavered,
moved with the wind under African clouds
In Canada, I said, we swam in the Pre-Cambrian
Shield, Lake of Bays,
in the glacial, ancestral bone of the earth
Lily pads were seen to grow
The lotus flourished

and I told her of the dark brown hunter
whose audience threw coins upon the wharf

when he came out, victorious
He was death's tangible, frangible self
with ribs like scimitars
and a bronze stomach
One day, his body greased for battle,
he plunged into the harbor, naked,
with a sharp knife,
San Juan's fastest
                under water

and the harbor bled as of a small wound
and the shark's fin surfaced
cutting red waters
silent as the sea-depths whence it came
into the harbor noon like solid fire

I'd rather talk of Canada, I said

                      whoosh   whoosh
                          the cars whooshed by
No one knows of the place down here,
                      she said

          Speak to us of sex
        so we can understand you

at which point
I spoke of nothing, trembled
my beard, full growth of two months,
three days, five hours,
                she stroked
said
          Pubic hair in public places

vanished
I went to bed with my pants down

                River of silver, river
out of my skin you surface, silver;
river of silver, river

The Bird Who Cleans the World

Our Mayan ancestors spoke of a great flood that covered and destroyed the whole world. They said that the waters rose and rose and rose, flooding the highest mountains and hills and killing everything that lived on the earth. Only one house stood above the flood. In that house all the species of animals entered and hid themselves.

The waters covered the earth for a long time. Then, very slowly, they began to recede, until finally the turbulent waters revealed the earth in its new freedom. When that house was still surrounded by water, they sent forth *Ho ch'ok,* the trumpet bird, to scout the horizon. Since the water was still high the trumpet bird returned quickly, its mission complete.

After a little time more they sent *Usmiq,* the buzzard, to find out how much the water was receding. The messenger, circling through the air, left the house. After a while he flew toward one of the newly uncovered hills and landed with a great hunger.

There he found a large number of dead and rotting animals. Forgetting his mission, he began to devour chunks of the meat until he satisfied his appetite.

When he returned to make his report, the other animals would not let him in among them because his smell was unbearable. And to punish him for his disobedience, *Usmiq* was condemned to eat only dead animals and to clean the world of stench and rottenness.

From that time on the buzzard has been called "The Bird Who Cleans the World" because his duty is to carry off in his beak all that might contaminate the land. *Usmiq,* the buzzard, had to be content with his fate, and thus he went away, forever flying and circling in the air or sitting on the bluffs looking for rotten things to eat.

How the Serpent Was Born

The care and devotion of a mother for her growing children is enormous. She denies herself and she pours forth the treasure of love from her heart in caring for her child. A mother is an angel. A mother is a treasure. A mother is a special being whom we ought to love every moment of our lives. But many of us do not have hearts big enough to repay her for all that we make her suffer.

There are some who insult and reject their mothers and make them suffer even when they are very old, even though the children ought to bless these women with love and care for all the great pleasures they have given.

So it was that once a certain mother wanted to visit her son's house and rest in the shade of his roof. Since he was her son, he might even give her some tortillas to quiet the great hunger raging in her stomach. But it was not to be so. When the son saw his mother approaching his house, he cursed her and ordered his wife to hide the bubbling pot full of chicken soup that she had cooked for dinner that day. The old lady sat on the doorstep and the son said, "Old woman, why do you come to my house?"

His mother answered, "Son, I only come to rest in the shade of your roof."

"Well, I don't believe I have anything to give you, and besides these visits bore me."

The son and his wife had to work hard to fight the appetites that made them want to devour the succulent chicken soup right in front of the old woman who would then want a share. The old woman grew tired of sitting on the doorstep with not a kind word from her son. She turned back toward her little house, saddened by the ingratitude and indifference of that self-centered and ungrateful son.

"Now the old woman has gone away," the son said to his mate. "Let's eat the chicken soup."

The wife brought out the pot that had been hidden from the old woman's eyes. She put it on the table and lifted off the lid.

"Huuuuuuyyy, oh Jesús!" she exclaimed.

"What? What's happening?" her husband asked.

The moment she had lifted the lid, instead of the chicken soup she saw a poisonous serpent, coiled in the pot, its head poised, ready to strike. They wanted to kill it, but the snake, shaking its rattles, slithered out to hide.

It is said that the serpent was born this way, the beginning of the bad things that lie waiting for us. It was born of the heart of a son who did not want to know the courage of a mother's saintly love.

The Disobedient Child

In old times in *Xaqla'* Jacaltenango there was a very disobedient child who often disappointed his parents. No matter how hard they tried to teach him, he never changed.

One afternoon the boy ran away from home looking for someone who would tolerate his mischief. Walking through the woods he discovered a lonely little house and ran up to it. On the porch of the straw-covered house sat an old man, smoking peacefully. The boy stood before him without saying hello or any other word of greeting.

When the old man noticed the boy's presence, he stopped smoking and asked him, "Where do you want to go, boy?"

"I am looking for someone who can give me something to eat," the boy answered.

The wise old man, who already knew the boy's story, said, "No one will love you if you continue being so bad."

The boy did not respond except to laugh.

Then the old man smiled and said, "You can stay with me. We will eat together."

The boy accepted his offer and stayed in the old man's house. On the following day, before going to work, the old man told the boy,

"You should stay in the house, and the only duty you will have is to put the beans to cook during the afternoon. But listen well. You should only throw thirteen beans in the pot and no more. Do you understand?"

The boy nodded that he understood the directions very well. Later, when the time arrived to cook the beans, the boy put the clay pot on the fire and threw in thirteen beans as he had been directed. But once he had done that he began to think that thirteen beans weren't very many for such a big pot. So, disobeying his orders, he threw in several more little fistfuls.

When the beans began to boil over the fire, the pot started to fill up, and it filled up until it overflowed. Very surprised, the boy quickly took an empty pot and divided the beans between the two pots. But the beans overflowed the new pot, too. Beans were pouring out of both pots.

When the old man returned home he found piles of beans, and the two clay pots lay broken on the floor.

"Why did you disobey my orders and cook more than I told you to?" the old man asked angrily.

The boy hung his head and said nothing. The old man then gave him instructions for the next day. "Tomorrow you will again cook the beans as I have told you. What's more, I forbid you to open that little door over there. Do you understand?"

The boy indicated that he understood very well.

The next day the old man left the house after warning the boy to take care to do exactly what he had been told. During the afternoon the boy put the beans on the fire to cook. Then he was filled with curiosity. What was behind the little door he had been forbidden to open?

Without any fear, the boy opened the door and discovered in the room three enormous covered water jars. Then he found three capes inside a large trunk. There was one green cape, one yellow cape, and one red cape. Not satisfied with these discoveries, the boy took the top off the first water jar to see what it contained.

Immediately the water jar began to emit great clouds that quickly hid the sky. Frightened and shivering with cold, the boy opened the trunk and put on the red cape. At that instant a clap of thunder exploded in the house. The boy was turned into thunder and lifted to the sky where he unleashed a great storm.

When the old man heard the thunder he guessed that something extraordinary had happened at home, and he hurried in that direction. There he discovered that the forbidden door was open and the top was off the jar of clouds from which churning mists still rose toward the sky.

The old man covered the jar and then approached the trunk with the capes. The red cape, the cape of storms, was missing. Quickly the old man put on the green cape and regained control over the sky, calming the great storm. Little by little the storm subsided, and soon the man returned to the house carrying the unconscious boy in his arms.

A little while later the old man uncapped the same jar and the clouds which had blackened the sky returned to their resting place, leaving the heavens bright and blue again. When he had done this the old man capped the jar again and put away the red and green capes.

Through all of this the boy remained stunned and soaked with the rains until the kind old man restored his spirit and brought him back to normal. When the boy was alert again and his fear had left, the old man said, "Your disobedience has almost killed you. You were lucky that I heard the storm and came to help. Otherwise you would have been lost forever among the clouds."

The boy was quiet and the old man continued:

"I am Qich Mam, the first father of all people and founder of *Xaqla'*, he who controls the rain and waters the community's fields when they are dry. Understand, then, that I wish you no harm and I forgive what you have done. Promise me that in the future you will not disobey your parents."

The boy smiled happily and answered, "I promise, Qich Mam, I promise." Qich Mam patted him gently and said, "Then return to your home and be useful to your parents and to your people."

From that time on the boy behaved differently. He was very grateful for the kindness of the old man who held the secret of the clouds, the rains, the wind, and the storms in his hands.

Casimiro Mendoza, the Improviser

Well then, since there are so many stories about the life of don Casimiro, all wrong, of course, here I'm going to tell you the real true story of the aforementioned Casi who died recently, may he rest in peace. Well, you probably already know that throughout his long life he enjoyed a special reputation; as a young man he was one heck of a good carpenter, and he even got it into his head to become a saint carver. Later on, he was one of our village's public scribes, and as a mature man, he was our soothsayer, healer, and adviser to all those who, fed up with life or sick in their soul, came to his little house to seek relief from their troubles. Because of the extraordinary and legendary things that happened to him, some of the townspeople ascribed to him a disreputable notoriety. Some used to say—in fact, some still say—that he was a liar, a phony, a fool, and all that, but others swear that he was a first-rate healer, a spiritual and wise man, and the best doctor that lived around these parts. Tall, thin, with long arms and legs, a bit stooped, nearsighted, wearing small, thick-lensed glasses, he looked like some sort of a strange bird when, as a young man, he crossed the plaza with his long strides, usually smoking and reading or staring right through you with his glistening eyes, his thoughts somewhere else. Although he never married, everyone used to say that he was always in love with one unmarried girl or another, or some widow, and from time to time, he'd even risk his life by paying special attention to a good-looking married woman who might go up to him in the plaza where he earned his living writing letters, or who came to his house to request some of his varied services.

Look, I had the occasion to hear some of the old men tell how young Casimiro made beautiful pine furniture, all carved with little birds and angels and hearts and flowers, and who knows what else. And also perhaps because of some spiritual rapture, or maybe because he simply needed the money, he carved, by special request, saints like Saint Judas Thaddeus, or if it was for women, images of Saint Barbara, who they say was the first feminist saint in history, or something like that—I don't know how to say that word they use nowadays. During those years when Casi was barely twenty-five or so, he was making plans to get married, building himself a little brick house, carving lovely furniture for when he married Genoveva, a really beautiful girl—I happened to know her, she had a very unusual way of looking at you, a bit cross-eyed, she was, and everybody said it made her look a lot more sensual than she might have been otherwise. But that wedding never took place. Two days before the ceremony, with everything ready, the beautiful Genoveva dropped dead—some said that it was some sort of stroke—leaving poor Casi in the deepest depression and despair, like without hope. After the funeral he went to bed and spent six months nearly motionless, not wanting to do anything, only wanting to die—he told me that. He didn't even bother with the house he'd just built, or the furniture. He even stopped carpentering, and his parents had to sell off all the things he'd been working on so lovingly for so long, or give them away.

He must have wanted to die so much that he got his wish, or, rather, that's what they say. In that depression he had an attack of meningitis, or however it's pronounced, and he went into a coma. His parents quickly took him to the General Hospital in El Paso, and they sent him by plane, unconscious, nearly dead, to San Antonio, and then, in another plane, to Dallas, and then to Houston where you find all those famous doctors who specialize in brains. All the doctors said there was nothing to be done, that he was going to die, and one of them even told the exact day and the exact time when Casi'd pass on to a better life. His grieved parents, who only a year earlier had buried their other son, Azaleo—I'm sure some of you remember that fine young musician—had no other choice than to bring him back to the village, and the poor dying guy arrived in an ambulance, on a stretcher, no less, with all the neighbors looking on and feeling sorry. Well, they started getting ready for Casimiro's inevitable death; the priest arrived and gave him extreme unction and all that, and they began to prepare for the wake with all the rosaries at the ready and the announcements out, and they even asked some of his friends to write obituaries to read at the funeral. One of the most beautiful eulogies, it really moved you, was the one written by don Salomón, the other carpenter, who, to be honest, had never been too fond of his talented competitor, but in the obituary he talked with a lot of feeling, just as if it had come out of the Bible, all about Casi's work and the deep friendship that had united the two carpenters and saint carvers. His parents and the neighbor women laid Casimiro out and put him in one of the rooms in his parents' house right there on the plaza, and his friends went by in a line and looked at him lying there, with his body in full view, all long and bony and his eyes shut tight; he had, for all practical purposes, really left this world. The women crossed themselves and said, "It's Genoveva come for him, she took him with her, you remember how jealous she always was," and the men peeked in at the window and saw him there motionless and took their hats off in respect and looked down at their boots, although some of them did say, "He's pretending, we all know him, he's been pretending all this time."

Now I couldn't say that that was true, but early the morning of Saturday, August 6, at daybreak, exactly the date that the doctors had said that he was going to die, Casimiro opened his eyes, and looking sort of furious at all those sobbing women carrying rosaries, said, "What the hell am I doing here again?" and the cynical ones said, "What did I tell you? He was trying to put another one over on us." Well, anyway, up jumped Casimiro from his bed, which was surrounded by candles, perfectly alert and healthy, you can't imagine, and took a bath to get rid of all the powders and ointments and all that oily stuff that Felícitas had rubbed him with, and then sat down and ate this humongous plate of vermicelli and meat and chile, and then began to read his obituaries, laughing boisterously from time to time or smiling dryly at some point in his reading. Well, who knows what got into him after that, because they say that the following morning, he left his parents' house with this little table and an old typewriter and sat in the shade under some trees in the plaza to wait for clients to ask him to write letters in English or Spanish—he could do both—like letters to the federal government asking about some check that had gotten lost, or to the mayor of Las Cruces complaining about the awful medical services in the village, or to someone's relative in Mexico about somebody being sick or dying, say, an uncle or aunt or brother-in-law; he even asked for girls' hands in marriage like they used to in those days, you'll probably remember, not like now when all they say is we're getting married, and that's it, with no respect for the nice customs we used to have. What Casi liked most, though, was writing love letters, and that was what he did best of all.

When I was still a kid, I used to see Casi writing those famous love letters. I'd go to the plaza on Sunday mornings to speak to others waiting around for their wives to come out of mass, and talking about the terrible state of the irrigation ditches and the high cost of fertilizers and that sort of thing. Frequently, to have a few laughs, I'd go to the corner where

Casi sat and always had a lot of customers gathered around waiting their turn, or just hanging around, because there's no two ways about it, when the fellow was inspired he'd really let go: he'd close his eyes with feeling and let his imagination run wild, reciting out loud and writing it all down at the same time, and, of course, you got a real good show right there on the plaza. Casi, in those days, was a real eccentric, a real weird one, so to speak. Now don't you go thinking he just wrote straight away. Oh, no, he first questioned his clients for a long time to get all the details; his clients were nearly always men who wished to give their mistresses or girlfriends or fiancéees or wives or what not a little poem or some written amorous declaration, something they wouldn't be caught dead doing in person.

Well, you can imagine, with young Casimiro's reputation, what sorts of things he asked the men, and, of course, what some of those cynical jokesters answered, because Casi wanted to know what color hair she had, what color her eyes were, and about her skin, and if she was tall or short, or if she had wide, sensuous lips and long, silky eyelashes, a lovely long neck and perfect feet, and any distinguishing mark like, say, a dimple or a birthmark, and if so, where was it, and what did she dream of. He even asked secret things that only the man could know, like some passionate quirk that she had, and so on and on, questions like that. What he always wanted to know, though, was if she was a bit cross-eyed, and there was always some guy who said yes. When that happened, boy, was he inspired! He was overcome with love, and he'd hit his typewriter and let it rip, composing and reciting and writing all at the same time. He always kept the carbon copy and gave the other to the customer who signed his name or made a little cross, and then Casi charged him a few dollars, and that was the end of the business transaction.

At the other side of the plaza don Secundino cursed and swore. He'd been working for years as the town scribe, and he saw how, day after day, Casimiro got all the customers with his flowery language and exaggerations and the show he put on in public. Some of the women who got letters said they were pure poetry, that they'd keep them forever, but there were others who wouldn't let their husbands or boyfriends get near Casi, you see, he got to know too much about their hidden secrets. Furthermore, they noticed that he started staring at them, you know, with that special kind of look, at the post office, at the shops, in church, as if he knew something very personal about them, as if he was in love with them even.

His being a scribe started, as I said, as a direct result of his strange experience in the world of the dead. Now another legend was added to his fame, that he had died and resurrected. So often did they ask him to tell them all he'd seen and who he'd talked to when he was dead that he ended up conducting special sessions, with an entry fee, of course, of one or two dollars, and he'd tell them all about his experiences in the world of the dead.

"Look here," he'd say, "the first thing I remember seeing is this big shining light that wrapped me all up; it brought peace and calm and made me go up, up, through some bright sunbeams, up, up, to a high place where you could see four mountains, each at the four points of the universe. The way up led to a brilliant white stone, and I saw a lot of people I knew up there, and they all smiled very serenely and said hi, very happy, and when I talked to them they seemed to know what was going on down here in the village. I even saw my younger brother, Azaleo, but everyone else was Azaleo, too, because it seemed that there wasn't any difference between one dead person and another up there. I was looking for Genoveva, of course, but all of the dead women were Genoveva, too. Well, when I spoke to her, or, rather, to one of the Genovevas, she seemed so happy that it made me quite angry, since I've been suffering so much for her, hour after hour, day after day, down here. I told her how I felt, and she said, real calm, 'If you're getting mad and jealous, that means you're not dead yet, so go back down there to earth. And be sure you say hello to Mama and Papa when you get down there.' I hardly had time to tell her how grieved I've been because she's not with me, and how I was going to dedicate the rest of my life writing love letters to her, and that I'd always love her throughout eternity, and that she should wait for me to join her so we could be together properly, and she then said, very quietlike, 'Forget it, man. There's none of that sort of thing up here. Get back to where your fate sends you.'"

Anyway, these sessions were real strange because Casimiro kept adding things and more and more details. As well as being a scribe and giving advice, a lot of people came to ask if he'd seen whatsisname and whatsername up there, and if they'd asked after them. Casimiro would always answer very seriouslike, "Your mama's keeping track of all the damn fool things you do when you get drunk on Saturday nights." And the patient would ask, "And does it make her sad? Is she suffering on my account?" And Casi, looking right into his eyes, would say, "It's you who're suffering, it's you who's sad with the pain you've got inside. Get rid of it."

Some continued to think that Casimiro was a big liar and that the best thing to do was to take no notice of him since he was probably doing more harm than good in his sessions on death with the village boozers, and with the young kids who smoked pot and took drugs and so on, stuff that at my old age I've never used. Take the case of Benito, remember? He'd been a drunkard for years, just like San Benito, patron saint of the drunks, for whom he'd been named and who, like his saint, gave up drinking. "What did he do?" they asked Benito. "How did that old buffoon cure you?" And Benito would answer, "Well, he didn't give me no drugs like the doctors in Las Cruces and El Paso. He just cured me with words. He had me recite poems and stories and that's how he cured me." And they said, "No, man, you gotta be kidding; you don't cure somebody like that. He must have given you something." But Benito would say, "No, that's how it was. I still know all those poems, I learned them by heart. Casimiro had me repeat after him just as if he was looking for the same thing I was.

"My Lord, if I, with my limitations and with my human weaknesses, forget Thee at times, Thou, oh Lord, do not forget me for one instant. Thou who are my creator, keep on loving me so I learn to love myself. Believe in me so I learn to believe in myself. Oh, my Creator who gave me life, help me to live."

"Now repeat it," don Casimiro would say, "repeat it until the words reach the corners of your heart, until they are the very breath of your soul. Repeat it when you feel like going off to join your friends at the bar because that's when you're suffering the pains of your illness. And if you still feel like drinking, get close to the powers of creation and re-create yourself. Start sawing wood and making furniture or saints, build houses, write or sing songs. Create paintings with whatever's in your heart and soul, and every day write a love poem which is to get close to the origins of reproduction. And if your true purity doesn't bloom, then get hold of a tree and don't let go, since the tree is the sacred symbol of a new life." And some of the neighbors, when they saw Benito crying and trembling from head to toe, holding onto a tree, would say, "Uuuu, that poor guy's nuttier now than his master." Anyway, that's how Benito described his treatment, and he always did say that what all those doctors with their diplomas and certificates on the walls of their offices were unable to do, Casi was able to do. Of course, I'm not saying that Casimiro was always successful, mind you, you've only to think of the recent case of Rigoberto, but, like they say, Beto didn't really want to create a new life for himself.

Up to this point, Casi would deal only with men in his healing business; he only cured men, that is, and he left the women to Felícitas.

In fact, some used to say—you know that there are always gossip mongers around—that Casi and Felícitas way back when were seen praying and meditating together in the desert, and God only knows what else they did, too, and one even heard the rumor that Casi was the father of Feli's daughter, Eduviges. Now nobody ever really knew if that was definitely true or not. The truth is that Felícitas, the herbalist, midwife, and layer on of hands, and Casi, our public scribe, adviser, and healer, were, in a certain way, competitors in the same business, so to speak, so some people refused to believe all those stories. Anyway, when Casi still attended to women, something really horrible happened, something really sad, and after that episode, he never let women into his house. Besides, that painful experience produced another change in his life, you might say.

Even though there are a lot of different versions of what happened, I know the exact truth because it was personally told to me this way: that one day this really pretty fifteen-year-old girl came into the plaza crying and sat down at Casi's side, who must have been about forty or so by then. Amid sobs and more sobs, tears and more tears, hiccups and more hiccups, and holding on to Casi's handkerchief, she told him how her husband had beaten her up, how he had abandoned her, how she didn't know what to do because she'd no money, and that she'd be better off dead. And Casimiro, completely stupefied by the beautiful dark-skinned girl with green eyes, curly hair down her back, didn't say anything at all because he didn't know what to say, but then, he pulled himself together a bit and started asking about her married life and cause and effect and all those things. After they'd talked several times in the plaza, this girl— Raquel she said was her name—and Casimiro became real good friends, and in a matter of a few days, Raquelita moved in with Casimiro, and on Saturdays you'd see them looking radiantly happy, walking through town arm in arm, heading for doña María's, the only restaurant we had in town. But you couldn't call it long-lasting happiness, since it took only four weeks for Raquel to take off unexpectedly with all the money Casimiro had hidden about his house, not that it was much, along with all his furniture and clothes and everything. Poor Casimiro got home from work in the plaza, and there was the house, all empty and dreadfully quiet. You can imagine what a terrible shock that must have been to see a healer like Casi yelling and foaming at the mouth, in a straitjacket and wrestling with the nurses who tried to hold him down and who finally took him straight to the lunatic asylum. And from then on, he wouldn't have anything to do with women and their ailments. "Go to Mesilla, go see Felícitas," he'd say and shut the door whenever somebody brought him a poor woman dying of sorrow or suffering from an attack of fury.

And as you know, there's always gossip; some of the guys who were nearby cutting alfalfa, as well as women neighbors, said that Raquelita was one of those loose women. I have to admit that that strange little girl never fooled me, no sir, not for a minute. They used to say that in the afternoons when Casimiro was in the plaza, a young man about twenty used to come and spend hours with her. I can't say anything about that since I never saw him. But I can tell you that when Casimiro got out of the hospital, all quiet and hurt, you could hear him at night in his darkened house sadly playing the guitar and singing the same song over and over again, which some said was one of the many things that the aforementioned Raquel taught him.

> Farewell, farewell, beloved,
> In this life I no longer want to be,
> Oh, how you've embittered it for me.
> When your ma bore you,
> And pushed you out into this world,
> A heart she failed to give you
> To love for even a second,
> To love for even a second.
> So look for another love
> Behind some other door.
> There look for another protector,
> Since for me you exist no more,
> Since for me you exist no more.
> Farewell, farewell, beloved,
> In this life I no longer want to be,
> Oh, how you've embittered it for me,
> Oh, how you've embittered it for me.

Some said he really learned a lot from her, that little girl, even those songs which they say come from Spain, or places like that, but I wouldn't know about those things. What I do know is that my eyes filled with tears every time I heard him singing in the darkness of his empty house. But who told him to get mixed up with a young girl like that? Not me. You wouldn't catch me doing a thing like that, no siree. Yes, yes, I know some say that all this is just a story, nothing but gossip, that that little girl was nobody else but doña Merceditas's daughter who lived in Anthony, and that nutty ol' Casimiro lost everything in crooked dealings and that he took all those songs from old books, and on and on, but I'm telling you the story I was told.

Well, anyway, as I was saying, when Casimiro got out of the hospital, you'd see him at first looking real tired and sad, all lost in his thoughts, very quietlike, staring into space as if he were trying to find an answer to something that didn't have one. And little by little, he stopped going to his place in the plaza, and you'd see him meditating in the desert or in front of his empty house which he never furnished again as long as he lived. We'd go visit him, poor guy, and we'd notice how his conversations weren't the same; they were going in other directions, you might say. To be more exact, he didn't really talk much anymore, he just said what was important, and that's all. Sitting on a little mat on the floor, with us sitting also on the floor, because, as I told you, there weren't any chairs around or anything else, he would tell us that he'd never really been able to forget the land of the dead, and that he wanted, while still alive, to reach that perfect calm and serenity that he'd seen in that other world. I think he meant it, too, because when he would talk to his patients, and even when he was talking to us, he used to say to himself, "All passes, all changes, let nothing disturb you, not the flight of the butterfly nor the storms of the earth, not the whispering of the wind nor the earth-quakes of the soul, because the center of the universe which is you and you and you and me is always in perfect peace and tranquillity." The fact is that more and more people started coming to consult him, from northern New Mexico, from Albuquerque, from Sierra Blanca, Texas, and even from Juárez, which was odd, because in Mexico, as you know, they've got healers and sorcerers coming out their ears. Well, just as I've said, he began to grow very famous as an adviser and healer, and we'd see him in front of his little house sitting on the ground with a patient looking at Casi very intenselike, as if the words were planting seeds in the depths of his soul. No two ways about it, his business certainly prospered, but, as I said before, Casimiro didn't just say strange things, he did them, too.

That was when he started painting those odd pictures with weird colors like you see in dreams sometimes, and he put those paintings all over his house; I say they were strange, because when we went to see him from time to time, we didn't know what we were looking at. "They're meditations," he'd tell us, "that's what they are." And we were still in the dark as to what they were. Some of them showed four mountains, one at each side, one up, one down, with a path that zigzagged across a rain of lightning until it reached the top where this shining stone was. "That's the divine quartz crystal," he would say, and down below was this thin old man with glasses on, and only a white loincloth and no shoes, all naked, going up the pathway, as if trying to get to the light. "That's the shaman's dream, and he's going to join the primary forces of creation," he said. And we'd say, "Oh yeah?" And we'd stare at the picture and still didn't understand anything. On the way home, all worried, we would say to each other, "The older he gets, the crazier he gets, no doubt about that. Maybe he picked up those crazy ideas when they locked him up with the other loonies." And as you know, he got worse as he got older, you all know that. What did he say? Well, it seems he didn't say much, he said less and less. In fact, he hardly talked at all anymore with friends and relatives, but he paid very special attention when he spoke to those who came to consult him; he knew exactly what he wanted to tell them. At least that's what Rogelio told me when he had this terrible depression that came upon him when his best friend Beto died. He said that according to Casimiro, the word is sacred and powerful and that the word is the creation of the cosmos or the universe, or something like that. Well, don't laugh, that's what Rogelio told me. What Casi did say to me one day though was, "If you say aloud what you are going to do, you've begun the process of creation." And I dunno why, but every time I start to tell the story of Casimiro, I remember that.

When Casimiro was real old, the neighbors started noticing that his little house was starting to collapse, adobe by adobe, along with the boards and beams and walls. The young folk came and offered to rebuild it for him, but, no, he didn't want that. It was then that he started moving from one room to another as the walls fell, until one day a flash of lightning like an electric zigzag, then a thunderbolt, and the roof fell in, leaving him outside under the sky, the sun, and the stars, his house just a heap of rubble, earth, and old sticks that bleached in the sun with the awful wind we have here and the cold of the desert. Well, man, and what were we to do, if that's the way he wanted it. He wouldn't let us come near, nutty old coot. And that was when he really did something nobody expected. He put on some old sandals and, all weak and trembling, the old man, naked with his white cloth like a diaper, went walking with his pilgrim's staff to Eduviges's house in Mesilla. He went up to her window and said, "Your moment has arrived. You, who have the experience of creating new living beings, come with me, you have much to do." And that's how they say Eduviges became the adviser-herbalist, the diviner-poet, midwife, layer on of hands, and the best doctor that has ever been known in all of these lands, even though there are so many young men who have asked Casi for instruction, wanting to become sorcerers and healers. But no, it was the quiet and serene Eduviges who perfected Casimiro's wisdom, his poems and stories, and the writings in which he jotted down the steps of his meditations. Well, that's what he called them, "steps and ladders," along with those weird pictures I mentioned, and piles of notebooks in which he daily composed love letters. And that was everything that had belonged to Casimiro. Yes, it's true that some people have told Eduviges to write books about her own meditations and her poems with which she cures women, men, and children or about the magic power of plants or the healing energy of her hands. They've even told her to get in touch with a Mexican writer like Juan José Arreola, I think that's his name, so he'll help her put all that in books. But you know how Eduviges is: she says that the spoken words are what really are important and are the ones that go straight to the heart and body. Something like that. Someday she'll write down all her wisdom, there's no doubt about that, but she's going to do it her way. Well, if you want to hear the story of Eduviges, go one of these days to see doña Serafina.

Well, anyway, one early Saturday morning, August 6, when he was ninety-two years old, Casimiro Mendoza woke up dead, completely naked, without a stitch on, flat out on the ground where his house had collapsed. He seemed to be sleeping, and he looked so peaceful that there were even some who said, "And what if he resurrects again? Maybe we'd better not be in a hurry to bury him." But Padre López, waving his hand a bit, as if giving him the benediction, said, "Well, let's hope he doesn't come back this time as San José de Cupertino, the patron saint of rockets, who according to the Acta Sanctorum was the saint who most frequently levitated and who went higher than anybody else."

But, no, as far as I know, that time Casimiro really did die, but by means of these words, every one true, I assure you, I've given you, and to all those who might ask in the future, the story of our beloved although eccentric friend. And that's the way it is, and ever shall be.

The Miracle

Candido Lopez had just gotten up. It was eight o'clock in the morning, but the sun was already beating down the pansies. He came out of his room wearing a pink kimono spotted with white irises; it was a gift doña Cipriana's husband had brought him from the capital. Candido was thirty years old but looked like eighteen. On his face he carried the innocence of a boy who had known only happiness. His face was that of a porcelain doll, white and smooth. His frame was slim and delicate.

In the kitchen, he opened a drawer and took out his mother's heart medicine. He made scrambled eggs for himself and heated some *rosquillas* for his mother. He drank coffee while he waited for his mother to get up.

When his mother came out of her room, Candido served her the *rosquillas* on a red tin plate with a glass of goat milk along with the two orange pills.

After eating breakfast his mother went back to her room to pray the morning rosary. Candido walked outside to wash the walls of their house. They lived next to the only whorehouse in town, and sometimes drunk men, tired of waiting in line to get in, would piss on their wall.

Candido still remembered the first time he had walked into that whorehouse a year ago. Women, from black to white, from blond to brunette, from tall to short, all looking the same, were absorbed in their clown faces. Cheap clothes, satin, rhinestones, almost no clothes, their breasts almost showing their nipples, teasing. And their red underwear, their red panties, their red . . . Hoarded like cows on their way to the slaughterhouse, some of them slept, others smoked, drank, chewed gum with the heaviness of their red lips. Smiling, caressing each other, grooming the fleas from one another's hair, complaining of last night's clientele, hiding the love bites on their necks, all dreaming. Candido sat in one corner, alone, smoking a long cigarette, until the mayor came in and sat with him.

"Are you new?" the mayor asked him, but Candido never answered him. He never spoke that night. He stared at the couples dancing to the rhythm of loud music, moving like monsters while the red-framed Holy Family hung on the wall between cutouts of naked women from old calendars.

When Candido finished washing the wall, he was covered in sweat. He came inside the house and lay down on the sofa doña Cipriana had given them twenty years ago. He held a book in his left hand and with his right he held a fan.

Every few minutes he fanned himself, sighing about the terrible heat. He could hear the tender whispering sound his mother made every time she prayed the rosary by herself. The wall that separated them was a folding screen made of thin plywood. Before turning each page, Candido would sigh again, fan himself, looking around the room at the things that brought him fond memories. He looked at the two plastic dolls sitting on a shelf, the little porcelain rabbit on the table, and the painting of Jesus the Good Shepherd surrounded by the sheep that appeared to be listening. Nearby was the wrinkled illustration he had cut out of a magazine depicting the birth of Venus, and next to it Marilyn Monroe on the cover of a magazine. He closed his eyes and fell asleep.

Minutes later, doña Cipriana walked into the house without making any noise. She walked to the sofa and discovered Candido sleeping. Doña Cipriana stared at his face, smiling. She had known him since he was a little baby. She touched his cheeks, stroked his hair slowly, and wondered what Candido was dreaming of.

"Candido," she said, whispering to his ear. "Candido."

"Uhh," he said, stretching himself. "Hello, doña Cipriana, how are you?"

"Fine. Fine. Is your mother awake?"

His mother walked into the room to greet doña Cipriana. Doña Lupita had worked as a maid during her youth for doña Cipriana's household.

"Hello, doña Cipriana, how are you?"

"Fine. Fine. How are you feeling today, doña Lupita?"

"Ahh, there. As usual. I have a pain in my liver, but sit down. Would you like some coffee?"

"Sure."

Candido stood up to give his place to doña Lupita and doña Cipriana.

"You didn't tell me you had a pain in your liver," he said to his mother.

"It was too early to talk about ailments, Candido. Bring us some coffee. Would you?"

Candido brought the coffee and went back to the kitchen to wash the dishes.

"Doña Lupita, I have to tell you something that I just can't believe," doña Cipriana said, after sipping her coffee and leaving a pink mark on the cup. "This new generation is doomed! You know what my son told me yesterday? I just can't believe it! He's here on vacation from school in the capital. You want to know what he told me? I just can't believe it! It might upset your heart."

Doña Lupita observed her, rolling her eyes, trying to imagine what doña Cipriana would say next. "Come on, go ahead and tell me. It won't upset me."

"Are you sure?" Doña Cipriana looked deep into her eyes. Then she got up from the sofa and went into the kitchen. Doña Lupita followed her with her eyes. "Candido, do you think she will get upset? I don't want your mother to get upset, you know."

Candido kept washing the dishes, looking at the pot of marigolds that Omar had given him on his birthday. "But what is it? If you tell me, dear, I might be able to tell you whether she will get upset or not," he said, placing his right hand on his hip and turning toward her.

"Oh, it's something terrible!" doña Cipriana said.

"Tell her. She's a strong woman. She survived a heart attack."

Doña Cipriana walked back to the small living room, producing a snapping sound with her heels. "My son said . . . oh, it's terrible! Terrible! He said that God does not exist!" She broke into tears—fat tears that smeared her black eyeliner around her eyes and brought it down to her chin. "It's terrible! He said that if I would take a deep look into my soul, I would find that there is nothing there. Nothing! It's terrible, doña Lupita. Terrible! He said that after that, I would be able to take a leap of freedom. I don't understand what he says, but those words are frightening." She held her head with her two hands and sobbed, "I feel like my heart is breaking," as she dropped limply onto the sofa.

"No, my darling. That's not good. Candido, bring me my heart medicine so that doña Cipriana doesn't have a heart attack. Hurry! Hurry!" Doña Lupita screamed, her head turned toward the kitchen.

Candido whisked into the living room with a glass of water and an orange pill.

"Candido, did you hear that?"

"I did. I did. That's so terrible!" He went around the sofa behind doña Cipriana and stroked her shoulders while she washed down the pill with the water. He leaned over and pressed his cheeks against hers. "I'm so sorry about that, dear, but cry, cry. The experts say that it's good for the soul and for the eyes too. You'll see better afterward."

"That's so terrible, doña Cipriana. Uhh, it gives me goose bumps. Look!" Doña Lupita pointed at her forearm. Doña Cipriana gave it a glance with her watery eyes and continued crying.

"I think those teachers are to be blamed. That's awful!"

"I know, and this is the Catholic university. I can't imagine what they tell them at the public university. It's terrible! And what can one do? Nothing."

Candido patted doña Cipriana's bunched shoulders. "Don't say that word, dear. That word should be censored by the government. I have to go finish the dishes," he said, walking toward the kitchen.

"You're right, Candido. Well, enough of this misery of mine." Doña Cipriana wiped off her tears with the palm of her hands. "How is your liver feeling right now, doña Lupita?"

"It's better now. Is your heart feeling better now?"

"Oh, yes. That medicine is good for the heart. It's incredible what progress has done lately. Isn't it? Before, in the old times, I would have died of a heart attack because of this son of mine who doesn't appreciate his parents."

"Oh, yes. The doctors are keeping me alive, too."

"Is Candido taking good care of you?"

"Oh, yes! He always does. I don't know what I would do without him. My only son has dedicated his whole life to taking care of me. He's almost a saint, you know. But that's what a son is for."

"I wish I could say the same about mine. The only thing he's given me is headaches."

"My boy has always been good. I knew he was going to be a good son since the day we fled La Rebusca, when half the babies on our block died of smallpox. He never cried, never complained, even though he was only a month old."

"It was like the flight to Egypt. I remember when you walked into Camoapa with little Candido wrapped in a blue sheet. It just broke my heart! Your son has been good to you, but mine . . ."

"It's just plain luck. Just plain luck. Sometimes God gives you a good one, sometimes He gives you a bad one."

"You know, doña Lupita, I think that Candido came out such a good son because you baptized him in the river. I'm sure that's the reason."

"Oh, no. That's nonsense."

"There were some signs, I remember. I know it was God saying, 'This is one of my sheep.' I saw the sun shining on top of his tiny head, then the toucans flew from one side of the river to the other, and the monkeys chirped away as if the jungle was afire."

"No, doña Cipriana. That's just the way the jungle is. There was no extraordinary sign that day."

"Excuse me," Candido interrupted them. "I have to get dressed and go." He kissed his mother and doña Cipriana. "It's terrible! I know how you feel," he said, patting doña Cipriana's shoulders.

"And where are you going, Candido?"

"I'm going to see the little boy Omar brought from the mountain. Omar says he has bad spirits inside of him. He talks like a parrot and has fever."

"Some offspring are just troublemakers, aren't they?" doña Cipriana said.

"Are they charging anything to go see him?"

"Uh-huh. Twenty-five cents."

"That's not bad at all," doña Cipriana said. "I might go see him myself."

"I want to see him too," said doña Lupita.

"Oh, good. Maybe we both go together and I'll treat you," doña Cipriana said.

Candido Lopez left his house, wearing a blue wide-brim hat with a red ribbon around the band. Next door, Margara, the owner of the whorehouse, was watering the dusty street with a bucket. "Adiós, Candido. I like your hat," she said, waving and smiling at him.

"Thank you. Isn't it hot today?" he said, fanning himself with his hands, walking toward her.

"Yeah. This sun feels like the flames from hell. Where are you going?"

"I'm going to see the boy who has the bad spirits."

"Who brought him to town?"

"Omar did. He said he found him in the jungle."

"Oh, really. How exciting! I'm gonna tell the girls about it. How much are they charging?"

"Twenty-five cents."

"That's not bad." She moved closer to his face and whispered in his ear, "You know that the mayor is coming to visit the establishment tonight for a government inspection. If you feel like it, you can sneak in again.

He said that he really liked the mute girl." She started giggling with him in complicity.

"I'll let you know when I come back," he said.

"Let me know soon so I can iron all the clothes."

"I will," he said, swishing away, leaving his friend giggling as she went back to watering the street.

On the way to the house where the boy with the bad spirits was, Candido thought about what Margara had told him. Today, he didn't feel like telling his mother he was going to the movie theater to see another rerun of *Gentlemen Prefer Blondes*. He didn't feel like putting on all that makeup and those tight dresses. He didn't feel like sneaking into the whorehouse that night to pretend he was a mute girl, waiting for the mayor to get drunk, before the mayor could do his thing. Today, he'd rather be watching the boy with the bad spirits and talking with Omar, his best friend.

Boys ran down the street as Candido walked to the other side of town. It was Saturday, and don Luis was killing his most precious pig. Candido remembered when he and Omar used to go there as kids. He remembered the pigs being carried to a rustic altar where don Luis and his son tied them up in a manner that looked like they were being crucified. Candido remembered the ax hitting the pigs' foreheads and the knife, bigger than the children, glittering in the air, then cutting the throats while the pigs howled in agony and the children stared and laughed. Hot blood spurted out of their throats, the dogs waited with their tails wagging. Then the bucket to catch the blood. The women in the kitchen, each giving directions to the other in a frenzied commotion, keeping the fire going, the pots and pans ready. And don Luis shaving the pigs' skin until it looked like his own. The time to collect all the precious treasures that rested inside the pigs came as the last ritual, and the kids would go back to their usual hide-and-seek.

How courageous of Omar to have brought this boy to town, Candido thought. Candido remembered the days when he went to Omar's house to play in the yard or to sneak into his room to play their forbidden games. He was always the housewife. Omar was married now and lived far away from town, but every time he came in, he visited Candido and brought him a gift.

When Candido got to the house, there was a line of people waiting to enter. He went around the crowd who didn't have any money to pay the fee but were hoping to catch a glance of the boy. Omar stood by the door holding a cardboard box where he put the money people paid to see the boy. He also made sure the crowd inside was no bigger than twenty and stayed no longer than half an hour. It was hot inside.

The boy lay on the dirt floor, without moving, surrounded by votive candles and flowers. He was about thirteen years old and was wearing only a ragged pair of underwear that didn't seem to be his. He had the belly of a starving child. Every five minutes the boy burped a sound that everybody interpreted as a parrot trying to talk. He trembled with fever, his cinnamon skin flecked with droplets.

People inside filed by the boy, looking at him, waiting for the burp. Then, after hearing him burp, they went on talking with the others. They asked each other questions. Had the priest come already? Yeah, he came in, threw some holy water on top of the body, and prayed something, but nothing happened. Who's the boy's father? No one knows. Who's his mother? Don't know either. Has he talked like a person? Not yet. What do you think this means? I don't know. I think this is a sign from God. It's a dilemma. What's a dilemma? I don't know. It sounds like something complicated.

Doña Catarina was selling hot coffee inside the house and went around the room offering her merchandise. "Hot coffee. Hot coffee." Everybody drank coffee, even though it was terribly hot inside. They couldn't say no to her: she was the owner of the house.

A woman inside who claimed to be able to decipher the boy's burps sat next to the body with one hand on the boy's belly and the other on her ear. She interpreted the burps right after they'd come out of his mouth. "He says he was bad with his parents." Five minutes later, "He says he disobeyed his parents." Five minutes later, "He says he knows this is a punishment, like the girl who became a spider because she didn't listen to her parents." Five minutes later, "I'm turning into a parrot," and everybody in the room got closer to the body and observed his skin, looking for feathers. They looked at his feet, waiting for them to turn into claws. They waited. Doña Catarina got so close to the body that her nose touched the tiny drops of sweat. She sneezed.

"A feather! I found a feather!" doña Catarina screamed, and everybody in the room crowded around her and looked where she was pointing.

"A feather? A feather!" people around the room murmured. But the feather turned out to be the boy's first pubic hair. Then they directed their attention to the boy's feet. They sat in chairs looking intensely at his feet, wishing the metamorphosis would happen before it was their time to leave the room. Doña Catarina went back to selling her coffee, telling people that the boy smelled like feathers.

"Time's up!" Omar screamed from the door. "Everybody out. Let the new round of people in. Everyone out."

The people who waited outside became more anxious. They pushed the ones who were in front of them. They craned their necks to see how close they were to the door. The ones who could count counted the people in line to make sure they would get in next. The first twenty in line reached into their pockets for some change.

Omar saw Candido waiting in the crowd of people who couldn't afford to get in. Omar whistled, and when Candido turned toward him, Omar signaled with his hand for him to come in. He didn't charge him. People in line complained. "He has to pay! That's not fair. He has to pay," they screamed, but Omar shut them up with "I'm the boss here!"

"How is it inside? How is it?" the people who waited in line asked those who were walking out. "Oh, it's terrible! A terrible thing, but he deserved it." "How so?" "Is it worth twenty-five cents?" someone asked. "Oh yeah, more than that. It's a terrible sight. It's worth it." "It's a lesson for the young," said an old woman.

After paying their fees, the twenty people entered the house in a slow and silent procession. When they were inside, they slunk to the corner where the boy was, looking at him as they would a deceased relative in a funeral box. Some of them placed fruits and *atol* around the candles and flowers, in case he'd awaken and be hungry.

"Poor thing. Look at him. He's suffering. He's gonna burp. Hush! Silence! Is there someone who can translate what he says?" Candido asked. People looked at each other, hoping there was someone who could. Doña Catarina, who was making a new pot of coffee, said from the kitchen, "The lady who knew had to leave. Her thirty minutes were up."

There was an air of sadness. The people felt the same way they had when they were at the church on Holy Friday keeping vigil over the body of Christ. "You could've let her stay longer, Omar," Candido said with a begging tone.

"I know, but she had to take some food to her man who's in jail for stealing."

"I know what we can do. We're all gonna touch him. He needs to be touched. I read a book that said that in some places they touch the person who is sick to heal him," Candido said, looking at the crowd.

"No, I don't want to touch him. What if the spell is transmittable?"

"I won't touch him. What if he bites?" "I can't touch him. The priest told me not to touch . . ." All those in the room gave their own excuses.

"The woman who was here deciphering the boy's burps said that he had been a bad boy, that he had misbehaved, that he had been doing something forbidden," doña Catarina told the crowd. "Hot coffee. Hot coffee."

"See, that's what will happen to you if you keep on disobeying me," a young mother said to her six-year-old.

"Oh, really? Is that true? It must be true. What a terrible thing! That happens," the people around the body commented to each other while they drank coffee and sat waiting.

Candido walked through the crowd to the front row. Poor little thing. Look at him, he's all sweaty. He must be in pain, Candido thought. "God, if I could help this poor little creature, let me do it," he said in a low voice. He placed his hands together and began the prayer of Saint Francis of Assisi as he sat on the floor next to the boy. People watched him.

He decided to lay his hands on the boy. He felt like he was an instrument of peace and healing. If the boy had misbehaved and this was his parents' curse, love was needed. If there was injury in him, pardon would heal him. If the boy had doubted, he would have faith. If the boy was in despair, he would show him hope. And where Darkness and sadness were, Light and joy. Candido felt the need to console him, to understand him, to love him, to give him what he needed, to pardon him, if his parents didn't. Candido felt the authority to do these things.

Candido took his wide-brim hat and placed his hands on the boy. He felt the tiny drops of sweat on the palm of his hands, and the fever. The boy trembled. People around got closer to the body. Silence took over the room. People pushed each other trying to see the boy and Candido. Some stood on chairs to see better.

When the boy opened his eyes, wobbled a little bit, and sat up, stretching as if waking from a long sleep, people around gasped in unison. They began whispering to each other. "It's a miracle! A miracle happened! It's incredible!" They knelt down in front of Candido and the boy. They stood up and walked around looking at each other in awe. The boy went directly to the food that lay on the floor and then walked to the kitchen, where doña Catarina was heating up some tamales to sell. People were too afraid to ask questions, but they wondered if what they had just seen was mere coincidence or an act of God. They talked about writing a letter to the pope, telling him what had happened and asking him to beatify Candido. They went on saying that it was all those years of taking care of his mother that had made Candido eligible to perform miracles. They gathered around Candido and told him of their ailments. They said that it was the everlasting love of God trying to teach a lesson to the young people present in that room that had made the miracle happen. Some regretted not having touched the boy.

The young boys and girls who were there were elbowed by their parents who wanted to remind them that if they always obeyed them they might be able to perform miracles too.

"But where is Candido? We need to ask him more questions about the miracle. Where is Candido?" they asked. But Candido had left already. He was in a hurry to tell Margara that he was going to sneak in that night.

"He went home to give the medication to his mother," Omar said to the crowd.

Mambo Love Poem

Carlos y Rebecca dance across the floor.
They move in mambo cha-cha
that causes the sweat of their bodies to swirl
in a circle of tropical love.

Carlos y Rebecca move
and the room fills with blazes of red.
Flaming pianos breezing spicy tunes as coconuts fall
from palm trees ancient to these children.
As coconuts fall from imaginary palm trees
ancient to Borinquen souls.
Imaginary coconuts fall to the beat of their feet
in rhythm with the talking African drum.

Rebecca y Carlos glide across the floor,
and two become one in the land of salsa.
The sweat of their bodies mingles with flute
blowing high over splintered wooden floors,
in notes that soar beyond the rooftops of El Barrio.

They forget their pain in this land of joy,
as the clave answers the singing African conga,
the dancing African drum,
the conga quintiando
the African tongue.
Rebecca y Carlos become one
like two birds flying through the open sky,
in mambo cha-cha to celebrate their joy,
their feet no longer touching the ground.

They dance
becoming jíbaros in eagle wings.
As Shango—Cabio Sile—enters their bodies
their sweat fuses with light.
Like thunderbolts in a fiery desert,
great wings galloping in flight.
The light in their feet dancing the African beat
with the singing African drum,
the conga quintiando the African tongue.
Marking the warrior's rhythym with the singing dancing drum,
Shango—Cabio Sile—enters their bodies,
they flow magically into one.

Autobiography of a Nuyorican

for Lela

Half blue, feet first
she battled into the world.
Hardly surviving the blood cord twice wrapped,
tense around her neck. Hanging.
Womb pressing, pushing,
pulling life from mother's child.
Fragile Flesh emerging perfect in blueness,
like the lifeline that sustained her,
yet limp, almost a corpse.

Her mother claims the virgin interceded.
Invoked through divine promise, in prayer,
that caused her dark eyes to open,
her tongue to taste air like fire,

as the blueness faded,
tracing death on the tail of an eclipse.

And as in birth from her darkness,
the free-giving sun inched slow to visibility,
revealing all color and form,
a great teacher, generous and awesome,
silent and reverent, loud and blasphemous,
constant,
sculpting edges of definition
in the shadow and light of multiple universes.

Half blue, feet first
she battled her way.
The world did not want another brown,
another slant-eyed-olive-indian-black-child.
Did not want another rainbow empowered song
added to repertoire in blue,
or azure, or indigo,
or caribbean crystal.
Did not want another mouth to feed,
especially another rock-the-boat poet,
another voice opened wide,
fixed on a global spectrum of defiance.

The meaning of war defined her. Gasping and innocent,
before she knew her mother,
before she discovered herself, barely alive,
gathering weapons into her being with each breath that filled her,
growing stronger,
determined
to beat all the odds.

Malinche's Rights

Dicen que no tengo duelo, Llorona
porque no me ven llorar.
Hay muertos que no hacen ruido, Llorona
Y es mas grande su penar.

They say I can't feel pain, Llorona
because they don't see me cry.
The dead are silent, Llorona
and their grief is even greater.

—"LA LLORONA"

I'm not here to apologize. After so many years, even our language has changed. This is what is possible: you won't understand me; or, my words may still be clotted in my throat. But I can't lose heart. As my grandmother used to say: *nunca es tarde cuando la dicha es buena,* it's never too late to say something good. I've come to bring you prickly pears. Look at them. So fresh. So red. Their juice slides over the letters of your name. Your tombstone needed this touch of blood. Now your nickname, *el papacito,* is more visible.

Father, last night I dreamt you again. In the movie of the dream, the whole family was at a party, a *quinceañera* or a baptism, some kind of initiation. You were sitting at a table, dressed in tails, a white silk shirt, a bow tie. You were older than fifty-two. You looked like a grandfather with gray hair and two long furrows on either side of your forehead where your scalp shone like wax. You seemed to be sleeping.

At a table next to yours, my brother was watching you, a look of terror and sadness on his face. I approached your table. I squatted beside you, my chin on the tablecloth, and watched you like my brother. Suddenly your face moved. A kind of painful grimace, a jerk of your lips, a twitch of your eyes, and I jumped and yelled to my brother.

"I know," said my brother. "That's what I've been watching."

I turned and looked at you again, and again your body moved. Now you stretched like a cat after a long nap. I ran to tell everyone that you were alive, that you were moving, but nobody listened.

I returned to your table. On a couch directly in front of you, my sister was breast-feeding her newborn. Your eyes opened like wounds. You gazed for a while at my sister, then you said, "*Hija,* bring me something to eat!"

My sister ignored you as if she hadn't heard. I felt a great pain knowing you were hungry, you who never ate, who made faces at the steaming plates of food that my grandmother would prepare for you to tempt you away from the brandy.

Seeing that my sister didn't respond to your request, you got to your feet and asked for food again, but as soon as you took the first step, your legs collapsed and you fell to the floor. You got up and fell two more times. By the second fall, your body had decomposed. Your clothes had rotted and your flesh looked like raw meat marbled with worms. Your legs were twisted, your knees to the back, and you had no lips left, only those white false teeth.

Some time passed in the dream, but afterward we all returned to that place, which had become an airplane with blue seats. You were sitting at the back of the plane, and I remember clearly hearing you say how hungry you were, but nobody, nobody but me, was listening. I went to the back and said, "But you're dead."

"Yes," you said, "the bad part is dead, but the good part is alive and hungry."

I ran up and down the plane, yelling to my aunts and uncles what you had said, but it was as though I were speaking to the dead.

I decided to give you something to eat. I took you a carton of milk and some butter cookies wrapped in wax paper. I served you a tall glass of creamy milk. You asked me to join you. I thought to myself that the milk was going to curdle with all the mescal I'd had to drink the night before, but I served myself a glass anyway. When I peeled the paper off one of the cookies, I noticed that the cookie was a host.

Suddenly I wanted to stroke you. You seemed so innocent sitting there with your milk and cookies, like a boy playing at holy communion. I closed my eyes and stroked your face, my cheek against your cheek, but .when I opened my eyes I saw that I was stroking the carton of milk.

Then I heard your voice. You told me to ask everyone in the plane to write something about you or about this situation. I distributed pencils and paper to everyone, and I begged them to do as you said, but nobody wanted to write. We'll be arriving at our destination soon, they said, we don't have time to write. I insulted all of them. I could no longer tolerate their indifference.

"You've always treated him like this," I shouted. "And you still have the nerve to criticize me for not having gone to his funeral. You can all go to hell. I'm going to write. I don't care where we're going or when we're getting there. I won't get off this plane until I finish my letter."

The angle of the camera focused on the paper, and I could clearly make out the words that I was writing, my handwriting that of a nine-year-old not yet fluent in script. Strangely, the letter was in English.

> *Dear Dad,*
> *if you want to heal your body, you have to rest a lot and you should hold this crystal pyramid in your right hand so that its energy can go up your arm and heal your body.*

Dad, you wrote to me only twice. On my sixth birthday, you sent me a letter telling me not to cut my hair. To obey my grandmother. To use the one-dollar check you had enclosed for candy and chocolates. Twenty-one years passed before I received the postcard you sent me from Las Vegas. You promised that now that you knew my address you were going to write more often. I never saw your handwriting again.

My grandmother says you were very bitter about what I had chosen, that "abnormal life," she said, that life without a man. Before me, the one responsible for your cirrhosis was my mother for having left you. Then my brother and sister for treating you *como un cero a la izquierda,* like a fool. Then I had to carry the cross. I wonder, Dad, did you ever notice that blame didn't stick to you? It's as if you pollinated us with your blame.

Instead of attending your funeral, I escaped to Mexico, but even there the cold dust of your breath reached me.

In Teotihuacán, on the Avenue of the Dead, an Indian woman was selling crystal amulets in the shape of pyramids. One in particular spoke to me. It was a miniature temple of the sun, its four sides reflecting the green light of the afternoon. I held it in my right hand and felt a rainbow arching through my arm. I knew this amulet would protect me from you.

Then, in Guanajuato, in the museum of dead bodies mummified by the very stones of the graveyard, bodies with tongues and pubic hair, each one laid out in a glass casket as if to await the kiss of Prince Charming, I stroked the toes of a Chinese mummy. I didn't do it for you. It was not meant to honor your death.

Understand me. I didn't come to the funeral because I didn't want to see you inside a box, surrounded by artificial flowers and tears like some king of the screen. They say you looked very handsome, *Papacito,* as always. That you wore a white suit and that the coffin was made of a very fine wood. My mother told me that a *compadre* of yours had brought you a bouquet of gardenias.

"It was a habit of my *compadre*'s," said your *compadre,* "on the nights we boys went out, to buy a bunch of gardenias from a *viejita* who was always on the corner of la Lerdo and el Malecón."

In Oaxaca, on a night heavy with mescal, my lover and I were sitting at the edge of the plaza, surrounded by children selling Chiclets and flowers, baskets and shoeshines. We listened to "La Llorona" twice in a row, and then I bought gardenias from the smallest saleswoman in the world. That night you came to visit me, just as you used to visit me every time I followed in your footsteps and got drunk. But I cast you out. I opened my mouth over the toilet and let you go, a thick and bitter substance that stuck to the bowl like the *atole* of death. It wasn't until the next day that I realized it was the gardenias that had brought you. For that reason, I have never again bought gardenias.

I'm not here to apologize. When I was told that you'd had an embolism, I felt a great calm. The clot of words in my throat at last began to loosen, and at last I could let the blood of your memory run free. That's why I've come to bring you prickly pears, the sacred fruit of Huitzilipochtli.

When the white man of the hairy face came to Malinche's cell, she was praying to Coatlicue, goddess of death. A man in a black dress and a white collar accompanied the bearded one. He was a man of her own blood, the same bronze face, slave's hands, traitor's eyes.

"What do you want?" Malintzin said to the traitor.

He spoke two languages, just as she did, and they had one in common.

"This man wants to know if you are the interpreter."

She looked at the bearded one. He had hair climbing up his arms, and his legs looked scrawny as a chicken's. The symbol of the new god hung over his groin.

She didn't mince words. "Yes, I'm the interpreter. But I'm busy."

The traitor translated her reply. The bearded one tossed his head back and a wild laugh came out of his mouth. His tongue was a pink snake coiled between his teeth. When he looked at her again, sparks of blood flew from his eyes. He held out his hand to her and said something that the traitor didn't bother translating.

"I'm busy," Malintzin repeated. "I'm praying."

Hearing the tone of her voice, the bearded one pulled his hand back. He exchanged words with the traitor, and then the traitor said:

"This man wants to know, where are your rosary and your crucifix? He says you can't pray without these things. He says you're a sinner, and he has come to save you."

Malintzin began to feel dizzy. An attack of words was coming on, strange words, words that she didn't know, secret words of the goddesses. She didn't want the stranger to hear her chant. That would be a real sin. Her stomach convulsed, and she shot a stream of bitter liquid at the feet of the bearded one. The first syllables were rising. She had to escape. She had to run. Those words could not be heard by any man, white or raza. She vomited again and a chameleon shot out. The bearded one jumped back, shouting in his strange tongue to the traitor. The chameleon grew and grew, a rattle shaking in its mouth, rattling in the bearded one's face.

"In the name of the Father, and of the Son, and of the Holy Spirit," intoned the traitor, casting on Malintzin drops of acid from a flask he carried.

Little by little the nausea stopped. The effort had exhausted her, but at least she had managed to save the words. She could barely breathe. Her body trembled, and the sweat that dripped from the hair under her arms burned her like the traitor's acid.

She felt something fresh against her lips. The bearded one had brought her the water jar. She looked at him for a moment before drinking, then, with hands of paper, with the bearded one's help, she lifted the jar and let the water of the well wash her inside and out. The bearded one seemed to know what she wanted, for he lifted the jar to let the water flow through her hair and down her forehead. He said something to the traitor and the traitor translated:

"He says that you are baptized now. Tomorrow he will come to take you to matins."

Malinche did not respond. She only moved her head up and down. In her temples she could hear a cacophony of rattles.

That night, Malinche prepared herself well. With the help of Coatlicue and Tonantzin, she rubbed the walls of her sex with the thorny skin of some prickly pears. She left the skins inside, and the red juice of the fruit spilled down her legs. Afterward, she decorated her hair with peacock plumes and then lay down on her *petate*.

The bearded one arrived with the first rooster's crow. Upon seeing that the woman bled, he felt his milk boil and he barely had time to pull down his hose. When he found himself inside that swollen space, that nest of thorns where his member had gotten trapped like a snake, his screams bubbled with his seed.

Never had doña Marina felt so much in control of her own destiny.

Do you remember, Father, the time you came home at dawn and tried to force my mother? I was three years old. I slept on a cot at the foot of your bed. It scared me when you spit that word at her: *Cabrona!* And later you tucked me in.

What about the time I saw you urinating through the bathroom window? You knew I was there. You even played with your *pirulí*.

I confess. One night in my grandmother's house I heard you panting, the same sound my boyfriend used to make when I masturbated him in the car.

When the bearded one poked at the skirts of la Malinche, she already knew what to expect. Her father, the chief of the Tabascans, had explained it to her the night before Moctezuma's tax collectors came to collect her. What happened with the bearded one was nothing more than another tribute to another conquistador. One hairless and heathen, the other bearded and baptized in the faith.

My grandmother always accused me of being a heathen. She used to say I was going to cook in hell because I never prayed the rosary and because I chewed on the host without having gone to confession. What she didn't know is that you, our father who art in heaven, took me to the matinee every Saturday and lifted my skirt and fed me our daily bread.

Unlike you, my boyfriend was a gringo and had a beard, but he also liked doing it at the movies. What happened with that bearded one was nothing more than another tribute to another conquistador.

And now, enough of all this homage. These prickly pears are the rights that you violated, the secret words I had to swallow.

I'm soaked to the marrow. A downpour has just flooded the desert. The rain has washed away the blood of the cactus that painted your name. Your stone is clean now. EL PAPACITO fresh as the cemetery grass. The rattles I hear are my own teeth.

Sonnets of Dark Love

IV

your hands are two hammers that joyfully
nail down and pry up the morning,
tender fists that unfold from earth,
sweet bunches of small bananas

your hands smell of the blackberries
you harvest in the fields that steal
your sweat at two dollars a bucket,
they are hard, warm, young and wise

hoes that bring bread to the tables,
dark stones that give light when struck,
pleasure, support, anchor of the world

I worship them as reliquaries
because like nesting sea gulls,
they console, delight, defend me

VI

asleep you become a continent—
long, mysterious, undiscovered,
the mountain ranges of your legs
encircle valleys and ravines

night slips past your eyelids,
your breath the swaying of the sea,
you stretch out so tenderly on the bed
like a dolphin beached on a shore

your mouth the mouth of a resting volcano,
o fragrant timber, what fire burns you?
you are so near, and yet so far

as you doze like a lily at my side,
I undo myself and invoke the moon:
now I am this dog watching over your sleep

VIII

you gave me a basket of apples
sweet as the sweetness of your gaze,
as I bit them, they began to complain
about the sacks your back has handled,

and the ladders you've climbed
trying to pick the most beautiful—
those shining on the highest branches
of the apple trees at Summer's end

the apples are like your songs:
filled with water, morning, and sun,
cool as the laughter in your throat

juicy, fragrant, pissed, they clamor:
"we belong to those sweating foreheads,
those hands that picked and gathered us"

XI

since I met you on the road,
I am no longer the same, a blind man
no more, tripping on his own shadow,
I am no longer deaf to landscapes

to follow you swiftly I've tossed aside
my cross, rid myself of those violins
always playing soap opera tunes,
I no longer walk, I run barefoot

ever since I heard the rumor of your voice,
all other words ring hollow to me—
useless, cumbersome, bewitching

this is why I no longer want to write poems
but live them with you: embers
blazing in a fire outside language

DIONISIO MARTINEZ

Across These Landscapes of Early Darkness

He is learning to play the elegant songs
again. By ear. By heart. He is picking

up a signal from America, a faint humming,
a plea. He doesn't understand it. The elegant

music will suffice for the moment. This
time he will listen for the diesels slicing

the fog as they come up each morning,
their headlights leaving trails like a

photograph's version of life. There is elegance
in this, too. But there is more. A sense

of decorum as motif for a whole generation.
He is learning to live in style again. Here's

the suit for the nights when all
the stars are out and closer than usual

and some tradition says that you must count them.
Here's the pale shirt with no purpose.

Here are all the pointed shoes, all
the hats, the ties with the wrong patterns.

It is no one else's style. This makes it
more solid somehow, more durable. This

makes him happy. He hasn't laughed this
hard in years. He is picking up signals from

countries where the last transmission
took place light years ago. This is how

he learns about light years and how time
equals distance and distance is a kind

of salvation. He wants to come to America,
home of the faint signal, land of stolen

elegance. By now he has caught on
to the way we package someone else's tradition,

the way we price each package. These days
he is in the market for a new tradition.

It is all so obvious—the way we manufacture
our legacies. We are not the best of

thieves. Our music is always holding something
back, always looking for its source. He is

willing—at last—to take us as we are.
He runs to catch up, but by the time he manages

to get his hands on the essence of a song,
the song itself is light years from his hands.

Cole Porter

Tell them something you can live with.

The world is a hyperbole of grief.

Say *Grief* and give them magic.
Your sleight of hand
is all they need to understand that magic
is its own hyperbole,
that the world they've been banking on
is going out of business—*Sale
of the Century* across each window,

the mannequins half stripped, the windows
half empty. You at the door, handing
out coupons for anything. You

at the door, talking the language
of the restless. Because it sounds good.
Or because there's always a market
for love in an age of discontent.

Let them bank on that.

Rob them clean. Sell them back
their own dreams and live on the profit.
Say *Bargain*. Say *Your money
or your heart*.

Pavane for Daddy Longlegs

Because they know that by this time tomorrow
Daddy Longlegs will be just another dead
man on the evening news, all the men in the world
are buying second-hand top hats and giving
their black shoes the necessary spit and polish
to tap down their streets. Each man
has a street of his own, a small stage
that doesn't end. Because it is the longest
day of the year, men in overalls will have
more time to change all the neon signs
in North America. By nightfall a single name
will flash outside every theater and hotel,
outside every soda shop. A single name
will light our lives for a moment. Even our very
lives will be called The Ritz. Or that part
of our lives that we carry like the last

vacancy of the off-season, the room
that remains empty and smells empty forever.
And now, because the future is common knowledge,
every man leaves a light at the window
and steps out to his own street and hears
music and holds his top hat at an angle
over his head. The lit windows
give certain neighborhoods the sense
of belonging elsewhere, like a Hopper seen
from a good distance. Daddy's framed
and clinging to this scenery.
He calls Irving Berlin and says:
Write me a song—half dirge, half pavane.
Tell Liza she can tap on the lid of my casket.
By now nearly every man in the world
has found a hat and a cane and half a reason
to meet another man who knows yet another man
who wants to tap his way through the night.
Even the longest day has a night. Even
my friend who almost killed Daddy Longlegs
is tapping his way out of his new house.
One afternoon my friend was driving
through Hollywood. Daddy Longlegs was crossing
the street, dreaming of Judy Garland and how
things might have been had she danced
with him from the beginning. My friend stopped just
in time. And Daddy Longlegs, apologizing in
silence in front of the car, tipped
his imaginary top hat and moved on.
My friend has rented a room in a mostly vacant
hotel by the sea. His wife is sleeping. He
turns away from her and goes to the window.
He leans on the sill and imagines a thousand
men passing by with top hats and tuxedos
and a smooth walk that leaves no trail.
Then he stares at the Pacific Ocean.
And he knows how little it takes to make a murderer.
His wife wakes up. A year goes by.
Daddy has forgotten my friend. Irving
Berlin has forgotten his own words.

Liza is beginning to get used
to the idea of a dead man tapping her
on the shoulder and saying: *Dance for me*.
All the rented tuxedos are walking
back to the shops on their own.
All the men in the world are returning
to their lit windows and their families.
All the neon is going out.
All the lights in the world are going out.
With the new day and the new light
we realize that the Hopper in the museum
was not a Hopper after all,
that no distance is ever safe and no house
is completely empty at dusk and nothing
is ever the same in the morning.
At first every man imagined that his legs
were long and thin, his movements flawless.
As the night ran out of room for these ideas,
the men began to believe in common
things like houses and pain,
and they invented simple explanations
for the dullness and the scratches on their
black shoes. But the next morning,
pretending to be waking up, they all
turn on their television sets to find
that the screens have turned black and
white and the sound is vintage Berlin.
And even weathermen cannot help themselves:
they start to tap out the forecasts: a heat
wave here, rain everywhere. Tap tap.
And all these men who have never believed
in anything begin to dress for another day of work.
And it begins to rain in the suburbs when
there seems to be nothing left but a song and
a prayer. And each man turns out the light he
has left on all night, and runs out saying half
to himself, half to no one in particular:
God bless the rain that rots my dancing shoes.

Maya

From *Dream*

The darkness is filled with whispers, as though a million secrets are being told at the same time. A deep humming begins all around me. A powerful sound. Like the end of the world. Or the beginning of the world.

A small, feeble glow makes me squint to the horizon, or what I think is the horizon. A line of black. It feels like the edge of the universe.

I begin to sweat with terror. I stand absolutely still. There's nothing I can do but stare into the feeble, glowing light as it rises, so slowly. So slowly. Each second, a million, million years.

Is it the end?

Is it death?

Or is it the sun? Rising.

I don't know, but I can't look away, I can't look away, I can't . . .

Maya's eyes flew open and searched her surroundings. Zorba lay, sprawled, to her left. The candle, to her right, flickered through the clear white candle holder. She got to her elbows and acknowledged herself in the wall mirror, through the broad green leaves that stretched themselves to hear her name in the silent, dark, empty air.

"Maya," she murmured, without knowing why. The small alarm clock said 3:48 A.M. She felt tempted to say his name, Zorba, out loud, but she didn't want to wake him. She wanted him to sleep. To remember her body, her hands, her mouth, her eyes. She wanted him to remember nothing else. She wanted him to forget everything she'd told him.

Today was the day. She'd told him everything but that. The truth. That she'd killed. Her father. Dead. That day. That night, Maya remembered, when the sun was farthest from the Earth. Solstice. Lara calls it Solstice. Mama says She walks to the horizon and back, and then She's new. She. The Virgin, Mother of God, Changing Woman. She who brings the new sun, Mama would say. And then, in the summer,

She who brings the new fire. In spring, She who brings birth, and in fall, She who brings death. Maya sighed, hearing her mother's voice, so clearly, in the silence.

"She who brings death," she whispered. And then she made herself say the impossible. The miracle that was possible today. "She who brings the new sun." Barely audible, but said.

Maya was grateful that no part of her body was touching Zorba's as she slid out of bed. She paused to watch his eyelids flicker with dreams. Irrationally, she wanted to enter his dreams. She envied them because he was there without her. She wanted to see them. She wanted to make love to him in his dreams. To make him remember her, so vividly, there, where there is no death. She savored her envy, mixed sharply with desire, as she dressed.

Lara's door was open, so that meant she was sleeping in X. J.'s room. Good, Maya thought, that means they're exhausted and will sleep in late, giving me a little time to get out before I have to talk to anyone, don't feel like it today, shit, today . . .

It was still dark outside as the faraway sun decided Earth's tiny fate, its billions of people clamoring for light and warmth. The sun. Would it rise? Again. Rise.

Instead of making coffee, which might wake them, Maya made a cup of tea. "The smell of coffee would wake the dead," she heard her mother say. It made her smile as a desolate stab of loneliness invaded her. She felt Zorba's thick, warm sperm seep out of her body, onto her panties, and it made her even lonelier (if that were possible). Usually she'd run to the bathroom to wipe herself clean, while feeling a slight revulsion at someone else's body fluids mingled with hers, *coming out of her body*. But not today. Today she mourned Zorba's sperm obeying the laws of gravity, leaving her body, forever.

Maya stood absolutely still, looking out the small kitchen window over the sink. She looked, hard, into the dark sky, feeling the warm sperm become cold and sticky, congealing onto her thighs.

"The law of gravity. The laws," Maya murmured to the reluctant sun. "The natural laws . . ." A bird began to sing, loudly, fully, making her pause. ". . . of everything."

She remembered the still, quiet, unnatural mornings after her mother had been beaten. A feeling, worse than a funeral (there was never a body, only the dark bruises on the body; the swollen, living face ashamed of itself; the dead weren't ashamed; only the living were ashamed, and the witnesses), much worse than a funeral, invaded the small, isolated house surrounded by desert. He'd chosen it for privacy. He'd chosen it so only his children could witness the shame. He'd chosen it to have no witnesses (they were his and didn't count in any hierarchy of importance; they didn't count at all).

She remembered Jim kneeling by her bed, shaking her gently but urgently, fastening his eyes on hers, silently commanding her, *Don't make a sound*. (Not that Jim would've woken up on those mornings, filled with alcohol, swimming in alcohol; he slept, dreamless, till past noon. And when he woke, his father's fists were on him, muttering, "Lazy fuckin chink bastard . . ." His mother cooked his father's breakfast. The fragrant, luxurious scents from the kitchen were never for him. As Luna Dulce—with a swollen, bruised face—fried the bacon, potatoes, eggs, made the coffee, strong, it was never for him. He was, forever, excluded from his own table, from his own food.)

She remembered the dark, cool desert air as they walked, quickly, from the house of their mother, their father. She and her brother always walked slightly apart, not touching, Jim walking a little ahead, she trying to keep up with him. When they could no longer see the house, Jim would slow his pace and ask, "Are you hungry, Maya?" "I'm starving. What did you bring?" "Oh, this and that, a surprise. You'll see." And he'd laugh as if they were going on a picnic rather than a journey through the dark to see if the sun would rise. Again.

They would get to Jim's favorite place, where the stones were; he used to say there was nothing more patient than stone and she would ask him how he knew and he would answer, "Mom says so and, besides, look at this." And she would look, seeing the feathery white lines and spirals of an ancient sea. Then she would sit, at peace, against the stones, waiting for her brother's shoulders to unhunch, for his face to unfrown —waiting for him to sit next to her on the cold hard ground. Then, together, they would wait for the miracle. The sun. To rise. Out of the dark. Again.

She remembered that almost always, as the pulse of unearthly light cracked itself like an egg on the far horizon, an immense black raven would perch on a giant saguaro and *caw caw caw*, with such authority, as though he were the messenger of the night allowing the sun to rise. To rise. Out of the dark. The miracle. Again.

Then they would eat.

Maya walked to the phone and dialed Jim's number, fighting the urge to hang up while she still had time. It rang six times.

"Yes?" It was Jim's voice thick with sleep.

"Jim, it's me, Maya, hey, I'm sorry to wake you up . . ."

"No, no." He yawned. "I expected you to call, you know, today, but I guess not at this hour." He laughed softly. "It's just a little after dawn, sis."

"Do you remember when we used to get up before dawn, after the bloodshed, and go out to the rocks and wait for the sun to rise?"

Jim sighed. "I sure as the hell do."

"I guess that's what I'm doing right now, you know?"

"Okay." His voice was gentle. "Is it still dark over there?"

"Yeah, it's still dark."

"Okay."

"I've got to ask you something."

"Sure, go ahead, sis."

"I've got to know—where, and how deep, did you bury him?"

"You know the stones?"

"Not there! Why there?"

"I guess—" Jim paused (she could hear him breathing, trying to find the right words). "I guess I thought if the ocean could forget the desert, you know, like the shells in the stones? I thought, like, maybe we could forget about him, shit . . ."

Maya's eyes filled with tears. "You're almost always right, Jim, I guess you did the right thing."

There was a long silence, and as Maya was about to tell Jim she could see a hint of light in the dark sky, he said, "I buried him at least five feet and covered it with rocks, very secure, so don't worry, Maya . . ."

"Here's the sun, I mean, I can't see it, just its light. Thanks for doing it . . ." Tears choked her voice. ". . . for me."

"Shit, you know you stopped him for me. I should've been there and done it my own damned self . . ."

"The sun is coming up, Jim, it's coming up, we did it, together, you know I love you." She felt like sobbing, like falling into her brother's arms through the phone wire, the invisible distance between them; to sob and sob until she was through. Instead, she caught herself, firmly, and asked, "How's the little guy, your very own son?"

"Oh, shit, Maya, he's so damned beautiful and new . . ."

The sun's light was thin and bright, pulsing in the clear, crisp sky. Sitting inside the warm restaurant, letting the sun hit her back, Maya imagined spring, then summer. She'd chosen a place Zorba and she never went to, in case he tried to find her. I should've written him a note, she thought, to make it seem okay that I left before he woke up, I never do that, leave like that. Maya sipped her coffee. Idiot, a few minutes, a few more lies, and he wouldn't worry. Now he might try to find me, he knows I'm not working today, I told him almost everything, but this, the truth, and I know he senses there's more, the way he looks at me, and when he asked me to meet his father I almost panicked with anxiety, *no fucking way,* no thanks, enough fatherly shit for a lifetime, all I need is *his* fucked-up father giving me any shit, no fucking thanks, I'll pass on that.

Maya turned to scan the street, dreading to see the man she loved, only she didn't know or, more accurately, accept the fact that she loved him. He made it so easy, and she was unconsciously, and wisely, afraid of the time he wouldn't make it so easy. The time she would admit to her love. All of her instincts held her back, when most women would joyfully gush forth their love, when most women would parade their love, when most women would wear their love like the first flower of spring; she stood on the scorching desert sand, saying to the man she loved: Be careful, it's noon, and the sun has no mercy at noon, and you have no water and know nothing of getting water in this place—you know nothing of the shade, of the small caves that I know, of the rattlers that slide, noiselessly—they don't scare me, but you know nothing of them, be careful—the sun, here, is deadly.

Trust, the word echoed behind her eyes as she looked for Zorba's face, his body, among strangers. Do I trust strangers more? she asked herself. They don't want anything from me, of course, but then, they don't give me anything. Why does it all come down to trust? What else is there? she answered herself, turning away from the window.

As Maya ate her scrambled eggs and potatoes, she took out the poem she'd typed up for her mother. Luna Dulce had bought the old, sturdy typewriter second hand for her junior year ("So your poems look nice and neat," she'd said rather sternly, but with obvious pleasure). It was manual and never gave her any trouble. She used a ribbon over and over, until she decided her words were becoming too faint and ghostly. She unfolded the poem and read it through once more.

Girlchild

Twilight. I walk by myself,
my feet in the cool, womb
water. She beckons me, but

I'm not that brave yet,
not at night. Purples, reds,
dark streaks, to the west, and

behind me darkness. No moon tonight.
New moon, tomorrow the crescent.
My mother taught me all this, and more,

in the desert air. At the end of the beach,
on some rocks, is a girlchild who asks,
"Do you know how spiders make the webs and everything?"

I say, "They pull the silky threads from their bodies and
then they weave the web." The girlchild laughs,
leaning over the spider's web. These are my childhood

mysteries. The delicate web spun from the dark.
I remembered them, answering a laughing
girlchild.

For you, Mama

Maya

She thought of what she was about to do: go to Zorba's sailboat, get his kayak, and paddle to the horizon. She wondered, idly, as though it had nothing to do with her, how long it would take to paddle to the horizon. Though, rationally, she knew better; she knew that the horizon would recede from her the closer she got; she also knew she would reach it. Only she didn't know if she could return. Maybe I'll die, she thought calmly. I wonder if Zorba will be pissed if the kayak is lost, that I took it without his permission, that I couldn't be trusted. This made her smile. I never told him he should trust me. If anything, I've repeatedly warned him about the dangers of trusting me, like a game, sure, but also in a serious way, and then he gets uncomfortable. Now he'll know he couldn't trust me, but maybe, today, I'll know if I can trust myself, maybe.

Maya stared at her name at the bottom of her poem: *Maya*. It seemed so alone, surrounded by emptiness, and she remembered what Jim had said about the ocean being able to forget the desert (the ancient traces of the ghostly shells in the stones, surrounded by the dry, indifferent desert sand). She wondered if the desert remembered the ocean. It must, she told herself—the shells. But does it care? Does it miss the ocean? Her thoughts came to an end. She received no answer in her body, in her mind. And if the ocean forgot the desert, Maya persisted, if the ocean forgot the desert . . .

Beside her typed-out name, "Maya," she wrote in "Mar" and added a short note to her mother: "My new last name, a kind of beginning. I know you'll like it. I'm serious. This is to be my new name. Don't forget. Never, ever, call me Thompson again, the name of the Barbarian. You should change your name too, Mama. Love you. Tu *Maya Mar.*"

She pinched off the head of a perfect white daisy, grouped in a small vase in front of her, and placed it in the poem, folded it, and slipped it into the envelope. She sealed it, carefully. I'll mail it, then start for the fucking horizon. Don't ever forget my name, Mama.

Luna Dulce sat by the fireplace, staring into the small, intense wood fire. She resisted the urge to add one more small piece and decided to let it burn down to glowing embers. She liked this stage of the fire, when it became a disintegrating structure of untouchable heat. She liked to rest her eyes on it and try to see the future; a hint of its naked intent as the wood was devoured and transformed into the purity of its flame. The moment, maybe a second, when the structure revealed itself to a patient eye.

Didn't I see his death? Didn't I believe it was I who would do it? Didn't I buy the gun, thinking I'd do it when he went too far? Luna Dulce sighed, harshly, with remorse and impatience for her failure; but her eyes stayed gazing on the dying fire. I should've slept with it, loaded and ready. I should've been prepared, yes, I should've known that to *see* isn't enough. Then, you stupid old fool, you must *do,* or your children will carry your sins, your destiny.

"Maya, *hija,*" she murmured. "Maya, *hija.*" *Tu hermano* tells me, she continued silently, that you called, that you were alone with your fear. He told me what you did as children, I never knew. Why did I stay? For you, for Jim, for him . . . for me? There are so many things I never told you or Jim, so many, many things.

The fire collapsed and shifted. She gazed, without staring, waiting to see a hint of things to come. Nothing. The fire had a life of its own, yes, but nothing.

I worked as a cleaning girl after *mi mamá y mi hermanito* were killed in the crossing, drowned in the fast, swollen spring river, *mi mamá* letting me go, to live. The men saved me and sold me to her, that woman with the sharp eyes of the dead, with her blond wig that fought with the darkness of her skin—but before she paid them, she made sure I was untouched, a virgin. And I cleaned, I cleaned, everything, in a whore-house, a house of whores, girls a little older than me, and then women old enough to be our mothers. I was thirteen, and one day a fat, stinking drunk offered the woman with dead eyes so much money, so much money, they made me, and they made me again and again. And that's how I met your father. You see, he paid for me, *Madre de Dios,* and I had no one else but him when he took me away at fifteen, and I was grateful, yes, I was grateful.

Luna Dulce didn't allow herself to weep. She would grieve without tears. It would be her penance. Tears were for the pure and the innocent. You don't deserve your tears, the voice inside her mind whipped her, you stupid old fool. You were always afraid to be alone with your fear and so your Maya must do it. . . . She thought of her dream last night—Maya, alone, on the ocean. I try to call her back, I scream to her to come back, but she doesn't hear me. She doesn't look back. Not once.

I'll go to Jim's tonight. I can't stay here. I have no courage, and so *mi hija* must have the courage for two of us. For all of us.

The fire shifted and fell, flat, as though trying to extinguish itself, but instead the flames rose higher with new energy. For an instant, the fire became the sea and Maya was alive in it—a small boat, with her hair on fire, facing away from her. "You'll live, mi Maya, you'll live. You have my mother's courage, the courage of one thousand women, and I know you'll live." She said this in a clear, loud voice, so that the spirits would hear her, as well as Maya's soul, so far away, alone, on the Mother Ocean.

Luna Dulce reached for a small, perfect piece of wood and placed it on the collapsed fire's center. "*Para la Mujer de Cambio. Mujer de sol y luna,*" she found herself saying. "*Para la Virgen, sin ningún Dios, que no necesita hombre para vivir, que se hace nueva otra vez.*" (To Changing Woman. Woman of sun and moon. To the Virgin, without even God, who needs no man to live, who makes herself new once again.) And then she remembered the Indian women, how they sometimes felt like dying from the shame of selling themselves, and they'd leave, early in the day, before dawn, not returning till nightfall. Once she'd dared to ask where one of them had been, and the young woman had told her, "To the horizon and back, and now I'm new." "Why?" Luna Dulce had persisted in spite of herself. The young woman had looked at her and laughed. "When Chang-ing Woman is old and tired and used up by life, she leaves everything and walks to the horizon, and when she returns she's a young virgin girl with new life." "Is she like God?" Luna Dulce had blurted out. "Yes, that's it." The young woman had laughed even louder. "She's like God, but she's a woman, and so she doesn't need him or any man. Run me a bath, girl, I'm not working tonight."

Luna Dulce stood up and walked to her back door. She opened it and was blinded by the glaring late-morning light of the desert that came from the sky, after the soft light of the knowing fire that came from the Earth. She closed her eyes and greeted the dark. Then she opened them and, squinting, she skimmed the horizon.

"I've never walked to the horizon." The sound of her own voice, alone, in the desert silence, was suddenly unbearable.

In the house the parrot let loose with a string of words and then tired of it, becoming quiet, and inched down toward her seed. She began to eat, slowly and deliberately, fluttering her wings from time to time as though trying to remember flight.

I know it's Maya. She's so small and far away. "Come back! Don't leave! Come back!" I yell. She doesn't turn. She's leaving me. She's becoming smaller. Smaller.

"Damn it," Zorba muttered as he opened his eyes. Maya was gone. He jumped to his feet and looked for a note on his bedside table. Nothing. The kitchen table. Nothing. He checked every room. Nothing. The feeling of the dream clutched him, but he couldn't remember any of the details. Loss was the tone. It rose and fell between his abdomen and his throat as though his body knew the meaning of loss better than he did. The loss of his mother, the loss of his wife, the loss of the others, the loss of love. Then, anger began to burn in his belly. You can't count on a fucking thing, he told himself. You can't make anyone stay, even if you give them everything. Did I give Maya everything? Did I really want to? "I sure did, I gave her her freedom." His anger mounted. He couldn't remember ever being this angry (I gave her her freedom—the words repeated in his head like a monotonous song, making him feel angrier, a little more robbed, each time he got to the word *freedom*).

Zorba picked up the phone, began to dial, and slammed it down. "I'll only get the fucking machine." Quickly, he dressed and sprinted to his car.

"I don't know if she came home. I mean, I thought she was at your place, though she might've come in and left before we got up." Lara could see the anger flickering in Zorba's eyes, his tense jaw, his teeth that wanted to clamp down on the object of his anger, bite it in two, and swallow it. "Do you want some breakfast, some coffee?"

"Yeah, man, plenty here. Hotcakes, ham." X. J. flipped a large round hotcake in an expert way. "Here, my man, this baby's for you. You sure as shit look like you need it." X. J. laughed, gently, as though to imply, we're all in the same damned boat.

Zorba poured himself some coffee and sat down. "It looks like I blew it on the be-in-charge shit. I just can't handle it. I'm not up to it. Like I know something's going on with Maya and she just won't crack."

"I know what you mean," Lara said, sipping her coffee. "I think it has to do with her family, she's pretty touchy about that, like she never talks about it."

"Well, so am I." X. J. rose to Maya's defense, instinctively. "There are things about my family I'll probably never tell you or anyone else. It's my own damned business. I'm not ashamed of it anymore, but I sure ain't proud of the shit." X. J. served Zorba the steaming hotcake, pushing a small pitcher of warm syrup toward him. "Eat."

"Are you sure she's not working?" Lara glared at X. J.

"No, she's off. I was going to surprise her with a coastal sail. I even ordered a lunch. I guess I should cancel it." Zorba took a bite of the pancake. "This is delicious. Hey, do you two want to go? You know how to sail, don't you, Lara?"

"Yeah, well, don't look at me, man, I ain't sailed in nothin bigger'n a tub."

"Oh, give me a break. Didn't you cross on some ferries in Europe and Greece?" Lara hated it when he made himself look simple. Simpler than he naturally was, which she loved. No, what she hated was when he played down his natural intelligence.

"Yeah, but those were big floatin things that *don't* sink because the wind's in a bad mood."

Zorba finally laughed. "Can I have another one of those? I didn't know I was this hungry. Where'd you learn to cook like this?"

"One of my down-and-dirty family secrets, like survival, and then I like to eat." X. J. flipped a hot fresh one onto Zorba's plate. "We're feedin you first, Mr. Z., so you don't make us walk the plank or nothin, like I ain't real smooth in no water."

"Oh, shit, X. J., you can wear a fucking life jacket and sit in the cabin and sip a beer. You don't have to do anything topside and I can help Zorba with the sailing. Come on, let's go . . ."

"Okay, okay, I'll be the cabin boy and butter the crumpets or whatever it is you all eat."

Lara's face flushed hot. "Will you *please* stop?"

"See, Zorba, man, I didn't even sign no be-in-charge papers and you can see what's what." X. J. flashed a wide white smile of pure mischief. "Yeah, sure, I'll come, but, believe me, the only thing I'll do is pop the beer open."

"Good enough, you're on." Suddenly Zorba wanted to see Maya's face, her hard and piercing eyes, so intensely that the sweet, delicious hotcakes in his stomach felt like cold cement.

Maya waved at Phil and thought, of course, someone's going to see me. "Oh, shit," she hissed, struggling with the kayak. She turned her back to Phil. Don't come, don't come, don't come, she chanted silently. Then she had it up and over and floating in the water, tied to the dock. She tugged on her life jacket. It felt secure.

"Are you going out by yourself?" Phil yelled.

"Yeah, but just a little bit toward Twin Lakes and back."

"Be careful, now." Phil smiled and waved.

Maya eased into the kayak as though it were made of glass, terrified of falling into the water right at the very beginning. As she connected to the scooped-out plastic seat, tilting a little crazily, back and forth, she let go of her held breath, sharply, with relief. And fear: *Here it is,* me and the fucking boat, this one measly oar, the big fucking ocean and the so-called horizon.

"What in the fuck am I doing?" she murmured. "I'm not Changing Woman. I don't even know if I'm Maya Mar. What do I know?" She dipped the right paddle into the water, then the left, right, left, the way Zorba had taught her, and she began to move, cleanly and soundlessly, through the gentle waves. Her visor kept the sun out of her eyes, and her yellow-tinted sunglasses made it look as though she were traveling through a movie of a woman in a kayak who was heading out to sea.

At the mouth of the harbor, however, the ocean opened wide, yawning, straight out to the horizon, and it woke her up, making her fully present. The horizon. There it was, stretched out to forever. "Changing Woman, my ass, more like Stupid Woman, but here I fucking go, I can't stand it anymore." . . . you in my head, she continued internally. The words seemed to be coming from her stomach rather than her head, yet when the words reached her head it translated everything into familiar language: I can't stand you in my eyes, in my brain, in my body, in my dreams, if you don't leave, "Father," she whispered, I'll go totally insane, I'm not strong enough for this, I'm just not strong enough for this, to carry you around for the rest of my life, *I can't stand it, why did you make me do it, why didn't you give me any choice, I know you wanted to die . . .* ". . . you bastard."

The water was fairly smooth and the swells in the distance were rounded and almost gentle. The paddle seemed to dip, rhythmically, of its own volition. Her body was in control—her hands, her arms, her legs, her back. Her mind was secondary. It limped along, hoping the body knew what it was doing. She cleared the swells, paddling furiously, yet it felt like such a minimal effort. "If everything were this easy." She grimaced at the sound of her voice. "Maybe the easiest thing is dying." . . . and someone doing it for you, the easiest way out. Make them responsible. Make them cook and serve the feast and then don't eat it. Tears ran down Maya's face. She saw him, again, throwing her mother up against the wall, choking her with one hand, covering her mouth with the other. She heard her mother struggling to breathe. She saw herself do it. Again. She killed him again. Her father. The man who should've been her father. Who lent his seed to her body. Who hated her body. Who hated her. Her body. Who hated.

"Did I hate you, Father?"

Maya fastened her eyes on the horizon, that mirage of the end. Limit. Still point. That long, dark line—shifting, receding, approaching—that stretched, left to right, endlessly, as she paddled left, right, left, right, toward the center. The water between her and it was alive with light and movement, and her arms were full of energy.

"Do I hate you, Father?"

The horizon pulled her whole body toward it, but mostly it pulled from her heart. It fastened onto her heart and wouldn't let go, but then, she didn't want it to let go. She wanted it to pull her and pull her until her heart broke open. Until her heart broke open with its own truth. Until her heart broke open with its own mute, and hidden, truth.

"Well, I'm sure glad I came," X. J. laughed, loading the food into the cabin. "And this nice padded seat here, this is mine for the day. I'll just watch you two break your asses, if that's all right with both a you."

"I'd watch the food, like do you get seasick?" Lara's voice was cheerful with the anticipation of sailing. She never got seasick.

"I'm eatin, no matter what this ocean decides, woman." X. J. drank Lara in with his eyes. He loved the strength of her legs, exposed in multicolored leggings, under black short shorts. The bulky white sweater hid her body, but he knew it by heart. His breath quickened. His groin softened with spread fire as his penis hardened, and he reminded himself, You are just a freedom phase, black boy.

Zorba jumped into the sailboat. His body was rigid and his face was distorted with anxiety. "Listen, I just talked to a friend of mine, and he tells me Maya took the kayak out about an hour ago. Like I thought someone stole the damned thing, but, no, she's out in it, somewhere . . ."

"You're kidding!" Lara gasped. "No, you're not kidding. Do you think she's okay out there?"

"No, she shouldn't be out there by herself. What in the *hell* is she thinking of, Lara? What do you think she's fucking doing out there *by herself*? Any ideas?" Zorba started the motor.

"Something heavy, man." X. J. put his hand on Zorba's shoulder. "Maya's no whiner, you know that. There's something pretty damned heavy happening to that beautiful woman, Zorba."

"She is beautiful, isn't she? Like not so much her face, but how she comes together . . ." Tears sprang to Zorba's eyes.

"Well, go and find her. I've got to go to the padded seat, I ain't no pirate. I'll keep an eye out with the binoculars."

"No, hand them to me."

"You've got it."

Maya looked back. The city looked like a miniature toy. A toy that children play with and accidentally destroy. She took out her juice bottle and sipped, looking around at the vast, pulsing water. "What must I look like?" A toy woman in a toy boat on the very real ocean, she answered herself, wedging the kayak into a thicket of seaweed. She placed the oar beside her, tucking it firmly under her left arm. Then she let her head fall back and extended her cramped legs into a stretch.

Well, do I go on? she asked herself. The bay ends soon, and the only way to the horizon is the open ocean. Do I go on? I'll probably kill myself out there. Is that it? Do I want to die? Am I out here to die? "Great, just great, the openfuckingocean . . ."

She took off her visor and sunglasses and shut her eyes, feeling the sun, like a perfect kiss, on her face. She began to see colors behind her eyes: yellow, red, purple, a deep, pulsing purple that changed shape, got large, shrunk, then large again. And then it seemed to become one solid circle, merging both of her eyes. On that circle, which pulsed violet now, she saw her mother, her brother, her girlhood friend Glenda, her first lover, Ron, her second, third, fourth, fifth, sixth . . . and then Zorba's face appeared and disappeared into the violet circle; and she felt their love. She felt love, period. Then she was swallowed, whole, by the sun.

She'd come to a place of decision and she had to decide which horizon would be hers: death or life. She was tired, but not exhausted. She slept, trusting the approach of the full noon sun. A dark young seal surfaced, stared at her, then rolled onto the seaweed and floated, awake, in the warming solstice sun.

Colors and shapes wash me as I float in the sunlight. I have no memory of pain. I'm fed and warm. A breast becomes the soft earth, then my mother's face. She never leaves me, I never forget her, my body, her body, lips to nipple, merged.

I'm being cradled. Held. The arms are strong and awkward. Hairy. But I'm not afraid. Of anything. I'm being cradled. Held. By my father. Father.

I'm grown. Bigger than him. He comes to my waist. I pick him up. I cradle him. He begins to grow. I can't hold him anymore. I can't hold him anymore. I'm not strong enough. Not strong enough. It hurts too much. It hurts. Too much. Hurts. Hurts. I have to let him go. I have to. I have to. It hurts. Too much. Too. Too. I have to. To. To. Hurts. It hurts. Hurts. Hurts. Too much. Too much. Much. Much. Hurts. I let him go. Go. Go. Go. Go. Him. Go. I let. Him go.

"Father! *I'm sorry! I loved you so much.* I love you, Papa!"

Maya woke with a start, her heart threatening to break free of her body. She felt the oar under her left arm. She looked out to the open ocean and it shone like an immense, living mirror. She sat up and stared into the slowly undulating water and saw the deep, thick tangle of darkest green seaweed, with fresh tendrils of translucent lime green seaweed that floated to the surface and filtered the sun, that had anchored her as she dreamt. The knot of tears in her throat made it difficult to breathe.

"I love you, Papa." She wailed, she sobbed, like a coyote at midnight, without shame or thought of being human. She wasn't human, she wasn't a woman—she was pure sorrow, pure grief, set free to roam the found horizon.

"I see a kayak!" Zorba yelled.

"Is it her?" Lara yelled back.

"I can't tell yet. Let's pick it up." But he knew it was Maya. He didn't know whether to be angry or ecstatic because he was both, simultaneously. "Goddamn you, Maya, I love you so goddamned much," he murmured.

X. J. stumbled out on deck, hanging onto the smooth wooden railing. He squinted to see the kayak and let out a whoop. "It's got be Maya. Yeah!"

Maya watched the sailboat approach. "Zorba," she whispered. "Oh, shit." She continued to paddle, left, right, left, right. She wore her visor, her sunglasses, but she no longer felt like a woman in a movie paddling on a kayak to the horizon. She felt, wholly, like herself. She felt quietly alive. The smell of the water and the air mixed and entered her nostrils, throat, lungs, her body, like some wondrous concoction she'd never known before. She wept and she smiled at the same time. How can I explain it? She could see Zorba, clearly, steering the sailboat. How can I tell him?

"How can I trust him?"

Now Lara was steering as he brought down the sails to bring them to a halt.

"I'll have to see." Maya paddled toward them, but first she wiped her face of tears. She began to smile a small smile of joy.

"*Eeeeehhhhhaaaaaa!*" X. J. yelled. "I'll pop some a that bubbly shit I found."

"Maybe we should pass on it," Lara said, trying to stop him.

"They can kill each other later, but right now I feel a celebration coming on, woman."

Lara shrugged her shoulders, but inwardly she smiled at X. J.'s runaway enthusiasm.

Zorba grabbed onto the kayak. "Throw me the rope."

"I'm paddling back in, Zorba," Maya said in a firm, distinct voice.

"You're *what?*"

"I said, I'm paddling back in, just the way I got here." Maya took off her sunglasses and looked at him. She saw worry, anger—love.

"Are you out of your mind, out here by yourself?" Zorba's voice was pitched to a firm control. Then he lost it. "Goddamn it, Maya, I don't want to lose you," he said, almost strangling with emotion. The words he should've said to his mother, he finally said to this woman, Maya. He felt naked, humiliated.

"You aren't going to lose me if you don't want to, I promise." She waited for his eyes to meet hers. His eyes were wounded and so were hers. They each looked at the other, at last, nakedly.

"Will you join us, at least, for some food?" There was a pleading tone to his voice, and his face was utterly somber as he waited for her reply.

"Sure, I'm fucking starved." As Zorba reached for her hand, it felt like the first human touch she'd ever known. It felt fleshy, strong, radiating warmth into her own hand. Her hand received his love, traveling up her arm, electrically, and straight into her heart. Her heart began pumping its message to every cell in her body as he enveloped her in his arms.

"Don't do this to me again, Maya," he murmured, tears running down his face and mingling with her dark, thick hair. "Please promise me, Maya."

"I can't promise you that, but I do love you."

He threw her to arm's length and shouted, "*You what?*"

The chill wind whipped her face. "I said I love you." Maya began to laugh her full-throated, rippling laugh that always announced the irrational.

He brought her back to his body, lifting her off the deck. He relished her weight, the feel of all of her, caught, in his arms. He put her back down, reluctantly, to the free will of her feet.

"Champagne, anyone?" X. J. approached with plastic glasses, holding a bottle of champagne. "I will now pop this baby if it's all right with you all."

"Pop it, pop it," Lara said semisarcastically. She was secretly enjoying the romantic drama unfolding before her eyes. She also admired Maya's guts (to paddle way the hell out here by herself). She caught Maya's eyes: I'm on your side, whatever it is, she tried to say with her own. For an instant, their friendship shimmered like a delicate silver bridge between them.

As the cork flew off into the restless sea, X. J. yelled, "To the newly-weds!" They all laughed, because that's exactly what it felt like.

The full, gusty late-afternoon wind had arrived, making the waves fast and choppy. Maya glanced back at the sailboat as her rhythm returned—left, right, left, right, left. The land looked so dark and far away. She hadn't realized she'd come this far. Suddenly she wanted to signal Zorba, to return to the sailboat. As she looked back at the boat, she saw Zorba, then beyond him the horizon, and the horizon said, *no, finish your journey.*

Slowly, very slowly, the dark land grew more distinct. It wiggled and danced as though she were witnessing an earthquake. "Destruction before creation, then after creation, destruction, law of the universe," Maya murmured.

Slowly, the land became larger, with points of light and color: her home. But she knew the sea (and the far horizon) would always be her haven, her teacher, her challenge.

"Maya Mar." Her breath joined the endless strength of the wind.

And then she knew that the sea had not forgotten the desert. Not ever.

The Last Dream

The place, as she called it, was a spacious, high-ceilinged Upper West Side apartment on Riverside Drive. They were lucky back then to find one so large. Eventually they had run out of children before they ran out of rooms for them, she often thought now. She had always marveled at the view of the park with the river below and the Jersey palisades beyond it; the sun going down behind them each day as if it was her very own pleasure; each season bringing something new; watching the snow drift slowly down from the darkness above or seeing the sky streaked yellow with lightning, the thunder exploding so close and the rain swirling madly so that it made her think of castle and vampire movies, and she laughed and told the children stories by candlelight.

Their perch, high above the sounds and smells of the city, had given her a sense of achieved grandness. It was their home, a canyon dwelling, free like an eagle's aerie from which she had seen the children fly, going farther out each year, learning and being frightened but returning to be fed and to cry and to complain and laugh through countless birthdays, each celebrated with the middle-class decorum of written invitations, favors for the invited, and a propriety which established a tradition, until soon now they'd be gone and the two of them would be left alone to do she knew not what.

"Dan, would you like more coffee?" she asked.

"Yes, please," he said, looking up from the sports section. The rest of the Sunday *Times* was strewn about at his feet. Their Sunday breakfast ritual, late and heavy, had been over an hour ago, and as soon as he finished the paper, predictably, he'd suggest a walk in the park.

She returned with the coffee and placed it on a small table next to him. Without looking up he thanked her.

"Dan, I had a dream last night," she said, retrieving the books section.

"What kind of dream?" he asked, absently.

"I'll tell you after you're finished with the paper," she said.

"I'll only be another minute," he said.

Two years ago the exchange would've turned into a long, involved argument. Why had she brought it up if she was willing to wait until he was finished? And it would go on from there until he exhausted her and she went off to lick her wounds and question her intelligence, even though her intellectual capacity had been validated in degrees and in published academic papers of relative importance. Then something had happened and suddenly there were no more arguments.

The change had left her lonely and wanting, feeling as if she'd eventually be forced to look elsewhere again and would hate herself because she couldn't relax completely with anyone but him. And then she had begun to understand what had happened, so that the last two years had brought her a freedom she'd never known. But with the freedom came new responsibilities and the old dread that one day things would be over between them. The change had come about gradually, balancing the relationship without the carefully arranged agreements from which they had suffered throughout their marriage. She began sensing the honesty around that time.

But it wasn't honesty in the old way, with every sexual fantasy or past infidelity dissected and every ounce of pleasure rendered empty of meaning so that the people, the rivals, their lean bodies and quick intelligence had withered and died and not even their ghosts dared trespass anymore. And it wasn't honesty in the simulated life-death adolescence of long-faded encounter groups which had caused her more pain than she thought possible to bear and forced him to adopt greater control over his emotions than he needed. It was a different type of honesty, akin, she suspected, to a code of honor, some chivalrous set of rules which had somehow filtered through the books or movies to find them while they were unguarded.

There was no longer suspicion between them, the one knowing that if the other lied he or she would have to live with the lie. They had both learned they could exist without guilt. And slowly, tentatively, mutually, they had given the new life form. This rebirth of their marriage had been accomplished less by analysis than by deeds until the deeds were like posted signs that said "Ladies" or "Exit" or "Dairy." Except that their signs said things like "Inveterate Romantic," "Amateur Painter," "College Graduate with Degree in Fine Arts," "Member of New York State Bar Association." And people began calling again to visit, and there were dinner parties and laughter once more.

"It's like the French," he'd said, one similar weekend morning after a small party last year. They had been lounging, trying to make up their minds how to start putting the house back in order. She'd asked, how like the French, and he'd said, abstracted from the conversation as if he were thinking out loud, "You know. Whatever a person does is his own affair, but not really, because one wouldn't take a chance lying. It wouldn't mean anything to the other. A confession would be bad manners."

"You don't sound French," she'd said. "You sound British. Cricket and all that," and had said the latter with what sounded to her like an English accent.

"Maybe that's what it's all about," he'd said. "Maybe we've finally caught up. It's all a matter of language."

"Caught up? Oh, Dan, if your clients heard you they'd strip you of your liberal standing. Your Kunstler rating would dip considerably." She'd ignored the sign that said, "Careful—Socially Conscious Lawyer with Love of American Literature." She wanted to wound him but knew before she'd finished that he wouldn't respond and instead would be saying something like, "Advantage, Mr. Cartagena."

A thread of anger had passed quickly through her. She was momentarily back in Dr. Lehrman's richly carpeted, soundproof living room, screaming vile things at Dan, trying to free herself of constraints and inhibitions, but watching herself so that she didn't use those forbidden words—words like *cabrón, maricón, hijo de la gran puta, mamalón, mierda,* which would give her away; she almost gave in one time when he called her a common whore, wishing to shame him by revealing that even though he had grown up in relative luxury and his own father had been a lawyer, she had grown up in the shadow of La Marqueta, and both of them had been raised speaking "Puertorican," as most of their friends said; her insides screaming with the rage of wanting to announce that she was one of those dreaded Puerto Ricans; cringing whenever the papers or television made the distinction between Blacks, Whites, and Puerto Ricans; wanting to state that there were white Puerto Ricans and instead keeping to safe ground and always announcing that they were Spanish, the children absolutely convinced of this fact.

She was immediately back to that time, the color coming on quickly; the other members of the group, watching, their faces contorted. And then the picture faded once again into the late winter weekend morning with the Hudson River wearing gray, dying, and she not the least bit concerned about ecology, that too having passed from their lives, along with health foods and cooperatives, baby-sitting pools, encounters, politics, the women's movement, the Thalia Theater art films, jazz, and even the Vietnam War—their very own war, like World War II had been their parents' war. All of it had faded and they still "endured," so that the word no longer belonged to Faulkner but had become their own. She was sure Dan would've liked that.

"I don't think what influences people is the spoken language," she'd said finally. "Spoken language is too fleeting to make a lasting impression. What really influences people is in the literature. The good stuff with real people struggling with themselves."

"Mailer and his cynicism?" he'd asked, amused by her sudden seriousness.

"Yes, even Mailer."

And she'd watched him pull back, ashamed because in agreeing to include Mailer she had truly conceded graciously after years of bitterness about her brief and innocent romantic episode with Marion Danzig; poor Marion who aspired to being a writer and who had stated at a small dinner party that she had known Mailer and that, besides being an ego-maniac, he would go down in history as a minor twentieth-century writer. Big, bad Dan Cartagena toying with Marion's emotions, intimidating her with his superior knowledge of literature until he had eventually chased Marion away. She, Frances Elizabeth Cartagena, née Cabrera, who did not fit the role of the dumb spic any more than he did, understood more than he'd hoped, and he had no right to ridicule her or demean himself by doing so.

"I'm sorry," he'd said. "I shouldn't have brought all that up."

"It's okay," she'd answered. "It's all pretty funny, anyway. The Dallas Orgasmic Repository."

"The what?" he said, hurt, as if he'd been left out of a private joke.

She'd repeated the phrase and laughed, tossing back her long black hair away from her face.

"That's where it all went. All the wasted love. Not lost out there in the vastness of the universe but stored in that book place and released in anger."

She'd tried sounding poetic and it made her laugh harder. She had finally rolled off the couch onto the carpeted floor and under the grand piano. He'd watched her curves fall slowly, her small, full body curling up fetally, her faded jeans and her New York University sweatshirt, the motto "Perstare et Praestare" all but gone from the seal; her body bare underneath; white; too white and vulnerable from winter and the cerebral existence of life on the Upper West Side.

He counted again and, like yesterday, in two years he would be fifty and she forty-six. Michael was nearly twenty-two and ready to enter law school; extremely serious, and as far as he knew hadn't touched drugs. Debby was eighteen and ready to enter college. She had the same luminescent skin, and from the rear he couldn't tell her and her mother apart, both bodies diminutive and incredibly beautifully shaped; discussing sexual issues with her friends, boys as well as girls, with ease; all of them worried sick about AIDS and relationships and he wondering what had happened to romance and afraid to ask.

"Fran, get up, for God's sake," he'd said.

She'd looked up from beneath the piano and her eyes mischievous, the gray green flashing in the winter sunlight, making her look younger than her years.

"I'm sorry," she'd said and got up. "Do you want something to eat? We can clean up later."

He'd looked at her and then she touched his face, the hand feeling unusually tender on his skin. He'd stood up and, placing a hand on her arm, steered her out of the living room, not with force but as a parody of someone being arrested or removed. Still smiling, she'd walked ahead of him, knowing what awaited her, down the hall in their bedroom; dark and warm, used to their arguments, a tired bedroom; unmade bed and reread books and clothes dangling like resting marionettes, not discarded in anger anymore but left there out of mutual respect because to pick up after the other was to insult.

"What are you doing?" she'd asked once they were inside the room and he'd closed the door, not feeling the excitement well up but knowing once they began she'd be totally for herself like he'd been these many years.

He didn't answer her but began undressing and she did the same. She waited for him, feeling his once lithe body search for her until he was there and she could join him, chase him, and, catching up to him, burst from consciousness; not romantically but like the son-of-a-bitch No. 2 Express roaring between Ninety-sixth and Seventy-second Streets when it races as if chased by demons so that it bounces and for a second seems to be airborne, floating free of the constraints of gravity, the rails a mere insinuation, flying without derailing as if the motorman, who was the conductor, loved and trusted the steel beneath him, talking Black to it: "Here we go, baby, one more time. God, yes." And when the train moved that way, the people bounced, their feet going up off the floor in that split second and down again, and it was enough New York thrills for one day because no matter how crazy they were and how starved for attention or tired of their anonymity, nobody wanted to be an "Eyewitness

News" casualty. And, oh, yes, Dan, but without saying the words, sucking on her own fingers when she couldn't reach his mouth, bursting all at once so that the second up off the tracks went on and on and left her outside of herself with no regrets, and if it wasn't love, then all right.

It had happened again two months later and a few more times in between, without the intensity and slowly, tenderly, for old times' sake, and then they both knew about the honesty and it was like a game. The rules were clear and were never discussed and it was boring to cheat, to break the rules overtly without intelligence, so that the challenge was gone. She knew now what it was about and no longer had to ask him to explain. It was like he'd said it was with sports and games and everything else. The rules created a framework, a set of parameters, and nothing really happened outside those boundaries, except that which went unseen or unproven, which everyone did and it wasn't really cheating.

And then one day in spring, of all times, with Riverside Park greening, cast anew with Columbia students and Haitian and Central American soccer players, and Dominicans and Cubans still resentful if thought to be Puerto Ricans, the park filled with new mothers and their English perambulators and English sheepdogs tied to them—God knew why they affected the damn things—he'd grown tired. Not old, she'd thought, but simply tired of the fight. She watched him closely, knowing in advance he was gone, the fire dampened, the spirit broken, and she was once again the trophy, mounted, dusted, and seldom admired. And she needed him more now than in the past twenty-five years. She never thought of divorce anymore. Not because she couldn't find someone else, but because she'd fought and won her own battle with herself and now that she understood, he didn't want to play.

She stepped away from her reverie, stood up, and placed the books section atop the piano. She watched him as he stood up and crossed the room to fill his pipe.

"Dan?"

"Yes, Fran," he said, without turning around.

"I had a dream last night," she said, making it sound like she was bringing it up for the first time. "Do you want to hear about it?"

"Yes, of course," he said. He held a lighter to the pipe and blew a large cloud of glittering smoke which drifted slowly through the sunlight. He returned to his soft, worn leather chair. It was his father's law office chair and he had insisted on keeping it after the old man's death. "Tell me about it."

"Well, we were on an airplane," she said, kneeling up on the couch across from him. "An old airplane. There was a young blond girl on it. You know, with her hair curly and soft and a beautiful body and she was wearing a jumpsuit and goggles. Well, she went out on the wing of the plane and did stunts and waved to you and you waved back and clapped. And then when we landed she came up and draped herself all over you and told you how glad she was to see you again. I was furious, Dan. I walked up to her and asked her how come she didn't say hello to me. And soft of offhand, bitchy like, she said, 'Oh, hi,' and hugged you and you kissed her. Not on the cheek but with your mouths open, and then the two of you walked off and left me standing there. When I woke up I was in a jealous rage."

By the time she had finished speaking he was laughing out loud. He set his pipe down and leaped to his feet, suddenly athletic and full of pep.

"That's quite a dream," he said.

"Please don't laugh, Dan," she said. "It was very real."

She described the girl to the last detail. "She must've been twenty-three or four and she had those incredibly pert breasts that don't need support, her body taut but full."

"And you were jealous?"

"Furious."

He looked at her and the fire had returned to his eyes, she thought. He took her hand and led her to the bedroom. But there was no express roaring beneath Broadway, no first time at his parents' home in Rockaway Beach when his family had left the city and he was studying for his senior exams. Back then she had been in love with life and intelligence and felt lucky to have found someone like him, whose Puertoricanness was not worn as a battlefield ribbon; someone who was going to be a lawyer.

There was a honeymoon in Europe and incredible summer nights on the Adriatic coast when they would make love over and over. They could not stop talking to each other about their lives and their dreams, and the memories still remained vividly with her after all those years; traveling through the canals of Amsterdam and letting her mind float back as she imagined Vermeer ambling through the city in the 1700s; forgetting that their parents had come from a small, poverty-stricken Caribbean island full of self-important people; walking the cobblestoned streets of Nürnberg, stopping off to visit Albrecht Dürer's house, which dated back to the sixteenth century and had survived the Allied bombing, and then stopping off at a biergarten to take long, cold draughts of wheat beer that made her feel as if she were washing away the squalor of her childhood; making their way westward on a train through the Swiss Alps to

France and then across the Pyrenees to Cataluña, spending the night in Barcelona and then going on to Madrid and the beauty of El Prado museum; the grand architecture of the capital putting her in touch with her true roots.

What was wrong with their saying they were Spanish; why was being Puerto Rican such a big deal? Why did they feel such pride? Why? Why couldn't they leave it alone? She was American. Dan was American. Their children were American. They were Spanish-American. There was no such thing as a Puerto Rican American. It was too long. It didn't make sense. Puerto Ricans couldn't be Something-Americans.

When it was over and he lay beside her, his breathing labored, she cried softly to herself and for herself and cursed the blond girl with the curly hair, wishing that she had truly dreamed her.

The Awakening

I

I did not think them to be
my kind and loving family.
They were cartoons, the
characters who swallowed
dynamite and after the blast
were scorched and sarcastic.

Not my family, no, for I
was just a child (what did
my spine know of evil?) and
if I had known then I'd
spend the rest of my life
making excuses, I would have

traveled back, avoided the
zygote, detached myself from
the placenta. It would have
been good-bye, adiós, auf
Wiedersehen. But knowledge
is not inherited. Stupidity

is and they tell me I am
the hope for a brave future.
I tell them I am no magazine
illustration, not one of
those kids like they see on
TV. No, my assault on the

world is this rope I lasso
about the legs of the
fleeing calf. I am the
fruition of the true dreams
of the mid-20th century.

2

I met him one night driving
through the humid Valley of
Texas. His arm was out the
window, one hand on the
wheel, a song on his lips,
sex on his mind. I know you

don't trust me. No matter,
I know what I witnessed and
I know you agree, we never
know how the almighty will
represent their divinity.
Wisdom says I should have
killed him then and there
and, no doubt, if I had,
I would be a hero in some
parts of this world. But
I am a coward and he meant
no harm.

3

I thought myself rootless,
no tendrils, no nutrition,
each police siren a song
to the arid night-time world
of grease and felt-made men,
products like the products
they buy. Oh, it was a
glorious machination to be
sitting as judge from a
window across the street from

a bar where telephone workers
met, then performed sex in

the alley. It was better than
TV, better than being a bird
or a bat, better than pictures
from Rio or North America. That's
when I realized I should have
murdered when I had the chance.

4

I tell my son, "It is your
responsibility never to forgive
or forget." He thinks I am
describing the plot of another
old movie, something in black
and white. Whether you have

children or not, each day we
sacrifice. Today I have made a
nylon net of my heart and I
listen for the song of the
Hmong women crushing cans in
the alley and wait for the

repercussion to rise straight
into the fog like scissors to
slice a path to the afternoon
sun and I will wave my arms out
the window and the streetcars
will stop and the constellations
will dance for my little boy.

Meetings with a Saint

All you bring with you
is a talent for alcohol,
but I don't complain.
I like the way
your thumb wipes
the sweat from your glass,
the way change accumulates
on the bar,
how you smile
so soft and cruel
at the pontificates
caught in the glare
of the Game of the Week.

If it's all you bring,
that's enough
because unmotivated companionship
is a rare commodity,
something to be praised
when men made plastic
grin from every corner,
their lips tight,
whether in exertion or rest.
No, you, my saint,
are someone to be revered,
someone who has transformed himself
into a hundred mouths
and two hundred ears.
I like the way you soak
yourself with noise and smoke
and settle into

the soft cushioning of alcohol.
I like that.
I know I'm not supposed to,
but I do.
I really do.

Jewel Lake

It was snowing when we reached Jewel Lake.
It was so cold our shovels
made no bite in the earth.
We had tents but no stakes or poles.
We slept like wolves
huddled against the night.

In the morning we marched,
the lake always to our left
until we reached the railhead
and were separated into groups of ten.

Spring passed, then summer,
and when I feel the cold
I remember my brother.
Do his calluses open like mine?
Does he tremble when he smells diesel?

When I hear the train
winding through the pass
above Jewel Lake
I remember the morning we were detained.
Twenty deep on the platform,
his chin on my shoulder,
promising nothing would happen to me.

OMAR S. CASTAÑEDA

Misunderstanding Prufrock, with Some Cummings

Long before Dian sleeps with him, she knows—she is certain of it!—all there is to know of him.

She kept him for weeks just under her tongue, his heat cupped in her palms, his softness behind her knees. She thought everyone could smell his scent on her. It trailed her to his class, perfumed out when she crossed her long, long—oh God, so long—legs. (White stockings suddenly looming brightly on the expanse of her thigh—like the sea foaming up, crashing, perhaps; the concussion of wild nature loud in the heart, loud in the empty chambers of our body. We could tell you—listen, where she walked, moons and Saturn rings, vast nebulae, whole clusters of galaxies sprinkled down like argentum, which we faithfully mined. But this is another story. A story that breaks our heart.)

Dr. Franco saw none of this. For Dian, the scent of him followed her everywhere down the hallways, to the bathrooms in Ballantine Hall where she scrubbed and scrubbed to remove her shame.

"My life is a nightmare of predictability," she told us.

She thought she might become a terrier, her toenails clicking in his kitchen, her head cocked expectantly at his door, her tongue flicking up. Once, sillily, she thought she would circle his mountain goat rug—of course, he would have one, a deep shag white, we were sure!—until curling comfortably at his feet.

She would accept a woman wanting him in front of the fire—their drinking of blood-red wines, their laughter, the woman's smooth, delicious throat. She would content herself with his fingers under her muzzle, scratching, his large hand stroking the arch of her back. All because someday he would make room for her on his bed, say in his husky, sonorous voice, "That's my good girl," or "Yeah-ess: Princess, Bay-bee, Sweet-ums." And there in his sheets, she would ascend into metamorphic dreams.

On Tuesdays, with the regularity of ash, she waited in the alcove beside his office, her back to the hall. Despite herself, she always imagined him coming out of his room, asking her for a piece of paper to write a quick note for another student. "Oh," she'd hear him say, "you got, maybe, a piece of scrap paper or something," his eyes not really looking, not really stopping, but scurrying over the flat surfaces of the alcove.

In this dream, she pulls out a Bic pen, blue, and places the thin blade in her hands. The ink bleeds through her skin and is siphoned up by his fingertips. She is perspiring, nibbling her inner lip, until she can't take it anymore and flees. "Hey!" he shouts. "I just wanted a goddamned scrap from you." His voice is very high; his forearms are veined with ink, his mouth dribbles blue. "Just something! Just a little bit of nothing!" But his voice is so far away, trailing, diminishing, like a tail of comet dust so that all of this dream is indecipherable, intractable.

On Wednesdays, she watched him from a campus park bench and found something of a dromedary in him: his long neck and reflective pose; his woolly chin-chin.

On Thursdays, she cracked pistachios between her knees and waited for him to appear and for her breath to disappear. Always, it was the secretive dip of his fingers into his inner coat pocket that sent her writhing: salty red spots dappling her knees.

On weekends, she imagined two hundred phone calls.

Courting? This?

When she finally sleeps with him—did we mention the heavens raining from her like angel dust?—it is *his* back that grows curly black hair. Yes. *He* growls into her ear. His face lengthens. His nose grows cold. He laps affectionately at her throat. He, ha-ha, *he!*

"Sit!" she says. "Heel!" She falls impatiently back into his pillow and lights a Camel Filter.

He whimpers away.

Blue smoke rises to the ceiling. She can hear him lapping his red thing, and wonders how she ever thought he was so?

He crouches in the corner.

Handsome? Dangerous?

One of his legs paddle-wheels at a flea and scritches against the blue shag rug. "God, Franco. It's not like we promised each other anything."

"Yip."

"I was honest with you from the start."

"Woof."

Another whorl of smoke blue above her. Her hand droops to the edge of the bed. She feels exhausted. The affair is already . . . "God. Okay," she says.

He comes trailing an ecstatic spray of pee. Yellow.

"I'm sorry," she says.

His tail slices the air.

There is power yet in those beagle eyes. Her heart unfrowns. "Was it anything I did?"

"No," he whispers, feeling the bones of his teeth shrink back. "No."

She is distracted. "Sure?"

"It was me."

"Hmm?" She watches his ears shorten; lobes begin to appear.

"I mean it was me."

"M-hmm?" She remembers the smell of a Baskin-Robbins, long ago. When? Where? One where *we* were whiling away time.

"I mean, why—that is *when*—I asked for, you know, you to lie down . . ."

She smiles distractedly. "Yes-ums?"

"Down, lie down," he said. "With the begonia over your ear. And the butter dribbled—"

"Better?"

"Butter. Are you deaf?"

"But you wanted it *melted*."

The word alone brings back his erection.

She giggles. "It was too hot."

His tongue flicks up against her earlobe.

"You're my professor!" she whines affectedly. Her long fingers curl lightly around him.

Frank shudders. He leans his head back to better feel her intimate caress. Ah, but something else take hold of him, and he suddenly crumples into her lap.

"What?" she asks.

He squirms.

"What?"

His fur reappears. His paws grow hard, curved nails.

"I'm afraid," he confesses.

Dian nods. "Me too." And softer, her voice bruised, her voice filling with something genuine, something that stings us: "Me too, Franco."

Because of this, a man stands humiliated atop a building, and looks down on the trees facing this Victorian literature professor's colonial house. "Aargh!" we hear. Or perhaps, "It's me! Why can't you see this?"

Or, "Oh! Oh! Oh!" It is a voice. Atop a brown building. That much is certain.

"What am I going to do?" she asks us.

Our throat is sore, hoarse. "Do you love him?"

"He wants everything so secret."

Our napkin is twisted into a grotesque ice-cream cone.

"I *was* his student."

"Is he . . . is he the most important thing to you?"

She looks over her shoulder. "Not now, though."

"Not now?"

Turning back: "Are you deaf? I'm not in his class anymore."

We do not like the small explosion of impatience in her throat.

"It's not like he's married or anything." The salt and pepper shakers collide in her hands.

"Perhaps you're just infatuated with him."

She rubs the holes of the silver shakers together. "We get along pretty well."

"Just a passing thing, perhaps. Meaningless."

"Odd how we can talk. You know, really talk."

"An infatuation of the body," we venture.

Her eyes glance at the door.

We venture again: "I always assumed that you and—"

"There are some moments with him that—"

"And us? What about us?"

"—are incredibly enlightening."

She did not hear. "Like lighting a kerosene-soaked cat!?"

The salt shakers are suspended in air. "I beg your pardon?"

We pull the shakers from her hands. "I think you do this too often."

"What are you talking about?" she says.

"This thing with authority figures."

"Oh, give me a—"

"No! You get all wrapped up in a professor and you think it's love or something."

"That's not—"

"It's a little embarrassing to see you do this." We look around the room for ears and eyes. "Do you think you may have a little problem here? I mean with really connecting, maybe? Being whole?"

"That's not—"

"What is it with you, anyway, that makes you have to be in a position of subservience? Of looking up to men? Why do you have to do this? It's humiliating. I mean—"

She is on her feet. "That is not it at all!"

"Then what is it?"

"Not at all!" she growls.

A veritable bang of asteroids, photinos, quasars, and redshifts, follow her out. We are certain she will go to him.

We see her next at three in the morning, saying she fell asleep in the library (it closes at ten). She spends an eternity with her tortoiseshell comb before going to sleep. We watch her in the mirror: eyes closed; arms undulating and entwining like broad sea plants; her face a blush of red; her breathing under a lunar spell; her hips grinding, grinding the soft white ottoman. Her nakedness becomes an exquisite tragedy of curves and shadows, a deep-set bowl of hips, thighs, abdomen, and—within this pale chalice—her dark-haired pudendum.

We cannot get angry. We cannot even speak. She is too?

—Suddenly we envision an impossibility: her body menstruating, filling that Grail of her hips and thighs with life-rich blood, and we on our knees before her, soul aching for redemption, tongue for mass—

Ethereal? Divine?

"I think we should end this," she says. Her eyes are on us.

We can barely swallow. We swipe a forearm across our vision-stained lips.

" 'Our now must come to then,' " she quotes from Cummings.

Her knees uncross, the bowl falls apart.

" 'Our then shall be some darkness.' "

"Can't I please stay forever in your pockets?"

"No."

"Just take me out when you want to, when you want to—"

"Really, no."

"It doesn't matter. I can wait, I can be there for you. Keep me in a drawer. That's all I ask."

She is pulling away.

"Under some sweaters, or old bras." We are driving her away. "It doesn't matter! I can wait. I'll stay out of your way, until you want me again."

"Look—"

"I can be alone until you're ready. Please. I won't even think of it as suffering."

"That's not—"

Suddenly, we are on our feet and screaming at the top of our lungs, "What do you want me to do!"

In an instant, finality molds across her face.

"I'm sorry," she states flatly. Her hands gather air toward her. "I'm really sorry, Alfred. Really."

But this is the other story.

Dian leaves us in the morning, bookbag clutched tight at her side. She will see him. Him. Him. At the head of the class, speaking out, book clutched tight in his mitt, correcting sophomoric understandings of Modernism, of "Prufrock," of mermaids singing. " 'I should have been a pair of claws scuttling across the floor of the sea,' " he says. She swooning at such unbridled passion, such denial of effete intellectualism. We mumbling, "You're damn right, asshole."

Here is the real story.

They meet furtively under the maples that shield his car. Drive away, her head held down as they pass campus security. Her laughter bubbles up at their escapade. Her hands open the knot of hair at her nape; she shakes free great cascades of deep, galactic black. She watches for his street. His house, with large scented bathtub, wide marble kitchen counters, four poster bed with four loose nooses, high-armed chairs for looping legs, pillows mushrooming on floors, large hanging baskets, oils, lotions, circular seats with holes, vibrating things, long, tickling ostrich things, feathers and boas, fuming incense, mist sprays, and silky, lavish protuberances.

Later, she wants to go to a movie. Or rent. "I don't know, something with Cary Grant, maybe."

He has to prepare for classes. There's a meeting. "Not this time, okay?"

She growls affectionately, barks, and they crash into each other again. And so it goes, in this minuscule story. Until finally, through the spray, she sees him for what he is.

We imagine them walking together on campus, pretending a seemly relationship. Deferential. Underneath, something quite different. Something boiling up. Something tied to his conspiratorial wave to a male colleague and his lighthearted scampering ahead.

"You're the most selfish man I've ever known!"

He turns on the steps of Ballantine Hall and glares back at her. Other students stop and stare. A window opens above them.

"All you want is someone who adores you! Someone who thinks you're special! What have you given me in return? Huh?"

Another window screeches open, old paint relenting. Then quickly, so that Dian backs away in momentary fear, he rushes headlong toward her, like a truck, a red and yellow pickup truck.

"Okay," he says. "Let's try this. I'm sorry. I see how I have done wrong. I have not given you enough power in this. I see how I have misunderstood."

Her mouth twists.

"But I can do better. I can. I know I've acted badly. Please. We can try. I can try. If you let me. That is." He pats his human legs as proof of sincerity.

She, of course, is a barnacle to hope. "Okay," she whispers. "Okay." She feels too many eyes upon them.

He spreads his arms to embrace the entire campus. His voice rises far above a whisper, far above propriety, and into a clear blue decision. "Let's go camping this weekend! Tomorrow, I mean. Right now, I mean!"

She laughs at his exuberance.

"I'm dead serious!"

"Oh, Franco."

"Just you and me," he whispers.

Already his hands are warming her shoulders.

"Tomorrow's fine," she answers, pouting shyly, forgiving him with upturned mouth, forgiving herself her submission.

But he will not kiss her unless she is absolutely certain that this is her decision, too. "I really do love you, you know?"

Her eyelids drop. Her shoulders slacken. Her knees grow hair.

He brings her mouth to his.

It isn't until their seventh day that she decides to shave his beard. Razor in hand, strop at the ready, the Coleman lamp casting rooster shadows, she approaches the cot. Far above the tent, a pair of bats jag through the night, the horned moon lows through grazing clouds. Frogs bark and pop.

The professor is dead drunk. He is spent.

She, in our story, has had enough of panfish, of small white scales, of campfires. Of getting. She has had enough of scrubbing the scent of fish from her body. She has had it with the minnows that swim through her pores when he falls on top of her. She wants a trimming.

So, in this story, when she finishes with his hairy face, it is as if she has cut off his?

Clippings fall onto a bag of Dick Loeb's Unsalted Peanuts.

Nose? Thumbs? Feet?

Hah! we hear. Hah! Atop a brown building.

El Rojo Esqueleto and La Negra Esqueleta Conduct My Examination

esqueleto—skeleton or death

El Rojo appears with a stethoscope, saying, *Listo?* Yes,
I'm ready, but I have to leave soon, I say. *Oh, I don't
think you have to, anywhere but here, Hombre. Disrobe.
We'll begin your examination from the bottom.*

THE FEET

He has me sit and takes one foot in his hands and closes
his eyes and runs his fingers over every inch. He does
the same with the other foot. *Medically, they're OK,* he
says, *but these are soft, pale feet that seldom leave
their shoes. They walked when they shouldn't have, and
stayed put when they should have been heading for the
road. A schoolboy's feet. No good when you really need
them, Hombre.*

THE KNEES

*I can see you haven't been in church, Mijo, no calluses.
What is this scar?* I had an operation, I tell him. He puts
the stethoscope to each knee and listens for a long time.
*The operation didn't work, Mijo, these will still buckle
under the weight of your own desire.*

THE GENITALS

El Rojo inspects the foreskin. *No circumcision, eh, Compadre, why not?* My mother wouldn't have it, said it was a Jewish custom, I answer. *Well there's a problem,* says Rojo, *Mama was controlling your dick from the start. Which way does it point?* What are you talking about? *When it's hard, which way does it point?* To the left. *Comunista! Well, I'm no good at this part, you know. I have to bring in a specialist, La Negra. They say women understand pricks better than we do, Compadre.* La Negra Esqueleta enters and approaches me. *Don't be afraid,* she says. Quietly singing to herself, she slowly examines my testicles and penis. Then she straightens up and stands close to me, her face next to mine. *The first time you had sex you got her pregnant, didn't you, Wedo?* Yes. *And you cried when she called you from Tijuana saying she was looking for an abortionist, didn't you, Wedo?* Yes, but she had the baby. *And do you know where your daughter is now, Wedo?* No. *Sex is a sad thing, isn't it?* Yes. And La Negra kissed me and stepped away.

THE STOMACH

El Rojo resumes the examination. He probes my belly with his red bones, and listens without the stethoscope. *Well, Chico, at least you eat like a Mexican. No problem, here.*

THE HEART

Rojo puts the stethoscope to my chest, moving the instrument around. He hums and mutters as he does this, his noises growing louder. Finally, he stops and tells La Negra, *You try.* She does the same, except after a time she throws off her stethoscope and puts her bare ear to me and listens patiently. *No,* she says, and they whisper and consult. Can't you hear my heart, I ask? I can hear it pounding myself. *Yes,* says La Negra, *we*

hear your heart fine. It's the others we can't find; where
is sweet Uncle Rudy's, your mother's, where are your
children's? Burt, do you hear my father's heart? Rojo and
Negra look at each other and laugh; *We couldn't hear
his when we examined him!*

THE HANDS

Rojo holds my hands like specimens, turning them over
delicately, and to La Negra says, *Mira, las manos, they're
full of stains.* What stains, I washed them, I say. *Oh,
they're clean now, Hermano, but they remember, don't
they?* La Negra takes my right hand and places it on her
shoulder saying, *For instance, the night you were drunk
and angry and pushed your wife hard against the wall
and saw the look in her eyes, recuerda?* Then walking
behind me, she wraps her black bones around me, *Or
when you held your son in your hands and rocked him
so long you both fell asleep and had the same dream,
recuerda?* Then laying my hand on her brow, *Or when
at 6:45 P.M. on April 2nd, your fingers closed your
mother's eyes against the darkness? Remember?*

THE HEAD

La Negra says, *The chin, as they say, is a little weak, but
the lips are full. Lips, labios, labia. You know some
men's sadness comes from having only one set of lips.
It makes some men so afraid, they cut those others out
of women. But you are not afraid, are you, Mijo?* Rojo
tells me to open my mouth and probes inside with his
bony finger. Tapping on my tongue, he says, *The word
must be born here before it can be written, Poeta.*
When he presses at the back of my tongue, I find myself
saying, La lengua. Then he presses at the tip, and I say
suddenly, This is my tongue. *There seems to be some
pathology here,* says Rojo, who now reaches far back,
nearly gagging me, and pushes hard, and I say, Leche.
Nearer the front, he pushes me again, and, in my mother's
voice, I say, You want milk, Mijo, not leche. *Oh,*

murmurs Rojo, *she who controlled the dick controlled the tongue.*

But your eyes are your own, whispers La Negra. She looks at them through a lighted scope that blinds me, and asks, *What do you see in the light?* And I see my mother burning in her beauty standing on the edge of a precipice overlooking the world laughing with Rojo and La Negra, then turning to me slowly and saying softly, *Tus ojos, Mijo, you have beautiful eyes; take care of your eyes.* And then La Negra turns out the light.

THE DOCTOR'S ORDERS

I'll write you a prescription I got from an old drunk. I read it, No se puede vivir sin amar. What has this to do with me, I ask. El Rojo turns to La Negra and says, *Pobrecito, he doesn't understand.* Turning to me, he sighs, *Well, if you can live without love, you don't need El Rojo.* With a stroke to my cheek, La Negra says, *See you next year.*

The Third Visit of El Rojo Esqueleto

In the dark, in a fever, I wake. In the corner of my room stands a red tree of bones, El Rojo Esqueleto with a skull's perpetual smile. Heat and damp, my body shivers and the sheets are wet. El Rojo paces at the foot of my bed, then turns and stares at me for a long time. Abruptly, El Rojo goes to my dresser, opens every drawer, lifting and turning everything, scooping and throwing things out, a low growling begins, El Rojo looks beneath the bed, then to the closet, where every shirt and suit is searched, pockets turned out, items examined, stubs, receipts, notes, read front and back, jackets rifled, a thin red bone examines hat linings, pokes into shoes, opens file boxes, pulls out letters, sent and received, drawings, bills, tax returns, the miscellanea of my life, photographs, bags and suitcases opened and shaken out, the growling grows louder, El Rojo goes to my desk and reads every paper, turns every page of my notebooks, goes to the bookshelf, flips through every page and reads every word scribbled in them, every forgotten note folded in. Finally, El Rojo stops. The room is inside out, all containers emptied, all contents examined and discarded. El Rojo walks slowly over to me, kneels by the bed, runs red bones over my brow, pulls up the covers, puts his mouth to my ear, says, *Your father sent me. He is looking for you. I will tell him I could not find you. You are not here.* El Rojo rises, leaves by the door to the hall, I hear the front door open, close, and last, the metal gate clang shut like a bell.

Banners

El monte, 1933

Our men drank water and never smoked
as they sat under the walnut tree,
green branches enfolding them,
green leaves flaming with sunlight.
They came each day as dawn approached,
tense dark men crowding together
and speaking low in the presence
of the morning star. We women
could hear the winds shifting south
over the empty fields.

Hours passed.
Our children chewed sticks
like ears of corn, dust devils
whirled and dissolved in the road.
At noon the sheriffs passed
in steaming black cars.
Nothing looked changed: the same
huddled shacks below the sun,
a yellow dog rising from a gully,
dungarees on a sagging clothesline.
So they passed on, riding out
the horizon as our singers
plucked a noisy chord.

When they emerged
stiff, morose, the evening rattle
had already begun in the trees.
Tomorrow we'll march to the fields, they said.

We brought them a sip of coffee
cooled by the breath of the night wind
and watched their faces screw up
as they said good night and turned homeward
over fields brimming with fruit.

* * *

In a week, the strikebreakers came.
Another week and the sheriffs
lured our men into the station
with lies, promises of good work.
And the Mexican consul there
sporting a pencil-stick mustache,
a solemn porky bastard who
sprouted among our dazzled men
calling them "reds." After that,
we kept up the daily pickets
and mass meetings and prayers.

The first time we drove our trucks
through town, forty women maybe,
shouting, making the place a beehive,
raw sunburnt faces stared at us
on every street. That was all right.
But one man, alone, swore at us.
Bracing his hips by the roadside,
hard blue eyes burning right through us,
he wished us bloodied and raped.
I never knew why the town existed,
but now I knew what I felt,
and that was my own heart staring
at itself, blood running not singing.

Returning at twilight, I stared
at the dark fields slipping past us,
the air hot and always doubled,
smell of young berries rotting . . .
Now I could no longer find hope
because we buried three small children
and put the sticks they chewed

upon that ground, one on each grave,
there in the summer harvest light.

*   *   *

I can still see those nameless stars
poking through the roof slats at night,
green and blue and plum-colored stars.
Eyes shut, I watched them holding still
while I rolled past them on a wave
as if the whole night were an ocean sea.
I never dreamed of food. That night
I woke at the sound of a small
tapping on the roof, the room cool
spread out around me like a wood.
My husband slept, his fine tangled head
on my arm, mouthing words that have
always stayed with me: *ya 'cabaron todo,*
the sticks an' all.

        The hour comes back
  in the dust thick with panicked men.
Harsh cries sang out from the workers
throwing their heads behind them,
a lightning flash through yellow clouds.
Three were blasted, rolling into
a ditch where they lay face down
licking the mossy earth. Some of us
were pulled away screaming, Murderers!
Brothers! Then we scattered
like a nightmare leaves over the valley.
In a windless orchard we began to cry.

Fire and Water

There was a fire once when they lived together
in the old house. He had cleaned the stove
with kerosene, then turned the burner on.
He would have been killed but for something
that loves a fool. My screaming uncle
ran through every room, *Quick, water!*
Grandfather, helpless and gentle in his wheelchair
laughed at uncle, *¿Pos cómo? ¡No puedo!*
He laughed so hard (he later told me)
that he almost found the strength to walk again.
That was years ago. I remember them now:
Grandfather, toothless, almost ninety,
laughing with all his years at uncle,
gaunt and shriveled and wild with cancer,
looking everywhere, nowhere, for water.
Water would have drowned the flames
and what they needed was fire—
fire for old broken railyard bones,
fire for diseased blackened packinghouse bones.
Sometime later, after uncle had died,
grandfather heard a voice one night
repeating slowly from the withered milpa.
A child? His dead wife calling?
He knew better than to answer the sound
of water rushing around the trees.

LUIS J. RODRIGUEZ

The Quiet Women

The quiet women roam in the din of belly screams.
They know rivers and caves and curbsides.
They know the advent of furled fists.
They are the quiet women, shadows on park bench,
pushed into needle grass, disheveled syllables
uttered between makeshift dreams. The burden
of memories are the salvage of fantasy flames,
the mossed-faced whose eyes stream through veins.
Here come the quiet women, blossoms in the womb of night.
The miracle-pulp in their hands. They swerve
around odors of hurt, odors of neglect,
of treachery and a lie. What's the smell of a poem?
The quiet women know; they breathe it in,
exhale it. Others take the naturalism away,
remove the tender; all that's left is facade
and caricature. All veneer and wordplay.
But for a quiet woman, a poem is a smile so open,
they're afraid of falling in.

To the police officer who refused to sit in the same room as my son because he's a "gang" member:

How dare you!
How dare you pull this mantle from your sloven
sleeve and think it worthy enough to cover my boy.
How dare you judge when you also wallow in this mud.
Somebody has turned over society's power to you,
a society relinquishing its rule, turned it over
to the man in the mask, whose face never changes,
always distorts, who does not live where I live,
but commands the corners, who does not have to await
the nightmares, the street chants, the bullets,
the early-morning calls, but looks over at us
and demeans, calls us animals, not worthy
of his presence, and I have to say: How dare you!
My son deserves to live as all young people.
He deserves a future and a job. He deserves
contemplation. I can't turn away as you.
Yet you govern us? Hear my son's talk.
Hear his plea within his pronouncement,
his cry from the crevices of his hard words.
My son speaks in two voices, one of a boy,
the other of a young man. One is breaking through,
the other just hangs. Listen, you who can turn away,
who can make such a choice, you who have sons
of your own, but do not hear them!
My son has a face too dark, features too foreign,

a tongue too tangled, yet he reveals, he truths,
he sings your demented rage, but he sings.
You have nothing to rage because it is outside of you.
He is inside of me. His horror is mine. I see what
he sees. And if he dreams, if he plays, if he smiles
in the mist of moon glow, it is me smiling
through the blackened, cluttered, and snarling pathway
toward your shriveled heart.

Reflection on El Train Glass

Gaze penetrates through the glass
of El train window. It infringes
& infiltrates, a misdemeanor
against silence. I turn toward it.
The face in the haze refracting light
in myriad directions, slicing into
working woman's tiredness, into
child's affront, into uniformed
man's wariness, into the uninterested
below city still-life.

A vise of sunrays grips a shape,
an innuendo of myself.
A caress of colors on the cheek.
I'm recalling the places I've been,
like flesh below the waters of a bath,
and I sleep into this transparent
world, sleep into a sort of flying,
into molds of day, into basic colors
and the feel which doesn't feel; into
the stupor deeper than reflection.

And on All Your Children

It was an infant, wailing.

But the story begins in the morning, that monsoon morning, waking up soaked, dishpan hands of an overworked housewife, dishpan feet too. Cookie, the radio man, pulls a pair of dry socks out of a plastic bag—as if they were going to keep his feet dry the rest of the day. In ten minutes they'll be as soaked as the ones he had on. But it's gotta help to at least go through the motions. And to actually have your feet nice and warm and hugged by a pair of calf-length, government-issue, olive-drab socks. I'm not that type though. Just taking my socks off and wringing them, wriggling some life back into my toes, is enough.

The damn rain won't stop. Didn't stop all night.

Rooks is on the radio from relay mountain asking for dry socks. "What does he need dry socks for?" asks Sergeant Gooch, incredulously. "He's in a warm shack up on relay mountain manning the radio."

Gooch is a stateside GI. Knows nothing but Rules & Regs, barracks inspections. Shit like that. He's gonna get us all killed out here in the boonies. Dumb motherfucking five-sided square. Dry socks is the code word for pot. When the supply chopper pays a visit today, Rooks, who's been up there a week already, will get a nice little package from Puckett, the cook. Inside a pair of dry socks.

An infant wailing for its mother's breast.

Sarge and his assistant, another fucking asshole, a buck sergeant who's into Rules & Regs (that's why Gooch chose him), check and recheck their maps and chart our course for the day. The last time we were out in the bush the dickheads had us walk about seven clicks in one day. This is a recon team, motherfuckers. We're supposed to observe the enemy's movements. Underline the word *observe*. Cookie got a call asking if that was us moving so fast. They not only have a gadget on choppers that can detect large amounts of urine, tell you exactly where ole Charley

Cong's been camping out, but they also have a sensor that picks up movement. We came pretty close to getting a shitload of artillery dumped right on top of us. Stupid fucks.

We down a quick breakfast of LRRPs. With cold water. You can't heat anything up out here. Charley will get a whiff of that butane burning and blow your shit clear back to Nantucket. Don't even think of slapping on after-shave before coming out here. Especially with only five other dudes besides you. And two of those being dumb stateside fucks. And one of those being a Wallace supporter from Alabama—that's Cookie. Now there's one dumb fuck, Congressional. But the damned thing didn't go off. It was a dud! So they gave him a Silver Star and a special R&R to Hong Kong instead. This is the dude who every time he was on guard duty back in base camp when we were brand-new in-country cherries claimed he saw gooks charging the perimeter. We would grab our gear and weapons and wait and wait—for nothing. The same dude who one time in an infil signaled he had seen some gooks and crouched down quickly in the tall grass and nearly got a punji stake right in the balls. He got a Purple Heart out of that. Along with a speech from some dry major who said the same thing to all the other GIs as he went from bed to bed, congratulating them all for their service and sacrifice, their country was proud of them.

But what's left for a southern boy nowadays? I mean you can't secede and have another Civil War. So you go squirrel hunting—on the other side of the big charco, as the World War II vets say.

And then there's Williams. Hard to tell about him. Goes around telling everybody he can't stand the silence out in the boonies—not being able to talk, communicating only by signals for days at a time. Well, shit, you can whisper out here, but I guess that's not quite the same. You have to be listening all the goddamned time, be on the lookout constantly. If you're the type that's gotta be running his mouth all the goddamned time this shit out here will drive you crazy. I mean you can catch yourself singing (silently, of course) shit like "Twinkle, Twinkle, Little Star" out here, and maybe even "Mary Had a Little Lamb," goddamn, because sometimes you can spend the whole day out here looking, looking for Charley, waiting, waiting for, and your mind will wander. It will definitely wander. Monsoon is worst because you can't hear Charley, the snap of twigs or the crackle of dry leaves. Of course, he can't hear you either. That's what it's like with Williams. You don't know whether you're ahead of him or he's ahead of you. Anyway I was talking about breakfast. You can have it three ways out here. With rainwater if that's your preference.

Or with rainwater with your purifying tabs thrown in. Or, if you're so inclined, you can have it with regular water. One good thing about monsoon is you don't run out of water. You can catch the runoff from a leaf and have a fresh, I repeat, fresh canteenful in no time at all.

We fold up our LRRP rations and stuff them in our packs (you don't bury anything out here and leave Charley traces of your visit), roll up our poncho liners (some guys carry a poncho, but that makes your load bulky and you can't get too comfortable out here), check our weapons (it's good to apply a fresh coat of oil), and saddle up. In less than ten minutes the straps are digging into your shoulders. In this rain we could pass for a small pack of burros, loaded-down burros climbing, tripping, sliding up and down hills and mountains. A pack of *pinche* burros. That's what we are. Who else would be out here slogging through this rain and mud but a goddamn burro?

Williams is walking point (paranoids make good point men 'cause they're overly careful), but I'm just not sure about this guy. Is he saying all this stuff so everybody'll think he's crazy and not want to go out with him, thinking he'll get sent to a shrink and get shipped back to the world? I mean, if you were going nuts would you be sharing your deepest and darkest thoughts so publicly? Practically broadcasting them? On the other hand, wouldn't that be a perfect sign of madness? Goddamnit, if he plays his cards right he'll have the U.S. Army snookered and be on that freedom bird (back to Birmingham) before me, and I'm at least six months shorter than he is. Ain't that a bitch? Making him walk point will keep him honest. If he fucks up Charley will blow his shit away.

Then there's Sarge. If this was a line outfit he would've been fragged a long time ago. Dusted. And the assistant squad leader, Garcia. He's a Chicano from L.A., a dry, stingy dude. Not much to say about him because there's not much to him. Except that he's engaged. Even has the wedding date set (the very week he gets home from the Nam). That's probably why he's so lifeless. He's scared to death. I hope (for his sake) he makes the army a career because I don't know how else he's gonna be able to put some food on the table.

And me. I walk drag. Bring up the rear. The opposite of point. Except that while you're brushing grass back into place you've also got to be watching out for Charley. Meanwhile your back is turned and your squad is moving away from you—and perhaps into something. So you're cleaning up, like the guy behind the horses in the Fourth of July parade. If you tarry too long you get left behind and break up the flow. Too little and you're bumping into traffic in front of you. It's an art, I tell you.

One hand holding the weapon, thumb on the safety ready to flick it on rock 'n' roll, full automatic at the slightest sound or movement, looking for Charley while at the same time looking to see if you've cleaned up well with your free hand, meanwhile glancing behind you to see what twists and turns the rest of the fellas have taken.

An infant, naked and screaming, and soft and loved like no other.

Last night I tried what the old sergeant in recondo school advised we could do in monsoon if we got cold: piss in your pants. Yeah, you get warm. For about five minutes maybe. Then it's back to cold again. And now I smell like piss. You'd think the rain would wash the smell off, but it doesn't.

I had an uncle I called Uncle Hoople (because he looked just like Major Hoople, the comic strip character). Hrrumphed and talked big just like the Major. He (and only he) knew how to cure the world's ills: los juvenile delinquents, increasing taxes, and the crooked politicians down at city hall who never got around to getting the potholes on the roads on our side of town repaired.

Uncle Hoople would stop by every morning after his shift in the mine to check on Grandma and Grandpa. I was living with my grandparents because my parents were divorced. I could hear Uncle Hoople roaring in the kitchen (*¡Sonamabisquete!*), complaining about the high cost of living or the inefficiency of our blundering sheriff, why the world was going to the dogs (*¡Sonamabisquete!*), and I'd wake up and immediately check to see if I was wet.

I was.

I'd swear I would stay in bed until Uncle Hoople left. Till noon. Sundown, if necessary.

But sooner or later I had to get up. Had to. Couldn't stand the smell. Or being soaked. Nothing left but to face Uncle Hoople.

I'd walk into the kitchen and his first words would be "*¿Como hace el gatito?*—What sound does a kitty make?" and then he'd quickly answer his own question: "Meow. Meow." Knowing full well that in Spanish "meow" sounded exactly like *mea'o,* a contraction for *meado,* which means "(one who has) peed on (himself)."

Every morning.

An infant wailing. Or was it the shriek of a man, unbelieving?

All morning working our way up mountains, down mountains, pulling ourselves up by grabbing trees, an outstretched hand, or a rifle sling and making our way down by sliding voluntarily, involuntarily, holding on to trees, roots, rocks. And for what?

You can't see shit out here in monsoon. Do these assholes really expect you to observe troop movements? Find a new bunker complex? A large weapons cache? All you can think about is sitting down and enduring the rain until the chopper comes to exfil us. There's fog in addition to rain out here. You'll see Charley only if he runs into you. And by the look of things that's exactly what he's gonna do. I saw four or five trees that had been whacked by a machete, all of them at about what would be shoulder high for Charley Cong. No more than a day old. Trail markings. Freshly cut—still white—not even beginning to turn yellow. We're gonna get dusted, man. But you can't tell these spit-shine soldiers a goddamned thing. If it isn't in the Rules & Reg they don't want to hear it. Okay, motherfuckers. But you just wait and see. Charley is going to hand us our ass. Up close and personal.

Let's see.
Are we following orders?
Are we following a trail?
Are we following a trail following orders?
And is Charley following orders?
Is Charley following his own trail?
Is he following his own trail following orders?
Or
Is Charley following us following him?
Twinkle, twinkle, little star.
Chingao, goddamn, and fuck it!

An infant. Nameless. Beloved of God. His. And ours.

We're in a circle, facing outward, in, of all places, an open field. Why we've stopped, why this has been chosen as an observation post, I don't know. Must be a new tactic they're teaching at the NCO academy these days. We're wearing camouflage fatigues and have camouflage stick all over our faces and hands so nobody can see us. We've cut irregular patterns of green tape and plastered them all over our weapons. We blend in perfectly with our surroundings. Not even Charley can find us, and we're right in his own backyard! Man, we're gonna get our ass handed to us.

The sarge signals for a lunch break. I stand up to remove my pack and I see the flashes of the muzzles and fall back down. (Later, Cookie will tell me he thought I had been shot.) (Later, much, much later, I will continue to wonder what the hell happened. Did Charley fire too hurriedly? Obviously, it just wasn't my time to go. There's just no explaining it.)

If we're not surrounded already we will be soon. Son of a bitch! So this is where it ends. (Later, I remember that I didn't have time to think of my entire life flashing before me as the heroes in films and novels say. No, just enough to quickly think that this isn't really the way you imagined it would end, time only to say good-bye not to everything (you notice the trees, the sky, briefly, this may be the last you see of this earth you've lived on for nineteen and one-half years) and to everybody (parents, sisters and brothers, yes, very quickly, but not to the crazy aunts, greedy uncles, old loves, the children you never had with that girl you secretly loved in third period English, the women you dreamed about out here). All the while you've flicked your weapons to full auto, scanning your slice of the horizon (hoping the rest of these motherfuckers are ever so vigilant about theirs). Something about laying down your life, a short phrase from the Bible or some sermon or catechism lesson runs through your head. Scanning. Scanning. You are going to die. Soon. You've accepted that. You are going to die. At the very least the odds are very high. And with no time to make your peace with the world. Only with yourself. And much too quickly to do you much good.

We wait. We are going to die. The one thing I fear is what happened to Jimmy. His team got surrounded and Charley dusted all of them except for him. Somehow he stayed alive until the choppers came and exfilled him. Sometimes you can't help but wonder if the guy wouldn't have been better off if they had dusted him too. He walked around the company area, green eyes shattered, a ghost, haunted. Nothing anybody would ever say or do would help piece him back together again. How do you award somebody his life back, Mr. President?

We wait.

But Charley must be waiting too. Waiting for us to make the first move.

Or, for some reason or another, he's gotten the hell out of here. Proof then this area is hot. If we get into a big firefight he knows we'll call in air support. But then why did he open fire on us? He could've bushwhacked us if he had had just a little more patience. Maybe Charley's got some NCOs that are at least as stupid as ours. I doubt it but you never know.

I pass the word on to Sarge. We need to didi mau, get the hell out of here fast. He thinks about it. We need to break out if Charley's trying to surround us. If he's waiting for reinforcements, we're helping him if we don't make a move to get out. There's no way a chopper could get in here to exfil us. Too many tall trees too close together. We better didi, carefully but fast, and find an LZ.

We begin to file our way north, away from where the shots came—as quickly as possible, staying as low as possible, crawling, slinking away as low as possible on all fours like hungry foxes raiding the chicken coop, knowing that one slipup and it's the farmer coming out with his shotgun, blasting away.

I'm a short-timer. Nine days and a wake up to go. I carry three bandoleers. Two across my chest, Zapatista style, and one around my waist (in addition to the two magazines, one in the weapon and the other taped upside down to it, ready to turn and jam in quickly). Everybody else carries two. I have a slipknot on the bandoleer around my waist. We get into any shit with Charley and I can lay it in front of me quickly, ready to pull out one magazine right after the other quickly, lay as much fire down as I need to. I'm short, man. I haven't come this far to let Charley get into my shit now. Nine goddamn days and a wake up.

We crawl and stumble until we're pretty sure we're safe. And then we wait. And then we crawl away again. And wait. Wait.

Nothing.

We have been spared. (For whatever reason, we have been spared.)

There is no other word for it.

It's a miracle. (A motherfucking, goddamn miracle!)

There's no greater miracle than having your life, your life granted back to you. Oh, if you could learn to live each day like that moment that you promised, promised, swore that you would never, never take it for granted ever, ever again! (A dude who had spent a year down in the delta had this engraved on his Zippo: YOU'VE NEVER REALLY LIVED UNTIL YOU'VE ALMOST DIED.) You have been allowed to be born again. Only the evil and the damned know the joyous chant of resurrection.

An infant. No, clearly there is no greater miracle than a newborn infant. An infant is you all over again (but, of course, not you) played out in front of you to love and worship and guide and inspire and dream for and change the world for.

We're able to make another click before the rain begins to come down hard, merciless. We can't be too far from the LZ where we'll be exfilled tomorrow. One more goddamned night out here. I'm short, man, getting shorter all the goddamned time.

We're forced to set up for the night on a slope. That means that it's going to be tough on the guys on the upper part to keep a sharp lookout. It's a very awkward position, trying to face uphill on your belly or on your side without your neck cramping up. Especially in monsoon with the rain whipping you in the face.

But the rain is coming down so hard that we are forced to sit huddled under our poncho liners, knees pressed tightly to our chests, trying desperately to keep warm. It's cold and the rain seems to be coming down even harder. Nobody's on guard duty. Huddled into ourselves, we try to dream of warmth, but it is impossible. It's as if that word *warm* has been removed from the dictionary by the book burners. You remember how to form the letters, how to spell it, pronounce it, but despite all that it doesn't exist, it's been driven from the world, like a leper, into the shadows, taking with it beloved synonyms such as hot and sizzling and scald and even torrid (as in kiss or lovemaking) and red-hot and scorching and blazing, smoldering (a woman, English class, third period) and blazing and boiling and roasting (the sweet smell of green chiles on the grill), flaming and blistering, the opposite of cold, icy, freezing, chilly, frosty and shit.

Finally the rain lets up. I stand up to stretch, to move a little, let the blood circulate after being hunched over for goddamned long. I'm short, man, short, I'm thinking, when I catch some movement out of the corner of my left eye. I turn and he swings toward me and for an instant, one long indefinable instant, we stand face to face, no more (and no less) than two feet away from one another, we are brothers, enemies, sons, soldiers, yin and yang, east and west, and we somehow don't see each other mainly because the rain has lulled us into a dull complacency: I've allowed myself to become totally involved with ridding the word *cold* from existence, of imagining myself (the possibility is becoming more and more real with each passing hour) back in a place long ago known as home; he is involved in getting someplace before nightfall, perhaps he has been thinking of a girl in his village, perhaps his dear old mother, aging father, his newborn child.

His weapon is unslung and mine is lying against my pack, on the ground. Nobody could have possibly seen us in this rain, and of course we couldn't have possibly seen anybody either. Unless, of course, either one of us runs right into the other. What the fuck are the odds of that happening out in the middle of a place that has been nicknamed Death Valley? I failed arithmetic in the fourth grade, so I couldn't possibly even come up with a formula that would provide an answer, but I goddamn guarantee the odds would have to be very high, like at least, what, 500,000 to 1? Nobody here would get that lucky at the poker tables or the slot machines in Las Vegas, I goddamn guarantee that. (I'm short, goddamnit!) I hit the ground instantly, see the file of soldiers making its way down the hill, each one swinging from the same tree to avoid slipping, sliding down the hill. I turn and see why nobody spotted Charley. Cookie and the rest are still under their poncho liners, facing the same direction as me. I signal them, and when they see the unending file they freeze. I put my index finger to my lips, urging them to be very quiet, and reach slowly, slowly for my weapon. How they haven't seen us God only knows.

God is important now. I beg for my life, my prayers never more sincere. All the praying I did back at St. Francis Xavier doesn't amount to shit compared to this. (Oh God, please. Please.) The column continues down the hill, like an unending, terrifying centipede.

God. *God. GOD!*

I promise that I will make my life worthwhile, that my life will serve your purpose. I will never stray from the path of righteousness.

I am shivering uncontrollably. There is nothing, absolutely nothing I can do to make my teeth stop chattering. I have never been, and will never be again, so terribly terrified. I can't hide it, not even from myself. There is a part of me, way down deep in the deepest part of me, wailing "Mother! Mother!" I can't hide that either.

An infant. Or was it its mother? Frightened beyond any measure of fear, wailing?

As soon as they've passed we move out toward the LZ. Cookie has hung back, providing cover. He cuts loose with a burst and then barks something into the phone. Evidently he's made contact with relay mountain because he's asking for gunships. Sergeant Gooch crawls to the radio, his map out, and begins calling out coordinates. Cookie cuts loose with another burst, an entire magazine, flicks it free, pounds another one in, locks and loads. It's hard to tell if that stupid peckerwood motherfucker is faking it in order to draw us into a firefight or if he's really seen a gook.

We move to a cluster of dead trees at the edge of the LZ. The gunships are on their way. I can hear the major telling somebody we can walk point when they drop the line company in. That means we're going in after Charley. The major wants a body count before nightfall.

The Cobras arrive and the sarge gives them the okay for their first run. The first one comes in fast and low, but the *grroaow* of the miniguns begins a second or two before the ship passes over us. The rounds hit and rip through the fallen trees, they splatter the mud around us, zip by our heads, missing us by inches and less. Gooch is having a hard time calling them off. He's stuttering, mumbling. He can't get enough saliva to grease his mouth; he's got a super case of the cottonmouth, worse than running laps under the hot August sun at the end of the first grueling practice of the football season. Luckily, the second gunship doesn't open fire until it's well beyond us. By the time they come around again for their second run the sarge is able to tell them not to open up until they get to the wood line. He's gulping down water, gulping and swishing and spitting like a buck private after his first desert skirmish in a French Foreign Legion flick.

The gunships make another run and then buzz around as we secure the LZ, and then the shithooks arrive full of line doggies.

We move out quickly. Too quickly. I don't like walking point for a line company. They move too fucking fast, make too much noise—give Charley all kinds of time to set up booby traps, time to get ready. The Man says we got to make contact before nightfall.

And we do. Within half an hour. It's possible that Charley is firing and moving back, slowing us down as much as possible so as to give the rest of his company or battalion or whatever time to didi. Or to set up.

I do not know, I cannot say, I'll never know if it was already there when we came up on the bunker. It may have been. It must have been. (Maybe I saw the mother place it there. That's possible.) How could anybody have placed it there in the middle of a firefight? Right on top of the bunker.

Screaming and wailing.

An infant.

Suddenly I heard the line sergeant call for a guy named Bazooka to get his ass up there on the double, but he got no answer. He hollered again. And again got no response. The line sergeant was cursing madly. Somebody told him that Bazooka was pinned down and he shouted that he didn't give a shit, he wanted Bazooka to get his ass up there or he was looking at some time in LBJ City. Then he shouted something to Sergeant Gooch and then Gooch yelled for me and when I got there he told me I had to go get Bazooka and bring him back. (Why the fuck me? I'm short. Just why the fuck me?) Gooch knows I'm short, the sorry motherfucker, but that doesn't stop him from asking me if I'm refusing an order. I hear a line doggie screaming his ass off for a medic. The machine gunner in the bunker is smoking us. Somebody yells that the medic's been hit. Charley's got us by the nuts and he knows it. We don't know what to do as long as that baby's on top of the bunker. If we dust the baby he wins, no matter if we wipe out the entire battalion, and another battalion, and another after that. Meanwhile, as we're weighing the consequences, he's ripping us to shreds.

I crawl off until I locate Bazooka. This guy (I learn later) can knock off a gnat's balls from as far away as a hundred meters. One look at him and I know why the sarge sent me after him. And why he didn't answer when the line sergeant called for him.

He too is from one of those little mountain villages in northern New Mexico. Obviously, I'm supposed to talk to him, convince him in Spanish to come with me and perform his duty for God and country. I notice his wedding band and I know, I know from the look in his eyes, he's carrying a picture of his new baby.

I don't know what the hell to say to him, and if I did, how to say it. There is nothing I can say or do to spare him.

We are *compadres* and *enemigos,* both (now) *hijos de la chingada madre,* greasers and the salt of the earth, *putos* and paratroopers, and wetbacks, both here and back home.

Finally, I ask him if he is from New Mexico. He nods and asks me, "*¿Y tu?*" We exchange information, where we're from, mutual acquaintances, and promise to get together for a beer back there (and maybe we will if we happen to run into each other, but I don't know that after something like this we're gonna seek each other out). This time of year back home they're opening the *compuertas* and the water from the melting snows comes coursing down the *acequia madre* and into the fields, the beginning of the growing season. We'll both be home to pick and roast and, of course, gorge ourselves on green chile three times and more a day. I tell him I have a can of green chile I'm going to cook with my rice and shrimp rations and share with him tonight. Finally I say to him that the sergeant wants to see him, and we crawl back toward the bunker.

The machine gunner, a young freckle-faced kid from Missouri named Tom, has managed to crawl close to the sergeant, and when Bazooka is ready with the rocket launcher the sergeant orders Tom to lay down some fire and give him plenty of cover. The ammo bearer gets ready to feed the belt and Tom opens up.

Bazooka aims, fires, and just as quickly slumps against the ground, his head buried in his arms, motionless.

An infant. The machine gunner swore it was a girl. Swore, all night, softly. All night.

———

After the line company sweeps the area, the sergeant gives Bazooka a hearty thumbs up, tells him he's gonna recommend him for a Silver Star. "Fuck you," Bazooka tells him, walking off, a raindrop, or is it a tear, coursing its way steadily down his dirty, hardened face.

It is a curse aimed not only at him, but a curse laid on him.

And on you, you masters of war.

And on all your children.

Homecoming

From *The Other Side: Fault Lines, Guerrilla
Saints and the True Heart of Rock 'n' Roll*

San Salvador, December 1987

The shadow of the plane darts across dusty fields that give off pale smoke
as they are burned before the sowing of winter's crops. Spontaneous
combustion and lightning strikes are also common during the long dry
season, and the brittle yellow remnants of the richly cultivated landscape
catch fire easily. I can't help but imagine the blazes that rise up where
rockets pound into the thickly forested hills along the Honduran
border—beyond the cultivated plains, beyond the volcanos and valleys,
somewhere beyond the horizon.

*Yet another homecoming. My second home. My first home. My no-
home* . . . I pass through the lightly guarded customs area without a
hitch—sometimes press credentials *can* help you in El Salvador. I had
told my family not to bother to pick me up, but as the automatic doors
that open onto the main lobby separate with a mechanical whoosh, I scan
the expectant faces anyway. A part of me wishes to see my grandparents
smiling widely, my nephews waving. But the eyes only glance at me, then
they are straining to find the familiar face behind me as the doors slam
shut.

Outside, I negotiate in vain for a cheap fare into town and end up
paying fifty colones ($10, an exorbitant fee here) to the driver of a mid-
seventies Toyota. As we speed along the open highway, I find myself
immediately looking for signs of the conflict. But of course there are
none. We are very far from the war of bullets and helicopters.

My driver fidgets with the radio, tuning it to a Top Forty station that
blares out the Miami Sound Machine. I gaze through the window. Men,
women, and children carry firewood, large baskets, water gourds alongside the road. There are some soldiers out on patrol, supposedly guarding

the highway, but it's been so long since the guerrillas have been in this part of the country that the soldiers look bored, expecting anything but an ambush.

I tell the driver that I was last here just after the earthquake. It had left San Salvador looking like the bombed-out towns of the remote countryside. Any progress?

"It's gone to hell."

I wince and grab onto the dashboard as he weaves in and out of the slower traffic. The Virgin Mary swings from the rearview mirror like a circus acrobat.

"Don't worry," says my driver, noticing my discomfort. "We're all experts at this."

We reach the end of the highway. The colonies of shacks built after the earthquake are still perched precariously on the hillsides below the middle-class homes; the dust still swirls about with the summer winds. As we move into downtown San Salvador, I see streets twice as congested with vendors as before. Their stalls of fruits and vegetables, clothing and cigarettes are spreading ever farther out from the Central Market. The city is rapidly becoming one huge, neurotic bazaar.

Every morning during the Christmas and New Year's holiday, my nephew, five years old, awakes at dawn, pulls out his toys, and turns on the TV at top volume. The adults, still in bed, grind their teeth. The only other person up at that hour is the maid, Nora, who loves to play pop radio, also at top volume, as she readies breakfast. A *cumbia* rhythm and the sounds of dishes clattering in the kitchen accompany the roosters that crow outside, and the dubbed voices of the cartoon characters GI Joe and the Masters of the Universe reverberate throughout the house.

In the rebuilt cottage adjacent to my uncle's large, comfortable home, my grandparents sleep. Grandfather is still alive, slowly losing his bout with cancer. Grandmother has been wishing that she might die with him. How I'd like to speak with Grandfather . . . about life and death and love and war. But he is even quieter now than he was when I was twelve and he occasionally broke his long silences to tell me his tall tales, and I can't seem to find the confidence to say what I must say.

I am the first of the grown-ups awake. Sleepily, I sip some coffee, look out through the bars across the windows at the peaceful greenery of the backyard. As I walk outside past my grandparents' silent cottage and take the cobblestone path toward the bus stop, I feel pangs of guilt: I'm going to betray my family by visiting my other family.

The last time I saw Pedro, about a year and a half ago, he was in exile in Mexico City and drunk, after more than a decade of sobriety. It was at a hotel in the Zócalo area downtown, a cavernous nineteenth-century palace with a skylight and a daunting interior patio. The Mexican authorities were using the building to house exiles from all over Latin America—everyone from shell-shocked FMLN combatants to anti-Castro Cubans. Pedro's drunken rants bounced off the thick cold walls and echoed throughout the building.

"This one's for the boys fighting the fascists in the mountains!" he toasts with the bottle of brandy. He passes me the bottle, then grabs it out of my hands to continue. "And this one's for the whores who suck the soldiers' cocks! This one's for us, the fucked-up poets whose petty bourgeois decadence is as tragic a story as the Crucifixion!" The bottle flies toward the mirror. Pedro looks at himself in a hundred shards, weeping.

I had originally met him at the National University in El Salvador— that "den of subversion" that succeeding governments have singled out for repression—where he led poetry workshops in the bullet-riddled extension building. In Pedro's case, there is no doubt that his sentiments fell into the "subversive" category, at least in the government's eyes: his poetry speaks of suffering and hope (*"The bloody rain soaks into the black earthland yet, the sunflowers manage to rise . . ."*), and sometimes outright militancy (*"The sons of the Conquest/will reconquer the land of the sun . . ."*). After collaborating with the rebels and publishing protest poetry in one of the country's major dailies, he was arrested and detained by the security forces.

In Mexico, with his usual hushed cadences, which faded in and out like a weak signal on a shortwave radio, he'd told me about the hideous poetry of that night: the soldiers' boots pounding on the roof . . . rifle butts smashing the floorboards . . . his daughters crying . . . bookshelves toppled . . . his wife stoically silent before the lieutenant's questioning . . . the leaves swirling about the house in the helicopter wind . . . the cockroaches skittering over his body in the dank cell.

He'd been lucky. Influential university authorities pulled diplomatic strings to get him off with a relative wrist slap: exile. But in Mexico City, the separation from home and family had driven him to the edge of insanity. (I imagine the bottle in one hand, a cigarette in the other: *"This is the first drink I've had in ten years, compañeros . . ."*) So he threw caution to the wind and risked returning, although there were no guarantees for his or his family's safety.

And so here he is, back in San Salvador, asleep after another late-night drinking session with his bohemian buddies when I arrive. His wife greets me, offers me coffee, and we chat quietly about Pedro's return while he showers. Yes, she says, it's a relief to have him home. But the anxiety remains, and no, she doesn't think the war will end soon, but what can one do?

When Pedro enters the room, shirtless, eyes reddened like coals, black hair unruly, a smile emerges from his deeply lined face. With his voice a whisper, on the verge of unintelligibility, he fills me in on the events of the last year. In Mexico, things had gone from bad to worse, he says. The pain of exile, coupled with his excessive drinking, had gotten him into more and more trouble.

One night, exasperated at not being able to contact his wife and daughters by telephone, the pressure became unbearable. He went on a rampage, bursting into his comrades' rooms and tearing the receivers off the telephones, which he deposited, one by one, in his room. None of his friends had been able to control him. When the police arrived, he was seated cross-legged on the bed, holding his head in his hands, surrounded by the black receivers and their severed cords.

The cry "*¡Felicidades!*" rings out in all directions. It is New Year's Eve and the house is filling with guests. My grandfather, the center of attention, seems happy: it is the first time in many years that his grandchildren from the United States have come to spend the holidays with him.

As ever, he comments on the political situation, which to him appears worse every day. He traces the trouble back to the late seventies and President Carter's emphasis on human rights. "This allowed the communists to gain strength."

An aunt chimes in. "What we need right now," she says, "is someone who isn't afraid of using force to get us out of this mess." (An image of Major Roberto D'Aubuisson flashes in my mind: he raises the machete and whacks the watermelon in half before a crowd of silent *campesinos.* "That's how the Christian Democrats are—green on the outside, but red on the inside! Communists!")

With the "human rights" stipulations, Grandfather continues, the war against the communists was checked. And just look at the country today. "Duarte is a socialist," he says. "And you know that between socialism and communism, there is only a very small step. And that's where this country is heading." Grandmother shudders. "This thing about communism scares me," she says. She's been complaining about my beard lately: "Looks too much like Che."

I say nothing, though I'd like to steer the conversation away from the politics, to hear once again Grandfather's stories. The one about the huge hacienda my family once owned comes to mind . . . *"Lands that stretched out as far as the horizon."* But all the memories have been truncated by the war.

I look at Grandfather's hands. I always marveled at them as a child —large and strong, capable of wielding a machete or pulling on a railroad brake. The hands retain some of their youthful strength, though they are now liver spotted. But his forearms, his chest, and the rest of his body have thinned. The guayabera hangs too loose over his sagging shoulders.

The family around him laughs, drinks, dances. Grandfather, his political speech over, gasps for breath.

"That hotel was full of phantoms—exiles from all over the world. I was one of the ghosts too," says Pedro, sipping a morning beer at a bar downtown. The waitress, a pretty young woman with a disquieting, distracted look, serves us *boquitas*—small chunks of cheese and pork. She returns to her post behind the counter, looking out over the empty tables.

This is Pedro's second homecoming. After his first return, it hadn't taken long to find out if he was welcome. He'd been in the country only a week when several armed security agents burst into his mother's house and asked for him by name. Fortunately, he wasn't there, but he went into hiding and left the country again shortly thereafter.

Six more months of exile had the same effect on him as his previous stint. He phoned his wife and told her that he'd do anything—stay inside, not visit any of his old communist friends, take not one sip of alcohol— anything to be home again. His wife relented, and during the summer school break he "visited" El Salvador once again. "The idea was to stay two weeks, to test the waters," he says, tousling his hair with a shaky hand. "I'm still living that two weeks, six months later."

During the first few months, he rarely went out, resisting the temptation to visit his colleagues. He spent endless hours working on his poetry. But as time passed and no rifle butts smashed down the door in the middle of the night, he gained confidence and gradually began venturing out onto the streets.

Still, it has been a bit much for me to take, to see him mentioned, lauded even, in the country's main right-wing paper by a columnist friend of his, who wrote a glowing commentary upon a new collection of poems by Pedro. He has also given a public reading at the Teatro Nacional, the plushly carpeted, chandeliered, government-run cultural center.

In effect, he is being toasted by the very government that two years ago kicked him out of the country, but Pedro reminds me that there still remain a couple of unknowns in the equation. Sure, there is more political space today—he probably wouldn't get busted for his poetic pamphlets now—but one could never trust the authorities that much . . . the fear is still there. And then there is the situation with his oldest daughter.

I give Pedro a querulous look.

"You haven't heard, I guess," he says, as he meticulously peels the label off the beer bottle. "Now we've got two troublemakers in the family. She's working full-time with a human rights organization. That could interest the authorities. Not just in her, but in my case again as well. It's a real family affair, now."

My uncle pours himself another vodka. It is still early in the evening, but my uncle Roger's New Year's "celebration" is more than well underway. We sit uncomfortably, next to each other, for a few minutes.

The years are most apparent in his balding pate, in his large belly, and in not just the rings under his eyes but the eyes themselves: they look down, away from you—too tired to meet your gaze straight on. But ever the responsible father, even though he's in the process of going through his second divorce, Roger gets up each morning, goes to work to support his children. No hangover has ever stopped him.

Finally, we hit upon a subject that animates him: business. He works for a Japanese-owned textile factory on the outskirts of the city, one of the largest in the country and among the few that has managed to hold its own during the war. Now in his element, Roger warms up to what sounds like a speech he's given many times.

Yes, it surely was one of the largest in the Central American market. These last few years have been ones of adversity though, no doubt about it. Lay-offs. Rebel sabotage. And the time the Japanese chief executive officer was kidnapped by the guerrillas. The FMLN asked for millions of dollars for his release. Endless negotiations for nothing: it all went awry in the end. Seems that an overzealous army commando unit attempted to ambush the guerrillas at the preappointed drop-off site. After the gun battle, the executive's bullet-riddled body was sent back home to Japan, and the ambassador asked for some military heads to roll. The FMLN, on the other hand, succeeded in getting the cash. An ex-guerrilla once told me about a mad shopping spree after the incident, eating out at expensive restaurants, hiring taxis even for short trips, renting out hotel rooms for romantic encounters. . . . *A crew of guerrillas disguised in white guayaberas at the Salvador Sheraton, wining and dining the daughters of the aristocracy . . .*

Roger's voice drifts back to me. The company's in a holding pattern these days, he says; no growth, no shrinkage. Everything stays the same. It's a depressing situation, you know?

He raises the glass to his lips, closing his eyes as he savors the drink. The ice cubes clink and some vodka spills over the rim as he sets the drink down too hard upon the glass table.

It is late in the afternoon at the National University, and I wait for Pedro's daughter, Soledad, to show up for our meeting. She is late, and I wonder about her new job, with the human rights organization.

The university is virtually unchanged: it lives up to its reputation as a "liberated zone," with FMLN recruitment propaganda blaring through speakers outside the psychology building, along with Cuban New Song by Silvio Rodríguez and Pablo Milanes. And the graffiti—ever since I can remember, almost every wall here has been covered with spray-painted slogans. Some walls sport several generations of them, dating back to the sixties. Each year there is a new set of slogans, but the theme never changes. *Duarte, ¡A la mierda!* is this year's favorite—"Duarte, to the shits!"

There do seem to be more student organizations (each slogan is signed by one group or another), though. The most radical have taken to taunting the security forces by throwing rocks, obviously wanting them to fire into the crowd and further radicalize the masses. But there are other students who tell me they feel this tactic is infantile. And there are significant numbers on the sidelines, genuinely interested in social change but utterly confused as to who is representing which faction and who is right.

Soledad arrives at the very moment when I'd given the date up for lost. She has many of her father's features: a prominent but pretty mole to the left of her nose, a mischievous smile, dark and radiant eyes.

"I'm not sure what to do," she tells me, as we sit down for coffee at an open-air campus café packed with students. The job with the organization has caused somewhat of a crisis in the family, she admits.

It was almost by chance that Soledad happened into the job. Only a few months ago, she had abandoned hope of finishing her studies in the unpredictable and dangerous environment of this university, where her father's notoriety (the poetry workshops) cast a peculiar shadow upon her. Last year she had visited a friend who was studying at Mexico City's finest university, and she began to consider completing school there instead, an idea her parents loathed. A short while later, however, she was offered the job and, she says, "Everything changed."

"I've been learning so much." Soledad flashes a smile. "I work a lot directly with the *campesinos,* and I've never had that experience before."

Again, her parents had objected—especially Pedro: *"What about school? You'll never be able to finish your studies with a full-time job! You know that we love you, but you have to understand my political situation, dear . . ."*

"Now, my parents say they want me to go to Mexico," Soledad says, smiling only slightly at the irony. She averts her gaze from me, out toward the gathering darkness. There are fewer students now and the waitresses are preparing to close down the café.

I find myself somewhat surprised that Soledad has gone so wholeheartedly into the political movement. When we first met, she had given me the impression that activism wasn't one of her ambitions. "I know what I'm doing," she stresses. "And to me, all politics is a dirty business. But there are some pure things. Like helping the *campesinos*. They're not ideologues. So I feel like I'm doing some good. At least . . . I'm not on the other side."

I step outside into the cool night air, under the canopy of the giant copinol tree in the backyard. Across the valley, roman candles toss rainbow colors into the air. Steadily, the sound of fireworks going off in the hills around us and in the city below has been increasing. An hour before midnight, we begin raising our voices to be heard over the multitudinous explosions.

"This is nothing," says Pablo, another one of my uncles, with his ironic smile, just a few minutes before midnight. "Back when people still had money, you could hear twice as much on New Year's." As with my uncle Roger, the economy is one of Pablo's favorite topics. He asks me about the Black Monday stock market crash in the States. "What in the hell is going on over there? How is it that your economy could seem so strong and then in one day, *pffft!?*"

Pablo has been dancing *cumbias* tirelessly, and everything he says is tinged with irony, but now it seems as if he's truly asking me to explain what went wrong with supply-side economics. "We haven't begun to feel it here yet. But we will," he says gravely.

Pablo goes on to relate an anecdote which, he says, will show just how bad things are in El Salvador now. He was walking downtown just the other day, in broad daylight, when an assailant tore a thick gold chain from his neck. "Six hundred dollars lost." But it's okay, he tells me. "Right afterward, I bought myself this." He thrusts up his arm, fist clenched, to show me his new gold bracelet. "Two hundred dollars."

The full fury of the fireworks is let loose at the stroke of midnight. All the sounds of the war are reproduced in the celebratory din. Strings of firecrackers imitate machine guns. Large dynamite-stick lookalikes boom out like mortar cannons. From dozens of different points around the city, skyrockets streak across the sky. There are so many detonations that the individual blasts become one solid hail of noise. It is that sound I will remember most: when I think back later and try to remember what people said in those moments, I will see the lips forming words, but there will be no sound other than explosions.

Later, the family gathers together in the living room for a toast to begin the New Year. Pablo is visibly drunk, but suddenly eloquent.

"We propose this toast, in honor of the entire family. But this toast, more than anything else, is a tribute to this couple," he says, motioning toward my grandparents, "who, through their example of longevity and loyalty, inspire all of us . . ."

The glasses clink all around the room. My grandfather, fatigued (he has already had to lie down once this evening to catch his breath), manages a smile.

Both Soledad and I shiver. Night has fallen upon the campus, and the cool breeze of the afternoon has given way to a stiff evening wind.

A small black monkey hops from table to empty table, vainly looking for scraps of food. Soledad is steeped in her thoughts. In a few moments, both the waitresses and monkey are gone.

Soledad knows she can't take the argument about her family's safety lightly. She recently attended the funeral of Herbert Anaya Sanabria, the slain leader of another human rights organization identified with the left. The death squads have been coming out of hiding lately, and as well as Sanabria's murder, there have been dozens of less-publicized "disappearances" of students and labor leaders.

Should she go to Mexico, as her family wants her to do, as she herself had felt was perfect only months ago? Stay on, working with the *campesinos*? Quit, but stay in El Salvador and study at the university?

"The thing is, I don't want to miss any of this history," she says, as a gust of wind plays with her thick curly hair (which is just like her father's). "Though I know there's more to the world than just El Salvador, and there's so much to see in Mexico City."

One thing is for certain: she can't continue at odds with her father. "When I was younger, he would play me his favorite music and read his poetry." She smiles at the memory. "But I didn't understand. I rejected him. And when he left the country, I . . ." She pauses, and her eyes, focused on the empty space between us, appear to conjure up his image again, and I see him too: *in the living room, reciting from a book before his bohemian friends . . . passed out in his study, his head resting over a furiously edited manuscript . . .* "I realized that the things he was trying to share with me were really beautiful. Those things began to mean so much to me while he was gone. And now that he's back . . . it's like he's not really here. Do you think he's really in danger?"

The full moon is rising above the horizon, and as we get up to leave the buildings of the university are silhouetted against the pale light. We walk into the darkness outside the glow of the café's lights.

"What would you do?" she asks.

Pedro and I are sharing a joint out on the patio. His youngest daughter, a cute four-year-old, bounds out to greet him, her black hair shiny and wet from a bath. The day is bright, the sun strong and warm. As the grass takes effect and my body relaxes, I gaze out at the neighborhood. Just a few blocks away is the National University. Pedro hasn't set foot on the campus in over two years, and he continues to resist the temptation to do so. Two blocks down in the opposite direction stands an army barracks.

I notice a dark band on the eastern horizon. Smoke? I ask Pedro. He peers at the phenomenon and shrugs his shoulders. "I've got my escape route all worked out," he jokes. "I hear them at the door, I jump over this wall, and I'm gone," he says, nodding his head at the five-foot wall that surrounds the narrow patio. Suddenly, as if on cue, we hear the sound of the doorbell. "There they are now," he says.

Agents in civilian clothes throw us against the wall for the body search. One of them is shouting obscenities, asking where the weapons are stashed. The bookshelves, Neruda, Vallejo ("¡Comunistas!" yells a soldier), tumble to the floor. Pedro's youngest daughter is screaming and his wife is trying to calm her down. One soldier is prodding Soledad with his rifle, telling her how "good she looks." And now they are asking what the hell an American journalist—a suspiciously Salvadoran-looking American journalist—is doing in the house of a "known communist terrorist." What am I going to tell my family? Then we're thrown into one of those red Cherokee jeeps with tinted windows. After a long ride, we are ordered out in the middle of nowhere. In an abandoned ranch house, the shots ring out . . .

"The risk is very real," says Pedro, snapping me out of the vision, and he passes me the joint. Back inside the house, he confides that his stay here feels "like a temporary one." He puts a shirt on, finishes off a cup of coffee, and searches for his cigarettes. Then he thinks out loud, muttering in fragments, "Maybe the best thing . . . Mexico again . . . fucking fascists . . ." (Later, when I ask his wife if she'll join him in exile should he leave again, she gives me a tired shake of the head. Will this moving never stop?)

As we are about to leave, Pedro's youngest daughter bounds into the living room. "Where are you going, daddy?" she asks, stretching her arms out to him for a good-bye hug and kiss on the cheek.

"I'm just going downtown for a little while, my love." After embracing her, Pedro turns toward me again. For a few moments, he gives me a wordless, troubled look, then we walk through the door and out onto the city streets.

In the rattling bus, on our way to different destinations (Pedro to check on the printing of his new book, I toward home for lunch with my family), Pedro invites me to spend New Year's Eve with him. "I'll show you what a real New Year's Eve celebration is like here," he tells me . . . *Communist party veterans and young radicals from the university dancing up a sweat, booze and grass, Soledad and me stealing a kiss in the backyard* . . . I can't, I tell Pedro, I have to spend time with my family.

The fireworks have begun to taper off, the battle sounds more distant. Outside on the patio, Roger sits before me, and between us is the bottle. A floodlight shines from the house behind him; his face is in perfect silhouette. "Look. I'll tell you something," he says, his mouth dry from the alcohol. "Some friends have approached me in the past and have said, 'Come on, let's join in the fight against the guerrillas.' But I told them no.

"There are many different ways of fighting. . . . I think the most important one is economic development. They have to let the middle class have a chance to right things." But he's too drunk to maintain his train of thought. Soon he's talking about the family.

Things never seem to turn out the way you dreamed they would, he says. Yes, the second divorce has been tough, but his kids still love him—nothing can break that bond. "Look. I'll tell you what's really the most important thing, more important than my money and your words and all that shit. Family, that's what." He appears to be on the verge of tears, but he holds it in. Then a sneer flashes across his face. "The fucking gringos don't know anything about family, and, unfortunately for you, you grew up with them.

"Without the family, we don't have anything. Because of business, I've had to travel a lot, you know. I've been alone in hotel rooms, so far from home, sad beyond words. Sure, I've had my flings, but without a family, what's it all worth? Family's what's important, damn it, so keep the family together!"

A few days later, I am on the highway that leads from San Salvador to the airport. Once again, I make the trip alone. It was a typical good-bye—wordless hugs on all sides. The highway stretches out before me; the Pacific appears as a gauzy blue ribbon on the horizon.

Grandfather, would you disown me if I joined up with the guerrillas? Uncle, why the fuck do you think there are young assailants after your gold? Pedro, I really should be with my family right now, this'll be the last beer, okay? By the way, Pedro, or Roger or Grandfather, are you certain that history is moving in a straight line here? A socialist utopia, a free market paradise, intervention, attrition, quake after quake? Soledad, you are my age and our generation faces these impossible choices, and how can I advise you when I can neither face nor turn away from my own family? Grandfather, I watch your chest struggling to rise against the weight of these years. Why are you so quiet, Grandfather? Maybe when the war is over, we can talk again. But you won't live that long . . .

The taxi rattles along the highway. The hot, humid sea air pours through the open windows as we pass by a column of soldiers marching along in sloppy formation before an expanse of charred cornfields. As we near the airport, I look back one last time through the rear window at the road that leads back to the hills, back to San Salvador, to the families that I am at once a part of and so distant from. Above those hills, towering, gleaming white clouds have gathered. But it's not going to rain, I tell myself. The rains are still months away . . .

RICHARD RODRIGUEZ

Mexico's Children

From *Days of Obligation*

When I was a boy it was still possible for Mexican farmworkers in California to commute between the past and the future.

The past returned every October. The white sky clarified to blue and fog opened white fissures in the landscape.

After the tomatoes and the melons and the grapes had been picked, it was time for Mexicans to load up their cars and head back into Mexico for the winter.

The schoolteacher said aloud to my mother what a shame it was the Mexicans did that—took their children out of school.

Like wandering Jews, Mexicans had no true home but the tabernacle of memory.

The schoolteacher was scandalized by what she took as the Mexicans' disregard of their children's future. The children failed their tests. They made no friends. What did it matter? Come November, they would be gone to some bright world that smelled like the cafeteria on Thursdays —Bean Days. Next spring they would be enrolled in some other school, in some other Valley town.

The schoolroom myth of America described an ocean—immigrants leaving behind several time zones and all the names for things.

Mexican-American memory described proximity. There are large Mexican-American populations in Seattle and Chicago and Kansas City, but the majority of Mexican Americans live, where most have always lived, in the southwestern United States, one or two hours from Mexico, which is within the possibility of recourse to Mexico or within the sound of her voice.

My father knew men in Sacramento who had walked up from Mexico.

There is confluence of earth. The cut of the land or its fold, the bleaching sky, the swath of the wind, the length of shadows—all these suggested Mexico. Mitigated was the sense of dislocation otherwise familiar to immigrant experience.

By November the fog would thicken, the roads would be dangerous. Better to be off by late October. Families in old trucks and cars headed south down two-lane highways, past browning fields. Rolls of toilet paper streaming from rolled-down windows. After submitting themselves to the vegetable cycle of California for a season, these Mexicans were free. They were Mexicans! And what better thing to be?

HAIIII-EEE. HAI. HAI. HAI.

There is confluence of history.

Cities, rivers, mountains retain Spanish names. California was once Mexico.

The fog closes in, condenses, and drips day and night from the bare limbs of trees. And my mother looks out the kitchen window and cannot see the neighbor's house.

Amnesia fixes the American regard of the past. I remember a graduate student at Columbia University during the Vietnam years; she might have been an ingenue out of Henry James. "After Vietnam, I'll never again believe that America is the good and pure country I once thought it to be," the young woman said.

Whereas Mexican Americans have paid a price for the clarity of their past.

Consider my father: when he decided to apply for American citizenship, my father told no one, none of his friends, those men with whom he had come to this country looking for work. American citizenship would have seemed a betrayal of Mexico, a sin against memory. One afternoon, like a man with something to hide, my father slipped away. He went downtown to the Federal Building in Sacramento and disappeared into America.

Now memory takes her revenge on the son.

VETE PERO NO ME OLVIDES.

Go, but do not forget me, someone has written on the side of a building near the border in Tijuana.

Mexicans may know their souls are imperiled in America, but they do not recognize the risk by its proper name.

Two Mexican teenagers say they are going to *los Estados Unidos* for a job. Nothing more.

For three or four generations now, Mexican villages have lived under the rumor of America, a rumor vaguer than paradise. America exists in thousands of maternal prayers and in thousands of pubescent dreams. Everyone knows someone who has been. Everyone knows someone who never came back.

What do you expect to find?

The answer is always an explanation for the journey: "I want money enough to be able to return to live with my family in Mexico."

Proofs of America's existence abound in Mexican villages—stereo equipment, for example, or broken-down cars—but these are things Americans picked up or put down, not America.

Mexicans know very little of the United States, though they have seen America, the TV show, and America, the movie. Mexico's pre-eminent poet, Octavio Paz, writes of the United States as an idea of no characteristic mansion or spice. Paz has traveled and taught in America, but his writings relegate America to ineluctability—a jut of optimism, an aerodynamic law.

To enter America, which is invisible, Mexicans must become invisible. Tonight, a summer night, five hundred Mexicans will become invisible at 8:34 P.M. While they wait, they do not discuss Tom Paine or Thomas Jefferson or the Bill of Rights. Someone has an uncle in Los Angeles who knows a peach farmer near Tracy who always hires this time of year.

Compared with pulpy Mexico, grave Mexico, sandstone Mexico, which takes the impression of time, the United States and its promise of the future must seem always hypothetical—occasion more than place.

I once had occasion to ask a middle-class Mexican what he admires about the United States (a provocative question because, according to Mexican history and proverb, there is nothing about the United States to admire). He found only one disembodied word: "organization." When I pressed the man to anthropomorphize further he said, "Deliveries get made, phones are answered, brakes are repaired" (indirect constructions all, as if by the consent of unseen hands).

Coming from Mexico, a country that is so thoroughly *there,* where things are not necessarily different from when your father was your age, Mexicans are unable to puncture the abstraction. For Mexicans, even death is less abstract than America.

Mexican teenagers waiting along the levee in Tijuana are bound to be fooled by the United States because they do not yet realize the future will be as binding as the past. The American job will introduce the Mexican to an industry, an optimism, a solitude nowhere described in Mexico's theology.

How can two Mexican teenagers know this, clutching the paper bags their mamas packed for them this morning? The past is already the future, for the bags contain only a change of underwear. These two may have seen "Dallas" on TV and they may think they are privy to the logic and locution of America. But that is not the same thing as having twenty American dollars in their own pockets.

Mexico, mad mother. She still does not know what to make of our leaving. For most of this century Mexico has seen her children flee the house of memory. During the Revolution 10 percent of the population picked up and moved to the United States; in the decades following the Revolution, Mexico has watched many more of her children cast their lots with the future; head north for work, for wages; north for life. Bad enough that so many left, worse that so many left her for the gringo.

America wanted cheap labor. American contractors reached down into Mexico for men to build America. Sons followed fathers north. It became a rite of passage for the poor Mexican male.

I will send for you or I will come home rich.

I would see them downtown on Sundays—men my age drunk in Plaza Park. I was still a boy at sixteen, but I was an American. At sixteen, I wrote a gossip column, "The Watchful Eye," for my school paper.

Or they would come into town on Monday nights for the wrestling matches or on Tuesday nights for boxing. They worked on ranches over in Yolo County. They were men with time on their hands. They were men without women. They were Mexicans without Mexico.

On Saturdays, Mexican men flooded the Western Union office, where they sent money—money turned into humming wire and then turned back into money—all the way down into Mexico. America was a monastery. America was a vow of poverty. They kept themselves poor for Mexico.

Fidel, the janitor at church, lived over the garage at the rectory. Fidel spoke Spanish and was Mexican. He had a wife down there, people said; some said he had grown children. But too many years had passed and he didn't go back. Fidel had to do for himself. Fidel had a clean piece of linoleum on the floor; he had an iron bed; he had a table and a chair; he had a frying pan and a knife and a fork and a spoon. Everything else Fidel sent back to Mexico. Sometimes, on summer nights, I would see his head through the bars of the little window over the garage of the rectory.

My parents left Mexico in the twenties: she as a girl with her family; he as a young man, alone. To tell different stories. Two Mexicos. At some celebration—we went to so many when I was a boy—a man in the crowd filled his lungs with American air to crow over all, ¡VIVA MEXICO! Everyone cheered. My parents cheered. The band played louder. Why VIVA MEXICO? The country that had betrayed them? The country that had forced them to live elsewhere?

I remember standing in the doorway of my parents' empty bedroom.

Mexico was memory—not mine. Mexico was mysteriously both he and she, like this, like my parents' bed. And over my parents' bed floated the Virgin of Guadalupe in a dime-store frame. In its most potent guise, Mexico was a mother like this queen. Her lips curved like a little boat. *Tú. Tú.* The suspirate vowel. *Tú.* The ruby pendant. The lemon tree. The song of the dove. Breathed through the nose, perched on the lips.

Two voices, two pronouns were given me as a child, like good and bad angels, like sweet and sour milks, like rank and clement weathers; one yielding, one austere.

In the sixteenth century, Spain bequeathed to Mexico two forms of address, two versions of "you": In Mexico there is *tú* and there is *usted*.

In Sacramento, California, everything outside our house was English, was "you"—hey you. My dog was you. My parents were you. The nuns were you. My best friend, my worst enemy was you. God was You.

Whereas the architecture of Mexico is the hardened shell of a Spanish distinction.

Treeless, open plazas abate at walls; walls yield to refreshment, to interior courtyards, to shuttered afternoons.

At the heart there is *tú*—the intimate voice—the familiar room in a world full of rooms. *Tú* is the condition, not so much of knowing, as of being known; of being recognized. *Tú* belongs within the family. *Tú* is spoken to children and dogs, to priests; among lovers and drunken friends; to servants; to statues; to the high court of heaven; to God Himself.

The shaded arcade yields once more to the plaza, to traffic and the light of day. *Usted,* the formal, the bloodless, the ornamental you, is spoken to the eyes of strangers. By servants to masters. *Usted* shows deference to propriety, to authority, to history. *Usted* is open to interpretation; therefore it is subject to corruption, a province of politicians. *Usted* is the language outside Eden.

In Mexico, one is most oneself in private. The very existence of *tú* must undermine the realm of *usted*. In America, one is most oneself in public.

In order to show you America I would have to take you out. I would take you to the restaurant—OPEN 24 HOURS—alongside a freeway, any freeway in the U.S.A. The waitress is a blonde or a redhead—not the same color as at her last job. She is divorced. Her eyebrows are jet-black migraines painted on, or relaxed, clownish domes of cinnamon brown. Morning and the bloom of youth are painted on her cheeks. She is at once antimaternal—the kind of woman you're not supposed to know— and supramaternal, the nurturer of lost boys.

She is the priestess of the short order, curator of the apple pie. She administers all the consolation of America. She has no illusions. She knows the score; she hands you the Bill of Rights printed on plastic, decorated with a heraldic tumble of french fries and drumsticks and steam.

Your table may yet be littered with bitten toast and spilled coffee and a dollar tip. Now you will see the greatness of America. As one complete gesture, the waitress pockets the tip, stacks dishes along one strong fore-arm, produces a damp rag soaked in lethe water, which she then passes over the Formica.

There! With that one swipe of the rag, the past has been obliterated. The Formica gleams like new. You can order anything you want.

If I were to show you Mexico, I would take you home; with the greatest reluctance I would take you home, where family snapshots crowd upon the mantel. For the Mexican, the past is firmly held from within. While outside, a few miles away in the American city, there is only loos-ening, unraveling; generations living apart. Old ladies living out their lives in fiercely flowered housedresses. Their sons are divorced; wear shorts, ride bikes; are not men, really; not really. Their granddaughters are not fresh, are not lovely or keen, are not even nice.

Seek the Mexican in the embrace of the family, where there is much noise. The family stands as a consolation, because in the certainty of generation there is protection against an uncertain future. At the center of this gravity the child is enshrined. He is not rock-a-bye baby at the very top of the family tree, as it is with American families. The child does not represent distance from the past, but reflux. She is not expected to fly away, to find herself. He is not expected to live his own life.

I will send for you or I will come home rich.

The culture of *tú* is guarded by the son, desired by the son, enforced by the son. Femininity is defined by the son as motherhood. Only a culture so cruel to the wife could sustain such a sentimental regard for *mamacita*. By contrast, much license is appropriated by the Mexican male. If the brother is taught to hover—he is guarding his sister's virginity—

the adolescent male is otherwise, elsewhere, schooled in seduction. For the male as for the female, sexuality is expressed as parenthood. The male, by definition, is father. The husband is always a son.

It is not coincidental that American feminists have borrowed the Spanish word *macho* to name their American antithesis. But in English, the macho is publicly playful, boorish, counterdomestic. American macho is drag—the false type for the male—as Mae West is the false type for the female.

Machismo in Mexican Spanish is more akin to the Latin *gravitas*. The male is serious. The male provides. The Mexican male never abandons those who depend upon him. The male remembers.

Mexican *machismo*, like Mexican politics, needs its mise-en-scène. In fair Verona, in doublet and hose, it might yet play. The male code derives less from efficacy than from valor. *Machismo* is less an assertion of power or potency than it is a rite of chivalry.

The *macho* is not urbane Gilbert Roland or the good guy Lee Trevino; he is more like Bobby Chacon, the slight, leathery, middle-aged boxer, going twelve rounds the night after his wife commits suicide. The *macho* holds his own ground. There is sobriety in the male, and silence, too— a severe limit on emotional range. The male isn't weak. The male wins a Purple Heart or he turns wife beater. The male doesn't cry.

Men sing in Mexico. In song, the male can admit longing, pain, desire, weakness.

HAIII-EEEE.

A cry like a comet rises over the song. A cry like mock weeping tickles the refrain of Mexican love songs. The cry is meant to encourage the balladeer—it is the raw edge of his sentiment. HAI-II-EEE. It is the man's sound. A ticklish arching of semen, a node wrung up a guitar string, until it bursts in a descending cascade of mockery. HAI. HAI. HAI. The cry of the jackal under the moon, the whistle of the phallus, the maniacal song of the skull.

So it may well be Mama who first realizes the liberation of the American "you," the American pan-*usted*, the excalibur "I" which will deliver her from the Islamic cloister of Mexico. (*Tú.*)

A true mother, Mexico would not distinguish among her children. Her protective arm extended not only to the Mexican nationals working in the United States, but to the larger number of Mexican Americans as well. Mexico was not interested in passports; Mexico was interested in blood. No matter how far away you moved, you were still related to her.

In 1943, American sailors in Los Angeles ventured into an evil vein of boredom. They crashed the east side of town, where they beat up barrio teenagers dressed in the punk costume of their day. "The Zoot Suit Riots" lasted several nights. City officials went to bed early, and the Los Angeles press encouraged what it termed high-spirited sailors. It required the diplomatic protest of the Mexican ambassador and the consequent intervention of the U.S. secretary of state to end the disturbances.

Mexico sent cables of protest to Washington whenever she heard of the mistreatment of Mexican nationals. In a city as small as Sacramento in the 1950s, there was a Mexican consulate—a small white building downtown, in all ways like an insurance office, except for the seal of Mexico over the door. For decades, at offices like this one, Mexicans would find a place of defense in the U.S.A.

In 1959, Octavio Paz, Mexico's sultan son, her clever one—philosopher, poet, statesman—published *The Labyrinth of Solitude,* his reflections on Mexico. Within his labyrinth, Paz places as well the Mexican American. He writes of the *pachuco,* the teenage gang member, and, by implication, of the Mexican American: "The *pachuco* does not want to become a Mexican again; at the same time he does not want to blend into the life of North America. His whole being is sheer negative impulse, a tangle of contradictions, an enigma."

This was Mother Mexico talking, her good son; this was Mexico's metropolitan version of Mexican Americans. Mexico had lost language, lost gods, lost ground. Mexico recognized historical confusion in us. We were Mexico's Mexicans.

When we return to Mexico as *turistas,* with our little wads of greenbacks, our credit cards, our Japanese cameras, our Bermuda shorts, our pauses for directions, and our pointing fingers, Mexico condescends to take our order (our order in halting Spanish), *claro señor.* But the table is not cleared; the table will never be cleared. Mexico prefers to reply in English, as a way of saying:

¡Pocho!

The Mexican American who forgets his true mother is a *pocho,* a person of no address, a child of no proper idiom.

But blood is blood, or perhaps, in this case, language is blood. Mexico worried. Mexico had seen her children lured by the gringo's offer of work. During the Great Depression, as the gringo's eyes slowly drained of sugar, thousands of Mexicans in the United States were rounded up and deported.

In 1938, my mother's brother returned to Mexico with only a curse for the United States of America. He had worked at construction sites throughout California and he was paid less than he had contracted for. At his stupefaction—the money in his hand—the contractor laughed.

What's the matter, babe, can't you Mesicans count?

And who took him back, shrieks Mexico, thumping her breast. Who?

No wonder that Mexico would not entertain the idea of a "Mexican American" except as a fiction, a bad joke of history. And most Mexican Americans lived in barrios, apart from gringos; many retained Spanish, as if in homage to her. We were still her children.

As long as we didn't marry.

His coming of age.

From his bed he watches Mama moving back and forth under the light. Outside, the bells of the church fly through the dark. Mama crosses herself. He pushes back the plastic curtain until his nostril catches air. He turns toward Mama. He studies her back—it is like a loaf of bread—as she bends over the things she is wrapping for him to take.

Today he becomes a man. His father has sent for him. His father has sent an address in the American city. That's what it means. His father is in the city with his uncle. He remembers his uncle remembering snow with his beer.

The boy dresses in the shadows. Then he moves toward the table, the circle of light. He sits down. He forces himself to eat. Mama stands over him to make the sign of the cross with her thumb on his forehead. He smiles for her. She puts a bag of food in his hands. She says she has told La Virgen to watch over him.

Yes, and he leaves quickly. Outside it is gray. He hears a little breeze. Or is it the rustle of old black Dueña, the dog—yes, it is she—taking her shortcuts through the weeds, crazy Dueña, her pads through the dust, following him. He passes the houses of the village; each window has a proper name. He passes Muñoz, the store. Old Rosa, the bar. The lighted window of the clinic where the pale medical student from Monterrey lives alone and reads his book full of sores late into the night.

The boy has just passed beyond the cemetery. His guardian breeze has died. The sky has begun to lighten. He turns and throws a rock back at La Dueña—it might be his heart that he throws. But no need. She will not go past the cemetery, not even for him. She will turn in circles like a loca and bite herself, Old Dueña, saying her rosary.

The dust takes on gravel, the path becomes a rutted road which leads to the highway. He walks north. The sky has turned white. Insects click in the fields. In time, there will be a bus.

The endurance of Mexico may be attributed to the realm of *tú,* wherein the family, the village, is held in immutable suspension; whereby the city—the government—is held in contempt.

Mexicans will remember this century as the century of loss. The land of Mexico will not sustain Mexicans. For generations, from Mexico City, came promises of land reform. *The land will be yours.*

What more seductive promise could there be to a nation haunted by the memory of dispossession?

The city broke most of its promises.

The city represents posture and hypocrisy to the average Mexican. The average Mexican imagination will weigh the city against the village and come up short. But the city represents the only possibility for survival. In the last half of this century, Mexicans have abandoned the village. And there is no turning back. After generations of ancestors asleep beneath the earth and awake above the sky, after roosters and priests and sleeping dogs, there is only the city.

The Goddess of Liberty—that stony schoolmarm—may well ask Mexicans why they are so resistant to change, to the interesting freedoms she offers. Mexicans are notorious in the United States for their skepticism regarding public life. Mexicans don't vote. Mexicans drop out of school.

Mexicans live in superstitious fear of the American diaspora. Mexican Americans are in awe of education, of getting too much schooling, of changing too much, of moving too far from home.

Well, now. Never to be outdone, Mother Mexico has got herself up in goddess cloth. She carries a torch, too, and it is the torch of memory. She is searching for her children.

A false mother, Mexico cares less for her children than for her pride. The exodus of so many Mexicans for the U.S. is not evidence of Mexico's failure; it is evidence, rather, of the emigrant's failure. After all, those who left were of the peasant, the lower classes—those who could not make it in Mexico.

The government of hurt pride is not above political drag. The government of Mexico impersonates the intimate genius of matriarchy in order to justify a political stranglehold.

In its male, in its public, in its city aspect, Mexico is an archtransvestite, a tragic buffoon. Dogs bark and babies cry when Mother Mexico walks abroad in the light of day. The policeman, the Marxist mayor—Mother

Mexico doesn't even bother to shave her mustachios. Swords and rifles and spurs and bags of money chink and clatter beneath her skirts. A chain of martyred priests dangles from her waist, for she is an austere, pious lady. Ay, how much—clutching her jangling bosoms; spilling cigars—how much she has suffered!

REMEMBER, THE STRENGTH OF MEXICO IS THE FAMILY. (A government billboard.)

In his glass apartment overlooking the Polanco district of Mexico City, the journalist says he does not mind in the least that I call myself an American. "But when I hear Mexicans in the United States talk about George Washington as the father of their country," he exhales a florid ellipsis of cigarette smoke.

America does not lend itself to sexual metaphor as easily as Mexico does. George Washington is the father of the country, we say. We speak of Founding Fathers. The legend ascribed to the Statue of Liberty is childlessness.

America is an immigrant country. Motherhood—parenthood—is less our point than adoption. If I had to assign gender to America, I would notice the consensus of the rest of the world. When America is burned in effigy, a male is burned. Americans themselves speak of Uncle Sam. Uncle Sam is the personification of conscription.

During World War II, hundreds of thousands of Mexican Americans were drafted to fight in Europe and in Asia. And they went, submitting themselves to a commonweal. Not a very Mexican thing to do, for Mexico had taught us always that we lived apart from history in the realm of *tú*.

It was Uncle Sam who shaved the sideburns from that generation of Mexican Americans. Like the Goddess of Liberty, Uncle Sam has no children of his own. In a way, Sam represents necessary evil to the American imagination. He steals children to make men of them, mocks all reticence, all modesty, all memory. Uncle Sam is a hectoring Yankee, a skinflint uncle, gaunt, uncouth, unloved. He is the American Savonarola—hater of moonshine, destroyer of stills, burner of cocaine. Free enterprise is curiously an evasion of Uncle Sam, as is sentimentality. Sam has no patience with mamas' boys. That includes Mama Mexico, ma'am.

You betray Uncle Sam by favoring private over public life, by seeking to exempt yourself: by cheating on your income taxes, by avoiding jury duty, by trying to keep your boy on the farm. These are legal offenses.

Betrayal of Mother Mexico, on the other hand, is a sin against the natural law, a failure of memory.

When the war was over, Mexican Americans returned home to a GI Bill and with the expectation of an improved future. By the 1950s, Mexican Americans throughout the Southwest were busy becoming middle-class. I would see them around Sacramento: a Mexican-American dentist; a shoe salesman at Weinstock's; the couple that ran the tiny Mexican food store that became, before I graduated from high school, a block-long electrified MEXICATESSEN. These were not "role models," exactly; they were people like my parents, making their way in America.

When I was in grammar school, they used to hit us for speaking Spanish. THEY.

Mexican Americans forfeit the public experience of America because we fear it. And for decades in the American Southwest, public life was withheld from us. America lay north of *usted,* beyond even formal direct address. America was the realm of *los norteamericanos*—They. We didn't have an adequate name for you. In private, you were the gringo. The ethnic albino. The goyim. The ghost. You were not us. In public we also said "Anglo"—an arcane usage of the nineteenth century—you-who-speak-English. If we withdrew from directly addressing you, you became *ellos*—They—as in: They kept us on the other side of town. They owned the land. They owned the banks. They ran the towns—They and their wives in their summer-print dresses. They kept wages low. They made us sit upstairs in the movie houses. Or downstairs.

Thus spoken memory becomes a kind of shorthand for some older, other outrage, the nineteenth-century affront. The land stolen. The Mexican scorned on land he had named. Spic. Greaser. Spanish, the great metropolitan language, reduced to a foreign tongue, a language of the outskirts, the language of the gibbering poor, thus gibberish; English, the triumphal, crushing metaphor.

I know Mexican Americans who have lived in this country for forty or fifty years and have never applied for citizenship or gathered more than a Montgomery Ward sense of English. Their refusal, lodged between *How much* and *Okay,* is not a linguistic dilemma primarily.

On the other hand, when we call ourselves Mexican Americans, Mexico is on the phone, long-distance: *So typical of the gringo's arrogance to appropriate the name of a hemisphere to himself—yes? But why should you repeat the folly?*

Mexico always can find a myth to account for us: Mexicans who go north are like the Chichimeca—a barbarous tribe antithetical to Mexico. But in the United States, Mexican Americans did not exist in the national imagination until the 1960s—years when the black civil rights movement prompted Americans to acknowledge "invisible minorities" in their midst. Then it was determined statistically that Mexican Americans constituted a disadvantaged society, living in worse conditions than most other Americans, having less education, facing bleaker sidewalks or Safeways.

Bueno. (Again Mother Mexico is on the phone.) *What kind of word is that—"minority"? Was the Mexican American*—she fries the term on the skillet of her tongue—*was the Mexican American content to say that his association with Mexico left him culturally disadvantaged?*

The sixties were years of romance for the American middle class. Americans competed with one another to play the role of society's victim. It was an age of T-shirts.

In those years, the national habit of Americans was to seek from the comparison with blacks a kind of analogy. Mexican-American political activists, especially student activists, insisted on a rough similarity between the two societies—black, Chicano—ignoring any complex factor of history or race that might disqualify the equation.

Black Americans had suffered relentless segregation and mistreatment, but blacks had been implicated in the public life of this country from the beginning. Oceans separated the black slave from any possibility of rescue or restoration. From the symbiosis of oppressor and the oppressed, blacks took a hard realism. They acquired the language of the white man, though they inflected it with refusal. And because racism fell upon all blacks, regardless of class, a bond developed between the poor and the bourgeoisie, thence the possibility of a leadership class able to speak for the entire group.

Mexican Americans of the generation of the sixties had no myth of themselves as Americans. So that when Mexican Americans won national notoriety, we could only refer the public gaze to the past. We are people of the land, we told ourselves. Middle-class college students took to wearing farmer-in-the-dell overalls and they took, as well, a rural slang to name themselves: Chicanos.

Chicanismo blended nostalgia with grievance to reinvent the mythic northern kingdom of Atzlán as corresponding to the southwestern American desert. Just as Mexico would only celebrate her Indian half, Chicanos determined to portray themselves as Indians in America, as indigenous people, thus casting the United States in the role of Spain.

Chicanos used the language of colonial Spain to declare to America that they would never give up their culture. And they said, in Spanish, that Spaniards had been oppressors of their people.

Left to ourselves in a Protestant land, Mexican Americans shored up our grievances, making of them altars to the past. *May my tongue cleave to my palate if I should forget thee. (Tú.)*

Ah, Mother, can you not realize how Mexican we have become?

But she hates us, she hates us.

Chicanismo offended Mexico. It was one thing for Mexico to play the victim among her children, but Mexico did not like it that Chicanos were playing the same role for the gringos.

By claiming too many exemptions, Chicanos also offended Americans. Chicanos seemed to violate a civic agreement that generations of other immigrants had honored: *My* grandparents had to learn English. . . .

Chicanos wanted more and less than they actually said. On the one hand, Chicanos were intent upon bringing America (as a way of bringing history) to some Act of Contrition. On the other hand, Chicanos sought pride, a restoration of face in America. And America might provide the symbolic solution to a Mexican dilemma: if one could learn public English while yet retaining family Spanish, *usted* might be reunited with *tú*, the future might be reconciled with the past.

Mexicans are a people of sacraments and symbols. I think few Chicanos ever expected Spanish to become a public language coequal with English. But by demanding Spanish in the two most symbolic places of American citizenship—the classroom and the voting booth—Chicanos were consoling themselves that they need not give up the past to participate in the American city. They were not less American for speaking Spanish; they were not less Mexican for succeeding in America.

America got bored with such altars—too Catholic for the likes of America. Protestant America is a literal culture.

SAY WHAT YOU WANT.

What was granted was a bureaucratic bilingualism—classrooms and voting booths—pragmatic concessions to a spiritual grievance.

I end up arguing about bilingualism with other Mexican Americans, middle-class like myself. As I am my father's son, I am skeptical, like Mexico; I play the heavy, which is to say I play America. We argue and argue, but not about pedagogy. We argue about desire's reach; we exchange a few platitudes (being richer for having two languages; being able to go home again). In the end, the argument reduces to somebody's childhood memory.

When I was in school, they used to hit us for speaking Spanish.

My father says the trouble with the bilingual voting ballot is that one ends up voting for the translator.

In the late 1960s, when César Chávez made the cover of *Time* as the most famous Mexican American anyone could name, he was already irrelevant to Mexican-American lives insofar as 90 percent of us lived in cities and we were more apt to work in construction than as farmworkers. My mother, who worked downtown, and my father, who worked downtown, nevertheless sent money to César Chávez, because the hardness of his struggle on the land reminded them of the hardness of their Mexican past.

I remember the farmworkers' "Lenten Pilgrimage" through California's Central Valley in 1966. Lines of men, women, and children passed beneath low, rolling clouds, beneath the red-and-black union flags and the flapping silk banners of the Virgin of Guadalupe. Their destination was the state capital, Sacramento, the city, Easter. They were private people praying in public. Here were the most compelling symbols of the pastoral past: life on the land (the farmworker); the flag, the procession in song (a people united, the village); the Virgin Mary (her consolation in sorrow).

Chávez wielded a spiritual authority that, if it was political at all, was not mundane and had to be exerted in large, priestly ways or it was squandered. By the late 1970s, Chávez had spent his energies in legislative maneuvers. His union got mixed up in a power struggle with the Teamsters. Criticized in the liberal press for allowing his union to unravel, Chávez became a quixotic figure; Gandhi without an India.

César Chávez was a folk hero. But the political example for my generation was Mayor Henry Cisneros of San Antonio. As a man of the city, Cisneros reflected our real lives in the America of *usted*. Cisneros attempted a reconciliation between the private and the public, between the family and the world. On the one hand, he belonged to the city. He spoke a metropolitan English, as well as Old Boy English; Cisneros spoke an international Spanish, as well as Tex-Mex. He chose to live in his grandfather's house on Monterey Street. The fiction was that he had never left home. Well, no—the fiction was that he had gone very far, but come home unchanged.

My mother saw Henry Cisneros twice on "60 Minutes." My mother said she would vote for Cisneros for any office.

The career of Henry Cisneros magnified the dilemma of other Mexican Americans within that first generation of affirmative action. Had it not been for CBS News, my mother would never have heard of Henry Cisneros. Though his success was unique—though his talent is personal—my mother assumed that his career was plural, that he represented Mexican Americans because that is what he was—and that is what he was because he was the first. Groomed for leadership by an Ivy League college and by Democratic party officials, Cisneros was then unveiled to the constituency he was supposed already to represent. He must henceforward use the plural voice on committees and boards and at conferences. We want. We need. The problem, in this case, is not with the candidate; it is with the constituency. Who are we? We who have been to Harvard? Or we who could not read English? Or we who could not read? Or we who have yet to take our last regard of the lemon tree in our mother's Mexican garden?

Politics can easily override irony. But, by the 1980s, the confusing "we" of Mexican Americanism was transposed an octave higher to the "we" of pan-American Hispanicism.

In the late 1980s, Henry Cisneros convened a conference of Hispanic leaders to formulate a national Hispanic political agenda.

Mexican Americans constituted the majority of the nation's Hispanic population. But Mexican Americans were in no position to define the latitude of the term "Hispanic"—the tumult of pigments and altars and memories there. "Hispanic" is not a racial or a cultural or a geographic or a linguistic or an economic description. "Hispanic" is a bureaucratic integer—a complete political fiction. How much does the Central American refugee have in common with the Mexican from Tijuana? What does the black Puerto Rican in New York have in common with the white Cuban in Miami? Those Mexican Americans who were in a position to speak for the group—whatever the group was—that is, those of us with access to microphones because of affirmative action, were not even able to account for our own success. Were we riding on some clement political tide? Or were we advancing on the backs of those who were drowning?

Think of earlier immigrants to this country. Think of the Jewish immigrants or the Italian. Many came, carefully observing Old World distinctions and rivalries. German Jews distinguished themselves from Russian Jews. The Venetian was adamant about not being taken for a Neapolitan. But to America, what did such claims matter? All Italians looked and sounded pretty much the same. A Jew was a Jew. And now America shrugs again. Palm trees or cactus, it's all the same. Hispanics are all the same.

I saw César Chávez again, a year ago, at a black-tie benefit in a hotel in San Jose. The organizers of the event ushered him into the crowded ballroom under a canopy of hush and tenderness and parked him at the center table, where he sat blinking. How fragile the great can seem. How much more substantial we of the ballroom seemed, the Mexican-American haute bourgeoisie, as we stood to pay our homage—orange women in fur coats, affirmative action officers from cigarette companies, filmmakers, investment bankers, fat cats and stuffed shirts and bleeding hearts—stood applauding our little saint. César Chávez reminded us that night of who our grandparents used to be.

Then Mexican waiters served champagne.

Success is a terrible dilemma for Mexican Americans, like being denied some soul-sustaining sacrament. Without the myth of victimization—who are we? We are no longer Mexicans. We are professional Mexicans. We hire Mexicans. After so many years spent vainly thinking of ourselves as exempt from some common myth of America, we might as well be Italians.

I am standing in my sister's backyard.

They are away. The air is golden; the garden is rising green, but beginning to fall. There is my nephew's sandbox, deserted, spilled. And all his compliant toys fallen where he threw them off after his gigantic lovemaking. Winnie-the-Pooh. The waist-coated frog. Refugees of some long English childhood have crossed the Atlantic, attached themselves to the court of this tyrannical dauphin.

Aserrín aserrán
Something something de San Juan . . .

I can remember sitting on my mother's lap as she chanted that little faraway rhyme.

Piden pan. No les dan. . . .

The rhyme ended with a little tickle under my chin. Whereas my nephew rides a cockhorse to Banbury Cross.

My youngest nephew. He has light hair; he stares at me with dark eyes. I think it is Mexico I see in his eyes, the unfathomable regard of the past, while ahead of him stretches Sesame Street. What will he know of his past, except that he has several? What will he know of Mexico, except that his ancestors lived on land he will never inherit?

The knowledge Mexico bequeaths to him passes silently through his heart, something to take with him as he disappears, like my father, into America.

In 1991, President Bush proposed the establishment of a free trade consortium among North American "neighbors." In fact, the new idea derived from old Mother Mexico. It was Mother Mexico, after all, who long ago mocked the notion of a border on the desert.

The United States shares with Mexico a two-thousand-mile connection—the skin of two heads. Everything that America wants to believe about himself—that he is innocent, that he is colorless, odorless, solitary, self-sufficient—is corrected, weighed upon, glossed by Mexico, the maternity of Mexico, the envy of Mexico, the grievance of Mexico.

Mexicans crossing the border are secret agents of matriarchy. Mexicans have slipped America a darker beer, a cuisine of *tú*. Mexicans have invaded American privacy to baby-sit or to watch the dying or to wash lipstick off the cocktail glasses. Mexicans have forced southwestern Americans to speak Spanish whenever they want their eggs fried or their roses pruned. Mexicans have overwhelmed the Church—eleven o'clock masses in most Valley towns are Spanish masses. By force of numbers, Mexicans have taken over grammar school classrooms. The Southwest is besotted with the culture of *tú*.

But Mexico was fooled by her own tragic knowledge of relationship. The desert is a tide. How could Mexico not have realized that tragedy would wash back on her, polluted with gringo optimism?

A young man leaves his Mexican village for Los Angeles in 1923. He returns one rainy night in 1925. He tells his family, next day he tells the village, that it is okay up there. The following spring, four village men accompany him back to L.A. They send money home. Mothers keep their sons' dollars in airtight jars, opening the jars only when someone is sick or someone is dying. The money is saturated with rumor.

Thus have Mexicans from America undermined the tranquillity of Mexican villages they thought only to preserve. The Mexican American became a revolutionary figure, more subversive than a Chichimeca, more subversive than Pancho Villa.

In the 1970s, President Luis Echeverría invited planeloads of "Chicano leaders" to visit Mexico with the apparent goal of creating a lobby for the interests of Mexico modeled on the Israeli lobby. Perhaps the Chicano was the key to Mexico's future? The Chicano, after all, defied assimilation in the United States, or said he did. The Chicano sought to retain his culture, his mother tongue. In the 1980s, the government ministry in Mexico City announced a policy of reconciliation (*acercamiento*) regarding Mexican Americans.

By the 1980s, Mexican Americans were, on average, older, wealthier, better educated than the average Mexican; we also had fewer children. In the 1980s, the proud house of Mexico was crumbling, the economy was folding, the wealthy of Mexico had begun their exodus, following the peasant's route north. Along the border, Mexican towns inclined toward America and away from Mexico City. And from the North came unclean enchantments of the gringo—the black music, the blond breasts, the drugged eyes of tourists.

How much is the gum?

Mexico worries about her own. What influence shall she have? The village is international now. Most of the men have been north; many of the women, too. Have seen. Everyone has heard stories.

Mexico cannot hold the attention of her children. The average age of the country descends into adolescence. More than half of Mexico is under fifteen years of age. What is the prognosis for memory in a country so young?

For Mexico is memory. . . .

On the television, suspended from the ceiling over the bar, is game four of the World Series. I am sitting with five Mexicans at a restaurant in Mexico City. Presiding is a woman in her thirties, a curator of the National Anthropology Museum. Others are a filmmaker, a cameraman, a location scout. We are all connected by the making of a television film.

The woman is scolding me—not severely—for not being as fluent in Spanish as she is in English. She will do most of the talking.

She has traveled, studied in Europe. I forget now whether she knows the United States—probably—but she has met enough Mexican Americans to mimic their embarrassment concerning Spanish.

Poquito, poquito (a double entendre, holding an inch of air between the lacquered bulbs of her thumb and index finger).

Peut-être je devrais parler français avec vous, Richard.

We will disagree about everything, Mexico and I.

Do I really call myself a Catholic, she asks in reaction to nothing I have said. She, of course, hates the Church for what it has done to Mexico.

(Of course.)

Where do you get your ideas about Mexico? From Graham Greene?

You have the opportunity to say something in public, and you go on and on about old churches and old mothers. You do a disservice with your reactionary dream of Mexico. Here, we are trying to progress. . . .

She has raised her own child—she has been married, oh yes—her own child is as free from the past as could be managed. Each generation must be free to discover its own identity, don't you think so. But, then, you have no children. Perhaps you have some Catholic malady, like sexual repression? She smiles.

I smile.

I feel I know them all; recognize the way their faces crease into smiles; recognize the ease of irony in a language so extravagant. Nothing is meant all that seriously, I suppose. They are speaking for my own benefit. They want to educate me.

I am not exactly bored, but I am demoralized.

They don't even seem like Mexicans. They are more like Americans of my generation. I would have avoided a dinner like this one, in a restaurant like this one, in California.

Do I have it all wrong? Was the Mexico I had imagined—the country of memory and faith—long past? Its curator a woman who reviles the past?

I lower my eyes. I say to Mexico, I say to my ice cubes:

I cannot understand you.

Do not pretend to understand me. I am but a figure of speech to you—a Mexican American.

What Richard needs to see, Alberto suggests, is . . . and then some Spanish name I don't catch. Titters all round.

We are drunk.

So, at one o'clock in the morning, we drive, five of us, crowded like clowns into a Volkswagen. I vote we go back to the hotel. The curator wants to listen to jazz. But the filmmaker is driving.

We end up at a nightclub on a quiet downtown street. The nightclub offers three kinds of therapy for sexual repression. We opt for the dinner theater. There is a small stage; twenty tables. Some Japanese businessmen at one table, some Mexicans at another. A drink costs a lot—ten American dollars.

A canned overture. Then two lines of dancers appear—"appear" cannot quite account for their corporeality. Twelve large vanilla flans, female; six samba shirts, male. The stage is so tiny the dancers must restrict their movements to the upper torso. After ten minutes of joust, a fog of dry ice is blasted from a funnel in the wings. The dancers fall to their knees and lift their arms to worship a tall, blond, goddessy woman who will sing of love.

The goddess's microphone is so revved up, her voice rides over our skulls like a metal lathe. Mid-routine, the goddess hesitates, evidently overcome with *nostalgie de la boue*. She descends two semicircular steps to ringside, her pink halo spilling after her. She stops at a table of Mexican men. She rests her hip against the shoulder of a man who has several rings on several of his fingers. He kisses her hand.

The filmmaker raises his arm, beckoning the goddess to our table, pointing at the crown of my head.

The goddess's eyes dart toward the filmmaker's hand. (There is a bank note caught like a butterfly between his fingers.) She lowers her forty lashes. Her pink penumbra shimmers tremulously; her lips curve upward. She begins to mash toward our table.

A cold hand caresses my cheek, a strong hand begins to tug at my necktie. The filmmaker giggles; the curator approves, lights a cigarette. The goddess makes sibilant remarks about me to the audience, little flatteries.

She begins to sing.

Tú. Tú. The song of the dove.

Tú the ruby pendant . . .

Suddenly she thrusts the microphone at my face.

The canned sound track rattles away in the distance, but the air, suddenly bereft of the concussion of the goddess's voice, seems a world without love.

I decline.

The goddess laughs—a detonation, like claps of thunder. The air is alive again, freighted with angels. She picks up the lyric, looping the cord of the microphone into a coil. . . .

> *Vete pero no me olvides.*
> *Vete, amor,*
> *Amor de mi vida,*
> *Toma la rosa,*
> *Tinta de vino. . . .*

Violins edge into the track. The refrain. My cue. Again, the microphone is in my face.

The goddess looks infinitely bored. She wets her lips with her tongue, hacks up a little phlegm.

I sing.

I sing to her of my undying love and of rural pleasures. *Tú. Tú.* The ruby pendant. *Tú.* The lemon tree. The song of the dove. Breathed through the nose. Perched on the lips.

Anything to make her go away.

I wrote:

I once met an old woman in Mexico who looked lonelier than anyone I have ever seen. She was a beggar woman in a slum market in Mexico City. The aisles of the market were covered with canvas; on either side of these tent aisles hung chickens and flowers and pineapples for sale. Within the transept of the market, against a stone wall, the old woman kept her anchor hold.

Hair grew out of her nose like winter breath. Her reply to every question was *no*. Nothing. Nobody. No husband. No sisters. No brother. Her only son dead.

If there was no one to claim her from the past, then she was unalterably separated from life. She lived in eternity. Even the poor neighborhood people, the poorest of the poor, could spare a few pesos for this mother of tragedy. People were in awe of her, for she was without grace, which in Mexico is children.

You stand around. You smoke. You spit. You are wearing your two shirts, two pants, two underpants. Jesús says, if they chase you throw that bag down. Your plastic bag is your mama, all you have left; the yellow cheese she wrapped has formed a translucent rind; the laminated scapular of the Sacred Heart nestles flame in its cleft. Put it in your pocket. The last hour of Mexico is twilight, the shuffling of feet. A fog is beginning to cover the ground. Jesús says they are able to see in the dark. They have X-rays and helicopters and search-lights. Jesús says wait, just wait, till he says. You can feel the hand of Jesús clamp your shoulder, fingers cold as ice. Venga, corre. *You run. All the rest happens without words. Your feet are tearing dry grass, your heart is lashed like a mare. You trip, you fall. You are now in the United States of America. You are a boy from a Mexican village. You have come into the country on your knees with your head down. You are a man.*

I went to a village in the state of Michoacán, on the far side of Lake Chapala.

A dusty road leads past eucalyptus, past the cemetery, to the village. For most of the year the village is empty—nearly. There are a few old people, quite a few hungry dogs. The sun comes up; the sun goes down.

Most of the villagers have left Mexico for the United States. January 23 is the feast day of the patron saint of the village, when the saint is accustomed to being rocked upon his hillock of velvet through the streets. On that day, the villagers—and lately the children of villagers—return. They come in caravans. Most come from Austin, Texas, from Hollister, California, and from Stockton, California. For a week every year, the village comes alive, a Mexican Brigadoon. Doors are unlocked. Shutters are opened. Floors are swept. Music is played. Beer is drunk. Expressed fragments of memory flow outward like cigarette smoke to tumble the dust of the dead.

Every night is carnival. Men who work at canneries or factories in California parade down the village street in black suits. Women who are waitresses in California put on high heels and evening gowns. The promenade under the Mexican stars becomes a celebration of American desire.

At the end of the week, the tabernacle of memory is dismantled, distributed among the villagers in their vans, and carried out of Mexico.

Winter of a Rose

1

Of America
record sprint through history
we talked and dreamed
racing down highways wider than oceans:
Buicks and apples,
high schools, phonographs,
super athletes and their women
sleek like cats;
suburbs young and green and open
where children tricycle
through dusk and housewives cook
slow steaming dinners as the sun goes down;

land of factories and lilacs
and locomotives churning through the snow
where bearded voices sing of everything growth
and the chest grows big with the self.

2

Five in the morning
New Year's my father charged
into the room his mouth
exploding with headlines:

"Batista's fallen
and gone to Spain!"

By midmorning the whole city
was a hurricane,
the mountains bristled
with beards and young men
like olive gods.

For the first time there was talk of peace and island,
talk of palm trees,
fierce faces,
smiles of future
droning in on tanks
garlanded with women and children
who saw their games reeling before them.

3

Some looked cautiously out of windows.
Behind the shutters slow old angers
pumped themselves into rock.
Wept diamonds cut glass
until it showed only the past:

Baccarat, Limoges, the ballerina
twirling stiffly in the drawing room,
servants glistening like teacups,
the sweet melancholy of cognac,

delicate wrists twisting gently
with the conversation of last fall's
European tour—and oh how brilliantly
they fear now and hide beneath their shawls.

4

There is a photograph
of my father, mother,
sister and me going up
the steps to the plane
all smiling, I holding
a book my great-uncle
had given me on Oriental art.

Be free to learn.
Only that is good.
He said.

It was cold in New York.
New words made dough in my ear.
The sky closed over my head.

When I made it to school
they thought I didn't
have a mind in English and if
you don't have a mind in English
you have a mind in nothing.

Secretly I read Poe in the ninth floor
of that hotel that smelled
of widows with their skirts up,
discovered dankness in closets,
tubed hands in a boring bathroom.

          5

Winter of concrete and brick,
winter of cars rumbling
desperately for love,
winter of whores like houses
painted over twenty times,
winter of the tear turned ice,
winter of a thousand urinals
and a man in a corner
with the whirling eye of need,
winter of subways rolling home,
scream and crash, scream and crash,
winter of frowns,
winter of sweats,
winter of a rose
                on a girl's coat
plastic
        and safe.

6

As far as you can go
in any direction
it is the same.
As if distance kept pulling itself
inside out, you are bound
to find yourself
eating dinner crosstown
copied right down
to the mole in your cheek,
or sunning yourself in a beach
and your face bloops out of waves
the same way in the other direction
and soon you realize
everything leaves you behind, always
the same looking at yourself
going home with a shovel
to dig for roots.

This place is full of dark holes
with the same frightened creature in them.

7

Enter the church.
Belief in rock,
in the flame of knowledge,
singe of flesh.

Pleasures sink,
the flame flickers:

every morning I loved
the only flesh allowed,
wood over the silence of marble.

Alone I wanted
bread to turn
human on the tongue.

The nave answered only its size,
waft of incense clouding the downturned face,
prayers brittle and cracked on the floor,
voices in a hollow skull:

Introibo ad altare mei.

8

Hunger for warmth
hunger for cold
hunger for history of candles
and the breasts they silhouette
hunger for the veins of virgins
and their fillets and their sweats
hunger for the lyres of spring
and suburban houses where accountants sing
and the breath of widows with their swollen shins

hunger for blindness and bishops and pens
hunger for whispers hunger for scents
and the dreams of janitors on the graveyard shift
and the housewife with a groaning mate
hunger for clocks and bathrooms and navels
and magazines and lentils

hunger for pubic clouds and pubic rain
hunger for wind and lanceolate leaves
and evergreen forests
and lips
and tongues
and gullets.

The city roars
the sun retreats
a child next door is weeping

9

Leaning against the steel
                              and glass
insurance building

<pre>
                     America
is the fluid
                   in that man's mind
that lusts
                 for elsewhere

and the trees wave their song
the girl chased
                            by her skirt
to where a wall stands
                        unclimbable and stark and
the trees wave their song
is a dark street
                          that clamps out hope
distance burgeoning
                         behind the wall
if she stops
                  the dress falls
naked and tender
                     and alone
the mind's man lusts
and the trees wave their song
</pre>

10

I ran
to lips so soft they smelled of clouds,
to the blindness of touch,
the welcome of brine.

I became water,
I became shore
rivered in until I lost myself:

trees, grass, hills
defining distance,
insects that devour it,
rain and birds
somewhere green,

a silent beautiful body
smiles of me:

sweet gash,
bone in my throat,
the farther I reach the more
I discover your winds,
your rabid storms,
gush of warmth,
tropic word

furrowing urge in
a wing's flight to long continents,
after the blind wreck
                           we
cloak with sleep
backs curved
to resemble ripe fruit

bite between us.

        II

Would it were definable this
weave past waves, this dolphin need
voyage home from a vast
stark solitude,
the vision straight
like the thin green edge
you sail to:
each discovery a gust of wind.

Let the night grow deep
like a church and see
the candle's wax in melting
pull the morning in

a word made a thin
fresh wafer on the lips

a landscape like a body
warming you:
                    morning
come window-crashing
on your loneliness.

Snuggle your shores
between oceans
stretch the tongue so
the sun never sets

on the island
like the arm of a lover asleep

on God who is light catechized

on the sea
that echoes back a dream:

I am alive.

Thirst

Secretly, he slipped out from between the bushes. I saw him out of the corner of my eye and had a foreboding that he would jump on me.... The first symptoms are like those of a common cold; general discomfort, periods of high fever followed by shivering, teeth chattering, and nausea. The nausea is oppressive; the patient experiences acute disgust at everything: the enticing smell of coffee in the morning, the penetrating odor of freshly baked bread—smells that normally give such pleasure now only further irritate the throat, which bleeds slightly each time the patient vomits, or attempts to vomit, with dry heaves that leave the person worn out, intensifying the general discomfort, so that the patient cannot sleep, can only doze. It is during this half-waking sleep that fantastic dreams occur.

Dogs appear in my dreams, sometimes many, sometimes only one. There was a dog, a lone dog that followed me and tried to bite me; then he would run and I too would run, always wondering how I could run so much. When I could go no further, I always awoke. In a corner of my mind there crouched the key question: if there comes a day when I don't wake up in time, what will happen?

I felt his fangs tearing my dress, my stocking, my thigh.... The infection which attacks the nervous system progresses rapidly, and if the patient is not treated within eleven days of being infected, death is unavoidable. The illness follows its implacable course; the general discomfort becomes overwhelming. Early symptoms become more acute. Salivation increases, together with the incapacity to control it; the patient regresses to a state of infantile dribbling from the mouth, since swallowing is no longer possible, with the irritation in the throat growing worse if any attempt is made to swallow the excess saliva. Saliva runs down the corners of the mouth, in threads down the neck, splashing the clothes of the patient, in whose lap a soaked handkerchief is held. Sharp changes in temperature cause extreme reactions, and the skin has now developed an acute sensitivity to heat and cold, making the patient shiver and cover up with heavy blankets one moment, only to throw them on the floor a moment later in reaction to what appears to be intense heat. The senses of sight and sound become heightened. The patient must withdraw to a place in the shade, since light, especially sunlight, now hurts the eyes; the fluttering of a moth threatens to burst the eardrums; the creaking in the walls is like a soft drilling to the temples. It is during this stage of the illness that any brusque change can cause a violent reaction in the patient, whose behavior becomes totally abnormal without apparent motivation.

The fantastic dogs of my morning dreams have wings and fly, though sometimes they simply run so fast they seem not to touch the ground. They are like a slow-motion film where action is held in suspense, or run so slowly that they seem to hover in the air like a hummingbird. In my dreams the dogs are gentle, faithful, and kind, the incarnation of the mythological man's-best-friend.

I raised my arm, covering my face, and screamed, my back against the cold metal rail. . . . In an earlier dream, one of many, there was always a dog following me, apparently a gentle dog, which came close and lay at my feet, trying to get me to pet it; I paid no attention, and when I turned my back, it became angered because I had treated it with contempt, and barked at me and began to chase me. I ran, forgetting sage or common-sense advice—never show them you're afraid; if you run they'll run after you and bite you—logic and panic inhabit different spheres of the brain, the information never crossed. I ran, and it ran after me; we ran across streets, through woods, between rivers; I could never explain to myself how we managed to run so much, the dog and I.

He turned and went back where he came from on hearing his master's voice: "Come, lie down, Chango. . . ." The end is near, the attacks that have given the illness its name, "hydrophobia," or "aversion to water," begin to take place. If the patient sees, hears, or even imagines liquid in any form, the throat constricts; all control of the arms and legs is lost, and the facial features contort. Instead of a human being, the patient becomes an object writhing on the ground, incapable of controlling the least body movement, the distorted face leaving a trail of slime like a snail.

It is only a matter now of waiting for the inevitable end, announced by a creeping paralysis which takes over the patient's body. Beginning with the legs and arms, this proceeds along the central nervous system which keeps the body alive. The heart stops beating, the lungs stop flexing, blood no longer runs through the veins when the heart stops functioning, and finally rest comes with the longed-for death that restores human dignity to the tortured being.

The other dream was of death, a dog's death. Finding a mad dog used to be like going to the circus. Word spread all through the town. You heard there was a mad dog on the corner of Jackson and Bandera, and everybody gathered, some with stones, some with dry branches, some with pieces of wood, anything that would kill the dog before it bit some Christian soul; killing a man or a woman with rabies isn't as easy as killing a dog.

It happened to the west of the freeway in the section called Guadalupe. It was a barrio filled with kids who played on the unsurfaced streets, without sidewalks, where one could listen to the chirp of the cicadas or the hum of pleasant conversation in the evenings. It happened in one of those barrios. And it happened to don Chema. Don Chema was a man from around there; he had no family, he ate where they fed him, and he slept where he could. Everyone knew him; he was no one's relation. One night when he went to sleep on his sack, huddled under a red blanket near the corner of the church, shielded from the cold and rain under a leafy avocado tree, the dog found him. From that moment on they were inseparable. They grew to be old friends. The dog always accompanied don Chema around the town. It went to work with him, to the park to take sun. The two spent their mornings there, don Chema dozing on a bench and the dog snoring at his feet. It was a black dog with a white spot in its face and four white socks. They called it Pantalón. Pantalón always wagged his tail to greet don Chema and ran back and forth until don Chema threw something for him. Then Pantalón would run off and bring back the thing don Chema had thrown for him and give it to don Chema as if it were a great treasure. Then they'd start on their daily rounds.

Pantalón disappeared unexpectedly for several days. When he didn't come back at night don Chema grew worried, but he knew the dog wandered off sometimes and always came back. The next day don Chema began making inquiries. Somebody had seen him the day before near the center of town knocking over trash cans; somebody else had seen him near the Greyhound station lifting his leg against the Greyhound bus tires. Don Chema stopped worrying; he'd come back at night. But he didn't come back that night or the next. He finally showed up a week later. He arrived at the corner of the church where don Chema was getting ready to spend the night. That night was different. Pantalón had come back in a bad mood; he grew angry when don Chema tried to cover him with his blanket. Pantalón could barely drag himself along on his four feet, but don Chema didn't see this, for he was more asleep than awake by then. When don Chema ran his hand along Pantalón's back to calm him down, the dog grew angry and bit him. Don Chema didn't tell anyone, but next morning Pantalón was quite stiff.

When the neighbors found don Chema crying because his dog had died, they began to ask why. Don Chema said he had no idea, and word got around it had rabies, since it had not been injured in any way; don Chema just shrugged. When they saw don Chema's hand wrapped in a dirty rag, they came to the conclusion the dog had bitten him. Everybody knew the two lost souls who slept there near the corner of the church had sought each other. It was hard to know what to do. They didn't just kill him like a mad dog, but they did see him die like his own dog had died. Although there isn't a vaccine against the illness yet, there's a way to treat it, a series of painful injections in the navel. But it was too late for don Chema, more than eleven days had gone by.

I lowered my hand and felt lightly where the dog had put his mouth. I felt the blood, sticky. . . . The dogs chased me last night. There were two, they seemed to be brothers; big ones, the same breed, the same size, one brown, the other black. I saw them coming from far off, running like deer. I saw them getting closer, and I couldn't move my feet. They were getting closer and closer, and I screamed, but I couldn't hear my screams. I could only see the silent grimace of the scream. They were upon me, they jumped, I closed my eyes and screamed.

Miami During the Reagan Years

From *Sonny Manteca's Blues*

Xavier Cuevas found himself stuck in bumper-to-bumper expressway traffic. The lunchtime rush hour in Miami. Exasperated, he changed lanes, taking chances in his 240GL Volvo. An accident, he suspected, cutting to the right-hand lane where the dense traffic moved at a faster pace. *Coagulate,* the word came to his mind. *Undo this coagulation!*

Xavier, the young-urban Cuban-American. The YUCA, the equivalent of yuppie. Business at hand at all times. In haste, no time to waste. Twenty-four hours a day not being enough time. Seven days a week. No time to rest, for in this magic city of Miami, the Sun Capital, there were many deals to be made, and whoever struck first struck big by making the money.

Into the center lane. Behind an eighteen-wheel Mobil Oil rig. Nobody budged to let him in. Nobody gave him a chance. Couldn't they see he was in a hurry? Stuck indeed. Caught. Missing in action in Miami. Driving had become too hectic. A time-consuming chore. Traffic, he thought, so much of it on the streets these days . . . going nowhere.

Traffic was being funneled to the only lane open on the right. Why must traffic always slow down to a halt on both sides of the expressway for an accident?

Nosy people. Either that, or bored.

Time, Xavier had come to understand the hard way, equaled money. It was that simple formula this country was founded upon. He remembered his high school history teacher telling the class: "The business of America is making money."

OF ALL THE THINGS I'VE LOST, read one bumper sticker on the car in front of him, I MISS MY MIND THE MOST. So many cars. Where was everybody going?

HE IS HERE! read another bumper sticker.

The accident up ahead looked serious. A yellow Ryder van had turned on its side and burst into flames. Black smoke rose over the long line of traffic. When your number came up, it was time to go. Thinking of death and dying made Xavier shudder, so to forget about it he reached for his cellular phone and dialed his office number.

It rang three times. The answering machine came on: "You have reached the insurance office of Xavier Cuevas." Darleen, his secretary, sounded scratchy on the tape. She had stepped out for lunch. The machine beeped, but he didn't leave a message. He pressed a code number to check for messages. While the machine rewound, he noted the time. He'd been stuck in traffic now for thirty-five minutes. So many things I need to do, he thought.

Lately his memory failed. His concentration waned. He constantly wrote little memos to himself to remember things. Sometimes he didn't remember them until Sarah, his wife, showed them to him before putting his clothes in the washing machine. Was this important? was what she always asked. By then it was too late, the need to remember specific things had passed. Sarah had gotten him one of those writing tablets that stick to the windshield and rest on the dashboard.

The machine whirred and clicked. Beeped.

A woman's husky voice came on. She needed quotes on the cheapest auto insurance. "If it's too expensive," she said, "I'll pay only P.I.P."

Xavier wrote "No money in it" on the tablet, then crossed it out.

The next message was a long silence. Xavier waited for a voice to speak, but no one did. Then the line clicked. Somebody'd been doing that a lot lately, calling his number and not leaving a message.

Next on was a client who was unhappy with his group health insurance premiums. The voice sounded familiar, and Xavier tried to figure out who he might be. The man said, "I am tired of leaving messages. Get back to me please, or I'm afraid I'll have to take my business someplace else!"

Familiar voice.

Another beep.

Then Eloisa, a client from way back when he had started to sell insurance, said, "Xavier"—she always pronounced his name with a *J* for *Javier*—"Izquierdo is not well. Not at all." There was a pause during which the faint sound of Eloisa's sobbing became audible. She continued, *"De malo a peor!* He wants to see you as soon as you can—" Then she hung up.

Izquierdo was dying of throat cancer from his sixty years of smoking cigars. Xavier made a note to make time to go by. Izquierdo and Eloisa lived in a condo in Kendall, which was in the opposite direction.

The last message was from Xavier's mother.

"*Cariño*," his mother said, "I need to talk to you. Come by if you can."

The machine clicked and whirred and beeped five times, signaling the end of all the messages.

As he returned the phone to its cradle between the front seats, Xavier noticed the driver in a beaten-up Falcon making strange gestures at him with his hands. What Xavier had done wrong, he didn't know. The man looked terribly upset; he flipped Xavier the middle finger.

"Same to you, buddy," Xavier said.

Once the opportunity opened, the Falcon cut in front of Xavier. The Falcon had New York plates.

Suddenly the man in the Falcon stepped on the brakes and stopped. Xavier wasn't paying attention, and when he realized he was going to crash he slammed his foot on the brake pedal. Then, almost voluntarily, the steering wheel moved under his hands and turned. His car swerved to the right, missing the fender of the Falcon. Close call, he thought, and took a deep breath. His heart beat in his throat. There was a throbbing at his temple.

Up ahead the lights of the police cars, ambulance, rescue units, and fire truck flashed. Firefighters doused the flames with a foam spray. Traffic gridlocked.

Finally, when his turn to pass the accident arrived, he turned to look at the foam frothing from the truck's charred and mangled chassis and stepped on the gas. In the rearview mirror he noticed that the flames had been extinguished. It didn't look as if the driver of the truck had made it. Hell, driving in this much traffic was too dangerous, but he, like everyone else, had to do it. Welcome to the hustle and bustle of Miami's daily life.

Now northbound on the 826 expressway, getting ready to engage in some heavy-duty cross-lane cutting, he wondered about his mother's call. She had sounded worried on the machine. On his way to see a prospective client, he decided to make a pit stop in Hialeah to find out what his mother wanted to talk to him about.

It was twelve minutes past one on a Monday afternoon. Blue Monday. Back-to-the-grind Monday. He hadn't eaten lunch. His stomach felt hollow. It growled. He'd been on the move since morning, taking care of business. Dropped off an insurance health application, answered calls, checked over the mail merge list Darleen had been compiling on the word processor. Pumped gas.

Calls and errands, no time for much else—such was his life.

Most of his clients were Latinos, and often, too often in fact, he couldn't help but feel like an inadequate go-between: an ill-equipped translator between two cultures, one which he worked hard to serve and understand and the other the source of his livelihood, which he needed to protect and respect.

As soon as he exited the expressway, traffic once again stopped. This time it was for a funeral caravan. A long string of cars with their headlights on was escorted by policemen on motorcycles. Traffic was stopped at a green light to let all the funeral cars pass. Xavier thought, They only let you run red lights when you're dead. What good was it then?

The funeral procession passed and traffic moved again. The phone rang and he picked it up.

"Hey, X," Wilfredo, his office partner, said.

"Where are you?" he asked him.

"Esplain later," Wilfredo said. It bothered Xavier that his partner spoke with such a thick accent when he was capable of speaking without one. They had grown up together, gone to the same schools, learned the same language. Whenever Xavier mentioned the accent, Wilfredo called him an *arrepentido,* embarrassed to be Cuban. Wilfredo believed he was as much Cuban as he was American, fitting right in the middle where the hyphen separated the two worlds.

"I've been running around like a chicken with its head chopped off," Xavier said.

Xavier stopped at a red light. WELCOME TO HIALEAH, THE CITY OF THE FUTURE, the sign on the median read. Cube city, U.S.A. *Bienvenidos a Hialeah, la ciudad que progresa y tropiesa,* the city that progressed and stumbled. This was the city where he had grown up after his family moved here from Cuba in 1960, when he was a year old.

"Monday is not my day," Wilfredo was saying.

"What day of the week is, pal?"

The light turned green, and Xavier made a right turn onto Forty-ninth Avenue, where the fruit, peanut, and flower vendors were out in full force, wearing tattered straw hats, weaving among the stopped cars.

"Where are you?" Wilfredo asked.

"On my way to see my mother."

"Say hi to her," Wilfredo said. Then, "You want me to meet you at the office?"

"I don't have the slightest clue when I'll be back." There was a client in Miami Lakes he had to see at two-thirty. That gave him enough time to wait out the lunch traffic at his mother's.

A Trans Am sports car with tinted windows cut in front of the Volvo. It was the kind of fast car Wilfredo called a Cuban Ferrari. Wilfredo drove a Camaro, which he called a Cuban Porsche.

"Can't believe this. Fucking traffic!" he said to Wilfredo. "Driving in Hialeah's like entering the Indianapolis 500 on horseback."

Wilfredo laughed.

A short, skinny man approached the Volvo and tapped on the window.

"Hold on," Xavier said.

The instant Xavier rolled down the window, the man slipped in a piece of paper which fell on Xavier's lap. The man walked away quickly. Xavier read the three-by-five index card aloud: " 'Phone call, while you were out. Re: personal. Hi lover; I hear you're an adventurous guy who really likes a good time. Call me. I have a personal message just for you. . . . My number is: 976-3231. Signed, The Foxx.' "

"Save that number," Wilfredo said.

"Two dollars for the first minute, fifty cents for each additional minute. Can you believe it, some jerk is making money with this crap?"

"Sex sells," Wilfredo said. "It's in the Constitution."

Xavier tsk-tsked.

"Hey, X," said Wilfredo, his voice full of excitement. Then he switched to Spanish: *"Si vieras la gringa que ligue anoche?"* Xavier should see the woman Wilfredo had picked up last night. "Hot, hot, hot. She's a marine biologist."

Wilfredo was so predictable, or was it because Xavier had known his partner for so long? "A couple of days ago it was an aerobics instructor."

"She told me this incredible story about how octopuses mate."

"How *what* mates?"

"Octopus," he said. "You know, the sea creature with all the arms."

"Okay, shoot."

"Listen. The female octopus has her vagina in her nose. If she's not in the mood, you know, and the male tries anything funny, she bites it off."

"Painful stuff."

"Thing is he's got eight penises. Eight tries, then he's out."

"I'd be more careful," he said to Wilfredo, making a note: "All the cars and they all need to be insured."

"I think I'm in love."

"Same thing you said last week."

"This time it's the real thing."

Xavier fought a strong urge to preach to him about the all-too-real risks of sleeping around. AIDS lurked behind every smiling face at bars and clubs—places Wilfredo frequented—and he was playing Russian roulette with five bullets in the barrel.

"Hey, bro, I better let you go," Wilfredo suggested.

Good idea, Xavier thought, then said, "Got to mom's."

"See you later, alleygator," Wilfredo told him. "I'm going to have my hands full right now, if you know what I mean."

"Watch out for hernias."

"Noses, *Cubiche,* it's noses I should worry about—"

The line clicked.

Xavier hung up and smiled. He couldn't believe his partner's energy—if he only had it for the business.

He turned the corner and pulled up behind his mother's blue Thunderbird in the driveway. The house was in need of paint—rust and mildew had turned the walls orange and green where the spray from the sprinklers hit. How many times had he offered to hire and pay someone to paint the house? Since his parents' divorce, his mother had let the outside of the house go. The lawn needed to be mowed and the hedges trimmed. The roses by the fence had dropped their petals, and now the ground was speckled with them.

Before climbing out of the car, Xavier removed his beeper from the sun visor and hooked it to his belt. Switching the vibration buzzer on, he stepped out of the air-conditioned cocoon into the humid, choking heat of the driveway.

Lizards scurried out of the way and hid as Xavier approached the front porch of the house he had grown up in. He rang the doorbell but there was no answer. He should have tried to reach her on the phone before driving out. Maybe she had called from work. Perhaps she was on the phone or taking a shower.

His childhood had been spent on these streets. He had lost track of how many years his parents had owned the house, having bought it in the early sixties.

He rang again, then he heard his mother's footsteps.

Opening the door, she said, "Got my message. Good."

She'd been cleaning. Her hair smelled of detergent and her skin, when he greeted her with a kiss, was moist with perspiration.

"I always get your messages," he said as he entered the house. "I didn't know whether to call you here or at work."

"Took the day off," she said. "Sometimes you've got to do that."

She worked as a buyer for Burdines department store in Westland Mall.

As she led the way to the kitchen, she said, "I don't know why I take days off. I always end up doing work."

From the rear of the house came the sound of music, a tune Xavier thought he knew because he had been hearing it most of his life. His mother was playing her old records, her prized possessions which she had paid a lot of money to sneak out of Cuba.

Mirna Alarcón was in her late fifties, tall and pretty, though her age showed in the wrinkled skin beneath her almond-colored eyes.

In the kitchen, he could hear the music better; it was the sound of congas going *tuc-tuc, tac, tac/truc-truc, truc-trac.*

"Welcome to the club," he said. "I've been at it since early this morning."

A wet mop leaned against the refrigerator in the corner of the kitchen. Soapsuds came up in the sink. The Windex and 409 spray bottles sat on top of the stove.

He told her about the impossible traffic and from habit opened the pantry.

"Are you hungry?" his mother asked.

"Hungry's not the word," he admitted, closing the sliding door.

"I ate lunch a while ago," she said. "I can fix you some leftovers."

"I'll pick up something on the way," he said and sat down on a stool behind the kitchen counter. "I don't want to trouble—"

"Nonsense. Shouldn't eat junk food. All that cholesterol."

He didn't want to ask her point-blank why she had asked him to come over. Obviously she was fine. There was something different about her appearance. It took a couple of glances to figure it out. A new hair style, cropped short on the sides, bobbed in the back. It made her look very young.

"All I have to do," she said, "is heat it up."

She took the chicken and yellow rice and fried plantain leftovers in Tupperware containers from the refrigerator, spooned them into a plate, and placed them in the microwave oven.

"How—" His mother stopped to press the START button. "How are Sarah and the children?" She sat on the stepladder on the other side of the counter.

"They're fine, mother. Lindy wants to have her ears pierced. She watched how it's done on television."

"Bring her by the store. I'll get someone in jewelry to pierce them for her," she told him.

"Sarah wants to wait until she's older."

Mirna gave him a look of disapproval, then said, "The longer she waits—" Again she stopped. "And you, how are you doing? How many policies did you sell last week?"

"Not enough."

"*La avaricia rompe el saco*," she said in her clear and soft-spoken Spanish. Avarice corrupts.

"Sink or swim," Xavier told her. "It's the nature of the business. I have to stay afloat or else."

Sink or swim. That was precisely the way he'd been living for the last few years. Always in a hurry, but never enough time. He felt the tugs and wondered if his time to sink had come.

"I suppose you want to know why I asked you to come," she said.

Xavier flashed her a what-could-be-so-urgent? look.

"I have good news."

At least someone did.

"I wanted to tell you before," she said. "But I had to wait for the right time."

"Did something happen?" he asked, checking the time on the kitchen clock and his watch. He was synchronized.

"Ready?"

"Ready."

"I'm getting married," she said.

He didn't know what to say. He was dumbfounded. *His mother getting married?* Why not? But to whom?

She started to say something but paused. "Well, I've been thinking it over."

"To whom?" he asked. He wondered what kind of expression he had on his face, since his mother was looking at him so strangely.

"This is really difficult for me, *hijo*." She placed a doily in front of him. From the cabinet drawer she pulled silverware, then she went down into the florida room and turned off the music.

"I am happy for you," he said finally. Why shouldn't she marry again? "Who is he?"

"I've always been honest with you, haven't I?" She returned to the kitchen, set the silverware down in front of him, then grabbed a glass from the cupboard and put ice in it.

He agreed.

The food's aroma filled the kitchen with a thick cumin-cilantro-and-chicken-in-yellow-rice smell.

"Well?" he asked.

"I told your father. We had lunch the other day."

"What did he say?" Xavier didn't know his parents still had lunch together.

She smiled. "You know how he is." She walked to the microwave to check the food. It was ready. Steam rose from the plate and swirled in front of him. Succumbing to its influence, he felt hungrier than ever.

"Really, what did he say to you? What does he think?" His father was living with a "friend," as Mirna put it, in Miami Beach, and Xavier didn't want to think about these living arrangements either.

"There's an avocado," she told him. "I can cut it and make you a salad."

Xavier told her not to bother. "Tell me what he said, for Christsakes!"

She got him a Diet Pepsi. She brought him a napkin. The pepper and salt were already on the counter. Xavier missed his mother's attention. Why didn't he come over more often?

"He wished me good luck," his mother said, returning to the fold-out stepladder. "He said to me, 'Why spend the rest of your life alone?' So I told him he was absolutely right."

"That's nice of him."

She smiled the way his children smiled when they had a trick up their sleeves, or a secret. "Your father's become an understanding man," she said, sarcasm thick in her voice. "We get along fine now that he under-stands himself better, now that he is—"

"You'll be happy now," Xavier interrupted her.

"Aren't *you* happy for me?" she asked.

"Of course I am."

"I want you to meet him."

"Tell me who he is," he said.

"You'll like him."

"How can I like him if you don't tell me who he is?"

"He styles my hair at the salon."

This caught Xavier off guard. "Your hairdresser? You are marrying your hairdresser?"

"Hair stylist."

Same thing. He grew quiet. His mood changed, plummeting to murky depths. He put the fork and knife down.

"What's the matter?" she asked.

"I've got to go, Mother," he said.

"I thought you were hungry."

"I'm late for an appointment," he lied. He was upset, but he didn't feel like explaining why. Besides, he didn't want to ruin his mother's mood.

It wasn't that he had anything against hairdressers/stylists. No, it wasn't anything like that. It was the idea of her getting married. After all these years . . .

"How about a *cafecito?*" she asked.

"No thanks."

Silence, then she looked at him and said, "Maybe it's my turn to have a middle-age crisis. You must promise me not to talk to your father about this."

"I thought you had told him."

"I have," she said. "But I don't want him to talk behind my back."

"Does he know who you are marrying?"

"It's none of his business."

"You are right," Xavier said and stood up.

"This man cares about me. Loves me."

His lunch was beginning to sour in his stomach already. He went to the bathroom, washed his hands, splashed cold water on his face, rinsed his mouth, and combed his hair in front of the medicine cabinet mirror. His was a tired face—tired eyes and a mouth tired from talking. Why don't people ever stop talking? he wondered as he stared at his bloodshot eyes. Sometimes he wished he didn't have to speak.

His mother's toiletries had taken over the bathroom completely. There was a bottle of Pierre Cardin men's cologne next to the toothbrushes. Was it his? Probably. Was he spending nights here?

What's going to happen to this house? he wondered. Would she live here among so many old memories and make her new marriage work?

Let her marry who she wanted, it was none of his business. Not his, or his father's. It was her happiness. He thought he could make himself understand.

Once again in the kitchen, he thanked his mother for the lunch and congratulated her. It isn't every day your mother announces an engagement.

"Will you be there?" she asked.

"Where?"

"At the wedding."

"When is it?"

"We haven't decided yet, but it'll be soon."

"Am I invited?"

She hugged and kissed him. "Don't be silly. Who do you think is giving me away?"

"Be serious, Mother."

"I am."

Xavier moved to the front door. She followed him there and put her hand on his arm as if to stop him.

She said, "I still care about your father. But I don't want to spend the rest of my life alone."

"You're not alone," Xavier said.

She's an adult, Xavier admitted to himself, as a way to form some sort of rationale, and she has a right to do as she sees fit. But what could she and this man have in common? He tried to imagine them sitting around, relaxing, and the man doing her hair all the time. Checking it. Combing it. Fiddling with it. Saying, "I've got to get it perfect. Look at your hair. Your hair's the reason why I married you, darling."

Xavier realized the unfairness of the stereotype.

"Good-bye, Mother."

"Keep in touch," she said. "I'll send you and Sarah an invitation."

Outside, the harsh midday sunshine made him squint. He got in the car. Putting on his shades, he pulled out of the driveway, waved to his mother, and drove on. He couldn't believe it, his mother getting married, and she wanted him to give her away. He wrote down, "Mother's marriage."

Warm air mixed with faint exhaust smells that came out of the Volvo's air vents. He loosened his tie and removed the beeper, hooking it to the usual place on the visor.

Date?

Twenty minutes to get to Miami Lakes to see his new client. At the corner of Sixtieth Street and Twelfth Avenue, he made a left and headed westward. School zones in this area slowed down traffic. No, sir, this city wasn't traffic friendly. But his appointments had to be kept, calls answered, errands run, and the bills for living paid.

A wedding gift for Mother? Sarah would know what to buy.

He turned the radio on, searched for easy-listening music. Without words. He scanned the stations. No luck. He changed his mind. Turned off the radio. Silence, he said to himself, was more gratifying.

Xavier leaned his head back against the headrest. A tension headache started behind his eyes, heartburn in his chest.

He was back in traffic.

Strange Planet

From *The Moviemaker*

We welcomed our Cuban guest with a Pinos Verdes feast: scrambled cholesterol-free eggs, high-fiber toast with margarine and sugar-free jelly, crisp strips of imitation bacon, a tall glass of seedless orange juice, and a cup of decaffeinated Maxwell House coffee sweetened with Ultrasweet.

"All this food for breakfast?" asked my grandmother as she nibbled at some of the offerings.

"Yes, rich in taste," commented Maman, as if promoting a product on TV, "but not in calories."

My grandmother—*abuela*—was here for one month; not enough time to explore the entire Southland, I thought, but we would at least be able to show her the world-famous tourist sites. During the course of the meal I described to her the American Studios, where she would see fantastic movie sets and special effects and famous actors. Fantasyland, where she would actually see ghosts and talking animals and jungles and pirates and prehistoric creatures. The Movie Star Wax Museum, which was packed with replicas of the greatest stars of all time. Sea World, where she'd be able to pet a whale and talk to a mermaid. And there were the local hangouts: Gala Mall, which was a shopping paradise, and the yo-gurt parlor and the Fifties Diner and Ramosa Beach and the video arcade and . . .

"Don't expect me to go with you," Maman interrupted. "I've had enough of those vulgar and collective fantasies."

"Your grandmother needs to get some rest," said Daddy. "She should spend a few days just relaxing."

"But I didn't come here to rest, Benito," Abuela protested. "Resting is for Galicians."

I didn't know what Galicians she was referring to, and I had no idea why they needed to rest, but the phrase sounded funny. *El descanso es para los gallegos.* Daddy and I started laughing.

"Gina," said my mother, trying to spoil our fun, as usual, "you must keep in mind that Estela can't run around with you like a teenager. She'll get to see what she can."

"What is this?" asked Abuela. "You people talk as if I were ready to stretch my leg already!"

Daddy was laughing again, but I wasn't getting it, so he deciphered the expression for me: "In Spanish you stretch your leg when you die. Your leg gets stiff. Get it?"

I got it: the first of many idioms of Cuban wisdom that I would gradually acquire from my grandma. People who died not only stretched their leg, I found out, but they also went out singing the "Peanut Vendor Song."

If you were called *mosquita muerta*, the little dead fly, in Cuban Spanish that meant you were cunning, conniving, and hypocritical. (But how could a dead bug be capable of so much evil?) If you "played the cadaver to see what kind of burial you get," that meant you didn't trust your friends. You'd be compared to a pussycat, *la gatica María*, if you did something awful and then tried to hide your crime. María the pussycat, according to Cuban legend, went around defecating in people's gardens and then carefully hiding the evidence.

Whenever reality got too mysterious or incomprehensible, Abuela would state that "a cat's locked up somewhere around here." You had to be assertive in life and always fight for your beliefs, said another one of Abuela's maxims, since "a baby who doesn't cry doesn't get milk." If you were not assertive and let people run all over you, you'd be like "the shrimp that fell asleep and got swept away by the stream."

Old age, in Cuban culture, was the best time of life because you knew everything. After all, the devil knows more from being old than from being the devil. People who lived to be very old were bad bugs, *bichos malos*, because a bad bug never dies. *Bicho malo nunca muere.*

There were surely more people at the mall than Abuela had ever seen during carnival time in Cuba. Gala Mall was an indoor world, with streets, stores, theaters, gyms, artificial sunshine, and dense vegetation—real flowering vines and miniature palm trees—that grew in enclosed gardens.

Shoppers were transported from one floor to another in a cylindrical object made of glass. "They look so helpless in there," remarked Abuela. No, she didn't want to travel in that "bubble" that went up and down incessantly. And she didn't care that the view from the elevator, once you reached the top floor, was spectacular.

Gala Mall had at least five stories, and each floor featured a large stage-shaped platform where several dapper men and lovely blond women stood modeling clothes, shoes, hats, and makeup. Were they human beings or mannequins? Abuela couldn't tell. She noticed they breathed and moved in slow motion, smiling, winking, waving. There was something human about them. But how could those people—if they *were* people—stand for hours, inert and lifeless, impersonating giant dolls? When and where and how did they do their "necessities"?

There were no private homes at the mall, but there were hundreds of restaurants decorated to look as if they belonged in the past or on another planet; boutiques where you could create your outfit on the spot, in a matter of seconds; rooms full of radiant whirling lights and machines that simulated other machines.

Gala Mall had clean and spacious restrooms; parks and playgrounds and even minizoos, places where animals were bred and raised and kept in cages for public viewing; where people went to buy—yes, *buy!*—dogs and cats and birds and monkeys and lizards and even snakes. And there were bakeries at the mall, and candy shops, and soundproof rooms where you could record a song—your voice with an orchestra!—and fulfill your fantasy of being a famous singer.

"You could live your entire life in here," I said, excited to be sharing my favorite hangout with Abuela. "Your entire life, yes," she replied. "But how do you keep track of time and reality when you're in this place?" And I thought, What do you mean "keep track"? This *is* reality.

Abuela and I browsed through at least half the stores at the mall while Daddy waited patiently outside. I bought a full wardrobe for her —most of which she said she didn't need—and some clothes for my cousins. After a late lunch at Sir Burger (her first real hamburger), we decided to head home. My grandmother had never spent so much time shopping; she was feeling overwhelmed and a little tired.

On our way out, Abuela observed, fascinated, the graffiti-spattered walls in the underground garage. VATOS BUENOS FOREVER. Handwritten signs, LOS BUENOS WANT YOU, gigantic and fanciful designs that resembled letters; perfectly round and ornamented words. VATOS BUENOS WERE HERE!

"They're everywhere," Daddy rued.

"Who?" asked Abuela. "Who is everywhere?"

I informed her that those fancy signs were messages from Santana gang members, *las pandillas;* and that they were meant to mark the Buenos' territory.

"How they managed to get past security is beyond me," said Daddy, sounding unusually defeated and concerned. "They're invading us, *coño!*"

I explained to Abuela that Santana was *la ciudad latina*. No, it wasn't all that far from Pinos Verdes. Most of the people who lived there were Mexican, yes, but most of the stores were owned by Cubans. In fact, it was in Santana where Daddy had one of his most profitable flower shops. Santana was supposedly hell on earth, a gang-infested city, and my mother wished that Daddy would rescue his Flores de Domingo from that infernal and dangerous zone. But Daddy liked to make money, and the Santaneros liked to buy his flowers.

Abuela wanted more details about those belligerent creatures who drew such dainty words, Los Buenos. "How can that writing be the mark of criminals?" she asked Daddy, who didn't elaborate. "They'll never get to Pinos Verdes," he stated. And silence ensued as we drove home from Gala Mall.

We went to Fantasyland on a weekday so we could avoid the lines. According to my mother, it shouldn't have made a difference to Abuela. "She must be used to waiting," scoffed Maman. "Isn't that how you spend your days in Cuba, Estela? Waiting in line?"

Abuela found the singing dolls in the Tiny World attraction too plump and round, too perfect and unbearably infantile. Yet she came out of the ride singing their song, which she loved: *"Es un mundo de muñecas . . ."*

Mister Fantasyland sure had a way with the music, she thought. She was deeply moved by Porky Lady, at the Big Pig Jubilee, when the female pig came down from a hole in the ceiling, wobbling on her swing, and sang her love ballad. Abuela couldn't understand a word of the song, but the melancholy tone of the animal's vibratos touched her. "Americans are capable of making pigs sing!" she cried out, in awe.

We enjoyed the boat ride in the Pirates of the Tropical Sea attraction. We got to sit up front, and when the boat lurched downward into the bowels of Fantasyland we were soaked to the skin. The vertigo was thrilling, but we didn't care for the rest of the ride. (I'd always hated it.) Why would anyone want to make a spectacle out of a town that's being pillaged and burned to the ground by savage men? Why would anyone want to witness such a tragedy? Battleships firing cannons in the middle of the ocean—the smell of gunpowder!—and beautiful homes being ransacked and women getting raped and filthy-looking drunkards wallowing in the mud of pigpens. You couldn't tell the men from the swine; they all had that same look of satiation and stupidity.

She refused to go on the Jungle Voyage because "I've been to enough jungles in my life." We also skipped the World of Dinosaurs because Abuela didn't care to see "those helpless monsters who'd been wiped out like ants."

In the Hawaiian Room, she was overcome by an attack of claustrophobia when the sunflowers started banging on the congas and the monkey flowers went wild, making strange, angry sounds, and the rain started to fall. "A mob of people trapped in here," Abuela complained, "all of us listening to a concert of artificial birds, and as if that weren't enough, a storm just broke out, with lightning!"

She wasn't afraid; she'd been annealed to bad weather in all its inclement tropical manifestations: cyclones, hurricanes, thunder squalls. It was just that she couldn't understand what was "attractive" about the Hawaiian attraction. Once outside, Abuela marveled at the cloudless sky. "This is truly magical," she said, finding it hard to believe that there wasn't a single drop of rain in sight.

The singing stone heads in the Ghost Mansion's cemetery fascinated her. "The way they play with your mind!" she shouted repeatedly as we went through the haunted house, surrounded by whispering, moaning voices; as we watched the dancing spirits cram the ballroom floor. "Even the smell is real," she remarked. "It reeks of death in this place."

She was tickled to discover a ghost sitting between her and me, in the car. As the vehicle moved and swiveled down the rail, toward the exit, it passed in front of a wall-size mirror. There we were, reflected, and there he was, the goofy-looking spirit of a young man.

"Look, Gina! He's so cute," Abuela said, giggling. "*Qué chulo!* Maybe you should ask him to be your boyfriend."

No way, I thought. I knew much too well what male spirits were capable of doing. . . .

I'm filming her against her will. She hates my camera. She hates seeing herself "duplicated," viewing that image of a woman who laughs and talks and looks just like her, Estela, on the screen, a woman who is herself and yet who isn't.

She's wearing faded blue jeans, fitted, with a wide black leather belt riding low on her hips; a pink tie-dyed T-shirt displaying the name of my favorite rock group, Remedy, and black flats. She faces her mirror reflection and discovers, incredulous, that she has turned into a replica of Gina. "Great!" she says. "Now your little boyfriend won't be able to tell us apart."

My little boyfriend, that's what she always called Robby, my *noviecito*. She liked him. She praised his attempts to speak to her in Spanish. She accepted with a kiss the flowers he gave her when they first met, and she even said, in a whisper, "Sank you, sank you." She was cool enough to smile approvingly whenever Robby and I held hands or kissed.

Robby and Abuela are playing Mintiendo at the video arcade. He's eating up tiny mechanical demons with his magic wand. She's driving her sports car at full speed, avoiding the bumps, the potholes, and the giant rocks along the road. Her tires screech as they burn down the freeway; her vehicle never explodes or goes up in flames—"and I've never driven a car in my entire life!"

Abuela's presence again, at the American Studios. She seems annoyed and unimpressed. She doesn't "give a cucumber" that prime-time shows and future box-office hits with megastars are being filmed a few feet away from us. "You go to this place to have fun," she says of the Studios' Earth Tremor, "and they throw you in a hole, *dígame usted!* And they make the earth move around you until you feel like coconut water, your stomach in your throat and your guts coming out of your nose. There is nothing fun about that."

"But it's good practice," I tell her, "for the real one that's coming." I'm so mean.

She despises the earthquake alerts and the false alarms, the preparations for the Big One (canned goods, stand in a door frame, and so on). It'll hit before the end of the century for sure; eight points on the Richter scale. And you have to know what to do, where to go to save your life. Yes, Abuela! People have lost their lives in previous earthquakes. Thousands of people.

She's been through one hundred cyclones and seventy-three hurricanes back in Cuba, but nothing has prepared her for this potential catastrophe. This invisible monster that will jolt and agitate the ground when you least expect it. Nowhere to go; you can't escape its claws. Mind you, it's only a threat and you're simply taking necessary measures. God willing, the monster will never show its ugly and omnipotent fangs. Hopefully she'll be back in her beautiful Cubita when it hits.

I see her at the Movie Star Wax Museum, again unimpressed. She hasn't seen most of the movies represented in those sets by those magically made-up and dressed-up dummies. She does recognize, however, some of the stars behind the frozen masks: Chaplin, Bogart, Monroe. "Imagine,

Gina," she whispers, "having your image cooped up in here for eternity, frozen forever playing a movie role. How sad."

So few visual traces of her; a handful of clips. Yet I see a woman who looks and talks just like Estela. I hear that woman laughing while she cooks. "I'll never learn my way around this maze," she'd say each time she entered the kitchen. She didn't like to use the microwave oven because the food placed in it for defrosting made strange explosive noises, as if it was refusing to accept its fate. She never tried to use the icemaker either. "When the machine produces the ice," she alleged, "it sounds like it's demolishing my bones."

She disliked the Mister PV coffee maker because it was the spitting image of a miniature spaceship, and it sounded like one when it was making that awful watered-down American version of *café*. She mistrusted the garbage disposal because it triggered an earthquake in the sink and could easily devour everything in sight. She'd rescued five pitiful-looking spoons and two crooked knives from its fangs. And the horrendous racket it had made trying to digest the silverware had brought my mother to the scene of the crime, fuming, "Estela! What catastrophe have you caused this time?"

Abuela was fascinated with our waste products, the things we considered trash, *basura*. How could we throw away so many valuable objects? Bottles, plastic glasses, cans, paper bags and plastic bags, newspapers, all to waste! (Recycling was a concept my parents never took seriously, in spite of all my nagging sermons about saving the planet.)

I wish I'd kept that bundle of burger boxes that she collected from our lunches at Sir Burger and that she had arranged into a knickknack. "Isn't it pretty?" she said, slightly embarrassed, when I found her trinket in one of the dresser drawers. I wish I'd kept the metal Loreo cookie box—Loreo cookies being my weakness—that she wanted to save in case we ever needed a strong container. And the milk cartons and the cereal boxes and the twist ties that she liked to make into make-believe rings, *anillos de mentirita*.

"Are those the presents you're taking to your family back home, Estela?" Maman would ask, sniggering, whenever she caught Abuela "saving" something.

My grandmother never took Maman's cattiness seriously. She'd react to my mother's snide remarks by staring at her. "Are you feeling sick, Elisa?" Abuela would ask her. "No, I am not feeling sick," Maman would always respond. To which Abuela would say, "Are you sure?" My mother would come back, glowering at Abuela, "Yes, I am sure!" To which Abuela would add, "I don't know. You have that look of sickness again on your face. Your nose and your lips are so contorted, Elisa. Are you sure you don't have a pain in your stomach?"

The time my mother found us in her French living room, eating pizza and drinking milk shakes and getting oozing red stuff all over her untouchable furniture. "*Mon Dieu!*" she wailed. "What are you two doing to my Louis Quinze?" After hearing about the "distasteful incident" from my mother, Daddy talked to me and Abuela over breakfast, half jokingly, reprimanding me for feeding her so much crap. Since when had I become a fast food junkie? I should know better, he said. And to his mother, "Eat all you want, Mamá. That's one of the reasons you're here, no? So you can eat. But please don't let Gina feed you junk. *Basura!*"

We are building a sand castle at Ramosa Beach. I am showing Abuela the secret to perfect tanning, describing to her the Ramosa dudes who walk by, the Surfer, the Yuppie, the Vato, the Neohippie, the Macho Latino, the Comecaca.

She complains about the gooey black stuff that got stuck on the soles of her feet when she walked down the shore. "It's the Blob, Abuela. *El Blobo,*" I tell her. But she doesn't know what I mean. She never saw the movie.

She reacts to the relentless waves. She feels assaulted, she fights them, tries to stay afloat but succumbs to them. No, Abuela, they won't stop. Believe me. This is not the Caribbean.

She had never been to the beach until now, this trip. But she had always dreamed about the Mar Caribe. She had tried to imagine it and, yes, she could almost touch its peaceful waters, its sand white and fine like sugar. So vivid were her visions that she talked about *la playa cubana* as if she'd actually been there, in Varadero, at the most beautiful beach that human eyes have ever seen.

In this other world—Pinos Verdes, Ramosa, the South Bay—Abuela felt like a shrimp swept away by the stream. There was a wondrous and menacing civilization growing beyond her country's shores, and she'd never known about it. This other world breathed and lived and grew and most of all it consumed. It had such big needs! This other world existed (and so did she) in a different dimension. She felt out of her element, a stranger on my strange planet.

"These people have built a wall around their city," Abuela observed, as she and I strolled down the Pinos Verdes hill one evening. "They have tried to force the dark side of life out of their patios and swimming pools," she said, pointing to the homes we were passing. The mansions were hidden in the trees, camouflaged and protected by radars and powerful electronic devices. The Pinos Verdes people lived in a machinelike world disguised as nature. "Blind," she noted, "to anything beyond their houses and their sunshine."

Down the crowded beach, under the smoggy Ramosa skies, Abuela told me of the village where she was born and raised, Piedrecita—the name means "little rock." She talked of the big city where she lived now, Florida, province of Camagüey, which forms the belly of the lizard-island. Her home was on the outskirts of town, Egusquiza Street, three blocks from the railroad and two blocks from Carretera Central, the only "free-way" in Cuba.

She said she loved and missed her house of impeccable white walls; the ceiba tree outside her window. And her neighbors, her *gente,* loud and spirited and driven to survive.

Baskets of Water

From *Dreaming in Cuban*

IVANITO

I started learning English from Abuelo Jorge's old grammar textbooks. I found them in Abuela Celia's closet. They date back to 1919, the first year he started working for the American Electric Broom Company. At school, only a few students were allowed to learn English, by special permission. The rest of us had to learn Russian. I liked the curves of the Cyrillic letters, their unexpected sounds. I liked the way my name looked: ИВАН. I took Russian for nearly two years at school. My teacher, Sergey Mikoyan, praised me highly. He said I had an ear for languages, that if I studied hard I could be a translator for world leaders. It was true I could repeat anything he said, even tongue twisters like *kolokololiteyshchiki perekolotili vikarabkavshihsya vihuholey,* "the church bell casters slaughtered the desmans that had scrambled out." He told me I had a gift, like playing the violin or mastering chess.

He used to embarrass me in front of the other boys. He'd call me up to the front of the class and ask me to recite a poem we had read only once. I'd pretend I couldn't remember it, but he insisted until I gave in, and I was secretly pleased. The words just came to me, clicked together like so many keys to locks. Afterward my schoolmates would tease me, "Teacher's pet!" "Show-off!" and shove me between them in the halls.

Mr. Mikoyan was a short man with shiny, ruddy cheeks like a baby's. He kept ice in a porcelain bowl on his desk. Every once in a while, he'd twist his handkerchief around a cube and press it to his temple. "The most civilized countries are the coldest ones," he told us many times. "Too much heat addles the brain."

I used to stay after class and wipe the blackboard for him with a wet rag. He'd talk of winter sleigh rides in the countryside, of lakes frozen solid enough to jump on, and snow that fell like crystal from the sky. He'd tell me stories of the czarevitch in Saint Petersburg, weak with hemophilia, his fate controlled by wicked forces. All the while, the ice would crackle in his bowl, as if to confirm his words.

I felt that I was meant to live in this colder world, a world that preserved history. In Cuba, everything seemed temporal, distorted by the sun.

Then Mr. Mikoyan would read me quotes from Tolstoy, whom he considered the greatest of all Russian authors, to copy onto the blackboard. My favorite was the first line in *Anna Karenina:* "Happy families are all alike; every unhappy family is unhappy in its own way."

"Perfect, it is perfect!" Mr. Mikoyan would say. He'd clap his hands, happy with Tolstoy and my perfect spelling. I liked to please him, to see his small, milky-marble teeth. He told me his wife was a chemist who worked with Cuban scientists on top-secret projects developing products from sugarcane. They had no children.

One afternoon, as I was wiping the blackboard, Mr. Mikoyan stood close behind me and told me that he was returning to Russia. He said that I would hear vile things about him.

I turned to look at him. His lips were dry and clung to each other as he spoke. I felt his sour little bursts of breath on my face. He looked as if he wanted to say something more, but then he clasped me to him suddenly and smoothed my hair, repeating my name. I pulled away from him, accidentally knocking the porcelain bowl from his desk. It shattered into a thousand pieces and crunched beneath my feet as I ran.

For a long time, I thought about Mr. Mikoyan, about his ruddy baby cheeks and the things he warned me I'd hear. A boy from an upper grade accused him of indiscretions. Everyone spoke of it like murder or treason, with fascination and revulsion. Then the jokes started, more and more cruel. They said I was his favorite, that I'd stayed with him after school. "Go join him in Siberia!" they taunted. "You'll keep each other warm!" I didn't want to understand.

(1978)

The *oddu,* the official *santería* prediction for this year, is mixed. Yes, believers can accomplish many things because the dead are benevolently inclined toward the living. On the other hand, nothing can be taken for granted because what the living desire will require great effort. Felicia del Pino is fortunate in that she knows unequivocally what she wants:

another husband. In this respect, at least, she will be twice more blessed.

In the second week of January, Felicia visits a *santero* known for his grace and power in reading the divining shells. Through the mouths of the cowries the gods speak to him in clear, unambiguous voices. The *santero* dips his middle finger in holy water and sprinkles it on the floor to refresh the shells. He begins to pray in Yoruba, asking for the blessings of the *orishas,* whom he honors one by one. Then, with the sixteen cowries, he touches Felicia's forehead, her hands, and her knees so that the gods may learn of the aching between her legs, of the hunger on her lips and the tips of each finger, of her breasts, taut with desire. The gods will tell her what to do.

The *santero* tosses and retosses the shells, but they foretell only misfortune. He enlists the aid of the sacred *ota* stone, as well as the shrunken head of a doll, a ball of powdered eggshell, and the *eggun,* a vertebra from the spine of a goat. But the reading does not change.

"Water cannot be carried in a basket," the *santero* says, shaking his head. "What you wish for, daughter, you cannot keep. It is the will of the gods."

He instructs Felicia to perform a rubbing ritual to cleanse herself of negative influences. This is easily done, he says, by smearing a piece of meat or a soup bone with palm oil, aspersing it with rum, curing it with cigar smoke, then placing it in a paper bag and rubbing herself from head to toe.

"The bag will absorb the evil that clings to you," the *santero* says. "Take it to the gates of the cemetery and leave it there. When you have done this, return to me for a final cleansing."

Felicia has every intention of following the *santero*'s advice. But on her way home she falls in love.

Not everyone would be attracted to Ernesto Brito. His most remarkable feature besides his paleness, a paleness that obliterates any possible expression, is his hair. He combs his flaxen strands meticulously from the lower left side of his head to his right temple, then swirls them round and round on his bald crown, securing them with a greasy pomade. When a stiff wind disarranges his lacquered locks, he looks panic-stricken, like a man who's just seen his own ghost.

Felicia first notices her second husband-to-be when he pedals by her furiously on a clunky Russian bicycle, his hair vertical as a sail.

At the end of the alleyway, Ernesto Brito, nervously attempting a sharp right turn, clatters to the ground.

Felicia approaches the bleached, crumpled heap that will be her husband. He looks like a colorless worm, writhing on his stomach in a synthetic tan suit with precisely matching socks, his steel glasses smashed against the pavement. Felicia is smitten. She helps him up and, without a word, pats his hair until his face flushes the color of beets. She takes him by the hand and leads him to her 1952 De Soto parked a few yards away.

It is late afternoon. There is a jowly woman hanging her wash across the alley with a trolling motion of rope. A bowlegged farmer unloads a crate of country chickens for the butcher. Two young mechanics in loose jumpsuits smoke cigarettes with oil-creased hands. Felicia opens the rear door of her vintage American car and slides across the backseat, gently tugging Ernesto with her. The windows are rolled down and a fly circles and drones above them. She pulls him toward her and it begins to rain, a hard afternoon rain that is rare in winter.

Four days later, before Ernesto can move his belongings from his mother's apartment to the house on Palmas Street, before Felicia's mother, children, and best friend, Herminia, can object to the suddenness of her marriage to Ernesto, before Felicia can heed the directives of the *santero*, whose advice she has not entirely forgotten, before she and her husband can celebrate their union with a clamorous party, Ernesto dies tragically in a grease fire at a seaside hotel.

Ernesto, her gentle Ernesto, had been a restaurant inspector, renowned for his refusal to take bribes (neither money nor pork loins could tempt him) and for his scrupulous campaign against mice feces. At his sparsely attended funeral, Felicia howls like a lonely she-wolf. "You killed him because he was honest!" she screams, tearing her hair. "He wouldn't tolerate a single dropping!"

Felicia relived their brief time together. Ernesto's pallid skin mottled with excitement, his tentative hands that quickly became assured under her encouragement, the way he laid his downy head between her breasts and slept contentedly, like a well-fed baby. Ernesto had been a virgin when Felicia coaxed him to the backseat of her car, and he displayed the profound gratitude of the unburdened. For three days they rocked in each other's arms, voracious and inseparable, speaking few words, but knowing all they needed to know.

After Ernesto died, Felicia learned from his mother that they'd been born minutes apart, on the same day of the same year.

Felicia writes a letter of protest to El Líder, demanding a full investigation into her husband's death. When she doesn't hear back from him, she becomes certain, with the surety of the white light illuminating her brain, that El Líder is to blame. Yes, he must have ordered her husband's murder personally. Others, too, are involved. They watch her bleary-eyed from behind their square black glasses, signaling to each other with coughs and claps. It is making sense to her now. Of course, it is finally clear. That is why the light is so bright. They refract it through their glasses so she cannot see, so she cannot identify the guilty ones. All the while, they are spectators to her wretchedness.

Felicia knows that Graciela Moreira is one of their spies. That is why she returns to the beauty shop, time and time again, to have her ringlets seared. She, too, wears the glasses. She, too, loves the fire. Felicia will trap her into a confession. She waits until the moon is propitious, then calls Graciela on the telephone, inviting her to the beauty shop for a free permanent.

"It's a special promotion, a new curling gel," Felicia coaxes. "I want you to be my model."

When Graciela appears an hour later, Felicia is prepared for her. She mixes lye with her own menstrual blood into a caustic brown paste, then thickly coats Graciela's head. Over it, she fastens a clear plastic bag with six evenly spaced hairpins, and waits. Felicia imagines the mixture melting through Graciela's frail scalp, penetrating the roots and bones of her skull until it eats her vicious brain like acid. Graciela cries out and pulls on the cap, hardened now like a helmet, but Felicia clamps it in place with her fists.

"You lying bitch! You killed him, didn't you?" Felicia shouts and knocks Graciela's glasses from her face.

That is the last thing Felicia remembers for many months.

Felicia notices the outdated calendars first, each month taped neatly to the ceiling. She is lying on her back in a bed that's not her own, in a room she doesn't recognize.

In the center of the ceiling, affixed with yellowed tape, is January 1959, the first month of the revolution. The glossy pages of succeeding months blossom around it: landscapes of fluted mountains for 1964; a curious collection of Irish setters and pugs in 1969; twelve varieties of jasmine for each month of 1973. The pages rustle slightly in the breeze. Felicia raises her head from the pillow. Three swivel-neck fans scan her with air. The sun glares through the paper window shades. Suddenly, the room vibrates with a deafening rattle and the Dopplerized screeches of children. A jingling music starts up and the air around her surges with the ricocheting voices of vendors hawking toasted corn and toy rockets.

It's as if Felicia's senses were clicking on one by one. First sight, then sound, then sight again.

She flaps open a shade and blinks unbelievingly at the carnival below her. The whirl of colors is unbearable, a jagged, unsettling choreography. It is summer and hot and well past noon, that much she can tell. A teenage boy in a baseball cap grins up at her nervously, and Felicia realizes she is standing naked in the window. She drops to her knees, wraps herself with a bed sheet, and lowers the shade.

A man's work clothes, stiff with dirt, hang oddly ballooned in the closet. There are two sets of barbells, a burlap sack of sand, a jump rope with red wooden handles, and a pear-shaped leather punching bag nailed to the closet ceiling. In the corner, a neat stack of American magazines features page after page of luridly sculpted men in contorted poses. In one centerfold, someone named Jack La Lanne tows a rowboat with a rope held between his teeth. The words in the caption look insect bristly. Felicia cannot understand them.

There's a straw shoulder bag on a hanger, and Felicia digs with her broken fingernails for clues. She finds eleven encrusted centavos, a rusted tube of orange lipstick, and, through a tear in the checkered lining, a soiled prayer card for La Virgen de la Caridad del Cobre. Nothing to tell her who she is, or where she is from.

Felicia pulls on the navy trousers. They fit her snugly about the hips, although the hems come up to her shins. The shirt billows over her breasts. She tries on a pair of rubber flip-flops that are just the right size. Felicia decides to fry an egg on a hot plate in the kitchenette. She eats only the yolk, dabbing it with a piece of stale bread she finds in the cupboard. Then she peels a tangerine. There's a gold band on her right ring finger. It's familiar to her. The whole place, in fact, is familiar, but she can't say how. She is not afraid, though. It's as if her body had inhabited this space for a time and pronounced it safe for her mind.

Felicia opens the room's only door and follows the hallway to a bathroom on the other end. She looks tanned and rested in the mirror, almost pretty. This reassures her. She combs her hair, spots a lone gray strand and plucks it with a flourish.

Outside, the air is thick and humid and crowded with noise. Are people watching her? It's hard for her to tell. She smooths her trousers with both hands and continues walking purposefully, to where she doesn't know.

"Excuse me, please, but where are we?" she asks a pudgy girl.

"Cienfuegos, señora."

"And what day is it?"

"July 26, 1978," she recites, as if Felicia were a teacher testing her history. "Is that your name?" she asks shyly, pointing to Felicia's left shoulder, where "Otto" is stitched in plain lettering. But Felicia does not answer.

There are many men in navy work clothes like hers. They wave and blow mock kisses from their candy stands and ticket booths and from the bumper-car rink. They all know her name. Felicia smiles wanly, waving back. Toward the far end of the amusement park, the roller coaster hovers above the other less-rhythmic rides. Rattle, rattle, rattle, swoosh. Rattle, rattle, rattle, swoosh.

"Come here, *mi reina,* come here!" a broad-chested man calls to her from behind a toolshed. He has a squeaky, inefficient voice that swallows syllables whole.

Felicia moves toward him, toward his tidy, ursine face. An ellipse of curly black hair is visible between the upper buttons of his shirt.

"You couldn't wait to come out, eh?" He laughs, patting her all over with hands solid and undefined as paws. His hair is frizzy, a woolly frame for his stubble-darkened cheeks. Felicia realizes with a start that he is carpeted with damp fur. She imagines him surviving freezing temperatures without so much as a sweater.

"I meant what I said last night," he says, lowering his voice. "We're going to Minnesota. It's the coldest state in the U.S. We'll open an ice-skating rink. I'll sleep naked on the ice. My own ice!"

He pulls her so close she can feel his hot breath on her throat.

"I spoke with Fernando today, and he said he could get us a boat to share with another family Sunday after next. We'll leave at night from the north coast. It's only ninety miles to Key West. He says they treat Cubans like kings there."

"Where are my clothes?" Felicia interrupts him sharply. She notices the stitching on his sweat-stained uniform, the gold band on his finger that matches hers.

"At the laundry, *mi reina.* Remember you asked me to take everything there? It'll be ready this afternoon. Don't worry, I'll bring them back to you."

During the following week, Felicia begins to assemble bits and pieces of her past. They stack up in her mind, soggily, arbitrarily, and she sorts through them like cherished belongings after a flood. She charts sequences and events with colored pencils, shuffling her diagrams until they start to make sense, a possible narrative. But the people remain faceless, nameless.

One evening right after dinner, as Otto is making love to her, her son's face appears in a vision on the ceiling, superimposed on the most recent calendar month.

"When are you coming home, Mami? When are you coming home?" Ivanito begs her in a wavering voice.

Felicia remembers her son's gangly body, his first stilted dancing steps, and begins to cry. Otto, mistaking his wife's sobs for pleasure, pushes his muscled hips against hers and shudders with relief.

Later that night, after the amusement park closes, Felicia urges her husband toward the roller coaster.

Otto Cruz thinks his wife is crazy and beautiful and mysterious, and he will do just about anything she asks. He can't believe his luck in finding her. She was wandering by herself behind the spare-parts warehouse last winter. An angel. Heaven-sent. And he'd only gone to get replacement bolts for the Ferris wheel.

"I'm here," she said simply. Then she shook her dark wavy hair and began unbuttoning her blouse. Her breasts shone like moon-polished marble. Otto's blood pumped so hard he thought he'd explode.

Otto knew he would never recover from his love for her and married Felicia the next morning. She stared at him innocently whenever he asked her where she came from, or where her family lived. "You're my family now," she'd say. "And I've come for you."

Thinking about the night he met Felicia makes Otto hard again. He turns on the switch for the roller coaster and pushes the first car, painted with laughing clowns, along the well-worn grooves. The platform is high above the ground and the electric generator trills and crackles beneath the winding tracks.

The cars lurch forward and Otto jumps in next to his wife. Her skin is smooth and white against her hair. He slides his hands beneath her gauzy skirt and rubs her warm thighs. The car climbs higher and higher, groaning up the rickety wooden tracks. Otto stands, unzips his pants with a fumbling hand, and pushes himself toward Felicia's lips, toward her miraculous tongue. The car stops for a split second at the peak of the first, the steepest crest. The sky is black, a cloudless blue black. Below them, the roller coaster is a jumble of angles.

Felicia closes her eyes as the car begins to fall. When she opens them, her husband is gone.

(1978)

The day after Felicia burns Graciela Moreira's scalp with lye, Celia's son returns from Czechoslovakia. Javier arrives before dawn in an unraveling tweed suit, his face sunken to flat angles, and collapses on his mother's back porch.

Celia falls on her son like a lover, kissing his face and his eyes and his broken-knuckled hands. His coarse graying hair is matted with salt air, and there's a lump the size of a baseball on the back of his neck. He cries deep soundless cries that make his thin body shiver like leaves in the wind. Celia half drags her son to her bed, the bed in which he was conceived, and for three days he sleeps, wrapped in blankets and his father's frayed pajamas. Celia pieces together his story from the torments he relives in delirium, between fevers and chills and a painful catarrh.

This is what Celia learns: that her son returned home from the university to find a note on the kitchen table, that the envelope was a buttery yellow and the handwriting tall, loopy, and confident, that his two pairs of trousers hung pressed with sharp creases in the closet, that his wife had made love to him the night before so he wouldn't get suspicious, that she'd left him for the visiting mathematics professor from Minsk, that the professor was a spindly crane of a man with a shaved head and goatee who liked to impersonate Lenin, that Javier's daughter, his beloved daughter, to whom Spanish was the language of lullabies, had left with her mother for good.

Celia ponders the lump on her son's neck and the curious scar on his back, a pulpy line just below his left shoulder blade. She finds $1,040 worth of U.S. twenty-dollar bills divided evenly among Javier's four pockets, and a receipt for nine cuff links.

In the following weeks, Celia boils mild chicken broths for her son, feeding him one spoonful at a time. He eats instinctively, without comprehension, and she reads him poetry from the clutter of books on her dresser, hoping to console him.

> *Me he perdido muchas veces por el mar*
> *con el oído lleno de flores recién cortadas,*
> *con la lengua llena de amor y de agonía.*

Muchas veces me he perdido por el mar,
como me pierdo en el corazón de algunos niños.

Could her son, Celia wonders, have inherited her habit of ruinous passion? Or is passion indiscriminate, incubating haphazardly like a cancer?

Celia hopes that the sea, with its sustaining rhythms and breezes from distant lands, will ease her son's heart as it once did hers. Late at night, she rocks on her wicker swing as Javier sleeps and wonders why it is so difficult to be happy.

Of her three children, Celia sympathizes most with her son. Javier's affliction, at least, has a name, even if it has no certain cure. Celia understands his suffering all too well. Perhaps that is why she is restless in its presence.

She understands, too, how Javier's anguish attracts the eligible women of Santa Teresa del Mar, who bring him casseroles covered with starched cloths and look into his night-sky eyes, imagining themselves as his bright constellations. Even the married women drop by to inquire about Javier's health, to hold his hands, warm as blood, and comfort him, when all the time they pray, "Oh, to be loved by this beautiful, sad boy!"

Celia remembers how her own eyes were once like her son's—hollow sockets that attracted despair like a magnet. But in her case, neighbors had kept their distance, believing she was destined for an early death and anyone she touched would be forced to accompany her. They were afraid of her disease as if it were fatal, like tuberculosis, but worse, much worse.

What they feared even more, Celia realized later, was that passion might spare them entirely, that they'd die conventionally, smug and purposeless, having never savored its blackness.

After two months in his mother's bed, Javier emerges from Celia's room. He dusts off the bottle of rum in the dining room cabinet, rinses a glass, chips ice from the freezer, and pours himself a long drink. Then he leans forward in the dining room chair as if expecting electricity to shoot through it and finishes the bottle in one sitting.

The next day he dresses in his mended tweed suit, takes a bill from his stash of American money, and buys a bottle of rum from a black-market dealer on the outskirts of town. He visits the dealer frequently, despite the rising prices, and buys one bottle after another after another. Javier can afford to be a drunk, Celia overhears her neighbors gossiping. The price of a liter of rum keeps most of them, with their monthly coupons and meager earnings, stone-cold sober.

As her son's condition deteriorates, Celia reluctantly cuts back on her revolutionary activities. She decides one last case before she resigns as a judge for the People's Court. Simón Córdoba, a boy of fifteen, has written a number of short stories considered to be antirevolutionary. His characters escape from Cuba on rafts of sticks and tires, refuse to harvest grapefruit, dream of singing in a rock-and-roll band in California. One of Simón's aunts found the stories stuffed under a sofa cushion and informed the neighborhood committee.

Celia suggests to the boy that he put down his pen for six months and work as an apprentice with the Escambray Theater, which educates peasants in the countryside. "I don't want to discourage your creativity, Simón," Celia tells the boy gently. "I just want to reorient it toward the revolution." After all, she thinks, artists have a vital role to play, no? Perhaps later, when the system has matured, more liberal policies may be permitted.

Celia's life resumes a stale, familiar air. She no longer volunteers for the microbrigades, and only guards her stretch of shore one night per month. The rest of the time, she tends to Javier's needs. She hadn't expected her son's illness to take this turn, and she feels helpless and angry, like the times Jorge had bullied Javier as a child. In fact, Javier is a small boy again. Celia helps dress him and combs his hair, reminds him to brush his teeth, and ties his shoelaces. She tucks him into her bed at night, absently stroking his brow. But when she holds her son's face in her hands, Celia sees only an opaque resentment. Is it his, she wonders, or her own?

Despite her care, Javier's skin turns sallow and thins until it looks as if she could strip it away in papery sheets. His knuckles heal poorly, and he is clumsy with everything but his tumbler of rum. Since Javier returned home, Celia has hardly thought of Felicia, who has been missing since winter, or of the twins or of Ivanito, away at boarding school, or of the faraway Pilar. Something tells Celia that if she can't save her son she won't be able to save herself, or Felicia, or anyone she loves.

With the help of some microbrigade friends in the capital, Celia tracks down the *santera* from east Havana who had diagnosed her in 1934, when she was dying of love for the Spaniard.

"I knew it was you," the *santera* says, clapping her hands with brittle twig fingers when she finds Celia on her doorstep. Her face is black and puckered and oily now and seems to breathe all at once like an undersea creature. But when she smiles, her skin pulls back like a curtain, stretching her features until they are as lineless as a young woman's.

She places her speckled hands over Celia's heart and nods solemnly as if to say, "I am here, *hija*. Speak to me." She listens closely to Celia, and they decide to travel together to Santa Teresa del Mar.

The *santera* looks up at the brick and cement house, bleached by the sun and the ocean air, and positions herself under the pawpaw tree in the front yard. She prays every Catholic prayer she knows in quick, calm succession. Hail Marys, Our Fathers, the Apostles' Creed. Her body starts to sway, and her clasped hands rock beneath her chin until it seems she is all loose, swinging angles. And then, as Celia watches, the little *santera's* moist eyes roll back in her dwarfish head until the white gleam from two pinpricks, and she trembles once, twice, and slides against Celia in a heap on the sidewalk, smoking like a wet fire, sweet and musky, until nothing is left of her but her fringed cotton shawl.

Celia, not knowing what else to do, folds the *santera's* shawl into her handbag and enters her home.

She knows by the stillness of the house that Javier is already gone. He'd talked of going to the mountains, of planting coffee on the forested slopes. He said he'd descend to Santiago for carnival and dance to the fifes and the *melé,* to the snare and the *batá* drums, that he'd die (in sequins and feathers) at the head of a conga line in Céspedes Park.

Celia reaches up and feels a lump in her chest, compact as a walnut. A week later, the doctors remove her left breast. In its place they leave a pink, pulpy scar like the one she'd discovered on her son's back.

The House on the Burial Mound

The dead, the forgettable dead
sank deeper and deeper beneath the house
and in the living room the baby
with her mother, who looked like an apple
with breasts and a kind face

But that was long ago.
Now mother looks more like a prune
and baby is the large dark woman
in the living room
increasingly mean to a mother
who dislikes her more and more.
The dead, the forgettable dead
keep absolutely neutral far below the house.

Wallace Stevens in Havana

He's at the old casino in the park.
His friends are losing their fathers'
money steadily at roulette.
"Brilliant gyrations
in privileged interiors,"
he says with mental lips.

He wants a theme, a music
requests an habanera
mispronounces, is misunderstood
misspells it on a crinkly menu.
Ah, sí, says the bandleader
making no move.
The ceiling fans hum gently
with a refreshing monotone.
He sweats as gently
sips his cool, diluted rum.
I'm having a grand time,
he tells a fellow American.

A Love Note

Due to circumstances beyond my control
this is an imperfect moment.
I was supposed to be myself
and touch you with words.
What is it that I have been squandering?
I will now include a butterfly
releasing a natural scent
over the tomb of a great lover.
If I call it an accident
in a perverse pastoral,
will you rush to the dictionary?
Go and return:
what I've left unsaid is waiting
in the white portions
of the page.

Guijuelo 1968

This is a happy land
where the largest
most prosperous houses
wear a faint smell of
oil or lard.

In the bedrooms
of such homesteads
the beds are laid
with icy, immaculate sheets
and woolen blankets;
silver crucifixes adorn the walls,
the floorboards creak and murmur,
the windows rattle.

This is a happy land
where the good boys and girls
of the largest,
most prosperous houses
marry young and multiply.

In the kitchens
of these houses
the pious ravenlike widows
and the menopausal mothers
dream and gossip over their rosaries.
Often some mad
or feeble-minded or deaf or blind
or stained old unmarried aunt
sits in a corner of one of these kitchens
knitting.

This is a happy land
where the men of the largest,
most prosperous houses
invest well, and eat well, and drink well.

There is an astounding abundance of hogs
as well as taverns,
millinery shops, churches, ghosts, saints, and misers.

This is a happy land
where young lovers slyly
wait for spring
when they fornicate, tumbling
in the grass, in the dark
under a moon—
the wind smelling faintly
of cow dung.

Riding on the #5

Past the Black
Cowboy's White House
and the dethroned madam queen
of the magenta cape
and the splayed toes
who sits to sip
sweet blackberry brandy
and the giant steel spectacles hanging
above the midtown Eye Shop
and the cool dudes
hip-hop
Adidas-shod
fast young gods
rappin' and jivin' dervishes

in gold and red
lovin' to the best
and blind windows
gardens of garbage
scrap monuments
and Beverly's Beauty Salon & Children's Boutique
and an old man
who stands on 12th
dancing to himself
a gooney minuet
like a creaky marionette
and the We
Abide in Thee Holy Jesus
One and Only
True Church of God
And purple yellow orange
bangled girls
who sway and sass
and bloated tired girls
who know where it's at
and the smells
of frying fish
wafting like glory
out the door
of Popeye's Paradise Inn
and an old hag
in feathers and blues
with sensible shoes
who scavenges telephone booths
and the lure of Mother Hope
Spiritual Consultations by Appointment
Tuesdays and Thursdays Reduced Rate

and a child who laughs
a child with a wrinkled face
a child with a buried smile
a child with a furrowed mask
and the bullhorn peddler
who screams
repent all you sinners

prepare to be cleansed
look at yourselves from within
and the stern long
white-robed aesthete
umbrella in hand
who proclaims
Arise mighty nation of Islam.

Brothers and sisters
watch your step
getting out
this is the end
of the line.

My Grandfather's Eye

Rey stepped back, focusing on his grandfather's pink left eye, which appeared to be turning itself inside out.

"Father Miller won't write me a letter."

"What are you talking about?"

Juan had once been tall, but now he was shorter than Rey. Rey himself wasn't short, but he'd always remembered Juan as towering over him. Although Juan sometimes claimed over one hundred years as his age—nobody in the family knew his actual birth year because he gave differing birth dates depending on whom he spoke with—he easily kept up with Rey on walks to the lake. Even in the heat of the Elsinore afternoon, he wore old gabardine slacks and a flannel shirt and a wool stocking cap over his head.

"A letter to keep me out of the draft."

"It's not up to Father Miller."

Juan, when in his teens, had crossed over the Mexican border and filtered south, all the way to the state of Morelos, where he'd joined with Zapata's troops. The family couldn't claim this particular part of Mexico as their homeland, for it seemed as if they had always been in California, having lost their familial connection to Mexico, if not their psychic one. And Juan had believed in the revolutions. But it had taken another war, in Europe this time, for Juan to forsake that particular folly. And it had been in Spain where Juan deserted the Catholic church.

"I don't want to go. I don't want to end up like Rudy." Rey hurt deep in his heart saying this.

"Don't go, then."

"Shit," Rey muttered.

Juan turned back to his sketch. "Can you see the lines already in the painting? I'm putting them in charcoal so you can see them."

Rey looked at the whitewashed section of wall. It was a large area, and Rey'd not seen his grandfather sketch directly on a wall before. The brush marks ended with a randomness that bothered him. But in the interior of the whitewashed area, he saw amphibian ghosts circling a shiny box that was on a chair. A strange bird with three wings held to the far left side of the charcoal, hovering next to a female ghost with long flowing hair.

"Yes," Rey lied.

"No, you don't." Juan stepped back from the drawing and looked at his work. "Now what's all this tragedy?"

The studio was small, cramped, and completely full of utensils for painting: turpentine; shiny number-10 cans holding brushes with the bristle ends up; two stools serving as palettes, separate universes of color; old, clunky easels holding paintings in various stages of completion. High up, a clerestory window covered in dirt and dust let in fading light. A stone fireplace once white was now covered in black all over the front, scarred from winter fires. Ashes swirled forward in small puffs as if the fireplace itself were alive.

"I'm in trouble."

Juan sighed. "Let's go out on the swing and enjoy the evening."

In the living room hens were settling in for the night, roosting on a couch, a chair, on a chest of drawers, on a painting.

"Damn," Rey muttered so that Juan wouldn't hear. He hated the fact that chickens lived in the house. He knew this wasn't the way you were supposed to live. None of his friends' families acted in this way.

But then, Rey no longer seemed to have friends. David, his best friend, had enlisted the summer after high school. He'd *wanted* to go to Vietnam, and, as luck would have it, wasn't able to. He'd been sent to Korea. And there, while on sentry duty at night, he'd been shot by a sniper. Hector and Joe were doing time for holding up a gas station with a rifle. The entire affair was a misunderstanding; the rifle was an unloaded pellet gun, and Hector and Joe had been drunk, acting on a stupid dare. But there you have it, they were at Terminal Island, doing hard time, but they would never face the draft. Billy, run down on graduation night by a hit-and-run driver. And Rudy, his brother, his closest friend, what could you say about that?

A movement from the trees surrounding the house gave Rey a slight shiver. The giant jacarandas wiggled. It wasn't quite dark.

"*Sientate, mijo,*" Juan said, motioning to the old swing. Rey sat on the frond-strewn cushions he'd sat on so many times before with his grandfather. But the dogs were gone. The Chihuahuas used to jump on Rey, sleep in his lap, growl with jealousy at each other. Juan hadn't replaced them as one by one they were stolen or hit by cars.

"What's that?" Rey asked, pointing to a lump on the patio.

"My opossum." Again Juan sighed, this time a huge one. The possum looked like a dead rat in the darkening light.

"Is it dead?"

"Yes."

"Where's your shovel?"

"What for?"

Rey stood up from the swing and moved toward the dead animal. "I'll throw it in the bushes." He scooted it away from the swing.

"It'll stink."

"I'll throw it across the street."

"It'll still stink."

"Let's cremate him."

"No!" Juan said. He walked to Rey, bent down, and scooped up the baby marsupial with large, bony hands, and Rey saw his grandfather's long fingernails, brittle with age, saw the big splotches of discolored skin contrasting with the thin fur of the possum. Rey backed up in fear of smelling something horrible.

"We'll bury it. I have a spot picked out." At the back of the house, the wind hit them full force. "When I die, I want you to bury me on the property."

"You're not dying, Pa."

They walked behind the weathered picket fence.

"I want you to wrap me in wet sheets."

Sure, everyone died. Rudy had died too, and Rey knew his grandfather would someday pass on, but death was the one thing Rey had thought about far too much lately. After Rudy anyway.

"You'll have to soak the sheets overnight so I don't dry out."

"Stop it, Pa."

"Feel the *viento?*"

Rey's lips were cracked and dry, but the air was alive with electricity. "You'll outlive us all."

Jacaranda fronds fell wholesale to the ground. Under the vine-covered carport, Rey found a shovel. The handle was worn smooth, and it felt slick, almost wet, in his hands as he began uncovering dirt.

The ground was hard and dry, and the loose dirt swirled in the gathering wind, making Rey squint, making him push back wisps of hair that escaped from his ponytail.

"Another foot," Juan whispered. He placed the possum on the ground. "I'll be back."

Rey leaned against the battered carport that housed the even more battered Volkswagen. He closed his eyes, letting the moisture soothe his mounting headache. Nearly all last night he'd been unable to sleep. Thinking about his action. Or inaction. He knew the priest, Father Miller, had been a last resort. A letter wouldn't have helped anyway.

He thought of Canada while digging again. Resisters went up north. Sweden was too far—Canada just right. Plus, they welcomed you. The end of the shovel hit a large, smooth river stone. He knelt and removed it.

As he dug deeper, he wondered why Rudy's body had never been found. Why they'd had that stupid memorial service that didn't satisfy anyone. And why the military had taken no responsibility. There had been no burial. Maybe that was the problem. No body. No Rudy.

Juan returned with a pail. "I'll show you how it's done. That's enough! The hole is big enough to put me in."

It wasn't that large, but without paying attention Rey had made the grave too deep.

"You set the sheets on the ground like this," Juan said, placing small, cut lengths on the ground. He placed the possum on the longest one. Then he wrapped it over and over. The blowing dust didn't bother Juan. "Mine will be much larger, and you'll have to soak them in the bathtub."

"Stop it!" Rey said emphatically while pushing strands of hair out of his face.

"You might need help. I asked Eddie across the way if you can't do it alone."

"I'm not burying you like this."

"Why not? I want to be close to the paintings."

Those fucking paintings. "You're not dying." Rey turned and looked down to the lake. It was a dark, rippled apparition, whitecaps whipped up in the center. Next to him, Juan had created a tiny mummy which he poured water over.

The problem with all the talk of burials was that the old man was serious. The older he became, the more disdain he held for convention. Rey knew there was little possibility of burying his grandfather in this way. Besides, Juan wasn't a marsupial.

When they finished, the night was dark black. One of those moonless, lightless Lake Elsinore nights. The air was hot and dry and the wind swirled uncontrollably.

———

The dream was water. And in the dream Rey's head burned. But the water was cool and it soothed his head. A shiny piece of metal was in a crevice. In water. Everything was fluid, slow motion, but Rey couldn't get to the metal, and it seemed that faces were watching him through the water. And sounds. Music, muffled by water. Louder. Clearer. It was radio music? No, children singing.

When he awoke to the strange sounds it was still dark. He heard voices in song, but they were far-off voices. The sounds faded, yet they were still slightly audible.

Groggy, he found himself at the doorway to his grandfather's studio. Inside, Juan sketched more figures on the wall. The three-winged bird now had two heads, one at each end of its body. The long-haired ghost woman smiled, her almond-shaped eyes squinting, her legs obscenely spread in flight. A salamander/dog ghost clawed escape from the scene. Rey wondered if his grandfather was the source of the sounds.

"Pa, did you hear the sounds?"

"What are you doing awake?"

"I heard sounds."

"What kind of sounds?"

"Like music."

"I heard nothing."

"Tell me about it."

"It's nothing."

"Does it come from you?"

"No."

"Where does it come from?"

"It's not important."

"Do you hear the same thing I hear?"

"I already told you, forget it. It's nothing. Go back to sleep." Juan turned back to his sketch.

Quietly, Rey walked outside to relieve himself. A full-blown windstorm tried to displace everything surrounding the house. Rey squinted to shield his eyes. His hair blew in a wild mess. He closed his eyes while pissing and then opened them a bit. The Big Dipper and the North Star beckoned to him through the dust.

In the morning Rey was awakened by the sound of a crash. He stood, still dressed in yesterday's clothes, and looked out the window. The birdbath had fallen. In the center of the birdbath Juan had placed a plaster statue of Saint Christopher. Saint Christopher held one hand up in greeting, in peace, like a phony movie Indian, but Rey saw the arm broken and lying on the ground.

Outside, the wind tried to push the jacarandas off their axes. Junipers on the other side of the street bounced to three o'clock, heading west, then popped back up to twelve o'clock. And the dust pushing through the air made his eyes feel gritty.

Placing the birdbath upright and leaning it against a dwarf walnut tree so that it wouldn't fall again, Rey closed his eyes and felt the energy from the wind. He picked up the statue and the broken arm.

Back inside, he shook his hair up and down to rid himself of the dust. Without thinking, he placed the saint on a pedestal that was attached to the wall. The pedestal was a flower cut in half, a bloom with a flat top that seemed perfect for holding Saint Christopher. All the colors on the saint had long since weathered so that the robe and hair were a pink plaster color. He placed the small arm in his pocket.

At the studio door he saw Juan asleep in a fetal position on the discolored old couch. Juan had covered himself with a newspaper. Rey knew the old man slept in snatches, rising during the night and painting, and then sleeping for hours during the day, and then rising, doing some chore, and then sleeping once again; Juan led an eccentrically disordered life.

"Good-bye, Pa," Rey whispered.

Once inside the car, he tied the arm of Saint Christopher to his rearview mirror. He didn't know which way to go, though he almost felt like driving to the huge induction center on Spring Street in Los Angeles and telling them he'd made a mistake—he'd forgotten the date of his induction physical, and could he take it now, please?

Straight ahead, he saw the outline of the Ortegas. The mountains were in silhouette, but the source of light was before them, not behind. The glare off the lake was blinding. Whitecaps frothed in the angry water.

Not knowing which way to go, Rey lit a joint, pushed a tape in the eight-track, turned up the volume, and slowly pulled away from his grandfather's house, watching the dangling arm of Saint Christopher, thinking how it was pink, like his grandfather's eye, and knowing, too, that the next move was already made.

Lost in Translation

My heart is in the East and I am at the edge of the West. Then how can I taste what I eat, how can I enjoy it? How can I fulfill my vows and pledges while Zion is in the domain of Edom, and I am in the bonds of Arabia?

—JUDAH HALEVI

Work of good prose has three steps: a musical stage when it is composed, an architectonic one when it is built, and a textile one when it is woven.

—WALTER BENJAMIN

I was born in Mexico City, 7 April 1961, on a cloudy day without major historical events. I am a descendant of Jews from Russia and Poland, businessmen and rabbis, who arrived by sheer chance in Veracruz, on the Atlantic coast next to the Yucatán peninsula. I am a sum of parts and thus lack purity of blood (what proud renaissance Iberians called *la pureza de sangre*): white Caucasian with a Mediterranean twist, much like the Enlightenment philosopher Moses Mendelssohn and only marginally like the Aztec poet Ollin Yollistli. My idols, not surprisingly, are Kafka and Spinoza, two exiles in their own land who chose to switch languages (Czech to German, Portuguese and Hebrew to Latin) in order to elevate themselves to a higher order and who, relentlessly, investigated their own spirituality beyond the realm of orthodox religion and routine. Ralph Waldo Emerson, in *Essays: Second Series* (1844), says that the reason we feel one man's presence and not another's is as simple as gravity. I have traveled from Spanish into Yiddish, Hebrew, and English; from my native home south of the Rio Grande far and away—to Europe, the Middle East, the United States, the Bahamas, and South America—always in search of the ultimate clue to the mysteries of my divided identity. What I found is doubt.

I grew up in an intellectually sophisticated middle class, in a secure, self-imposed Jewish ghetto (a treasure island) where gentiles hardly existed. Money and comfort, books, theater and art. Since early on, I was sent to Yiddish day school, Colegio Israelita de México in Colonia

Narvarte, where the heroes were Sholom Aleichem and Theodor Herzl, while people like José Joaquín Fernández de Lizardi, Agustín Yáñez, Juan Rulfo, and Octavio Paz were almost unknown; that is, we lived in an oasis, completely uninvolved with things Mexican. In fact, when it came to knowledge of the outside world, students were far better off talking about U.S. products (Hollywood, TV, junk food, technology) than about matters native—an artificial capsule, our ghetto, much like the magical sphere imagined by Blaise Pascal: its diameter everywhere and its center nowhere.

Mother tongue. The expression crashed into my mind at age twenty, perhaps a bit later. The father tongue, I assumed, was the adopted, alternative, and illegitimate language (Henry James preferred the term "wife tongue"), whereas the mother tongue is genuine and authentic—a uterus: the original source. I was educated in (into) four idioms: Spanish, Yiddish, Hebrew, and English. Spanish was the public venue; Hebrew was a channel toward Zionism and not toward the sacredness of the synagogue; Yiddish symbolized the Holocaust and past struggles of the eastern European labor movement; and English was the entrance door to redemption: the United States. Abba Eban said it better: Jews are like everybody else . . . except a little bit more. A polyglot, of course, has as many loyalties as homes. Spanish is my right eye, English my left; Yiddish my background and Hebrew my conscience. Or, better, each four represents a different set of spectacles (near sight, bifocal, night reading, et cetera) through which the universe is seen.

THE ABUNDANCE OF SELF

This multifarious (is there such word?) upbringing often brought me difficulties. Around the neighborhood, I was always *el güerito* and *el ruso*. Annoyingly, my complete name is Ilan Stavchansky Slomianski; nobody, except for Yiddish teachers, knew how to pronounce it. (I get mail addressed to Ivan Starlominsky, Isvan Estafchansky, and Allan Stevens.) After graduating from high school, most of my friends, members of richer families, were sent abroad, to the United States or Israel, to study. Those who remained, including me, were forced to go to college at home, to face Mexico *tété a tété*. The shock was tremendous. Suddenly, I (we) recognized the artificiality of our oasis. What to do? I, for one, rejected my background. I felt Judaism made me a pariah. I wanted to be an authentic Mexican and thus foolishly joined the Communist cause, but the result wasn't pleasing. Among the *camaradas,* I was also "the blondy" and "the Jew." No hope, no escape. So I decided to investigate my ethnic and religious past obsessively and made it my duty to fully understand guys like Maimonides, Arthur Koestler, Mendelssohn, Judah Halevi, Hasdai Crescas, Spinoza, Walter Benjamin, Gershom Scholem, Martin Buber, Franz Rosenzweig, Abraham Joshua Heschel . . . It helped, at least temporarily. Nothing lasts forever.

Years later, while I was teaching medieval philosophy at Universidad Iberoamericana, a Jesuit college in downtown Mexico City, during the 1982 Lebanon invasion, a group of Palestinian sympathizers threw rotten tomatoes at me and my students (99 percent gentiles). Eager to manifest their anger and protest, they had to find an easy target, and I was the closest link to Israel around. The whole thing reminded me of a scene that took place when I was fourteen, sitting in Yiddish class at Colegio Israelita. Mr. Lockier, the teacher, was reading from I. J. Singer's *The Family Carnovsky*—the story of three generations in a German-Jewish family enchanted with the nineteenth-century Enlightenment, slowly but surely becoming assimilated into German society until the tragic rise of Nazism brought unthinkable consequences. The monotonous rhythm of the recitation was boring and nobody was paying much attention. Suddenly, a segment of the story truly captivated me: the moment when Jegor, eldest son of Dr. David Carnovsky's mixed marriage to Teresa Holbeck, is ridiculed in class by Professor Kirchenmeier, a newly appointed principal at the Goethe Gymnasium in Berlin. Singer describes the event meticulously: Nazism is on the rise; the aristocracy, and more specifically the Jews, is anxious to know the overall outcome of the violent acts taking place daily on the city streets. Racial theories are being discussed and Aryans glorified. Feverishly anti-Jewish, Kirchenmeier, while delivering a lecture, calls Jegor to the front to use him as a guinea pig in illustrating his theories. With compass and calipers, he measures the length and width of the boy's skull, writing the figures on the board. He then measures the distance from ear to ear, from the top of the head to the chin, and the length of the nose. A packed auditorium is silently watching. Jegor is then asked to undress. He is terrified and hesitates, of course; he is ashamed and feels conspicuous because of his circumcision. Eventually other students, persuaded by Kirchenmeier, help undress the Jew, and the teacher proceeds to show in the "inferior" Jewish strain the marks of the rib structure. He finishes by calling attention to Jegor's genitalia, whose premature development shows "the degenerate sexuality of the Semitic race."

Astonishment. What troubled me most was Jegor's inaction. I suppose it was natural to be petrified in such a situation, but I refused to justify his immobility. So I interrupted Mr. Lockier to ask why the boy didn't escape. A deadly silence invaded the classroom. It was clear I had disturbed the other students' sleep and the teacher's rhythm. "Because . . . he couldn't. He simply couldn't," was the answer I got. "Because that's the way lives are written . . ." I don't know or care what happened next. As the years went by, I came to understand that concept, the almighty Author of Authors, as intriguing, and the scene in Yiddish class as an allegory of myself and Mexican Jews as an easy and palatable target of animosity. At the Jesuit college almost a decade later, I was the marionette holder's Jegor Carnovsky—God's joy and toy: the Jew.

KALEIDOSCOPE

Bizarre combination—Mexican Jews: some fifty thousand frontier dwellers and hyphen people like Dr. Jekyll and Mr. Hyde, a sum of sum of parts, a multiplicity of multiplicities. Although settlers from Germany began to arrive in "Aztec Country" around 1830, the very first synagogue was not built in the nation's capital until some fifty-five years later. From then on, waves of Jewish immigrants came from Russia and central and eastern Europe, Ashkenazim whose goal was to make it big in New York (the Golden Land), but since an immigration quota was imposed in the United States in 1921, a little detour placed them in Cuba, Puerto Rico, or the Gulf of Mexico (the Rotten Land). Most were Yiddish-speaking Bundists: hardworking peasants, businessmen, and teachers, nonreligious and entrepreneurial, escaping Church-sponsored pogroms and government persecution. Their primary dream was never Palestine. Hardly anything physical or ideological differentiated them from the relatives who did make it north, to Chicago, Detroit, Pittsburgh, and the Lower East Side—except, of course, the fact that they, disoriented immigrants, couldn't settle where they pleased. And this sense of displacement colored our future.

Migration and its discontent. I have often imagined the culture shock, surely not too drastic, my forefathers experienced at their arrival: from *mujik* to *campesino,* similar types in different milieus. Mexico was packed with colonial monasteries where fanatical nuns prayed day and night. Around 1910, Emiliano Zapata and Pancho Villa were making their socialist Revolution, and an anti-Church feeling (known in Mexico as *La Cristiada* and masterfully examined in Graham Greene's *The Power and the Glory*) was rampant. Aztecs, the legend claimed, once sacrificed daughters to their idols in sky-high pyramids and perhaps were cannibals. Undoubtedly this was to be a transitory stop, it had to. It was humid and, at least in the nation's capital, nature remained in an eternal autumn.

I must confess never to have learned to love Mexico. I was taught to retain a sense of foreignness—as a tourist without a home. The best literature I know about Mexico is by Europeans and U.S. writers: Italo Calvino, André Breton, Jack Kerouac, Greene, Joseph Brodsky, Antonin Artaud, Katherine Anne Porter, Malcolm Lowry, Harriet Doerr . . . I only love my country when I am far and away. Elsewhere—that's where I belong: the vast diaspora. Nowhere and everywhere.

OUT OF THE BASEMENT

When the Mexican edition of *Talia in Heaven* (1990) came out, my publisher, Fernando Valdés, at a reception, talked about the merits of this, my first (and so far only) novel. He applauded this and that ingredient, spoke highly of the innovative style, and congratulated the author for his precocious artistic maturity. Memory has deleted most of his comments. I no longer remember what he liked and why. The only sentence that still sticks in my mind, the one capable of overcoming the passing of time, came at the end of his speech, when he said, "For many centuries, Latin America has had Jews living in its basement, great writers creating out of the shadow. And Ilan Stavans is the one I kept hidden until now." A frightening metaphor.

For the past five hundred years, Jews in the Hispanic world have been forced to convert to Christianity or somehow to mask or feel ashamed of their ancestral faith. Their intellectual contribution, notwithstanding, has been enormous. Spanish letters cannot be understood without Fray Luis de León and Ludovicus Vives, without Fernando de Roja's *La Celestina* and the anti-Semitic poetry of Francisco de Quevedo, author of the infamous sonnet "A man stuck to a nose." (*Erase un hombre a una nariz pegado, érase una nariz superlativa, érase una alquitara medio viva, érase un peje espada mal barbado . . .*) In the Americas, a safe haven for refugees from the inquisition and later on for eastern Europeans running away from the Nazis, Jewish writers have been active since 1910, when Alberto Gerchunoff, a Russian immigrant, published in Spanish his collection of interrelated vignettes, *The Jewish Gauchos of La Pampa,* to commemorate Argentina's independence. He switched from one language to another to seek individual freedom, to validate his democratic spirit, to embrace a dream of plurality and progress: Yiddish, the tongue of Mendel Mojer Sforim and Sholom Aleichem, was left behind; Spanish, Cervantes's vehicle of communication—Gerchunoff was an admirer of *Don Quixote*—became the new tool, the channel to entertain, educate, and redeem the masses. Like Spinoza, Kafka, Nabokov, and Joseph Brodsky, he was the ultimate translator: a bridge between idiosyncrasies.

The abyss and the bridge. Many decades later, some fifty astonishing writers from Buenos Aires and Mexico to Lima and Guatemala, including Moacyr Scliar, Isaac Goldemberg himself, Clarise Lispector, and Mario Szichman, continue to carry Gerchunoff's torch . . . but the world knows little about them. The narrative boom that catapulted Gabriel García Márquez, Carlos Fuentes, and others from south of the Rio Grande to international stardom in the sixties managed to sell a monolithic, suffocatingly uniform image of the entire continent as a banana republic crowded with clairvoyant prostitutes and forgotten generals, never a multicultural society. To such a degree were ethnic voices left in the margin that readers today know much more about Brazilian and Argentine Jews thanks to Borges's short stories "Emma Zunz" and "The Secret Miracle" and to Vargas Llosa's novel *The Storyteller* than to anything written by Gerchunoff or his followers. Sadly, and in spite of his anti-Semitic tone, my Mexican publisher was right: in the baroque architecture of Latin American letters, Jews inhabit the basement. And yet, *la pureza de sangre* in the Hispanic world is but an abstraction: native Indians, Jews, Arabs, Africans, Christians . . . the collective identity is always in need of a hyphen. In spite of the "official" image stubbornly promoted by governments from time immemorial, Octavio Paz and Julio Cortázar have convincingly used the salamander, the *axólotl*, as a symbol to describe Latin America's popular soul, always ambiguous and in mutation.

AMERICA, AMERICA

I honestly never imagined I could one day pick up my suitcases to leave home once and for all. And yet, at twenty-five I moved to New York. I was awarded a scholarship to study for a master's at the Jewish Theological Seminary and, afterward, perhaps a doctorate at Columbia University or elsewhere. I fled Mexico (and Spanish) mainly because as a secular Jew —what Freud would call "a psychological Jew"—I felt marginalized, a stereotype. (Little did I know!) A true chameleon, a bit parochial and nearsighted, a nonconformist with big dreams and few possibilities. Like my globe-trotting Hebraic ancestors, I had been raised to build an ivory tower, an individual ghetto. By choosing to leave, I turned my past into remembrance: I left the basement and ceased to be a pariah. *Talia in*

Heaven exemplified that existential dilemma: its message simultaneously encourages Jews to integrate and openly invites them to escape; it alternates between life and memory. Paraphrasing Lionel Trilling, its cast of characters, victims of an obsessive God (much like the Bible's) who enjoys ridiculing them, is at the bloody crossroad where politics, theology, and literature meet.

To be or not: to be. The moment I crossed the border, I became somebody else: a new person. In *Chromos: A Parody of Truth,* Felipe Alfau says, "The moment one learns English, complications set in. Try as one may, one cannot elude this conclusion, one must inevitably come back to it." While hoping to master the English language during sleepless nights, I understood James Baldwin, who, already exiled in Paris and quoting Henry James, claimed it is a complex fate to be an American. "America's history," wrote the black author of *Nobody Knows My Name,* "her aspirations, her peculiar triumphs, her even more peculiar defeats, and her position in the world—yesterday and today—are all so profoundly and stubbornly unique that the very word 'America' remains a new, almost completely undefined and extremely controversial proper noun. No one in the world seems to know exactly what it describes." To be honest, the rise of multiculturalism, which perceives the melting pot as a soup of diverse and at times incompatible backgrounds, has made the word "America" even more troublesome, more evasive and abstract: Is America a compact whole, a unity? Is it a sum of ethnic groups unified by a single language and a handful of patriotic symbols? Is it a quixotic dream where total assimilation is impossible, where multiculturalism is to lead to disintegration? And Baldwin's statement acquires a totally different connotation when one goes one step beyond, realizing that "America" is not only a nation (a state of mind) but also a vast continent. From Alaska to the Argentine pampa, from Rio de Janeiro to East Los Angeles, the geography Christopher Columbus mistakenly encountered in 1492 and Amerigo Vespucci baptized a few years later is also a linguistic and cultural addition: America the nation and America the continent. America, America: I wanted to find a room of my own in the two; or two rooms, perhaps?

ON BEING A WHITE HISPANIC AND MORE

Once settled, I suddenly began to be perceived as Hispanic (i.e., Latino)—an identity totally alien to me before. (My knowledge of spoken

Latin is minimal.) To make matters worse, my name (once again?), accent, and skin color were exceptions to what gringos had as "the Hispanic prototype." In other words, in Mexico I was perceived as Jewish; and now, across the border, I was Mexican. Funny, isn't it? (In fact, according to official papers I qualify as a white Hispanic, an unpleasant term if there ever was one.) Once again, an impostor, an echo. (An impostor, says Ambrose Bierce in *The Devil's Dictionary,* is a rival aspirant to public honors.)

Themselves, myself. Hispanics in the United States—some 22,254,059, according to the 1990 census: white, black, yellow, green, blue, red . . . , twice Americans, once in spite of themselves. They have been in the territories north of the Rio Grande even before the Pilgrims of the May-flower; and with the Guadalupe Hidalgo Treaty signed in 1848, in which Generalissimo Antonio López de Santa Ana gave away and subsequently sold half of Mexico to the White House (why only half?), many of them unexpectedly, even unwillingly, became a part of an Anglo-Saxon, English-speaking reality. Today, after decades of neglect and silence, de-cades of anonymity and ignorance, Latinos are finally receiving the atten-tion they deserve. The second fastest growing ethnic group after the Asians, their diversity of roots—Caribbean, Mexican, Central and South American, Iberian, and so on—makes them a difficult collectivity to describe. Are the Cuban migrations from Holguín, Matanzas, and Havana similar in their idiosyncratic attitudes to those of Managua, San Salvador, and Santo Domingo? Is the Spanish they speak, their true *lingua franca,* the only unifying factor? Is their immigrant experience in any way different from that of previous minorities—Irish, Italian, Jewish, what have you? How do they understand and assimilate the complexities of what it means to be American? And where do I, a "white Hispanic," fit in?

Nowhere and everywhere. In 1985 I was assigned by a Spanish mag-azine to interview Isaac Goldemberg, a famous Jewish-Peruvian novelist, who wrote *The Fragmented Life of Don Jacobo Lerner.* When we met at the Hungarian Pastry Shop at Amsterdam Avenue and 110th Street, he told me, among many other things, that he had been living in New York for over two decades without mastering the English language because he didn't want his Spanish to suffer and ultimately evaporate. Borges wrote in his short story "The Life of Tadeo Isidoro Cruz (1829–1874)," "Any life, no matter how long or complex it may be, is made up essentially of *a single moment*—the moment in which a man finds out, once and for all, who he is." That summer day I understood my linguistic future to lie in the opposite direction from Goldemberg's: I would perfect my English and thus become a New York Jew, an intellectual in the proud tradition celebrated by Alfred Kazin. . . . And I did. In just a single moment I understood who I could be.

White Birch

for Katherine, December 28, 1991

A strong dark wood
swirls at the core of white birch,
beneath white bark a darkened tree
older than the sawmill,
black roots drinking years of snow.

Two decades ago rye whiskey
scalded your father's throat,
stinking from the mouth
as he stamped his shoe
in the groove between your hips,
dizzy flailing cartwheel down the stairs.
The tail of your spine split,
became a scraping hook.
For twenty years a fire raced
across the boughs of your bones,
his drunken mouth a movie
flashing with every stabbed gesture.

Now the white room of birth is throbbing
the number palpitating red on the screen of machinery
tentacled to your arm; the oxygen mask wedged
in a wheeze on your face; the numbing medication
injected through the spine.
The boy was snagged on that spiraling bone.
Medical fingers prodded your raw pink center
while you stared at a horizon of water
no one else could see, creatures leaping silver
with tails that slashed the air
like your agonized tongue.

You were born in the river valley,
hard green checkerboard of farms,
a town of white birches
and a churchyard from the workhorse time,
weathered headstones naming women
drained of blood with infants coiled inside
the caging hips, hymns swaying
as if lanterns over the mounded earth.

Then the white birch of your bones,
resilient and yielding, yielded again,
root snapped as the boy spilled out of you
into hands burst open by beckoning
and voices pouring praise like water,
two beings tangled in exhaustion,
blood-painted, but full of breath.

After a generation of burning
the hook unfurled in your body,
the crack in the bone dissolved:
One day you stood, expected again
the branch of nerves
fanning across your back to flame,
and felt only the grace of birches.

The Hidalgo's Hat and a Hawk's Bell of Gold

Columbus hallucinated gold
wherever sunlight darted
from rock to water, spelled the world
slowly in his logbook

so that the Lord might see
and blow his ship
into a storm of gleaming dust.
When God would not puff his cheeks
for trade winds of gold, the Admiral flourished
a decree on parchment: a hawk's bell
full of gold from every Indio
where the rivers gilded the soil
of Española, 1495.

The Indios could only load the bells
with mirrored sunlight. For bells
without gold, the hands were pressed together
as if in prayer, gripped on the block,
then the knobs of wrists were splintered
by a bright and heavy sword.
Their stumps became torches
seething flames of blood,
the vowels of their language
lamentations flattening the tongue.

While the Admiral slept
in the exhaustion of dysentery,
or amused the Queen
with his zoo of shackled caciques,
the town he named Isabela
dissolved into the stones
like a rumor of gold, deserted swampground.
There is a spirit legend:
that the moans of men in rusting helmets
would radiate from the vine-matted walls,
starved with a mouthful of bark
or mad with a brain soaking in syphilis,
or digging an arrowhead from the eye
fired by an Indio with two hands.

Someone saw the hidalgos there, ghosts of noblemen
bowing in a row, a swirl of velvet cloaks.
As each swept off his feathered hat
in greeting, his head unscrewed
from the hollow between caped shoulders,

swinging in the hat
like a cannonball in a sack.

The Other Alamo

San Antonio, Texas, 1990

In the Crockett Hotel dining room,
a chalk-faced man in medaled uniform
growls a prayer
at the head of the veteran's table.
Throughout the map of this saint-hungry city,
hands strain for the touch of shrines,
genuflection before cannon and memorial plaque,
grasping the talisman of Bowie knife replica
at the souvenir shop, visitors
in white Biblical quote T-shirts.

The stones in the walls are smaller
than the fist of Texas martyrs;
their cavernous mouths could drink the canal to mud.
The Daughters of the Republic
print brochures dancing with Mexican demons,
Santa Anna's leg still hopping
to conjunto accordions.
The lawyers who conquered farmland
by scratching on parchment in an oil lamp haze,
the cotton growers who kept the time
of Mexican peasant lives dangling from their watchchains,
the vigilantes hooded like blind angels
hunting with torches for men the color of night,
gathering at church, the capitol, or the porch
for a century all said this: Alamo.

In 1949, three boys
in Air Force dress khaki
ignored the whites-only sign
at the diner by the bus station.
A soldier from Baltimore, who heard nigger sung here
more often than his name, but would not glance away;
another blond and solemn as his Tennessee of whitewashed spires;
another from distant Puerto Rico, cap tipped at an angle
in a country where brown skin
could be boiled for the leather of a vigilante's wallet.

The waitress squinted a glare and refused their contamination,
the manager lost his crew-cut politeness
and blustered about local customs,
the police, with surrounding faces,
jeered about tacos and señoritas
on the Mexican side of town.
"We're not leaving," they said,
and hunched at their stools
till the manager ordered the cook,
sweat-burnished black man unable to hide his grin,
to slide cheeseburgers on plates
across the counter.
"We're not hungry," they said,
and left a week's pay for the cook.
One was my father; his word for fury
is Texas.

This afternoon, the heat clouds the air like bothered gnats.
The lunch counter was wrecked for the dump years ago.
In the newspapers, a report of vandals
scarring the wooden doors
of the Alamo
in black streaks of fire.

La Ermita (the Hermitage)— El Cedro, Gomera

A woman with white and silver hair
nestles in the deepest curve
of this forest floor. She is the mist
when she stirs
and loves that way of
the other woman
who welcomes her here. The forest
is her confidante. They sleep together
in the mystery of what it is
to be so beautiful and forgotten.
What they dream
enchants this night and I
hear their breathing as my own.
I have wandered here to kneel
beside the stream of their sadnesses
wet my mouth
and drink like a sister.
They offer me watercress
and I taste their delicate sweetness
like my own.
Tonight there are no words
but our thoughts
create this pleasure
as we speak together
in the gestures of the tree limbs
and her hair softly
softly sweeping our faces.

Gathering the Wild Figs—
Vizcaina, Gomera

They are plump
and deeply purple.
Hungry and hot
we gorge ourselves
on their rich, red sweetnesses
that break into our mouths
like last and urgent kisses.
They are how this island rewards
our loving her so well
our venturing into the ache
of all her beauty
and abiding the gaze
of her myriad faces
with our myriad faces.
She was broken
but pieced herself together again
from the shards of the lava flow
from the destruction
she grew beautiful and strong.
Today we have paid the price
for her unveiling.
We have seen her scars
and she is not pleased
but ay
how she wanted us to see.
Ay, how we have hungered and thirsted to see.
And here her bounty.
We will taste her wild figs forever.

When we are old
our breaths will be scented with her wildness.
When we die we will know where we go.

In My House—Wasiniypi

En mi casa
I am the second daughter
of the curandero's first born son.

My father, Guillermo Chota Paredes
born in Urimaguas
Departamento Loreto, Peru 1926
tells stories of how it was
days, weeks of seeing no one, except
jaguar, boa, wild boar
pues hija, era la gloria
arto ganado, paiches pero enormes
parecia que nunca
acabaria sound of Loretano sound
of sweet water fish and porpoise.

1991 near Eureka, California
my father gathers kindling by the Eel river
and does not forget. Once
he took me to a tributary of the Amazon
Nanay, Quechua for sorrow
and this river, *hija, mis lágrimas*
our tears compose a river
a father and his child watch
Nanay, swift and innocent
thick with plankton, algae, silt.

Maita muskanqui songokirishka?
Donde haz ido mi triste corazón?
Where have you gone, my sad heart?

Dive papa into your river
sweet, sorrowing river, swim
in your tears, your feet
one fine tail, your hands, fins
until that longing
hurls you to the surface
gasping for memory.
Papa, no matter what they do
she will not be defiled.

In my house
are many mansions
of virgin forest
rosewood, cedar
mahogany, rubber tree
mi palo rosa, mi cedro
mi aguano, mi leche caspi
mi mama coca
I am not pure
not white gold
in my house
these have been sacrificed
to the god of survival
for generations
so that through the sweat
rubble and blood
one fragrant *lirio*
might bloom.
I am not virgin gold
my eyes dark
as the place between my legs.
Mama Pacha, Tierra Sagrada
tears in her eyes
naked and beautiful.

El cielo esta nublado
quiere llover y no puede
asi esta mi corazon
quiere llorar, y no puede

The sky is overcast
it wants to rain, but can't
so it is with my heart
it wants to weep, but can't

Pa' ahi que si, pa' ahi que no
pa' ahi que si, pa' ahi que no
estando quieriendo me dices que no
estando quieriendo me dices que no

There you say, yes, there you say, no
you say, yes, you say, no
even in your wanting, you tell me no
even in your wanting, you tell me no*

My eyes dark as selva
watch your steel glare swords
slash roots and vines
my mouth. I choke
on your language, your god
again and again, my maiden body
not ripe for your seed
your child haunts my belly
half victor, half vanquished.

Perú, they called her
hija del demonio
devil's daughter
because her thin air
humbled them
because her mosquitoes
plagued their dreams
because they feared
what her eyes told them.

In my house, her name
Tuahuantinsuyo means
land of four worlds
la costa, la selva, los Andes
and the seasons between them.
In 1548, eight million people
worked, made love
warred and worshipped.
After 13 years
of the spaniard's solution

*Huayno-Andean song/rhythm/dance.

one million people survived
to mourn our dead.
Those who would not die
would not be counted or redefined
fled our home for other lands.
On the banks of the *Apurimac* river
our spirits spin gold thread from sunrays
in the fevered minds of greedy men
then gather what is yet sacred
to the sun, Inti, sol.

I want to go home.
No hay donde ir
there is no where to go
except to excavate
this body
this smooth, brown skin
an offering to the sun, *Inti*
Inti raymi, Inti, Inti, sol, sun
rise and set, in my house
there is dancing
all night long because
before the *Huacrachucos, Mochica, Chavín*
before the *Inca, Maya, Azteca*
before *Pizarro, Cortés,* Columbus:

Inti, sol, sun, *Inti*
Inti raymi, Inti, Inti, sol, Inti, sun
ignite our dreams
seas and rivers, *la tierra sagrada.*
your light burns and soothes
illumines everything
what the spider has spun
between infinities
what the pampas grass hides
what the bird sees.
your fire pure, fierce
flame of condor
jaguar, puma
speaks, when all others
are silent.

Papá, no matter what they do
she will not be defiled. . . .

El río Nanay
mirrors the starless
night coiled in my limbs
a seething want
I part the tangle
of your dreams
with my red tongue
lick the sweat
from your brow
and soothe you
with the heat
of my feral breath
in the dark of my eyes
the stars emerge
my eyes
will always find you.

Rattlesnake Dreams

From *Memory Fever:*
A Journey Beyond El Paso del Norte

I have dreamed about rattlesnakes for many years, which has resulted in a sequence of poems written over those same years. I do not know why I dream about snakes or why I am fascinated by rattlers, those powerful, elusive creatures few people see in the desert. They are out there, even though their habitat has been reduced by suburban growth. As time and civilization pass through the deserts of the Southwest, fewer humans will encounter them, except in zoos or movies.

How many people who live in New Mexico, Arizona, or west Texas have recurring dreams about diamondback rattlesnakes? Do the dreams have to do with growing up in the desert and having killed rattlesnakes as a boy? Do my dreams and snake poems have to do with the myths of my ancestors, who came from northern Mexico and settled in the Sonora desert of Arizona, their houses and working environment surrounded by those elusive, unpredictable reptiles?

Rattlesnake Dream

I thought the rattlesnake was dead
and I stuck my finger in its mouth,
felt the fangs bite down,
penetrate me without letting go,
the fire removing my eyes,
replacing them with green light
of the reptile that illuminated my hand.

It entered my bone and blood,
until my whole arm was green and damp,
my whole left side turning
slick and cool as

I tried to pull it
out of my body.

I peeled my skin back
to find my veins were green
and held tightly what I believed,
what forced itself into me,
what I allowed to be given
without knowing

I would carry that secret,
crawl over the ground,
become a fusion of muscle
only the sun steps on.
I leaned against a huge boulder,
sweated, waited, slept,
and, by morning, found a new way
of embracing that rock,
new life in the green flesh
of the world.

This was the first snake dream in which I touched a snake. In earlier dreams, I walk across the desert and the Rio Grande River. The ground is seething with snakes, dozens of them coming out of the earth, but none bite or threaten me. I walk through the twisting, moving shapes without fear. This new version of my reptilian journey marks the first time I approached a snake to touch it.

I am standing in someone's front yard. There is an old adobe house a few yards away. A giant cottonwood tree with its huge trunk and limbs parts above my head. A dark-skinned man stands by the tree, holding a rattlesnake in his hands. I do not know him. I cannot see his face clearly. He holds the snake like an experienced snake handler. I walk up to him and see that the snake is dead. He cradles it in his arms without fear. I reach out and run my fingers over the cool, slick head of the rattler. Its eyes are closed.

I carefully move a finger to the tip of its head and then quickly stick my finger inside its mouth. I am not afraid. I know the mouth of the dead rattler will open for me, and it does. I push my finger deeper to feel the fangs.

Suddenly the snake comes to life and clamps down hard on my finger. But I do not scream or jump back; the snake handler does not pull the snake away. I feel a strange kind of contentment. The snake will not let go. I am not surprised. The man disappears. The snake dangles in the air, hooked onto my hand.

The dream shifts, and changes pace and scene. I am walking along the river. It is near nightfall. I wander somewhere in La Mesilla Valley, north of El Paso. The snake has entered my body through my hand and fist. It has become my arm. As I walk, I peel back the shedding skin on my left hand to expose the bright green veins and muscles of my flesh. The snake has traveled up my bones and blood to become a part of me. I keep walking along the river. My whole body is damp and cool, as if I had crawled out of the river, out of a dark place. I feel no pain, do not suffer, do not panic. This is not a nightmare. It is a trance of motion; I hear low rattling and have the sense that more snakes are about to crawl out of the ground at my feet. I keep walking along the river.

Then I wake up.

It is a peaceful awakening, but I cannot get the dream out of my mind. I think about it for several days and then write the poem. The questions return. I go through my notebooks to read earlier snake poems, trying to find a clue as to why I absorbed this snake when my earlier dreams were passive. Were my questions about rattlesnakes being answered? Did this dream take me back to my childhood, when I first encountered baby rattlesnakes? When I killed several of them, once in our neighbor's front yard, and one in a crucial encounter behind my house?

Several of my snake poems are about these killings, the only times I chanced getting bitten as a kid who played and wandered in the desert for many years. I was twelve years old when our neighbor Martha came to our door and told me there were three or four baby rattlers in her flower box. Her sons and husband were not home. She was afraid the snakes were going to get into the house or bite someone. She asked if I would take the shovel that she held in her hands and kill them for her. She thrust the long wooden handle of the shovel at me. Hesitant, I stood in the doorway.

I don't recall if my mother was home, or who else was around, but I took the shovel and carefully walked back to Martha's house with her. I had seen a few snakes in the desert hills across the street and heard a few rattles in the tumbleweeds, but I had never tried to kill or confront any of them.

I spotted three snakes curled around each other under one of Martha's rosebushes. They looked like thick pieces of string, each one not more than ten inches long. The baby rattlers were a pale, fleshy color with their heads almost invisible. They had not developed their rattles yet. I could see the rattle's nub at the end of their bodies.

I stood about six feet away and did not move for several seconds. I was not really afraid, but what would a twelve-year-old with a big shovel do at a moment like this? Charge and chop everything to pieces? I stood there with Martha saying, "Go on, kill them!" She backed off and waited for me to do something. The snakes moved and continued to wrap themselves around each other, becoming a single creature.

"Go on, kill them!"

I turned to look at Martha and noticed how quiet the neighborhood was in the middle of the afternoon. How did she know that I didn't go to school that day? I saw one of the snakes separate itself from the other two, and I stepped forward, using the shovel as a spear. Without aiming or pausing, I lanced the snake behind the head and watched it come apart. The two pieces split into the ground. The other snakes reacted by separating from each other. I hacked at the second one. The shovel pushed the head into the dirt. The third snake disappeared under another bush. I moved back a few feet, watching the writhing, dying snakes. I expected lots of blood but did not see any. The baby rattlers soon stopped squirming.

"How many did you kill?" Martha asked me, her hands covering her mouth. She could clearly see I had gotten two. We couldn't find the third one.

I turned to her but didn't say a word. I still recall staring at her in silence. I did not know what to say as I handed her the shovel. She took it and watched me leave, the expression on my face preventing her from saying anything else to me. I cannot recall what else happened that day. That was more than twenty-six years ago. Killing the two snakes contributes to my not remembering the rest of the day, how I was able to kill the snakes with a rare bravery, a recklessness that could have gotten me bitten.

My second encounter with snakes may be the crucial doorway into my dreams. A couple of summers later, my mother saw four baby rattlers in our backyard. She closed the sliding doors leading to the porch and told me not to go out. She panicked and wanted to call pest control. I knew it was up to me, and I was less hesitant this time.

I used a shovel again. This time, I was more careful and noticed that the four snakes looked similar to the ones at Martha's house. I hacked at one, cutting it into pieces. I killed two more with one swing and loud thud of the shovel. Their bodies remained knotted together, their entrails streaking across the metal head of the shovel, one of the tiny snakes opening its jaws at me as it came apart in the grass. With my heart racing and sweat running down my forehead onto my eyeglasses, I looked wildly for the fourth rattler. Through the wet, distorted vision of my lenses, I saw the snake crawl up the bricks of the house to disappear into a crack in the overhanging roof. Before I knew it, it vanished into the wall of the house. My mother was going to be horrified.

I stood there and stared at the dead snakes. I couldn't take my eyes off the head of the one that died with its miniature white fangs bared to the sun and pointed at me, the jaws wide open as if to swallow my bravery completely. I could see the beautiful diamond patterns starting to develop on its torn skin. I did not want to tell my mother one of the snakes had slithered into the wall. My failure was not so much in losing a snake, but in the fact that its turning toward my mother's place of safety would create resentment on her part. This only added to my shame, my sense of failure about confronting these mysterious creatures.

I dug a hole near a dry spot in the flower box and shoveled the dead snakes into it. The sweat ran down my glasses, so I couldn't see clearly what was left of the snakes. I did not stop to wipe my glasses until I covered the hole with dirt and packed it down. I wanted this mutilation to disappear into the safe ground.

When I told her what happened, my mother called pest control. The man came out and said the snake would die inside the walls. He didn't think it could actually come into the house. My mother worried for several days. I remember her asking me in an anguished voice, "Why didn't you kill them all? What are we going to do with a snake loose in the house?"

Without realizing it at the time, I was consumed with guilt. I had done something terribly wrong by letting the snake get into the wall. What was a fourteen-year-old supposed to do? I was good with the shovel, but what was I doing killing snakes for other people and not completing the job, letting two of them get away?

I have never forgotten the snake that rushed up the bricks to escape my attack. It could be the seed planted for my recurring dreams. Part six of my poem "Rattlesnake Dance, Coronado Hills, 1966" reads:

> After killing three of them
> I saw the fourth one climb up the porch,
> squeeze into the bricks and disappear
> into a corner of the house, its sleek body

vanishing into the wall,
becoming a part of our home.

I never saw it, again,
but lay awake at night,
knowing it was inside the house,
trapped between wood and mortar,
moving from room to room without rattling,
waiting for the walls to crumble in years,
waiting for the boy to press his hands
against the wall above his bed,
and push in the dark,
tap and push,
the silence of life
a falling black wall
that smothered every breath I took
as I waited and waited.

When I dream about snakes, there is a house nearby. I never go inside, but know it is my childhood home. It is the house the snake entered—to leave something with me—the snake I did not kill because it was quick and fast. Instinct told it where to go. Instinct saved it—and instinct shapes my snake dreams.

In his book *Symbols of Transformation,* Carl Jung writes about snakes coming from the world of instinct, involved with the vital processes of life that are not always apparent to us. He feels snake dreams personify hidden conflicts within us. An appearance by a green snake in a dream could mean danger.

In my early dreams, there is no sense of danger, only the house somewhere in the scene. The ground is covered with snakes, hundreds of them moving between my legs as I walk peacefully along the river on a bright, sunny day. The snakes keep coming out of the ground. In one dream, they come out of a freshly dug pit. Where is my shovel?

Suddenly I am in the most recent dream. The veins and muscles in my left arm have turned green. In other dreams, I cannot identify the colors of the rattlers—there are so many snakes, the darkness of their numbers makes it impossible to recall colors. The one time I can identify a color, it becomes the green snake of danger and has entered my body.

What danger is this? As I try to relive those incidents of killing the baby rattlers, I know I overcame my fear. The harder thing to bring back is the guilt and sense of failure that I did not kill every snake that was threatening those women and the tranquillity of their homes. The ones that got away inhabit my dreams. If there is a danger, it is the fact that I have been stuck in the cycle of wandering over ground covered with snakes—the desert of my lonely childhood experiences as an only son.

This sets off the recurring dreams and the snake poems that tell me that I did not finish my job as the snake killer. I sleep and go back to the snakes, but I do not kill them. I do not lift shovels and tear baby rattlers apart. The snakes are alive to be a part of my dreams, even the one that pretends it is dead, so that I can come to it. The green snake that is becoming my arm is consuming me in order to force me to complete the cycle and get the job done. But I do not dream killing dreams. Death is not a part of the fertile ground covered with thick diamondback rattlesnakes.

Of course, I will not go out and find a real snake, kill it, and rid myself of the baby rattlers that became grown snakes in my dreams. Instead, I complete the cycle by writing poems, allowing myself to go back to the killings I carried out for the women. I must accept the fact that I did what I could, and let the river of living snakes flow in my dreams.

What about the green snake in my body? It is the snake that entered my house through the wall. I hacked those rattlers with a strong swing of my left arm. I am right-handed.

My conscious mind says that I was told to kill the snakes by two women who were frightened, though they must have known that snakes are a hazard of living in the desert. I cut the snakes without much hesitation. Who could ask more from a teenaged boy who had never killed snakes before? For several weeks, my mother could not get over the fact that there was a snake in the walls. I lay awake at night, listening through the walls of my bedroom to see if I could hear the rattle, find out if the snake was going to get its revenge against the young killer. Instinct tells me that I became the snake that got away. It becomes my being by traveling through my body, reaching my heart, letting me open the earth to allow newborn rattlers to emerge into the light.

If the green snake brings any other signs of danger, they point to my family and our personal history. Killing the snakes for my mother meant I was a good boy defending my home. Letting one of them enter the house meant that I was not quite what she expected me to be. My mother eventually forgot the snake incident and life went on. I do not recall seeing snakes in our yard again. As a matter of fact, it was the last time I saw any rattlers in my twenty-five years of living in El Paso.

I started having snake dreams after I left El Paso and moved to Denver. I was gone from the desert and lived a different life. The dreams began. Distance and time, and my intense separation from the desert, triggered the release of those snakes. The dreams happen three or four times a year. They never come as nightmares. I wake in a peaceful state and never see the dreams as signs of danger. If Jung is correct, the dreams are speaking of an unsettled killing, a flawed act of bravery, an incomplete hunt before the matriarchal audience, a family history shaped in the desert to turn out in ways I could not foresee.

The Navajo believe snake dreams are not serious or threatening, unless you are bitten in the dream. When I stuck my finger into the snake's mouth, I did not feel a real bite, even though the snake took hold of me. It was a feeling of pressure, a slow evolution up my arm, a sudden, energetic flowing—an awakening within my reptilian sleep. Was it a bite? According to Navajo belief, this is the most serious dream, the one that led me to ponder this as I continue writing my snake poems.

> I leave after searching each stall,
> but the boa and copperhead have a long way
> to go before turning blue, neither one
> knowing me when I killed blue lightning
> to prevent a storm of open flesh,
> drove metal through muscled ground
> in search of blood that never came,
> my wonder over the clean pieces
> sending the snake on its way
> before I could enter the glass,
> find the hidden blue eyes sparkling
> off the wire where the rattle
> misses a beat for me.
>
> (from "The Blue Snake")

I remember the color blue when I think of the baby rattlers, never the color green from my later dream. Baby rattlers have a pale sheen. I see their quick bodies in flashes of blue. "The Blue Snake" refers to a dream in which I find myself in a zoo reptile house, searching for the snakes I killed and the ones that got away.

A couple of years ago, after one of the dreams in which I walked in a swampy area near the river, the ground covered with harmless rattle-snakes, I woke and lay quietly in the dark. I thought back to killing the baby rattlers. I could still feel the sensation of snakes crawling between my legs without harming me, dozens of them sliding in and out of the river. I was not afraid, and I lay there knowing that I had not felt threatened at the age of twelve when I first killed the snakes. I was simply doing a favor for someone. The later killings helped a more immediate person and involved my house. After several of these dreams, I admitted that I was fascinated by the surviving snake crawling into the wall. I was curious as to how a snake could survive or die inside the walls. That was more important than pleasing my mother. As I lay in my bed, breathing after the latest dream, I could finally admit it to myself.

The dream of walking along the river occurred earlier than the most recent one in which the snake becomes my arm. The first dream took my fear away. The second dream made me reach out to the snakes for the first time. It was a cycle in completion, closing upon the circle like a snake devouring its own body, consuming my arm to settle within me in a startling, nonthreatening way.

I accept the dream about the green snake as a sign that the baby rattler that got away grew beyond the walls of the house to be spared by fate and the actions of a boy responding to command. I had to spare the snakes. As I relive the images of hacking at them with the shovel, I know the baby rattlers were fast, but I could have killed them all. As I dream, I let some of them go—I have an inner need to not kill everything threatening the neighborhood, my mother, our house!

Native American people have a general taboo against killing snakes. Tuscarora Indians are afraid to kill rattlers out of fear that the snake's relatives will return to seek revenge. The Tarahumara Indians of Mexico believe that the rattlers are companions of sorcerers, who meet and talk with them. Meskwaki Indians believe in the rattlesnake as an instrument of punishment. The Chiricahua Apaches of Arizona have a dread of rattlers that goes beyond the fear of snakebite. They address rattlesnakes as "mother's mother" and have a restriction among their people against talking about snakes. I find this amazing for a tribe of the Sonora desert, one of the richest habitats of giant diamondback rattlers, the most poisonous of the twenty-five species of rattlesnakes in the United States.

The only other time I came close to confronting a rattlesnake was in 1986, on a hike with my poet-mentor Robert Burlingame. I was visiting my family in El Paso. Whenever I could, I would look up the wise old poet and we would take long walks in the Franklin Mountains. We were climbing back down a narrow canyon on the eastern face of the Franklins after resting at the top.

He was walking in front of me and turned the corner around a huge boulder that lay in the narrow trail to the bottom. The rocks and dirt our feet rolled down warned the huge diamondback sunning itself ten yards from Robert. We stopped immediately as the powerful rattle echoed against the steep red walls of the canyon. We froze for a second, and then he pointed to it.

I could not see the snake clearly because it lay under a mesquite bush, but I could make out the thick roll as it slowly coiled back, ready to strike. Robert said quietly, "It's one of the biggest I have ever seen." I didn't say anything. Without hurry or panic, we stepped back and went around the snake from several yards away. We hopped over rough mesquite and Spanish dagger cactus, then moved back onto the smooth trail cut in the avalanche of rocks. I could hear the rattle as we left the snake behind, but I did not think about the snake dreams I had already had. I was too immersed in the pleasure of good company, hiking through the desert I loved, wondering why I didn't visit often enough; I did not think about the snake until later, when the canyon encounter would result in my first snake poem, a piece I never knew would be the start of a long sequence of poems.

Diamondback on the Trail

We were climbing
down the canyon
when the sudden head
and rattle moved in the sun.

We froze in awe and respect
as it turned to us,
the enormous, poised body
revealing its claim
to the desert, its reason
for waking to challenge us,
to let us stand suspended
among the cactus and red rocks.

We stepped back as you said
it was one of the biggest
rattlers you had ever seen,
your years in the canyons

flashing in memory
like the snake's quick tongue
flicking at the crossing of time
and the way we all meet,
darting at the breathless way
we stumble upon the slithering heart,
the cold, slow muscle,
and the way we listen
to the loud rattling,
its blood in beauty one beat,
its bone and body
one movement into rock,
one sudden grasp at the earth.

Years and dreams later, the sudden grasp becomes the boy walking along the river, then my finger in the snake's mouth, forming itself into my arm in a cool, slow dream—a trance in which the house stands there, creatures hidden in the walls, its history of being constructed in the desert, the story of people entering their own walls, trying to find their way over the constantly moving ground.

My snake dreams may never go away. I don't know how long the snake poem sequence will be. I continue to learn more about rattlesnakes. I wonder if boys today, living in desert towns like El Paso, will encounter snakes the way I did. Now Southwest streets in the 1990s have nothing to do with the waiting desert and its inhabitants. The baby rattlers have gone underground, away from brick walls and suburbs. They rise near the river where there are no houses, no chance to mistake neighborhoods for the fresh ground of the desert, the fertile, hot soil where muscled bone rises to shake a beat for those who dream and wonder.

From *Alburquerque*

"I'm going to fight," he told Sara the following Sunday.

He had been nervous all day about telling her, and as he stood next to her while she prepared a salad he suddenly blurted out the news.

She paused and looked at him. "You're going to box?"

"Yes. In a few weeks."

"But why?"

He told her about Dominic's offer. She listened, but in the end shook her head. "I feel like Lucinda," she said. "I just don't like it. Isn't there another way? Maybe I could go to Mr. Johnson—"

"No, Mamá! I don't want you to have to beg from that man. If he knows, he won't say anything. Look, it's just one fight."

She knew how much he had suffered when Junior died, and how hard it was for him to go back into the ring, and it was natural for him to want to know his father. But she didn't like his being mixed up with the attorney who was so rich and always in the papers. Being mixed up with the rich could only bring trouble. She didn't like it, but for her son she would bear it without complaint.

"Go and get Lucinda, I'll finish here," she said calmly. He handed her the vegetables he had cut, and washed his hands.

"It's going to be all right, *jefita*. It's something I have to do." He kissed her.

"I know, I know," she answered. "Go on, the enchiladas will be ready when you return."

He drove to Lucinda's. She was radiant in a white summer dress. She kissed him and whispered, "*Tú eres tú*. You're all I want."

Sara had prepared red chile enchiladas, beans, and tortillas. For dessert she served sopa, a sweet bread pudding topped with melted cheese. It felt good to have Lucinda in her home. This was what Abrán needed, not the boxing and not the running around and making deals with the big-shot lawyer.

Time was the most valuable ingredient in life, and for Sara it was to be enjoyed with family and friends. She sipped wine and enjoyed the warmth of their company as they ate. Lucinda talked about her life in the mountain village of Córdova. Sara had asked her about her family. *Quien es tu familia?* was one of the first questions that was always asked. One was known by one's family.

Lucinda told about her father and how he came to be a *santero,* and she told them about her mother and many of the old customs in the isolated villages of the Sangre de Cristo. She wanted Abrán to visit her family, she said with a glance at Sara. "That would be good for Abrán," Sara agreed. "He's a city boy. He needs to see the villages."

"How about the training?" Lucinda asked.

"I can jog up and down the mountain," Abrán said. "We'll go on Good Friday, come back after Easter. The doctor gave me a physical, said I'm in great shape."

"I knew that," Lucinda teased him.

"He is in good shape," Sara said as she cleaned up the dishes. "He runs every day, he doesn't smoke, but he drinks beer," she said with a mock frown. "*Bueno,* let's go in the living room. Lucinda, help me get the coffee and sopa. Then I want Abrán to read the beautiful story Cynthia wrote. She was not only an artist, she could write like a poet."

They gathered in the front room for dessert. Abrán flipped through Cynthia's diary. "This is an old entry, and it's as close as she comes to describing my father. They went to a *matanza* in the South Valley, near Los Padillas. It was the day they discovered the bower where we buried her ashes. She never mentions his name. She refers to him only as '*mi árabe.*'"

"So he is dark," Sara said. A dark and handsome Mexicano was her son's father, an indio like Ramiro, a dark, curly-haired *árabe.* She looked at her son and admired him. Yes, he would find his father, it was best to believe that. He had been bound by destiny long enough, now he had to break those old ropes and create his own future.

Abrán smiled at his mother. "Yes. *Bueno, aquí 'stá.*"

He read Cynthia's "*la matanza,*" the entry that described the killing of the hogs for winter meat:

It was in the fiestas of the people that I discovered the essence of my people, the Mexican heritage of my mother. Other painters had concentrated on the Indians; I went to the small, out-of-the-way family fiestas of the Mexicanos. There is a chronicle of life in the fiestas, beginning with baptism. La fiesta de bautismo. I painted the padrinos at church as they held the baby over the font for the priest to bless el niño with holy water. In the faces of the padrino and madrina I saw and understood the godparents' role. The padrinos would become the child's second parents, and the familial kinship in the village or in the barrio would be extended. La familia would grow. I painted a scene where the baby was returned from church by the padrinos, the joy of the parents, the song of entriego, the return of the child, the food and drink, the hopeful, gay faces of family and neighbors.

And I painted wedding scenes. Gloria has my favorite. She has the painting that captures the moment when two of the groom's friends grab the bride and stand ready to spirit her away. The bridegroom is caught off guard, someone is pouring him a glass of champagne. The fiddler is leaning low, playing away, his eyes laughing. The other músicos join in the polka, drawing attention away from the traditional "stealing of the bride."

Fiestas, I loved the fiestas. There is a series: "Spring Planting," "Cleaning the Acequias," "Misa del Gallo," "Los Matachines." I did the Bernalillo Matachines, although my favorite were the Jémez Pueblo Matachines. I painted los hermanos penitentes on Good Friday, the holy communion of Easter Sunday, the little-known dances of Los Abuelos and Los Comanches. I painted a triptych of Los Pastores at the Trampas church one Christmas. And the Christmas Posadas. All the fiestas of life that might die as the viejitos die.

I painted the fiestas of the Río Grande, the fiestas of your people, mi amor, the fiestas my mother used to tell me about when I was a child, because if life had not been so cruel, we would have shared these fiestas.

Do you remember la Matanza in Los Padillas, mi árabe moreno? We were invited by your friend Isidro. His family was having a matanza. We had fallen in love that summer, and suddenly it was October, a more brilliant October I never saw again. The entire river was golden, the álamos had turned the color of fire. Long strings of geese flew south and filled the valley with their call, and we, too, drove south along Isleta. Farmers lined the road, their trucks filled with bushels of green chile, red chile ristras, corn and pumpkins, apples. It was autumn, and the fiesta of the harvest drew people together.

It was my first trip into the South Valley. I was a gringita from the Country Club; I had been protected from the world. But the valley was to become my valley. I would visit the villages of the Río Grande again and again, until the old residents got to know well the sunburned gringa who tramped around with easel, paint, and brushes. I earned their respect. They invited me into their homes, and later they invited me to their fiestas. Their acceptance kept me alive.

The night had been cold, and the thin ice of morning cracked like a fresh apple bitten. The sun rising over Tijeras Canyon melted the frost. Gloria helped, as usual. She picked me up. I told my parents I was spending the day with her. Without her help we could never have had time together. Why did she marry F? What a pity.

The colors of autumn were like a bright colcha, a warm and timeless beauty covering the earth. The sounds carried in the morning air, and all was vibrant with life before the cold of winter. Oh, if we had only known that the wrath of parents can kill!

The matanza was beginning when we arrived. Cars and trucks filled the gravel driveway. Family, friends, and neighbors filled the backyard of the old adobe home. Isidro greeted us.

"Just in time," he said, and we followed him to the back where the women were serving breakfast. They had set a board over barrels to use as a table, and on it rested the steaming plates of eggs, bacon, potatoes, chile stew, hot tortillas, and coffee. The men were stuffing down the food. Somebody had already called for the first pig to be brought out of the pen. Whiskey bottles were passed around; those who had gotten up early to help the women start the fires and heat the huge vats of lye water had been drinking for hours.

A very handsome, but very troubled, young man held a rifle in one hand and a bottle of whiskey in the other. Remember Marcos? I will never forget him; he learned a lesson that day. We all did. At the pigpen the frightened sow was being roped and wrestled out.

The women watched; they goaded the men. My mother was a woman of great strength, I always knew, and I saw that same strength in those women of the valley.

"Ya no pueden," they teased the men wrestling with the sow. The worst thing to tell a macho, especially when he's drinking and doing the "bringing the meat home" business. But it was a fiesta, and the teasing was part of it.

"¡Andale! ¡Con ganas!"

"¡Qué ganas, con huevos!"

They laughed; the men cursed and grunted as they lassoed the pig.

"Don't shoot yourself, Marcos!"

"Don't stab yourself, Jerry!" they said to the young man who held the knife.

Isidro told us that Marcos was an attorney in town and Jerry was a computer man at Sandia Labs. Like other young men who had left the valley for a middle-class life in the city, they only returned once in a while to visit the parents and grandparents. Or they returned for the fiestas. They had almost forgotten the old ways, and so the older aunts teased them.

Who remembered the old ways? The old men standing along the adobe wall warming themselves in the morning sun. With them stood don Pedro, Isidro's grandfather, the old patriarch of the clan. These were the vecinos, the neighbors who had worked together all their lives. Men from Los Padillas and Pajarito and Isleta Pueblo. Now they were too old to kill the pigs, so they had handed over the task to their grandsons. They warmed their bones in the morning sun and watched as the young men drank and strutted about in their new shirts and Levi's. Those old men knew the old ways. Maybe it was that day that I vowed to paint them, to preserve their faces and their way of life for posterity. They would all die soon.

"Hispano Gothic," I called the painting I did of those old men. The last patriarchs of the valley. And their women, las viejitas, las jefitas of the large families, stood next to their men and watched. These old men and women remembered the proper way of the fiestas, and so they watched with great patience as their uprooted grandsons struggled to prove their manhood. What a chorus of wisdom and strength shone in their eyes. What will happen to our people when those viejitos are gone? Will our ceremonies disappear from the face of the earth? Is that what drives me to paint them with such urgency?

Time has been like a wind swirling around me, my love, since I last touched you. Time will scatter my paintings, but the seed planted that autumn day will survive. Our seed will grow, but we were not destined to nourish it.

The children were always present at the fiestas, and they were there that day. They laughed and played tag, chased each other, the boys shot baskets through a hoop, a baby nursed at his mother's breast. As the squealing, struggling pig was pulled out of the pen, the children paused to watch. Here was the link between past and future generations, this is how the young would learn the old ways.

Near the fire a large wood plank was set over two barrels. The dead pig would be hoisted up onto the rough table to be gutted and cleaned. A huge cauldron sat over the hot fire that had been lighted before the sun was up. Boiling water laced with lye let off wisps of steam; a thin scum clouded the surface. When the dead pig was raised onto the plank, it would be covered with gunnysacks and the hot water poured over the sacks. The bristle would be softened and easy to scrape off with knives.

The shouts of the men grew agitated, the sow was big and nervous. The men pulled with ropes, others poked and pushed from behind. "¡Nalgona!" one cursed. The women laughed. "That's the way you like them, Freddie!"

Don Pedro and his compadres watched patiently.

"¡Sonamagon! ¡Pinche! ¡Muevete!" the young men cursed the pig.

"Come on!" Marcos shouted. "A little closer!" He aimed the rifle. He was drunk.

Marcos's wife stood in the circle of people around the pig. She was a Northeast Heights gringa, and she didn't like what they were doing. She wished they *hadn't come. Marcos was making a fool of himself, she thought, and he was going to muddy the new boots and Levi's she had bought him for the state fair. Too much pagan ritual in the air for her taste.*

"Hold him still," Marcos shouted.

They had frightened the pig, made it nervous, now they couldn't hold the struggling animal that pulled from side to side.

"Watch out, Marcos!"

"He's going to shoot someone!"

"Ramona. Take the gun away," someone said to the oldest aunt. She was in charge of the fire and the cleaning, and tough enough to keep the men in line.

"Marcos?" she called.

"I'm okay," he answered angrily. He threw the empty bottle aside and cocked the rifle.

"No tiene huevos," somebody shouted. Marcos heard. He turned and glared at his cousins, those who had not left the valley.

"Sonofabitches!" he spat. They'd been razzing him all morning, now they came out and said he didn't have the balls to do the job. He was a drugstore cowboy playing at being a macho man. He'd show them.

Then his wife whined, "Marcos, let somebody else do it. You're ruining your boots."

His face grew livid. I painted anger in his eyes, for it was there. Bitch, he wanted to scream, I'll show you.

"Grandpa," Ramona said, and for a moment everyone glanced at don Pedro. Would he stop the charade before someone got hurt? The old man looked at Marcos's father. The father shrugged; it was up to don Pedro to decide.

The old man nodded. Continue. He held up a finger. Make a clean kill with one shot, he said.

"You damn right, daddy-o." Marcos grinned. Somebody handed him a just-opened bottle of Jim Beam and he took a big swig.

"Don't give him any more to drink, he's going to shoot somebody." The women were worried, they had known of matanzas that turned deadly.

The men heaved and pushed the pig in front of Marcos. He aimed, the rifle wavering.

"¡Cuidado!" one man shouted and jumped aside.

"Behind the ear! Behind the ear!"

"Between the eyes!"

"Watch out!"

"He's drunk!"

"Get back!"

The men jumped away from the pig, and a deafening explosion filled the air. The baby cried, the children screamed, the crows in the giant cottonwoods by the ditch rose cawing into the air. Dogs barked, and the air echoed with the report of the rifle. The smell of gunpowder filled the clean morning air.

The pig gave a shrill cry and reared up. The bullet had only grazed it. Marcos fired again, wildly, and the second bullet entered above the left shoulder. The sow hit the ground, turning round and round in the dirt, crying shrilly as blood spurted from its wound.

"You missed, cabrón!"

"Shoot!"

"No! The knife!"

The men pulled at the ropes around the pig's feet and held it. But Marcos would not take the knife. The pig's hot blood made him turn away and vomit, the stuff splattering his new boots.

Tío Mateo took the knife and pounced on the screaming sow. He grabbed an ear for leverage, then plunged the knife into the throat as hard and deep as he could. The wounded sow thrashed and turned.

"Hol'im! Goddamnit hold him!"

The men held, dirtying themselves with mud and blood as the knife found an artery and the blood rushed out. Then the pig grew still. The men got up slowly, covered with filth and blood, wiped their hands on their Levi's and cursed Marcos. They spit out the bitter taste in their mouths and reached for a drink.

Against the wall the old men stood quietly. They shook their heads; it was not good. The frightened children had turned to the women, hiding in folds of skirts. This is not how it should be.

"Pinche marrano," Marcos cursed and kicked the dead pig at his feet. "You sonofbitches didn't hold it," he blamed the men.

"Fuck you," one of the men answered, "you're a lousy shot!"

They faced each other, angry that it had not gone right. They blamed Marcos, he blamed them. None looked at the old men along the wall.

"Bring the other one! I'll show you who's a good shot!" Marcos bragged and wiped the vomit from his mouth. He cocked the rifle.

"Put the gun away, Marcos, you're drunk," tía Ramona said. She was angry, too. She remembered matanzas that were done right, not crazy and dirty like the one she had just seen. She looked at the children; they shouldn't be frightened, they should be learning to value this old custom.

"Stay out of this, tía!" Marcos insisted. "Bring the other pig!" he shouted, waving the rifle. "I'm gonna blow his brains out!"

"No!" A stern voice broke the tension in the air. We turned to see don Pedro step forward, bent with age but resolute. He had stayed out of the argument as long as he could, but now he had to set things right. I think it was the frightened children who compelled him to stop the debacle.

He walked right up to Marcos and looked squarely at his grandson. "Ya no valen ni para matar un marrano," he said.

Marcos and the other men stiffened. It was an insult, and if any other man had said that, there would have been a fight, but this was their grandfather so they swallowed their pride.

Don Pedro, still sinewy and tough, was the patriarch of the family, and respect for elders was still a value in the family. He took the rifle from Marcos.

"You call yourselves men," he said firmly, "and look at this mess. You can't even kill a pig."

His words stung. His sons and grandsons looked at their dirtied clothes and the mess of blood on the ground and knew he was right.

"Ah, come on, Grandpa," one of his grandsons said, "don't take it so serious. We're just killing a pig, it's no big deal, ese."

"It is a big deal," the old man retorted. "It has to be done right."

Marcos's eyes narrowed, but he tried to make amends. "Come on, Grandpa, have a drink. . . ."

"I don't drink with boys," don Pedro answered, a hardness in his voice. He stood unwavering, strong as an old tree of the river.

The silence was deadly. Marcos clenched his jaws in anger.

They were young men full of booze, and the smell of blood had made their own blood boil. I felt something terrible was about to happen.

So did don Pedro's wife, because she stepped forward and put her hand on his arm, trying to coax him back. The arena of blood and drunk young men was no place for an old man. Better to stand with his compadres at the wall and warm his bones in safety. But don Pedro wouldn't budge.

"Okay, Grandpa." Marcos spit out the bile in his mouth. "If you're such a man, why don't you do it."

It was the grandfather's turn to be stung. He looked around and saw the men nod. Yes, if you're such a man, you show us how it's done.

"Grandpa likes to talk," Marcos continued, "but he's too old to cut the mustard."

The young men smiled.

"¿Qué pasa, Grandpa?" a grandson said, and slapped the old man on the back.

"No puede," Marcos snickered. They stood facing each other, Marcos and don Pedro, the young and the old. Their veins bulged with tension, their eyes glared.

The old woman whispered, "Anda, Pedro, vente." Come away, leave this to the young men. The old man straightened his shoulders, looked at her, and smiled. Then he turned to the old compadres who stood along the wall.

"Secundino," he said softly, "el martillo."

The old man Secundino thought he hadn't heard, then he smiled and nodded. It was the call to the matanza, an old calling, something they knew in their blood, something they had done surely and swiftly all their lives. The right way. He hobbled to the shed and returned with a ten-pound, short-handled sledgehammer.

"Procopio, ponle filo a la navaja," the old man said as he rolled up his sleeves.

"Con mucho gusto." Procopio spat a quick stream of chewing tobacco through yellow-stained teeth and smiled. He took the long knife and began sharpening it on a small whetstone. "Lana sube, lana baja," he whispered as the blade swished back and forth on the stone.

"Compadres," don Pedro whispered, "la marrana." The old men ambled silently but quickly toward the pen.

"Wait, Grandpa," Marcos said, "you don't have to—" But it was too late, the old man's eyes were fixed on the huge sow that the men moved out of the pen by softly clicking their tongues. They needed no ropes to move the pig. Secundino slipped the big hammer into don Pedro's hand. Then Procopio handed don Pedro the sharpened knife, so now the old man balanced the hammer in one hand and the knife in the other.

The young men had only heard these stories, that long ago when rifles and bullets were scarce, the matanza was done like this. Like a bullfighter meeting a bull with just a cape, the old man met the two-hundred-pound pig with just a blade and hammer.

Don Pedro moved in a circle, keeping his eye on the pig as it came closer and closer to him. There was no noise, no ropes, no fast motions to spook the pig, just the circle of men getting smaller.

The compadres smiled and remembered all the years of their lives when they had done this. It was a ceremony, the taking of the animal's life to provide meat for the family. The young men needed to be reminded that it was not sport, it was a tradition as old as the first Hispanos who settled along the river.

This is how we have lived along the river, the viejos said. We have raised generations on this earth along the Río Grande, and we have done it with pride and honor. Each new generation must accept the custom and likewise pass it on.

The air grew still, we stood transfixed. The circle closed in, until the animal was only an arm's length away.

Crows called from the cottonwoods of the river, a dog whined, the wood embers popped, the wisps of steam hissed and rose from the lye water in the cauldron.

When don Pedro had come face-to-face with the pig, he raised his hammer, and with the speed of a matador, there was a brief glint in the sunlight, the arc of his arm, a dull thud, and the pig jerked back and stiffened. The kill was complete and clean.

It had taken all the old man's strength to make the kill, but he had done it with grace. There was no loud thunder of the rifle, no crying children or barking dogs, just a clean kill. We stood hypnotized as don Pedro dropped to his knees in front of the quivering pig. Two of the men held the pig by the ears as don Pedro plunged the knife into the pig's heart. The blood flowed swiftly.

Tía Ramona stepped forward with a pan to save the hot, gushing blood. Not a drop was wasted. She would mix it with water in a bowl, then slowly stir it with her hand until the thick coagulants were removed and only the pure blood remained. This she would fry with onion and pieces of liver as a blood pudding, a delicacy for the guests.

When don Pedro withdrew the knife it seemed to come out spotless, un-bloodied, and his hands were clean. Then the old man stood, and a shudder of fatigue passed through his frail body. He took a deep breath and then sipped from the tin cup of water his wife handed him. He smiled at her, and when he looked at us, there was a serene beauty in his face. A noble look on the faces of the old men of the clan.

His compadres nodded, slapped him gently on the back. That's the way we used to do it, their nods said.

"Chingao," one of the grandsons exclaimed, breaking the silence.

"Did you see that?"

"Damn, Grandpa."

They moved forward to touch the old man. One handed him a bottle so he could drink. They were filled with admiration. Even Marcos reached out to touch the grandfather, as if to share in the old man's valor.

"You're too old to be killing pigs," his wife scolded. She took his arm, and together they walked back to the safety of the warm adobe wall.

"A man's never too old," he winked, willing to withdraw. Let the young men lift the hog and begin the gutting and cleaning, he would sit with his old vecinos and watch. They had done their duty, they had shown the young people the right way to perform the ceremony.

The pig was gutted and the liver was thrown on the hot coals. When it was baked, the first slice was served on hot tortillas with green chile and offered to don Pedro, a tribute to the old warrior. Then he and the rest of the men *ate, drank wine, and talked about the old days when the people of the valley lived in harmony with the earth and their neighbors.*

"We will die and all this will pass away," I remember don Pedro saying.

That is why I had to paint. I wanted to preserve the beauty of those moments. That was the gift and the commitment which came to rest in my soul that day. The life and love of the old people opened my eyes, and I wanted to share that gift.

Love filled that entire space of time, the people and the golden colors of the river. Love consumed us, and we thought time would never change. We drove south and walked along the river bosque. There we found our bower. Do you remember, mi amor? The warmth of the brilliant October sun, the love we shared? The beauty of your bronze body was so new and pure that I couldn't get enough of you. That bower became our place of love, it will always be my home. I return there to be with you.

Abrán finished reading and placed the diary on his lap. Sara sighed, and Lucinda's eyes were filled with tears.

"It's beautiful."

"Yes, it is."

"Such a gifted woman," Sara whispered. She looked at Abrán. So this was her son, the child of that woman. Ah well, life is passed on like that, not to own and possess, but to nurture for a while. The woman had given him the gift of life, but she had given Abrán love all these years. Each had offered what she could, and at that instant Sara felt very satisfied and content.

I Never Even Seen My Father

From *In Nueva York*

"Okay then, Lillian . . . you tell me, what kind of person is he? A pervert, right? He's gotta be one." Yolanda puffed on a cigarette waiting for an answer.

Lillian sat in the small booth facing Yolanda, trying earnestly to answer.

"Look, I think all he meant was it's more of a subconscious wish on your part. Not like you really wanted to do it."

"But he said it was something I wanted. Can you imagine? I wanted it! Like I never even thought of such a thing . . . never, I swear."

"Yeah, but that's it, maybe you don't know that. But deep down inside your head, you don't know what your mind is thinking. Right? Nobody does, like dreams—you can't control dreams. Right? That's what psychology is all about, you see . . . getting way back in there down in your mind." Lillian put her hand on the nape of her own neck, then rubbed the back of her head. "And seeing what makes people tick . . . mentally. That's what the doctor is talking about."

"All right then, you talking about dreams, right? And getting inside your head? Well, what about somebody like doña Digna over on Rivington Street? What about her? She gets into people's heads and explains their dreams too, right? Do you believe what she says? A lotta people do!"

"Wait, Yolanda; now you're talking about *espiritismo*. . . . That's something else. That's not science."

"But people believe in it, and they say she cures them."

"That's not science. There's no proof. You are comparing the science of psychology, something that is altogether different, to *espiritismo*, where you got no proof. The psychiatrist interprets your dreams and your subconscious to cure you of your problems, based on facts."

"Okay, you talking about facts, so let's say that doña Digna tells you there is a *muerto,* a dead person, a ghost that is causing your problems, right? Then she'll get in touch with this ghost, who could be an evil spirit. . . . Somehow, she's got the power to fix things and cure your problems. People believe in that, Lillian. And you know I'm saying it right too!"

"First of all, there have been many, many books written on the science of psychology, and a doctor can tell you what's wrong—"

"What about all the dream books they sell? I seen them all over and so do you."

"Yolanda, you know them books are no proof; they are not scientific. With the right books a doctor can tell you what is wrong and cure you and—"

"He ain't gonna cure me. Because he's a sicko . . . really. He's putting things in my head I never even thought of."

"What will you girls have?" Rudi called out from behind the counter. The luncheonette was quiet during the early evening. Except for another customer at the counter, the store was practically empty. In about an hour the place would be busy with night customers. Rudi sipped a cup of coffee, enjoying the break.

"Gimme a coffee and . . . you got a piece of coconut cream pie? Good, I'll take a piece. Go on, Lil, order what you want. It's my treat."

"No, I'll buy." Lillian stood up and looked over at the glass display case against the wall behind the counter. She examined the pies, cakes, and puddings inside. "Gimme a root beer and a flan."

"Hey, Lil, I'm treating. I called you, remember?"

"But you gotta save your money now."

"Forget it. I insist, Lil, otherwise I'm gonna feel bad. Okay?"

Lillian smiled and nodded.

"Listen, Yolanda, I'm really glad you called me."

"It's been a long time since we seen each other privately and talked, huh, Lil?"

They smiled somewhat shyly as they remembered what good friends they once were. Lillian and Yolanda had been classmates and friends through grammar school and most of junior high. Then they went separate ways. Lillian was a good student and liked school. She found that most of her friends were good students like herself. Yolanda had never been very interested in school, and as the work became more difficult for her, she found that friends outside in the street were easier to be with.

"But you know you was always my ace! I respect you because you're smart and you always knew the answers. Everybody knows how smart you are, Lil." Yolanda hesitated. Nervously she put a cigarette in her mouth, then offered one to Lillian. "Smoke?"

"I don't smoke. Thanks."

Yolanda lit her cigarette, then bit her lip apprehensively. "Like I was saying, I know how smart you are and . . . well, that's why I had to talk to you about this. I know you could help me figure this out. Part of being out on probation is that I gotta stay in therapy with this jive-turkey doctor. And look, I know there's something wrong with me. Maybe a lotta things are wrong with me. Or else I wouldn't of messed up so badly. But, what he's talking about, it's . . . it's not my problem. And I'm not admitting to something like that. No way."

"Look, Yolanda, you feel like that because you don't understand what he means. I'm gonna major in psychology when I graduate next June. So I'm into that. What the psychiatrist means is that it's a symbolic meaning, not a reality, you see? Just a symbol."

"What do you mean, a symbol? What does—"

"Wait. For instance, something that stands for something but doesn't actually look like or mean that something. Like an idea or a suggestion of a concept . . ."

"Lil, I don't know what you're talking about."

"Okay. The psychiatrist says you have"—Lillian lowered her voice and leaned over toward Yolanda—"a desire to go to bed with your father and you hate your mother. But he don't mean that really."

"What the hell does he mean, then?"

"Wait, let me explain. He means that you act out your guilt about this desire and you punish yourself by being self-destructive."

"That's a joke. What guilt? Lillian, you know me and my family since we was kids, right? You know I never even seen my father! All I know is that when I was a baby he split and left my mother with three kids, and that's it. So then I got a desire to go to bed with somebody I ain't even seen? Come on." Yolanda inhaled deeply and vigorously blew out the smoke. "And then, I wanna do this or that because I'm guilty. So that means I'm punishing myself. . . . Man, that's ridiculous!"

Rudi set down the orders. "Enjoy yourself, girls." He went over to the other booths, carefully wiping down each table and seat with a clean damp cloth.

"One good thing about this place, Rudi still keeps it spotless."

"That's right, and he keeps out the bums too. I can't stand when they come in here all drunk, moaning and smelling."

"You're right, Lil, phooey!" They both laughed. "But it's good to be back." Yolanda sighed and drank her coffee. "You know, I missed the old neighborhood even though I thought I never would. It's funny, but I did."

"It must of been rough on you."

"Well." Yolanda put out her cigarette and began to eat. "Actually I was in a bad way, you know? . . . Girl, really wasted. Drugs messed me up bad . . . so I was better off in a rehab center than outside like I was. And I could've been in worse placcs. Anyway, I gotta lotta catching up to do. I gotta take some tests now to see where I fit back into school. I quit when I was fifteen, remember? You told me not to. You said, don't do it, stick it out, don't quit. You were right, Lil, you're smart, I always knew that."

Lillian and Yolanda ate in silence for a few moments.

"You see, Lil, I gotta figure this business out first because I know that the doctor is wrong, and I'm not gonna admit to anything like he's asking."

"That's only because you don't understand." Lillian sipped her root beer. "He's trying to help, Yolanda."

"Understand what? Go on, you're smart. Tell me how he's trying to help me. I'm gonna tell you something I wish I could tell him. But I know I'll make it worse on myself because he don't wanna know about it. And that's that there's a lot going on out there he, and even you, don't know about. You might read about it or see it on TV, but that don't mean you know anything about what it's like to be hustling, stealing, mugging in a dog-eat-dog world . . . that's right, for survival, baby, in a sewer! Why don't he ask that? Why don't he ask me about the world I'm trying to split from? All he gives me is some jive talk about my sexual desire for somebody I ain't never seen or met really. In fact, if I think of it, somebody I got me no use for."

"Okay." Lillian ate her last spoonful of flan, then took a deep breath. "I'm gonna tell you something. I'm gonna tell you a story about a Greek myth. Just listen to me, Yolanda. I've got my reasons. Just listen." Lillian stopped and waited until she was positive Yolanda wouldn't argue. "You see, the doctor's theory is based on a myth that was used by Sigmund Freud. He was a very famous doctor, a psychiatrist from Vienna. Now, this myth tells the story of a king back in ancient Greece, his name was

King Oedipus. When he was born, the prophets said that he would grow up and kill his father, marry his own mother, and have children with her. When his mother heard this, she decided to have the baby killed. So she gives it to a servant to kill. But he feels sorry for the baby and gives it to a nobleman in another town, far away. When this baby grows up, he meets a blind man who is really a prophet, you know, someone that can tell the future? So this here prophet tells him about what is going to happen. That he will kill his father, marry his mother, and have kids with her. He leaves his town and runs away from his adopted parents, thinking that he don't want to do this to them, not knowing of course that he's not really their kid. Well, on his travels, he meets a man on the highway; they get into a fight, and he kills this man. Guess what? This man he just killed happens to be his real father! Now . . . he goes into the town where this man lives and he takes his place, marries this man's wife. And who is she? His real mother! They have kids and the whole thing comes true after all."

"Hey, wait a second, isn't his mother a little too old to marry such a young dude?"

"Well . . . maybe, but not that old, and probably in the old days it didn't make too much difference."

"What happened to his kids?"

"Wait . . . there's more. Somebody tells him the truth about his wife, you know, that she's his mother and that he killed his father and all. Well, he gets so upset and guilty that he pokes out his own eyes and goes blind. Then his wife kills herself because she's also very guilty."

"And what about his kids? Do they die too?"

"No, he goes away to an island in exile, and his kids just go to live with him."

"Yugh! That's some story."

"Right. So, from this myth is the theory of the Oedipus complex. See? That's what they call the subconscious desire for one's father or mother. The Oedipus complex, for King Oedipus. Now, because you feel very guilty for this desire, you punish yourself. It's a theory for treatment. Sigmund Freud discovered it."

"The doctor never explained it to me that way."

"There, you see then?" Lillian smiled, satisfied.

"Look." Yolanda lit another cigarette. "I gotta ask you something. Is that a true story?"

"I don't really know. I don't think so . . . it's more like a myth. You know, from ancient Greece."

"Do you believe this story really happened then?"

"Well, that's not important, whether it's true or not."

"It is to me. Just answer me if you believe it?"

"Yolanda, I already told you, my major in college is going to be psychology, and I've done a lot of homework on this already. Believe me, these things are facts."

"How can it be a fact if it ain't true? Now you tell me."

"The truth is the guilt . . . that's the facts—guilt and punishment."

"Okay, Lillian, guilt about what? Something that's not a true story?"

"You don't wanna understand, Yolanda . . . you don't!"

"All right." Yolanda hesitated. She pushed away her empty coffee cup and half-finished piece of coconut cream pie and leaned forward, placing her arms on the table directly in front of Lillian. "I'll tell you a story that really happened. Okay? Doña Digna did a cure for my mother once. My mother was suffering from migraine headaches so bad she couldn't work, sleep, or nothing. When she went to doña Digna for help, she said the cause of these headaches was that an evil spirit was leading my mother's guardian angel away from her. Now, this evil spirit was actually my mother's dead mother. That's right! Because when she was alive she had promised the Virgin Mary a novena and a sacrifice for a favor that the Virgin done for her. Somehow, her mother, you know, my grandmother, never kept her promise. So the Virgin Mary was making her pay her dues by sending her out to take her own daughter's guardian angel. The headaches were being caused by the guardian angel, who didn't wanna leave my mother because that's where the angel belonged. All right, so then doña Digna tells my mother to complete the novena and do the sacrifice, you know, like wearing no shoes for six months or walking up to the altar on your knees eighty times—something like that. This way, her mother, my grandmother, will get off her back and leave her guardian angel alone. In the meantime, doña Digna says her prayers and does her thing . . . man, and guess what? After my mother does all of this and doña Digna finishes, my mother's headaches are all gone. And she don't get them no more. All right?"

"All right what?"

"All right, do you believe that story? It's true, you know . . . I mean it's true my mother's headaches went away. She got cured."

"It's not the same thing, Yolanda."

"It's a cure, ain't it?"

"The headaches got cured because they were psychosomatic."

"What's that?"

"That's where you give yourself an illness for psychological reasons. The cause is psychosomatic, mental and not physical."

"She still had bad migraine headaches even if they were . . . psy— psychromatic. And they went away. She got cured after doña Digna solved her problem."

"You know, Yolanda, you are not giving the doctor a chance to cure you. I can see that. He's a scientist and doña Digna is a—a spiritualist; that has nothing to do with science. You just won't listen and accept facts."

"What facts? So far you ain't told me no facts and neither did he."

"Guilt, for one thing. Yes, that's a fact. People who are guilty because of things they can't face punish themselves. That way they keep from being successful and have an excuse for not living up to their potential."

"Why should I punish myself for something I never even thought of? You tell me."

Rudi approached them. "Hey, you want something else? You two looking so serious, eh? Cheer up, you young and good looking. What more you girls want?"

"Have another soda, Lil . . . go on."

"It's okay, no thanks, I'm fine."

"Go on, give her another root beer and me another coffee." She smiled at Rudi and winked.

"*Mira,* there you go, that's better. You don't wanna go around looking like you have to carry the world's problems around with you, do you?" He walked back behind the counter.

"Well?" Yolanda leaned back in her seat and waited.

"Look, Yolanda, it don't matter if the story is true or not. Don't you see that? You just refuse to understand that! The doctor is only trying to find out why you do the things you do and"—Lillian lowered her voice, avoiding Yolanda's eyes—"got messed up and went to a . . . a place to get rehabilitated."

"But I wanna know why I did them things too. It does matter to me. Hey, Lil, it matters a lot! But what's a story about the olden Greek days got to do with me and the streets out there? Look, maybe I started on drugs because of a lotta things that might be wrong with me. Right? First of all, drugs are out there, available for anybody who wants to get high. And being high is a ball. You must think I'm sick to say that. But it's true, I swear it! And at the beginning everybody out there is real willing to get you high. Junkies want company, believe me, I'm saying it right. When you're high, it's beautiful, because you got no worries, man. You feel fabulous, you ain't scared of nothing and nobody. Your problems are over because you don't see where you live and you don't see what you ain't got and what you look like, and you don't miss what you can't see. Everything's perfect. But then you need more and more shit to keep you going. You don't get high so easy no more. You got to hang on to that feeling and you chase it like mad . . . you're not about to lose it. And the chase is a nightmare. Where you gonna get the money? Because by this time your body can't live without drugs . . . and you need shit just to feel normal, never mind being high. Just feeling normal and not dying becomes your problem. And, you know, like my mother ain't got a cent, right? I can't even steal from her if I wanted to. I'm not smart like you, right? School turns me off. So what's left? Stealing and hustling. All your friends are junkies. You know you never gonna earn enough at no factory or being a salesclerk to support your habit. Because by now, it's taking several hundred dollars a day. A day! That's right. So you steal and you turn a few tricks and then you get yourself a man for protection. A pimp, so you got more rights on the street. Then you got more troubles than you need, right? Because now you got more than one habit to support, right? And there you are, part of that whole life scene, and it's got nothing to do with wanting to sleep with my father, who I never even seen, or some olden Greek times." Yolanda stopped. She realized that Lillian's face was flushed and her cheeks were beet red. "Lillian, I'm sorry. I offended you. Look, I didn't mean it that way."

Lillian turned away and reached into her handbag for a tissue. She blew her nose.

Yolanda reached over and touched Lillian lightly. "Please, Lil . . . it's . . ." A scowl crossed Lillian's face as she looked at Yolanda. Yolanda withdrew her hand. "I said I'm sorry if I offended you. I shouldn't of talked out of turn."

"I'm not offended. It's all right; don't be silly."

"You see, Lil, it's very important to me that you know something. During my worst days, even on the street . . . when I had to—to, well, when it was real bad—and I done things I don't wanna remember, I never, never, I swear to you that in my whole life, I never wanted to go to bed with my father. In fact, I don't remember even any dream like that. Please—please believe me. I ain't sick that way, not like that!"

"Yolanda, yes, of course, but you still don't understand, do you? What—"

"Lil, just answer me one thing. Do you believe me? What I just said. Do you? Just answer me if you believe me, that's all."

They looked at each other silently for a moment, then Lillian whispered, "Yes, I believe you."

"Good." Yolanda sighed.

"Here you are, young ladies." Rudi set down the drinks. "You want something else?"

"That's it. Thanks, Rudi. I get the bill."

"Just pay me when you're going out." The door opened. "Here they come." Rudi greeted his customers. "I got some delicious carne guisada con papitas tonight, just cooked fresh." He pushed his blue-plate special before taking orders.

The luncheonette was beginning to fill up with customers. The counter was almost full and the three tiny booths were occupied. A young woman walked out of the back kitchen and began to work at the grill. She worked rapidly, trying to fill the orders almost as quickly as she got them.

"Who's she?"

"Oh, you don't know her. That's Lali, Rudi's new wife. He brought her back with him from Puerto Rico, less than a year ago, I think."

"She's so young." Yolanda whistled softly. "How about that horny old goat!"

"Isn't that something? You know he went to P.R. to get a wife, don't you? Because he knew he's not gonna find nothing like that here, right? My mother says he works her to death. You know, they could use some more help here with the business he's got, but . . ." Lillian shrugged. "Poor Lali, she's a little *jibarita,* a hick, from the mountains, so I guess to her this is living."

The door opened and Rudi called out.

"Hey! Chiquitín, come on, *bendito.* You're late. Let's go."

William hurried by. He smiled and greeted Lillian. His shoulders brushed past the edge of their table.

"Who the hell is that?" Yolanda looked astonished after William.

"Oh, that's right, you don't know him either. Well, he's Old Mary's son, from the building next door. You know, Old Mary?"

"Yeah. She's still hitting the beer, I bet. Really? He's her son?"

"He came from Puerto Rico a few months ago to live with his mother. His name is William, but everyone calls him Chiquitín . . . on account of, well, his size . . . you know, he's so tiny."

"I can see why, wow! He's a dwarf, ain't he?"

Lillian nodded.

"But he's really nice, you know, like anybody else. He works here at night, part-time, for Rudi."

"Far out! Weird." Yolanda shook her head. "How old is he?"

"I don't know, but he don't look all that young. He must be like around thirty."

"What does he do, I mean besides work?"

"I don't know too much about him. I see him around. My mother says that he's trying to learn English. Taking a course at the high school or something. He works with Ramón, Old Mary's husband. He helps out on the truck. They say he's very strong."

"Yeah, he's got some shoulders. Beautiful hair too. It's so golden. I wish I had hair that color."

"Me too."

William walked over to their table and began to stack the dirty dishes in a large plastic basin he carried. His blue workshirt fit snugly around his shoulders. The sleeves had been cut, and his well-developed biceps bulged out, exposing a large tattoo on his left arm, just above the elbow, and a smaller tattoo on his right forearm. The large tattoo showed a colorful butterfly and the word MOTHER inscribed in each wing. The smaller tattoo was a decal of the Puerto Rican flag with the words MI PATRIA printed boldly underneath.

"*Acabaron?* Finish?" he asked, smiling.

"Sure." Yolanda took a cigarette and held it out to William. "Smoke? Go on, take it."

"Later—*después,* after work—yo—me smoke." He put the cigarette in his shirt pocket. "*Gracias,* thank you." He smiled.

"Hey, it's okay. You're welcome. Enjoy it." Yolanda smiled and nodded as she watched him clear away the dishes and carry the large basin back into the kitchen.

"I told you he's nice."

"Man, I think I got problems and then I look at him." She shivered slightly, as if shaking off a chill. "Anyway, he ain't afraid to smoke and stunt his growth."

They laughed out loud.

"Shh . . . ," Lillian said, unable to stop laughing. Yolanda would stop laughing and then look at Lillian and they would begin to giggle again. They remembered how they used to laugh this way in school. It was as if they had a private joke no one else knew about, and when they looked at each other, only they could know how funny it was. After a while they stopped laughing and were silent.

The luncheonette was bustling with customers. Rudi hurried in and out behind the counter, serving and working the cash register. He called the orders to Lali in Spanish. She worked without interruption, as if she didn't hear him. The jukebox played a loud rock ballad.

"I gotta split, Lillian. I got me a date tonight."

"Yolanda, where are you staying? At your mother's? You didn't tell me."

"Well, right now I am with my mother, but she's got more problems than me. Like it's still the same there, so I don't know how long I'm gonna stay. Besides, I'd rather be on my own. I'm looking for a place around here on the Lower East Side. You know, I'm used to it here and I got friends here. My probation officer is a pretty nice woman; she's trying to get me into a school-work program. This way I can make some bread. You know, under one of the antipoverty programs. And, like I told her, I been a poverty program all my life, right? So what else is new?"

Lillian laughed. "You're still the same Yolanda. Listen, come to see us, okay? You haven't been up to my house for a long time."

"Yeah, sure."

"I mean it. I know, you think my mother would mind, but you're wrong. She knows I'm seeing you tonight and it's cool. Honest. Besides, we're the same age, you know. I'm not a baby."

"I dig. Lil, thanks."

They stood up. Yolanda paid the bill.

"Okay, Yolanda, you take it easy?" Rudi handed her the change. "The fast life slowed you up, eh?"

"That's right, Rudi. I slowed up, and you"—Yolanda gestured toward Lali—"started making double time."

"*Bueno,* I gotta do the best I can, eh? For an old guy, *me defiendo!* I'm holding my own."

"Take it easy, Rudi, you know what they say about old dogs learning new tricks." Yolanda winked at him.

"Don't worry about this old dog." Rudi laughed. "Ave María, Yolanda, you still the same, eh? *Mira,* take care of yourself. It's good to see you back looking so good."

"It's good to be back."

"Take care . . ."

"I'm trying, Rudi. I'm doing my best."

Outside it was cold and windy.

Yolanda leaned over and put her arms around Lillian.

"You're still my ace, girl. Keep on being smart and stay in school."

Abruptly she turned and walked by the old orange cat sitting at the curb near the garbage cans.

Yolanda stopped for an instant and chuckled.

"You still around, eh? You old mother . . ."

The old cat blinked as it watched her dart across the street.

Lillian looked after Yolanda until she disappeared around the corner, then she started back home. As she walked she had a desire to run after Yolanda, to tell her once more that she must listen to the doctor; it was for her own good! She stopped for a moment and looked back in Yolanda's direction. Traffic rolled by steadily on the avenue. The head-lights on the cars created bright silhouettes and long shadows in the darkness as they slipped in and out of sight. Lillian reached the stoop steps of her building. She stopped once more, thinking that Yolanda might never call again. This is silly. She'll call, why not? After all, she called tonight, right? I tried to help. I told her how it was. But, yes, Lillian sighed, she already knew Yolanda wouldn't call her. Shrugging, she ran up the steps, feeling, for some reason, and she couldn't figure out why, an enormous sense of relief.

Shabbat Shalom

for Felipe, my brother

Grandma would tell Grandpa that it was 7:45 A.M. when it was really 8:15, so we always arrived at the synagogue halfway through the Saturday morning reading of the haftorah. She did this for us, knowing how little we understood of the service and how bored we were spending Saturday mornings listening to old men praying in Hebrew. Doña Sofia was an obedient wife to her husband, but in the summer, when we spent six weeks with them, there were other priorities: Henry and I should sleep till seven; the chauffeur, Joaquin, was entitled to a *pan francés* and coffee before the Saturday morning synagogue drive. Had Grandpa not been nearly blind, she herself—crippled though she was—would've dragged her bad leg up a ladder to change the time on the clock above the dining room breakfront, just to please us.

Back then, in 1963, the Magen David was the only synagogue in Guatemala. Its entrance on the Septima Avenida was protected by two large bronze lions peering alertly from granite slabs at either side of the entrance gate. When we were younger, while the adults gossiped during the kiddush breakfast after services, we played King of the Mountain on the lions. This was fun until Jaime Sultan flew from one lion to the next, crashed into a paw, and knocked out two teeth.

The synagogue's swinging front door was so heavy that Henry and I had to take a running start to push it open. Once inside, an old and musty blue curtain enveloped us as if to underscore how difficult it was to make any headway with Adonai. The synagogue was huge and airy, the way I imagined a barn to be, only it was painted all white and the sunlight streamed through the two roseate Stars of David on its eastern flank, drenching the marble floor in a swirl of color. Immediately to the right of the entrance was the small women's section and beyond, on both sides of the bimah, sat the men. Each family had its assigned seats, identified by bronze plaques, which the elders insisted had to be purchased.

These seats were hard, like the benches for the mourners who sat shiva for the dead. Believe me, after three hours of almost nonstop Hebrew, our young little *tuches* were sore.

Services, like the last weeks of school, were interminable. Henry and I actually believed that the old men plotted to extend the prayers, just to test the limit of our patience. We couldn't read Hebrew, so we stared blankly for hours at the prayer book our grandfather had memorized before losing his sight. Whenever don Samuel stood up, we stood up; when he sat back down, so did we. Don Samuel was a serious Jew: he smoked like a fiend, but never on Saturdays, no matter how deeply the desire burned within him.

When it was his turn to read from the bimah, Henry and I proudly escorted him up the steps and remained standing loyally at his side till he had finished reciting the prayers. Our only other exercise was when Alfredo Cohen carried the Torah from the bimah back to the ark and we could move out of our seats and kiss the sacred scrolls with the *tzitzits* of our *talet*.

Haham Musan, a tubular man with a growth the size of a peach pit on his forehead, was the spiritual leader of our congregation. His tongue slipped in and out of his mouth a hundred times during the service, which he conducted in a dictatorial manner, even though he was not an officially ordained rabbi. He was the one who decided who could read from the Torah and for how long, and this, we suspected, was determined by the size of the contribution to the synagogue. The Haham's wife was equally controlling, deciding when and where the women's teas and card games would be held. She was also memorable, at least to us, since we swore she ruled the women's auxiliary because her breasts were so much bigger than those of the other women. Henry and I noticed these things: without exaggeration, each breast was the size of Alfredo Cohen's head.

The Haham's sermon was always delivered in Spanish, which one might expect would have been more interesting to us, since we at least understood the language. Wrong. First of all, he always began by castigating those Jews who opened their stores on Saturday morning instead of coming to pray. "It says in the Torah that on the seventh day Adonai rested." But his comments were pointless: he was preaching to the converted, to the people who did close up shop. What, did he think Marcos Yarhi would go tell Bernardo Berkowitz that he shouldn't open up his toy store on Saturday? And since Musan sold cloth by the bolt, and Saturday was the best selling day, he would proclaim that commerce was permitted after noon: "God is practical. He wants Jews to succeed, not fail." Then he'd cite a letter he had received in 1948 from Aleppo's chief rabbi backing his theory. Grandpa groaned during this part of the sermon, knowing full well it was another of the Haham's inventions.

Haham Musan's sermons touched on all the major tenets of Judaism: the need to be honest and forthright, the importance of mitzvahs, the sanctity of the covenants and the Ten Commandments, etc., etc., etc.— all delivered in the broadest of terms, without humor or insight. Sometimes he mentioned the Indians, 60 percent of the Guatemalan population, stressing the need to treat them—particularly the maids and the gardeners—with familial care and affection: "We have an obligation to care for their children, to make sure they are healthy and receive a proper education."

Every Saturday Uncle Abie would pop in around 10:00 A.M., before the sermon began, with a wide grin on his face. He'd cover his eyes with his *talet,* chant the blessing out loud, then swing it like a cape around his shoulders. The Haham pretended not to notice, but he would always look to our side of the bimah when Uncle Abie's voice sang the prayers, with such passion that his voice rose to the top of the synagogue's vaulted ceilings. Never mind that his eyes were bloodshot, that he had spent most of Friday night drinking and screwing. And not with his wife, certainly.

After the sermon, he, the repentant Jew, would ceremoniously accompany his father downstairs for breakfast. As soon as he had deposited don Samuel around the kiddush wine cup, he'd go around the breakfast room wishing everyone Shabbat shalom. Then he'd scoop up a few cheese *sambusaks,* walk over to us, and say something along the lines of "Hi, boys. The way everyone's smiling, I think I must have missed one of the Haham's jokes."

And if we shrugged, he'd say, "You mean Musan didn't explain how his wife's breasts got so big?"

He loved to get us laughing.

And if I said something like "We thought you were coming over last night for Shabbat dinner. Grandma made a special *hamad* soup for you," he'd counter with:

"I had some important business to tend to last night."

And if Henry kidded him back by saying, "Yeah, a serious appointment in Puerto Barrios," the smile would disappear from Uncle Abie's lips.

"You boys have no respect," he'd say, his feelings truly hurt.

———

One Saturday in August, Uncle Abie gave each of us five quetzales —five dollars—on the synagogue steps. "So you won't tell your mother that only your Uncle Aaron gives you an allowance."

"Wow, thanks, Uncle Abie," I said, stuffing the bill into my right front pocket. "Uncle Aaron gives us only a quarter each week."

"You don't say," he answered, knowing full well that in one fell swoop he had outdone his brother. "You boys have to remember he also gives allowances to his four children."

"I'm going to spend this at the fair," said Henry, but before he could put the bill away Uncle Abie pinched it. "No gambling, Henry. This money is for food and rides."

"But, Uncle Abie, the rides are for babies—"

"I don't care. It's Shabbat. If I find out you were playing the slots or roulette at the fair, I'll never talk to you again. I mean it!"

"But you yourself—"

"I don't want to discuss it, Henry."

Of course he didn't. It was well known in the Jewish community— Lonia, Aaron's wife, made sure everyone knew—that last year Uncle Abie had spent a week in jail because he had run up a debt of over a thousand quetzales to the fair operators. Uncle Aaron had bailed him out, and rumor had it that this hadn't been the first time. Money, like women, slipped easily through Uncle Abie's fingers. He certainly didn't want any nephew reprobates. Not on Shabbat.

That afternoon, while our grandparents took their siesta, Henry and I stole off to the Hippodrome, where the fair was held. Blocks before even reaching it, still on the bus, our mouths were salivating from the aroma of the cooked food: two-for-a-nickel pork tacos, crisp and covered with tomatoes, and the burritos—Indian tamales wrapped in corn husks. We'd get off the bus on Avenida Simeon Cañas and run to the metal grill arcade that marked the fair's entrance. All around were vendors selling food, all sorts of trinkets, Indian handicrafts, *trenzas de azúcar*—braids of wrapped sweets—sugared fruits, pink doughnuts, and my favorite canillas de leche.

"Let's go to the rifles," said Henry, as we stopped to buy tacos from a vendor. We had gobbled them up, almost without breathing, by the time we reached the rifle stall.

The object of the game was simple: to fire a rifle at hundreds of burned-out light bulbs whose sockets had been wedged between nails on a wooden pegboard. If you hit a bulb with a colored dot on the socket, you'd win a prize. Sometimes we'd walk around to the side of the stalls and spy which sockets were marked, but we never won anything of value.

Henry started firing away, at a nickel a shot. After ten shots all he had to show for his fifty-cent investment was a painted tumbler for hitting a bulb with a yellow dot. I took my turn and came up with a green dot, a plastic magnifying glass.

"Why don't you try to break the string holding up that bottle of wine? It's yours if you break it," said the clerk. The bottle would fall on a cushion of sawdust.

"No way," said Henry. "The sights on these rifles are curved. You couldn't hit a cow in the ass at ten feet. And none of these sockets have any of the decent prizes. All I ever win is a glass."

"What do you know?" asked the clerk.

"I know what I see."

The clerk reached under the counter. "Just yesterday a lady hit this bulb," he said, showing us a socket with a red dot, "and won a Swiss Army knife made in El Salvador. And this morning a policeman won a watch with an authentic metal band. So you better watch what you say. I can call the policeman back to prove it."

Henry could be cocky. "I'm sure that *chonte* is your uncle," he answered, walking away and laughing. "Where to, douche?" he said to me.

"Want to play the gerbil game?" I asked, referring to a game where you had to predict which of twenty cubbyholes a gerbil would enter. In this game the prizes were more substantial: six glasses, a frying pan, or a pewter coffee pot. The operator would release the gerbil at the center of a ring, and the *cuyo* would sniff around till it found a hole it liked. Trick was the operator would choose the gerbil after all the bets were down and he knew which hole—naturally the one with no bets—was its favorite. He would keep changing *cuyos* to throw the public off, but if you stayed and watched long enough, you could figure out which gerbil went where. In this way we had outfitted our grandma's kitchen with pewter pots and pans.

"We don't have time," said Henry. "Let's go play roulette."

"Henry, you heard what Uncle Abie said."

"He's not going to find out unless you squeal on me."

"You know I won't tell him."

"That's my douche."

The roulette wheel was out-and-out gambling. For a quetzal you picked a number, and if the dart landed on it you won thirty quetzales.

There were thirty-six colored numbers in all, and once bets were placed, the wheel was spun and a dart thrown.

"I'll take the eight and twenty-three," said Henry, giving two quetzales to the game clerk, who put blue chips on those numbers.

"That's almost half your money."

"Hey, douche, you don't win unless you gamble. Gonna play?"

I took out a quetzal and picked number fifteen.

About ten more people made bets. Naturally, no one selected the winning number. No one, not even Uncle Abie, had figured out how we were being cheated, though it seemed that the wheel had odd scratches on the cardinal points.

"Dammit," I said.

Henry kicked the stall. "Rigged, man."

"How is it that Uncle Abie won two hundred quetzales the other night?"

"He doesn't play this shitty game. He goes inside the tent to gamble. You have to be eighteen to get in. There they don't cheat—at least Uncle Abie doesn't think so."

"That's why he's such a winner."

It had begun to drizzle. We went over to the covered food area and ordered *atol de elote,* corn porridge topped with kernels. "What are we going to do now?" I asked, blowing in my glass before taking my first sip.

Henry had spent all his money, and I had two quetzales left. "What about the spinning wheel?" he said.

I took a second drink of my *atol.* "I don't want to spend all my money. I thought we could go see *From Russia with Love* at the Reforma."

"Yeah, well, I think we can get money for that from our grandparents. After all, tomorrow is my half-birthday. Let's blow it now."

"Easy for you to say. It's my money."

"Come on, douche, if I had won on the roulette, you know I would've given you some of my winnings."

I drank down the rest of my *atol,* letting the kernels slide whole down my throat. "You always say that after you've lost."

"Danny, you're so selfish."

"I'm not."

"You are."

I shook my head. "It's four o'clock already. Grandpa will be worried sick. Besides, it's raining harder now."

"Don't be such a pussy."

Henry knew just what to say. It was easy enough for me to say no, but whenever he challenged my manhood, I seemed to lose my resistance. I was his trained gerbil.

We went over to the spinning wheel. It was divided into nine parts and was spun flat. Nails separated the colored wedges, each of which had a prize on top: a glass, a penknife, a deck of cards, a bar of soap, a five-quetzal bill, sometimes a comb, and the two top prizes: a bottle of wine and a watch. A feather that flicked against the nails determined the winning color. Once a man had won a watch, and we were convinced he was a confederate of the operator because no matter how many colors we covered, the feather always stopped on the bar of soap.

"What do you want?" asked the game operator as we approached. He had a small face which jerked about nervously. His teeth were small and sharp like a rat's. He wore a short-sleeved white shirt, brown around the collar, that stuck to his skin wherever the raindrops had fallen.

"We want to play," said Henry, wiping the rain from his face with his shirt.

"Both of you?"

"No, just one of us."

"The game's a quetzal a spin."

"That's a lot of money! Last year it cost fifty cents."

"If you can get five other people to play, I'll cut the cost. Otherwise I lose money every time. Or you can wait for more players."

We waited for a minute, but as it was raining hard now, few people were walking about. Henry lost his patience and said to me, "Give him the quetzal or we'll be here all afternoon."

I handed the clerk a quetzal, and he gave the wheel a soft spin. Objects started going around but not so fast that I couldn't see what they were. After three turns the wheel began slowing, and I could see the objects passing by the feather marker. The clerk suddenly rested his hands on the table and looked about disinterestedly.

When the wheel was about to stop, Henry shouted, "The watch, the watch, you've won the watch, douche!"

At that moment the wheel stopped short, on the wedge before the watch: I had won a comb, my fourth of the summer.

"Unbelievable! Henry, I thought I had the watch."

"Damnit, so did I."

The clerk let out a sigh and said, "Nice try, boys. Do you want another turn?"

"Sure," Henry said to the man. Then to me, in English, "Did you see what he did?"

"We lost, Henry."

"He jerked us, man. Didn't you see that after he spun the wheel he put his hands on the table? As it was about to stop on the watch, the fucker pushed down hard and the wheel just stopped. I'm going to get him, watch."

Again we waited for a few seconds, but no one else came to play.

"Last call," shouted the clerk. He then gave the wheel an even spin.

When the clerk put his palms down on the table after two turns, Henry shouted to him, "Take them off, take your hands off."

"Whaat?"

"Don't put your hands on the table!"

"What's wrong with you?"

Henry leaned into the operator. "You press on the table so that the wheel stops where you want it to stop."

"Are you accusing me of cheating?"

"I just want you not to put your hands down."

"—or else we get to put our hands on the table, too," I added.

"Yeah," said Henry, slapping me on the back.

The operator looked at us one at a time. His face was creased like a wet brown paper bag. He threw up his hands and locked them behind him.

The wheel slowed on its own till it stopped on the bottle of wine.

"We won, we won, we won!"

"Luck," the operator whispered, giving us the bottle. "You two fuck off. If you try and come back I'll call the *chontes*. You're too young for this game. And you keep real people from coming to play. Now take your bottle and scat."

Henry and I whooped it up: he with his tumbler and I with my bottle of wine.

"What'll we do with the wine?"

"We'll give it to Grandpa. He can use it for next week's kiddush."

By now it was five o'clock, and we were not only soaked through but an hour late. We took the number-seven bus back home, got off on Sixth Avenue, and rushed home. As we opened the garage door, Uncle Abie pounced on us.

"Where have you two been?" he asked with a knotted brow. "Don Samuel called me to come over, he was so worried about you."

"You knew we went to the fair, Uncle Abie. Here, this is for you," said Henry, giving him my wine bottle.

"You were gambling, weren't you? After I told you not to. You gave me your word of honor and you broke it. On Shabbat."

"We didn't gamble," Henry began.

"Like hell you didn't. You played the slots, roulette. And you won this shitty wine betting on the gerbils—"

"Not the gerbils, the spinning wheel," I said before I could stop myself.

"Aha. And I'm sure you, Henry, were behind Danny."

"I didn't do anything!" he countered, looking at me as if I had just betrayed him.

Uncle Abie whacked us both on the neck. "Go to your rooms and change your clothes. Not only are you two grounded for a week, but I'll never talk to you both ever again."

Henry and I walked away. "You blew it, douche."

"Me? It was your idea, not mine."

"If it hadn't been for me you wouldn't have won anything—"

"Yeah, and we wouldn't have gotten in trouble."

Henry's eyes burned with hurt and anger. "You always blow things, you know that, Danny? You and your fucking big mouth!"

From "Angelitos Negros: A Salsa Ballet"

for Willie Colon

Willie Colon, Composer
Marty Sheller, Conductor

2 trumpets
1 trombone
2 saxophones/alto and baritone
1 bass
1 piano
1 guitar
1 trap drum
1 bongo
1 conga
1 timbalero
6 violins
1 flute and piccolo

PROLOGUE

Good Vibrations Sound Studio,
the date is for three
but we arrive at 2:30 P.M.,
the occasion: the first recording
of Willie Colon's score of "A Salsa Ballet":
the studio is refrigerator cool,
the vibes are mellow,
the rhythm is sleepy slow,
the set is slowly pulling together,
musicians arrive, slapping hands
talking through months of absence
into hugs and tightly held hands,

they are coming together
                    to invent
the sound that Willie
has in his head,
musicians are Willie's brush,
musicians are Willie's sound partners,
today's the day for an orgy of sounds,
today is the day for the birth
of a new latin perception
of sound,
Willie walks around,
four months into his pregnancy,
I see prenatal rhythmic juices pour
out of his pores as notes shoot
pitches of sounds high into the atmosphere,
musicians come together in a holy
trust, the bond of marriage for
a trumpet and a saxophone
is the listening
that they do to one another,
there in the listening,
there is hope.

Taos Pueblo Indians: 700 strong according to Bobby's last census

It costs $1.50 for my van to enter
Taos Pueblo Indian land,
adobe huts, brown tanned Indian red skin
reminding me of brown Nuyorican people,

young Taos Pueblo Indians
ride the back of a pickup truck
with no memories of mustangs
controlled by their naked calves and thighs,
rocky, unpaved roads, red brown dirt,
a stream bridged by wide trunk planks,
young warriors unloading thick trunks
for the village drum makers to work,
tourists bringing the greens,
Indian women fry flour and bake bread,
older men attend curio shops,
the center of the village is a parking lot
into which America's mobile homes
pour in with their air-conditioned cabins, color
TV, fully equipped kitchens, bathrooms
with flushing toilets and showers,
AM & FM quadraphonic stereo sound,
cameras, geiger counters, tents,
hiking boots, fishing gear and mobile telephones,
"restricted" signs are posted round the parking lot
making the final stage for the zoo
where the natives approach selling
American jewelry made in Phoenix
by a foster American Indian from Brooklyn
who runs a missionary profit making turquoise jewelry shop
"Ma, is this clean water?
do the Indians drink out of this water?
is it all right for me to drink it?"
the young white substitute teacher's daughter
wants to drink some Indian water,
young village schoolchildren recognize her,
and in her presence the children snap
quick attentive looks that melt into
"boy am I glad I'm not in school"
gestures as we pass,
but past, past this living room zoo,
out there on that ridge,
over there, over that ridge,
on the other side of that mountain,
is that Indian land too?

are there leaders and governments over that ridge?
does Indian law exist there?
who would the Pueblo Indian send
to a formal state meeting
with the heads of street government,
who would we plan war with?
can we transport arms earmarked for ghetto
warriors, can we construct our street
government constitutions on your land?
when orthodox Jews from Crown Heights
receive arms from Israel in their territorial struggle
with local Brooklyn Blacks,
can we raise your flag
in the Lower East Side
as a sign of our mutual treaty of protection?
"hey you you're not supposed to walk in our water,"
"stay back we're busy making bread,"
these were besides your "restricted zones"
the most authoritative words
spoken by your native tongue,
the girl's worry about the drinking water
made Raúl remove his Brazilian made shoes
from the Pueblo Indian drinking cup,
the old woman's bread warning
froze me dead on the spot
"go buy something in the shop,
you understand me, go buy something,"
I didn't buy I just strolled on by the curio shops
till I came across Bobby the police officer,
taught at Santa Fe, though he could've gone on to Albuquerque,
Taos Pueblo Indians
sending their officers of the law to be trained
in neighboring but foreign cities like in New Mexico
proves that Taos Pueblo Indians
ignore that a soldier belongs to his trainer
that his discipline, his habitual muscle response
belongs to his drill sergeant master:
"our laws are the same as up in town"
too bad Bobby! they could be your laws,
it's your land!

then flashing past as I leave Taos Bobby speeds
toward the reservation in a 1978 GMC van with two red flashers
on top bringing Red Cross survival rations to the Taos Pueblo Indians
respectfully frying bread for tourists
behind their sovereign borders.

Lucky Alley

I never understood why they called this graffiti-scarred alley lucky. Still the same as when I lived here—littered with abandoned shopping carts, broken-spring couches, pools of dirty oil, and a million shards of glass. *Vatos* living in parked cars swigging beer and dealing dope, clouds of black flies buzzing over mounds of garbage, and stray cats under stoops with yellow fear in their eyes. Piss smell so thick in the air, even weeds, sprouting through cracks in the asphalt, look like they want out of this place. At sundown, the hazy light filtering between Victorian-vintage tenements makes even the dust motes seem dangerous, and you know nothing but bad luck is going to happen here.

Going by Lucky Alley always reminds me of Catarino Maraña—drove a pearl white sports car, a '60 Triumph with canvas top. I sold him the top after wrecking my own Triumph. Funny that when I think of other people's bad luck I think of my own. During my bad days I wrecked plenty of cars; the last one, a signal-red TR3, happened one Saturday night when I turned, piss-drunk, into Lucky Alley and never saw the street light step in front of me—I woke up in General Hospital, an intern stitching my forehead like he was mending a sock, leaving this crescent scar to remind me.

I wrecked the Triumph after an all-night celebration drinking shots of tequila with beer chasers. My girlfriend, Alba, had agreed to move into my studio apartment, 25 Lucky Alley. I'd just left her old flat, and her face was the last thing I flashed on before the pinwheel of nausea exploded in my head; then, like in a movie, everything faded to darkness.

Alba is the most beautiful woman in the Mission. She has brows that are charcoal smudges and eyes like a pampas night. She's Argentine, elegant as a pedestal, and can't stand stereotypes—hates tangos, Juan Perón, and the films of Armando Bo and Isabel Sarli. Perón kicked her family out of Argentina, and she's lived her whole life here in La Mission, like everyone else I know. Her main love is films. Always with a

Super-8 camera, she'd film a sparrow's burial if she could. But I'd been into movies way before I met her.

She appeared one day at the Ribeltad Vorden—that place across Precita Park where I tended bar—a red beret cocked over one ear, a light meter around her neck, asking if she could film the poets, locos, revolutionaries, and anarchists who hang out there. Why not? I said, and offered her an Anchor Steam.

She filmed the junkies nodding in the park, the drunken poets reading from up on the little stage, even me, pouring a draft. I got her number before she left and a week later took her to dinner, then a double feature at the New Mission, *El Santo Contra el Medico Asesino* and another one I forget. El Santo, the Mexican wrestler with white mask and tights, *el enmascarado de plata,* in one scene he drives a white Corvette into an alley and about seven thugs jump him. The bad guys attack with two-by-fours, chains, and clubs while El Santo fights back with all his champion wrestler moves, flying kicks and all. Cut to the next scene: El Santo is having dinner at someone's house and you never know how he escaped. We laughed it was so bad.

Later that night we wound up at my studio in Lucky Alley, a couple of blue candles lit for atmosphere. We were fooling around on the mattress when she picked my hand off her breast.

"Would you ever lie to me?"

Her mouth was so beautiful I felt I was in a foreign movie, something by Lina Wertmuller.

"Never," I said, and meant it.

"Not telling is also lying," she said.

My tongue was already dipping into her navel, and her words were lost on me. I grunted what sounded like agreement.

"Good," she said, "because I never forgive a liar."

That's how our affair began.

When I met Alba she was a film student at the Art Institute and worked nights at El Gaucho on Mission Street, serving drinks in a fluffy skirt and low-cut blouse. I could never reconcile to that part of her. In those days Alba wore spike-heeled shoes, red ones, looked like one of those Helmut Newton models, all legs. Would wear them when we made love. Even after everything that's happened between us—the deal with Catarino, and her chasing other men—I can't stop loving her, not even now when things aren't so good for us and there's no art or glory in our lives. She burns steady, just enough and every day; I like to fire up both ends and the middle. I guess our contradictions unite us.

I didn't know Catarino in those days I was wrecking cars, but he lived on Folsom Street, around the corner from Lucky Alley. I met Catarino a few months after my last wreck. I'd gone to the North Beach office of Revolutionary Films, a foreign film distributor, to rent *Mexico, the Frozen Revolution,* about government corruption after the 1910 Revolution. I wanted to impress Alba by starting a Latino film society in the Mission, a *cine* club to bring underground classics like *Memorias de Sub-desarollo* and *Reed-México Insurgente,* something really political, to the barrio, an alternative to the telenovela mentality.

Catarino was sitting in their snazzy offices, at the edge of the front desk, rapping a mile a minute on the phone, a huge orange-and-brown poster of Zapata on a wall behind him. He sported wire-rimmed glasses, a big mustache, the tips waxed and curled to a fine point, and a tie loosely knotted and looped around his neck like a strip of film, or a noose. He cupped the receiver on his thigh to greet me, pushed the glasses back with one finger, then asked the receptionist to send a memo. He set the receiver down while he stuffed an envelope with publicity flyers and explained the hardships of the movie business to me. The problem was cash flow, he said. In three seconds he returned to his phone conversation like I wasn't there. He smoked as he talked, mouthing his words around a cigarette stub like Bogart in *Treasure of the Sierra Madre.* I barely got a word in before he rushed out for a business lunch, telling the receptionist he'd taken a twenty from petty cash.

My father started me on movies. His addiction goes back to the first reels carried on muleback over narrow trails to his small town in Jalisco. At dusk, silent movies on a stretched cotton sheet hung in the open-air plaza, the flickering projector light blinding the fruit bats swooping through the royal palms. Later, in Mexico City, the classic leading men of the golden age of Mexican cinema were his idols, but in particular that scowling film-noir legend, Pedro Armendáriz. My father fashioned his life after those Mexican matinee idols, except he didn't sing or ride a horse. Rigid in his honor, brave around men, courteous to women. That's where I got my code of honor that a man's word is worth his life. And about women—if she leaves you for another man, burn every scrap of her memory like Cortés torching Tenochtitlán. I didn't know any other way. That's how I'd been since that movie with Pedro Armendáriz where María Félix tells him she's been raped by a troop of soldiers, and he responds with utter contempt, "You should have let yourself be killed instead." That was me.

The third *cine* club night at the Precita Community Center some sprockets tore while I was on the phone with Alba; by the time I heard the audience howling, several hundred feet of good film lay piled on the floor like black spaghetti. I refunded the gate to placate the mob. What money was left I used to pay for the damaged film. Somehow it didn't seem right to continue with the *cine* club, so I filed away the idea and chalked it up to experience.

A couple of weeks after the last *cine* club showing, a pearl white Triumph pulled up outside the Ribeltad Vorden. But a Triumph without the top isn't so hot.

Right away I recognized Catarino when he slid up to the long mahogany bar and ordered an Anchor Steam. I said hello, reminded him about our meeting at Revolutionary Films, and slipped him a draught on the house—but hell, I did that for everyone. No one I knew ever went thirsty when I worked the plank.

Catarino's voice was like a rasp file, the words scraped from deep in his chest where the cigarette smoke collected. At thirty-seven, he was fifteen years older than me, he knew plenty about the movie business, and spoke with authority about films, directors, and life. You'd maybe not guess he'd spent ten years in the joint, but he had, for possession of heroin—a kilo and a half. When he told me I wasn't shook by it. Cat, as he liked to be called, never sat still, always moving around the bar, beer in hand, sleek and intense, always ready. I liked that about him. You might call him a hustler—*vivo,* my father would say. Neither would be wrong.

Catarino came from El Paso, where he learned early about girls, *mota,* and Johnny Law. In and out of Texas reform schools, he survived by hustling and dealing. After the ten-year stint in Huntsville picking cotton for the Texas Rangers, he came out to the Coast and settled in the Mission.

I offered him the white canvas top, the only thing I salvaged from the Triumph I wrecked in Lucky Alley. I asked a hundred but took eighty and got fifty, the rest an IOU I still have. That's when I learned Cat was often a little short, light in the wallet, he'd say with a sly smile. Glen, who managed the Ribeltad and was an old friend of Cat's, often let him run up a tab. Glen used to say: Forgive your friends their sins or you'll live a lonely life.

When Revolutionary Films folded, literally went under, Cat started hanging out more often at the Ribeltad. The times when he appeared flush with cash—I never asked where it came from since it wasn't my business—he always paid off his tab and left a nice tip.

One slow night Cat cruised into the Ribeltad and invited me to the storage room. There, among stacked beer cases, he fired up a wheat-paper rolled joint. After a couple of tokes, he laid a pair of tickets on me to a special screening of Les Blank's, *Chulas Fronteras*. "For the free beers, Felix," he said. High on that purple smoke, I figured Cat a *vato* who'd give you the last sip of beer in his mug.

A few nights later Cat dropped in near closing time and helped me shoo out the last customers. I dimmed the bar lights so cruising cop cars wouldn't see us, and, with the bar closed up, we drank free till four in the morning and talked films—Fellini, Herzog, Buñuel. The burning ember of Cat's cigarette reflected in his deep-set, beer-bottle-colored eyes.

This became our ritual. Two, three times a week, Cat would appear around closing time, and after I'd shut down the plank, we'd sit in the dark sharing a pitcher or two of steam beer. One of those nights, well into our third pitcher, I'm not sure which of us had the idea to lease the York Theater on Twenty-fourth Street in the heart of the Mission. The York had been closed for years, but as a kid I'd spent many Saturdays mesmerized in the plush-velvet seats, and during intermission I'd sit back and, looking up at the ceiling, trace every curlicue on the gold-leaf design. To this day, the smell of roasting popcorn conjures up the York Theater and those Saturday afternoons.

At first I wasn't sure, but little by little, night after night, in the empty bar draining pitchers of Anchor Steam with Cat, I started going for the idea. I knew the theater was an architectural gem, and a gala premier featuring the golden age of Mexican cinema, movies like *Los Olvidados, Nosotros los Pobres, La Mujer del Puerto,* would blow everyone away.

Cat located the owner of the York, a guy in Hollywood named Brody. We needed a five-grand deposit for a one-year lease. Cat said he had a thousand, could I raise the rest? I had to think about this. Alba and I had two grand saved for her to finish school, we'd even mentioned getting married. Alba really wanted her degree more than she wanted marriage. But it was something to think about, since my studio in Lucky Alley was tightly crammed. Every Saturday we'd go looking for a bigger flat; we looked at some real dogs and some nice ones we couldn't afford.

Those nights after drinking and talking with Cat, I'd come home to Lucky Alley, my head full of ideas about the York, and I'd lie awake thinking how to tell Alba. I knew already what she'd say. Alba is a practical, food-on-the-table, all-the-bills-paid kind of woman. Like her mother. Don't come to her with get-rich schemes 'cause she'll tell you every reason why they'll fail.

So, I called this one alone—and took the two grand from the savings. It was my money, too, and I figured it'd be better not to give Alba a choice, just present her with the done deal. Glen cosigned for the other two grand from a loan company at 22 percent so we could make the deposit. That was the biggest debt I'd ever had in my life, and when I signed on the dotted line the pen was trembling.

The next day Cat came into the Ribeltad Vorden with ten crisp hundred-dollar bills, and I turned over my share in a white envelope. We called Brody from the bar phone and he agreed to fly in on Saturday to show us the theater and sign the papers. Cat said he'd get a cashier's check for Brody. We toasted to success with a pitcher of Anchor Steam, on the house.

The rest of the week I'm so high I can barely eat. I'm bursting inside to tell Alba, 'cause I want this for her just as much as I want it myself. I know she's tired of waitressing at El Gaucho, tired of the cheap tips and lewd comments. And her negatives piled in boxes. So each night while she's sleeping I'm thinking of running the York, of that moment we throw open the doors for the grand premiere and the house lights dim, the credits come on, and the faces light up. Alba can even show her own films. One of her *cinema vérité* black-and-whites that haunt you days later with their powerful images. That's what film is all about—subliminal messages. Film is also about forgetting, just sitting in a darkened theater losing yourself in those evanescent images, forgetting everything. You should see Alba's Super-8s, very much influenced by Shirley Clarke. They showed one last year at the Roxie, an interview with a woman who'd been waitressing twenty-four years, and they gave her a standing ovation. Alba still talks of making feature films, and she will, but for now she's editing commercials for Channel 5. She hates it, says she wants to do subversive work, not this garbage.

All this happened in the middle of that seven-year drought. Newspapers said the planets were lined up all wrong or something. Winters came dry as parchment, with no rain but a few pissy storms. And summers like tinder, radiators would suddenly blow, and a spark would incite riots. At night, young *cholas* strolled the sidewalks on Twenty-fourth Street in scanty shorts, the half-moon of their *nalgitas* showing, and *vatos* low-riding behind them, tooting "La Cucaracha" on those insane car horns.

And drunken fights at the Ribeltad all the time. Nights so wild I had to use the little bat behind the bar. And gunshots in Lucky Alley and around the corner keeping us up till four in the morning, like all hell wanted to bust loose that summer. I knew things had to change or I'd get my skull cracked one night trying to stop a fight at the Ribeltad or walking home through Lucky Alley.

That's when Alba and I found a flat on Twenty-fourth and San Bruno, next to Tede Wong's Chinese laundry. The walls soaked up gallons of paint and Lysol, but it was our first real place together, big enough for Alba to set up an editing table in a corner of the living room. But at night before sleep crept over us, we'd hear mice loud as horses between the walls.

By the end of that summer I was so worn out with the drunks and the fights at the Ribeltad, I gave up that gig.

After laying the money on Cat, I waited all week, tense as a death row inmate, jumping each time the phone rang. Every glance I stole at Alba tied loops in my stomach.

Alba keeps house so clean you can eat off the floor, but that Thursday night for some reason there's a *cucaracha* poking two thin feelers around the edge of the kitchen table, unsure whether to come out into the light. I had one eye on Alba, one eye on the *cuca,* but I was thinking of Cat.

Finally, like I'd just learned to talk, the words came and I told Alba where I'd put all our money. She thought I was kidding. No, I said, I'm serious as the Ten Commandments. She stared at me like I had burned her negatives and smashed her cameras, her eyes pinpoints of black light. "How could you without telling me?" is what she said. "And if it doesn't work out, can you trust Catarino?"

Trying to hide my doubts, I kept talking about things taking off for us. Then I stopped. She had me pinned with those Argentine eyes of hers, but she wasn't seeing me, she was seeing her dreams slipping away like a boat from the dock.

Then she locked herself in the bedroom and wouldn't open the door, but I could hear her smashing things. The lamp. A framed picture of us when we first met. I slumped in the kitchen, my scar throbbing like an open vein, feeling like I had slept with another woman, or worse, and nothing since has made me feel as bad.

For a long time I stared at the bubbled-up linoleum floor, followed the cracks across the kitchen wall. The sour odors in the woodwork we tried so hard to scrub away seemed to rise up and mock me. When the lousy cockroach finally made a dash across the kitchen table, I put my thumb on it and squashed it into the next world.

Friday morning, the brown egg yolk of the sun tried to break through the dirty industrial haze of the city. Glen, the manager of the Ribeltad, woke me with an urgent call. He wanted to meet at the Hall of Justice on Seventh Street. Something urgent. Wouldn't say what it's about till we're going down the hot, piss-smelling elevator to the morgue. At the mention of Catarino's name, my heart wrinkled up like a balloon without air.

A sheriff, pale as a maggot, led us to a walk-in freezer that smelled of chrome and formaldehyde. He pulled back the white sheet on a corpse laid out on a gurney and there's Cat—dead and naked, one eye closed and one partly open, face and chest a gray, pasty color. Death had stripped away his cool-as-ice look. There's a smudge of gunpowder and a little burn hole on Cat's forehead like the dot on a question mark. Anger, rage, I don't know, made the scar on my forehead want to burst.

Can we identify the body? It's Catarino all right, that's his mustache still waxed and curled, though the tips looked a bit singed. In a monotone voice, the sheriff told us the district attorney would be holding an inquiry, but it was pretty much a routine case. Catarino and a partner were scoring some Mexican heroin, but the deal was a setup, the dealer an undercover narcotics agent.

There wasn't much I could do for Catarino, he seemed at peace, much more at peace than I was. I wondered what movie his eyes were looking at now. *Pobrecito.* Then I thought, why should I feel sorry for him when I have Alba and myself to feel sorry for? Then I got angry, thinking— damn it, Cat, what were you doing? And what about your friends, did you ever think of them? Anger pulled me one way, betrayal another.

We tried to claim the body, but they wouldn't release it till after the autopsy and the inquiry. They did turn over a manila envelope with Catarino's belongings—a wristwatch with a worn leather band, an empty wallet, his wire-rimmed glasses with one lens busted.

Days later, still unable to accept what had gone down, I went to the sixth floor of the city jail to visit Catarino's partner in the deal-gone-bad.

Pablo Damian, on the other side of the glass, was a guy I didn't know, had never seen before. The little mustache in his fat face looked run over by a truck. Bruises still showed from the beating, lots of purple around the bloodshot eyes and a red lump on the jaw.

Damian was up for hard time, so I think he told the truth—why bother lying when you're facing twenty years? This is his story: He and Catarino were scoring a kilo of Mexican tar in Lucky Alley to resell the same day. An easy hundred percent profit, Damian said. I just listened. They came up to a blue car where the connection, a Mexican, was waiting with a paddy guy. Cat, holding the money, leaned in to check out the goods and found a gun pointed at him. Oh, no, Cat said, stepping back from the window. Then the two guys jumped out, guns drawn, no badges, nothing. While the one narco pistol-whipped Damian, Cat scuffled with the Mexican, thinking it was a rip-off. Cat fell, wrestled to the ground, then the narco blasted him in the head, point-blank. And that was that.

What about the money Cat had on him? I asked Damian. Narcos kept it, never turned it in. Only about three hundred appeared as evidence in the report. I don't know why I asked if Cat had ever mentioned the York Theater. *Chale*—not to me, Damian said. That's all I needed to hear. I took the elevator down. Out on the street, not a breeze or leaf stirred, flocks of blackbirds perched on the chestnut trees in front of the city jail like mourners. Walking down Bryant Street, the sky gray as cinders, rage boiled inside me—I wanted to hurl stones at windows and shoot every cop that passed. By the time I reached home I felt worse than a piece of liver thrown to dogs, and I just didn't care anymore about a lot of things.

Life took a turn after that. Alba walked around for days like nothing was the matter, but I could tell she was seething inside.

But the worst was yet to come.

Weeks later, after I'd left the Ribeltad and thought we had healed from this disaster, Alba volunteered as an usher for the San Francisco Film Festival, where she met this Brazilian filmmaker. She wound up serving him as camerawoman, secretary, and lover. When I found out, a great fight exploded between us. I came home one day and her cameras were gone. That's all she took, and she moved to Project Artaud with a girlfriend. What could I do? I slipped deep into darkness and bad dreams. I'd show the film she'd taken of me at the Ribeltad over and over, trying to see what she'd seen, and I couldn't see a damn thing. All I saw were black-and-white images on her little editing machine. Light and darkness. Then just the darkness. And one peek at her red spike-heeled shoes, which I kept under our once-happy bed, and I'd walk around torn up for days. Still, I was glad she wasn't wearing them for the Brazilian.

After the Brazilian dumped her, we ran into each other one night at the Roxie at a showing of *La Hora de los Hornos*. We went out for coffee afterward, and she said she'd never really loved the Brazilian, the affair was just revenge for betraying her. Betraying her how, I asked? By lying to her about the York deal. Too late I remembered her definition of a lie—not telling when you should is also lying—and I saw how I'd killed something between us when I lost that money, something I can't repay or splice back in.

She moved back a week later. I just don't know if she feels the same as before, though she eats and sleeps with me—sometimes I catch her singing to herself in Portuguese, and her eyes focus on my forehead when we're talking. She keeps saying we're so different because we're from opposite ends of the continent. I guess it's only a matter of time, I don't know what else to do. You make peace in your head, but there's a piece of your heart that never heals.

I hadn't thought about Catarino and Lucky Alley in a long time. Usually I take my bus on Potrero—today, for some reason, I walked down Twenty-fourth Street to Mission and passed by the York Theater all boarded up and still dying for affection. This set me thinking how sometimes you work so hard for something, still the results turn out just the opposite. When I came to Lucky Alley I remembered Catarino—I wish I could forgive him, wish I could believe in friendship, honor, and law, but I can't. True, Cat paid the ultimate price—but he also gave me his word with no intention of keeping it. In the barrio a man has only his word, and if his word is no good, he's nothing.

Sometimes, at four, five in the morning, when I've crawled in from the *jale* and have slipped quietly under the blankets not to wake Alba who is toasty next to me, I don't sleep but stare at the striped shadows cast by the venetian blinds on the bedroom wall and listen to the rumbling buses below my window and the occasional whoosh of a car going by— the only sounds in the city—then the welt from that old scar starts pounding on my forehead like a drum with an urgent message, and I think maybe I should have followed up with Brody anyway, tried raising more cash, maybe I quit too soon. Then I figure—hell, the theater's still empty and available, no reason why I can't do it, right? And just before I fall asleep a cozy feeling comes over me and everything seems possible, like the world will spin my way. But the next morning, in the cruel, unforgiving light of day, those dreams burn off like fog.

Today, when I passed by Lucky Alley and started thinking about Catarino and how different my life is now with Alba, who seems to be in a movie of her own, her resentment rich as silver dollars, and how all we do is argue about the bills and that two-thousand-dollar loan that burned my credit forever 'cause I couldn't pay it back, I knew—definitely and forever—I would never open the York Theater. It's all just theory now.

I kept walking to Mission Street and waited for the bus. I don't drive anymore, not since I wrecked in Lucky Alley. I don't drink either, ever since Alba came back; I don't want to fall into *parandas*. I don't miss it 'cept it's hard having to smell it all the time, that's the worst part of my job, the stink of spilled booze and urine. I should look for something else, but for now I work the plank in a downtown bar, the night run, six days a week till two in the morning—doesn't leave much time for the movies.

But I'm not complaining. My love for Alba is something I wouldn't trade for an Oscar. You have to forgive your lovers their sins; how else will you know you love them? It's important to move on, even if it's a half-step at a time. Next year, if we're still together, the plan is for Alba to finish school and get her degree. At last. Then maybe she can get out of Channel 5 and into something she really loves. She's never stopped dreaming of making films, you know, and it would be a shame to waste her talent. We have rolls of her film we look at once in a while. Sometimes I mention kids, having some together, then Alba falls into moods when she won't talk to me, and I know she's brooding about how I betrayed her. That's when I feel like we're in a foreign movie with all the subtitles missing. Even though it's been a long time since we've mentioned Catarino, and we avoid Brazilian movies, you can understand why, I can't help feeling these mistakes have led to our present unhappiness, no matter how hard we try, and have tried, to forget the past.

So on Mission Street the number-14 Mission pulls to the curb and I'm pushed forward by the crowd. I'm in the middle of a mob of high schoolers with their starter jackets, their baseball hats turned backward. They're all laughing, shouting, shoving, and I make some way so this little old lady, looks like your *abuela* in Mexico, can get on with her two hand-held bags. I mean, big deal.

I move to the back of the bus and I'm looking out the graffiti-tagged windows as we go by the New Mission Theater where big red letters on the marquee announce *Corrupción Encadenada* starring Hugo Stiglitz and Patricia Santos, "La Tumbahombres." To me, all these young people are oblivious to the real world. It's like they're waiting for the curtain to rise, the lights to dim, waiting for the credits to start rolling. Life to them is a Saturday night flick, something starring themselves, and they're the hero in a fancy car who gets the girl, or they're dreaming of doing an *ingrata* number, cold-hearted yet they want jewels, a new house, and the leading man, anyway. They're dreaming. They think life is a movie with El Santo waiting in the wings. You can't blame them, you believe what you want to believe. Who wants to hear there's betrayal around every corner, that honor and friendship are lies, that somewhere, someplace, someone's got your name on their knife. But believe me, I know. So watch yourself in Lucky Alley, *carnal*.

Voz de la Gente

I went to the river last night,
sat on a sandbar, cross-legged,
played my drum. My third hour,
tum—tum-tum, I noticed four young boys
waist-high in water, quarter mile down river,
staring at me. Tum—tum-tum. . . .
I stared, tum'd louder, stronger,
pads of my hands stung with each slap
on deerskin drum,
sound radiating ancient tribal rap
into night, an ancient heartbeat.
      Where the shore doglegs
      to the middle of the river,
      group of men and women stood.
Their silhouettes
defined in metallic moonlight,
gleaming in brown murky water.
I slapped harder, faster,
wild weed doctor covering night with my cure,
with *matachines* handstep, slow, then fast,
brown notes smoked and misted
close to sleeping children's lips,
curled in their hair, in adobe houses
along La Vega, Vito Romero road, and Atrisco.
      There would be no tomorrow,
      no mountains, no *llano*,
      no me,
and my drum softened its speech to whisper
sleeping to the shores,
singing us all together.

I heard rattling branches
crackle
as thousands of *la gente* pushed through the bosque,
lining the Río Grande shore.
Standing knee-high in water, crowds swooped
out into the shallows,
drawn by the ancient voice of their beginnings.

            Then I awoke.
And now this morning I run five miles
to Bridge street and back,
the dream clings to my ankles like leg-irons
a prisoner drags, and there is a pain
in the pads of my hands
that will not subside,
                until I play the drum.

Mi Tío Baca el Poeta de Socorro

Antonio Ce De Baca
chiseled on stone chunk gravemarker,
propped against a white wooden cross.
Dust storms faded the birth and death numbers.
Poet de Socorro,
whose poems roused *la gente*
to demand their land rights back,
'til one night—that terrible night,
hooves shook your earthen-floor
one-room adobe, lantern flame
flickered shadowy omens on walls,

and you scrawled across the page,
"*¡Aquí vienen! ¡Aquí vienen!*
Here they come!"
Hooves clawed your front yard,
guns glimmering blue
angrily beating at your door.
                    You rose.
Black boots scurried round four adobe walls,
trampling flower beds.
They burst through the door.
It was a warm night, and carried the scent
of their tobacco, sulphur, and leather.
Faces masked in dusty hankies,
men wearing remnants of Rinche uniforms,
arms pitchforked you out,
where arrogant young boys on horses
held torches and shouted,
"Shoot the Mexican! Shoot him!"
Saliva flew from bits
as horses reared from you,
while red-knuckled recruits held reins tight,
drunkenly pouring whiskey over you,
kicking you up the hill by the yucca,
where you turned, and met the scream
of rifles with your silence.

            Your house still stands.
Black burnt tin covers window openings,
weeds grow on the dirt roof
that leans like an old man's hand
on a cane *viga*. . . .
I walk to the church a mile away,
a prayer on my lips bridges
years of disaster between us.
Maybe things will get better.
Maybe our struggle to speak and be
as we are, will come about.
For now, I drink in your spirit, Antonio,
to nourish me as I descend
into dangerous abysses of the future.

I came here this morning
at 4:30 to walk over my history.
Sat by the yucca, and then imagined you again,
walking up to me
face sour with tortuous hooks
pulling your brow down in wrinkles,
cheeks weary with defeat,
face steady with implacable dignity.
The softness in your brown eyes
said you could take no more.
You will speak with the angels now.
I followed behind you to the church,
your great bulky field-working shoulders
lean forward in haste
as if angels really did await us.
Your remorseful footsteps
in crackly weeds
sound the last time
I will hear and see you. Resolve is engraved
in each step. I want to believe
whatever problems we have, time will take
its course, they'll be endured and consumed.
Church slumps on a hill, somber and elegant.
After you, I firmly pull the solid core door back.
You kneel before La Virgen de Guadalupe,
bloody lips moving slightly,
your great gray head poised in listening,
old jacket perforated with bloody bullet holes.
I close the door, and search the prairie,
considering the words *faith, prayer,* and *forgiveness,*
wishing, like you, I could believe them.

Imagine My Life

One afternoon, as I was editing video footage shot in the village where I spent part of my childhood, my grandmother's face appeared on the monitor, and shock waves of hurt erupted in me. Her image revived the unbearable pain of leaving her when I was a child. I always thought my childhood was savage, beautiful in parts, but mostly full of hurt. Seeing her face, ravaged leather cracked and burned by the sun, her silver, squash-blossom eyes, it came back to me how much she had loved me and how warm and nurturing my childhood had been because of her love.

On the film, her mouth pursed into wrinkles as she said in Spanish, "You ran every day to the railroad, and no matter how we spanked and scolded you, you would run to play on the tracks. You spent so many afternoons there. You loved waving to the caboose engineers, and throwing rocks at the cattle cars to see if you could hit them between the slats. You had a fascination for things that went away, that traveled and came by in a whoosh and then were gone. You wanted to go with them, and it was hard to bring you back, to bring you home, especially after you had seen a train. You wanted to go after those trains, and I was scared when you ran alongside them. Once you threw your rosary on top of one of those flatcars and waved it good-bye. Yes, how you loved things that ran and went on and on."

I didn't remember any of that. It hurt to have forgotten so much, and I wondered why I had imagined my life so destitute and deprived.

My grandmother had an old-world decency. She would offer food first to the guest, offer the best chair, offer whatever the guest lacked: comfort, a bed, change from her penny purse. She would share anything she had, listen in consoling silence for hours, give of herself unstintingly, and pray every night for those less fortunate than she. I would fall asleep to that mumbling drone of prayers, like a Buddhist monastery chant. They calmed me and I fell into tranquil dreams.

My grandmother's face has a powerful dignity, like that of an old female eagle on a craggy peak, whose world is eternal. Her gestures are restrained, tentative and soft, as if the world around her, the innocent earth and flowers, were a child easily bruised. Her silence is sunlight sparkling in a freshwater snowmelt stream.

The memories of her suffering, evoked by those film images, were too much for me. I stopped the monitor, pulled on my oilskin jacket, and left the house. As I walked, a dark remorse brimmed in me. If I had not left our village, if I had stayed all these years with her, I could have learned from her; I could have been a better man than I am today. My life seemed to me a fool's jig of drunken jesters dancing for the deaf and blind. I fled from her face because it was too strong a telling of undeserved suffering. As I thought these things, my rage burst out in savage sounds of grief.

Those who cannot see might take my grandmother's kindness and caring for weakness. She has lived with hunger—beans, tortillas, and chile her daily bread; worn frayed and faded clothes, mended a thousand times over. Yet never has she extended her hands for help, those hands always reaching to help others. For more than eighty-five years she has risen before daybreak to prepare the breakfast for her family. Her meals are offerings of the highest graces from her heart—food like spring flowers, to those who know how to savor the fragrant scents of fermenting earth and the magic of dew and sunlight. Her aged body is bent as if in perpetual homage to the earth. Those aspects of goodness that she embodies—truth, kindness, giving, and compassion—are virtues of high wisdom that the hurrying world derides.

I wish I had sat with her longer to listen to the stories of the history of our people that she carried inside her frail rib cage as a morning dove carries the song that awakens dreamers to the dawn. On rare visits after I left home, we would sit in her kitchen, happy to be together, and I would make her laugh, so hard she would cry, at my *vato loco* jokes, pulling her handkerchief from her sleeve and dabbing her wrinkled cheeks. She loved my wordplay. To her I was still the little boy who obeyed no one, who after getting spanked would rush to a grown-up's knees and hug them, who needed to be loved and was afraid to love. I was still the angel who tripped over his wings and loved running more than being still and good, who loved laughter and men's conversations in bars more than prayers in church.

When I would tell her how difficult it was to pay my bills, she would smile gently and say, "Poverty in the pockets brims riches in the imagination, that's why you are a poet."

Those images of my grandmother's anguished face impacted the deepest reserves of my feelings and made me understand the misery of her life as something criminal. How distant she is from my world, how much truer and more sustained is her world in grounded work of the spirit. As I mourned the distance, it seemed as if my life, a boat halfway across the lake, was capsizing.

Yet as a child I had lived in her world and drawn from her spirit, the mirror that gave me my face. When I was near her, I too was gentle and caring, and raucous with joy as a yearling colt cavorting on canyon slab rocks, outrunning the wind. With gusto and reverence, I lapped up hot chile and bean soup, slurped the goat's milk that fed my young strength. Leaping up from the table, I would roll on the ground, intoxicated with laughter.

In those early days, I used to watch the men of our barrio build adobe and clapboard houses for neighbors, how their hands worked the earth with love, with such dignified attention to their tasks. The rigors of life were themselves occasions of praise for the sustaining life force that allowed us to breathe and wake and work. Work became a celebration of hands, of fingers that could move and bend, grip and push. Intelligence, wood, mud, voice, eye, were all precious, all gifts, but laughter was the highest gift, and courage and endurance. When the men worked there was much laughter, but long spells of silence, too, before the talk would start up again, so quietly. They did with words what Bach could do with musical notes: they composed the most beautiful improvised poems from everyday talk. And, as I listened, the red seed of my young heart took root and blossomed under the prairie moon.

These men always followed careful pathways through their days, following ways where they would not be obstructed, avoiding foreigners who might question them or block their passage. They refused promotions that would compromise their cultural values, preferring to work with friends and earn less than to work with strangers at a higher status and wage. Work of the hands, with the earth, was to them holy work, good for the spirit, that allowed a man to feel his life lived on earth was shared with others. And there is much good to say about leaving your house at dawn, in your trusty jacket, and breathing in the cold air, walking down a familiar path to meet friends who wait for you, noticing the changes in the fields around you, and feeling the rising sun on your cheeks and brow.

It was a mythic life they lived. Yet these gentle heroes were regarded as ignorant and vicious by those who did not know their hearts. Outsiders provoked them to fight to enhance their own machismo. They treated these kind men as if they were knife-carrying savages, every one, against whom you had to strike the first blow. When they came around looking for trouble, or arrogant tourists snooped around our yard, my uncles would ask them politely to leave. But then, if they still hung around, treating the place as if it was their own, my uncles would get angry. Without a word they would lift these intruders off the ground and toss them into the pickup bed, or drag them out of the yard by the collar and throw them in the dirt road.

The time came for me to leave the pueblo and go to school. There I learned hard lessons not to be found in books. The Anglo boys mocked me and hurled insults at me. I felt ashamed and lowered my head, trying to hide my face. When they beat me up they were heroes; but when I struck back, defending myself and knocking them down, I got the name of troublemaker. Their blows boosted their self-esteem, while, for a time, my defenseless silence assured my survival.

Looking at the monitor, hearing my grandmother talk and seeing her gestures, brought back to me what I had lost. Because I was too fragile and sensitive to endure the abuse, eventually I struck back. And, in so doing, I lost the inner balance of my elders, rejecting their wisdom and becoming lost to their ways.

At first I withdrew into silence, searching out others like me, brown children from rural towns whose confidence had been crushed; outsiders, unwanted, scorned, and condemned to lives of servitude. But later I rebelled, refusing to do anything I was told to do. Yet fighting was against my deepest instincts. When I raised a fist, my other hand stretched out, pleading for peace. I was caught in a conflict not of my making that squeezed from me every drop of my childhood's sweetness.

I soon realized that, to many, I was just a *mestizo* boy destined for a life of hard work in the fields or mines, and nothing more. But that was a judgment I couldn't accept. Knowing no other way to refuse, I found myself falling into the dark worlds where the winos and ex-cons live, a gypsy child in the urban wasteland, hanging under neon lights and on hopeless street corners. I began to drink and take drugs.

I was becoming what society told me I was—prone to drugs and alcohol, unable to control my own life, needing a master to order my affairs, unworthy of opportunity and justice—a senseless beast of labor. I drugged my pain and drowned my self-hatred in drink, seeking oblivion. I had no future, no plans, no destiny, no regard for my life; I was free-falling into bottomless despair. Death seemed the only way out.

Finally, I found myself hoping for death in a fight with the police or the Anglos; or that a security guard would shoot me when I tried to rob his building. Or that one night while driving my car I'd be so high I would sail off a cliff and explode in a rage of bursting petroleum and gnarled iron, my misery ending in a smoldering, lifeless mound of pulverized bone and burning flesh at the bottom of a canyon.

Now I had become the coauthor, with society, of my own oppression. The system that wanted to destroy me had taught me self-destruction. I had become my own jailer and racist judge, my own brutal policeman. I was ruthless to myself and murdered all my hopes and dreams. I was in hell.

They told me I was violent and I became violent, they told me I was ignorant and I feigned ignorance. It was taken for granted I would work for slave rations at the most foul and filthy jobs, and I did. It was taken for granted I could not resolve my own problems, and I relinquished control of my life to society's masters.

I was still young, a teenager, tormented because none of what I did was who I was. I was screaming for release, I was afraid. My dreams for a good life, a life I would make for myself, had been strangled at birth or were stillborn.

They sent me to prison for drug possession. And there, out of suffering, I found a reprieve from my chaos, found language, and it led me back to the teachings and conduct of my elders. I discovered a reason for living, for breathing, and I could love myself again, trust again what my heart dreamed and find the strength to pursue those dreams.

Language has the power to transform, to strip you of what is not truly yourself. In language I have burned my old selves and improvised myself into a new being. Language has fertilized the womb of my soul with embryos of new being.

When I left prison, I went to see my sister, who showed me photographs of a teenager leaning against a Studebaker, his foot on the bumper, a bottle of wine in his hand. In the background a park, mildly subdued in afternoon sunlight. It was me, my sister said, at Highland Park. I remember my amazement and pain that I had no recollection of ever being this person I was looking at.

The mistral singer I am, whose hand-clapping, heel-kicking love dances celebrate every living moment, has always found it hard to go back home. The place of humble origins exposes the illusions of my life. My loss thunders with fountains of memories, and I want to reach out to the paths, the alleys, the leaning fences, the adobe bricks, the ground, and kiss them all, rub my face in the grass and inhale the sweet earth and mesquite fragrance of my innocence.

Going back, there is so much hurt to overcome.

Recently, I visited our village again. My grandmother's house there is a very lonely house, filled with spirit shadows, spiritual presences, lingering echoes of ancient drumbeats. In the yard, the golden yield of spring in all its millions of shoots is evocations of the returning dead, breaking dirt to smell and taste and bathe again in the warm sunlight.

My grandmother is hunchbacked and disfigured now with age, a bronzed anchor, her hooked fingers refusing to loosen their grip on the *llano*. Her wrinkles are encrusted watermarks on canyon walls, telling of almost a century of living. So many years after her birth, she still stands in her back doorway to welcome friends.

Pools of silence float in the rooms where her children, my uncles and aunts, once lived. People were born and grew up there and went away, leaving their spirit prints on the air. There is something in quiet rooms where old grandfathers and grandmothers have lived and died that vibrates with sanctity. Some of these presences do not want something to be touched or revealed. Others want something to be remembered. These spirits mourn lives filled with struggle, pain, solitude, and love, mourn the moments when they felt truly one with all earth and all people. And now there is empty space, the great vertigo of nothingness, of chairs and beds, rugs and old photos, and curtains and wood and windows falling into a meaningless abyss of motionless silence.

So few things make sense to me. I have lived on the dark side of life so long, nosing my way into patches of rotting life to find my answers; the side of life where I wear my coat without sleeves, where sometimes I wake up in the morning and shave only one side of my face, where I wear a hat with a brim and no crown. I furnish my life with what I can find on the road or in trash cans—books, chairs, and shoes that have known other lives, picked up by the waysides on my journey. I am fool and king, genius and imbecile, for this is what it is to be a poet. In my poems, whatever has been crippled in me, my hope and love and trust and endurance, rises again in spume of fire, unleashing bird wings and jungle howls. My poems beckon those who are dry into the rain, those without love into lovers' beds, call those who are silent to cry out and moan in revery.

Who can say why one day I take my shotgun and shoot the newspaper, bits of paper floating on the air as the little dog whines and scampers for cover? The poor telephone rings, and it, too, goes up in an explosion of black plastic pieces, and I am howling and laughing. The next thing I know, I am sitting cross-legged in a tepee under a pine tree in the forest off South 14, fasting and meditating. This to me is normal.

How can I contain this violent bursting of canoes that white-water in my blood and vault into the world laden with songs and flowers? Such joy will not be confined in prisons of nine-to-five. There is too much life and too much flint in my blood, and the crazy and wild light in a boy's eyes, the innocence in a small girl's whisper need all my life to tell and to praise.

And so my grandmother. How her image hit me with a jolt of lightning, and how her way of living, so different from mine, makes so much sense to me now, and I understand her gift to me. In her presence I can be anyone. I am a scuttling lizard scurrying from tin can to tin can, under boards, into weeds; then I jerk my praying mantis head and my right eyeball stares in one direction while my left eyeball swivels askance. My heart is a cow's tongue slowly licking a block of ice. My legs want to catch the train the way a cat catches a mouse in the cupboards. I flick on the light in the midnight of my life, and cockroaches skitter everywhere on these pages, on the fingers of the reader, along the woman's dress, up the man's arm and neck and into his nose, to nest in his heart that touches the life around him with cockroach antennae, testing the floors in filthy housing projects. In the French Quarter, I am that woman at the table by a window drinking her cappuccino, her suffering concentrated in her ankles like cold iron anvils pounded with sledgehammers, her life a red-hot iron sizzling in a bucket of black water.

And on the Lower East Side, down a dingy street, in crack dealer alleys, I howl and mutter in unknown sacred tongues. In a small mountain town in Arkansas, I am the woman screaming because her parakeet got stuck under the refrigerator and died, green shit smearing his once-sleek feathers. I am the field worker in south Texas whose showered-off dirt forms the image of Christ's face on the floor of the stall. Thousands of people arrive to pay homage to the miracle, kneeling with candles and rosaries, cripples crowding the bathroom with their crutches and braces and bottles of pills, it's a sanctuary; while the president's son in the Rose Garden snares a butterfly into his net and rips off its wings. Some day he will command great armies.

———

A poet in the forests of the Sangre de Cristo Mountains stares at a placid pond frozen over with crust ice, where a bluebird flits across the steamy, cold fog simmering off the surface. And I walk out and take off my clothes and start to sing and flowers appear on the air, blue and red and green and yellow flowers, and the ice cracks and fish spin in glittering swirls and catch the flowers. And in other places millions of things are happening, equally absurd, equally heartbreaking and marvelous. How incredible our life is! How much there is that we do not understand. How honorable and full of heart has been my grandmother's life.

My grandmother does not understand what a Chicano is. She does not read newspapers, listen to radios, watch TV. Her life is lived elsewhere: thirty years meditating on the pebbles in her yard, fifty years smelling the dawn, eighty years listening to the silence at dusk, ninety years waiting for the two hummingbirds that come each spring to her unpainted picket fence—if they arrive she will live another year to await their arrival again. Forgiveness rises in her heart as she watches them whirr around the yard and hum at her screen door. She understands how they are truly flowers given wings and a beak, and how she is truly an old female turtle lumbering on wide, wrinkled footpads, raising her head with the millennial slowness of a diamond forming in the coal mines of dark years, ocean moaning in her blood vessels, returning home. While the image of a young boy chasing a train visits her, a boy as new as a just-hatched baby turtle, stumbling toward the ocean for the very first time.

BENJAMIN ALIRE SÁENZ

I Want to Write an American Poem

ON BEING A CHICANO POET IN
POST-COLUMBIAN AMERICA

There is no "degree zero" of culture, just as there is no "degree zero" of history.
—EDUARDO GALEANO

I

In the world of late-twentieth-century postcolonial, postdeconstruction-ist, postmodern American letters, I occupy an unenviable, liminal space both as a poet and as a Chicano. "Poet" is a difficult role for anyone to play, especially in an era where the possibility of meaning has been thrown into question. What does being a poet "mean" in an age when words and concrete, sensible realities abide in separate worlds?

Untrained in the academy when the idea of writing occurred to me, I naively began with the simple premise that I was going to represent aspects of my culture that were all but absent in the literature to which I was exposed. When I began writing, I implicitly believed that (1) I could legitimately "represent" some of the "realities" of Chicano culture, and (2) that writing necessarily had a social and moral function. But through my experiences in the educational institutions of this country—from El Paso to Iowa to Stanford—I became aware of the literary traditions that I would be measured against, and I began to suspect that everything that had ever been written could and would be used against me.

It is impossible for me to apply the word "poet" to myself without wincing. I become embarrassed. I put my hands in my pockets and look down at the ground as if I have stolen something that does not belong to me. "Poet" is a difficult role for anyone to play, especially someone who was not trained to play the part. (Some people grow up with a tremendous sense of entitlement; others do not. I belong to the latter group, whose psychology was formed in part by race and class—issues we find troubling to speak about in this country because race and class differences are not supposed to exist.) "Poet" brings with it too many expectations of high culture and/or academic traditions—poet as maker, poet as prophet, poet as the literary personage par excellence, poet as "unacknowledged legislator of the world"—expectations that will always be foreign property. You can take the boy out of his neighborhood, but you cannot take the neighborhood out of the boy, and in my neighborhood, the great literature of the world was not something that any of us aspired to write—it was not even something we aspired to read.

I may not always know what I am, but I know what I am not: I am not an Ovid; I am not an Alexander Pope; I am not a T. S. Eliot; I am not an Emily Dickinson; I am not a Gertrude Stein. I do not feel myself to be a true heir to Walt Whitman, to William Carlos Williams, to Ezra Pound, to W. H. Auden, to Wallace Stevens. I do not feel that I have inherited the literary traditions of García Lorca, of Pablo Neruda, of Octavio Paz, of Rosario Castallenos. Am I an heir, then, to the indigenous writings of the Aztecs and the Mayans? Can I rightfully claim the *Popol Vuh* as mine? The *Chilam Balam*? Do the writings, oral traditions, and myths of the North American Indians properly belong *to me*? What can I legitimately, morally, and honestly claim? The ancient Greeks? In short, who are my forefathers and foremothers? Whose son am I? What is my genealogy?

But if I wear the garb of "Poet" uncomfortably—like an ill-fitting oxford shirt—then I wear the robe "Chicano" quite differently. If I am uneasy about making large claims as to my literary identity and lineage, then I am in no such uncertainty when it comes to my cultural identity. Chicano is a realm where I live comfortably (which is not to say painlessly). Chicano is skin: you can touch it, can smell it. The skin sweats. The skin has known work, has been scarred, and it will keep sweating, keep working far into another century. Chicano: 64 percent will not graduate from high school, will keep working, will keep sweating. Chicano works at Burger King in Palo Alto—Chicano is service economy. Chicana is maid. Chicana is farm worker. Chicano is janitor. Chicano is *corrido*:

> *Ya mataron a Cortez,*
> *Ya se acabo la cuestion,*
> *La pobre de su familia,*
> *La lleva en el corazon.*

But Chicano is not opera. Chicano dies—it is not tragedy: Chicano is not Achilles, is not Hamlet, is not King Lear, does not have far to fall, cannot be measured by *The Poetics*. Chicano is trickster; Chicano is coyote. Chicano sings: *sin musica no hay vida, sin musica no hay vida*. Chicana is neither Mexican nor North American, but Chicana is both. Chicana is neither truly European nor truly Indian. Chicana is conquered. Chicana is exile. Chicana is desert. Chicana is Rachel grieving for the thousands who are no more, who had no names, the cannon fodder, the grape pickers, the imported *brazeros* who came to farm during World War II, but were deported soon as the war was over. Chicana is Magdalena at the tomb rolling back the stone with her rough bare hands demanding to know where they have taken her dead. *Where have they taken my dead?* It is a scream, a lament, a demand. No answer is given. Chicano is child: product of a violent fuck. European desire meets savage, indigenous, noble Eve. Chicano is incarnation of rape. In turn, he rapes. In turn, he is raped. Chicano is macho, but Chicano is feminized. Chicano is not Puritan, does not keep the words of Jonathan Edwards in his books. Chicana finds herself in the image of Guadalupe, in the paintings of Frida Kahlo and Remedios Varo, in the altars she builds in her house. Chicano speaks impurely, makes up words. They call what he speaks "Tex-Mex," "Calo," "Code Switching." Defenders of the pure call it corrupted, call it corrupting. Chicano corrupts the integrity of the Spanish language. Chicano corrupts the integrity of the English language. Chicana's integrity is this: she has no respect for borders. She knows why borders are there.

II

Several years ago, the Russian poet Joseph Brodsky came to visit our writing workshop at Stanford. When it came time to discuss the poem I had written, he remarked that my poem was the "most regrettable of the lot." One of the pieces of advice he gave me was to keep foreign languages out of my poems, since I was working in an "English tradition." (I had used a childhood poem rendered in Spanish, since Spanish was the predominant language of my childhood.) He later went on to recite a poem with a Latin phrase in it. What Mr. Brodsky was objecting to was not my use of a foreign language per se, but my use of Spanish—a language that has not traditionally held an esteemed place in American letters— unlike Latin, Greek, and French. Clearly, in the "English tradition," some languages are more foreign than others. Mr. Brodsky also warned me about expressing my politics via my poetry. As it turns out, I came to the same conclusion as Brodsky regarding my poem—I eventually threw it out. But I have since spent a great deal of time pondering Brodsky's attitudes toward American "poetics" (if that is what they are). Brodsky assumes that an American poet is *necessarily and by definition* working in the Anglo-American tradition. It never occurred to Brodsky that there are many literary and cultural traditions that coexist in America, and not every poet who writes "in English" is necessarily enamored of the Anglo-American tradition. Brodsky's attitude suggests that I set aside my culture, my working-class roots, and my bilingual heritage if I wish to be an American poet.

Brodsky asks the impossible. I cling to my culture because it is my memory—and what is a poet without memory? I cling to my culture because it is my skin, because it is my heart, because it is my voice, because it breathes my mother's mother's mother into me. My culture is the genesis and the center of my writing—the most authentic space I have to write from. I am blind without the lenses of my culture. Robert Frost's New England is not even a remote possibility for me, nor is Pablo Neruda's Isla Negra. Paterson, New Jersey, was no Paris, but it was a big enough place to give William Carlos Williams his wonderful and particular vision of the world—but Paterson is not my city. What I have is a desert—and it is all I have—and it is a big enough place to write from for a lifetime. Like every poet, I would like to be read and appreciated—and not just by other Chicanos. By refusing to write out of any other space, I run the risk of being labeled nothing more than an "ethnic writer"—applauded by some for no other reason than my "ethnicity" and held in contempt by others for the same reason.

This is the truth of the matter: I have no choice. I cannot write out of a white space, and this for the obvious reason that I am not white. It is true that my writing wears a sign: THIS POEM WAS WRITTEN BY A CHICANO, but it is also true that almost everything I read also wears a sign that ANNOUNCES ITS AUTHOR'S CULTURE, GENDER, AND CLASS. Robert Lowell's poetry is filled with his very male obsessions, his Yankee history, his Catholic/Puritan angst, his academic, formal training—none of these qualities validates or invalidates his poetry. Every writer has his obsessions, and there are very real personal, psychological, historical, and political backgrounds for those obsessions. My particular obsession is my culture—a culture less familiar to most audiences in the United States than Robert Lowell's, but no less "American." Often, people do not read Chicano, Native American, or African-American poets because they are not interested in "ethnic" subject matters. But, as a Chicano, I do not read non-Chicano poets merely because I am necessarily enamored of the cultures from which they come and which they represent, but because I am interested in learning about the different poetic traditions that form and inform the broader culture around me. If Wallace Stevens's formal verse is complex and formidable, is it honest to dismiss the poetry of Langston Hughes because it fails to meet Stevens's poetics? Hughes himself once said, "I believe that poetry should be direct, comprehensible, and the epitome of simplicity"—a far different goal from Stevens's—a goal I find completely genuine and admirable. Hughes attempted to develop a poetics that was based on the music and life of black culture—a poetry that included his own people as part of the audience for his work. He could not afford to ignore the racism confronting the circumstances of his people. This very knowledge became a part of his aesthetic. Hughes's position in society (a position defined by his "blackness") became central to his poetics, just as Stevens's position in *his* culture was central to his formation as a poet. Like Stevens and Hughes, I too have a particular position vis-à-vis American culture, and it would be impossible to escape this position, even if I wanted to. I've learned to embrace the space out of which I write. It is a curse. But it is also a blessing.

III

I write to document what has largely remained undocumented, under-represented, and misrepresented in American literature. I write a poetry of witness. This does not mean that I consider myself to be *the* voice of the Chicano experience—this would not only be egotistical, it would be impossible. We are not a homogeneous people. All one need do is read a sampling of Chicano and Chicana poetry to realize how very diverse we are. There is no such thing as the Chicano voice: there are only Chicano and Chicana voic*es*. The definitive Chicano writer does not exist, and never will exist. The more Chicana and Chicano writers there are, the better chance outsiders will have to gain fuller, broader, and deeper insights into our culture, and history. I am but one of many voices that seek to bear witness to a history that has remained hidden. What I write out of is my own particular and historical experiences, my own particular psychology, my own particular vocabulary.

   I do not know how important my work is. I only know that it is important to me. I certainly do not write because I am convinced that my work is indispensable to American letters. To me, this would be ridiculous. Aesthetically speaking, I am not likely to threaten the position of the "important" poets of my century. But, as far as I am concerned, this is not a cause for weeping or gnashing of teeth. I am more than a little aloof from my North American predecessors (if, in fact, they are my predecessors). Much of the canonical poetry (that is, the poetry appropriated by the academy) is preoccupied with aesthetic concerns. More often than not, the poetry that comes to us via the centers of higher learning is a poetry filled with references to other writings—which is to say there is a preoccupation with established literary traditions, the self-conscious act of writing, and intertextuality. The academy has a penchant for poets who refer to other poets, writers, or philosophers (by working either *in* or *against* the traditions of their intellectual peers and predecessors). The study of poetry becomes a dialogue with the poetry that has come before it. Poetry becomes the property of intellectuals—a society where the virtues of subtlety, irony, distance, and complexity reign supreme. A poetry that seeks an audience outside the society of the academy is relegated to that purgatory referred to as popular culture—which is to say "lowbrow"—which is to say that it will be written out of poetic history. Given the poetic demands of the academy, what becomes of the poetry and the lived experiences of much of the American population?

Since I have spent so much time in academic institutions, it would be ludicrous to claim that I am completely unaffected by what is taught in those institutions, but I have remained close enough to my identity and distant enough from my education to remain critical of how the idea of literature is produced and reproduced. The representation of my culture has always remained at the core of my writing. If I have a muse, then it is my culture. The impulse behind my work has more to do with *my experience of America* than it has to do with the poetic traditions passed down from generation to generation in American universities. I am busy documenting the undocumented. (On the border, the *Migra* stop "aliens" and ask them for their "papers." Despite centuries of our presence in this country, we are still being asked to provide "papers." Providing papers is precisely what my poems are about.) I try deliberately to remain as aloof as possible from aesthetic debates. My work is political on a more basic level. I will not go so far as to say that aesthetic concerns have no relevant politics: I will say only that that particular battle is not mine to fight. There are many different aesthetic traditions—a writer ought to be free to work in the aesthetic he or she is most comfortable with without being condemned. I do not assume that a writer is necessarily conservative because he or she writes in traditional English metrics, nor do I assume

"postmodern" avant-garde poetry is politically intelligent and more relevant merely because of the aesthetics in which it participates. If I am
critical of an elitist notion of art, then I am equally critical of a poetics
that champions popular culture without acknowledging that much of
popular culture in the United States is based on rampant commercialism
and is, more often than not, misogynistic and ethnocentric. Very often I
get the distinct feeling that aesthetic debates only serve to further remove
us from the historical and political issues that affect the peoples of our
society. If I wish to be distracted from the world, I will spend the evening
watching television.

I believe that art is more than a decoration, that it is a cultural
necessity, that it is indicative of the mystery of the imagination—the ritual
expressions of our complex emotional lives. But I do not believe in defending the integrity of art above the integrity of people whose lives I
seek to represent in my poems. To work with words is to necessarily work
in an aesthetic. But "to aestheticize" should not imply "to anesthetize."
I find it impossible to engage in a poetics divorced from the history that
constitutes my memory and that produced me. I understand exactly what
James Joyce meant when he spoke of his Ireland: "This race and this
country and this life produced me. I shall express myself as I am." My
cultural position does not allow me the mobility of many white writers.
Being conscious of the poverty out of which I arose, and being acutely
aware of the poverty in which so many members of my family remain,
what choices do I have if I am to keep a necessary connection to my past
in order to maintain some integrity? I cannot abandon the cultural and
historical circumstances that are my only true inheritances. I do not claim
that everything I write is "real." Like every writer, I mythologize. But if
I mythologize about the southwestern desert, I can do so only because
of my *very real* relationship to a *very real* place.

When my mother was in the ninth grade, she was awarded a medal
for outstanding academic achievement. A few years ago, she handed me
her medal. It reads, "For God and Country." That same year she dropped
out of school to help support her large family because her mother was
sick. At fifteen she became a maid and part-time mother to her brothers
and sisters. My father experienced such racism in West Texas that he still
says bitterly, "I wouldn't shit in the best part of Texas." In the early 1960s
what passed for plumbing in the "house" I lived in was one pipe that
brought in cold water. My mother would rise in the morning and heat
water to scrub us before we went to school. I sometimes still feel her
washcloth rubbing my skin raw. She wanted us to be clean; she would

not have her children be called "dirty." I am not likely to privilege what I have learned in educational institutions over the experiences of my family. For too many years I have seen the cycle of poverty of our people. All of my life I have seen more wasted minds and lives than Allen Ginsberg ever dreamed of seeing. I could launch into full and graphic descriptions—to do so would be to utter an endless litany of despair. I write to fight despair.

Though I work in language, language is not my primary concern (which is not to say that I am disconnected from and unconcerned about the language I work in—the words I choose). According to Alexander Pope, "Language is the dress of thought." I have always struggled to "dress" my thoughts appropriately. When I say that language is not my main concern, I am not implying that I do not pay attention to sound, rhythms, line breaks, imagery, metaphors, similes, and the rest of the poetic and literary devices available to me as a poet—this goes without saying. No poet is exempt from learning his craft. No artist is exempt from immersing himself in his discipline. But it should be remembered that a poet ought to be judged according to his own particular tradition. It is disingenuous, inappropriate, and chauvinistic to judge the poetry of the indigenous peoples of the Americas by the poetic standards of English culture. (In the United States, the English literary tradition has been constructed as the central poetic tradition—but it is not central to many poets who find that particular tradition culturally and artistically foreign.) I am primarily concerned—perhaps even obsessed—with the desire to write the unwritten into history—into time. We have bled. We have died unnecessarily. We have lived. *We live now.* We are worthy of being represented in history, in art, in poetry (and not merely assigned to be studied by cultural anthropologists and social scientists).

In Joyce's *A Portrait of the Artist as a Young Man,* Stephen Dedalus is speaking to an *English* Jesuit. As he does so, he reflects about his relationship to the English language because of his Irishness. He writes:

> The language in which we are speaking is his before it is mine. How different are the words *home, Christ, ale, master,* on his lips and on mine! I cannot speak or write these words without unrest of spirit. His language, so familiar and so foreign, will always be for me an acquired speech. I have not made or accepted its words. My voice holds them at bay. My soul frets in the shadow of his language.

My soul, too, frets in the shadow of those who take for granted their ownership of the English language. Because the language of my family was Spanish and not English, I have always had an ambivalent relationship to the language of my country. The language I am writing in will always be someone else's before it is mine. English was the language of my education; it was the language of power—of empowerment—of intelligence. To speak Spanish, when I entered grade school in 1960, was to be dumb in every sense of that word. If "in the beginning was the word," then the word belonged to the gods who spoke English. The word was not mine—the word was the possession of the gringo. It was my task as a student to receive the word and, having received it, to forget the language of the home. But to erase a language is to erase a culture. We were treated as inferior and we knew it, though we did not know the word "inferior." We learned shame early, and despite my mother's efforts *we were* looked upon as dirty.

But a child knows more than he can say in language. James Baldwin spoke for many when he wrote:

> All this enters the child's consciousness much sooner than we as adults would like to think it does. As adults, we are easily fooled because we are anxious to be fooled. But children are very different. . . . They don't have the vocabulary to express what they see, and we, their elders, know how to intimidate them very easily and very soon. But a black child, looking out at the world around him, though he cannot quite know what to make of it, is aware there is a reason why his mother works so hard, why his father is always on the edge. . . . He is aware that there is some terrible weight on his parents' shoulders which menaces him. And it isn't long—in fact it begins when he is in school—before he discovers the shape of oppression.

A child senses all the splits of his universe though he cannot give them names. Often, he does not even learn the names of the many oppressions and inequalities from the adults around him because the adults are all trying very hard to deny that they exist. Silence is a difficult habit to break. I did not have a word for racism and cultural domination until I was much older—and even then, I first thought it applied only to what whites felt for blacks. It was only much later that I understood that in southern New Mexico, it was we who were the blacks.

When I speak of my self, if it is not obvious already, I speak of a historical self—a self that is immersed in a specific cultural context. The self I speak of is obsessed with history precisely because in the writing of history, so many Chicanos (not to mention Native Americans) have occupied almost no space, and this from a culture that has been present in North America for centuries. I do not need Fredric Jameson to implore me to "always historicize." I would like to think that the self I bring to my poetry is much more than a self-indulgent, confessional individualist whose emotional life is the center of his universe. The self that I bring to my writing is not an individual self that seeks to divorce himself from the polis. I agree wholeheartedly with Denise Levertov when she responds to Wordsworth by writing, "The world is not with us enough." I must keep myself close to the world and its concerns, the earth and its peoples, if my poetry is to be a bridge (however small) between clashing cultures and ideologies.

In the United States we have evolved into a fractured culture of individualists. We have lost interest in building community and are becoming less and less capable of critiquing the self-interest of the upper classes and multinational business firms who have broken with the community of humankind. We must stop fetishizing the "rich and famous"—they are not worthy of our attention or admiration. We must break with the very rich because the very rich have broken with the common people of the earth. We must stop showering the Donald Trumps of the world with affection. He, and individualists like him, have no valuable vision to offer the Americas. We must turn to those who have a vision of community (and by community I do not mean a nationalism supported by militarism) and learn (perhaps for the first time) that our differences with each other need not be threatening, and that, despite everything, we all belong and must return to the earth—we all belong and must return to each other. As Dorothy Day, the founder of the Catholic worker movement, once wrote, "We have all known the long loneliness and we have learned that the only solution is love and that love only comes with community."

IV

We often speak about American history as if it were something real. But I do not believe in American history: I only believe in American histories. But histories are written constructions of those in possession of the word, and I object to the way history has been constructed, sanitized, and glorified. Dick Fool Bull was a witness to the events at Wounded Knee:

> There were dead people all over, mostly women and child-
> ren, in a ravine near a stream called Chanke-opi Wakpala,
> Wounded Knee Creek. The people were frozen, lying there in
> all kinds of postures, their motion frozen too. The soldiers, who
> were stacking up bodies like firewood, did not like us passing
> by. They told us to leave there, double-quick or else. . . . So
> we went on toward Pine Ridge, but I had seen. I had seen a
> dead mother with a dead baby sucking at her breast. The little
> baby had on a tiny beaded cap with the design of the American
> flag.

American history has much to do with slavery, with the European genocide of indigenous populations, with the creation of myths that served
an ideology of occupation. American history has much to do with in-
dustrialization and the ensuing exploitation of workers and the pollution
of the earth. American history is sordid and bloody and disgusting, and
nothing will ever convince me that our national past has been heroic.
Our politicians are enamored of speaking of "traditional American values," but *the* traditional American value is war—killing—and it seems to
me that this country has always been able to create the illusion of community by engaging in wars (the U.S. invasion of Panama and Desert
Storm being but the latest examples). Wars create an *us*—*us* against them.
This is a very false community. It takes more than waving yellow ribbons
and flags in a parade to create an authentic community—it takes a commitment to create a climate where all the peoples of the Americas can
enter into dialogue.

Walt Whitman once wrote:

> We Americans have yet to really learn our own antecedents,
> and sort them, to unify them. They will be found ampler than
> has been supposed, and in widely different sources. Thus far,
> impress'd by New England writers and schoolmasters, we
> tacitly abandon ourselves to the notion that our United States
> have been fashion'd from the British Islands only, and
> essentially form a second England only—which is a very great
> mistake. Many leading traits for our future national
> personality, and some of the best ones, will certainly prove to
> have originated from other than English stock.

"Many of the leading traits for our future national personality" should come from our indigenous peoples—their attitudes toward the land, their sense of community, their myths (which ought to be as well known to us as Greek and Roman myths), their spiritualities. The European sense of superiority we have inherited has shown itself to be militant and uncivil.

Since Columbus set foot on the Americas five hundred years ago, and had the audacity to rename everything he saw and claim every piece of land he set foot on for Spain, the indigenous peoples have been struggling for their place in American society. They are still waiting. What kind of a civilization are we?

The story of America is chaos. The European-Americans who colonized and appropriated this land have fought war after war, piled up violences upon violences. Our American past is a mass grave with bodies stacked up taller than the tower of Babel. The living stare at the bones looking for meaning. I confess that I cannot walk through life unless there is some kind of meaning: this is not only at the heart of constructing history, but it is also at the heart of constructing poems. In his last interview, Arturo Islas said, "Life has no shape. We impose shape on it so we can deal with it. It's scary to think that it's all chaos. And what artists do to the nth degree, what writers do to the nth degree, without seeming to do it, this is the trick you see, is to give shape to things that have no shape. The human heart has no shape. Emotions have no shape. It's the writer who gives them a form." Our history *is* chaos. Others have been giving it form for centuries. I refuse to sit back and merely curse the darkness. I have decided to enter the debate for the heart of America.

Eduardo Galeano, in his preface to his trilogy, *Memory of Fire*, makes the following observations:

> I was a wretched history student. History classes were like visits to the waxworks or the Regions of the Dead. The past was lifeless, hollow, dumb. They taught us about the past so that we should resign with drained consciousness to the present: not to make history, which was already made, but to accept it. Poor history had stopped breathing: betrayed in academic texts, lied about in classrooms, drowned in dates, they had imprisoned her in museums and buried her, with floral wreaths, beneath statuary bronze and monumental marble. . . . Through the centuries, Latin America has been despoiled of gold and silver, nitrates and rubber, copper and oil: its memory has also been usurped. From the outset it has been condemned to

amnesia by those who have prevented it from being. Official American history boils down to a military parade of bigwigs in uniforms fresh from the dry cleaners. I am not a historian. I am a writer who would like to contribute to the rescue of the kidnapped memory of America, but above all of Latin America, that despised and beloved land: I would like to talk to her, share her secrets, ask her of what difficult clays she was born, from what acts of love and violation she comes.

Galeano's monumental work, a fragmented representation of the history of the Americas, has become for me a model for what I wish to do through my poetry. Like him, I want to breathe something of my people into history. I remind myself that we are not so much the products of history as we are the products of our interpretations or constructions of history. History is not so much something that has been written as it is something that we continually and necessarily must rewrite. What has been lost must be recovered. I write to recover. I write to proclaim. I write to explain. I write to declaim. I write because I love, because I am sad. I write because I am a part of the universe of the living and the dead, and it is a joy to be a part of it. I write because I am angry, and my anger is legitimate. *I write because I remember.* Some Chicanos, unfortunately, feel the price they have to pay for success is to relinquish their culture. We give up our altars, our processions, our prayers, our traditions, and immerse ourselves in the great White Protestant culture of North America. But I do not call that success; I do not call that "integration." I call it erasure. I call it the great forgetting. I call it death. There are many people who suffer from cultural and historical amnesia—it is one of the great ailments of our age, and why we so often and stupidly repeat mistakes over and over again. Memory is the most important tool at the disposal of a writer—any writer—and without it, she not only cannot be a writer, she cannot be alive. As Luis Buñuel reflected, "You have to begin to lose your memory, if only in bits and pieces, to realize that memory is what makes our lives. Life without memory is not life at all."

We often think of 1492 as the year Columbus "discovered" America. We think of the discovery of the North and South American continents as a *fait accompli*. In fact, the Americas have yet to be discovered. It is false to think of "the age of discovery" as being over—we are still in the midst of the age of discovery. We must keep searching until we get closer to the heart of what America is. Five hundred years and we are still in search of our communal identity. Human beings are slow to learn. The tensions in our society are everywhere to be seen, and they point to our arrested development: the tensions between the ancestors of the European colonists and the indigenous peoples they displaced; the tensions between rich and poor, the homed and the homeless; the tensions between races, between peoples who speak different languages, between genders, between sexual identities, between peoples who think in different grammars. I believe our violent and contentious present is symptomatic of the fact that we have never come to terms with the truth of our past. We have never come to terms with our impulse to enslave, our drive to prove our cultural and military superiority, our compulsion to dominate other peoples and the earth that gives us life. Part of our national psychology has always been to aspire to be "the greatest nation on the face of the earth," but that greatness has *always* had more to do with power than it has had to do with the spiritual and emotional development of our civilization. We must exorcise this sickness. We have remained far too interested in defending and glorifying the colonialist and militaristic enterprise that made possible the European conquest of the Americas—so much so that we have never been able to effectively critique our own history. We have remained mortgaged to European culture and European standards for far too long. In doing so, we have sacrificed the art, literature, and culture of the peoples of the Americas.

I am a Chicano poet, which makes me an American poet—and by American I am not speaking exclusively of the United States. I am a citizen of the Americas, and I want my poetry to reflect it. Like William Carlos Williams, I believe we must keep searching for "an American idiom"—a language truly American (not merely North American but *pan* American). In his seminal essay, *In Defense of the Word*, Eduardo Galeano expresses what he sees as his responsibility as an American writer:

> It seems to me that the possibility of contribution depends to a large extent on the level of intensity of the writer's responsiveness to his or her people—their roots, their vicissitudes, their destiny—and the ability to perceive the heartbeat, the sound and rhythm, of the authentic counterculture, which is on the rise. That which is considered "uncultured" often contains the seeds or fruits of *another* culture, which confronts the dominant one and does not share its values or its rhetoric. . . . The testimonies of the people as they express in a thousand ways their tribulations and their hopes are more eloquent and beautiful than the books written "in the name of the people."

Our authentic collective identity is born out of the past and is nourished by it—our feet tread where others trod before us; the steps we take were prefigured—but this identity is not frozen into nostalgia. We are not, to be sure, going to discover our hidden countenance in the artificial perpetuation of customs, clothing, and curios which tourists demand of conquered peoples. *We are what we do, especially what we do to change what we are:* our identity resides in action and in struggle. . . . A literature born in the process of crisis and change, and deeply immersed in the risks and events of its time, can indeed help to create the symbols of the new reality, and perhaps—if talent and courage are not lacking—throw light on the signs along the road. It is not futile to sing the pain and the beauty of having been born in America.

What does it mean to be a Poet? What does it mean to be a Chicano? What does it mean to be an American? It is the nexus between these realities that forms my poetry and my identity. I know America has not yet been discovered. I want to help sing her into being. I want to write an American poem. But to do so I must learn the chants of her peoples and repeat them until they are written in my heart: *May it be beautiful behind me / May it be beautiful below me / May it be beautiful above me. Happily on the trail of pollen, may I walk.* Whitman's impulse to sing himself into America seems absolutely right to me: "I celebrate myself and sing myself." He was not celebrating an individual divorced from his community—he was celebrating a love that he had claimed as his—*America.* Much later, Langston Hughes wrote, "I, too, sing America." Corky Gonzalez, the Chicano activist and poet, once asserted, "I am Joaquin." He had to proclaim himself back into the land of the living. Long buried—and buried precisely because of his race—he had to find the strength to unbury himself. They knew what Galeano knows, and what I know now, too: *It is not futile to sing the pain and the beauty of having been born in America.*

Undocumented Anguish

Insatiable harpies
    the skyscrapers
    devour the stars
    eating their fill of the moon
    caging the wind
    which in turn wreaks vengeance
    on flowers and umbrellas
    appeased only
    when its great, transparent tongue
    savors again
    the smooth skin of the water.

The fog rolls in then
    full of countless wandering
    hands and birds,
    flowing among the trodden leaves
    muting groans and the crack of whips,
    quieting the undocumented anguish
    of the man living illegally in his own land,
    plunging its fingers into the moon
    and into the distance without harbors,
    without beacons.

Fugue

to Norma Alarcón

Tired of bearing in my eyes
light, wall and silence
and in my ears
a rustle of wings and rain,
between farewell and unexpected door
I chose fire
and in its promise of rich harvest
my heart burned
one winter night.

I crossed the insolent geometry
your hands had constructed
on the grim latitudes of February.

Your fabrication of lurking tigers I threw
to the rebellious ecology of the wind

Washed from my lips the fearsome
flavor of your skin

Cauterized motive, cause and sentiment

Scrubbed your gaze off my body

And closed the doors of the past
against the memory of your name and mine.

Outside
in the winter of the gods
with trembling hand I uncovered silence

Conjured the seeds of fire
Felt them beating in my temples and my breasts.

In the spaces between my fingers they turned to

    blood

        wheat

            June light

the thousand eyes of night

    twilight

        pain

            song

and the wheatstalk lying in the field

    cliff

        delta

            golden fish

star secrets in the sand

    fishscale

        seafoam

            salt

and the mournful song of the whale
heralding the calm expanse
of a boreal equinox.

Abstract

The sighs of burning wood filled the air
and in the sky a single star shone;
the moon rode on a silver saddle
alone through the early morning hours,
and in a carriage made of water
small dead leaves were borne
toward the common grave of the sewer;
the sun dried the traces of nostalgia
left in the byways of my memory
by Sarasate's gypsies
and from deep inside my belly
came the hesitant voice of Marina my daughter:
"Mamá, if I should die this autumn morning . . ."
Outside
the day rose triumphant
through the keening of the wind.

Al-Haram

(THE RED ONE)

The red one will come through letter and number
As I flip the Spanish cards linked to the
Egyptian Tarot
She will be an equestrian
Galloping upon a flying horse

The hidden
Red pepper
In a stew
Not the thing itself
But the shadow

She sometimes appears in green
but I know it is a disguise
For I come from the land of
Interior decorators
I have spotted her pushing
Her way out of purple and pink
A clear sign that she is going home
She is nowhere if she is not there
There is only one place

That place is protected by the
Sound the color makes
A red drum from Loíza Aldea
Directs traffic at the corner

It's in fowl play too:
What came first the chicken or
The egg

Answer: The rooster
Who entered quietly into the
Chicken coop
To deplume red feathers
It is night tight
The best time
Half in dream
She goes under
The Red Sea

She is coming through the
Undercurrent
Its pull irresistible
An echo becomes form in space
There is no water for the thirst
For the satisfaction is fire

She is walking 8,000 miles away
from where I am airing
Out of a window
She is in Cidra walking down
one of its small streets
Each step she takes
Drops a piece of her body
Till finally she is only
The virtues of the hue
Crimson on the great horizon

Glances and walks
Of the pensamiento
Come to the cherry entrance
Where they bow
with the rest of the aspirants

The red face is turning
Like dice turning onto four
Multiplication brings it to
Me more
It is raining blood
In the town between two
Mountains

Al-Haram lives there—
Find her door and bring
Midnight serenade
Lyrics and guitars below
Balcony
Minds disappear from the present
Go for walks under orange trees
Passage through sea coast
Red sails to Red

Al-Haram
Travels like pollen
Grows in invisibility
Notice at night
Starring into the darkness

That she comes
As a shrimp taken by the river
Is history
As prescribed by the doctors

Succumb to my painting
For there are no exits
The red fog is coming down from
The hills to suffocate us—

As the hands of a thief of calling
Seizes the gold
So will my hands
Open the portón of the red one's
Balcony

Its combination
The number
The code
Broken

A brown hand leans upon a white
Wall
As if pushing it away—
The body making a house
Where the guest enters

To find ferocious animals
Tamed and loose in the backyard.

Problems with Hurricanes

A campesino looked at the air
And told me:
With hurricanes it's not the wind
or the noise or the water.
I'll tell you he said:
it's the mangoes, avocados
Green plantains and bananas
flying into town like projectiles.

How would your family
feel if they had to tell
The generations that you
got killed by a flying
Banana.

Death by drowning has honor
If the wind picked you up
and slammed you
Against a mountain boulder
This would not carry shame
But
to suffer a mango smashing
Your skull
or a plantain hitting your
Temple at 70 miles per hour
is the ultimate disgrace.

The campesino takes off his hat—
As a sign of respect
toward the fury of the wind
And says:
Don't worry about the noise
Don't worry about the water
Don't worry about the wind—
If you are going out
beware of mangoes
And all such beautiful
sweet things.

Igneris

Air is raining upon the organs
of reproduction
From heaven the color spectrum
into your pelvis
Raining a ceremony of structures
Upon the joys of the winds.

This is the drum of my island
The coast of an eternal circle
I sea it in the wheres I follow
Hear it in the hands that designate
Upon the skin of a goat stretched
In the sun maps for the knee and ankles
To join the trunk of the trees
That the barrel was made from.

El Yunque is falling into necks
and waists appearing in dreams.
With nature you dance
Get in rhythm Catalan, Galician,

Asturians bow to the vegetable
Instruments that rattle indigenous
Joints to sour and disappear
Through doors found in echoes.

That's the juice
Before Spain the snake dance
The waist in the river woman
Bells and flute caracoles
Caracoles sipping the dawn
Guayaba painting the insect wings
Flavor colors
Earth Igneri
AguasBuenas
Guesbuenas
Agueybanás

Deep in the caves I grow
In light light
Where rodents fly
Oxygen to fish that shell
Their coats and hats
Radios in their bellies
Where lightning falls

Phosphorous La Parquera is
a light bulb in the mar
When she was a virgin
It was seen from the moon

She knew how to melt rocks for
Perfume
Importing it beyond registered
frequencies—
To make a brown so round
That before it was seen
Shape was heard

Sonadora was not cement and cal
boxes
It was just an opening
A musical

A song is heard out of the flora
The hum of love
The moan of two
Tree comes in fauna

Now Igneris flames upon cement
the trail of a soul
Religion is a God that moves the
Feet
Scratches backs and tabs shoulders
Up on the stage presents
Itself in costumes
Which shows how to progress
Walking inside.

I got source and can shake it off
To sprinkle the designs
That hide the patterns
Of the lord of movement
I am the explosion of the fiesta
The timing of feet and elbows
The moisture of lips sacrosanct
Manifesting the evidence of presence
The heart speaking in the hands
Before it grows wings to land again
Upon the supply.

Santa Cruz

So what of our sputtering names,
unhinged. So what of blank
seasons, blistered and shot
from the cannons of our slow desires.

And what of summer's pestilence,
our worried flies on sweat sand?
What of the harbor where we fished
our love seals into mute extinction?

What will become of the kiss
I give you, the spit on my lip,
the lips of my vulva pushing
fins and flash? Twelve bushels

of silt and salt, this year
I rivet on a tide as gray
as winter and it stops
my catch. What about the graves

where the suds first dug apart
the sloughs of our nesting?
See the slit-throat pelicans,
the dumbed whales beached on cape foam?

What of this poet
reading season's end?
My worm heart, overwrought
as a slacked line, loses.

Flatirons

for the Ute and Arapaho

The mountains are there like ghosts
of slaughtered mules, the whites of my
ancestors rest on the glaciers, veiled
and haloed with the desire of electrical
storms. Marginal feasts corral the young
to the cave walls, purple smoke wafts up
a chimney of shedding sundown. Statuesque
and exquisitely barren, my seed shines
in the dying rays. The rich earth of the wealthy
splays the legs of heaven in my view. Monstrous
and sullen, the slabs of death let loose their
hikers, let fall with an old snow. My harmony
of blood and ash, fire on the mound, I feel
them shuffling in the aspen, their vague ahems
marry the sucking fish in a derelict river. The
winter of their genocide still Ghost Dances
with a dream where the bison and mammoth unite,
where the story of their streams is as long
as the sabers of northern ice. The mountains
are the conquest of the sea, the belly of gems,
her fossil stays, her solicitudes. The glass
before the angel fish, she stands royal in
her invisible captivity, the impassibility of her
element, elemental and efficient. She is there
in the silent baying, in the memory of a native
and the dripping pursuance of thawing babies—
specters in a sunset of The Heights—after massacre.

Shooting the Wren

For ten centuries I want to be birdless
—JAY GRISWOLD

He sends trophies from Sunday's kill: a China
pheasant—feathers despicable starling coal,
backs the color of Chilean copper. They shimmer
in the distance, a beautiful expectancy of only 2.2
years so who could feel bad about the downing
of another rooster? The species about wiped out
for the hats of the thirties are plentiful
game now. They succumb to harsh winters,
feral cats, coyotes, wild dogs, farmers. The hens
preen in the spattered leaves. A speckle of blood,
nearly unnoticed, backs the wolf-down, and at
the quill's tip, a dark tangling in the fluff
of a ringneck's queue. They gleam iridescence,
what was more precious than gold to an extinguished
race. I walk among the ghosts of history, the
agony of the tortured condemned to their barracks
of serene mustard slopes. In California: China
berry, manzanita, wild boar imported from Europe.
My ancestors leached acorns, hollowed granite
at river beds with kindness kneading in a steady
procession. My grandmother knew only one
constellation, the Seven Sisters, and she would
ask them to help her remember her grandmother's
story of how they descended to earth from
a fusion of difference. But it's an unremembered
song cut off at slavery's beck and call. Her
eleven year old hands deadened at the hard
sale of cash, unlikely, untutored, caring.

She taught me the rights of a hunter are inalienable,
spinning the head of a chicken. It is true.
We are the fallen angels returned to teach
the tenderness of hands, the tough choice
of heart. My grandmother's heart was pure as topaz.
She knew what gives out comes back quantum.
She taught her babies patience with the eye
of a feather smudged with honey. A day's work
could get done as the plume was passed from hand
to hand in the brilliance of sunlight, bright
as it is now as I finger the fray
and nap of this gift.
                            You are of the tender
heart. I know nothing of your hands but what
they write down, what graphite is bound between
horizons of blue, what nature of carbon skin
of dead birds coats the page. It is true. You can
buy the lean meat of plucked birds. You can buy
fresh hens at the market, quail the color of
chardonnay grapes. You have reservations where
you can purchase the tokens of the dead. They bear
their own speeches, these silent ones
trading the winds, their own histories and stories.
Tell me a few. Give it 2.2 years to come to life
and tell a tale of triggers and steel, of tumblers
and the slut peg of the chamber; mail me a silver
bullet from the mountains of your memory.
Your trophies bear witness to gunfire in the
numbed trees of eternity's forests, of winter
in the eastern plains—while I fashion
these feathers into the fragile art of my tribe.
I will wear them when the black of white
never dies, this gift of intent woven in a silent
bead. I'll let it blow through my matted
locks, the weight of a kiss. What you kill
I will pay for, what you let live
we will praise, ignore it, and eat.

PEDRO PIETRI

The First Day of Spring

Sweating in the midnight snow
Laughing and crying, actually dying
Lost in the after effects of affection,
Sinking deeply into the highest level
Of delirium, sleepwalking backward
In the process of becoming transparent
Extra holy and extremely excellent

Elated casualty of abstract emotions
Reaching for the safe side of oblivion
To celebrate the art of fulfillment
In the opposite direction of reality
Where the correct age of the universe
Is learned and forgotten immediately

To be reborn making no sense whatsoever
Talking the foreign language of dreams
Misunderstanding simple conversations
In the confusion of drowning peacefully
Seriously sober and tremendously stoned

Staggering proudly through the shadows
Of the unknown seeking remarkable state
Of no mind, ecstatic to be bewildered,
Drifting out of the future into the past,
Protecting my principles from perfection
After rising from the dead in the arms
Of the woman who will write my epitaph

The Night Is Out of Sight

In a dream I wasn't having yet
My father was expelled
From heaven and hell for walking
Through a few thousand walls
Under the influence of alcohol

Assured me everything was real
And unreal enough to frighten
Those who are dead serious about
What they are going to laugh at
The next time they get uptight

We sat down on bar stools to talk
About our magnificent mother
Whose hair has become a bouquet
Of flowers that are endless
In the smile of sad expressions

We got very drunk staying sober
And when daylight was finally over
We came to the sane conclusion
All conversations end with hello
& all greetings begin with farewell

He congratulated me for refusing
To remove my hat & stop dressing
In black regardless of the weather
Or the occasion—there is nothing
Anyone alive can do right or wrong

He said before deciding the time
Had come to discontinue talking
& continue walking through walls

To be discovered by other days &
Nights that make metaphor possible

So we departed to poetry forever
& ever to never again listen
To the ringing of alarm clocks
Reminding us nothing ever happens
If we must keep track of time

ROSARIO MORALES AND
AURORA LEVINS MORALES

Ending Poem

I am what I am.
A child of the Americas.
A light-skinned mestiza of the Caribbean.
A child of many diaspora, born into this continent at a crossroads.
I am Puerto Rican. I am U.S. American.
I am New York Manhattan and the Bronx.
A mountain-born, country-bred, homegrown jíbara child,
up from the shtetl, a California Puerto Rican Jew
A product of the New York ghettos I have never known.
I am an immigrant
and the daughter and granddaughter of immigrants.
We didn't know our forbears' names with a certainty.
They aren't written anywhere.
First names only or mija, negra, ne, honey, sugar, dear

I come from the dirt where the cane was grown.
My people didn't go to dinner parties. They weren't invited.
I am caribeña, island grown.
Spanish is in my flesh, ripples from my tongue, lodges in my hips,
the language of garlic and mangoes.
Boricua. As Boricuas come from the isle of Manhattan.
I am of latinoamerica, rooted in the history of my continent.
I speak from that body. Just brown and pink and full of drums inside.

I am not African.
Africa waters the roots of my tree, but I cannot return.

I am not Taína.
I am a late leaf of that ancient tree,
and my roots reach into the soil of two Americas.
Taíno is in me, but there is no way back.

I am not European, though I have dreamt of those cities.
Each plate is different.
wood, clay, papier mâché, metals basketry, a leaf, a coconut shell.
Europe lives in me but I have no home there.

The table has a cloth woven by one, dyed by another,
embroidered by another still.
I am a child of many mothers.
They have kept it all going

All the civilizations erected on their backs.
All the dinner parties given with their labor.

We are new.
They gave us life, kept us going,
brought us to where we are.
Born at a crossroads.
Come, lay that dishcloth down. Eat, dear, eat.
History made us.
We will not eat ourselves up inside anymore.

And we are whole.

Contributors to
Currents from the Dancing River

JACK AGUEROS is the author of a book of poetry, *Correspondence Between the Stone Haulers* (Hanging Loose Press), and a book of short stories, *Dominoes and Other Stories from the Puerto Rican* (Curbstone Press). He lives in New York City.

FRANCISCO ALARCON is the author of numerous books of poetry, including *Body in Flames* and an American Book Award winner, *The Snake Poems* (both from Chronicle Books). He teaches at the University of California at Davis.

ALICIA GASPAR DE ALBA is a native of El Paso, Texas, and has worked as a transcriber of children's books into Braille. Her first poetry collection was part of *Three Times a Woman,* an anthology of three women poets published by Bilingual Press. Her first book of short stories, *The Mystery of Survival and Other Stories,* was also released by Bilingual Press. She is completing her Ph.D. work in Santa Barbara, California.

MIGUEL ALGARÍN is the founder of the renowned performance space, the Nuyorican Poets Café, in New York City. His books of poetry are *Mongo Affair* (Nuyorican Press) and three from Arte Publico, *On Call, Body Bee Calling from the 21st Century,* and *Times Now/Ya es tiempo.* He lives in New York City.

RUDOLFO ANAYA is the author of several novels, including *Bless Me, Ultima, Heart of Atzlan,* and *Alburquerque. Zia Summer,* a mystery, will be published in 1995 by Warner Books. He has also published short stories, nonfiction, plays, and children's stories. He lives in Tortuga, New Mexico.

GLORIA ANZALDÚA is the editor of the legendary women's anthology *This Bridge Called My Back: Writings by Radical Women of Color*

(Women's Kitchen Press). She is also the author of a book of poetry and prose, *Borderlands/La Frontera: The New Mestiza* (Spinster Aunt Lute Books). She lives in Santa Cruz, California.

ROSA MARIA ARENAS has published poetry in the *Kenyon Review, The Americas Review, Blue Mesa Review,* and other magazines. She graduated from the Master of Fine Arts program at Washington University in Saint Louis.

JIMMY SANTIAGO BACA is the author of five books of poetry, including *Immigrants in Our Own Land, Martin and Meditations on the South Valley,* and *Black Mesa Poems,* all published by New Directions. His first collection of essays, *Working in the Dark,* was published by Red Crane Books in 1993. He lives in Albuquerque, New Mexico.

RAFAEL BARRETO-RIVERA is a member of the performance poetry group The Four Horsemen, who have collaborated on two books, *Horse d'Oeuvres* and *The Prose Tattoo.* His book of poetry is *Voices, Noises* (Coach House Press). He lives in San Francisco.

BERTHA SANCHEZ BELLO has published poetry in *Ball Peen, Linden Lane Magazine, Black Swan Review,* and other journals. She lives in Elizabeth, New Jersey.

ARISTEO BRITO is the author of a novel, *The Devil in Texas* (Bilingual Press), the winner of a Western States Book Award in fiction. He teaches at Pima College in Tucson, Arizona.

RAFAEL CAMPO's first collection of poetry, *The Other Man Was Me* (Arte Publico Press), was selected in the 1993 National Poetry Series. He is a resident in primary care medicine at the University of California at San Francisco.

OMAR S. CASTAÑEDA is the author of three novels, *Among the Volcanoes* (Dutton), *Cunuman* (Pineapple Press), and *Sudden and Uncommon Acts* (Dutton). Lee and Low Books published his first children's book, *Abuela's Weave,* in 1993. He is coeditor of *New Visions: Fiction by Florida Writers* (Arbiter Press). He teaches at Western Washington University in Bellingham.

ROSEMARY CATACALOS is the director of the Poetry Center at San Francisco State University and received a National Endowment for the Arts fellowship in poetry in 1993. Her book of poetry, *Again for the First*

Time (Tooth of Time Books), won the Texas Institute of Letters Award in 1984.

LORNA DEE CERVANTES is the editor of *Red Dirt,* a literary journal. Her two books of poetry are *Emplumada* (University of Pittsburgh Press) and *From the Cables of Genocide: Poems on Love and Hunger* (Arte Publico Press), the winner of a Paterson Poetry Prize. She teaches at the University of Colorado in Boulder.

JUDITH ORTIZ COFER is the author of a novel, *The Line of the Sun* (University of Georgia Press), a memoir, *Silent Dancing* (Arte Publico Press), two books of poetry, and a poetry-prose collection, *The Latin Deli* (University of Georgia Press). She has received fellowships from the National Endowment for the Arts and the Witter Bynner Foundation. She teaches at the University of Georgia in Athens.

LUCHA CORPI is the author of two novels from Arte Publico Press, *Delia's Song* and *Requiem for a Brown Beret.* Her book of poetry is *Variations on a Storm* (Third Woman Press). She lives in Oakland, California.

VICTOR HERNANDEZ CRUZ is the author of several books of poetry, including *Selected Poems* (Arte Publico Press) and *Red Beans* (Coffee House Press). He teaches at the University of California at San Diego.

SILVIA CURBELO has received creative writing fellowships from the National Endowment for the Arts and the Florida Arts Council. Her poems have appeared in numerous journals. She is the author of a chapbook of poetry, *The Geography of Leaving* (Silverfish Review Press). She lives in Tampa, Florida.

MARTIN ESPADA received the Paterson Poetry Prize for his second book of poetry, *Rebellion Is the Circle of a Lover's Hands* (Curbstone Press). His other books of poetry include *Trumpets from the Islands of Their Eviction* (Bilingual Press). He is the editor of *Poetry Like Bread: An Anthology of Political Poets* (Curbstone Press). He teaches at the University of Massachusetts at Amherst.

SANDRA MARIA ESTEVES conducts writing workshops through community organizations in New York City. Her two books of poetry are *Yerba Buena* (Greenfield Review Press) and *Bluestown Mockingbird Mambo* (Arte Publico Press).

ENRIQUE FERNÁNDEZ is a columnist for the *New York Daily News.*

KLEYA FORTE-ESCAMILLA is the author of a book of short stories, *Barrio Stories,* and a novel, *Daughter of the Mountain,* both published by Spinster Aunt Lute Books. She lives in Aptos, California.

CRISTINA GARCIA is the author of a first novel, *Dreaming in Cuban* (Knopf). She is a correspondent for *Time* magazine and lives in Los Angeles.

RICHARD GARCIA is the author of a book of poetry, *The Flying Garcias* (University of Pittsburgh Press), and a bilingual children's book, *My Aunt Otilia's Spirits.* He lives in Los Angeles, where he is poet-in-residence at Children's Hospital.

DAGOBERTO GILB was born and raised in Los Angeles. He is the author of two collections of short stories, *Winners on the Pass Line* (Cinco Puntos Press) and *The Magic of Blood* (University of New Mexico Press). He received a 1993 Whiting Award for fiction. He lives in El Paso, Texas.

RAY GONZALEZ is the author of three books of poetry, including *The Heat of Arrivals,* and a book of essays, *Memory Fever: A Journey Beyond El Paso del Norte* (both from Broken Moon Press). He is the editor of fourteen anthologies and received a 1993 Before Columbus Foundation American Book Award for Excellence in Editing. He lives in San Antonio, Texas.

JORGE GUITART is the author of *Foreigner's Notebook* (Shuffaloff Press). His work has appeared in numerous anthologies, including *Los Atrevidos: Cuban American Writers* (Linden Lane Press). He teaches at the State University of New York at Buffalo.

JUAN FELIPE HERRERA is the author of eight books of poetry, including *Facegames* (As Is, So & So Press)—winner of a Before Columbus American Book Award—*Akrilica* (Alcatraz Editions), *Night Train to Tuxtla* (University of Arizona Press), and *Days of Invasion* (Curbstone Press). His memoir, *Indian Journeys,* was published by Broken Moon Press. He teaches at Fresno State University in California.

ARTURO ISLAS was the author of three novels, *The Rain God* (Alexandrian Press), *Migrant Souls* (William Morrow), and the posthumous *La Molly and the King of Tears* (Broken Moon Press). He taught at Stanford University for over twenty years. He died in 1991.

JACK LOPEZ has published short stories in a number of important Latino anthologies, including *Pieces of the Heart: Chicano Short Stories*

(Chronicle Books), *Iguana Dreams: New Latino Fiction* (HarperCollins), and *Mirrors Beneath the Earth: Chicano Short Fiction* (Curbstone Press). He lives in Costa Mesa, California.

DIONISIO MARTINEZ received a 1993 Whiting Award in Poetry. His two books of poetry are *History as a Second Language* (Ohio State University Press) and *Bad Alchemy* (Norton). He teaches in the artists-in-residence program in the Tampa, Florida, public schools.

RUBEN MARTINEZ is a columnist for the *L.A. Weekly* in Los Angeles. His memoir, *The Other Side: Fault Lines, Guerrilla Saints and the True Heart of Rock n' Roll,* was published by Verso Books in 1992.

VICTOR MARTINEZ is the author of a book of poetry, *Caring for a House* (Chusma House Publications). His manuscript of essays on Chicano artists and poets received a John McCarron New Writing in Arts Criticism grant and will be published by the University of Arizona Press. He works as a laborer in San Francisco.

JULIO MARZÁN is a poet and fiction writer whose work includes a book of poetry, *Translations Without Originals,* and a collection of short stories, *Unforgettable Tangos, Indelible Pagodas.* He lives in New York City.

PABLO MEDINA's poetry, prose, and translations have appeared in many journals and anthologies. He is the author of two books of poetry, *Pork Rind and Cuban Songs* and *Arching into the Afterlife* (Bilingual Press). His collection of essays is *Exiled Memories: A Cuban Childhood.* He teaches at Mercer County Community College in Trenton, New Jersey.

NICHOLASA MOHR is the author of several books of fiction and nonfiction and books for young adults. Among them are *In Nueva York, Nilda,* and *El Bronx Remembered* (all from Arte Publico Press). *El Bronx Remembered* was a finalist for the National Book Award. She lives in New York City.

VICTOR MONTEJO is the author of *The Bird Who Cleans the World,* a collection of Mayan folk tales, and the nonfiction *Testimony: Death of a Guatemalan Village* (Curbstone Press). He lives in Connecticut.

PAT MORA has numerous children's books forthcoming from Knopf, Macmillan, and Clarion. Her first one, *A Birthday Basket for Tia,* was published by Macmillan in 1992. She is the author of three books of poetry, *Chants, Borders,* and *Communion,* all published by Arte Publico Press. Her first collection of essays, *Nepantla: Essays from the Land in the*

Middle, was published by the University of New Mexico Press in 1993. She lives in Cincinnati, Ohio.

AURORA LEVINS MORALES has published poetry and prose in numerous journals and anthologies, including *Puerto Rican Writers in the U.S.A.* (University of Puerto Rico Press). She lives in New York City.

ROSARIO MORALES is the coauthor of *Getting Home Alive* (Arte Publico Press). She lives in New York City.

ELÍAS MIGUEL MUÑOZ is the author of four novels, including *Crazy Love* and *The Greatest Performance* (both from Arte Publico Press). He is the author of two books of criticism, two collections of poetry, and several plays that have been performed Off Broadway in New York City, where he lives.

ALEJANDRO MURGUIA received a Before Columbus American Book Award for his second collection of short stories, *Southern Front* (Bilingual Press). His first is *Farewell to the Coast* (Heirs Press). He was the editor of the legendary Chicano magazine of the seventies, *Tin-Tan.* He lives in San Francisco.

ROBERT NAVARRO is an attorney in San Francisco. His poetry has appeared in *Equinoz* and *Guadalupe Review.*

EMILIA PAREDES received her first publication in *New Chicano Writing II* (University of Arizona Press). She works as a psychiatric social worker for the HIV program at San Francisco City Clinic.

RICARDO PAU-LLOSA is an art critic specializing in modern Latin American art and is a contributing editor to *Art International.* His three books of poetry are *Sorting Metaphors* (Anhinga Press), *Bread of the Imagined* (Bilingual Press), and *Havana* (Carnegie Mellon University Press). He lives in Miami, Florida.

PEDRO PIETRI'S two books of poetry are *Puerto Rican Obituary* (Monthly Review Press) and *Traffic Violations* (Waterfront Press). He is the author of a collection of stories, *Lost in the Museum of Natural History* (Rio Pedras Press), and a play, *The Masses Are Asses* (Waterfront Press). He lives in New York City.

MIGUEL PIÑERO was the author of eight books of poetry, including *La Bodega Sold Dreams* (Arte Publico Press), and coeditor of the anthology *Nuyorican Poetry: An Anthology of Puerto Rican Words and Feelings* (William

Morrow). He was also a highly acclaimed playwright with three collections of plays, *Short Eyes, Outrageous and Other One-Act Plays,* and *The Sun Always Shines for the Cool* (all from Arte Publico Press). He died in 1989.

MARY HELEN PONCE is the author of two novels, *Taking Control* and *The Wedding,* both from Arte Publico Press. Her memoir, *Hoyt Street: An Autobiography,* was published by the University of New Mexico Press. She teaches at the University of California at Santa Barbara.

LEROY QUINTANA is a two-time winner of the Before Columbus Foundation American Book Award in poetry for *Sangre* and *The History of Home* (both from Bilingual Press). He teaches at Mesa College in San Diego.

ORLANDO RAMÍREZ has published poetry in *Quarry West, Berkeley Poetry Review, Zyzzyva,* and the anthologies *New Chicano Writing,* volumes 1 and 3. He won the 1979 Chicano Literary Contest at the University of California at Irvine. He lives in San Diego.

ALBERTO RIOS received the 1982 Walt Whitman Award in poetry for his first book, *Whistling to Fool the Wind* (Sheep Meadow Press). His other books of poetry include *Lime Orchard Woman, Five Indiscretions* (both from Sheep Meadow), and *Teodore Luna's Two Kisses* (Norton). He received a Western States Book Award in fiction for his first collection of short stories, *The Iguana Killer* (Confluence Press). He teaches at Arizona State University in Tempe.

MARGARITA TAVERA RIVERA grew up in a migrant family in the Rio Grande Valley of Texas and dropped out of school in the tenth grade, only to return and eventually earn three M.A. degrees. Her work appeared for the first time in *New Chicano Writing II* (University of Arizona Press). She lives in Tucson.

ROWENA A. RIVERA coauthored *Penitente Self-government: Brotherhood and Councils, 1797–1947* (Ancient City Press). Her fiction has appeared in numerous journals and anthologies, including *New Chicano Writing* (University of Arizona Press). She lives in Albuquerque, New Mexico.

ABRAHAM RODRIGUEZ, JR., is the author of a book of short stories, *The Boy Without a Flag* (Milkweed Editions), and the novel *Spidertown* (Hyperion Books). He lives in New York City.

ANDRÉS RODRÍGUEZ's poetry has appeared in *Wilderness, Quarry West,* and *New Chicano Writing* (University of Arizona Press). He teaches at the University of Arizona in Tucson.

LUIS J. RODRIGUEZ is the author of the best-selling memoir, *Always Running: La Vida Loca: Gang Days in L.A.* (Curbstone Press). His books of poetry are *Poems from the Pavement* (Tia Chucha Press) and *The Concrete River* (Curbstone Press). He received a Lannan Foundation fellowship in 1992 and lives in Chicago.

RICHARD RODRIGUEZ works as an editor at Pacific News Service in Los Angeles and is a contributing editor for *Harper's* and the *Los Angeles Times.* He is the author of two collections of nonfiction, *Hunger of Memory* (David R. Godine) and *Days of Obligation: An Argument with My Mexican Father* (Viking).

LEO ROMERO's first collection of short stories, *Rita and Los Angeles,* is forthcoming from Bilingual Press. He is the author of five books of poetry, including *Going Home Away Indian, Agua Negra* (both from Ahsahta Press), and *Celso* (Arte Publico Press). He owns Books and More Books, a used-book store in Santa Fe, New Mexico.

BENJAMIN ALIRE SÁENZ received a 1993 Lannan Literary Fellowship. His two books of poetry, from Broken Moon Press, are *Calendar of Dust* and *Dark and Perfect Angels.* He is also the author of a book of short stories, *Flowers for the Broken* (also from Broken Moon Press). He teaches in the bilingual Masters of Fine Arts program at the University of Texas at El Paso.

LUIS OMAR SALINAS is the author of seven books of poetry, including *Crazy Gypsy, Walking Behind the Spanish* (both from the University of California Chicano Studies Library Publications), and *Sadness of Days: Selected Poems* (Arte Publico Press). Among the numerous awards he has received are the Earl Lyon Award, the Stanley Kunitz Award for Poetry, and a 1983 General Electric Foundation award. He works as an interpreter in Sanger, California.

JOSE SEQUEIRA, a native of Nicaragua, has published poetry in *Blue Unicorn, The California State Poetry Quarterly, The Evergreen Chronicles,* and other journals. His short stories have been featured in *The Americas Review* and *Mala Leche.* He lives in Welches, Oregon.

GARY SOTO is the author of twenty books of essays, poetry, young adult fiction, and books for children. Some of them include *Black Hair* (University of Pittsburgh Press), *Living Up the Street* (Dell), *Home Course in Religion* (Chronicle Books), and *Too Many Tamales* (Putnam). He lives in Berkeley, California.

ILAN STAVANS coedited *Growing Up Latino: Memoirs and Short Stories* (Houghton Mifflin). His forthcoming books include *The Stranger Within* (HarperCollins), a look at Latino culture in the United States. He teaches at the University of Massachusetts at Amherst.

VIRGIL SUAREZ is coeditor of several anthologies, including *Iguana Dreams: New Latino Fiction* (HarperCollins). He is the author of two novels, *The Cutter* (Ballantine) and *Latin Jazz* (William Morrow). His first collection of short stories, *Welcome to the Oasis,* was published by Arte Publico Press in 1992. He teaches at Florida State University in Tallahassee.

DAVID UNGER is the author of *Neither Caterpillar nor Butterfly* (Es Que Somos Muy Podres Press) and an unpublished novel, *Life in the Damn Tropics*. He was born in Guatemala and lives in New York City.

LUIS ALBERTO URREA is the author of the highly acclaimed memoir, *Across the Wire: Hard Times on the U.S.-Mexican Border* (Anchor Books). His first novel, *Searching for Snow,* was published in 1993 by HarperCollins. He lives in Boulder, Colorado.

ED VEGA is the pen name of Edgardo Vega Yunqué. He was born in Puerto Rico and is a resident of New York City. He is the author of *The Comeback*, *Mendoza's Dreams*, and *Casualty Report*, originally published by Arte Publico Press. His new novel, *No Matter How Much You Promise to Cook or Pay the Rent You Blew It Cauze Bill Bailey Ain't Never Coming Home Again*, will be published by Ballantine in 1995. He teaches writing at The New School for Social Research and has won NEA and NYFA fellowships in literature.

MARISELLA VEIGA has published her short stories and poetry in the *Mid-American Review* and *Ploughshares,* in the collections *Looking for Home: Women Writing About Exile* (Milkweed Editions) and *Iguana Dreams: Latino Short Fiction* (HarperCollins), and in various other journals. She teaches in the artists-in-residence program of the Miami, Florida, public schools.

ALMA LUZ VILLANUEVA is the author of numerous books of poetry, including *Bloodroot* (Place of Heron Press) and *Planet* (Bilingual Press). Her novel *The Ultraviolet Sky* (Bilingual Press) received a Before Columbus Foundation American Book Award. Bilingual Press also published her second novel, *Naked Ladies,* and her collection of short stories, *La Llorona/Weeping Woman.* She lives in Santa Cruz, California.

HELENA MARÍA VIRAMONTES is the author of two collections of short stories, *The Moths and Other Stories* (Arte Publico Press) and *Paris Rats in East L.A.* She teaches in the Spanish department at the University of California at Irvine.

RUTH WARAT has published poetry in *Cornfield Review, The Antigonish Review, Chelsea, Kansas Quarterly,* and other journals. She lives in Charlotte, North Carolina.

Permissions

lished by Hanging Loose Press, 1991. Copyright © by Jack Agueros, 1991. Reprinted by permission of the publisher.

"Look on the Bright Side" by Dagoberto Gilb. The story first appeared in *The Magic of Blood*, published by the University of New Mexico Press, 1993. Copyright © by Dagoberto Gilb, 1993. Reprinted by permission of the publisher.

"The Graduation" by Marisella Veiga. Copyright © by Marisella Veiga, 1994. Used by permission of the author.

"Gravity," "The Seed Must Kill," "A Letter from My Mother" by Victor Martinez. The poems first appeared in *Caring for a House*, published by Chusma House Publications, 1992. Copyright © by Victor Martinez, 1992. Reprinted by permission of the publisher.

"Miguelito, Miguelito," "Backward Facing Man" by Leo Romero. Copyright © by Leo Romero, 1994. Used by permission of the author.

"The Devil in Texas" by Aristeo Brito. The excerpt is from *The Devil in Texas*, published by Bilingual Press, 1991. Copyright © by Aristeo Brito, 1991. Reprinted by permission of the publisher.

"The Day Rito Died" by Mary Helen Ponce. The chapter first appeared in *Hoyt Street: An Autobiography*, published by the University of New Mexico Press, 1993. Copyright © by Mary Helen Ponce, 1993. Reprinted by permission of the publisher.

"Black Hair" by Gary Soto. The essay first appeared in *Living up the Street*, published by Strawberry Hill Press, 1985. Copyright © by Gary Soto, 1985. Reprinted by permission of the publisher.

"Dear Frida" by Pat Mora. Copyright © by Pat Mora, 1994. Used by permission of the author.

"The Itch" by Pat Mora. Copyright © by Pat Mora, 1994. Used by permission of the author.

"Seals," "Swirling Lines," "Minas de Cobre" by Ricardo Pau-Llosa. "Seals" and "Swirling Lines" first appeared in *Bread of the Imagined*, published by Bilingual Review Press, 1992. Copyright © by Ricardo Pau-Llosa. Reprinted by permission of the publisher. "Minas de Cobre" first appeared in *Cuba*, published by Carnegie Mellon University Press, 1993. Copyright © by Ricardo Pau-Llosa, 1993. Reprinted by permission of the publisher.

"Love and Hunt in the Dark Room," "Inquisitors, Dead and in Power" by Ruth Warat. Copyright © by Ruth Warat, 1994. Used by permission of the author.

"The Marriage of the Prostitute in Puerto Rican Folklore" by Rafael Barreto-Rivera. The poem first appeared in *Voices, Noises*, published by the Coach House Press, 1982. Copyright © by Rafael Barreto-Rivera, 1982. Reprinted by permission of the author.

"The Bird Who Cleans the World," "How the Serpent Was Born," "The Disobedient Child" by Victor Montejo. The fables first appeared in *The Bird Who Cleans the*

by Arte Publico Press, 1991. Copyright © by Lorna Dee Cervantes, 1991. Reprinted by permission of the publisher.

"The First Day of Spring," "The Night Is Out of Sight" by Pedro Pietri. Copyright © by Pedro Pietri, 1994. Used by permission of the author.

"Ending Poem" by Rosario Morales and Aurora Levins Morales. The poem first appeared in *Getting Home Alive*, published by Firebrand Books, 1986. Copyright © by Rosario Morales and Aurora Levins Morales, 1986. Reprinted by permission of the publisher.